MASSACHUSETTS REAL ESTATE

Third Edition

Volume 5

Robert L. Marzelli
Jon D. Witten

LexisNexis™
Matthew Bender®

QUESTIONS ABOUT THIS PUBLICATION?

For questions about the **Editorial Content** appearing in these volumes or reprint permission, please call:

Patricia A. Valentine at .... 1-800-252-9257 (ext. 2286)
Internet Address: .... patricia.a.valentine@lexisnexis.com

For assistance with replacement pages, shipment, billing or other customer service matters, please call:

Customer Services Department at..(800)833-9844
Outside the United States and Canada, please call ....(518)487-3000
Fax Number ....(518)487-3584

For information on other Matthew Bender publications, please call
Your account manager or ....(800)223-1940
Outside the United States and Canada, please call ....(518)487-3000

Library of Congress Card Number: 20–05014238

ISBN: 0-8205-7481-3

Editorial Offices
744 Broad Street, Newark, NJ 07102 (973) 820-2000
201 Mission St., San Francisco, CA 94105-1831 (415) 908-3200
www.lexisnexis.com

MATTHEW◆BENDER

Statement on Fair Use

Matthew Bender recognizes the balance that must be achieved between the operation of the fair use doctrine, whose basis is to avoid the rigid application of the copyright statute, and the protection of the creative rights and economic interests of authors, publishers and other copyright holders.

We are also aware of the countervailing forces that exist between the ever greater technological advances for making both print and electronic copies and the reduction in the value of copyrighted works that must result from a consistent and pervasive reliance on these new copying technologies. It is Matthew Bender's position that if the "progress of science and useful arts" is promoted by granting copyright protection to authors, such progress may well be impeded if copyright protection is diminished in the name of fair use. (See Nimmer on Copyright § 13.05[E][1].) This holds true whether the parameters of the fair use doctrine are considered in either the print or the electronic environment as it is the integrity of the copyright that is at issue, not the media under which the protected work may become available. Therefore, the fair use guidelines we propose apply equally to our print and electronic information, and apply, within §§ 107 and 108 of the Copyright Act, regardless of the professional status of the user.

Our draft guidelines would allow for the copying of limited materials, which would include synopses and tables of contents, primary source and government materials that may have a minimal amount of editorial enhancements, individual forms to aid in the drafting of applications and pleadings, and miscellaneous pages from any of our newsletters, treatises and practice guides. This copying would be permitted provided it is performed for internal use and solely for the purpose of facilitating individual research or for creating documents produced in the course of the user's professional practice, and the original from which the copy is made has been purchased or licensed as part of the user's existing in-house collection.

Matthew Bender fully supports educational awareness programs designed to increase the public's recognition of its fair use rights. We also support the operation of collective licensing organizations with regard to our print and electronic information.

Table of Contents

CHAPTER 1   **PURCHASE AND SALE OF RESIDENTIAL REAL ESTATE—LAW AND PRACTICE**

PART I   THE LAW

§ 1.01   Preliminary Matters

§ 1.02   The Purchase and Sale Agreement; Statute of Frauds

§ 1.02[1]   Use of Written Offers to Purchase

§ 1.03   The Purchase Price

§ 1.03[1]   The Deposit

§ 1.04   The Quality of Title

§ 1.05   Time for Performance

§ 1.06   Risk of Loss

§ 1.07   Clearing Encumbrances

§ 1.07[1]   Correcting Defects in Premises

§ 1.08   Insurance

§ 1.09   Adjustments

§ 1.10   Closing Costs

§ 1.11   Broker's Commission

§ 1.11[1]   Seller's Duty to Disclose

§ 1.12   Remedies on Default

§ 1.13   Disclaimers

§ 1.14   Smoke Detectors

§ 1.15   Lead Paint Disclosures

§ 1.16   Contingency Clauses

§ 1.17   Common Contingency Clauses

§ 1.17[1]   The Financing Contingency

§ 1.17[2]   Contingencies Relating to Condition of the Premises

§ 1.17[3]   On Site Septic System Inspections (Title V)

§ 1.17[4]   Mortgage Plot Plans

§ 1.18   Merger by Acceptance

§ 1.19   Deed Drafting

§ 1.20   Registered Land: Special Considerations

§ 1.21   Condominiums: Special Considerations

§ 1.21[1]   Condominiums: Liens for Common Charges

§ 1.21[2]   Condominiums: Unit Deeds

§ 1.21[3]   Condominiums: Master Deed

v

Table of Contents

§ 1.21[4]   Condominiums: Management

§ 1.22   Title 5—State Environmental Code—Detailed Outline of Inspection and Upgrade Requirements

§ 1.23   Preliminary Information Gathering

§ 1.24   Make Contact with Broker and Other Attorneys

§ 1.25   Draw or Review and Revise Purchase and Sale Agreement—Diary Expiration Date

§ 1.26   Secure List of Liens and Encumbrances

§ 1.27   If Corporate Client Check On Vote

§ 1.28   Draw Deed

§ 1.29   Certificate of Occupancy

§ 1.29[1]   Smoke Detector Certificate

§ 1.29[2]   Lead Paint Disclosures Form

§ 1.29[3]   Release of Tax Lien

§ 1.30   Certificate of Title

§ 1.31   Draw Discharges Where Necessary

§ 1.32   Obtain Payoff Figure and Per Diem

§ 1.33   Double Check Documents and Do Preliminary Closing Adjustments

§ 1.34   Property Insurance

§ 1.35   Utilities and Fuel

§ 1.36   Registered Land—Special Problems

§ 1.36[1]   Limited Partnership and Other Special Entities

§ 1.37   Condominiums—Special Tasks

§ 1.38   The Closing

§ 1.39   Preliminary Information Gathering

§ 1.40   Make Contact with Broker and Other Attorneys

§ 1.41   Draw or Review and Revise Purchase and Sale Agreement—Diary Expiration Date

§ 1.42   Property Inspection

§ 1.43   Financing Contingency

§ 1.44   Title Examination—Evaluating a Real Estate Title as to Marketability

§ 1.44[1]   Have the Title Examined and Abstract Prepared

§ 1.45   Get an Overview of the State of the Title

§ 1.46   Make a Detailed Analysis of the Report

§ 1.47   Report Your Findings to Your Client and Other Interested Parties

Table of Contents

§ 1.48   Certified Plot Plan

§ 1.49   Municipal Lien Certificate

§ 1.50   Prepare List of Liens and Encumbrances

§ 1.51   Property Insurance Binders

§ 1.52   Obtain Payoff Figures and Per Diem From Each Mortgagee

§ 1.53   Utility Meters, Fuel Tank and Smoke Detectors

     § 1.53[1]   Lead Paint Notification to Tenants

§ 1.54   Review Proposed Deed and Other Instruments

§ 1.55   Title Insurance

§ 1.56   Double Check Documents and Do Preliminary Closing Adjustments—Advise Client

§ 1.57   Registered Land

§ 1.58   Condominiums—Special Problems

§ 1.59   The Closing

CHAPTER 2   **ZONING—PLANNING AND THE PLAN**

§ 2.01   CONTROL OF THE PROCESS IN GENERAL PLAN STATES

     § 2.01[1]   Use of the Plan in the United States

     § 2.01[2]   The California Model

     § 2.01[3]   Other States

     § 2.01[4]   The Massachusetts "Model"

     § 2.01[5]   Exceptions to the Massachusetts Model on Cape Cod and Martha's Vineyard

CHAPTER 3   **ZONING—REGULATORY TAKINGS**

PART I   THE LAW

§ 3.01   Introduction

§ 3.02   Physical Invasions of Real Property and Complete Deprivations of Value: "Always a Taking"

§ 3.03   Nuisance Preclusion: "Never a Taking"

§ 3.04   Balancing "Too Far" in Reviewing a Regulatory Takings Claim

     § 3.04[1]   Legislative Actions

     § 3.04[2]   Adjudicative Actions

Table of Contents

CHAPTER 4   **ZONING—THE COMPREHENSIVE PERMIT LAW**

PART I   THE LAW and PRACTICE

§ 4.01   Introduction
§ 4.02   The Statute in Summary Form
§ 4.03   Qualified Comprehensive Permit Applicants
§ 4.04   The Project Eligibility Letter
§ 4.05   The Application to the Board of Appeals
§ 4.06   The Hearing before the Board of Appeals
§ 4.07   The Board of Appeals' Decision
§ 4.08   Appeal to the Housing Appeals Committee
  § 4.08[1]   What is "Uneconomic"?
  § 4.08[2]   What is "Consistent with Local Needs"?
§ 4.09   Intervention by Abutters at the Housing Appeals Committee
§ 4.10   Appeal to Superior Court
§ 4.11   Appeal of Housing Appeals Committee Decisions
§ 4.12   The Comprehensive Permit Statute and the Cape Cod Commission
                 Act
§ 4.13   The Comprehensive Permit Statute in Cities and Towns Consistent
                 with Local Needs

CHAPTER 5   **ZONING—GENERAL PRINCIPLES OF LAW**

§ 5.01   Introduction
§ 5.02   Determining Applicable Zoning
§ 5.03   Zoning Changes
§ 5.04   Board of Appeals: Composition and Powers
§ 5.05   Filing; Public Hearing and Notice Requirements
§ 5.06   Withdrawal of Petitions; Reconsideration by Board
§ 5.07   Variances
  § 5.07[1]   Introduction and the Purposes of Variances
  § 5.07[2]   Required Findings for Granting a Variance
    § 5.07[2][a]   *Required Finding #1*: Soil Conditions, Shape or Topography
      § 5.07[2][a][i]   Soil Conditions
      § 5.07[2][a][ii]   Shape
      § 5.07[2][a][iii]   Topography

Table of Contents

§ 5.07[2][b]   *Required Finding #2*: Hardship

§ 5.07[2][c]   *Required Finding #3*: Public Good

§ 5.07[3]   Use Variances

§ 5.07[4]   Conditional Variances

§ 5.07[5]   Lapsed Variances

§ 5.07[6]   Procedural Issues and Grants of a Variance

 § 5.07[6][a]   Filing Requirements

§ 5.07[7]   Public Notice Requirements

§ 5.07[8]   Public Hearing and Voting Requirements

§ 5.07[9]   Decisions of the Board of Appeals

§ 5.07[10]   Decision Filing and Notification Requirements

§ 5.07[11]   Decision Recording Requirements

§ 5.07[12]   Use of Variances While Awaiting Appeals

§ 5.07[13]   Constructive Grant of Variances

§ 5.07[14]   Board of Appeals Liability

§ 5.08   Special Permits

 § 5.08[1]   Introduction and Purpose

 § 5.08[2]   Special Permits in Practice

§ 5.09   Judicial Appeals

§ 5.10   Commonly Encountered Problems in Zoning Practice

 § 5.10[1]   Protections for Nonconforming Structures and Uses

 § 5.10[2]   Vested Rights ("Grandfathering")

  § 5.10[2][a]   Introduction

  § 5.10[2][b]   The Seven Protections of G.L. c. 40A, § 6

   § 5.10[2][b][i]   Preexisting Structure or Use

   § 5.10[2][b][ii]   Building or Special Permit "in hand"

   § 5.10[2][b][iii]   Single Lot: 50/5,000

   § 5.10[2][b][iv]   Common Lot: 75/7,500

    § 5.10[2][b][iv][A]   Common Lots and the "Merger Theory"

   § 5.10[2][b][v]   Preliminary Plan

   § 5.10[2][b][vi]   Definitive Plan

   § 5.10[2][b][vii]   Approval Not Required Plan

   § 5.10[2][b][viii]   Vested Rights, the Martha's Vineyard, and the Cape Cod Commission Acts

§ 5.11   Nonconforming Uses and Structures

 § 5.11[1]   Introduction

 § 5.11[2]   What are Nonconforming Uses and Structures?

Table of Contents

§ 5.11[2][a]   The Use or Structure is Existing When the First Advertisement Appears

§ 5.11[2][b]   The Lot is Existing and Protected

§ 5.11[3]   The Protections Afforded to Nonconforming Uses and Structures

§ 5.11[4]   Extensions and Alterations to Nonconforming Uses and Structures

§ 5.11[5]   Extensions and Alterations to Nonconforming Uses and Structures: Signs

§ 5.11[6]   Extensions and Alterations to Nonconforming Uses and Structures: The Second "Except" Clause (Single and Two–Family Residential)

§ 5.11[7]   Changes to Nonconforming Uses

§ 5.11[7][a]   Does the Use Reflect the Nature and Purpose of the Nonconforming Use Prevailing When the Zoning Took Effect?

§ 5.11[7][b]   Is There a Difference in the Quality, Character and/or Degree of the Resulting Use?

§ 5.11[7][c]   Is the Current Use Different in Kind in its Effect Upon the Neighborhood?

§ 5.11[8]   Abandonment of Nonconforming Uses and Structures

§ 5.12   Spot Zoning

§ 5.13   Contract Zoning and Development Agreements

§ 5.14   Availability of Declaratory Judgment in Zoning Cases

§ 5.15   Failure of Building Inspector to Act

§ 5.16   When Does a Zoning Hearing End?

§ 5.17   Regulating Form of Ownership as Opposed to Use: Condominium and Time Share Conversions

§ 5.18   Access Roadways—Different Zones

§ 5.19   The Site Plan Review Process

§ 5.20   Constructive Grant of Variances, Special Permits and Appeals

§ 5.21   Open Meeting, Quorum Requirements and Voting in Zoning Cases

§ 5.22   Judicial Enforcement of Zoning

§ 5.23   Split Lots (Lots Transected By a Zoning Boundary)

§ 5.24   Perimeter Plans—Entitlement to Approval Not Required Endorsement

§ 5.25   Who is 'Aggrieved' Party for Purposes of Zoning Appeal

§ 5.26   Modification of Board's Decision

§ 5.27   Permit Conditions Requiring Off-Site Improvements

Table of Contents

§ 5.28   Earth Removal

§ 5.29   Growth Management

§ 5.30   Inclusionary Zoning

§ 5.31   Regulation of Adult Entertainment Businesses

§ 5.32   Additional Zoning Techniques

§ 5.33   Due Process Claims in Zoning and Subdivision Appeals

§ 5.34   Creation of Conforming Lot Resulting in Zoning Violation by Another Lot (Infectious Invalidity)

§ 5.35   What Use Qualifies As Accessory

§ 5.36   Expiration and Extension of Special Permits

CHAPTER 6   ZONING—EXEMPTIONS FROM LOCAL REGULATION

§ 6.01   Introduction

§ 6.02   Exemptions Under the State Building Code

§ 6.03   Exemptions for Agricultural, Religious and Educational Uses

   § 6.03[1]   Exemptions for Agricultural Uses

     § 6.03[1][a]   Definition of Agriculture

     § 6.03[1][b]   "Primarily for Agriculture"

       § 6.03[1][b][i]   "Majority of Such Products:" The 50 Percent Rule

       § 6.03[1][b][ii]   Parcels Less Than Five Acres

   § 6.03[2]   Exemptions for Religious Uses and Educational Uses

     § 6.03[2][a]   Definition of Religious and Educational Use

     § 6.03[2][b]   To What Extent Can the Protected Activity Be Regulated?

   § 6.03[3]   Exemptions for Governmental Uses

   § 6.03[4]   Exemptions for Public Service Uses

   § 6.03[5]   Exemptions for Child Care Facilities and Family Day Care Homes

   § 6.03[6]   Exemptions for Hazardous Waste, Refuse Treatment and Disposal Facilities

   § 6.03[7]   Exemptions for Scientific Research Facilities

   § 6.03[8]   Exemptions for Amateur Radio Operators

   § 6.03[9]   Telecommunications Act

   § 6.03[10]   Exemptions for Solar Energy Systems

   § 6.03[11]   Exemptions for Handicapped Access Ramps

   § 6.03[12]   Exemptions for Temporary Mobile Homes

   § 6.03[13]   Conclusion

Table of Contents

CHAPTER 7 ZONING—THE PRACTICE

§ 7.01   Obtaining Building and Use Permits, Comprehensive Permits, Zoning Variances and Zoning Changes

§ 7.01[1]   Preliminary Information Gathering

§ 7.01[2]   Determine Applicable Zoning

§ 7.01[3]   Decide Whether a Variance, Special Permit or Zoning Change is Necessary

§ 7.01[3][a]   To Obtain a Variance

§ 7.01[3][b]   To Obtain Special Permit

§ 7.01[3][c]   To Obtain a Zoning Change in a Town

§ 7.01[3][d]   To Obtain a Zoning Change in a City

§ 7.01[3][e]   Obtain Board of Health Approval Where Necessary

§ 7.01[3][f]   Obtain Additional Planning Board or Appeals Board Approval Where Necessary

§ 7.01[3][g]   Obtain Conservation Commission Approval Where Necessary

§ 7.01[3][h]   To Obtain A Comprehensive Permit

§ 7.01[3][i]   Obtain Building Permit

§ 7.01[3][j]   Advise Client of Period of Validity of Permit

§ 7.01[3][k]   Flow Charts

CHAPTER 8 REGULATIONS PROTECTING NATURAL RESOURCES—IN GENERAL

§ 8.01   Introduction

§ 8.02   Regulations Protecting Natural Resources in Massachusetts

§ 8.02[1]   National Pollution Discharge Elimination System

§ 8.02[2]   Massachusetts Endangered Species Act

§ 8.02[3]   Massachusetts Environmental Policy Act

§ 8.02[4]   Historic Resources

§ 8.02[5]   State Environmental Code

§ 8.03   Wetland Resources

§ 8.03[1]   The Scientific Framework for Wetland Protection

§ 8.03[2]   Types of Wetland Protection Regulation

§ 8.04   Wetland Protection—Zoning Ordinances and Bylaws

§ 8.05   State Inland and Coastal Wetland Protection Statutes

§ 8.06   Wetland Protection—General Bylaws

Table of Contents

§ 8.07   "Chapter 91 License Requirements"—Filled or Flowed Tidelands and the Public Trust Doctrine

§ 8.08   Federal Wetlands Regulation

CHAPTER 9   **WETLANDS PROTECTION—THE PRACTICE**

PART II   THE PRACTICE

§ 9.01   Applying for State and Local Wetland Permits

CHAPTER 10   **SUBDIVISION CONTROL—GENERAL PRINCIPLES OF LAW**

§ 10.01   Determining Applicability of Subdivision Control Law

     § 10.01[1]   G.L. c. 41, § 81-L: What Is a Subdivision?

§ 10.02   Approval Not Required Plans

§ 10.03.   Subdivision Plans; Preliminary

§ 10.04.   Subdivision Plans; Definitive

§ 10.05.   Modification, Amendment, or Recission of Previously Approved Plan (G.L. c. 41, § 81-W)

§ 10.06.   Judicial Review Under Subdivision Control Law

§ 10.07   Commonly Encountered Problems in Subdivision Control Law

     § 10.07[1]   Approval Not Required Plans (§ 81P) Which Show Zoning Violations

     § 10.07[2]   Entitlement to Approval Not Required Endorsement—Judicial Guidelines

     § 10.07[3]   Creation of Lots With Inadequate Frontage By Means of a Plan

     § 10.07[4]   Refusal of Planning Board to Accept Plan

     § 10.07[5]   Disapproval of Preliminary Plan—Effect

     § 10.07[6]   Consideration By Planning Board of Matters Outside the Proposed Subdivision

     § 10.07[7]   Dead End Streets—The Double Bubble and Issues Related to G.L. c. 41, § 81-R

     § 10.07[8]   The Practical Role of the Board of Health in Subdivision Approval Process

     § 10.07[9]   Adequacy of Statement of Reasons for Planning Board's Disapproval of Plan

     § 10.07[10]   Conditional Approval of Plan Limited as to Time

Table of Contents

§ 10.07[11]   Amendments to Previously Approved, or Disapproved, Plans After an Intervening Zoning Change

§ 10.07[12]   Constructive Approval of Plans

§ 10.07[13]   Effect of Restrictive Notes

§ 10.07[14]   Effect of Pre-existing Easements on Approvals of Plan

§ 10.07[15]   Problems Relative to Long-Term Maintenance of Engineering Structures

§ 10.07[16]   Development In or Near Historically or Archaeologically Significant Sites

§ 10.07[17]   Requirement of Connection to Abutting Land

§ 10.07[18]   Resubmission of Disapproved Plans

§ 10.07[19]   Plan Approval Conditioned on Subsequent Compliance with Rules and Regulations

§ 10.07[20]   Subdivision of Single Lot Containing Two or More Buildings

CHAPTER 11   **SUBDIVISION CONTROL—THE PRACTICE**

§ 11.01   Applying for Subdivision Approval

§ 11.01[1]   Preliminary Information

§ 11.01[2]   Approval Not Required Plans

§ 11.01[3]   Decide Whether to Submit a Preliminary Plan

§ 11.01[4]   Submit Definitive Plan

§ 11.01[5]   Prepare for Public Hearing

§ 11.01[6]   After the Hearing, Follow-up

§ 11.01[7]   Flow Chart—The Process of Securing Approval of Subdivision

§ 11.01[8]   Controlling Subdivision Appearance and Amenities-Restrictive Covenants

CHAPTER 12   **FORECLOSURE OF REAL ESTATE MORTGAGES—LAW AND PRACTICE**

§ 12.01   Matters Preliminary to Instituting Foreclosure

§ 12.02   Prerequisites to Instituting Foreclosure Proceedings

§ 12.03   Court Proceedings

§ 12.04   The Foreclosure—Notice and Sale

§ 12.04[1]   Deeds In Lieu of Foreclosure

§ 12.05   Redemption

Table of Contents

§ 12.06   Bankruptcy

§ 12.07   Default and Foreclosure

  § 12.07[1]   Actions Prior to Foreclosure Sale

  § 12.07[2]   Actions Taken at Foreclosure Sale

  § 12.07[3]   Actions Taken After Foreclosure Sale

CHAPTER 13   SUMMARY PROCESS—GENERAL PRINCIPLES OF LAW

§ 13.01   Generally

§ 13.02   Plaintiffs in Summary Process Action

§ 13.03   Defendants in Summary Process Action

§ 13.04   Grounds

§ 13.05   Notice

§ 13.06   Defenses to Summary Process

§ 13.07   Procedure

  § 13.07[1]   Execution

§ 13.08   Stay of Execution

§ 13.09   Appeals

§ 13.10   Security Deposits

  § 13.10[1]   Statutory Security Deposit and Advance Rental Requirements Respecting Residential Real Estate

CHAPTER 14   SUMMARY PROCESS—THE PRACTICE

§ 14.01   Insuring Compliance with Security Deposit and Advance Rent Requirements Imposed on Residential Landlords

  § 14.01[1]   Obtain Required Information

  § 14.01[2]   Send Proper Notices to Tenant

  § 14.01[3]   Maintain Proper Documentation

  § 14.01[4]   Transfer Security Deposit and Accrued Interest to New Owner

§ 14.02   Summary Process/Evictions Representing the Landlord

  § 14.02[1]   Prior to Hearing in Court

  § 14.02[2]   At the Court Hearing

  § 14.02[3]   After the Hearing

§ 14.03   Summary Process/Evictions Representing the Tenant

  § 14.03[1]   Prior to Court Hearing

  § 14.03[2]   At the Court Hearing

Table of Contents

§ 14.03[3]   After the Court Hearing

CHAPTER 15   **THE CHARACTERISTICS AND USES OF NOMINEE REALTY TRUSTS—GENERAL PRINCIPLES OF LAW**

§ 15.01   Generally
§ 15.02   Common Provisions of Nominee Trusts
§ 15.03   Reasons for Using Nominee Trust
§ 15.04   Liability to Third Persons
 § 15.04[1]   Liability of Trustees
 § 15.04[2]   Liability of Beneficiaries
§ 15.05   Relationship Between Trustee and Beneficiary
§ 15.06   Maintaining Pass-Through Tax Status of Nominee Trusts

CHAPTER 16   **THE CHARACTERISTICS AND USES OF NOMINEE TRUSTS—THE PRACTICE**

§ 16.01   Drafting a Nominee Trust
 § 16.01[1]   Introduction
 § 16.01[2]   Establishment of Trust
 § 16.01[3]   Trustees' Powers
 § 16.01[4]   Termination of the Trust
 § 16.01[5]   Trustee Succession
 § 16.01[6]   Relations Between Trust and Third Persons
 § 16.01[7]   Limitation on Liability to Third Persons
 § 16.01[8]   Ancillary Documents

CHAPTER 17   **REAL ESTATE TAX ABATEMENTS AND EXEMPTIONS**

§ 17.01   Generally
 § 17.01[1]   Definition of Real Property
 § 17.01[2]   Owner with Multiple Parcels
 § 17.01[3]   Land and Buildings Are Taxed Together
 § 17.01[4]   Real Estate Under "Permanent Restriction"
 § 17.01[5]   Property with Multiple Owners of Fractional Interests
 § 17.01[6]   Taxation of "Brownfields" Property
 § 17.01[7]   Generally
 § 17.01[8]   If Tax Is Invalidated by Error or Irregularity

Table of Contents

§ 17.01[9]   Effect of Clerical Errors

§ 17.01[10]   If Property Is Omitted from Annual Assessments

§ 17.01[11]   Generally

§ 17.01[12]   Personal Liability for Tax

§ 17.01[13]   If Real Estate Is Divided or Sold Before Tax Is Paid

§ 17.01[14]   Deceased Persons or Persons Unknown

§ 17.01[15]   Mortgagees

§ 17.01[16]   Condominium Owners

§ 17.01[17]   Planned Unit or Cluster Developments

§ 17.01[18]   Lessees of Public Property

§ 17.01[19]   Returns Filed by All Taxpayers

§ 17.01[20]   Returns by Organizations Claiming Charitable Exemption

§ 17.01[21]   Returns by Other Persons Claiming Exemptions

§ 17.01[22]   Effect of Failure to Furnish List

§ 17.01[23]   Assessors' Right to Question Taxpayers by Questionnaire

§ 17.01[24]   Assessors' Right to Question Businesses As to Profit/Loss

§ 17.01[25]   Generally

§ 17.01[26]   Public Access to Records of Assessors

§ 17.02   Introduction

§ 17.02[1]   Time for Application and Qualification

§ 17.02[2]   Generally

§ 17.02[3]   The United States

§ 17.02[4]   The Commonwealth

§ 17.02[5]   One Municipality Owning Property Located in Another

§ 17.02[6]   Generally

§ 17.02[7]   Definition of Charitable Organization

§ 17.02[8]   Use of Property for Noncharitable Purposes

§ 17.02[9]   Generally

§ 17.02[10]   Houses of Worship and Effect of Non-religious Use on Exemption

§ 17.02[11]   Parsonages

§ 17.02[12]   Cemeteries

§ 17.02[13]   Nonprofit Hospitals and Other Medical Organizations

§ 17.02[14]   Urban Redevelopment Corporations

§ 7.02[14][a]   Payments by Urban Redevelopment Corporation in Lieu of Taxes

§ 7.02[14][b]   Project Developed in Separate Stages

Table of Contents

§ 7.02[14][c]		Valuation of Property—Right to Appeal
§ 7.02[14][d]		Determination of Fair Cash Value Prior to Construction
§ 17.02[15]	Housing and Redevelopment Authorities
§ 17.02[16]	Veterans
§ 17.02[17]	Surviving Spouses, Orphans and Poor Persons
§ 17.02[18]	Aged Homeowners
§ 17.02[19]	Living in Multi–family Dwellings
§ 17.02[20]	Owning Less than Entire Property
§ 17.02[21]	Deferral of Tax
§ 17.02[22]	Manufactured Homes
§ 17.02[23]	Forest Land
§ 17.02[24]	Obtaining the Exemption
§ 17.02[25]	Appeal of State Forester's Decisions
§ 17.02[26]	Keeping the Exemption
§ 17.02[27]	Taxation of Classified Forest Land
§ 17.02[28]	Appeal of Assessment of Tax
§ 17.02[29]	Withdrawal From Classification
§ 17.02[30]	Conversion to Nonforest Use: First Refusal Option
§ 17.02[31]	Agricultural and Horticultural Land
§ 17.02[32]	Agricultural Land—Definition
§ 17.02[33]	Horticultural Land—Definition
§ 17.02[34]	Minimum Area and Dollar Sales
§ 17.02[35]	Application for Eligibility
§ 17.02[36]	Valuation
§ 7.02[36][a]	Taxation of Farmhouses and Other Structures
§ 7.02[36][b]	Special or Betterment Assessments
§ 7.02[36][c]	Valuation for Other than Assessments Purposes
§ 17.02[37]	Effect of Sale or Change of Use
§ 17.02[37][a]	Conveyance Tax
§ 17.02[37][b]	Roll-back Tax
§ 17.02[37][c]	Conveyance and Roll-back Taxes—Relationship to One Another
§ 17.02[38]	Municipality's Option to Purchase Upon Sale or Conversion
§ 17.02[39]	Sale or Conversion of a Portion of Qualified Lands
§ 17.02[40]	Appeals from Determination of Assessors
§ 17.02[41]	Agricultural Preservation Restrictions
§ 17.02[42]	Recreational Land

Table of Contents

§ 17.02[43]   Recreational Land—Definition

§ 17.02[44]   Application for Eligibility

§ 17.02[45]   Valuation

   § 17.02[45][a]   Taxation of Dwelling Houses and Associated Structures

   § 17.02[45][b]   Special or Betterment Assessments

§ 17.02[46]   Effect of Sale or Change of Use

   § 17.02[46][a]   Conveyance Tax

   § 17.02[46][b]   Roll-back Tax

   § 17.02[46][c]   Conveyance and Roll-back Taxes—Relationship to One Another

§ 17.02[47]   Municipality's Option to Purchase Upon Sale or Conversion

§ 17.02[48]   Sale or Conversion of a Portion of Qualified Land

§ 17.02[49]   Appeals from Determinations of Assessors

§ 17.02[50]   Other Exempt Classes of Property

§ 17.02[51]   Generally

§ 17.03   Generally

   § 17.03[1]   Who Applies

   § 17.03[2]   When

   § 17.03[3]   Unusual Relief for Late Applications

   § 17.03[4]   To Whom—Form of Application

   § 17.03[5]   Assessors' Right to Inspection and Information Prior to Hearing

   § 17.03[6]   Hearings—Evidence Taxpayer Should Introduce

   § 17.03[7]   Non-income Producing Property

   § 17.03[8]   Income Producing Property

   § 17.03[9]   Notice of Decision or Non-action

   § 17.03[10]   General Rules for Appeals

   § 17.03[11]   Late Appeals

   § 17.03[12]   Payment of Tax as Prerequisite to Appeal

   § 17.03[13]   Inability to Pay Tax—Effect on Appeal

   § 17.03[14]   Assessors' Right to Remove From County Commissioners

   § 17.03[15]   Interest on Abated Taxes

   § 17.03[16]   Taxpayer's Right to Certificate of Abatement

   § 17.03[17]   Effect If Property Sold or Taken for Non-payment of Taxes During Pendency Appeal

§ 17.04   Generally

   § 17.04[1]   Structure of the Board

   § 17.04[2]   Publication of Decisions

Table of Contents

§ 17.04[3]   Right of Appeal to the Board
§ 17.04[4]   Jurisdiction
§ 17.04[5]   The Formal Procedure—Taxpayer's Petition
§ 17.04[6]   Assessors' Answer
§ 17.04[7]   The Informal Procedure—Taxpayer's Statement
§ 17.04[8]   Assessors' Answer
§ 17.04[9]   Assessors' Right to Elect the Formal Procedure
§ 17.04[10]   Discovery
§ 17.04[11]   Motion Practice
§ 17.04[12]   Telephone Motions
§ 17.04[13]   Continuances
§ 17.04[14]   Pre-hearing Conferences
§ 17.04[15]   Hearings
§ 17.04[16]   Taking of Views
§ 17.04[17]   Stenographic Reports of Proceedings
§ 17.04[18]   Costs of Suit
§ 17.04[19]   Appeals from Decisions of the Appellate Tax Board
§ 17.04[20]   Insuring Full Review on Appeal
§ 17.04[21]   Evidence Necessary to Sustain the Decision of the Board on
                        Appeal
§ 17.05   Introduction
§ 17.05[1]   The Concept of Highest and Best Use
§ 17.05[2]   Replacement Cost
§ 17.05[3]   Generally
§ 17.05[4]   The Market Sales Comparison Method
§ 17.05[5]   The   Cost   Minus   Depreciation   Method   (Depreciated
                        Reproduction Cost)
§ 17.05[6]   Replacement Cost
§ 17.05[7]   Accrued Depreciation
§ 17.05[8]   The Capitalization of Income Method
§ 17.05[8][a]   Capitalization Rate
§ 17.05[8][b]   Interest Rate
§ 17.05[8][c]   Depreciation Rate
§ 17.05[8][c][i]   Straight Line Depreciation
§ 17.05[8][c][ii]   Sinking Fund Depreciation
§ 17.05[8][c][iii]   Annuity Depreciation
§ 17.05[8][c][iv]   Relative Merits of Three Depreciation Methods

Table of Contents

§ 17.06   The Generally Accepted Valuation Methods
  § 17.06[1]   Definition
  § 17.06[2]   Rental Value as Evidence of Fair Cash Value
  § 17.06[3]   Rental Value of Owner-occupied Property
  § 17.06[4]   Rental Value of Other, Comparable Properties
  § 17.06[5]   Capitalizing Net Rental Value for Tax Purposes
  § 17.06[6]   Original Cost of Property as Evidence of Fair Cash Value
  § 17.06[7]   Sales of Other Comparable Properties as Evidence of Fair Cash
                      Value
  § 17.06[8]   Depreciated Reproduction or Replacement Cost as Evidence of
                      Fair Cash Value
  § 17.06[9]   Valuing Contaminated Property For Tax Purposes
  § 17.06[10]   Generally
  § 17.06[11]   Owners
  § 17.06[12]   Expert Witnesses
  § 17.06[13]   Other Persons
§ 17.07   Generally
  § 17.07[1]   Assessment in Excess of Fair Market Value
  § 17.07[2]   Proving Assessment in Excess of Fair Market Value
  § 17.07[3]   Assessment of Different Kinds of Property at Different
                      Percentages of Value (Disproportion)
  § 17.07[4]   Proving Disproportion
    § 17.07[4][a]   Can There Be a Class Within a Class?
  § 17.07[5]   Improper Classification
§ 17.08   Generally
  § 17.08[1]   How Classification Works
  § 17.08[2]   The Residential Exemption
  § 17.08[3]   The Small Commercial Exemption
  § 17.08[4]   Effect of Classification on Abatements and Exemptions

CHAPTER 18   REAL ESTATE TAX ABATEMENTS AND
                    EXEMPTIONS—THE PRACTICE

§ 18.01   Obtaining Real Estate Tax Abatements
  § 18.01[1]   Preliminary Information
  § 18.01[2]   Evaluate the Case
  § 18.01[3]   File the Appropriate Applications

Table of Contents

§ 18.01[4]   Appeal Unfavorable Action By Assessors to the Appellate Tax
                    Board
§ 18.01[5]   Determine Whether to Utilize the Limited Discovery Available
§ 18.01[6]   The Hearing
§ 18.01[7]   Real Estate Tax Abatement Timetable For Lawyers

CHAPTER 19   DRAFTING A COMMERCIAL LEASE—THE PRACTICE

§ 19.01   Introduction
§ 19.02   Identify Parties
§ 19.03   Describe Premises and Appurtenances Fully
§ 19.04   Set Forth Warranties of Title and Authority
§ 19.05   Set Forth Lease Term and Base Rent With Specificity
§ 19.06   Define Conditions Under Which Lease Agreement May Be
                 Extended or Renewed
§ 19.07   Include Provisions for Any Automatic Rent Escalators Agreed to
                 By Parties
§ 19.08   Provide for Security Deposit to be Held by Lessor
§ 19.09   Provide for Payment of Utilities
§ 19.10   Describe Any Limitations on Use of Premises
§ 19.11   Describe Any Limitations on Assignment or Sublease
§ 19.12   Define Duties of the Parties with Respect to Maintenance and
                 Repair
§ 19.13   Signs
§ 19.14   Define Rights of the Parties with Respect to Structural Alteration or
                 Additions to Premises
§ 19.15   Set Forth Respective Obligations of Parties To Make Repairs
§ 19.16   Set Forth the Responsibilities of Parties With Respect to Indemnity
                 and Insurance
§ 19.17   Define Rights of the Parties in Event Property is Partially
                 Destroyed or Taken by Eminent Domain
§ 19.18   Subrogation in Event of Casualty Loss
§ 19.19   Set Forth Events of Default Under Lease
§ 19.20   Subordination of Subsequent Mortgages
§ 19.21   Miscellaneous Provisions

Table of Contents

CHAPTER 20 **REGISTRATION AND CONFIRMATION OF TITLE TO REAL ESTATE—THE PRACTICE**

§ 20.01   Preliminary Considerations—Registration or Confirmation
§ 20.02   Prepare to File Complaint
§ 20.03   Prepare Filing Documents
§ 20.04   File Documents in Court
§ 20.05   Follow Up Regularly with the Court
§ 20.06   Petitions Subsequent to Registration
§ 20.07   Voluntary Withdrawal of Land from Registration

About the Authors

Robert L. Marzelli

Robert L. Marzelli is an attorney with the firm of Billingham and Marzelli. He has practiced real estate, land use and municipal law in Massachusetts for the past 35 years. He is a graduate of Brown University and Georgetown University Law Center.

Jon D. Witten

Jonathan D. Witten is a land use planner and an attorney with the law firm of Daley and Witten, LLC. He is on the faculty of Tufts University Department of Urban and Environmental Policy and Planning and the Boston College Law School.

Preface to the Third Edition

Massachusetts Real Estate, Third Edition, is written as a reference for counsel practicing real estate and land use law. The substantive areas covered are those that public and private counsel are most likely to encounter. Practice suggestions, checklists and forms are provided to summarize key issues. Several topical areas, including for example a discussion of takings law, are summaries of evolving principles of law within Massachusetts and at the federal level.

The laws governing Massachusetts real estate have evolved dramatically over the past several years. Municipal and private counsel must be familiar with a broad range of transactional, land use and environmental regulations, procedural details and confusing appellate procedures. Most notably, Massachusetts' land use regulatory system-an influential driver of the state's real estate market-remains one of the nation's most incomprehensible, and is predictable only for its unpredictability.

As this edition goes to print, Massachusetts continues to experience a dramatic real estate development boom that includes extensive transactional activity. One result of this surge in real estate development and record setting sales prices has been intensification over the battle for the state's remaining un-developed and "under-developed" lands; a battle that is no longer limited to the eastern portion of the state. Whereas development pressures have historically been confined to land areas within the Route 128 corridor and Cape Cod, the state as a whole has witnessed an unprecedented expansion of residential, commercial and industrial development. It is no longer surprising for municipal or private counsel in the Berkshires to encounter the same real estate and land use challenges as counsel in a suburb of Boston.

Massachusetts Real Estate, Third Edition is written to address common and complex problems encountered by public and private counsel throughout the Commonwealth in today's complex real estate environment. We hope you find the text helpful.

Robert L. Marzelli
Jon D. Witten

Dedication

To Alexandra and James and Bernice and Carl.

CHAPTER 1

PURCHASE AND SALE OF RESIDENTIAL REAL ESTATE—LAW AND PRACTICE

Synopsis

§ 1.01   **Preliminary Matters**

§ 1.02   **The Purchase and Sale Agreement; Statute of Frauds**
         § 1.02[1]   Use of Written Offers to Purchase

§ 1.03   **The Purchase Price**
         § 1.03[1]   The Deposit

§ 1.04   **The Quality of Title**

§ 1.05   **Time for Performance**

§ 1.06   **Risk of Loss**

§ 1.07   **Clearing Encumbrances**
         § 1.07[1]   Correcting Defects in Premises

§ 1.08   **Insurance**

§ 1.09   **Adjustments**

§ 1.10   **Closing Costs**

§ 1.11   **Broker's Commission**
         § 1.11[1]   Seller's Duty to Disclose

§ 1.12   **Remedies on Default**

§ 1.13   **Disclaimers**

§ 1.14   **Smoke Detectors**

§ 1.15   **Lead Paint Disclosures**

§ 1.16   **Contingency Clauses**

§ 1.17   **Common Contingency Clauses**
         § 1.17[1]   The Financing Contingency
         § 1.17[2]   Contingencies Relating to Condition of the Premises
         § 1.17[3]   On Site Septic System Inspections (Title V)
         § 1.17[4]   Mortgage Plot Plans

§ 1.18   **Merger by Acceptance**

§ 1.19   Deed Drafting

§ 1.20   Registered Land: Special Considerations

§ 1.21   Condominiums: Special Considerations
          § 1.21[1]   Condominiums: Liens for Common Charges
          § 1.21[2]   Condominiums: Unit Deeds
          § 1.21[3]   Condominiums: Master Deed
          § 1.21[4]   Condominiums: Management

§ 1.22   Title 5—State Environmental Code—Detailed Outline of Inspection and Upgrade Requirements

§ 1.23   Preliminary Information Gathering

§ 1.24   Make Contact with Broker and Other Attorneys

§ 1.25   Draw or Review and Revise Purchase and Sale Agreement—Diary Expiration Date

§ 1.26   Secure List of Liens and Encumbrances

§ 1.27   If Corporate Client Check On Vote

§ 1.28   Draw Deed

§ 1.29   Certificate of Occupancy
          § 1.29[1]   Smoke Detector Certificate
          § 1.29[2]   Lead Paint Disclosures Form
          § 1.29[3]   Release of Tax Lien

§ 1.30   Certificate of Title

§ 1.31   Draw Discharges Where Necessary

§ 1.32   Obtain Payoff Figure and Per Diem

§ 1.33   Double Check Documents and Do Preliminary Closing Adjustments

§ 1.34   Property Insurance

§ 1.35   Utilities and Fuel

§ 1.36   Registered Land—Special Problems
          § 1.36[1]   Limited Partnership and Other Special Entities

§ 1.37   Condominiums—Special Tasks

§ 1.38   The Closing

§ 1.39   Preliminary Information Gathering

§ 1.40   Make Contact with Broker and Other Attorneys

§ 1.41   Draw or Review and Revise Purchase and Sale Agreement—Diary Expiration Date

§ 1.42   Property Inspection

§ 1.43   Financing Contingency

§ 1.44   Title Examination
          § 1.44[1]   Have the Title Examined and Abstract Prepared

§ 1.45   Get an Overview of the State of the Title

§ 1.46   **Make a Detailed Analysis of the Report**

§ 1.47   **Report Your Findings to Your Client and Other Interested Parties**

§ 1.48   **Certified Plot Plan**

§ 1.49   **Municipal Lien Certificate**

§ 1.50   **Prepare List of Liens and Encumbrances**

§ 1.51   **Property Insurance Binders**

§ 1.52   **Obtain Payoff Figures and Per Diem From Each Mortgagee**

§ 1.53   **Utility Meters, Fuel Tank and Smoke Detectors**
           § 1.53[1]   **Lead Paint notification to Tenants**

§ 1.54   **Review Proposed Deed and Other Instruments**

§ 1.55   **Title Insurance**

§ 1.56   **Double Check Documents and Do Preliminary Closing Adjustments—Advise Client**

§ 1.57   **Registered Land**

§ 1.58   **Condominiums—Special Problems**

§ 1.59   **The Closing**

PURCHASE AND SALE OF RESIDENTIAL REAL ESTATE
THE LAW

§ 1.01 Preliminary Matters

It seems that nearly every lawyer more than one week out of law school considers himself or herself fully qualified to represent a buyer or seller of residential real estate. Yet these transactions are probably one of the more fertile sources of legal malpractice claims. One reason for this is the cavalier attitude taken by many lawyers toward these "simple" transactions, and the absolute necessity for planning and attention to detail, which they require if they are to be properly handled.

Further, over the past several years, Massachusetts' courts have become more inclined to recognize a duty by attorneys in real estate transactions which extends to non-clients involved in the transaction. Previously, the supreme judicial court had held that a lender's attorney was not liable to a buyer for an erroneous title reference which resulted in no clear title because that attorney had an independent and conflicting duty to his lender client.[1] But more recently, the courts have demonstrated a possible relaxing of this position respecting liability to non-clients. In one such case, an owner who attempted to refinance his home to avoid foreclosure sued the closing attorney for malpractice after the closing attorney, erroneously believing that the closing had not occurred (the parties were in different states), did not discharge the earlier mortgage.[2] The court recognized that an attorney can owe a duty to a non-client but such duty was a question of fact. The court explained that the duty can exist if it is foreseeable they would rely on closing attorney to pay off and record and there is no conflict in the closing attorney duties.

Your first conversation with your client will likely involve a discussion of the fee you will charge. Clients buying or selling single-family residential properties do not expect to pay large fees. Indeed, the downward pressure on fees charged by lawyers in residential real estate transactions has been relentless in recent years. You will be asked to state a flat fee rather than merely quoting a per-hour rate. Therefore you should have an amount in mind that you need to charge to be fairly compensated for the "average" transaction. This amount should be quoted to the client with the caveat that if unusual problem arise in the negotiation of the purchase and sale agreement or the services required leading up to closing, then the fee will be higher. If such problems do arise the client should be notified immediately and should receive an explanation of the problem and the estimated additional fees that it will cause.

The most important general rule to be observed by the lawyer who wishes to

---

[1] Page v. Frazier, 388 Mass. 5, 445 N.E.2d 148 (1983).
[2] Nickerson v. Walsh, 13 Mass. L. Rptr. 2 (2000); Memorandum of Decision on Motion for Summary Judgment.

handle real estate sales efficiently and without error is that everything should be thought out in advance, a diary and checklist system should be used, and everything should be double checked prior to the closing.

§ 1.02   The Purchase and Sale Agreement; Statute of Frauds

Contracts for the sale of real estate must be in writing and must be signed by the party against whom enforcement is sought or by his or her expressly or impliedly authorized agent.[1]

The contract must also describe the property to be conveyed with sufficient particularity that it can be located and distinguished with certainty.[2] Although it is not good practice, in many cases a description of the property by street and number may be sufficient.[3]

However, a casual approach to the matter of describing the property can come back to haunt the parties or their counsel if one party decides it wants out of the contract.[4]

The contract need not contain the time for performance, as the law will imply that a reasonable time was intended.[5]

Normally the purchase price is considered an element, which must be included in the writing in order for the contract to satisfy the Statute of Frauds; but there are certain types of circumstances where the price need not be expressly stated.[6]

Of course, the parties to the contract must be specified with sufficient certainty.[7] Where the property is owned by more than one person all owners must be identified and must sign the agreement.[8]

Part performance of an oral agreement to sell land has been traditionally held to take the agreement out of the Statute of Frauds and make it enforceable.[9] The older cases tended to require a significant part performance of the contract before invoking the rule. But recent cases have shown a tendency on the part of courts

---

[1] G.L. c. 259, § 1; Michelson v. Sherman, 310 Mass. 774, 39 N.E.2d 633, 139 A.L.R. 960 (1942).

[2] Des Brisay v. Foss, 264 Mass. 102, 162 N.E. 4 (1928); Epdee Corp. v Richmond, 321 Mass. 673, 75 N.E.2d 238 (1947).

[3] Epdee Corp. v. Richmond, 321 Mass. 673, 75 N.E.2d 238 (1947).

[4] Foster v. Bartolomeo, 31 Mass. App. 592 (1991); Michelson v. Sherman, 310 Mass. 774 (1942).

[5] Michelson v. Sherman, 310 Mass. 774, 39 N.E.2d 633, 139 A.L.R. 960 (1942).

[6] Shayeb v. Holland, 321 Mass. 429, 73 N.E.2d 731 (1947).

[7] Lewis v. Wood, 153 Mass. 321, 26 N.E. 862 (1891).

[8] Cluff v. Picardi, 331 Mass. 320, 118 N.E.2d 753 (1954).

[9] Andrews v. Charon, 289 Mass. 1, 193 N.E. 737 (1935).

to specifically enforce the contract wherever the buyer changes position in reliance on the oral agreement.[10]

A line of Massachusetts cases also holds that a written contract that satisfies the Statute of Frauds may be modified orally as to the "time and manner of performance."[11]

§ 1.02[1]   Use of Written Offers to Purchase

Although conventional wisdom, and ordinary prudence, militate against the use of written "Offer to Purchase" forms, they continue to be widely employed, particularly by real estate brokers. This is largely because of the desire of both seller and buyer for some kind of formal commitment during the period between the time a deal is struck and a formal Purchase and Sale Agreement can be prepared and signed.

Whether these "offer" forms will themselves be enforced as binding purchase and sale agreements seems to depend on a combination of the language of the offer form and the particular factual circumstances surrounding its use, including the intent of the parties as manifested by their conduct.[12] The most commonly used form, a pre-printed one generated by the Greater Boston Real Estate Board, provides for the execution of a purchase and sale agreement within a specific time, which agreement shall then be the agreement of the parties. It also warns that it creates binding legal obligations. Where the purchase and sale agreement is not in fact signed within the time set out in the Offer these two provisions appear to conflict. The Supreme Judicial Court has held that where the Offer to Purchase contains all the material terms of the agreement, along with a statement that it is binding, it is enforceable. It has further warned that persons who do not intend to be bound by offers to purchase should make this explicitly clear in the text of the offer.[13]

A superior court case has applied this rule to a commercial sale, holding that the offer to purchase was binding since it contained all material terms. The provision referring to a purchase and sale agreement to be executed by a later date was held to be a condition subsequent, the failure to satisfy which would render the contract void. However, where the parties continued to negotiate the purchase and sale

---

[10] Parker v. Page, 270 Mass. 167, 169 N.E. 915 (1930); Fisher v. MacDonald, 332 Mass. 727, 127 N.E.2d 484 (1955); Orlando v Ottaviani, 337 Mass. 157, 148 N.E.2d 373 (1958); Hickey v. Green, 14 Mass. App. 671, 442 N.E.2d 37, *appeal denied*, 388 Mass. 1102, 445 N.E.2d 156 (1982).

[11] McKinley Investments, Inc. v. Middleborough Land, LLC, 62 Mass. App. Ct. 616, 620 (2004), and cases cited.

[12] Germagian v. Berrini, 60 Mass. App. Ct. 456 (2004); Nelsen v. Rebello, 26 Mass. App. 270, 526 N.E.2d 262 (1988), rereported (Mass. App.) 530 N.E.2d 798, *review denied*, 403 Mass. 1103, 529 N.E.2d 1345.

[13] McCarthy v. Tobin, 429 Mass. 84 (1999).

agreement terms beyond the deadline for signing contained in the offer, the condition was held to have been waived.[14]

If contacted early enough, it would be wise for buyer's counsel to include an inspection, sewage disposal and mortgage financing contingency, and a recitation that the purchase and sale agreement shall be mutually acceptable to the parties "after advice of counsel", to the standard form Offer to Purchase. If the purchase is of a condominium unit, a contingency should be added to the offer permitting the prospective buyer adequate time to review the condominium documents, including most importantly the budget, and to withdraw the offer if dissatisfied. If representing the Seller, it is recommend that a provision be added to the offer to purchase as follows:

> "If Seller does not fulfill his obligations under this Offer, Buyer's sole and exclusive remedy against Seller shall be the refund of all deposits paid hereunder plus interest."

§ 1.03   The Purchase Price

Unless the Agreement specifies otherwise the purchase price must be paid in cash at the time of closing. However the use of certified checks or bank treasurers or cashiers checks is the usual method of payment and the Agreement should, and usually does, so provide.[1]

§ 1.03[1]   The Deposit

The standard Greater Boston Real Estate Board form of purchase and sale agreement provides as follows with respect to the disposition of the deposit pending closing:

> "All deposits made hereunder shall be held in escrow by [ ] as escrow agent subject to the terms of this agreement and shall be duly accounted for at the time for performance of this agreement. In the event of any disagreement between the parties, the escrow agent may retain all deposits made under this agreement pending instructions mutually given by the seller and the buyer."

Most commonly the broker holds the deposit, although it is not infrequent for the deposit to be held by seller's attorney, and many seller's attorneys will insist on holding it. The standard form clause is notable for failing to provide where the

---

[14] First General Realty Corp. v. Carpinteri, 13 Mass. L. Rptr. 39 (2001).

[1] Epdee Corp. v. Richmond, 321 Mass. 673, 75 N.E.2d 238 (1947); Minsky v. Zieve, 255 Mass. 542, 152 N.E. 41, 51 A.L.R. 391 (1926).

deposit is to be held, if it is to be in an interest-bearing account and what happens to the interest if it is held in such an account. Where the funds are held by the escrow agent for a short period they are typically not held in interest-bearing accounts. Where the time between signing of the agreement and the closing is more than a three or four weeks the seller's attorney may want to at least raise the issue with his client as to whether the funds should be in an interest-bearing account. This involves substantially more trouble than deposit in an existing escrow or clients' funds account. When bank rates are very low this can all be a non-issue in practice. At any rate the agreement should provide for deposit in an insured account in a Massachusetts financial institution and that any interest will follow the deposit.

The legislature recently amended G.L. c. 184, § 17A to add a paragraph reading:

> "If an individual, firm or corporation holds funds entrusted to him pursuant to a written agreement for the sale of real property and the written agreement expressly authorizes the individual, firm or corporation, as escrow agent, to continue to hold the funds in the event of a dispute between the buyer and seller concerning entitlement to the funds, no claim shall be maintained against the individual, firm or corporation, as escrow agent, whether as trustee, stakeholder or otherwise, if the escrow agent has complied with the mutual written instructions of the buyer and seller, if any, and any order or judgment of a court or final decision of an arbitrator with regard to accounting for or disbursing the funds. In an action commenced with regard to entitlement to such escrowed funds, a party to the action may file a motion seeking an order to have the funds paid into court by the escrow agent. Written notice of the motion shall be given by the moving party to all other parties and to the escrow agent. The escrow agent shall pay the funds into court within ten days of receipt of such order or within such other time as provided by the court."

§ 1.04   The Quality of Title

In the absence of express terms in the Agreement, the law will imply the obligation to convey a "marketable" title. This is a term susceptible to various interpretations, so the well-drafted Agreement will usually contain a provision requiring that a title "good and clear of record," as well as marketable, be conveyed. With the requirement that the title be clear of record the obligation of the seller becomes much less ambiguous.[1]

Defects in title can take various forms. In some cases, a defect may occur when

---

[1] First African M.E. Church v. Brown, 147 Mass. 296, 17 N.E. 549 (1888); Smith v. McMahon, 197 Mass. 16, 83 N.E. 9 (1907); Close v. Martin, 208 Mass. 236, 94 N.E. 388 (1911).

there is a death in the chain of title and the estate needs to be probated. Frequently, a real estate tax lien may have been satisfied but no release recorded. Other problems include zoning issues, such as land conditions which require a variance, the existence of undischarged but paid off mortgages, structures built without a building permit, building encroachments and easements that run through improvements on the property. All such problems must be handled prior to closing. The lender's or buyer's attorney will look to seller's attorney to resolve problems of this type. When they arise the agreement will usually require written notices between the parties. Counsel should be aware of these requirements in the agreement and be sure they are complied with.

Most purchase and sale agreements list exceptions to the seller's obligation to convey clear title. Examples of such exceptions would be easements, restrictions, mortgages to be assumed by the purchaser, betterments assessed after the date of the Agreement, and so on. Unless an encumbrance is listed as an exception in the Agreement, its presence at the time of closing will enable the buyer to avoid the contract.[2]

Sellers will frequently want to include language such as "all easements and restrictions of record insofar as in force and applicable" in the list of exceptions. Buyers should resist this language most strenuously since the title has not yet been examined and there is no way of knowing what encumbrances may be on it. Buyers should require that all encumbrances be listed. If this is not possible then language should be included which will define just which kinds of encumbrances will make the title unacceptable.[3]

§ 1.05   Time for Performance

If the contract does not specify a time for its performance the law will imply a reasonable time.[1] However, it is customary for the contract to provide for a time and to provide that time is of the essence.[2] But it is also customary for closing dates to be extended, and for them to be extended orally in the face of contract language providing that modifications must be in writing. Where this happens a court may hold that the right to require strict adherence to the time for performance provisions has been waived while the remainder of the contract remains binding.[3]

It has also been held that an attorney or other agent may have real or apparent

---

[2] Gossels v. Belluschi, 4 Mass. App. 810, 348 N.E.2d 115 (1976).
[3] Hershorn v. Rubenstein, 259 Mass. 288, 156 N.E. 251 (1927); Siegel v. Shaw, 337 Mass. 170, 148 N.E.2d 393 (1958).
[1] Kattor v. Adams, 323 Mass. 686, 84 N.E.2d 124 (1949).
[2] Porter v. Harrington, 262 Mass. 203, 159 N.E. 530 (1928).
[3] Church of God in Christ, Inc. v. Congregation Kehillath Jacob, 370 Mass. 828, 353 N.E.2d 669 (1976).

authority to grant an oral extension of the time for performance of the contract, even against the wishes of his principal.[4] This problem can be avoided by utilizing written extensions in each instance.

At the time the buyer pays the purchase price and accepts a deed the buyer is entitled to actual possession of the property.[5]

§ 1.06 Risk of Loss

During the time between the signing of the Agreement and the closing the risk of loss remains on the seller. If the property is substantially destroyed during this period then the buyer is excused from performance.[1] But if the damage is found to be less than substantial the buyer may have to complete the contract with appropriate reduction in the price.[2] This problem is usually dealt with in the agreement by giving the buyer the right to require that the premises be delivered at the closing in the same condition they are in at the time of signing of the Agreement.

§ 1.07 Clearing Encumbrances

It is customary for Agreements to contain a clause allowing sellers a short period of time, usually 30 to 90 days, to correct any last minute damage to the premises or to cure any lately discovered title defect. If such a right is not included in the Agreement then the buyer will have a right to avoid the contract if such a contingency should arise and not be cleared up prior to the closing date.

However, the existence of a title defect will not excuse tender of performance by the buyer and allow it to avoid the contract where the failure of tender was due to lack of funds or some other cause unrelated to the defect. That is, the defect cannot be brought in as an afterthought to excuse nonperformance by the buyer.[1] Similarly the title defect clause will not allow the seller to avoid the agreement where the failure to clear encumbrances is the result of his or her inaction, collusion, bad faith or other fault. That is, where the sellers have the ability to clear the encumbrance and simply fail to do so out of a desire to terminate the agreement the courts will enforce the contract.[2]

The common practice at real estate closings is for the seller to apply a part of the purchase price to clear off any mortgages or other liens on the property. Unless the Agreement so provides, he has no right to do this and the existence of the

---

[4] Res Lumber Co. v. Acton Block Company, Inc., 29 Mass. App. 510 (1990).
[5] Barrell v. Britton, 252 Mass. 504, 148 N.E. 134 (1925).
[1] Libman v. Levenson, 236 Mass. 221, 128 N.E. 13 (1920).
[2] Hawkes v. Kehoe, 193 Mass. 419, 79 N.E. 766 (1907).
[1] Karll v. Minot Light, Inc. 30 Mass. App. 166 (1991).
[2] Hastings v. Gay, 55 Mass. App. Ct. 157 (2002).

encumbrances will put the seller in breach of the Agreement.[3] The usual provision gives the seller the right to use the purchase money to clear encumbrances provided the instruments of discharge are recorded simultaneously with the delivery of the deed.

However, in most cases, any mortgage given by the seller which is outstanding at the time of closing will not be cleared of record simultaneously with delivery of the deed. Instead, the conveyancing attorney will obtain a payoff figure from the mortgagee bank as of the estimated closing date along with a so-called per diem amount, to be added for each day after that in the event that the closing is delayed. The amount so calculated is then withheld from the sale proceeds at closing and forwarded immediately to the mortgagee bank, which then returns a discharge for recording.

The effect of all this is that buyers and sellers routinely ignore the provisions of the purchase and sale agreement relating to the clearing of encumbrances. It would appear that, under the usual contract language, the buyer could avoid the agreement whenever the property being sold is not cleared of encumbrances simultaneously with the delivery of the deed; in other words, most of the time. Sellers' attorneys should probably add language to the agreement to reflect more accurately the intentions of the parties in this area, although simply striking the simultaneity provisions of the standard form relating to the clearing of encumbrances may accomplish the same thing in a more rough-hewn way.[4]

The Appeals Court has read into the standard form purchase and sale contract, by implication, the requirement that the buyer have a chance to examine the title right up to the moment of recording and to assure that it is clear, prior to being obliged to hand over the purchase price.[5]

§ 1.07[1] Correcting Defects in Premises

Typically, purchase and sale agreements contain a provision requiring the seller to deliver the premises in the condition they are at the time of signing the agreement, and a provision that allows the seller to extend the closing for a fixed period of time to enable him to correct any deficiencies in the condition of the premises. An interesting tension can arise between these two provisions when in the course of exercising the right to correct a defect in one part of the premises the seller makes significant changes in another part of the premises. The Appeals Court has held that if the premises are "significantly changed or ... materially altered" in the course

---

[3] Greenberg v. Lannigan, 263 Mass. 594, 167 N.E. 882 (1928).

[4] Auclair v. Thomas, 39 Mass. App. 344, 656 N.E.2d 321 (1995). But this solution, while simpler, may create the mirror image problem by leaving the time for clearing encumbrances open ended.

[5] Lee v. Dattilo, 26 Mass. App. 185 (1988).

of correcting a defect then the buyer is justified in refusing to go through with the sale.[6] Buyers' counsel will typically want an escape clause allowing buyer to terminate the agreement if buyer's loan commitment would expire during the extension period, unless the commitment can be extended on substantially the same terms.

§ 1.08   Insurance

Most Agreements require that the property be kept insured between the time the Agreement is signed and the closing. The seller customarily maintains this insurance. Disagreement sometimes arises over the amount of such insurance. Since in the event of serious casualty loss the buyer usually has the option to take title along with an assignment of the insurance proceeds, the buyer will normally want the premises to be insured at market value. The seller on the other hand, particularly in the case of residential real estate, is reluctant to go to the trouble and expense of increasing his or her insurance coverage a few weeks before selling the property. This problem simply has to be worked out between the parties. Although many forms of agreement provide for assignment of insurance on the property from seller to buyer, such assignments are quite rare in residential real estate transactions.

Note however, that unless the buyer is able to close without bank financing the insurance clause will have little practical significance. If there is a serious casualty loss the buyer's lender will not usually agree to lend the amount committed prior to the repair of the property. So even though buyer has the right to take a deed and an assignment of the insurance proceeds he will not typically be able to finance the portion of the purchase price over and above the insurance proceeds. There will often be other practical problems as well if buyer was planning to live in the property right after closing.

§ 1.09   Adjustments

At the closing it is usual to have to make adjustments between the parties with respect to current local property taxes, fuel bills, or oil present in tanks, water, sewer charges, and rents. (In the days of cheap fuel, when fuel adjustments were either insignificant or ignored, one could remember the needed adjustments by the key word WRITS (water, rents, insurance, taxes, sewer).)

Agreements usually provide that these costs be assigned proportionately to buyer and seller as of the closing date. Thus, for example, if the closing is held on January 1, the real estate tax is to be assigned 50% to the seller and 50% to the buyer. Sometimes it is possible to avoid certain utility adjustments by having meters read as of the day before the closing. Where the tax rate has not been set at the time

---

[6] Breuning v. Callahan, 50 Mass. App. Ct. 359, 363 (2000).

of closing adjustment is based on the prior year with a provision for readjustment after the rate is set.

§ 1.10   Closing Costs

Agreements do not normally address the question of who will pay which closing costs. This is of course subject to oral agreement between the parties before or at closing. Customarily, the seller pays the recording fee to discharge any mortgage or other encumbrance on the property as well as the cost of obtaining State Excise Tax Stamps. The buyer pays the recording fee for the deed and for any mortgage he or she is giving on the property and for the municipal lien certificate.

§ 1.11   Broker's Commission

Since 1975,[1] the law in Massachusetts has been that a broker is entitled to a commission only if the property is actually sold to a buyer produced by the broker, such sale being on terms agreed to by the seller. Provided, however, that if the failure of performance by the buyer is caused by the wrongful act of the seller then the broker is entitled to his or her commission nonetheless. Agreements between brokers and other parties which vary these rules will be carefully examined before they are enforced by the courts, the bias being against enforcement. Such agreements must be made with enough specificity to alert the seller to the situations in which she can be liable for a broker's commission even if a sale is not consummated.[2]

Often the seller and broker will enter into an exclusive agency agreement for a period of days, usually between 90 and 180 days. During the exclusive agency period the broker will usually be entitled to a commission if the property is sold to anyone. Such agreements usually provide that a sale after the exclusive period has expired to someone "introduced" to the property by the broker during the exclusive period. What constitutes introduction can and does result in disagreements between sellers and brokers. The Appeals Court has held that a buyer was introduced to property by the broker when the buyer first became aware the property was for sale by seeing the broker's sign posted on it.[3] "To create an exclusive brokerage, ... the parties must expressly and unambiguously indicate such an intent in the contract [citations omitted]."[4] Sellers who enter into exclusive agency

---

[1] Tristram's Landing, Inc. v. Wait, 367 Mass. 622, 327 N.E.2d 727 (1975).

[2] Currier v. Kosinski, 24 Mass. App. Ct.106, 107 (1987).

[3] Upper Cape Realty Corp. v. Morris, 53 Mass. App. Ct. 53 (2001).

[4] Samuel Nichols, Inc. v. Molway, 25 Mass. App. 913, 515 N.E.2d 598 (1987), *review denied*, 401 Mass. 1104, 519 N.E.2d 595. *See also* Upper Cape Realty Corp. v. Morris, 53 Mass. App. Ct. 53, 756 N.E.2d 1193 (2001), *review denied*, 435 Mass. 1109, 762 N.E.2d 324 (2002) (where broker explicitly agreed to make "reasonable effort" to sell property, agreement was bilateral and irrevocable during its term).

agreements should require language in the agreement that obliges the broker to provide a list of the names and addresses of all persons the broker claims to have introduced to the property.

Where the brokerage agreement is nonexclusive, a broker is not entitled to a commission unless "(a) he produces a purchaser ready, willing and able to buy on the terms fixed by the owner, (b) the purchaser enters into a binding contract with the owner ... and (c) the purchaser completes the transaction ..."[5]

There is an exception to this rule where the failure of completion of the contract results from the "wrongful act or interference of the seller."[6] In such cases, the broker is entitled to a commission even though the sale does not go through. However, in order for the broker to take advantage of this exception there must be a written agreement of sale signed by the seller.[7]

The *Capezzuto* and *Hunneman* cases suggest however that the rule requiring a writing may not be applicable where the seller has engaged in "bad faith dealing, or some other misconduct which prevents an agreement between the broker's client and the seller." It is clear from the cases, however, that favoring one broker over another (e.g. Capezzuto), or simply refusing to sign a written agreement when a ready, willing and able buyer is produced (e.g., Hunneman), are not such "bad faith" or "other misconduct."[8] Neither is it such misconduct for the seller to sell to a third party holding a right of first refusal after the broker has produced a ready, willing and able buyer, even if the seller had never told the broker of the existence of the right of first refusal.[9]

A fairly recent Federal case, applying Massachusetts law, held that the broker was entitled to a commission where the sale failed due to an unknown defect in the seller's title.[10]

Where the seller falsely represented that he had releases needed for the consummation of a sale of property and the broker relied on that representation, the failure of the sale based on the seller's failure to produce the releases will not defeat the broker's right to a commission.[11] Two superior court cases have held that

---

[5] Kelley v. Neilson, 433 Mass. 706, 745 N.E.2d 952 (2001).

[6] Tristram's Landing, Inc. v. Wait, 367 Mass. 622, 629, 327 N.E.2d 727 (1975).

[7] Capezzuto v. John Hancock Mut. Life Ins. Co., 394 Mass. 399, 404, 476 N.E.2d 188 (1985); Hunneman & Co. v. Lo Presti, 394 Mass. 406, 409, 476 N.E.2d 191 (1985).

[8] Currier v. Kosinski, 24 Mass. App. 106, 107, 506 N.E.2d 895 (1987).

[9] De Pasquale v. App, 27 Mass. App. 1185, 542 N.E.2d 309 (1989).

[10] Bennett v. McCabe, 808 F.2d 178 (1987, CA1 Mass.). *But see* Hillis v. Lake, 421 Mass. 537, 658 N.E.2d 687 (1995), *specifically disapproving the rule in Bennett v. McCabe,* insofar as it fails to require misconduct by the seller under Massachusetts law.

[11] Discover Realty Corporation v. Stephen T. David, 49 Mass. App. Ct. 535, 731 N.E.2d 79 (2000).

negligence by seller, or other misconduct not amounting to bad faith, that causes the sale to miscarry will not entitle the broker to a commission under the rule in *Hillis v. Lake*.[12] It is common for purchase and sale agreements to be amended to provide that the broker's commission shall not be deemed earned until the full purchase price is paid and a deed is accepted and recorded by buyer.

§ 1.11[1] Seller's Duty to Disclose

As a general rule, a seller only has a duty to disclose defects in property under limited circumstances. Courts have stated that liability may be imposed in cases where the buyer is induced to enter into the transaction because of seller's: (1) false statements; (2) misrepresentation; (3) bad faith. Courts have also considered whether the parties had a fiduciary relationship or whether the seller was in a position of confidence with the potential of abuse. Omission or concealment of a fact does not suffice.[13] In *Greenery*, the court found that it would be unreasonable to require every seller to disclose a nonapparent defect in the property which materially reduces its value and which the buyer failed to discover. Correspondingly, the court stated that no buyer would be liable who fails to disclose any nonapparent virtue known to him about the property which materially enhances its value and of which the seller is ignorant.[14] In explaining its rationale, it stated, "the law has not yet, we believe, reached the point of imposing upon the frailties of human nature a standard so idealistic as this.... . The buyers may have been careless, indifferent, or merely overeager to close the deal during the negotiating process, but any such manifestation of lack of business acumen does not entitle them to seek relief through the judicial process."[15] However, the courts have recognized that if a buyer asks the seller about the condition of something in the property, the seller has a duty to disclose fully the extent of his or her knowledge. A statement by seller that is clearly an expression of his opinion or belief that turns out to be false is not actionable, where the same statement made as one of definite fact may be.[16] For example, the Appeals Court has upheld the recission of a sale when the buyer relied upon a seller's alleged engineering estimates as to the cost of repairing a septic system and such estimate fell significantly short.[17] However when a dispute arises after the fact it can be difficult to sort out expressions of opinion from statements of fact.

---

[12] Real Advantage v. Hood, 12 Mass. L. Rptr. 70 (2000).

[13] Greenery Rehabilitation Group v. Antaramian, 36 Mass. App. Ct. 73 (1994); Province Securities Corp. v. Maryland Casualty Corp., 269 Mass. 75 (1929); Underwood v. Risman, 414 Mass. 96, 100 (1993).

[14] *See* Goodwin v. Agassiz, 283 Mass. 358 (1933).

[15] Greenery Rehabilitation Group v. Antaramian, 36 Mass. App. Ct. 73, 80 (1994).

[16] Moran v. Levin, 318 Mass. 770 (1945); Snyder v. Sperry and Hutchinson Co., 332 Mass. 368 (1955).

[17] Zimmerman v. Kent, 31 Mass. App. Ct. 72, 77 (1991).

§ 1.12 Remedies on Default

In the absence of contractual provisions, both the seller and the buyer have the right to bring suit for specific performance or for damages in the event of default.[1]

The measure of damages is the difference between the fair market value and the contract price as of the date of default.[2] Where the buyer elects to take an encumbered or defective title the measure of damages in proper cases is the amount necessary to clear the title.[3]

Note however that this manner of fixing damages is the usual rule, but not the invariable rule. Where application of this rule will place the wronged party in a better position at the conclusion of the lawsuit than if the contract had been consummated the usual rule will not be applied. Instead the court may apply a different measure of damages more consistent with the dominant principle of making the wronged party whole.[4]

However, the foregoing common law rules respecting damages are almost invariably modified by the Agreement. Seller's attorney will often seek a provision requiring that the buyer's remedies upon seller's default be limited to a return of the deposit. Similarly, buyer's attorney will nearly always require a provision that forfeiture of the deposit shall be the seller's sole and exclusive remedy for buyer's default.[5]

Liquidated damages provisions, such as forfeiture of the deposit are always subject to attack on the ground that they constitute a penalty. For many years there was some ambiguity as to the proper methodology to be employed by a reviewing court in determining whether or not a liquidated damages provision should be enforced in any particular case. The Appeals Court, beginning in 1989, adhered to the so-called "second look" doctrine. Under this doctrine the court examined both the circumstances at the time of contract formation, and the actual damages suffered by the plaintiff when the breach occurred, to determine whether the liquidated damages clause was an unenforceable penalty.[6] The second look doctrine has now been firmly rejected by the Supreme Judicial Court. A liquidated

---

[1] Olszewski v. Sardynski, 316 Mass. 715, 56 N.E.2d 607 (1944); Noyes v. Bragg, 220 Mass. 106, 107 N.E. 669 (1915); Kelley v. Neilson, 433 Mass. 706, 745 N.E.2d 952 (2001) (G.L. c. 204, § 1 authorizes judge, at request of buyer to order specific performance of purchase and sale agreement entered into by a person before death; statute extends time for performance beyond death of testatrix in accordance with terms of purchase and sale agreement).

[2] Widebeck v. Sullivan, 327 Mass. 429, 99 N.E.2d 165 (1951).

[3] Boyden v. Hill, 198 Mass. 477, 85 N.E. 413 (1908).

[4] Foster v. Bartolomeo, 31 Mass. App. 592 (1991).

[5] Old Colony Trust Co. v. Chauncey, 214 Mass. 271, 101 N.E. 423 (1913); Rigs v. Sokol, 318 Mass. 337, 61 N.E.2d 538 (1945).

[6] Shapiro v. Grinspoon, 27 Mass. App. 825 (1989).

damages clause in a purchase and sale agreement will be enforced where, at the time the agreement was made, potential damages were difficult to determine and the clause was a reasonable forecast of damages expected to occur in the event of a breach.[7]

§ 1.13 Disclaimers

Many purchase and sale agreements contain a clause expressly disclaiming any warranties or representations, by the seller and/or the broker, which are not contained in the Agreement. Since the passage of the Massachusetts Consumer Protection Act (G.L. c. 93A) it has also become common for brokers to attach a standard clause to the Agreement which recites that the buyer has had an opportunity to inspect the premises and is not relying on any representations except those set out in the clause. Usually the word "none" is inserted after the clause. It is never certain how well these disclaimers will stand up in court.

It is clear that often conduct which makes out a common law action of misrepresentation will not be obviated by a disclaimer clause, because the wronged party may sue to have the contract, including the disclaimer, rescinded in its entirety.[1] Nevertheless, courts have turned aside suits seeking such equitable remedies and given effect to the disclaimer where the clause itself was the product of "deliberate, uncoerced and businesslike negotiations" between the parties.[2]

§ 1.14 Smoke Detectors

Any building used for residential purposes, in whole or in part, must, upon its sale or transfer be equipped with smoke detectors. Such detectors must be present on every floor, including the basement.[1] It is the seller's responsibility to insure that this statutory requirement is complied with, and he or she must produce at closing a certificate of compliance from the local fire department. Most purchase and sale agreements now contain a provision setting out the seller's obligations in this regard.

§ 1.15 Lead Paint Disclosures

Under the Massachusetts Lead Paint Law,[1] prospective purchasers of residential properties built before 1978 must be notified about the hazards of lead in paint,

---

[7] Kelly v. Marx, 428 Mass. 877 (1999).

[1] Zimmerman v. Kent, 31 Mass. App. 72 (1991). *See however* Sound Techniques v. Hoffman, 50 Mass. App. 425 (2000) (holding that a disclaimer clause will avoid liability for negligent, as opposed to intentional, misrepresentation).

[2] Cone v. Ellis, 59 Mass. App. Ct. 748 (2003).

[1] G.L. c. 148, § 26F.

[1] G.L. c. 111, § 197A.

plaster, soil or other material in residential premises and the requirements for their removal or covering. This notification consists primarily of forms and other materials prepared by the director of the childhood lead poisoning prevention program which are designed to inform prospective purchasers about the possible presence of lead, the symptoms and treatment of lead poisoning, and the requirements of the lead paint law and the regulations issued thereunder.[2]

Prior to the signing of a purchase and sale agreement, the seller must provide a copy of the materials prepared by the director to the prospective purchaser. The seller and any broker involved in the sale must also each disclose to the prospective purchaser any information known to them about the presence of lead in the premises. At the time of making such disclosure the seller must provide the purchaser with any letter of interim control or letter of compliance under G.L. c. 111, § 197 which applies to the premises.

Further, the seller and broker must also inform the prospective purchaser about the availability of inspections for dangerous levels of lead. If, after receiving such notice the purchaser chooses to have an inspection done, the seller must agree to allow the purchaser at least ten days to have the inspection performed, either through a contingency clause in the agreement or otherwise.

Finally, where the information and materials described above have been provided to the prospective purchaser by the real estate broker, he or she must also verbally inform the purchaser about the possible presence of dangerous levels of lead and the provisions of the lead paint law and regulations.

The broker must obtain, either at the time of making the required disclosures, or at least prior to the signing of the purchase and sale agreement, a certification from the prospective purchaser that he or she has received the required disclosures.[3] The foregoing requirements also apply to persons leasing premises with an option to purchase. Purchasers of residential rental properties should:

- determine if the tenants have received the required notices under the Lead Paint Law,
- obtain the Tenant Certification Form for each existing tenant who will remain after the purchase, and
- notify those who have not received the proper notification.

Where a rental portion of the property is vacant the tenant notification requirements of the Lead Paint Law and its regulations will apply as and when the premises are rented by the new owner.[4]

---

[2] *See* Volume 6, Appendix D for material issued by the director.
[3] *Id. See generally* Samuels v. Brooks, 25 Mass. App. 421, 519 N.E.2d 605 (1988).
[4] 105 CMR 460.725.

§ 1.16   Contingency Clauses

It is not uncommon for Agreements to be made contingent upon the fulfillment of some condition, for example the obtaining of financing by the buyer, or the sale of buyer's house, or the obtaining of some local regulatory approval. Such provisions are frequent sources of litigation and it is in the interest of all parties that they be written as explicitly as possible.[1]

Much of the litigation has turned on the question of whether there is an affirmative obligation on the seller to bring about or help bring about the contingency, and, if so, how much effort on his part is enough. Two relatively recent Appeals Court cases have reviewed and discussed the case law on these points and are recommended reading for lawyers advising clients about to enter into agreements containing such clauses.[2]

If the buyer wishes to use the failure of a contingency as a reason for refusing to close on the property, he or she must comply scrupulously with the terms of the contingency clause.[3]

§ 1.17   Common Contingency Clauses

§ 1.17[1]   The Financing Contingency

A mortgage financing contingency is found in most purchase and sale agreements, especially those relating to single-family homes. They typically provide that the buyer's duty to close is contingent upon obtaining financing in a specified minimum amount at a specified maximum interest rate on or before a specified date. The buyer is required to notify the seller if he or she has been unable to obtain financing. Such notice usually must be in writing and be given no later than a date set out in the contract. If the notice is not timely given then the financing contingency expires and the agreement is binding without reference to the buyer's ability to obtain a mortgage. The Appeals Court has described the mortgage financing contingency "as containing two conditions, one relating to the terms of the mortgage and the other relating to the time for obtaining the mortgage commitment."[1] The first condition is for the benefit of the buyer and the second for the benefit of the seller.

§ 1.17[2]   Contingencies Relating to Condition of the Premises

Most Offers to Purchase contain inspection contingencies that allow the pro-

---

[1] Livoli v. Stoneman, 332 Mass. 473, 125 N.E.2d 785 (1955); Stabile v. McCarthy, 336 Mass. 399, 145 N.E.2d 821 (1957); Russo v. Enterprise Realty Co., 347 Mass. 655, 199 N.E.2d 689 (1964).

[2] McCarthy v. Mills, 26 Mass. App. 223 (1988); Durkin v. Ferreira, 21 Mass. App. 771, 490 N.E.2d 498 (1986), *review denied*, 397 Mass. 1104, 494 N.E.2d 388 (1986).

[3] Churgin v. Hobbie, 39 Mass. App. Ct. 302 (1995).

[1] Bossi v. Whalen, 19 Mass. App. Ct. 966 (1985).

spective purchaser a limited period of time, usually 10 days, to have the property inspected to ascertain that it is structurally and mechanically sound, free of mold or other evidence of water intrusion, free of wood-destroying pests and free of lead-based paint or other unhealthful contaminants. Where the property is not served by a public sewer there is also a provision for a septic system inspection. And, in the relatively infrequent case where the property is served by an on-site drinking water well there should be a provision for a water quality analysis and pressure test. These inspections are usually on the basis that any deficiencies which, in the purchaser's sole discretion are unsatisfactory, are grounds to terminate the transaction. It is usually most economical and sensible for all concerned for these inspections to be done before the trouble and expense of preparing a purchase and sale agreement is undertaken. However, if such inspections have not occurred prior to preparation of the agreement, then the appropriate contingency language should be added to that agreement. Where the inspection reveals significant problems the buyer will often ask for price concessions. The seller may respond by offering repairs. The latter course is very liable to cause problems for both parties, because seller will want to have the repair done as quickly and cheaply as possible, while buyer will be very interested in quality and thoroughness. Inspection should always occur as early in the transaction as is feasible so that problems that threaten the viability of the transaction are discovered early.

It is customary, either by terms of the Agreement or by custom, for there to be a "walk-through" of the premises by the buyers just prior to closing to verify that all contingencies have been satisfied and that there has been no significant decline in the condition of the premises between the time of initial inspections and the closing.

§ 1.17[3]   On Site Septic System Inspections (Title V)

Since the adoption of the so-called "new" Title V by the State Department of Environmental Protection, the inspection of the septic system has become a very important part of most real estate transactions in unsewered areas. Under the current regulations, when title to a residential property served by an on site septic system is to be transferred that system must be inspected at, or within two years prior to, the transfer of title. There are certain limited exceptions to this general rule:

- If the system has been inspected up to three years prior to the transfer of title and the inspection report is accompanied by system pumping records demonstrating that the system has been pumped at least once a year during the intervening period, no further inspection will be required.

- If the system must be inspected at the time of transfer and weather conditions preclude such inspection, the inspection may be completed as soon as weather permits, but no later than six months after the transfer of title, provided the seller notifies the buyer in writing of the inspection and upgrade requirements contained in Title 5 of the State Environmental Code (310 CMR 15.300 through 15.305).

- Transfers of title which merely change the form of ownership among the same owners, intra-family transactions and financing transactions such as the granting of security interests do not invoke the inspection requirement.

- The appropriate authority has issued a certificate of compliance for the system within two years prior to the transfer of title.

- The seller or buyer has signed an enforceable agreement with the appropriate authority to upgrade the system or connect the system to a public or private treatment works or shared septic system within two years following transfer of title. Where the seller has signed such an agreement it must be disclosed to, and enforceable against, the buyer.

- The property is subject to a comprehensive local plan of on-site septic system inspection approved in writing by the Department of Environmental Protection and administered by a local or regional governmental entity, and the system has been inspected at the most recent time required by the plan.

Where the system fails the inspection, it is common for lenders to require escrows of up to 150% of the estimated cost of bringing the system into compliance if the repairs are not to be completed prior to closing. A detailed discussion of Title 5 upgrade requirements and procedures is contained in Sec. 1.22.

§ 1.17[4]   Mortgage Plot Plans

It is common for purchase and sale agreements to provide that the premises will not be deemed to comply with the title provisions unless all buildings and appurtenances and accessories thereto are contained entirely within the lot lines and do not violate building and/or zoning laws. The primary way that compliance with these types of provisions is ensured is by means of the mortgage plot plans. These are plans that are routinely required by lenders, and should be routinely required by cash buyers. They are prepared by registered land surveyors using rough estimation techniques rather than instrument surveys. Typically the surveyor examines an existing deed and/or plan of the lot, locates two or more boundaries or monuments, then uses a tape measure to estimate the distance of any structures from the various lot lines. The fee for such plans is quite modest and they are certainly worth the money as long as persons using them realize their limitations.

§ 1.18   Merger by Acceptance

The traditional common law rule has been that upon acceptance of a deed by the buyer, pursuant to a purchase and sale agreement, the agreement merges into the deed and the deed is deemed to be the final contract between the parties, except where the Agreement provides that certain provisions will survive delivery of the deed.[1]

Many purchase and sale agreements attempt to specifically incorporate the traditional rule by including provisions like the following: "The acceptance of a deed by the Buyer or his nominee as the case may be shall be deemed to be a full performance and discharge of every agreement and obligation herein contained or expressed except such as are, by the terms hereof, to be performed after delivery of said deed." This type of clause has generally been given effect by the courts only with respect to title matters. Indeed, the more correct modern formulation of the traditional rule is that promises which are collateral or additional to the delivery of title, and which are not inconsistent with the deed as given, survive delivery of the deed even in the face of a clause such as the above.[2]

The doctrine of merger by acceptance also does not apply to defects in a building on the premises where the seller contracts to construct a building on the premises by a collateral contract with the buyer. Thus the usual contract and tort rights of the buyer arising out of the collateral construction agreement are not swallowed up by the merger doctrine upon deliver of the deed.[3] Further, the Supreme Judicial Court has now held that an implied warranty of habitability attaches to the sale of a new home by a builder-vendor, which warranty cannot be waived.[4]

§ 1.19   Deed Drafting

There are two forms of deeds in common use today in Massachusetts, the quitclaim deed which is prevalent in the eastern part of the state, and the warranty deed, which is prevalent in the western part of the state. Except in certain special situations, such as deeds from fiduciaries, one of these two forms will invariably be used.

The statutory short forms of both quitclaim and warranty deeds, which appear in the Massachusetts General Laws, eliminate the need for the extensive recitations found in older deeds.[1]

The words "warranty covenants" when used in a deed constitute a promise on the part of the grantor that at the time of delivery of the deed the grantor was the fee simple owner of the premises, the premises were free from all encumbrances, that the grantor had a right to convey the premises, and that the grantor and the

---

[1] Pybus v. Grasso, 317 Mass. 716, 59 N.E.2d 289 (1945); Fanger v. Leeder, 327 Mass. 501, 99 N.E.2d 533 (1951); Gainsboro v. Shaffer, 339 Mass. 1, 157 N.E.2d 536 (1959); Schrank v. County Sav. Bank, 298 Mass. 30, 9 N.E.2d 559 (1937).

[2] Pedersen v. Leahy, 397 Mass. 689, 493 N.E.2d 486 (1986).

[3] Solomon v. Birger, 19 Mass. App. Ct. 634, 642 (1985).

[4] Albrecht v. Clifford, 436 Mass. 706 (2002).

[1] G.L. c. 183, § 8-28 and Appendix.

grantor's heirs will defend the title against all persons claiming against the right of the grantee or the grantee's assigns.[2]

The words "quitclaim covenants" when used in a deed constitute a promise on the part of the grantor that the premises are free from all encumbrances made by the grantor and that the grantor and the grantor's heirs will defend the title against all persons claiming by, through, or under the grantor, but against no others.[3]

On occasion, a deed is used which contains no covenants at all. These are normally used only in specialized situations such as sales by fiduciaries, by foreclosing mortgagees, by sheriffs on execution, and, where a minor, questionable or contingent interest is being surrendered.[4]

Deeds from corporations should recite that the corporation is duly organized and existing under the laws of a particular jurisdiction and give the location of its usual place of business. The deed should be accompanied by a certificate of corporate vote authorizing the conveyance or should be signed by both the president or a vice president and the treasurer or an assistant treasurer.[5]

Some conveyancers require that a deed from a corporation state that the land conveyed is not all or substantially all of the assets of the corporation, since such a conveyance would require a waiver of the Commonwealth's lien for corporate excise taxes.[6] Conservative practice would be to obtain the waiver wherever there is a doubt as to whether the conveyance constitutes all or substantially all of the assets of the grantor corporation. However, delays in obtaining such waivers from the Department of Revenue often make this impracticable.

Massachusetts has authorized the creation of limited liability companies[7] which may largely supplant the use of small, closely held business corporations. The authorizing statute provides in detail for the execution of deeds and other conveyances of real estate. The deed from such a company should be signed by a person identified on the certificate of organization of a domestic company, or on the application for registration of a foreign company, as a manager or as a person authorized to execute, acknowledge, deliver and record instruments affecting the company's interest in real property. The statute further provides that any person identified on the certificate of organization or application for registration as a manager, or person authorized to execute documents to be filed with the office of the secretary of state, may certify as to the incumbency or authority of any person,

---

[2] G.L. c. 183, § 10, 16.

[3] G.L. c. 183, § 11, 17.

[4] See G.L. c. 183, Appendix.

[5] G.L. c. 156B, § 115.

[6] See G.L. c. 62C, § 51.

[7] G.L. c. 156C; see §§ 66 through 68 in particular.

whether or not that person is identified on the certificate of organization. This certificate should follow roughly the form of a corporate vote, and would only seem to have any practical utility where the signing manager is not identified in the certificate of organization or application for registration. It may be expected that counsel for lenders and buyers will want a certificate from the Secretary of State certifying to the existence of the limited liability company and the authority of the officers of the company signing any documents intended to be recorded.

In the case of residential real estate, the grantee(s) will usually take in fee simple under a single name, or as trustee under a trust, or if married as tenants by the entirety. Occasionally the grantee(s) will wish to take as joint tenants or tenants in common. The tenancy by the entirety usually makes the most sense for married people since it provides maximum protection against creditors and allows for automatic descent to the surviving spouse without the necessity of probate. Attorneys representing buyers will want to explain the attributes of the various forms of tenancy to their clients.[8]

§ 1.20 Registered Land: Special Considerations

Registered land is land that has been made the subject of proceedings in the Land Court pursuant to G.L. c. 185.[1] The effect of these proceedings is that the plaintiff obtains a Certificate of Title which is in effect a judgment of the court that he or she holds title to the land described in the certificate subject only to the encumbrances recited in the certificate and to the following possible encumbrances:

- Liens, claims or rights arising or existing under the laws or constitutions of the United States or of Massachusetts which are not by law required to appear of record in the registry of deeds in order to be valid against subsequent purchasers or encumbrances of record.

- Taxes, within two years after they have been committed to the collector.

- Any highway, town way, or any private way laid out under G.L. c. 82, § 21, if the certificate of title does not state that the boundary of such a way has been determined.

- Any lease for a term not exceeding seven years.

- Any liability to assessment for betterments or other statutory liability, except for taxes payable to the Commonwealth, which attaches to land as a lien.

- Liens in favor of the United States for unpaid taxes arising or existing under the Internal Revenue Code.[2]

---

[8] For discussion of attributes of various tenancies, *see* Moynihan, *Introduction to the Law of Real Property* (1962) and *Tenancy by the Entirety in Massachusetts*, 59 Mass. L.Q. 53 (1974).

[1] Note the amendment to G.L. c. 185, § 52, effective April 12, 2001.

[2] G.L. c. 185, § 46. Note that registered land may have appurtenant rights that are not

With the exception of the foregoing the judgment of registration is conclusive on all parties and quiets title. The judgment may not be reopened except on complaint of a person alleging he was deprived of land by fraud. This kind of complaint is required by statute to be brought within one year of the entry of the judgment of registration.[3] However this area has been clouded by recent decisions holding that even after a year a complaint to impose a constructive trust on the property may be brought based on a claim of fraud even where there is no fraudulent intent on the part of the person procuring the registration.[4] The intervention of a good faith purchaser for value will cut off the right to bring this type of complaint.

Once title to land has been registered no interest therein can be acquired by prescription or adverse possession, nor can an easement by implication or necessity arise on the conveyance of registered land.[5]

As a practical matter registered land can be sold, mortgaged, leased, and so on, in the same manner as unregistered land. Technically speaking the change in ownership in the land does not occur on delivery of the instrument but upon registration of the same by the Land Court Recorder. Prior to registration the deed, mortgage, or other instruments is considered only a contract between the parties giving the Assistant Recorder authority to make the registration.[6]

Each piece of registered land is evidenced by a title certificate held by the Assistant Recorder. When the property is conveyed the deed is presented to the Assistant Recorder who makes out a new certificate of title in the name of the new owner and inserts it in the books kept at the appropriate registry of deeds. The old certificate is then marked canceled. The deed is also kept by the Assistant Recorder, marked with the number of the new certificate of title. (The old method of issuing, and requiring the surrender of owners' duplicate certificates of title has been discontinued).[7]

§ 1.21   Condominiums: Special Considerations

A condominium is a creature of statute in Massachusetts, and is created when the owner or owners of land execute and record a master deed containing a statement to the effect that they intend to create a condominium to be governed by and subject to the provisions of G.L. c. 183A.[1]

---

themselves registered. Registration will not extinguish these rights.

[3] G.L. c. 185, § 45; Wareham Sav. Bank v. Partridge, 317 Mass. 83, 56 N.E.2d 867 (1944).

[4] State Street Bank & Trust Co. v. Beale, 353 Mass. 103, 227 N.E.2d 924 (1967); Kozdras v. Land/Vest Properties, Inc., 1980 Adv. Sheets 2409, 413 N.E.2d 1105 (Mass. 1980).

[5] G.L. c. 185, § 53.

[6] G.L. c. 185, § 57.

[7] G.L. c. 185, § 64.

[1] G.L. c. 183A, § 2.

Once the condominium is created each unit thereof together with its undivided interest in the common areas and facilities is treated as a separate parcel of real estate with respect to sale, lease and other incidents of ownership. Except:

- no unit may be used for a purpose prohibited in the master deed;
- the unit owners' organization and its agents shall have the right of access to each unit for maintenance, repair and replacement of common facilities and for emergency repairs in the unit itself necessary to prevent damage to common facilities; and
- the unit owner must comply with the bylaws, rules and regulations of the condominium and with the covenants and restrictions contained in the master deed or the deed to his or her unit.[2]

Each unit owner has an undivided interest in the common areas in the percentage set forth in the master deed. This percentage must approximate the relation between the value of the unit and the aggregate value of all units as of the date of the master deed. The percentage of each unit owner in the common areas and facilities, as expressed in the master deed, may not be altered without the consent of all unit owners whose percentage of the undivided interest is affected, expressed in an amended master deed duly recorded. This should be taken to require affected owners to sign the amended master deed.[3] The interest in the common areas may not be separated from the unit to which it is appurtenant and is deemed to have been conveyed or encumbered along with the unit whether or not it is expressly mentioned in the relevant instrument.[4]

The common areas and facilities remain undivided and equally available to use by all owners subject to the bylaws, rules, and regulations. However, Master Deeds or bylaws can and often do create exclusive use rights in parking, storage or other common areas on the part of specific units. The rights of the unit owners respecting maintenance, repair, and replacement of common areas and facilities are defined in the bylaws of the organization.[5]

§ 1.21[1]   Condominiums: Liens for Common Charges

The statute provides for a lien upon each unit for its proportionate share of the common expenses, which lien has priority over all other liens except municipal liens and recorded first mortgages. The lien also attaches with respect to fees, attorneys' fees, charges, late charges fines, costs of collection and enforcement, court costs, interest, and expenses incurred by the unit owners' organization as a result of the unit owner's failure to abide by the terms of the condominium law

---

[2] G.L. c. 183A, §§ 3, 4.
[3] Kaplan v. Boudreaux, 410 Mass. 435 (1991).
[4] G.L. c. 183A, § 5.
[5] G.L. c. 183A, § 5.

or condominium documents. If certain procedures set out in the statute are followed, the lien takes precedence over prior first mortgages to the extent of common expense assessments made during the six months immediately preceding the institution of a suit to enforce the lien, and to the extent of any costs and reasonable attorneys' fees incurred in such enforcement action. Because the language of the statute as first enacted effectively required the unit owners' organization to institute suit in order to fix its super-priority lien as against a first mortgagee, such mortgagees complained that unnecessary litigation costs were generated, which they were then required to pay. As a result, the statute was amended in 1998 to provide a procedure whereby first mortgagees could avoid these costs.

The amended lien statute provides as follows. After receipt of a notice of delinquency, the first mortgagee agrees in writing that a priority lien exists without the requirement of suit, and pays within 60 days of that agreement the following amounts:

- any delinquent assessments of common expenses applicable to the six months immediately preceding the notice by the unit owners' organization to the mortgagee to the extent such amounts would have had priority over the mortgage if suit had been commenced on the date of the notice; and
- costs and reasonable attorney's fees incurred by the organization in attempting to collect the delinquent amounts, prior to receiving the mortgagee's written acknowledgment of the lien.

The first mortgagee also agrees to pay within 30 days of their due date all future assessments of common expenses and special assessments assessed against the unit, except assessments for capital improvements to the common areas under G.L. c. 183A. The first mortgagee is not required to pay any amounts attributable to late charges, fines, penalties or interest assessed by the organization against the unit. The mortgagee's obligation under its agreement ends when it assigns or forecloses the mortgage, or it otherwise ceases to encumber the unit. A successful bidder at foreclosure takes subject to the agreement of the mortgagee with respect to all amounts coming due prior to the foreclosure. Other successors in interest take subject to the agreement for all amounts due until the mortgage is foreclosed or no longer encumbers the unit. The mechanics of the process are as follows:

(1) Within 10 days of receipt of a written request from the first mortgagee, the organization must provide the mortgagee with a detailed written statement of the amounts it must pay to avoid the commencement of suit.

(2) The mortgagee then has 14 days following mailing of the statement of amounts due to enter into the written payment agreement described above.

(3) Once it has received the mortgagee's written request, the organization may not file suit to enforce its lien for a period of 24 days from receipt

of the request or 14 days following the mailing of the statement of amounts due, whichever is less.

(4) If the organization fails to send the statement of amounts due to the first mortgagee, it loses its super priority lien for attorneys' fees and costs of collection when it brings suit.[6]

The statute also provides for the issuance of a statement of unpaid common expenses by the owners' organization relative to each unit owner. When such a statement is recorded it operates to discharge the owner's unit from any lien for sums which are not shown on the statement. The statement is required to be furnished within ten business days after a written request and is binding on the unit owner and the unit owners' organization.[7]

§ 1.21[2]   Condominiums: Unit Deeds

Specific requirements as to the contents of both master deed and deeds of units are laid out by G.L. c. 183A.[8] Unit deeds must contain:

- Reference to the fact that deed relates to a condominium subject to G.L. c. 183A;
- A description of the land or its post office address, and the book, page, and date of recording of the master deed;
- The unit designation of the unit in the master deed and any other data necessary for its identification;
- A statement of the use for which the unit is intended and the restrictions on its use;
- The percentage undivided interest in the common areas and facilities; and
- In the case of the first deed of a unit, a certified plan showing the unit in the form described in G.L. c. 183A, § 9.

§ 1.21[3]   Condominiums: Master Deed

Master Deeds must contain:

- a statement that the owner(s) of the land proposes to create a condominium to be governed by and subject to the provisions of G.L. c. 183A;
- a description of the land on which the buildings and/or improvements is located;
- a description of each building stating: the number of stories, the number

---

[6] G.L. c. 183A, § 6.
[7] G.L. c. 183A, § 6.
[8] G.L. c. 183A, §§ 8, 9.

of units, the principal material of which constructed;

- the unit designation of each unit, and a statement of its location, approximate area, number of rooms, the immediate common area to which it has access, and any other data necessary for proper identification of the unit;
- a description of the common areas and facilities and the proportionate interest of each unit therein;
- an as-built floor plan of the entire condominium, certified by a registered architect, professional engineer, or land surveyor;
- a statement of the purpose for which the building and each of the units are intended and any restrictions as to their use;
- the method by which the master deed may be amended; and
- the names and mailing address of the unit owners' organization, together with a statement that the organization has adopted bylaws pursuant to G.L. c. 183A. If the organization is not a corporation, the deed must contain the names of the trustees or managing board.[9]

§ 1.21[4]   Condominiums: Management

The common areas and facilities of a condominium are controlled and managed by the unit owners' organization. This organization may be either a corporation, a trust, or an unincorporated association. Each unit owner has an interest in the organization equal to his percentage interest in the common areas and facilities, as set forth in the master deed. The statute gives the owners' organization fairly broad powers to deal with the common facilities and to manage the affairs of the condominiums as a whole, and it requires that the organization keep proper financial and other records, which records shall be available for inspection and photocopying by the unit owners.[10]

Unit owners' organizations are required by law to adopt bylaws which provide for at least the following:

- The method of providing for the necessary work of maintenance, repair and replacement of the common areas and facilities and payments therefor, including the method of approving payment vouchers.
- The manner of collecting from the unit owners their share of the common expenses.
- The procedure for hiring all personnel, including whether or not a manager or managing agent may be engaged.
- The method of adopting and of amending administrative rules and regu-

---

[9] G.L. c. 183A, § 8.
[10] G.L. c. 183A, § 10.

lations governing the details of the operation and use of the common areas
and facilities.

- Such restrictions on and requirements respecting the use and maintenance
  of the units and the use of the common areas and facilities, not set forth
  in the master deed, as are designed to prevent unreasonable interference
  with the use of their respective units and of the common areas and facilities
  by the several units owners.

In addition, the bylaws may contain such other lawful provisions as are deemed
necessary for the proper management of the organization.[11] One such optional
bylaw provisions often adopted provides for a 30 day right of first refusal on behalf
of the organization with respect to the sale of any unit.

A condominium unit and its appurtenant percentage interest in the common areas
and facilities is taxed as a single unit by the municipality. The real estate tax is billed
to the owner but, except as provided by G.L. c. 111, § 127B 1/2, water, sewer, and
like municipal charges may be billed to the unit owners organization, although any
lien associated with such charges will attach proportionately to each unit. The use
of the word "may" suggests that the statute is permissive and that municipalities
can also meter and bill unit owners directly for water actually used by that unit.[12]
Where a septic system that is part of the common facilities of a residential
condominium needs repair, replacement or upgrade, the unit owners' organization
may petition the municipal board of health to enter into a betterment agreement
to finance the needed improvements. A notice of such agreement is then recorded
in the registry of deeds and becomes a lien only upon the units identified in the
notice as being benefited by the repairs. The amount of the lien on each benefited
unit is prorated based on the percentage interest of that unit in the common areas
and facilities.

If more than fifty percent but less than seventy five percent of the unit owners
agree to make improvements to the common facilities then only the persons so
agreeing may be assessed the cost of such improvements. Where more than seventy
five percent of the owners agree to the improvement then the cost is assessed to
all owners. However if the improvement costs more than 10 percent of the then
value of the condominium, any owner who dissents may petition the court for an
order requiring the owners' organization to buy his or her unit at fair market value.[13]

---

[11] G.L. c. 183A, §§ 11, 12.

[12] G.L. c. 183A, § 14.

[13] G.L. c. 183A, § 18.

THE PRACTICE

§ 1.22   Title 5—State Environmental Code—Detailed Outline of Inspection and Upgrade Requirements

INSPECTIONS

I. What Systems Must Be Aligned

All existing on-site septic systems which are governed by the provisions of Title 5 of the State Environmental Code (310 CMR 15.00 et seq.), that is those whose design flows (310 CMR 15.203) are less than 15,000 gallons per day, are subject to the inspection requirements of the code.

II. When Must They Be Inspected

1. Subject to certain very limited exceptions, (which are discussed below), when title to a property served by an on site septic system is to be transferred that system must be inspected at, or within two years prior to, the transfer of title. 310 CMR 15.301(1).

2. A system must also be inspected upon any change in use or expansion of use of the property served, for which change or expansion a building permit or occupancy permit from the local building inspector is required.

3. Properties where the total design flow generated at full build out equals or exceeds 10,000 gallons per day must be inspected according to a schedule contained in the code, which schedule is based on the geographical location of the system. After the initial inspection, such systems must be inspected every five years. 310 CMR 15.301(6).

4. A system serving more than one property, or more than one dwelling on the same property, (shared system) must be inspected annually.

5. Where properties with existing systems are either divided or combined, all systems serving the property or properties must be inspected.

6. Systems serving condominiums consisting of five or more units must be inspected at least once every three years, with all existing systems having been initially inspected by December 1, 1996. (If the system has a design flow of at least 10,000 gallons per day the deadlines in paragraph 3, above, will apply instead). Where the condominium consists of fewer than five units, it may defer inspections until the time of title transfer of each unit, at which time the system serving that unit must be inspected.

7. Regardless of whether or not any other inspection requirement in the code is applicable, a system must be inspected when such inspection is ordered by

the Board of Health, the DEP or a court.[1]

III. Who Must Have The Inspection Done

The persons owning or having charge or control of the property served by the system are responsible for having the required inspections done. 310 CMR 15.300(4).

In the case of condominiums, the condominium association is responsible for inspections, maintenance and upgrade of the system(s) serving the units, unless otherwise provided in the condominium documents. 310 CMR 15.301(3).

IV. Who Can Do The Inspection

The inspections of on-site systems must be performed by System Inspectors who are approved by the Department of Environmental Protection. The DEP maintains a list of all approved System Inspectors which is available to anyone. In order to be approved, an Inspector must be:

1. A Massachusetts Registered Professional Engineer with a concentration in civil, sanitary or environmental engineering, a Massachusetts Registered Sanitarian, a Certified Health Officer, or

2. A Board of Health member or agent, engineer in training with a concentration in one of the above listed disciplines, professional home inspector, licensed septage hauler or system installer, or other individual with at least one year of experience in septic system inspection who has attended and passed an examination authorized by the DEP. 310 CMR 15.340.

V. What Must Be Inspected

The System Inspector must, at a minimum, collect and record the following information (310 CMR 15.302):

1. A general description of the system components and layout;

2. Quantification of the source/type of sanitary sewage, including type of use, design flow and whether or not the property is occupied at the time of inspection;

3. An analysis of whether the system exhibits any of the "failure criteria" set out in the code for small systems (310 CMR 15.303) or "threats to public health and environment" for larger systems (310 CMR 15.304);

---

[1] Special rules apply to non-market transactions such as foreclosure, inheritance and the like. *See* 310 CMR 15.301(3).

4. Water use records for the previous two years for properties served by a public water supply, if available from the supplier;

5. A description of the physical characteristics and condition of the septic tank, distribution box and dosing tanks, if any, along with certain other observations which indicate how well each is functioning;

6. A description of the condition of the soil absorption system along with certain other observations which indicate how well it is functioning. Sometimes, particularly in older systems, all of the components of the system cannot be located. In such cases, the Inspector must, at a minimum, locate and inspect the septic tank and distribution box, or the cesspool, and make a reasonable professional effort to determine the location and condition of the other system components. The code describes what constitutes a reasonable professional effort. 310 CMR 15.302(3).

VI. What Records of Inspection Must Be Made

The results of any required system inspection must be entered on the DEP approved Subsurface Sewage Disposal System Inspection Form by the approved System Inspector and submitted to the local Board of Health. (*See* Volume 6, Chapter 1, Form 28.4). However the results of an inspection made by the owner voluntarily, rather than to comply with a mandate of the code, need not be submitted to the Board of Health. Inspections of systems with design flows over 10,000 gallons per day must be submitted by the System Inspector and the owner to the DEP, apparently whether they are voluntary or not.

VII. What Exemptions Are There From The Inspection Requirements

There are certain limited exceptions to the general rules requiring inspections. Inspections are not required:

1. If the system has been inspected up to three years prior to the transfer of title and the inspection report is accompanied by system pumping records demonstrating that the system has been pumped at least once a year during the intervening period;

2. If the system must be inspected at the time of transfer and weather conditions preclude such inspection, the inspection may be completed as soon as weather permits, but no later than six months after the transfer of title, provided the seller notifies the buyer in writing of the inspection and upgrade requirements contained in Title 5 of the State Environmental Code (310 CMR 15.300 through 15.305);

3. In the case of transfers of title which merely change the form of ownership among the same owners, intra-family transactions, financing transactions such

as the granting of security interests and fiduciary transactions such as the appointment of a guardian or trustee;

4. Where a certificate of compliance for the system has been issued by the appropriate authority within two years prior to the transfer of title;

5. Where the seller or buyer has signed an enforceable agreement with the appropriate authority to upgrade the system or connect the system to a public or private treatment works or shared septic system within two years following transfer of title. If it is the seller who has signed such an agreement it must be disclosed to and enforceable against the buyer;

6. Where the property is subject to a comprehensive local plan of on-site septic system inspection approved in writing by the Department of Environmental Protection and administered by a local or regional governmental entity, and the system has been inspected at the most recent time required by the plan; or

7. When the system inspection is occasioned by a proposed addition to an existing structure which changes the footprint of the structure with no increase in design flow, the system inspection is limited to determining the location of all system components, including the reserve area, in order to ensure that the proposed construction will not be placed upon any of the system components. If official records are available to make a determination regarding location of system components, an on site inspection will not be required. (310 CMR 15.301).

UPGRADES

I. What Is A System Upgrade For Title 5 Purposes

The word "upgrade" is a term of art in Title 5. It is defined as the modification of one or more components of an on-site system, or the design and construction of a new on-site system, which is intended to bring a nonconforming system into conformance with Title 5 "to the maximum feasible extent." 310 CMR 15.002. However, the code also provides that where a system failure is solely due to the failure of one of its components, that component alone may be brought up to full compliance with Title 5, provided the upgraded component functions properly with the other system components. 310 CMR 15.404(1).

II. When Must A System Be Upgraded

An on-site septic system must be upgraded when, after an inspection by an approved System Inspector utilizing the criteria for inspection set out in the code, the system is found to be failing to protect the public health safety and the environment. 310 CMR 15.303. Any system which exhibits one or more of the following characteristics has failed for Title 5 purposes and must be upgraded:

1. there is a backup of sewage into the facility served by the system or any component of the system as a result of an overloaded and/or clogged soil absorption system or cesspool;

2. there is a discharge of effluent directly or indirectly to the surface of the ground through ponding, surface breakout or damp soils above the disposal area or to a surface water of the Commonwealth;

3. the static liquid level in the distribution box is above the level of the outlet invert;

4. the liquid depth in a cesspool is less than six inches from the inlet pipe invert or the remaining available volume within a cesspool above the liquid depth is less than of one day's design flow;

5. the septic tank or cesspool requires pumping more than four times a year;

6. the septic tank is made of metal, unless the property owner has provided the System Inspector with a copy of a Certificate of Compliance indicating that the tank was installed within the twenty year period prior to the inspection;

7. the septic tank is cracked or is otherwise structurally unsound, indicating that substantial infiltration or exfiltration is occurring or is imminent;

8. a cesspool, privy or any portion of the soil absorption system extends below the high groundwater e elevation.

There are special additional criteria applicable to cesspools, privies, septic tanks and soil absorption systems within certain distances from public or private drinking water supplies. Such systems may be found to have failed even if the above listed conditions are not found to exist. 310 CMR 15.303(1)(b-c).

In the case of so-called large systems, those with design flows of 10,000 gallons per day or greater, there are also additional criteria applied which may cause them to fail inspection even if the above conditions are not found to exist. If such a system is located within 400 feet of a surface water supply or within 200 feet of a tributary to a surface water supply, or, is located within a nitrogen sensitive area, such as the wellhead protection area of a public water supply, its owner may be required to upgrade beyond the requirements of Title 5 and install an on-site treatment plant. 310 CMR 15.304.

If the actual or design flow to any system is to be increased above its existing approved capacity, the system must be upgraded.

The code also contains a kind of fail/safe provision which allows the DEP or the local Board of Health to order an upgrade if it "determines that a specific circumstance exists by which any system threatens public health, safety or the environment or causes or threatens to cause damage to property or creates a nuisance ..." 310 CMR 15.303(2).

III. To What Extent Must A System Be Upgraded

Where an upgrade is required, the overall goal of Title 5 is that the system be brought into full compliance through the installation of one or more of the following:

1. a system which is in full compliance with all provisions of the code;

2. a so-called "alternative system" which has been approved by the DEP;

3. an approved shared system;

4. connection to a sewer system.

Where full compliance in accordance with the above standards is not "feasible" then the upgrade must be designed with the goal of "maximizing protection of public health and safety and the environment to the maximum extent feasible." 310 CMR 15.404(2). In determining whether full compliance is feasible, the code directs that the approving authority shall consider not only "physical possibility as dictated by the conditions of the site, but also the economic feasibility of the upgrade costs." Lest property owners take too much heart from this admonition, the code goes on to state that protection of water resources and treatment of the sewage are to be emphasized and that the requirements of the code should be varied "to the least degree necessary." 310 CMR 15.405. The Board of Health is allowed to diverge from the goal of full compliance only to the extent necessary to achieve a "feasible upgrade."

Certain Title 5 standards cannot be reduced by the Board of Health in the context of the maximum feasible upgrade process. The code also provides a hierarchy of options which the Board should consider in developing the maximum feasible upgrade. 310 CMR 404–405.

If the nonconforming system cannot be upgraded in accordance with the foregoing standards the owner must

1. install a treatment plant on the site, or

2. apply to the DEP for permission to install a tight tank or modified tight tank (a system which holds waste until it can be pumped out and disposed of rather than discharging it into the ground), or

3. apply for a variance from the provisions of Title 5, or

4. abandon the failed system. 310 CMR 405(3).

IV. What Are The Time Limits For Completing Required Upgrades

A system which has actually failed must be upgraded within two years of discovery unless (1) a shorter time is set by the Board of Health of DEP based on the existence of "an imminent health hazard", or (2) the continued use of the failed system is permitted by the Board of Health in accordance with the provisions of an enforceable, scheduled upgrade plan. Such a plan must provide for completion of the upgrade within a maximum of five years and include interim measures to be taken by the owner to minimize damage to the environment. Failure of the owner to take agreed upon measures or to meet any interim goals will automatically terminate the right to delay upgrade of the system. The DEP may in writing allow a longer period of time where the municipality has made a financial commitment to a sewering or shared system plan. 310 CMR 15.305(1).

A large system (flow greater than 10,000 gpd) which is deemed to be a threat to public health and safety or the environment solely because of it location in relation to ground or surface drinking water supplies must be upgraded within five years unless (1) a shorter time is set by the DEP based on the existence of "an imminent health hazard", or (2) the continued use of the system is allowed by the DEP because it is necessary to allow implementation of an environmentally superior solution. Such continued use may be for a maximum of seven years. Failure of the owner to take agreed upon measures or to meet any interim goals will automatically terminate the right to delay upgrade of the system. 310 CMR 15.305(2).

Where an owner has been given permission to delay upgrade, during the period of the delay he/she must take appropriate measures to ensure that there is no backup or direct discharge of sewage or effluent to buildings, to the surface of the ground or to surface waters.

V. How Does One Secure Approval Of An Upgrade

The owner or operator of a property served by a system which has actually failed may apply to the local Board of Health for permission to upgrade the system in accordance with the standards set out above.

Permission to upgrade a system owned by the federal or state governments, or a large system (flow greater than 10,000 gpd) which is deemed to be a threat to public health and safety or the environment solely because of it location in relation to ground or surface drinking water supplies must be obtained from the DEP. 310 CMR 15.403.

The application for upgrade approval must be made on a form approved by the DEP. Certified mail notice of the application must be provided to all abutters. Where approval is given by the local Board of Health, the system owner must provide a copy of the approval to the DEP upon issuance and before commencement of construction. 310 CMR 15.403.

VI. What Exemptions Are There From Compliance With The Upgrade Requirements

There are no exemptions from the Title 5 requirement that systems which are failing to protect the public health safety and the environment must be upgraded within the time periods set out in the code, except through the variance process. Both the local Board of Health and the DEP have the power to grant variances from the upgrade requirements of the code, but only when the applicant has established (1) that enforcement of the provision of Title 5 from which a variance is sought would be manifestly unjust considering all the facts and circumstances of the case, and (2) that a level of environmental protection that is at least equivalent to that provided under Title 5 can be achieved without strict application of the code provision from which a variance is sought. 310 CMR 15.410.

Every request for variance must be in writing, make reference to the provision from which a variance is sought, and assert that the requirements set out in the preceding two paragraphs have been met. Ten days' notice of the variance request and the hearing date must be given by the applicant to all abutters by certified mail. 310 CMR 15.411(1).

Any variance allowed shall be in writing. A copy must be conspicuously posted for 30 days following its issuance, and must be made available to the public through the office of the town clerk or board of health while it is in effect. 310 CMR 15.411(3).

A request for variance which relates to a residential structure with four or fewer units is deemed constructively approved by the Board of Health if it is not acted upon within 45 days from the receipt of a complete application. 310 CMR 15.411(4), G.L. c. 111, § 31E.

If the local Board of Health approves the requested variance the applicant must file a copy of it with the DEP, along with the appropriate filing fee. The DEP has 30 days to approve, modify or disapprove the variance, or to request additional information. (The 30-day period begins running again once the DEP has received the requested information). No work authorized by the variance may begin until the DEP has approved the variance or the 30 day period has elapsed without comment from it. 310 CMR 15.412. (*See also* 310 CMR 15.415, Provisions From Which No Variance May Be Granted).

VII. Use of Alternative Systems

The DEP has approved the use of certain so-called "alternative systems" for use in upgrades and remediation. 310 CMR 282. These are systems which contain components different from, or in addition to, the septic tank, distribution box and soil absorption system found in the traditional on-site system. Proposed additions to the list of approved alternative systems are under review. The DEP is required to maintain and publish at least annually in the MEPA Environmental Monitor a complete list of the status of systems approved, conditionally approved and pending approval under this program. 310 CMR 15.289.

PURCHASE AND SALE OF RESIDENTIAL REAL ESTATE

THE PRACTICE

§ 1.23   Preliminary Information Gathering

Representation of Seller in Residential Real Estate Transactions

Step 1. Obtain the basic initial information from the client which is required to complete the Information Checklist—Representation of Seller/Buyer in Residential Real Estate Transaction, Volume 6, Chapter 1.

Step 2. Find out if the Purchase and Sale Agreement has been executed by your client. Usually it will have been prepared by the real estate broker. Your client may or may not have signed it. In any case, your client will almost certainly have signed a standard form Binder or Offer to Purchase which will be sufficient in most cases to lock your client into the sale, although not perhaps as irrevocably as a long form Purchase and Sale Agreement.

Step 3. Get a feel for what the client believes are the main points of his or her agreement with the buyer. If the client is vague on any major points such as time, price, occupancy, etc., question the client closely on these points.

Step 4. If the client has not brought the Purchase and Sale Agreement and/or any Binder or Offer to Purchase signed by the client, make arrangements to obtain these from the client or broker.

§ 1.24   Make Contact with Broker and Other Attorneys

Step 5. Either ask the client to have the broker call you or get the broker's name and call him or her. There seems to be a natural animosity between lawyer and broker in Massachusetts, that really serves no one's interest. Establishing a reasonable unpatronizing relationship with the broker where possible can be helpful to both parties. Also obtain names of other attorneys, if any.

§ 1.25   Draw   or   Review   and   Revise   Purchase   and   Sale Agreement—Diary Expiration Date

Step 6. Usually you will find that you are using the printed form prepared by the Greater Boston Real Estate Board or a form nearly identical thereto prepared by a local or county real estate board. While this form used to be severely slanted toward the Seller it has been modified to the point where it is reasonably even-handed. At any rate everyone in the real estate business feels more comfortable with it than with a completely original form that you might prepare. (Volume 6, Chapter 1, Form 2).

Step 7. Where the agreement has not yet been signed by your client review the proposed form prepared by the broker. Take careful note that the printed form has not been modified in any way from the standard one. Also take note of any typed or written changes to the form and of any addenda or riders prepared by the broker.

Step 8. During review of the agreement pay particular attention to the following:

(a) Are all parties clearly and correctly identified?

(b) Is the legal status of any of the parties such that you should require further assurance of the signing person's authority to bind that party?

(c) Has the property been sufficiently described so as to avoid later problems on this point? A description by street and number is very common, although many attorneys consider this poor practice. Copying the description from the seller's own deed should be easy enough. In any case, be sure that if easements or other appurtenant rights are to be conveyed this fact is spelled out.

(d) The agreement should specify which fixtures and personal property are to pass with the property and which are to be kept by the Seller. This is a common area of disagreement. You should find out from your client his or her views on this point, particularly respecting those items of property the status of which as attachments to the realty is ambiguous. Where significant amounts of personal property are being sold it may be useful to divide the purchase price between realty and personalty in order to save on tax stamps.

(e) The clause relating to the quality of title to be conveyed often causes problems. Sellers commonly wish to have inserted language such as "subject to any and all easements and restrictions of record insofar as the same are in force and applicable." Because the buyer has no way of knowing the state of the record title this language is objectionable to the buyer. When representing the seller you must insist on some similar language since otherwise a utility easement on the title will be sufficient to allow the buyer to avoid the contract. (Volume 6, Chapter 1, Form 3).

(f) A question may arise on the point of how large a deposit is to be made by the buyer at the time of signing the agreement, and who should hold the deposit. Deposits of between three and ten percent are the rule with individual circumstances controlling each case. As the representative of the seller you may request that the seller hold the deposit. However, both the buyer's attorney and the broker will object to this. In fact, unless the seller is a builder or regular dealer in real estate, it is more usual for the broker to hold the deposit.

(g)   Occasionally the seller will find that he or she is for some reason unable to move to his or her new home by the time for closing set in the agreement. In such cases, the seller wishes to stay on in possession after the closing. If this is a possibility, it may be useful to deal with it in the agreement, for example by an automatic extension or holdover clause. (Volume 6, Chapter 1, Form 4).

(h)   You should modify the standard contract to provide that the broker is to be entitled to his or her commission only if the sale is actually consummated. (Volume 6, Chapter 1, Form 5). Also, an attempt should be made to modify or eliminate the standard form language giving the broker the right to one-half of the deposit retained by the seller in the event of buyer's default.

(i)   Although such adjustments are routinely made at closing, you should be sure that the agreement provides for the apportionment of current real estate taxes, since otherwise the seller is legally liable for them. The same might be said of other closing adjustments like fuel and water/sewer bills which are often not touched on in agreements. (Volume 6, Chapter 1, Form 6,).

(j)   Add a provision that the agreement will be void if assigned or recorded (Volume 6, Chapter 1, Form 7).

(k)   If no broker is involved delete references to a broker in the agreement and seek to add an indemnity clause. (Volume 6, Chapter 1, Form 8).

(l)   Resist the insertion of liberal financing and inspection contingency clauses in the agreement, and where they are necessary, be sure the buyer is required to use reasonable efforts within a fixed time to satisfy the contingency. (Volume 6, Chapter 1, Forms 9 and 10).

(m)   A clause disclaiming any warranties or representations not included in the written Purchase and Sale Agreement should be added.

(n)   In older residential structures, consider adding a Lead Paint Law disclaimer clause. (Volume 6, Chapter 1, Form 10.1).

(o)   where the property is served by an on-site wastewater system the buyer will typically request an inspection contingency clause specifically directed to whether the system complies with Title 5 of the State Environmental Code. (*See* Volume 6, Chapter 1, Form 10.2, for seller's form of such a clause). If a system fails inspection, either the agreement is terminated, or the closing is postponed until the seller can have the system repaired, or the sale closes with an escrow held from the sale proceeds. In some agreements, the escrow fund can be applied to paying the contractor making the repairs, in some it is held purely as security, to be used only if the seller defaults on his/her obligation to repair. A Lender will usually have a form of escrow agreement which it will want signed. (*See* Volume 6, Chapter 1, Form 28.3 for an example). A sample of the current DEP inspection form is included (Volume 6, Chapter 1, Form 28.4), as is a sample of the Application for

Disposal System Construction Permit and Certificate of Compliance which would pertain if repairs are needed (Volume 6, Chapter 1, Form 28.5).

(p)   It is no longer common for the insurance policy on the premises to be assigned at sale. However there is often discussion over the amount of insurance to be maintained during the time between signing the agreement and closing. This is important because the usual agreement gives the buyer a right to take a conveyance of casualty damaged premises and an assignment of any insurance proceeds. The seller will want to avoid any expense for additional insurance prior to the closing.

(q)   Be sure that each page of the agreement as well as any riders are initialed by each party.

(r)   Get one fully executed copy for your file.

(s)   Diary the expiration date of agreement.

§ 1.26   Secure List of Liens and Encumbrances

Step 9. Ask your client what mortgages, liens, attachments, or other encumbrances there are on the title, to his or her knowledge.

Step 10. Contact the attorney for buyer and mortgagee as applicable and ask that they present you with a list of encumbrances on the title which must be cleared prior to or at the closing. Make sure you know who is expected to draft relevant documents. (Volume 6, Chapter 1, Form 11). Remember discharge of these encumbrances are ultimately the responsibility of the seller even though the bank attorney often takes care of this.

§ 1.27   If Corporate Client Check On Vote

Step 11. In the case of a corporate seller, it must be clear that the individual who signs has the authority to bind the corporation.

Although a vote is no longer an absolute necessity where the proper officers sign, many conveyancers will require one anyway. A two-thirds or unanimous stockholder vote is advised. (Volume 6, Chapter 1, Form 12).

Where seller is a Trust, examine the Trust Indenture to see if all trustees must sign. Determine if the trust has been recorded in the appropriate Registry of Deeds.

§ 1.28   Draw Deed

Step 12. Find out how the buyer wishes to take title, and draw the deed.

Married couples usually take as tenants by the entirety but do not take this for granted. Show professional courtesy to the buyer's attorney, and avoid the possibility of having to redraft the deed by checking with his or her office first.

If the seller is a Corporation refer to date, and book and page where corporate vote is recorded, if relying on vote for authority to convey. If seller is a Trust refer to the book and page where recorded and the date of instrument of Trust. If the deed is from a limited liability company it should be signed by a person identified on the certificate of organization of a domestic company, or on the application for registration of a foreign company, as a manager or as a person authorized to execute, acknowledge, deliver and record instruments affecting the company's interest in real property. Or, any person identified on the certificate of organization or application for registration as a manager, or person authorized to execute documents to be filed with the office of the secretary of state, may certify as to the incumbency or authority of any person to sign deeds, whether or not that person is identified on the certificate of organization.

Remember that the amount of consideration in dollars, and the full name, residence, and post office address of the grantee must appear on the deed. Or, if non-monetary consideration is involved it must be described.

Also, in the case of unregistered land, the deed must contain a title reference by book and page, or must refer to a recorded plan, or must state that it does not create any new boundaries.

The street address of the property be included in the margin of the deed, but the failure to do so will not prevent the instrument from being recorded under the statute, as will the preceding requirements. However you may find that counter personnel at the registry of deeds will not accept a deed lacking this information. (Volume 6, Chapter 1, Forms 13 and 14).

§ 1.29 Certificate of Occupancy

Step 13. Where the property being sold is new construction, or where a change of use for zoning purposes is involved, then it is necessary to secure a certificate of occupancy from the local building department. It is the seller's responsibility to obtain this.

§ 1.29[1] Smoke Detector Certificate

Step 13A. Seller is responsible for obtaining an inspection of the property by the local fire department to determine if appropriate smoke detectors are in place and operational. After inspection the department will provide a certificate of approval, which should be brought to the closing by the seller.

§ 1.29[2] Lead Paint Disclosures Form

Step 13C. If the property was constructed before 1978, be sure that your client makes, or has made, any disclosures required by the lead paint law.

If the premises have been previously de-leaded, you should provide the prospective buyer with a letter of interim control or full compliance under G.L. c. 111,

§ 197A. This should all be done prior to the signing of the purchase and sale agreement. If it has not been done, immediate curative action is recommended. (*See* Volume 6, Appendix D, for required form and excerpt from regulations relating to notification requirements.)

§ 1.29[3]   Release of Tax Lien

Step 13D. Where the seller is a surviving joint tenant or tenant by the entirety you must obtain and record:

    i) Death certificates for deceased tenants,

    ii) Release of estate tax lien,

    iii) in the case of registered land, a certificate of no divorce in appropriate cases.

For deaths between 1997 and 2002, a certificate by the Executor, Administrator or person in possession of the decedent's property to the effect that no Federal Estate Tax is due on the estate may be substituted for the Form M-792, Release of Massachusetts Estate Tax Lien. For deaths on and after January 1, 2003, the certificate should state that the decedent's estate does not necessitate the filing of a Massachusetts Estate Tax Return.[1] *See* Volume 6, Chapter 1, Form 14.1.

§ 1.30   Certificate of Title

Step 14. As Owner's Duplicate Certificates of Title are no longer used, existing Duplicates need not be surrendered when registered land is sold.

§ 1.31   Draw Discharges Where Necessary

Step 15. Ultimately it is the responsibility of the seller to clear encumbrances off the title. This would include as a natural concomitant the duty to draw any documents necessary to accomplish this. It may happen in fact that the attorney for the mortgagee or buyer will draw one or all of these instruments, but this fact should be clearly ascertained prior to closing.

Where the property is subject to a first mortgage the mortgagee bank will usually prepare its own discharge which it will release upon receipt of the amount due. Where there is a second mortgage it will usually be seller's attorney who draws the discharge. There may also be releases of conditions to be obtained from the planning board or conservation commission where new construction is involved.

§ 1.32   Obtain Payoff Figure and Per Diem

Step 16. You should obtain a payoff figure for all mortgages as of the scheduled

---

[1] G.L. c. 65C, §§ 6(a) & 14(a); DOR Directive 03-02.

closing date and also a per diem figure in the event the closing occurs earlier or later than planned.

This should be done even though it will probably be duplicative of work done by the attorney for mortgagee or buyer since the money withheld to pay off these mortgages is subtracted from amounts payable to seller and he has the greatest interest in accuracy.

Lender or buyer attorneys will usually close a sale based on a written payoff figure from an institutional lender. But where a mortgage or other encumbrance is held by another type of entity the discharge itself will have to be obtained and escrowed prior to closing.

Where your client has an outstanding home equity loan of the revolving type it will be necessary to notify the lender to terminate the right of withdrawal from the line of credit at least 14 days before the closing. The lender should be asked to note the termination date in any payoff letter to the attorney representing the new lender or the buyer.

§ 1.33   Double Check Documents and Do Preliminary Closing Adjustments

Step 17. Go over the list of encumbrances be sure you have cleared or are prepared to clear them at the closing. Take a blank closing memo and work through a preliminary closing adjustment. You should have most of the figures needed at this point. (Volume 6, Chapter 1, Form 15).

You might consider sending the preliminary closing memo to the attorneys for lender and buyer asking for any problems or comments. (Volume 6, Chapter 1, Form 16).

§ 1.34   Property Insurance

Step 18. Remind client to call insurance agent or company to have property insurance cancelled after closing. Be sure to allow sufficient leeway in case the closing is late. Or tell the agent you will call after closing. It is assumed, of course, that the policy is not being assigned to the buyer. (Volume 6, Chapter 1, Form 17).

§ 1.35   Utilities and Fuel

Step 19. Have client notify utility companies to have meters read as of the closing day, also arrange to have telephone service discontinued as of that day. (Volume 6, Chapter 1, Form 18).

Step 20. In case of fuel tank, the increase in price per gallon and the growing prevalence of large tanks makes this an important item. An easy solution is to have the tank filled at or near the closing day and give the seller a credit for this amount.

Otherwise, one must estimate the fuel in the tank. (Volume 6, Chapter 1, Form 19).

§ 1.36   Registered Land—Special Problems

Step 21. If the land is registered, then approval by the court of a deed prior to recording is needed in certain cases, as follows:

(a) if a copy of the plan has not been forwarded to the Registry;

(b) if deed is coming out of an estate;

(c) in certain cases, if seller is a limited partnership.

§ 1.36[1]   Limited Partnership and Other Special Entities

Where a limited partnership is involved, in addition to the executed documents to be registered, you will need a long form certificate, not over thirty days old and bearing the seal of the Commonwealth, from the Secretary of State attesting the name of the general partner and certifying that the limited partnership has not filed a Certificate of Cancellation (or if the limited partnership is a foreign one, that its application for registration has not been cancelled and that it has not filed a Certificate of Withdrawal). As to foreign limited partnerships organized in any of the other forty-nine states, if it is not registered with the Massachusetts Secretary of State you will need an original certificate, not over thirty days old, of legal existence from the secretary of state of the foreign jurisdiction stating the name of the limited partnership, the names of its general partners and the fact that the partnership has not filed a Certificate of Cancellation. If you cannot meet these requirements then you will not be able to record the deed without prior land court approval. The deed can be signed by any one general partner. If the general partner is a corporation the usual requirements as to execution of corporate deeds will apply.

Where necessary, begin to seek court approval sufficiently in advance of the closing.

Where a deed from a probate court fiduciary is involved, you will need, in addition to the deed,

i) if under license from the probate court, an attested copy of the license no more than one year old,

ii) if pursuant to a power of sale in the Will, an attested copy of the will, certificate of appointment of executor not more than 90 days old, and a tax release from the Department of Revenue.

Where the deed is coming from a limited liability company (LLC) you will need,

i) the certificate of organization of a domestic LLC or the application for registration of a foreign LLC, and

ii) a certificate of the Secretary of State's office, dated within 60 days of the date presented for filing, that there have been no amendments, or a certificate that there have been amendments accompanied by copies thereof, or

iii) a good standing certificate under G.L. c. 156C, § 68 dated within 60 days of the date presented for filing, or

iv) a certification under G.L. c. 156C, § 67 by someone whose authority is established under (i) or (ii) above, of the authority of some other person to act.

The deed will have to be executed by a person appearing on the certificate of organization or application for registration as authorized to sign, acknowledge, deliver and record instruments affecting real property, or a manager or other authorized person appearing on a good standing certificate, or a person named on the certificate of an manager or other authorized person as being authorized to execute real estate instruments.

Where the deed is coming from a bankrupt you will need an attested copy of the certificate of title, the usual instruments from the Bankruptcy Court, and a certificate of no appeal.

Where the deed is out of a trust and the trust is not recorded in the same registry you will need court approval to record the deed. Where the deed from the trustee recites less than full consideration it must be approved by the court prior to recording. You will need a certificate from the trustee that beneficiaries are of full age and have assented.

Where the seller is a surviving tenant by the entirety the Land Court requires an "Affidavit of no Divorce" before it will issue a new certificate based on a deed from the survivor. The affidavit must be signed by a child of the deceased tenant or by the attorney for the survivor, and must state that the owners had not been divorced prior to the death.

As Owner's Duplicate Certificates of Title are no longer used, existing Duplicates need not be surrendered when registered land is sold.

§ 1.37 Condominiums—Special Tasks

Step 22. Make appropriate adjustments to the agreement where necessary to show a condominium is involved. Be sure the list of encumbrances in the agreement includes condominium laws, bylaws, and regulations. Be sure the agreement provides for adjustment of common expenses.

Be sure the title examiner runs the unit owners' organization for betterments. Also be sure to check this name with the tax collector for the same reason.

Step 23. The buyer's attorney will probably wish to see, and you should be prepared to obtain:

(a) copy of Master Deed;

(b) instrument creating unit owners' organization, and its bylaws, rules, and regulations;

(c) site and floor plans;

(d) current budget of owners organization, income, and expense statements;

(e) any applicable title and property insurance policy;

(f) proposed Unit Deed.

Step 24. Obtain a certificate relating to unpaid common expenses from the unit owners' organization.

Step 25. Where applicable obtain a waiver of right of first refusal from owners' organization.

Step 26. Consult G.L. c. 183A, § 9 which specifies in detail the special requirements of condominium unit deeds. Be sure you comply. Note that the first deed of each unit must have attached thereto a certified plan of the unit being conveyed. (Volume 6, Chapter 1, Form 20).

For situations where the seller is the initial developer of the condominium, a set of condominium documents is enclosed which include Forms 19.1 *et seq.* (Volume 6, Chapter 1). The documents include Master Deed and Unit Owners' Trust, and sample Rules and Regulations. The latter are usually adopted and amended from time to time by the managers of the unit owners' organization and often are not recorded. Also, the comprehensive building plan required by G.L. c. 183A, § 8(f) is not included, nor is a budget or statement of financial condition of the unit owners' organization.

§ 1.38 The Closing

Step 27. Seller's attorney has a very limited role at the closing, particularly if the seller's attorney has done his or her preliminary work well.

Step 28. You need merely appear with the documents you were required to produce and be prepared to oversee and confirm the actions of the lawyer conducting the closing.

§ 1.39 Preliminary Information Gathering

Representation of Buyer in Residential Real Estate Transaction

Step 1. Obtain the basic initial information from the client which is required to complete the Information Checklist—Representation of Seller/Buyer in Residential Real Estate Transaction (Volume 6, Chapter 1).

Step 2. Find out if the Purchase and Sale Agreement has been executed by your client. Usually it will have been prepared by the real estate broker. Your client may or may not have signed it. In any case, your client will almost certainly have signed a standard form Binder or Offer to Purchase which will be sufficient in most cases to lock your client into the sale, although not perhaps as irrevocably as a long form Purchase and Sale Agreement. Although the use of Binder's or Offers to Purchase is not good practice from a legal standpoint, clients will sometimes insist on using them because of their speed and convenience in establishing that a deal is truly made. In such cases, it is a good idea to have the Binder clearly reflect the intention of the parties not to be irrevocably bound until a detailed Purchase and Sale Agreement is signed. *See* Form 20.2 in Volume 6, Chapter 1, which contains suggested language to be added to the usual form of pre-printed Binder.

Step 3. Get a feel for what the client believes are the main points of his or her agreement with the seller. If the client is vague on any major points such as time, price, occupancy, etc., question the client closely on these points.

Step 4. If the client has not brought the Purchase and Sale Agreement and/or any Binder of Offer to Purchase signed by the client, make arrangements to obtain these from the client or broker.

§ 1.40 Make Contact with Broker and Other Attorneys

Step 5. Either ask the client to have the broker call you or get the broker's name and call him or her. There seems to be a natural animosity between lawyer and broker in Massachusetts that really serves no one's interest. Establishing a reasonable unpatronizing relationship with the broker where possible can be helpful to both parties. Also obtain names of other attorneys if any.

§ 1.41 Draw or Review and Revise Purchase and Sale Agreement—Diary Expiration Date

Step 6. Usually you will find that you are using the printed form prepared by the Greater Boston Real Estate Board or a form nearly identical thereto prepared by a local or county real estate board. (*See* Volume 6, Chapter 1, Form 2.) While this form used to be slanted toward the Seller it has been modified to the point where it is reasonably even-handed. At any rate everyone in the real estate business feels more comfortable with it than with a completely original form that you might prepare.

Step 7. Where the agreement has not yet been signed by your client, review the proposed form prepared by the broker. Take careful note as to how the printed form may have been modified from the standard one, of any typed or written changes to the form, and of any addenda or riders prepared by the broker.

Step 8. During review of the agreement pay particular attention to the following:

(a) Are all parties clearly and correctly identified?

(b) Is the legal status of any of the parties such that you should require further assurance of the signing person's authority to bind that party?

(c) Has the property been sufficiently described so as to avoid later problems on this point? A description by street and number is very common, although many attorneys consider this poor practice. Copying the description from the seller's own deed should be easy enough. In any case, be sure that if easements or other appurtenant rights are to be conveyed this fact is spelled out.

(d) The agreement should specify which fixtures and personal property are to pass with the property and which are to be kept by the seller. This is a common area of disagreement. You should find out from your client his or her understanding of just what is to come with the house, particularly with respect to items such as carpeting, lighting fixtures, dishwashers, appliances, and television antennas.

(e) The clause relating to the quality of title to be conveyed often causes problems. Sellers commonly wish to have inserted language which excepts from their obligation to give marketable title, clear of record, "any and all easements and restrictions of record insofar as the same are in force and applicable."

There would be no problem with this language if the buyer's attorney could see the title record before his or her client signs the agreement. However this is not possible. The ideal from the buyer's point of view is simply to strike this language. Regrettably, the seller's attorney will usually object strenuously to this.

From the sellers point of view the elimination of this language often turns the agreement into an option since it can be avoided if even a utility easement is on the record.

As buyer's attorney you must be concerned lest some truly onerous easement or restriction burden the property and your client be nevertheless required to take title and pay full price.

If the seller insists on some language of this kind you may be able to convince the seller to accept language requiring that the restrictions be listed in the agreement or that some less onerous language be substituted. (Volume 6, Chapter 1, Forms 22, 23).

(f) A question may arise on the point of how large a deposit is to be made by the buyer at the time of signing the agreement, and who should hold the deposit. Deposits of from three to ten percent of the contract price are common, with five percent deposits being very common. The amount depends on a number of factors, not the least of which is the relative bargaining power of the parties. The seller may request that he or she hold it. The broker will also wish to hold it. If the seller is represented by an attorney you should request that he or she hold the deposit in escrow. If the seller is unrepresented the next best choice is the broker if he or she is a well known and substantial business person. Builders and real estate dealers will insist on holding the deposit themselves. The attorney for buyer should not agree to this because the funds will often be commingled with other funds of seller and may be lost if the seller encounters financial difficulties before closing.

(g) Occasionally the buyer will not have completed sale of his or her old home by the time set for closing on the new home. In such cases, he or she may wish to delay the closing. If this is a possibility it may be wise to deal with it in the agreement by an automatic extension clause. (Volume 6, Chapter 1, Form 24).

(h) Although such adjustments are routinely made at closing you should be sure that the agreement provides for the apportionment of current real estate taxes. The same might be said of other closing adjustments like fuel and water/sewer bills which are often not touched on in agreements. (Volume 6, Chapter 1, Form 25).

(i) If the buyer is going to execute a second mortgage it may be wise to have the form of note and mortgage attached to the agreement or, failing this, to have the essential terms set out in the agreement.

(j) Be sure that the agreement contains a reasonable financing contingency unless buyer has a guaranteed commitment for financing. (Volume 6, Chapter 1, Form 26).

(k) It is no longer common for the insurance policy on the premises to be assigned at sale. However there is often discussion over the amount of insurance to be maintained during the time between signing the agreement and closing. This may important because the usual agreement gives the buyer a right to take a conveyance of casualty damaged premises and an assignment of any insurance proceeds. The buyer should require that the premises be kept fully insured during the period prior to closing. It may be expected that the seller will resist increasing the insurance. (Unless your client is a cash buyer this may be an argument not worth having, since the lender will not usually close if there is substantial damage to the premises.)

(l) Be sure that the liquidated damages clause in the agreement provides that in the event of buyer's default retention of the deposit shall be seller's sole remedy. (Volume 6, Chapter 1, Form 27).

(m) Contingency clauses relating to termite and lead paint inspections and inspections for construction defects should be inserted. (Volume 6, Chapter 1, Form 28). In the case of the purchase of vacant land intended for use as a building site, some buyer's attorneys are beginning to ask for a so-called "21E" or hazardous waste contingency clause where the history or location of the property suggests that this is appropriate. (Volume 6, Chapter 1, Form 27.1). Also in vacant land sales a site suitability contingency clause is often requested. (Volume 6, Chapter 1, Form 27.2). In the provisions providing for these contingencies, you should try to obtain as long a time as possible for your client to accomplish these things.

(n) If the sale is of vacant land contingent upon buyer actually obtaining necessary building and related permits, rather than the suitability of the site for obtaining such permits, the agreement should explicitly so provide. The Buyer may also wish to limit how much he/she has to spend to obtain such permits. (*See* Volume 6, Chapter 1, Form 28.1).

(o) Where the property is served by an on-site wastewater system it is now customary for purchase and sale agreements to include inspection contingency clauses specifically directed to whether or not the system complies with Title 5 of the State Environmental Code. (*See* Volume 6, Chapter 1, Form 28.2). If a system fails inspection, either the agreement is terminated, or the closing is postponed until the seller can have the system repaired, or the sale closes with an escrow held from the sale proceeds. In some agreements, the escrow fund can be applied to paying the contractor making the repairs, in some it is held purely as security, to be used only if the seller defaults on his/her obligation to repair. A Lender will usually have a form of escrow agreement which it will want signed. (*See* Volume 6, Chapter 1, Form 28.3 for an example). Obviously the use of an escrow poses certain risks to the buyer if the escrow turns out to be insufficient. A sample of the current DEP inspection form is included (Volume 6, Chapter 1, Form 28.4), as is a sample of the Application for Disposal System Construction Permit and Certificate of Compliance which would pertain if repairs are needed (Volume 6, Chapter 1, Form 28.5).

(p) If seller will agree to warrant heating, roof or water-free basement, or zoning compliance, the appropriate language should be included. (Volume 6, Chapter 1, Forms 29 and 30). In a few cases, the property may be served by an on site water well rather than by municipal water. If so, language should be added to Form 29 to the effect that the well water has been tested within the past year by a DEP certified testing laboratory and the test results are attached to the Agreement. The Buyer should be given ten days after receipt of the well test results to terminate the Agreement without penalty. Notice should be taken by the Buyer of any contaminants or high salt levels shown by the tests. Even results below state-established minimum contamination levels could indicate progressively greater contamination in the future.

(q) If your client is purchasing a property constructed prior to 1978, with rental units in which existing tenants will continue to live after the purchase, the agreement should provide that the seller will provide at the closing the Tenant Certification Form or other evidence satisfactory to buyer's counsel that the tenant notice requirements of the Lead Paint Law and regulations have been complied with.

(r) Be sure that each page of the agreement as well as any riders or addenda are initialed by each party.

(s) Be sure to get one fully executed copy of the agreement for your file. This is often overlooked.

(t) Diary the expiration date of the agreement.

§ 1.42   Property Inspection

Step 9. Arrange as quickly as possible to have the relevant inspections done by reliable and reputable persons. There will normally be a fairly limited time to have these inspections done before the agreement becomes unconditionally binding.

§ 1.43   Financing Contingency

Step 10. Have your client proceed immediately to apply for financing at a rate consistent with the limitations provided for in the contingency clause in the agreement. Application at more than one bank is advised to show good faith attempt at compliance, although in times of tight money some banks charge hefty application fees.

§ 1.44   Title Examination—Evaluating a Real Estate Title as to Marketability[1]

§ 1.44[1]   Have the Title Examined and Abstract Prepared

Step 11. Choose an experienced and respected title examiner to do the title

---

[1] If lender's counsel will be certifying title to your client, or providing your client with title insurance, Steps 11 through 21 may be eliminated. Be sure your client understands what you are, and are not, doing.

abstract. Unless you have experience in this work do not try to do the abstract yourself.

If you do not know the name of a reliable person call a prominent conveyancer in the area and he or she will usually be happy to make a recommendation.

§ 1.45   Get an Overview of the State of the Title

Step 12. Read the examiner's report carefully. It should point you to problem areas, if any. But do not rely on this alone. Go over the entire abstract. Your reputation and malpractice insurance are on the line.

Step 13. Read the abstract backwards from the title reference instrument first.

Step 14. Now read the abstract forward from the first instrument to the present.

Step 15. As you proceed forward make a chart or diagram, or merely shorthand notes, which will help you trace the history of the parcel through time. There is reproduced at the end of this chapter an illustration of the type of chart of title chain referred to.

§ 1.46   Make a Detailed Analysis of the Report

Step 16. Make notes of any problems you find beside the appropriate stage in your chart. Prepare a list of these problems.

Step 17. If you have questions of interpretation on the abstract, discuss these with your examiner. Remember he or she will have a better "feel" for the title having researched it than you will get just reading the abstract.

Step 18. Have a standard list of common defects that you check for. This list is not exclusive, but covers most common problems:

(a) Be sure the examiner has gone back 50 years to a warranty deed or to a quitclaim deed which does not suggest any defects on its face.

(b) Follow the description of the parcel through the entire chain of title. It is sometimes very difficult, but be reasonably certain that you have the right parcel throughout. Take particular care when the description changes because of subdivision or whatever.

(c) Where there is a corporation in the chain of title be sure to see that certificate of vote is on record. The affirmative vote should be of at least 2/3 of each class of stock entitled to vote. By statute, a deed signed by the president or vice president and the treasurer or assistant treasurer is a substitute for a vote in most cases.

(d) If there is a deed from a corporation within 3 years of the date of the title report you should request that the seller provide a tax waiver from the Dept. of Revenue unless it is clear from the record that the sale did not involve substantially all of the corporation's assets and/or was made in the ordinary course of business. There can be delays in getting these waivers from the Department such that requiring them may not be practicable and a warranty to the same effect by the seller will have to suffice.

(e) If there is a low value tax title in the chain, the property will have to be put through registration or confirmation proceedings before the title is accepted. *But see* G.L. c. 60, § 80C relating to cases where 20 years or more have elapsed after the date of recording of an instrument purporting to convey land under the so-called "land of low value" procedure. Decide for yourself if this statute obviates the need for Land Court proceedings.

(f) Until fairly recently it had been generally agreed that if there is a sheriff's deed in the chain of title within 21 years from the date of examination, the property must be registered or confirmed. Some conveyancers will insist on land court procedures regardless of the age of the sheriff's deed. However, Title Standard 20 of the Massachusetts Real Estate Bar Association has been recently modified to provide that title based on a sheriff's deed is not defective where the record discloses clearly that there has been full and complete compliance with the procedural requirements of G.L. c. 236, notice has been given to the record owner and all junior lien holders as of the date of sale, and more than one year has passed since the date of sale. Notwithstanding, the more conservative practice is certainly to require the land court confirmation of the title. Where there has only been an attachment or levy by the sheriff, but no sale, this will expire in 6 years unless further proceedings have been had to bring it forward.

(g) If there is a mortgage foreclosure in the chain of title examine all documents carefully to see that the requirements of G.L. c. 244 and the Soldiers' and Sailors' Civil Relief Act have been met.

(h) Where there is a deed from the heirs of an intestate or the devisees of a testator great care must be taken.

(1) If the sale is within one year of the time the executor or administrator has his or her bond approved there should be a license to sell from the court. Review the documents to be sure that statutory procedures were scrupulously followed.

(2) If the sale is after one year, but at the date of examination less than six years have passed from approval of the bond, there should be a final account showing payment of all debts, legacies and expenses.

(3) If the sale is after six years from approval of the bond then no action can

be brought to reach the real estate and the assurances of (1) and (2) above are not needed.

(i) Where an owner or joint owner in the chain of title has died while title was in his or her name, be sure there has been a release of the estate tax lien or an affidavit by the executor, administrator or person in possession that no estate tax return was required to be filed. Where the estate tax lien has not been released by the department of revenue, it will expire 10 years after the date of death, or in the case of future interests, 10 years after the right to possession or enjoyment accrues. The lien is also cut off by a sale of the property under license of the probate court.

(j) Restrictions should be read very carefully to see if they might interfere with client's proposed use of property. Most restrictions unlimited as to time expire in either 50 or 30 years if created prior to 1/1/62, in 30 years if created thereafter. *See* G.L. c. 184, § 28 *et seq.*

(k) A deed from a trustee should refer to the book and page where the trust instrument is recorded. Be sure that the instrument gives the trustee sufficient power to sell, execute, and deliver a deed. A sale by the trustee to himself free of trust will usually make the title defective. Sales by trustees obviously for less than full consideration should also be scrutinized further. Federal and state tax liens other than estate tax liens expire 10 years 30 days and 6 years, respectively, from the date of assessment of the tax.

(l) Where there is a deed from a municipality in the chain of title be sure the official signing had proper authority from the legislative body. (*But see* G.L. 40, § 3A.)

(m) Where there is a deed from a general partnership in the title be sure that you know the identity of all the partners at the time of the deed and that all have signed. If less than all the partners have signed you must get evidence of signing partners' authority to bind the partnership. An affidavit may resolve this kind of problem.

(n) Where there is a deed from a limited partnership in the title check the certificate on file with the secretary of state as of the time of the deed to ascertain the identity of the general partners and their authority unless such information is of record in the registry of deeds. (*See* G.L. c. 109).

(o) Where there is a deed from a limited liability company (LLC) be sure that the record demonstrates that it has been signed by a person with authority to sign real estate instruments or verify such authority through the records of the secretary of state.

(p) Where there is a deed from an attorney or agent under a written power of attorney, there are problems as to whether the power has been revoked prior to execution of the deed. For deeds after January 1, 1978, an affidavit pursuant to G.L. c. 201, § 50 can often be of help here.

(q) Be sure that each grantor has been run in the grantor indices for 4 years beyond the year in which he or she conveyed to see if there were any tax takings.

(r) If there is a transfer from a bankruptcy trustee in the title, examine the recorded documents to see if there is a certified copy of the motion for approval of sale, certificate of service on lienholders if, as is usual, their rights are to be affected and an order of court allowing the motion and approving the sale. If these matters are not of record the docket at the Bankruptcy Court can be examined for the same information. The examiner should be satisfied by examination of registry and court records that the court approved the conveyance after proceedings in which the trustee gave interested parties notice, and that all appeal periods have expired. Note that the applications and orders authorizing and confirming the conveyance are sometimes merged in one set of documents.

(s) Check the abstract of each individual instrument to see if there are any formal defects. Minor clerical or scrivener's errors should not be of great concern. Also, certain specific formal defects are cured by statute after 10 years from date of recording. (*See* G.L. c. 184, §§ 24 and 25).

(t) In the case of condominiums, examine the abstract of the Master Deed to be sure it contains: a particular description of the land, buildings, units and common areas, floor plans, statement of purpose and restrictions on use, method by which Master Deed may be amended, the name of the unit owners organization, and a statement that the organization has enacted bylaws. If a trust or unincorporated association is named then the deed must set forth the names of the trustees or managing board. (G.L. c. 183A, § 8).

(u) Be sure any deed transferring a condominium unit complies with G.L. c. 183A, § 9.

(v) Be certain that the bylaws of the unit owners organization have been abstracted and comply with G.L. c. 183A, § 11. Check the bylaws for restrictions on use.

(x) Be sure there is a certificate relating to the lien for unpaid common expenses on file for each transfer of the unit.

(y) Note whether the examiner has run the name of the unit owners' organization in the indices to pick up any betterments or other charges made against the organization which are liens against the individual units.

§ 1.47 Report Your Findings to Your Client and Other Interested Parties

Step 19. If the title is clear and acceptable to you then so notify your client and the other interested parties. If there are problems then contact the attorney for the seller, or the broker if seller is unrepresented, and notify him or her as to any flaws you have discovered in the title.

Step 20. Where necessary, explain to your client that certain problems have arisen which must be resolved before you can certify the title. Explain the exact nature of the problem in simple terms.

Step 21. Determine what is necessary to correct any title problems and indicate to seller's attorney the nature and form of the documents he or she will have to prepare and have executed before you will accept title. Where Seller is not represented either you or lender's counsel, if there is one, will have to prepare the necessary documents.

If a land court proceeding is necessary to clear the title, explain this to your client giving your client an indication of the likely time and expense involved.

Illustrative Form of Chain of Title Chart

[SEE CHART IN ORIGINAL]

§ 1.48 Certified Plot Plan

Step 22. A certified plot plan is a measured, scale drawing by a registered land surveyor or engineer which depicts the location of all property lines and buildings on the subject property. Its primary purpose is to assure that structures are located entirely on the parcel and do not encroach on other property, and that there has been compliance with applicable zoning bylaws. Although these were not commonly obtained in the past, more and more banks are requiring them. As attorney for the buyer you may wish to require them whenever the lender does not, in order to assure the full protection of your client. This is particularly appropriate with older properties.

It should be remembered however that mortgage plot plans are not precise and detailed as are on the ground instrument surveys. They are typically based on a review of an existing plan by the surveyor, the location of one or more bounds shown on the plan, and a rather brief tape measuring of the property. A modest fee is charged and the plan is well worth the fee if property prepared.

§ 1.49 Municipal Lien Certificate

Step 23. Obtain from the municipal tax collector's office a Municipal Lien Certificate. Take note of any liens which will require adjustment at closing. Be sure to take the certificate to the closing and to record it when you record the deed. The recording of the lien certificate discharges the property from the lien for municipal taxes and charges due on or before the date of the certificate if such taxes and charges are not shown on the certificate. This discharge will not occur with respect to liens shown on other previously recorded instruments, (i.e.) elderly taxpayer deferral liens under G.L. c. 59, § 5(41A). The certificate must be recorded within one hundred fifty (150) days from issuance in order for the discharge to be effective.

§ 1.50 Prepare List of Liens and Encumbrances

Step 24. Using the title examiner's report and municipal lien certificate prepare a list of liens and encumbrances on property. Send a copy of same to the seller's attorney. (Volume 6, Chapter 1, Form 31).

§ 1.51 Property Insurance Binders

Step 25. Secure or have your client secure a property insurance binder covering the property effective as of the closing date.

§ 1.52 Obtain Payoff Figures and Per Diem From Each Mortgagee

Step 26. Call each mortgagee and lien holder and obtain payoff figures from them, including a per diem payment rate.

§ 1.53 Utility Meters, Fuel Tank and Smoke Detectors

Step 27. Call seller's attorney or representative and ask if he or she will arrange to have the meters read as of the day of closing. Discuss the problem of fuel tank adjustments and see if his or her client will fill the tank just prior to closing. Also find out if arrangements have been made to obtain a smoke detector inspection and certificate from the local fire department.

§ 1.53[1] Lead Paint Notification to Tenants

If your client is purchasing a property constructed prior to 1978, with rental units in which existing tenants will continue to live after the purchase, you should:

(1) determine if the tenants have received the required notices under the Lead Paint Law,

(2) obtain the Tenant Certification Form for each existing tenant who will remain after the purchase, and

(3) advise your client that at the time of lease renewal, he/she will be

required to notify those who have not received the proper notification.

At will and multi-year lease tenants may be notified at any time. Where the rental portion of the property is vacant, the tenant notification requirements of the Lead Paint Law and its regulations will apply as and when the premises are rented by your client. The notification requirement is a burden which properly belongs on the seller in the case of existing tenants.

§ 1.54 Review Proposed Deed and Other Instruments

Step 28. Good practice suggests that you should request copies of the mortgage, note and any other instruments which your client will be expected to sign at the closing. You should also review the form of deed and/or plan you will be asked to accept to be sure they meet legal and registry requirements. Refer to § 1.51, where the seller is a limited partnership, limited liability company or a surviving joint tenant the documents which the land court requires before it will record the deed in the case of registered land. You should require the seller to provide the same instruments in recordable form, even in the case of unregistered land. While this is often not done in practice it seems clearly the better procedure.

Step 29. It very often happens that the buyer for some reason cannot be present at the closing. Given the many disclosure and other documents which must be signed by buyer the bank attorney will very often insist on a detailed special power of attorney running to buyer's attorney or other representative before scheduling the closing. A sample of such a form is included in Volume 6, Chapter 1, Form 31.1.

§ 1.55 Title Insurance

Step 30. If title insurance is being obtained and you are not an authorized agent for a title insurance company, be sure that the application has been submitted and the binder obtained. (Volume 6, Chapter 1, Form 32).

§ 1.56 Double Check Documents and Do Preliminary Closing Adjustments—Advise Client

Step 31. Check the encumbrances on the title record and lien certificate, contact the seller's attorney to be sure he is prepared to clear all encumbrances on or before the closing. If seller is unrepresented you should find out who is taking care of this and offer to do it yourself if needed. Where seller has an outstanding home equity loan of the revolving type it will be necessary to notify the lender to terminate the right of withdrawal from the line of credit at least 14 days before the closing. The lender should be asked to note the termination in any payoff letter. You need to be sure that all outstanding amounts on the equity loan are accounted for as of closing in order to be sure that a discharge will be obtainable with the funds withheld.

Step 32. Where there is no lender's counsel involved, take a blank closing memo and work through a preliminary closing adjustment. You should have just about all of the figures needed at this point. (Volume 6, Chapter 1, Form 15). Since most municipalities issue preliminary tax bills during the first half of the fiscal year, July 1 to December 31, the actual amount of real estate taxes may not be known until after the closing. The typical purchase and sale agreement provides for reapportionment once the 'real' tax bill is issued. In practice, the differences between preliminary and actual tax are so small, and buyer sophistication so low, that reapportionment rarely occurs. However, in the case of new construction or substantial additions to property occurring just prior to sale the difference between the preliminary and actual tax will be substantial. You and your client should both be aware of this when the closing adjustments are prepared. A discussion of this issue should also occur at the closing, with appropriate follow up when the actual tax bill is later issued.

You might consider sending the preliminary closing memo to the attorney buyer asking for any problems or comments. (Volume 6, Chapter 1, Form 16). Where lender's counsel is involved ask for a draft of the settlement statement as soon in advance of the closing as it is prepared. Tell your client approximately how much he or she will need to bring to the closing. This is a good opportunity to discuss with your client the advantages of filing a Declaration of Homestead, if a purchase of a primary residence is involved. People often will put off this kind of thing, but are receptive when it is included in the whole package of paper work and inconvenience that goes along with the purchase of a home. Also, with respect to Declarations of Homestead the amounts of exemption for each type of Homestead is now $500,000 (*See* Volume 6, Chapter 1, Forms 34.1, 34.2, and 34.3, for forms of standard, elderly/disabled and manufactured home homestead declarations).

§ 1.57 Registered Land

Step 33. If the land being sold is registered then approval by the Land Court of the deed prior to recording is needed in certain cases, as follows:

(a) if a copy of the plan has not been forwarded to the registry;

(b) if the deed is coming out of an estate;

(c) in certain cases, if seller is limited partnership.

Where a limited partnership is involved, in addition to the executed documents to be registered, you will need a long form certificate, not over thirty days old and bearing the seal of the Commonwealth, from the Secretary of State attesting the name of the general partner and certifying that the limited partnership has not filed a Certificate of Cancellation (or if the limited partnership is a foreign one, that its application for registration has not been canceled and that it has not filed a

Certificate of Withdrawal). As to foreign limited partnerships organized in any of the other forty nine states, if it is not registered with the Massachusetts Secretary of State you will need an original certificate, not over thirty days old, of legal existence from the secretary of state of the foreign jurisdiction stating the name of the limited partnership, the names of its general partners and the fact that the partnership has not filed a Certificate of Cancellation. If you cannot meet these requirements then you will not be able to record the deed without prior land court approval. The deed can be signed by any one general partner. If the general partner is a corporation the usual requirements as to execution of corporate deeds will apply.

Where a deed from a probate court fiduciary is involved, you will need, in addition to the deed,

  i) if under license from the probate court, an attested copy of the license no more than one year old,

  ii) if pursuant to a power of sale in the Will, an attested copy of the will, certificate of appointment of executor not more than 90 days old, and a tax release from the Department of Revenue.

Where the deed is coming from a bankrupt you will need an attested copy of the certificate of title, the usual instruments from the Bankruptcy Court and a certificate of no appeal.

Where the deed is out of a trust and the trust is not recorded in the same registry you will need court approval to record the deed. Where the deed from the trustee recites less than full consideration it must be approved by the court prior to recording. You will need a certificate from the trustee that beneficiaries are of full age and have assented.

If seller is unrepresented, it will be necessary for either you or lender's attorney to undertake land court procedures. Be sure everyone is aware of this problem and someone is working on it sufficiently in advance of the closing.

Where the seller is a surviving joint tenant or tenant by the entirety you must obtain and record:

  i) death certificates for deceased tenants,

  ii) Release of estate tax lien,

  iii) in the case of registered land, a certificate of no divorce in appropriate cases.

Where the seller is a surviving tenant by the entirety the Land Court requires an

"Affidavit of no Divorce" before it will issue a new certificate based on a deed from the survivor. The affidavit must be signed by a child of the deceased tenant or by the attorney for the survivor, and must state that the owners had not been divorced prior to the death.

If a new plan is to be recorded with the deed you will need prior approval from the Land Court engineering department of the plan in most cases. This approval is obtained at the Boston office of the court and needs to be obtained ahead of the closing date.

As Owner's Duplicate Certificates of Title are no longer used, existing Duplicates need not be surrendered when registered land is sold.

Checking with the Land Court section of the registry to be certain as exactly what documents or pre-approvals will be needed well in advance of closing can avoid aggravation, delay and embarrassment for counsel.

§ 1.58   Condominiums—Special Problems

Step 34. Read G.L. c. 183A. It is very brief.

Step 35. When reviewing the purchase and sale agreement, be sure it has appropriate modifications to reflect the fact that a condominium unit is involved. Particularly:

(a) be sure unit is described with sufficient particularity along with description of all appurtenant rights and interests in common facilities (Volume 6, Chapter 1, Form 33);

(b) where registered land is involved, the agreement should provide that the seller will deliver documents sufficient to entitle the buyer to a Memorandum of Unit Ownership from the Land Court;

(c) the agreement should provide for the adjustment of condominium charges for the current month at the time of sale;

(d) the seller should be required to provide a certificate of no unpaid common charges signed by the unit owners' organization, and where appropriate a waiver of right of first refusal by the organization;

(e) the seller should obtain proper endorsements to the master property insurance policy on the common facilities running to the buyer and his or her mortgagee, as of the closing date;

(f) if there is a policy of casualty/liability insurance on the property seller should obtain a binder running to buyer as of closing date (Volume 6, Chapter 1, Form 32).

Step 36. Request that prior to closing you be provided with:

(a) copy of Master Deed;

(b) instrument creating unit owner's organization, its bylaws, rules and regulations;

(c) site and floor plans of unit and adjacent areas with nearest entrance and common area displayed;

(d) current budget of owners' organization with recent income and expense statement;

(e) any applicable title and property insurance policy; (Volume 6, Chapter 1, Form 33.1)

(f) the proposed Unit Deed.

Step 37. Review all documents to be sure they comply with relevant law relating to condominiums. Note powers given to representatives of unit owners' organization. Check the Master Deed and Bylaws to see if any rights to use common facilities or areas, or other common rights, are limited to fewer than all of the unit owners. If so, discuss this with your client.

Step 38. Review rules and regulations of owners' organization and any covenants and restrictions in the master deed to see if they conflict with your client's objectives in purchasing the unit.

Step 39. Review the financial status of the owners' organization with particular note of nature and size of expenses.

Step 40. Be sure the form of proposed deed conforms to G.L. c. 183A, § 9, and that any plan meets local registry requirements.

Step 41. At the closing, in addition to your usual procedures be sure you have obtained a certificate of no unpaid charges, waiver of right of first refusal, title and property insurance binders.

§ 1.59   The Closing

Step 42. If you have done your work properly in advance, the closing itself should be very quick and routine. Lender's attorney usually conducts the closing.

Where there is no mortgagee you will be required to conduct the closing. You must be sure that all the proper documents have been produced, are in the proper form and are properly executed.

Remember that if you conduct the closing you must prepare and file Form 1099B with the Internal Revenue Service, with a copy to the seller (Volume 6, Chapter 1, Form 80.2).

Where you are conducting the closing it is recommended that copies of all closing documents be indexed and bound together. A sample form of closing document index is included in Volume 6, Chapter 1, as Form 34.4.

Step 43. Using a blank closing memo and the preliminary memo you had prepared earlier make the final closing adjustments (Volume 6, Chapter 1, Form 15).

Step 44. Explain to all parties the adjustments you have made and be sure everyone, especially your client understands what has been done.

Step 45. If you are at the registry of deeds, run the title from the date your examiner ended his or her report up to the last document to be recorded prior to yours. Then record your documents.

If you are closing elsewhere than at the registry, all funds must be held in escrow until the documents are recorded.

Step 46. Disburse funds.

Step 47. Where a bank or insurance company has a mortgage on the premises they will usually provide a discharge only when paid. So send them their money, and receive and record the discharge. Be sure you have withheld enough at the closing to cover a few days mail delay in getting their money to them. (Volume 6, Chapter 1, Form 34). In the case of lien holders other than financial institutions, it is customary to have discharges signed ahead of the closing and held in escrow until sufficient funds are withheld from the proceeds to pay them off.

CHAPTER 2

ZONING—PLANNING AND THE PLAN

Synopsis

§ 2.01   CONTROL OF THE PROCESS IN GENERAL
          PLAN STATES
          § 2.01[1]   Use of the Plan in the United States
          § 2.01[2]   The California Model
          § 2.01[3]   Other States
          § 2.01[4]   The Massachusetts "Model"
          § 2.01[5]   Exceptions to the Massachusetts Model
                       on Cape Cod and Martha's Vineyard

§ 2.01 CONTROL OF THE PROCESS IN GENERAL PLAN STATES

While the Subdivision Control Law requires the preparation of a master plan (G.L. c. 41, § 81-D), a community that fails to do so is not penalized. Nor does the Subdivision Control Law or the Zoning Act require that subdivision rules and regulations or zoning amendments be based on the direction, goals or policies of the plan, if one is prepared. Municipal and private counsel are advised to consider the ramifications of cities and towns that are free to rezone without adherence to a plan or document that provides rational support for the legislative act. It has long been alleged that states that do not require a link between zoning and planning are subject to an attack that the zoning is arbitrary, as it has no rational basis. Planners generally refer to the master or comprehensive plan as a "blueprint" for the community's future; a guidance document that prevents zoning and other land use regulations from simply becoming a "Gallup poll."[1]

A brief discussion of the linkage requirements of "plan states" as a comparison to the Massachusetts "non-plan state" model is presented below.

The importance of the comprehensive plan or general plan[2] sprang from the model legislation for planning and zoning promulgated in 1926 and 1928 by the U.S. Department of Commerce. They were labeled the Standard State Zoning Enabling Act—1926 ("SZEA") and the Standard Planning Enabling Act—1928 ("SPEA"). Section 3 of SZEA stated that zoning and other regulations are "in accordance with a Comprehensive plan."

§ 2.01[1] Use of the Plan in the United States[3]

Regulation of land use in the United States occurs almost exclusively at the local level. Consequently, regulations and procedures vary widely from jurisdiction to jurisdiction, with varying degrees of success. From a national perspective, it is highly unlikely that Congress will undertake either land use regulation or an effort to standardize land use processes across the country. Massachusetts has long since

---

[1] *See*, for example, Town of East Greenwich v. Narragansett Electric Co., 651 A.2d 725, 727 (R.I. 1994), where the Rhode Island Supreme Court stated that the comprehensive plan "establishes a binding framework or blueprint that dictates tow and city promulgation of conforming zoning and planning ordinances" and Udell v. Haas, 21 N.Y. 2d 463, 469 (1968), where the New York Court of Appeals stated, "The comprehensive plan is the essence of zoning. Without it, there can be no rational allocation of land use. It is the insurance that the public welfare is being served and that zoning does not become nothing more than just a Gallup poll."

[2] The term "comprehensive plan" is commonly called the "general plan" or "master plan." The term "general plan" is being more commonly used today.

[3] Portions of this discussion are based upon an article by Daniel Curtin, Jr. and Jonathan Witten, *Windfalls and Wipeouts, Givings and Takings in Dramatic Urban Redevelopment Projects* (Boston College Environmental Affairs Law Review, Vol. 32.01, 2005.

resisted "regional authority" and with the exceptions of the Cape Cod Commission and Martha's Vineyard Commission, little regional regulatory authority exists in the state. Consequently, at least in the Commonwealth, reforms to deal with common land use problems will likely continue to develop at the local level.

Increasingly, outside of Massachusetts, local jurisdictions are implementing the comprehensive plan as part of their land use planning process. Although specifics vary widely, most jurisdictions with a comprehensive plan view it as the "constitution" for development within that community. Typically, all subsequent land use decisions must be "consistent" with the vision for growth and development reflected in the comprehensive plan.

§ 2.01[2]   The California Model

In California, land use regulations and approvals must, in most instances, be consistent with the general plan. The general plan[4] has been declared by the California Supreme Court as the single most important document and the "constitution for all future development." *Lesher Communications, Inc. v. City of Walnut Creek*, 52 Cal. 3d 531 (1990). Since the general plan is the constitution for all future development, any decision of a city or county affecting land use, development and public works projects must be consistent with the general plan. *Citizens of Goleta Valley v. Board of Supervisors,* 52 Cal. 3d 553 (1990). Under Government Code section 65860(a), for example, a zoning ordinance is consistent with such plans only if:

- The city or county has officially adopted such a plan; and
- The various land uses authorized by the zoning ordinance are compatible with the objectives, policies, general land uses, and programs specified in such a plan.

In *City of Irvine v. Irvine Citizens Against Overdevelopment*,[5] the California Court of Appeal held that a land use regulation is consistent with a city's general plan where, considering all of its aspects, the ordinance furthers the objectives and policies of the general plan and does not obstruct their attainment. A city's findings that a land use regulation is consistent with its general plan can be reversed only if it is based on evidence from which no reasonable person could have reached the same conclusion.[6]

The California courts have stated that a land use regulation inconsistent with the general plan at the time of enactment is "*void ab initio*," meaning it was invalid

---

[4] Cal. Gov't Code § 65700 *et seq.*

[5] 25 Cal. App. 4th 868, 879 (1994).

[6] A Local and Reg'l Monitor (ALARM) v. City of Los Angeles, 16 Cal. App. 4th 630, 648 (1993).

when passed. *Lesher Communications, Inc. v. City of Walnut Creek*, 52 Cal. 3d 531 (1990); *City of Irvine v. Irvine Citizens Against Overdevelopment*, 25 Cal. App. 4th 868 (1994); *Building Indus. Ass'n v. City of Oceanside,* 27 Cal. App. 4th 744 (1994); *deBottari v. City Council*, 171 Cal. App. 3d 1204 (1985). If a land use regulation becomes inconsistent with a general plan due to an amendment to the plan, or to any element of the plan, the regulation must be amended within a reasonable time so that it is consistent with the amended general plan. *See, e.g.,* Government Code § 65860(c) (zoning ordinances). Since general plan consistency is required, the absence of a valid general plan, or the failure of any relevant elements thereof to meet statutory criteria, precludes the enactment of zoning ordinances and the like. *Resource Defense Fund v. County of Santa Cruz,* 133 Cal. App. 3d 800, 806 (1982).

To ensure that a Machiavellian community cannot avoid the planning requirements embodied in the statute by repeatedly and routinely amending their plan to achieve their zoning objectives, the legislation limits to four the number of times the plan may be amended per year. *See* Government Code § 65358(b).[7]

§ 2.01[3]   Other States

Nearly all states require that zoning take place "in accordance with" some sort of comprehensive or master plan. The states vary, however, in the use of the comprehensive plan as a significant or decisive factor in evaluating land use regulations, although over time, there has been slow and incremental increase nationwide in the quasi-constitutional status of the comprehensive plan. As labeled by one of the nation's foremost commentators on the comprehensive plan,[8] currently the states fall into three major categories in terms of the role of the comprehensive plan in the land use regulatory process.

The first category, the "unitary view," probably reflects the majority of the states—the comprehensive plan is accorded no special significance; i.e., there is no requirement that local governments prepare a plan that is separate from the zoning regulations. Examples of states falling into this category with recent judicial

---

[7] In addition, plan amendments are subject to detailed review pursuant to the California Environmental Quality Act and public hearings before the local planning commission and local legislative body. California Public Resources Code, Section 21000, *et seq.* and Government Code § 65360 *et seq. See also* Curtin's California Land Use and Planning Law, (Solano Press Books, 24th Ed., 2004), page 29.

[8] *See* Sullivan and Michel, *Ramapo Plus Thirty: The Changing Role of the Plan in Land Use Regulation*, 35 Urban Law. 75, 81 (2003). This article traces developments in the role of the comprehensive plan since a 1975 article was published. *See also* Edward J. Sullivan, *2003 Comprehensive Planning Law Update*, The Urban Lawyer, Vol. 36, No. 3, pg. 541 (2004); Daniel J. Curtin, Jr., *Ramapo's Impact on the Comprehensive Plan*, The Urban Lawyer. Vol. 35, No. 1 (Winter 2003).

decisions upholding this "unitary view" are Arkansas,[9] Connecticut,[10] Illinois,[11] New York,[12] and as discussed below, Massachusetts.

States in the second category, "planning factor," give some significance to the comprehensive plan, if it exists, as a factor in evaluating land use regulations, but do not make it the exclusive factor. The weight to be given the plan varies from state to state. Examples of states in this category are Missouri,[13] Montana,[14] and New Jersey.[15]

The third category of states, "plan as the constitution or the law," are those, like California, which grant the general plan quasi-constitutional status regulating ordinances and other actions of the local government in implementing the plan. Other states within this category include Rhode Island,[16] Florida,[17] Oregon,[18] and Washington.[19]

Clear cut policies and goals in a city or county's general plan which guide all developments and approval of development agreements would assure, hopefully, that the bargaining for land use entitlements adhere to the public goals and policies in the adopted general plan and thus preventing piecemeal, ad hoc, arbitrary and capricious decisions.

In California and other plan states, the general plan is the most important legal planning tool for city and county officials to utilize in their efforts to regulate development. It is clearly the constitution for all future development. The goals and policies of the general plan can be used not only in managing growth, regulating development, imposing land use regulations, but also in imposing dedications and impact fees on new projects, rezoning and other approvals especially those not directly authorized under state law. Examples in California include dedications for libraries, police stations, and fire station sites, and fees for affordable housing or child day care centers, provided there is a legally established nexus.

---

[9] Rolling Pines Ltd. Partnership v. City of Little Rock, 40 S.W.3d 828 (2001).

[10] Heithaus v. Planning and Zoning Comm'n, 779 A.2d 750 (2001).

[11] City of Chicago Heights v. Living Word Outreach Full Gospel Church and Ministries, Inc., 749 N.E.2d 916 (2001).

[12] Yellow Lantern Kampground v. Town of Cortlandville, 716 N.Y.S.2d 786 (2000).

[13] Fairview Enterprises, Inc. v. City of Kansas City, 62 S.W.3d 71, 2001 Mo. App. LEXIS 1430 (Mo. Ct. App. 2001).

[14] Greater Yellowstone Coalition, Inc. v. Board of County Comm's of Gallatin County, 25 P.3d 168 (2001).

[15] Medical Center at Princeton v. Township of Princeton Board of Adjustment, 778 A.2d 482 (2001).

[16] Town of East Greenwich v. Narragansett Electric Co., 651 A.2d 725 (1994).

[17] Buck Lake Alliance v. Board of County Comm's, 765 So. 2d 124 (2000).

[18] Jackson County Citizens' League v. Jackson County, 15 P.3d 42 (2000).

[19] Ahamann-Yamane, LLC v. Tabler, 19 P.3d 436 (2001).

In states such as California, Rhode Island, Florida, Oregon, and Washington, for example, since the general plan is the controlling document, it provides protection against "knee jerk" land rezonings, insures appropriate due process, and leads to better thought-out planning to achieve the goals and policies of the local agency. Therefore, when specific issues or individual projects are being considered, they must be weighed against the goals and policies of the plan as a whole. This holistic approach is very different from that encouraged by the Commonwealth of Massachusetts.

§ 2.01[4]   The Massachusetts "Model"

Unlike each of the states discussed above (and many, many others), Massachusetts does not require or even encourage cities and towns to plan. Planning in Massachusetts is an oxymoron.[20] The Courts have responded to challenges to rezonings or the issuance of adjudicative permits that argue "inconsistency with a plan" summarily: a master plan has no legal meaning in Massachusetts.[21]

The American Planning Association has criticized the Massachusetts Zoning Act as "contradictory," "confusing," and "outdated"[22] and the Massachusetts Appeals Court has characterized the vested rights portion of the Act as "infelicitous."[23]

The results of such an "anti-planning" platform are broad:

The Massachusetts Courts have held that cities and towns:

---

[20] Two notable exceptions exist. The Martha's Vineyard Commission Act, 1974 Mass. Acts. 808 and the Cape Cod Commission Act, 1989 Mass. Act 716 (see Mass. Gen. Laws. Ch.40B, § 4) provide for planning consistency among the Island's six towns and Cape Cod's fifteen municipalities. The Cape Cod Commission Act provides that if a town prepares a plan consistent with the regional plan prepared by the Cape Cod Commission, the town may elect to impose impact fees and enter into development agreements. Towns wishing to execute development agreements must then adopt the terms and conditions of the Commission's Model Development Agreement Bylaw, at http://www.capecodcommission.org/bylaws/.

[21] "Neither the master plan itself nor the law requires that zoning be in strict accordance with a master plan." Rando v. Town of North Attleborough, 44 Mass. App. Ct. 603, 612 (1998). G.L. c. 41, § 81-D requires planning boards to "make a master plan" but provides no requirement that regulations adopted by the city or town be consistent with the plan. The plan is adopted by a majority of the members of the planning board, not the local legislative body. The verb "planning" does not appear once in the entirety of the Massachusetts Zoning Act (G.L. c. 40A) or the Subdivision Control Law (G.L. c. 41, § 81L, et seq.).

[22] American Planning Association, "Planning for Smart Growth", 2002 State of States, page 71.

[23] Fitzsimonds .v Board of Appeals of Chatham, 21 Mass. App. Ct. 53, 55–56 (1985). See also Joel Russell and Jonathan D. Witten, "Massachusetts Land Use Law—Time for A Change" and "Affordable Housing—At What Price?" in Land Use Law & Zoning Digest, January 2002, wherein the authors label the Massachusetts land use system as "highly dysfunctional," "Byzantine," and "promoting anarchy."

- are free to rezone property conditioned upon the payment of money (lots of money);[24]
- are free to rezone property conditioned upon completion of specific public improvements;[25]
- are not bound by the goals or policies of a locally adopted plan (if one exists) in their legislative or adjudicative decision making;[26]
- cannot impose long-term growth management devices with or without a planning basis.[27]

The ramifications of the anti-planning approach taken in Massachusetts benefit neither the landowner, the real estate developer nor the community at large. As discussed throughout this text, Massachusetts' land use regulations are confusing and the outcome of a petition before the legislative body, planning board, conservation commission or board of appeals is far from predictable. Counsel representing applicants before local boards should bear in mind that virtually no policy guidance exists—beyond their advocacy and the vexing language of the Zoning Act and Subdivision Control Law—to direct a legislative body or adjudicative board during their deliberations.

§ 2.01[5]   Exceptions to the Massachusetts Model on Cape Cod and Martha's Vineyard

On Cape Cod, by virtue of the Cape Cod Commission Act (Act), the Cape's fifteen towns have strong incentives for the completion of a local comprehensive plan. As of 2005, nine of the fifteen towns have completed and certified plans on record.

The Cape Cod Commission Act establishes a regional planning agency with regulatory powers without parallel in the Commonwealth.

First, the Act provides a strong incentive for the Cape's towns to develop a comprehensive plan in compliance and concert with the Regional Policy Plan prepared for Cape Cod. Once the Cape Cod Commission has certified the town plan, the municipality is authorized to enact both impact fees and development agreements. Neither tool is available to cities and towns elsewhere in Massachusetts. A discussion of impact fees and development agreements is found in Chapter Five.

The purpose of the plan—to provide a vision for the community in concert with plans for neighboring towns and the Cape in general—establishes a process by which zoning, subdivision control, health and wetlands regulations are consistent

---

[24] Durand v. IDC Bellingham, LLC, 440 Mass. 45 (2003).
[25] McClean Hospital Corporation v. Belmont, 56 Mass. App. Ct. 540 (2002).
[26] Rando v. Town of North Attleborough, 44 Mass. App. Ct. 603, 612 (1998).
[27] Zuckerman v. Town of Hadley, 442 Mass. 511 (2004).

with the plan and each other.[28] As discussed, this principle of consistency is the hallmark of comprehensive planning.

On Cape Cod, the grant of a development permit or a rezoning, for example, should be consistent with the town's adopted comprehensive plan. For example, while the board of appeals in Fitchburg must comply with the required findings pertaining the grant of a variance, as discussed in Chapter Five, Falmouth, by virtue of its location on Cape Cod and its relationship to the Act, must do more. In addition to complying with the required findings pursuant to G.L. c. 40A, § 10, the Falmouth board of appeals must also ensure that the grant of a variance is not in conflict with its Comprehensive Plan, certified by the Cape Cod Commission in 1998.[29]

Second, the Act and its predecessor, the Martha's Vineyard Commission Act,[30] establish a process for designating "districts of critical planning concern" (DCPC). These districts, by virtue of their "critical nature", allow the respective Commissions' additional review authority and limit many of the protections otherwise afforded a landowner by the Zoning Act.[31] In the variance example noted above, the Falmouth board of appeals would be required to ensure that the grant of the variance complies with the local comprehensive plan as well as ensure that the grant will not conflict with a DCPC designation.[32] In addition, as discussed below, the board must ensure that the grant will not, or could not, become categorized as a development of regional impact.

---

[28] Many commentators have referred to this consistency as both vertical and horizontal. Vertical meaning, for example, that new subdivision regulations are consistent with zoning controls and zoning regulations consistent with the comprehensive plan. Horizontal meaning that within the zoning ordinance, for example, use regulations are consistent with dimensional requirements.

[29] Although the Act is silent on this point, it seems reasonable to conclude that a town that grants variances inconsistent with their Plan is in violation of the Act and therefore runs the risk that their Certification will be revoked. "The commission may revoke the certification of a municipality's local comprehensive plan if the municipality fails to make its development by-laws consistent with said plan within the time allowed under this section." Cape Cod Commission Act, Section 9. This interpretation is consistent with case law from jurisdictions that mandate comprehensive plans.

[30] Chapter 831 of the Mass. Acts of 1977.

[31] For example, and as discussed in detail in Chapter 5, G.L. c. 40A § 6 provides seven broad protections to property owners from subsequent zoning changes. The Act's DCPC regulations supersede these protections.

[32] Such a conflict could occur in one of two ways on Cape Cod, for example. First, upon nomination of an area as a DCPC and the subsequent notice provisions specified in the Act, "no municipality may grant a development permit within the nominated district until the commission has decided not to accept the nomination or has denied a designation... ." Section 11(b). A variance is included in the Act's broad definition of a "development permit." Second, if the DCPC nomination is accepted by the Cape Cod Commission, "no municipal agency may grant a development permit for a development in a district of critical planning concern unless the proposed development is consistent with the municipality's approved implementing regulations or implementing regulations adopted by the assembly of delegates for the district of critical planning concern." Section 11(g).

Third, both Acts establish thresholds, so-called "developments of regional impact (DRI)," for which projects of a certain size or impact require review and approval by the Cape Cod or Martha's Vineyard Commission as a condition precedent to project approval. Both Acts articulate which projects, and what types of development will require regional review. In addition, the Cape Cod Commission Act allows local towns to request regional review of projects that do not categorically fit within the prescribed thresholds. These "discretionary reviews" can be based on one of several relevant criteria pertaining to regional impacts.

DRIs are projects that are presumed to present regional impacts due to their size or character. For example, as a presumptive threshold, the Commission must approve or deny "development, including the expansion of existing developments that is planned to create or add thirty or more residential dwelling units."[33] In addition, projects subject to MEPA review may be required to obtain DRI approval from the Commission.[34]

To obtain DRI approval the applicant must demonstrate the following:

1. The probable benefit from the proposed development is greater than the probable detriment;

2. The proposed development is consistent with the regional policy plan and with the local comprehensive plan of the town in which the development is proposed;

3. The proposed development is consistent with municipal development bylaws, or, if not consistent, the inconsistency is necessary to enable a substantial segment of the population to secure adequate opportunities for housing, conservation, environmental protection, education, recreation or balanced economic growth;

4. The proposed development is consistent with implementing regulations for applicable districts of critical planning concern.[35]

In reviewing DRIs, the Commission relies heavily on the Minimum Performance Standards ("MPS") set forth in the Cape Cod Regional Policy Plan (the "RPP"). These MPSs touch on a wide range of planning topics, including but not limited to protection of water resources, coastal resources, natural resources, transportation impacts, affordable housing, land use impacts, and historic and community character.

---

[33] Code of Cape Cod Commission Regulations, Barnstable County Ordinance 90-14, as amended, Chapter A, Section 3(d).

[34] MEPA is the acronym for the Massachusetts Environmental Policy Act, G.L., Chapter 30, §§ 1—62H. Under Sections 12(i) and 13(b) of the Act, projects filing an Environmental Impact Report with MEPA must obtain DRI approval; projects filing only an Environmental Notification Form with MEPA may be reviewed as a DRI at the discretion of the Commission.

[35] Act, Section 13(d)(1–4).

The RPP's Minimum Performance Standards are mandatory. Hence, each DRI applicant must demonstrate conformance with all applicable MPSs. In the event a project does not comply, it may only be approved if the applicant can show that "the interests protected by a given Minimum Performance Standard can be achieved by an alternative approach including appropriate mitigation."[36] To allow this flexibility, the Commission must find that "the proposed use must not be more detrimental to the protected resource than would be allowable under the applicable Minimum Performance Standard."[37]

---

[36] Cape Cod Regional Policy Plan, 2002, p. 6

[37] *Id.*

CHAPTER 3

ZONING—REGULATORY TAKINGS

Synopsis

§ 3.01   Introduction

§ 3.02   Physical Invasions of Real Property and Complete
          Deprivations of Value: "Always a Taking"

§ 3.03   Nuisance Preclusion: "Never a Taking"

§ 3.04   Balancing "Too Far" in Reviewing a Regulatory
          Takings Claim

          § 3.04[1]   Legislative Actions
          § 3.04[2]   Adjudicative Actions

THE LAW

§ 3.01 Introduction

The point at which a land use regulation "goes too far" and thus constitutes a compensable taking, is often debated and is the subject of numerous articles, texts and weekday planning board and commission hearings across the Commonwealth. While the subject makes for interesting dialogue, the methodology for assessing when a regulation goes too far is well accepted.

Before analyzing whether the claimed regulation or adjudicative action triggers the takings clause, counsel should first ensure that the case is ripe for judicial review. A case is not ripe for review, and thus a takings claim cannot be effectively asserted, until all administrative remedies have been exhausted.[1] Note that exhaustion of administrative remedies differs greatly in Massachusetts land use practice. Special permits, for example, have no exhaustion requirement. The issuance or denial of the special permit is the final action required before an appeal.[2] A denial of a building permit, however, requires an appeal to the board of appeals pursuant to G.L. c. 40A, § 15 to complete the ripeness requirement.

Note that in some instances, a takings claim may be brought pursuant to an argument that the ordinance violates due process principles "facially," obviating the need to exhaust all traditional remedies such as applying for a variance or building permit.[3] The law regarding exhaustion of remedies prior to filing a takings claim is complex and counsel is well advised to ensure that their claim is ripe.[4] Whereas the Courts have traditionally upheld facial attacks against a zoning

---

[1] *See*, for example, United States v. Riverside Bayview Homes, 474 U.S. 121 (1985), Williamson County Regional Planning Commission v. Hamilton Bank of Johnston City, 473 U.S. 172 (1985), MacDonald, Sommer & Frates v. Yolo County, 477 U.S. 340, 348 (1986) ("A court cannot determine whether a regulation has gone "too far" unless it knows how far the regulation goes"), Wilson v. Commonwealth, 413 Mass. 352 (1992), and FIC Homes of Blackstone, Inc. v. Conservation Commission of Blackstone, 41 Mass. App. Ct. 681 (1996).

[2] *See* G.L. c. 40A, § 17.

[3] *See*, for example, Agins v. City of Tiburon, 447 U.S. 255 (1980) and Grenier v. Zoning Board of Appeals of Chatham, 62 Mass. App. Ct. 62 (2004), where the Court reviewed the merits of a regulatory takings claim even though the plaintiff sought and was denied a building permit. "However, given the unconditional nature of the zoning bylaw's prohibitions against erecting a house on lot 93, we conclude that the question presented, whether a single family house can be erected on lot 93 is one of law and that any request by Gove to build on lot 93 would have been futile." 62 Mass. App. Ct. 62 (2004), at 66, *citing* Wilson v. Commonwealth, 31 Mass. App. Ct. 757 (1992); Trust Ins. Co. v. Commissioner of Ins., 48 Mass. App. Ct. 617 (2000); Daddario v. Cape Cod Comm., 56 Mass. App. Ct. 764 (2002), *cert. denied*, 540 U.S. 1005 (2003).

[4] "Dismissal is proper disposition where, because of failure to exhaust administrative remedies, party had no right to seek declaration... ." Commonwealth v. Blair, 60 Mass. App. Ct. 741, 752 (2004), *citing* The St. Paul Cos. v. TIG Premier Ins. Co., 58 Mass. App. Ct. 650, 657 n.12 (2003).

regulation pursuant to the "futility" exception of the exhaustion doctrine, in some cases, usually where the permit granting authority is an administrative agency, the Courts have ruled that a regulatory taking claim does not ripen until "the government entity charged with implementing the regulations has reached a final decision regarding the application of the regulations to the property at issue."[5] As the U.S. Supreme Court stated, "A court cannot determine whether a regulation has gone 'too far' unless it knows how far the regulation goes."[6] In addition and in general, the mere denial of development plan or development proposal does not, by itself, constitute a taking.

Several Massachusetts decisions[7] have focused upon regulatory takings claims, although the most instructive decisions have, not surprisingly, been those of the United States Supreme Court. Takings claims are emotional: a landowner has alleged that government has so over-regulated her property that it is "as if" government has used its eminent domain powers and seized her land. The fundamental difference between government's use of eminent domain and regulation, however is that the former always requires compensation and the later, rarely does. Thus, a skeptic would argue that government, if left unchallenged, would always seek to regulate private property and avoid paying compensation as opposed to the compulsory payment of compensation through use of the government's eminent domain powers.

The line at which government "goes too far" is the focus of this Chapter.

For the purposes of determining whether a land use regulation "goes too far" and thus constitutes an impermissible regulatory taking, it is recommended that counsel analyze the regulation according to the following three questions:

- First, does the regulation, either facially or as applied, constitute a "physical invasion or "physical appropriation" of real property or, does the regulation deprive the landowner of all economic value. With the exception of appropriations permissible in exchange for the grant of an adjudicative permit

---

[5] Daddario v. Cape Cod Comm., 56 Mass. App. Ct. 764 (2002), *cert. denied*, 540 U.S. 1005, (2003).

[6] MacDonald, Sommer & Frates v. County of Yolo, 477 U.S. 340, 348 (1986).

[7] *See*, for example, Lopes v. City of Peabody, 417 Mass. 299 (1994), where the Supreme Judicial Court remanded the case to Land Court to determine whether the City of Peabody's zoning ordinance regulating wetland resources (*See* Chapter XXX for further discussion on the pitfalls of using zoning to regulate wetland resources) was a categorical taking as an economic "wipeout." Before remand, however, the Court announced the ruling that subsequent purchasers of real property obtain the right to the challenge burdensome regulations imposed on the real property's prior owners. This ruling foreshadowed the United States Supreme Court's holding in Palazzolo v. Rhode Island, 533 U.S. 606 (2001). In *Palazzolo*, the Court held that regulatory takings claims are not barred simply because a prior owner of real property failed to challenge the regulation as confiscatory.

(special permit and to some degree, approval of a subdivision plan pursuant
to the Subdivision Control Law), a physical invasion as well as a complete
deprivation of value (an economic "wipeout") always constitutes a taking.
A physical invasion or complete deprivation of value are considered "categorical takings" as they are always—categorically—considered regulatory takings.

- Second, does the regulation preclude the use of private property that would
  otherwise constitute a nuisance pursuant to Massachusetts law? Nuisance
  preclusion is never a taking and therefore compensation is not required
  simply because no one has the right to use her property such that it would
  constitute a public or private nuisance. If the landowner never had the right
  to operate a nuisance in the first instance, prohibition of an unallowable use
  could hardly be deemed a taking. Counsel is advised to put forth the
  nuisance argument carefully. Precisely because government may lawfully
  preclude a nuisance without having to pay compensation, the nuisance
  preclusion argument should be used sparingly and only in those cases where
  the facts truly support the argument that alleged activities is a common law
  nuisance.

The above two questions frame the "ends" of the takings analysis. On one end,
governmental actions that always constitute a taking: physical invasions and
complete economic wipeouts. On the other, governmental actions that never constitute a taking: prohibition of a nuisance.

- The more common problem encountered by public and private counsel is
  in the area best described as between these two ends, and defined by the
  third question: Does the regulation "go too far"?

In *Leonard v. Town of Brimfield*,[8] the Massachusetts Supreme Judicial Court
reviewed the Town of Brimfield's zoning bylaw-regulating development within
designated floodplains against a complaint that the bylaw precluded the full development of the plaintiff's real property. Concluding that the bylaw did not
constitute a physical invasion or complete deprivation of economic value of the
plaintiff's property, the Court stated, "When a regulatory taking involves neither
a physical invasion nor a complete deprivation of use…Federal law has established
several interrelated factors which are to be considered in determining whether a
compensable taking has occurred… ."[9] The Court went on to cite the three "*Penn
Central*" factors discussed below.

In *Grenier v. Board of Appeals of Chatham*,[10] the Appeals Court concluded that

---

[8] 423 Mass. 152 (1996).
[9] Leonard v. Town of Brimfield, 423 Mass. 152, at 153.
[10] 62 Mass. App. Ct. 62 (2004).

where a zoning bylaw does not strip a landowner of all economic value—even where the remaining economic value is measured for "recreational value"—the bylaw does not constitute a categorical taking. *Grenier* provides an excellent summary of several federal and Massachusetts takings cases highlighting the current state of the law today: "…a land use regulation 'may deprive an owner of a beneficial property use—even the most beneficial such use—without rendering the regulation an unconstitutional taking."[11]

Leonard and *Grenier* are also instructive as the SJC concluded that the zoning bylaws under attack did not constitute a regulatory taking as the property was purchased after the bylaw was adopted. The landowner could not, therefore, have suffered from an interference with her investment backed expectations, nor "complain about the loss of a right she never acquired."[12]

Discussed more fully in Section 3.04, determining if a land use regulation that is neither a physical invasion nor an economic wipeout "goes too far" hinges on an additional level of analysis: whether the regulation is "legislative" or "adjudicative."

§ 3.02 Physical Invasions of Real Property and Complete Deprivations of Value: "Always a Taking"

A physical invasion of real property—government's taking of real property, in fee or easement—is always a taking as the action is tantamount to government's use of its eminent domain powers. Land belonging to a private party that either was physically taken (as in an eminent domain action) or the private parties' ability to exclude others has been stripped by government's actions (e.g. taking an easement to install water mains on private property) are categorical takings. In either case and regardless of how noble or important the government's claimed purpose, compensation is required. This latter point is critical. The Court will not apply a balancing test between the benefit conveyed to the public by the government's action and the harm suffered by the landowner (even if the harm is minor) in a physical invasion case. The underlying principle is that whenever government seeks to acquire private property or deprive that property owner of a fundamental attribute of ownership, government must pay for the acquired right, regardless of the public benefit supporting the acquisition.

Lorreto v. Teleprompter Manhattan CATV Corp., 458 U.S. 419 (1982), high-

---

[11] 62 Mass. App. Ct. 62, at 70–71, *citing* Lovequist v. Conservation Commission of Dennis, 379 Mass. 7, 19–20 (1979).

[12] Leonard, 423 Mass. at 155. In *Grenier*, the Court concluded that the plaintiffs could have made more profitable use of the land prior to the enactment of the offending bylaw and that even after the bylaw's adoption, the property had a value for "recreational pursuits" of $23,000. 62 Mass. App. Ct. 62, at 70.

lights the bright line established by the Supreme Court in physical invasion cases. In *Lorreto*, the U.S. Supreme Court reviewed a challenge by a building owner in Manhattan that the City's ordinance mandating property owners to allow the installation of a cable television connection plate on the outside of the buildings was a physical invasion. The Court concluded that despite the otherwise insignificant invasion, it was nonetheless an invasion in violation of the Fifth Amendment to the Constitution. *Loretto* is instructive guidance for private and municipal counsel alike. Regardless of the areal extent of the invasion, cities and towns simply cannot take or otherwise strip landowners of their fundamental rights of property ownership without compensation.

Loretto is also instructive as to the distinction between a physical invasion and permissible regulation. Had the City of New York required that all property owners install the connection plate on their own by a date certain, justified on a public health or safety basis; it is highly unlikely that the Court would have concluded that a taking had occurred. As discussed below, the test for whether a regulation constitutes a taking is far different from the test that was at issue in *Loretto*. The former analysis provides government with significant leeway and discretion; the latter does not.

A second categorical taking—government's action that will always be a taking—is where government's action deprives a landowner of all economic value. Thus, a zoning regulation that leaves the landowner with no—zero—economic value has been ruled a categorical taking. The underlying premise is straightforward: government should not be allowed to accomplish through regulation what it should be required to pay for using its eminent domain powers.

While it is generally apparent when government violates the rule against physical invasions (and therefore these violations can be readily avoided), government's violation of the rule against economic wipeouts is less obvious. In many cases, the local legislature's adoption of a zoning ordinance or wetlands bylaw does not automatically signal the likelihood of an as applied regulatory takings claim. The difficulty lies in the fact that the zoning ordinance, for example, may seek to limit the density of development or the placement of a development within a generalized zoning district. On its face, the ordinance complies with the due process requirements of *Agins* (discussed below) and the basic and unconstrained requirements applicable to Massachusetts land use law. However, as applied to a particular parcel, the same ordinance could render a parcel economically valueless and trigger a regulatory takings claim.

§ 3.03   Nuisance Preclusion: "Never a Taking"

Whereas a physical invasion is "always" a compensable action, precluding a nuisance "never" requires compensation. The distinction is simply the opposite side of the same coin. Whereas a physical invasion is the removal of a fundamental element of property ownership (e.g. the right to exclude), preclusion of a nuisance activity is prohibiting a use that common law never permitted in the first place. As a landowner could never lawfully violate the common law nuisance principle that of using her land to the unreasonable detriment to another, government's prohibition of the already proscribed activity does not require compensation. "Clearly the government is not required to compensate an individual for denying him the right to use that which he has never owned."[1]

§ 3.04   Balancing "Too Far" in Reviewing a Regulatory Takings Claim

The outcome of a takings analysis differs if the action being challenged is the result of a legislative or adjudicative act. A legislative act is one adopted by the local legislature (e.g. city council, town council or town meeting) and typically involves a new or amended zoning ordinance or bylaw, wetlands bylaw more restrictive than the Wetlands Protection Act, historic district regulation and related regulations. An adjudicative action is one rendered by an adjudicative body, including any municipal board or commission that is empowered with adjudicative functions. (Note that the enabling authority for the adjudicative action must first be provided by the local legislature, e.g. the authority to grant a special permit within a specified zoning district). The distinction between the two categories for the purposes of a takings analysis, however, is that while a legislative action such as the adoption of a zoning ordinance is granted broad deference by a reviewing Court, the deference is narrowed where the legislation is applied and enforced by an adjudicative body. The courts' overriding concern is best witnessed by even the casual observer at planning board, board of appeals and conservation commission hearings throughout the state: the fear of an abuse of adjudicative powers.

While most litigation focuses on claims of regulatory takings as the result of decisions by boards of appeals and planning boards, conservation commissions, boards of health, city councils, boards of selectmen and historic district commissions may each, from time to time, have adjudicative functions. Any municipal entity that has discretionary permit granting authority has the potential of triggering a regulatory takings claim.

While the distinction between adjudicative and legislative actions is clear—only the legislature (town meeting, town council or city council) can act in a legislative capacity, determining when a local board is acting in an adjudicative capacity is not always as apparent. The determinative factor is discretion. Where the municipal agency, board or commission has discretionary powers, the city or town must act according to the takings rules discussed below.

---

[1]   Flynn v. Cambridge, 383 Mass. 152, 160 (1981).

If the agency, board, or commission does not have discretionary powers, the actor is functioning in a ministerial capacity and, accordingly cannot (or should not) run afoul of takings jurisprudence simply because the actor has no discretion in its decision-making. Therefore, the actor has no ability to "go too far." In this later case, the aggrieved landowner may very well challenge the effect of the regulation, but the landowner would not have a claim that the city or town abused its discretionary powers.

§ 3.04[1] Legislative Actions

The U.S. Supreme Court succinctly stated the regulatory takings analysis for legislative decisions in *Agins v. City of Tiburon*, 447 U.S. 255 (1980). The Court explained that a regulatory taking occurs where government's action fails to advance a legitimate governmental interest (prong one) or denies the landowner economically viable use of his land (prong two). *Agins* "simplified" the Court's earlier holding in *Penn Central Transp. Co. v. New York City*, 438 U.S. 104 (1978).

The *Penn Central* Court reviewed a New York City regulation designed to prohibit additional construction above the landmark Grand Central Terminal. The Court concluded that the City's ordinance did not violate what was labeled a "multi-factor inquiry." First, what is the character of the government action? Second, what is the economic impact of the government's action? Third, does the regulation interfere with "distinct, investment backed expectations?"

Note that the three *Penn Central* tests are mostly synonymous with the tests discussed above. For example, by referring to the "character of the government action, the *Penn Central* Court was referring to the three questions noted previously. Was, for example, the government physically invading private property? If so, the "character" of the governmental action would automatically trigger the compensation clause. By referring to the "economic impact" of the governmental action, the Court was referring to what has become the second prong of *Agins*: does the regulation strip the landowner of all economic value? The third prong of *Penn Central* adds an equitable estoppel element to takings jurisprudence; an element difficult to prove. The "investment backed expectations" prong requires the plaintiff to prove that he was somehow led along by government—led to believe—that the development proposal was acceptable and permissible and that armed with this knowledge, government intentionally (or negligently) changed the regulatory rules to the plaintiff's detriment. While such a fact pattern is possible, it is highly unlikely in an early vesting state such as Massachusetts.[1] (See Chapter 5.10 for a detailed discussion on vesting rules in Massachusetts).

---

[1] Even late vesting states rarely apply the equitable doctrine of "investment backed expectations" suggested by the Court in *Penn Central*. *See*, for example, Avco Community Developers, Inc. v. South Coastal Regional Commission, 17 Cal. 3d 785 (1976).

Counsel is advised to apply the *Agins* tests in evaluating a regulatory takings claim in Massachusetts. If the facts present themselves, an investment backed expectations argument is possible, but as noted, highly unlikely in Massachusetts given the ease at which a landowner can protect herself from regulatory changes.

In evaluating a regulatory takings claim pursuant to *Agins*, first analyze the validity of the zoning regulation, subdivision rule and regulation, health regulation or local wetlands ordinance at issue. While these regulations usually meet the very broad "public purpose test," it is worthwhile scrutinizing the regulation itself. Is it outdated? Does it protect the very built or natural resource it is intended to preserve? Is the scale of the map referenced in the ordinance appropriate for the resource targeted by the ordinance? Does the ordinance constitute "spot zoning," "contract zoning," or otherwise violate due process requirements?

The second prong of *Agins*, based on the principles set forth in *Penn Central*, is violated only where the landowner is left with no reasonable economic value.[2] A mere diminution in value has not been held to constitute a regulatory taking.[3] This prong is often referred to as the "whole parcel" doctrine. The doctrine looks at "what is left over" not at "what was taken." In other words, the doctrine forces the landowner to demonstrate that the value of the land after the regulation is applied is negligible as opposed to analyzing the value that the regulation stripped away. The whole parcel doctrine remains the law in Massachusetts today.[4]

For example, a regulation that deprives a landowner of the development density allowed under previous zoning regulations, adjusted to comport with the city or town's goals, would not be considered a taking as there has not been a total deprivation of economic value. As the new regulation presumably allows (or have allowed) some level of development, it is unlikely that the regulation would be tantamount to a total economic wipeout. As only a complete diminution in value—a

---

    [2] 438 U.S. 104 (1978). "...appellants, focusing on the character and impact of the New York City law, argue that it effects a 'taking' because its operation has significantly diminished the value of the Terminal site. Appellants concede that the decisions sustaining other land-use regulations, which, like the New York City law, are reasonably related to the promotion of general welfare, uniformly reject the proposition that diminution in property value, standing alone, can establish a 'taking.'" . 438 U.S. 104, at 131, *citing* Euclid v. Ambler Realty Co., 272 U.S. 365 (1926) and Hadacheck v. Sebastian, 239 U.S. 394 (1915).

    [3] *See*, for example, William Haas & Co. v. City and County of San Francisco, 605 F.2d 1117 (9th Cir. 1979), where the U.S. Court of Appeals upheld a city zoning regulation that effectively reduced the plaintiff's property value from $2 million to less than $100,000, but did not constitute a compensable taking.

    [4] The whole parcel doctrine is a product of federal law and as a result, could be made less burdensome on landowners by state courts or state constitutions. *See*, for example, Coast Range Conifers, LLC v. State of Oregon, 189 Or. App. 531 (2003), where the Oregon Appeals Court states that the whole parcel doctrine has been "rejected." 189 Or. App. 531, at 546.

complete wipeout—would render a parcel susceptible to the second prong of *Agins*, regulations that reduce real property value as a consequence to public health protection are unlikely to constitute a regulatory taking.[5]

Note that while the *Agins* test traditionally inserts the word "or" between the first and second prongs, a violation of the first prong of *Agins* will be a violation of substantive due process principles and not takings law. Thus, a zoning ordinance or bylaw that failed to protect public health or welfare, would not necessarily trigger the compensation clause. The ordinance or bylaw would also have to violate the second prong of *Agins* by virtue of its economic impact on the plaintiff's property.[6] A violation of the first prong would lead to invalidation of the ordinance or bylaw. A violation of the second prong would require compensation.

A challenge under the *Agins* test remains however. Assume that a zoning bylaw is in place that limits the number of dwelling units based upon nitrogen loading calculations.[7] Is it a regulatory taking if a landowner seeks to develop her property within a wellhead protection area, but the area's carrying capacity for nitrogen loading has been exceeded? In other words, previous development applicants have assumed the capacity for nitrogen loading and no new development permits will be granted within the wellhead protection area.

The landowner, citing the U.S. Supreme Court's holding in *Lucas v. South Carolina Coastal Council,* 112 S. Ct. 2886 (1992)[8] and reiterating the holding in

---

[5] This statement presumes that state law does not more narrowly define a regulatory taking. In an extraordinary case given the State's historic and aggressive restrictions on development, *see*, for example, Oregon Revised Statutes Chapter 197, adopted in November 2004. This ballot initiative, referred to as "Measure 37," requires the payment of compensation to a property owner where a land use regulation "reduces" the property's value. *See also* Harvey Jacobs, "*The Impact of State Property Rights Laws: Those Laws and My Land,* Land Use L. & Zoning Digest, Vol. 50, No.3 (1998).

[6] *See* Lingle v. Chevron USA, Inc., 125 S. Ct. 2074 (2005).

[7] It is increasingly common to find these ordinances and bylaws across the Commonwealth. Many are derivatives of nitrogen loading restrictions found in Title 5 (310 CMR 15.00) and the state's wellhead protection regulations (310 CMR 22.00).

[8] In *Lucas*, the Supreme Court stated a new categorical takings rule: when a landowner is subject to total deprivation of all economically viable use of her land, a taking has occurred regardless of the purpose or effect of the regulation. Thus a regulation that was designed to protect public health, but left the landowner with no economic value, would constitute an unconstitutional regulatory taking. Although Justice Scalia narrowed the scope of this categorical taking rule (allowing for some instances where a complete deprivation could be justified without compensation), the Court's holding in *Lucas* reversed the long held position that in some instances, private property could be regulated without compensation afforded, no matter how aggressive the regulation. Citing cases dating back to Mugler v. Kansas, 123 U.S. 623 (1887), Justice Blackmun's strong dissent provides numerous cases where a landowner's property value was destroyed, yet no compensation was awarded. "These cases rest on the principle that the State has full power to prohibit an owner's use of property if it is harmful to the public…It would make no sense under this

Agins, will claim that the carrying capacity regulation renders her property devoid of all economically beneficial uses and requires compensation.

In *Zanghi v. Board of Appeals of Bedford*,[9] the Massachusetts Appeals Court was faced with a challenge to a local zoning bylaw that, the landowner claimed, affected a regulatory taking as one of the lots in a multi-lot subdivision could not comply with the bylaw's minimum lot size requirement. Citing *Agins*, *Lucas*, *Penn Central*, and several Massachusetts cases, the Court concluded that the bylaw did not trigger the compensation requirement as the "property has not been deprived of all economically beneficial use."[10]

The Appeals Court cited a four-step test in determining whether a legislative action constituted a regulatory taking. Note that the four steps suggested by the Court are a restatement of the tests announced by the U.S. Supreme Court in *Penn Central* and *Agins*. Citing *FIC Homes of Blackstone, Inc. v. Conservation Commission of Blackstone*,[11] the Court stated that a regulatory taking that is not a categorical taking (e.g. not a physical invasion or a complete economic wipeout as announced in *Lucas*) must be evaluated by a review of four factors: (1) the validity of the bylaw as applied to the plaintiff's property,[12] (2) the plaintiff's reasonable investment backed expectations, (3) the economic impact of the regulation on the plaintiff's property, and (4) the character of the governmental action.[13]

Zanghi's reaffirmation of federal takings law provides as "bright" a line as possible in takings litigation without creating a definitive list of what will be a categorical taking.

Based upon the federal and Massachusetts cases noted above, municipal counsel facing a claim that a legislative action constitutes a regulatory taking has three clear options. First, compensation can be granted and the real property acquired and preserved. For example, the acquisition and protection of real property in a well-head protection area or other natural resource habitat provides the strongest level of protection available, the landowner will be fairly compensated for her property and claims of unfair or discriminatory regulatory controls will be resolved.

A second option is for the local government to defend the regulation under the

---

theory to suggest that an owner has a constitutionally protected right to harm others, if only he makes the proper showing of economic loss." Lucas, 112 S. Ct. 2886, at 2912.

[9] 61 Mass. App. Ct. 82 (2004).

[10] 61 Mass. App. Ct. 82, at 90.

[11] 61 Mass. App. Ct. 82, at 90.

[12] As a threshold matter, the plaintiff bears "…the burden of demonstrating that the bylaw as applied to [his] property does not 'substantially advance legitimate State interests." FIC Homes of Blackstone, Inc. v. Conservation Commission of Blackstone, 41 Mass. App. Ct. 681, 690, *quoting* Lopes v. Peabody, 417 Mass. 299, 305 (1994).

[13] 61 Mass. App. Ct. 82, at 87.

holding in *Lucas* by demonstrating that the regulation and thus the development prohibition is supported by common-law nuisance principles found in state law.[14]

Third, local government can defend the regulations insofar as they will not constitute a complete or even moderate destruction of all economically viable property uses, consistent with *Agins*, *Penn Central*, and *Zanghi*.

Counsel's response to a regulatory takings challenge is likely to differ depending upon the purpose of the regulation under attack. For example, if the ordinance is designed to limit the impacts of growth upon built systems by instituting a temporary moratorium on new building permits (e.g. the municipal wastewater treatment plant is at capacity), plaintiff's counsel may need to argue that the regulation's temporal standards are, de facto, a complete economic wipeout (a temporary taking that simply lasts too long). Municipal counsel is likely to respond that the temporary nature of the regulation does not conflict with any of the tests discussed above.

If the ordinance is designed to limit the impacts upon natural resources, however, plaintiff's counsel's argument is more complicated. A well-written "carrying capacity" regulation that prohibits additional development within a specified area (e.g., a wellhead protection area as used in the previous example) need not stipulate that *no development* be allowed (thus potentially running afoul of *Agins*, *Lucas* and *Zanghi*). Regulations designed to protect natural resources can (and should) be tailored to regulate specific contaminants of concern rather than a complete ban on all contaminants or portions of a parcel as opposed to the entire parcel, if possible. For example, a fresh water body is limited by phosphorus but not typically by nitrogen. A coastal estuary that is well flushed is limited by nitrogen, but not phosphorus. A drinking water supply is threatened by nitrogen, but not phosphorus.[15] Therefore, the above noted regulation intending on protecting a wellhead protection area could be tailored to prohibit additional *nitrogen* loading. It is left to the landowner to propose land uses that do not generate additional nitrogen.

Where the regulation is designed to protect wetland resources, the ordinance could focus on wetland resources of greatest concern (e.g. vernal pools or bordering vegetated wetlands) and emphasize the protection of these areas over other wetland resources that while deserving of protection, are less vulnerable than others. Massachusetts courts have reviewed numerous claims by landowners that a wet-

---

[14] This option is the least desirable given the Court's requirement that support for use prohibition under a common law nuisance theory "must inhere in the title itself, in the restrictions already placed upon land ownership." Lucas, 112 S. Ct. 2886, at 2900.

[15] *See*, for example, Hughto, R., Nelson, M., and Witten, J., *Environmental Science and Engineering for Lawyers*, Massachusetts Continuing Legal Education, Boston, MA. 2000 and Hopkinson, C. and Vallino, J., *The Relationship Among Man's Activities in Watersheds and Estuaries: A Model of Runoff Effects on Patterns of Estuarine Community Metabolism*, Estuaries, Vol. 18, No. 4, p. 598–621, December 1995.

lands protection regulation constitutes a regulatory taking. The Courts have routinely ruled consistent with the discussion noted above.[16]

While it is possible that a landowner's development options will be curtailed by the regulation, it is unlikely that they will be eliminated. Thus, carrying capacity regulations that are targeted to specific threats should benefit from the highly deferential judicial review given to legislative actions.

Legislative actions are imprecise in their abilities to protect complicated natural resources from the negative impacts of development, however. While a legislative action, based on the findings of a comprehensive plan, can ensure appropriate zoning and land use regulatory controls, the fine-tuning often needed to protect a water body or wetland resource from development impacts demands a close, site-specific analysis. Massachusetts cities and towns have, therefore, relied on the discretionary nature of a special permit pursuant to G.L. c. 40A, § 9 (discussed further in Section 5.08[2]) and its ability to provide for the type of ad hoc analysis needed to evaluate site-specific impacts of individual projects.

§ 3.04[2]   Adjudicative Actions

As discussed above, legislative actions can attempt to establish appropriate use requirements and minimum lot sizes under zoning, but are generally too "clumsy" to assure the precise protection of a natural resource sufficient to ensure that established standards or carrying capacity thresholds are not exceeded.

Thus, the role of special permits pursuant to G.L. c. 40A, § 9. With a special permit, a planning board, board of selectmen, city council or board of appeals can fine-tune a development application to ensure that the specific purpose of the regulation (using the above noted example, carrying capacity of an affected resource) will be respected.[17]

Nevertheless, relative to takings claims, special permits must be used with caution and a relatively recent host of cases have helped clarify the rules applying to these permits.

First, the permit conditions—extractions—must relate to the harm posed by the

---

[16] *See*, for example, Englander v. Department of Environmental Management, 16 Mass. App. Ct. 943 (1983), *review denied*, 390 Mass. 1102 (1983) and Moskow v. Commissioner of Environmental Management, 384 Mass. 530 (1981).

[17] Special permits are generally required for uses that the jurisdiction encourages or, at a minimum, will support, but nevertheless require some level of scrutiny by a municipal board or commission. This distinguishes an adjudicative permit from a use "by right." It also distinguishes an adjudicative permit from a variance. Whereas adjudicative permits are obtainable provided that the applicant's development does not, for example, exceed the carrying capacity of the affected resources, a variance is specifically reserved for uses or structural construction that the zoning ordinance does not allow.

new or expanded development. This relationship—nexus—has always been an integral piece of substantive due process requirements, but made "headlines" following the U.S. Supreme Court's decision in *Nollan v. California Coastal Commission*.[18] Thus, in applying a local carrying capacity ordinance, the permit granting authority must ensure that the conditions imposed (e.g. reduction in density, use of denitrifying septic systems and so on are directly related to the threats to an identified built or natural resource posed by the new development).

Second, the breadth—extent—of the permit conditions must be in proportion to the harm posed by the new or expanded development. As with the nexus requirement, proportionality has been an historic due process mandate.[19] It received renewed public attention following the U.S. Supreme Court's decision in *Dolan v. City of Tigard*.[20] In applying a local carrying capacity ordinance, the permit granting authority must ensure that the nexus requirement is satisfied and that the extent of the conditions imposed are proportional to the likely impacts.

Third, the tests established above will always apply where real property is surrendered and may apply where public benefits are required in addition to fee (or less than fee) dedication of real property.[21]

A conservative recommendation is for adjudicative boards to apply the *Nollan/Dolan* standard to all extractions brokered during the special permit process. In other words, and for example, if the carrying capacity of a water resource will be exceeded unless the development density of a proposed project is reduced by 15%, the special permit's requirement that the development reduce by 15% of its housing units likely complies with the *Nollan/Dolan* tests. First, a substantive basis for the required reduction exists, thus satisfying the *Nollan* requirement (but for the reduction, the integrity of the resource will be threatened). Second, the 15%

---

[18] 483 U.S. 825 (1987). Referring to the decisions in *Nollan* and Dolan v. City of Tigard, 512 U.S. 374 (1994), the California Supreme Court noted, "Scholarly comment on the two cases is almost unmanageably large." Ehrlich v. City of Culver City, 12 Cal. 4th 854, 868 (1996). The Court then cited seventeen references to the two cases and the issues of nexus and proportionality. *Id.*

[19] "The Fifth Amendment guarantee…was designed to bar the Government from forcing some people alone to bear public burdens which, in all fairness and justice, should be borne by the public as a whole… ." Armstrong v. United States, 364 U.S. 40, 49 (1960).

[20] 512 U.S. 374 (1994).

[21] For example, in Ehrlich v. City of Culver City, 12 Cal. 4th 854 (1996), the California Supreme Court held that the nexus and proportionality requirements of *Nollan* and *Dolan* are *not* limited solely to land and, in the facts presented, apply to monetary exactions. *Id.* at 860. Notwithstanding *Ehrlich*, and relying on *Nollan*, *Dolan* and the U.S. Supreme Court's decision in City of Monterey v. Del Monte Dunes At Monterey, LTD., 526 U.S. 687 (1999) and others (for example, Eastern Enterprises v. Apfel, 118 S. Ct. 2121 (1998)), case law seems to narrow the limitations of the nexus and proportionality requirements to only real property "takings." *See* F. Bosselman, *Dolan's Mysteries Explained?*, Land Use Law & Zoning Digest, Vol. 51, No. 1, January 1999.

reduction mandate is based upon analytical and defensible findings and represents no less than the reduction needed to preserve the resource. The *Dolan* proportionality requirement is thus satisfied.

As the extraction is not real property, some commentators, relying on *Nollan*, *Dolan* and their progeny, may argue that issues of nexus and proportionality do not apply. However, that argument seems risky.[22] A safer approach is to analyze the relationship and extent of the extraction to the carrying capacity regulation, and focus less on whether the extraction was land, money, or off-site improvements, and more on the relationship and extent of the extraction relative to the harm the community seeks to minimize. The point is to ensure that the regulations are enforced as intended, an exercise that stands a strong chance of surviving court scrutiny where the due process rules of nexus and proportionality are consistently applied.

As noted in the introduction of this Chapter, takings discussions are frequent and often emotional. The landowner claims that the regulation or adjudication is tantamount to a "take." The city or town argues that the regulation or adjudication is needed to protect the public good. Massachusetts law remains consistent with federal law; a regulatory taking occurs rarely and only where a city or town legislative or adjudicative action violates the principles noted above. Given that Massachusetts has established bright lines for when a taking has occurred, it should be relatively easy for cities and towns to avoid crossing that line and obvious to landowner's counsel when the line is impermissibly crossed.

---

[22] *See*, for example, Isla Verde Intl. Holdings, Inc. v. City of Camas, 990 P.2d 429 (Wash. Ct. App. 1999) (petition for review granted by the Supreme Court of Washington, September 5, 2000, 10 P.3d 1071), where the Washington Appeals Court held that a 30% land dedication imposed regardless of the impact of the new development failed the proportionality test of *Dolan*. The Court went further, however, stating that the U.S. Supreme Court's holding in City of Monterrey v. Del Monte Dunes at Monterey, 119 S. Ct. 1624 (1999), regarding impermissible land takings was "nonbinding dicta." 990 P.2d 429, at 436. "...the City must show a reasonable relationship between the 30 percent set-aside ordinance and Dove Hill's impact on open space. But unlike *Trimen*, the record here is devoid of evidence of studies or formulas showing a reasonable relationship between the impact of Dove Hill and the 30 percent set-aside requirement." 990 P.2d 429, at 437.

CHAPTER 4

ZONING—THE COMPREHENSIVE PERMIT LAW

I. THE LAW AND PRACTICE

Synopsis

§ 4.01   Introduction

§ 4.02   The Statute in Summary Form

§ 4.03   Qualified Comprehensive Permit Applicants

§ 4.04   The Project Eligibility Letter

§ 4.05   The Application to the Board of Appeals

§ 4.06   The Hearing before the Board of Appeals

§ 4.07   The Board of Appeals' Decision

§ 4.08   Appeal to the Housing Appeals Committee
    § 4.08[1]   What is "Uneconomic"?
    § 4.08[2]   What is "Consistent with Local Needs"?

§ 4.09   Intervention by Abutters at the Housing Appeals Committee

§ 4.10   Appeal to Superior Court

§ 4.11   Appeal of Housing Appeals Committee Decisions

§ 4.12   The Comprehensive Permit Statute and the Cape Cod Commission Act

§ 4.13   The Comprehensive Permit Statute in Cities and Towns Consistent with Local Needs

§ 4.01 Introduction

The Massachusetts comprehensive permit statute, codified as G.L. c. 40B, § 20–23 is often referred to as the "Anti-Snob Zoning Act[1] This chapter provides guidance for municipal and private counsel reviewing or applying for, permits under the statute. The statute is unusually brief for the power it grants. However, brevity and power are not often compatible and as a result, the statute in practice is exceedingly complicated.

Unlike other chapters in this text, the present discussion is as much a critique as it is a guidance document on interpreting the statute. This critique is not directed at the fact that the affordable housing units have been constructed or at the fact that the structures are occupied by needing residents. This chapter does not contend that affordable housing development has any impact, positive or negative, on abutting or municipal property values. Thus, this chapter does not criticize the "end result."

Rather, the focus of this chapter is that the means of producing affordable housing is as important as the resulting production. To ensure an equitable result—to guarantee that the ends do justify the means—this chapter takes the position that affordable housing is best created consistent with a municipal comprehensive plan and not through the tactics permitted by the statute in issue.

As discussed in detail below, a successful affordable housing program is, by definition, one that is consistent with the city or town or regional plan for growth and development. Unfortunately, and as discussed in Chapter 2, the Massachusetts model has no foundation in plans or planning principles.[2] The result is that while the program may facilitate the construction of affordable housing units, its reliance upon an "end justifies the means" methodology challenges historic notions of due process, ignores so-called "smart growth" principles[3] and clouds an otherwise clear and addressable problem.[4]

---

[1] Chapter 774 of the Acts of 1969 was referred to in the original House Bill (5429) as the "Anti-Snob Zoning Act." The phrase and its attendant implications have stuck and in fact remains a title of choice among the statute's supporters. *See*, for example, "Snob Zoning Alert," The Boston Globe, May 18, 2001.

[2] As discussed below, the Massachusetts approach to affordable housing development fosters an "end justifies the means" approach. The relevant statute and regulations mandate that where a city or town does not have a requisite number of dwelling units defined as subsidized, an applicant proposing to build twenty-five percent of a project's dwelling units as "affordable" can override all local rules and regulations.

[3] "Provisions in Massachusetts' current planning statutes would allow plans for new development to circumvent smart growth measures by: …allowing construction of affordable housing in unsuitable locations through a "comprehensive permit" which effectively bypasses local planning and zoning requirements." *Planning for Smart Growth: 2002 State of the States*, American Planning Association, 2002, p.22.

[4] The clear problem is the need to create more dwelling units that sell or rent below market rates.

§ 4.02　The Statute in Summary Form

G.L. c. 40B, § 20–23 has remained unaltered since its adoption in 1969. The intended goal[1] of the statute remains the same as it was when adopted: to require that no less than 10% of the housing stock within every city and town be subsidized with or by, a federal or state subsidy.

Applications pursuant to the statute are required to sell or rent twenty-five percent of the dwelling units in their proposed development project at 80% of the median income for the community. If this offer is made, the Massachusetts statute permits a developer of raw, under-developed or previously developed land to seek approval of a development density unconstrained by local rules, regulations, ordinances or policies. Put another way, in exchange for offering twenty-five percent of total number of dwelling units as "affordable," no density restrictions are imposed, subdivision rules and regulations, health regulations, historic district requirements and any and all other local rules or requirements can be suspended—waived—by the local board of appeals.

Thus, a parcel of land zoned four dwelling units to the acre can now contain twelve or fourteen or forty units to the acre. A parcel prohibiting structures greater than 40 feet in height can contain structures 100 feet in height. Structures otherwise required to be set back at least twenty feet from a neighboring sideline can now be constructed on the neighboring sideline.

In short, the only applicable local regulations are those "negotiated"[2] between the board of appeals and the applicant.[3] In yet another ironic aspect of the statute,

---

The problem is best addressed, as discussed below, not by destroying the basic building blocks of local government—land use controls—but rather through a logical and legally defensible planning and regulatory process that assures dwelling unit construction in an equitable and logical process.

[1] The 10% requirement under G.L. c. 40B, § 20–23 can hardly be considered a "goal" however. First, the "goal" is not tied to a plan or statewide process to matching housing needs with housing development. Second, the "goal" presumes that every city or town has the same housing needs and thus the same needs for housing production, regardless of where the municipality is located, the historic development patterns of the community or demands placed upon housing due to economic expansion or contraction. Third, the "goal" exists in a complete vacuum. It is oxymoronic to articulate a goal that is not linked, in some way, to any one of a variety of issues and concerns that face city and town government on a daily basis.

[2] It is freely admitted that negotiation is a productive activity when applied to executing a treaty between otherwise hostile nations, for example, or when attempting to secure a fair deal from a used car dealership. But when applied to land use regulations, negotiation leads to unpredictable results and anarchy. Referring to the connection between planning and zoning, the New York Court of Appeals cautioned that without a rational foundation for land use decision-making, decisions "…become nothing more than just a Gallup poll." Udell v. Haas, 21 N.Y.2d 463, 469 (1968).

[3] The board of appeals is required to hear and rule upon the application on an expedited basis. A public hearing must be commenced within thirty days of receipt of the comprehensive permit application and a decision rendered within forty days of the close of the public hearing. G.L. c. 40B,

whereas the board of appeals can waive rules and regulations adopted locally,[4] regulations promulgated by the state, even if implemented locally, cannot be waived. Thus, the state Building Code,[5] Wetlands Protection Act,[6] Environmental Policy Act,[7] and wastewater disposal regulations[8] apply to comprehensive permit and market rate projects alike.

The logic of this fact should be called into question. On one hand, the Commonwealth has promulgated minimum standards for the protection of public health and welfare, including ground, surface and drinking water supplies[9] and wetland resources.[10]

---

§ 21. Intrepid board of appeals have learned that since virtually no comprehensive permit applicant ever presents a complete application to the board, they can prolong rendering a final decision by extending the public hearing process. This strategy is fraught with risk, however and the Housing Appeals Committee has signaled an available remedy. "When the local hearing has been unduly protracted, this Committee will entertain an appeal on the theory that the permit has been constructively denied." Transformations, Inc. v. Townsend Board of Appeals, Ruling on Motion for Summary Judgment, (Mass. Housing Appeals Committee, No.02-14, September 23, 2002, footnote 3, referencing Milton Commons Assoc. v. Board of Appeals of Milton, 14 Mass. App. Ct. 111 (1982) and Pheasant Ridge Assoc. v. Town of Burlington, 399 Mass. 771 (1987).

[4] For example, the regulations governing subsurface disposal of wastewater are "minimum regulations." G.L. c. 111, § 31. Therefore, to protect locally specific resources from the impacts of viruses, nitrogen or phosphorus found in wastewater effluent, a city or town may choose to expand the minimum setback between drinking water supplies and wastewater disposal systems (set by the state at 100 feet). Notwithstanding the fact that this local regulation has a firm rational basis, the board of appeals can waive the additional setback imposed by the local regulation beyond the state requirement of 100 feet. Similarly, whereas the state Wetlands Protection Act grants review authority to the local conservation commission for activities occurring with one hundred feet of a wetland resource, a local ordinance could grant authority within a greater distance (e.g. one hundred and fifty feet). It is presumed that the board of appeals may waive the difference between the state requirement and the local, more restrictive requirement. Note, however, that G.L. c. 40B, § 20 clearly omits the phrase "conservation commission" from the list of local boards whose regulations can be waived.

[5] 780 CMR 100 et seq.

[6] 310 CMR 10.00 et seq.

[7] See 301 CMR 11.00 et seq. (Massachusetts Environmental Policy Act). See also Executive Order 385, "Planning for Growth," signed by Governor William Weld in 1996. EO 385 strongly discourages the use of state financing for projects that will develop previously undeveloped land or encourage land development in areas without adequate infrastructure. Although the phrase "sprawl" is not found within EO 385, it was clearly intended to minimize the use of state funds to encourage sprawl. See, for example, Jay Wickersham, Managing Growth Without a Growth Management Statute: The Uses of MEPA, New England Planning, April, 2001. EO 385 applies to both the admission ticket to the board of appeals and the funding obtained to develop the comprehensive permit project.

[8] See 310 CMR 15.00 (Title 5 of the State Sanitary Code) and 314 CMR 4.00, 5.00 and 6.00 (Surface Water and Groundwater Discharge Permit Regulations).

[9] See, for example, 314 CMR 2.00, 4.00, 5.00 and 6.00.

[10] See, for example, 310 CMR 10.00.

On the other hand, the comprehensive permit statute demands a "one size fits all" approach apply to the state's 351 municipalities. Septic system regulations applicable in communities with geologic deposits of bedrock, for example, cannot be more restrictive than in communities with geologic deposits of sand and gravel.[11] Wetland regulations in communities with extensive vernal pools and wildlife habitat cannot be more restrictive than in communities with limited and degraded wetland systems.[12]

§ 4.03   Qualified Comprehensive Permit Applicants

Eligible applicants for a comprehensive permit include (1) a city or town, (2) a non-profit organization, or (3) a limited dividend organization. The first two categories are self-explanatory. The limited dividend organization (LDO) is solely a creature of this statute. Many have confused the entity with a limited liability corporation or other traditional organizational arrangements permitted by corporate law. An LDO is a fictional organization with no corporate status or requirements. The only requirement—a condition subsequent to claiming LDO status—is the agreement of the individuals or entities that have created the LDO to restrict the profits they take from the project to that limited by the subsidizing agency. Discussion as to the limits placed on profit by the subsidizing agency is discussed below.

An important question is whether the LDO must be formed prior to applying for the comprehensive permit, during the application process or subsequent to the grant of the permit. Despite the fact that the statute clearly requires the LDO be formed as a condition precedent to application ("Any public agency or limited dividend or nonprofit organization proposing to build... ." G.L. c. 40B, § 21), the Courts and the Housing Appeals Committee have concluded that the LDO requirement is merely a demand that the development organization agrees to restrict its profit. That agreement can, and usually is, not executed until the permit has been issued.

---

[11] Contaminants behave differently in the subsurface depending upon the geologic environment. Whereas contaminant pathways are predictable in a sand and gravel aquifer, for example on Cape Cod, contaminant pathways are grossly unpredictable in bedrock environments, for example on Boston's north shore on in the Berkshire communities. *See*, for example, Sanjay Jeer et al., *Nonpoint Source Pollution: A Handbook for Local Governments*, American Planning Association, PAS No. 476 (1997).

[12] "There are several good reasons for increasing protection [beyond the state act]. The Wetlands Protection Act [the state act] is limited to protecting only eight wetland values...Communities may wish to regulate work over a broader geographic area including wetlands not linked to water bodies and also including adjacent upland areas, work on which may affect wetlands and floodplains." Alexandra Dawson and Sally Zielinski, *"Environmental Handbook for Massachusetts Conservation Commissioners,* Massachusetts Association of Conservation Commissioners, 2000, p. 194–195.

§ 4.04   The Project Eligibility Letter

An application for a comprehensive permit requires a qualified applicant (as discussed above) and a "ticket" to the board of appeals.[1] The "ticket" is a project eligibility letter. The issuer of the project eligibility letter is a subsidizing agency, historically a federal or state agency. More recently, most project eligibility letters are issued by MassHousing (formerly the Massachusetts Housing Finance Agency) pursuant to 760 CMR 31.01(2).

A presumed purpose of the project eligibility letter is to ensure that only bona fide applicants will be able to engage the board of appeals and that the board "will not spend time reviewing a proposal that is unlikely to be realized."[2]

---

[1] 760 CMR 31.01 (1) states in relevant part, "To be eligible to submit an application for a comprehensive permit…the applicant and the project shall fulfill the following jurisdictional requirements…(b) The project shall be fundable by a subsidizing agency under a low and moderate income housing subsidy program." 760 CMR 31.01(2) states in relevant part, "Fundability shall be established by submission of a written determination of Project Eligibility by a subsidizing agency… ." The board of appeals is the adjudicative body with responsibility under the Massachusetts Zoning Act (G.L. c. 40A) to hear petitions for special permits (an adjudicative permit), variances and appeals for relief from decisions made by the building inspector. G.L. c. 40A, § 8. It is the body responsible for adjudication of applications made under the comprehensive permit statute. G.L. c. 40B, § 20–23.

[2] Commonwealth of Massachusetts, Department of Housing and Community Development, Housing Appeals Committee, "Guidelines for Local Review of Comprehensive Permits," October 1999, p.4. *See also* Board of Appeals of Hanover v. Housing Appeals Committee, 363 Mass. 339 (1973). "The board's and the committee's power to require full disclosure of the applicant's present or planned property interest, and their power to grant conditional permits that do not become operative until the applicant has satisfied the funding agency's property interest requirements, provide ample protection against the unlikely possibility of frivolous applicants who have no present or potential property interest in the site." *See* 363 Mass. 339, at 378. One wonders what the Court meant by the use of the word "potential" as noted above. Any and all applicants have the potential of acquiring the necessary property interest in the site to be judged, according to the standards established by the regulations, as having sufficient property interest in the locus. 760 CMR 31.01(3) specifies the extent of the property interest. "Either a preliminary determination in writing by the subsidizing agency that the applicant has sufficient interest in the site, or a showing that the applicant or any entity 50% or more of which is owned by the applicant, owns a 50% or greater interest, legal or equitable, in the proposed site, or holds any option or contract to purchase the proposed site, shall be considered by the Board or the Committee to be conclusive evidence of the applicant's interest in the site." The Court neglected to foresee how entrepreneurial applicants would satisfy this requirement. The requirement is presumably satisfied if a purchase and sales agreement is executed with terms highly favorable to the offeror. For example, a speculator executes a purchase and sales agreement with the owner of developed, underdeveloped or marginal land contingent upon the receipt of a comprehensive permit for a density 8 or 10 times the underlying zoning. No deposit is made, no expiration date is included, no penalties imposed for breach by the offeror. This will satisfy the requirements of 760 CMR 31.01(3). In the alternative, a landowner executes a purchase and sales agreement or a deed to herself as trustee of a trust. The beneficiary of the trust is herself. This purchase and sales agreement and/or deed will satisfy the requirements of 760 CMR 31.01(3).

The gatekeeper strategy is, theoretically, a good one. Rogue applicants seeking nothing more than to develop on a parcel of marginal land, land that heretofore had been deemed undevelopable, would be rejected and would not receive the eligibility ticket needed to apply for a comprehensive permit. Thus, the gatekeeper could be considered some sort of trustee.

In fact, the Supreme Judicial Court and the Housing Appeals Committee have elevated the role of the gatekeeper to nothing short of trustee status. Because of the trust imputed to the subsidizing agency in their review of applications for project eligibility status, the Court and the Housing Appeals Committee have established the principle that a local government has extremely limited authority to review or comment upon the matters contained within the project eligibility approval.[3]

This point is worth restating. The Court and the Housing Appeals Committee presume that the subsidizing agency is professional, thorough and diligent in its investigation of applications for project eligibility status. The presumption presumes that the agency has, among other things, investigated the parcel subject to the application, investigated the qualifications of the applicant and assured that the proposal is consistent with neighborhood characteristics.[4]

The importance of the thoroughness and perhaps a basis for the Court's and the Housing Appeals Committee's reliance on the word of the subsidizing agency is that once issued, the ticket becomes not just a ticket to the local board of appeals, but also to the Housing Appeals Committee. Moreover, a ticket to the Housing Appeals Committee usually assures a successful outcome for the applicant/developer.[5]

In fact, the gatekeeper responsible for issuing the majority of project eligibility letters, MassHousing, rejects any notion that it is obligated to comport with any rule or regulation promulgated by the Department of Housing and Community Development.[6]

---

[3] "Prior to applying for a comprehensive permit, a proposal must be submitted to a subsidizing agency for preliminary approval, it is then "presumed fundable if a subsidizing agency makes a written determination of project eligibility… ." Welch v. Easton Board of Appeals, (Mass. Housing Appeals Committee, No. 94-06, Feb, 28, 1995), *citing* 760 CMR 31.01(2) and Hanover v. Housing Appeals Committee, 363 Mass. 339, 379–380 (1973).

[4] 760 CMR 31.01(2)(b).

[5] "The pattern of decisions by the HAC is striking: local zoning board decisions have been upheld in only 18 cases and overruled in 94 cases." Sharon Perlman Krefetz, *The Impact and Evolution of the Massachusetts Comprehensive Permit and Zoning Appeals Act: Thirty Years of Experience with A State Legislative Effort to Overcome Exclusionary Zoning*, 22 W. New Eng. L. Rev. 381, 397–398 (2001).

[6] *See* Civil Action No. PLCV2002-00298, Town of Duxbury et al. v. Massachusetts Housing Finance Agency (MassHousing), et al., wherein the Town of Duxbury alleged that MassHousing

Without the assurance that the applicant is a bona fide developer and the land sought for development is appropriate for the density proposed, the comprehensive permit process, as envisioned by the framers of the statute and regulations, and by the courts, loses an essential underpinning. As the statute and regulations are currently applied, cities and towns cannot rely on the subsidy agents to weed out inappropriate applications. At the same time they are estopped from doing so themselves.[7]

§ 4.05   The Application to the Board of Appeals

Once the project eligibility letter has been obtained, an application may be made to the board of appeals. The minimum filing requirements established by 760 CMR 31.02(2) may be supplemented by the board of appeals, but only if the local board has adopted regulations pursuant to 760 CMR 31.02(3). It is strongly recommended to counsel for municipalities that boards of appeals be encouraged to adopt regulations that articulate local needs and concerns. Note that while the board should be careful to avoid requiring the submission of materials that, de facto, render the project uneconomic, a comprehensive permit applicant would be ill advised to take an appeal on the basis of burdensome local regulations alone. This fact heightens the tension between the board and the applicant. Whereas the regulations suggest that very little must be filed by an applicant, the local board may permissibly require more, if "more" does not, by itself, render the project uneconomic.

Note further that a board that fails to adopt local regulations is deemed to have "adopted" the model rules promulgated by the Department of Housing and Community Development. The model rules merely recite portions of the regulations. They are not considered by most municipal counsel to be protective of local interests or customs, regional or local needs or concerns. The only option for cities

---

failed to comply with the "gatekeeper" requirements of 760 CMR 31.01. MassHousing's Answer denies that the relevant regulations are "binding upon MassHousing." *See also* MassHousing's Memorandum in Support of its Motion for Summary Judgment (Dec. 18, 2002, withdrawn) in the same matter. "It should be noted at the outset, that MHFA is not, in any technical sense, bound to obey the rules promulgated by the HAC pursuant to Chapter 40B." *Id..* at 7.

[7] This fact raises the question as to the true underlying purpose of the statute. If, for example, the purpose of the statute were to create affordable housing units, units of housing that were affordable would count toward the required quota. Mobile homes, generally more affordable than "stick built" homes would thus qualify toward the municipal requirement. Mobile rental certificates, often referred to as Section 8 vouchers, would also qualify. But the state's leading advocate for affordable housing, the Citizens Housing and Planning Association has continually opposed the counting of mobile homes and Section 8 vouchers toward the requirement. "If the Legislature agrees to count mobile homes and Section 8 vouchers, 67 communities will immediately go over the 10% affordable housing goal without building one new unit of housing." Citizens Housing and Planning Association, *The Impact of Counting Mobile Homes and Vouchers under Chapter 40B*, Massachusetts Continuing Legal Education, 2002, p.141.

and towns to avoid having the model rules being "adopted for them" is to adopt locally tailored regulations as discussed above.

§ 4.06   The Hearing before the Board of Appeals

The board of appeals must open a public hearing on the submitted comprehensive permit application within thirty (30) days of the application's submission. Note at the outset that unlike special permit or variance applications, the comprehensive permit statute is silent as to whether the application must also be submitted to the city or town clerk. Private counsel should nevertheless file a copy of the application submitted to the board of appeals with the city or town clerk. Note further that whereas an incomplete special permit or variance application might empower the board of appeals to "reject" the application as not consistent with the board's or the municipality's filing requirements, such "rejection" of a comprehensive permit application is an invitation to the applicant to appeal this to the Housing Appeals Committee as a denial of the application. Such a procedural posture is not considered advantageous from the point of view of the board. Prudent advice to municipal counsel is to always open the public hearing within the statutory period, take some evidence, and then inform the applicant that the application is deficient during the opening hearing session.

§ 4.07   The Board of Appeals' Decision

The board's decision must be "rendered" within forty (40) days of the close of the public hearing. The requirement that a decision be rendered within a time following the close of the public hearing is vastly different from the requirements governing special permits, variances or even subdivision applications. In each of these examples, the time for rendering a decision is built into the statute: a date certain is provided. In a comprehensive permit application however, the board of appeals has no date certain; it and only it determines when the public hearing is closed and when the forty day clock begins to run.

Not surprisingly, disputes have arisen between a comprehensive permit applicant who believes that the board is abusing the lack of a date certain requirement and a board of appeals which believes that the applicant has not submitted sufficient information or that specific issues have not been properly vetted such that the decision clock should begin to run. "Public hearings end when the right of interested parties to present information and argue is cut off."[1] While the Appeals Court did not provide a bright line test as to when a public hearing has been concluded, private and municipal counsel should apply common sense. For example, has the board asked for and received relevant information such that it can make an informed

---

[1] Milton Commons Associates v. Board of Appeals of Milton, 14 Mass. App. Ct. 111, 115 (1982).

decision? Has the board asked for and received the minimum information required by 760 CMR 31.02(2) and the board's local rules? Has the public had an opportunity to review, comment upon and have its experts testify in regard to information submitted by the applicant? If the answers to any of these questions is "no," it is doubtful that the board could render an informed decision and the public hearing should, therefore, not be closed.

Remember, an applicant who believes that all the information required for submission has been submitted or, more defiantly, simply refuses to submit additional information, is posturing for an appeal to the Housing Appeals Committee. Without a final decision from the board of appeals, the applicant will need to plead that the board's failure to close the hearing and render the decision is tantamount to a "constructive approval." While not impossible, this is nevertheless a difficult case to argue. First, no decision has been rendered and the date for rendering a decision has not expired, making it pragmatically difficult to appeal. Second, the Housing Appeals Committee's regulations require that the applicant has first submitted the materials identified in 760 CMR 31.02(2) to the board of appeals. The applicant is at risk that the board's counsel will simply argue that the appeal must be remanded back to the board of appeals for a hearing consistent with the requirements of 760 CMR 31.02(2). While it is true that the case will now be under the "supervision" of the Housing Appeals Committee, the applicant has lost both time and good faith with the local board of appeals. In hindsight, and where the board was acting itself on good faith, the applicant is likely to wish she had complied with the board's requests for information.

Finally, once a decision has been reached—rendered—an open question has remained: does the decision need to be reduced to a writing and filed with the city or town clerk by a date certain? The Appeals Court concluded "no" a written decision is not required, if the board of appeals renders its decision in a timely fashion.[2] This holding, combined with the SJC's conclusion that a written decision need not be filed with the city or town clerk[3] poses traps for both developer and abutter counsel.

Without the requirement for a written decision, it is important that every meeting of the board of appeals be observed to determine the exact date the decision is rendered. This is especially important for abutter's counsel as the normal reliance on the records of the city or town clerk is not necessarily available in comprehensive

---

[2] Cardwell v. Board of Appeals of Woburn, 61 Mass. App. Ct. 118 (2004). "We conclude that any requirement for written notice of a decision of the board of appeals on an application for a comprehensive permit is directory rather than mandatory." 61 Mass. App. Ct. 118, at 121.

[3] Milton Commons Associates v. Board of Appeals of Milton, 14 Mass. App. Ct. 111, 118 (1982).

permit disputes.[4] Abutter's counsel needs to know when their appeal period commences pursuant to G.L. c. 40B, § 21 and may receive no other indication of that appeal period other than by listening for the board's vote on the final decision.

Developer's counsel should likewise be concerned about the actual decision date, although pursuant to 760 CMR 30.06(8), the developer's time within which to appeal to the HAC does not commence until the decision is "filed in the office of the city or town clerk." Thus while an appeal brought by an abutter must be commenced within twenty days of the board's vote, the developer's appeal period might not commence until considerably later. This fact provides the developer with a significant strategic advantage: she can refrain from appealing to the HAC until after the abutter's appeal period has expired. Where the board of appeals' decision is favorable and no abutter appeal is forthcoming, she may choose to accept the board's decision without appeal. But if the abutter's appeal, she then has the option of bringing an appeal to the HAC seeking the full number of units applied for; a number likely far more than what the board approved and far greater than tolerable to the appealing abutters.

§ 4.08   Appeal to the Housing Appeals Committee

In cities or towns that are not "consistent with local needs" (see § 4.08[2], infra), if an applicant's comprehensive permit application is denied or approved with too many conditions, he may take an appeal to the Housing Appeals Committee.[1] The

---

[4] While the SJC stated that a filing with the city or town clerk is not required by the statute, it is nevertheless recommended that boards of appeals file comprehensive permit decisions with the clerk's office as the board would a special permit or variance pursuant to G.L. c. 40A, §§ 9 and 10.

[1] Two recent affirmations of denials by the Dennis and Barnstable (Cape Cod), Massachusetts board of appeals have received significant attention. In one case, a developer proposed 50 dwelling units within the Town of Dennis' historic district on 3.2 acres of land, constrained by wetlands and stormwater runoff. Much of the open space proposed for the parcel consisted of a parking lot and stormwater drainage basin. Dennis Housing Corporation v. Dennis Board of Appeals, (Mass. Housing Appeals Committee, No. 01-02, May 7, 2002). The second case involved a proposal to develop multi-family housing on a waterfront parcel of land in Barnstable Harbor zoned "Marine Business." Stuborn Ltd. Partnership v. Barnstable Board of Appeals, (Mass. Housing Appeals Committee, No. 98-01, Sept. 18, 2002). The Town argued that this was one of the last remaining marine related parcels in the Village. In addition, and perhaps more relevant, the town of Barnstable has embarked on an aggressive and on-going campaign to build town-sponsored affordable housing developments in each of the town's villages. The 3-2 decision supporting the town's denial put much weight on the town's comprehensive plan. Id. at 7–10. This is relevant in that nine of the Cape's fifteen towns have adopted comprehensive plans in accordance with the Cape Cod Commission Act. Given that the HAC cannot overrule state legislation, (see, for example, Board of Appeals of North Andover v. Housing Appeals Committee, 4 Mass. App. Ct. 676 (1976)), the Barnstable decision could be read as precluding any interference by the HAC in decisions rendered by Cape Cod towns that have properly promulgated a comprehensive plan. At issue is how much noblesse oblige should be afforded the Housing Appeals Committee by these decisions. One view is that the HAC was

Housing Appeals Committee is established by G.L. c. 23B, § 5A.[2]

The Housing Appeals Committee, through rules promulgated by the Department of Housing and Community Development,[3] has overseen the appeal process with unceasing commitment to the primary intent of the statute to increase the supply of affordable housing in the Commonwealth. The Massachusetts Courts have supported this commitment, deferring to the state regulators and suggesting or, arguably demanding that the Legislature respond where municipalities have sought what they perceive as a righting of the imbalance in the process.[4]

In decision after decision, the HAC has dismissed local offers of proof and/or

---

aware of the overwhelming evidence that the Cape Cod towns (through the Cape Cod Commission Act) have been developing affordable housing at a faster pace and more equitably through the inclusionary requirements of the Act. A reversal by the HAC would have too transparently illustrated that the comprehensive permit statute cares little about municipal efforts to build affordable housing and far more about getting housing built, anywhere, without regard to promulgated rules or regulations.

[2] "It is quite significant that in cases appealed to the HAC, the Committee rarely has found that the local decision was 'reasonable and consistent with local needs." Krefetz, p.397–398, *supra*.

[3] 760 CMR 30.00 *et seq.* and 760 CMR 31.00 *et seq.*

[4] Judicial support for the decisions of the Housing Appeals Committee and the statute in general is perplexing given the Supreme Judicial Court's (SJC) decision in Vazza v. Board of Appeals of Brockton, 359 Mass. 256 (1971). The Court noted, "Purchasers of real estate are entitled to rely on the applicable zoning ordinances or bylaws in determining the uses which may be made of the parcel they are buying…For many persons, particularly those purchasing houses, this is the largest single investment of their lives. It is important that such purchasers be able to determine with reasonable accuracy, before making that investment, just what the applicable zoning ordinances and bylaws are, and what uses they permit or prohibit." *Id.* at 263. The Court's concern for the due process rights—the ability to predict with some certainty the allowable uses on a parcel of land—is noticeably absent in its support for the comprehensive permit statute. The statute provides no "reasonable accuracy," as was deemed so important in *Vazza* for property owners, neighborhoods, cities or towns to determine what will happen on the parcel of land next door, down the street or within the corporate boundaries. The comprehensive permit process is predictable only in its unpredictability. Any and all parcels of land are subject to it, at anytime and at any density. The SJC may be signaling the Legislature that reform is due, however. In Wellesley v. Ardemore Apartments Limited Partnership, 436 Mass. 811 (2002), the SJC ruled that unless otherwise permitted by the city or town, the affordable dwelling units within a comprehensive permit project must remain affordable in perpetuity where the comprehensive permit violates local zoning regulations. "It may be that a comprehensive permit is essential for the construction of some affordable housing projects because of local zoning restrictions, and it may be that, in those situations, the absence of an affordability restriction expiration operates as an economic disincentive to developers to build affordable housing. The solution to that problem, however, lies with the Legislature." 436 Mass. 811, at 828. In Planning Board of Hingham v. Hingham Campus, LLC, 438 Mass. 364, 780 N.E.2d 902 (2003), the SJC ruled that G.L. c. 40B, § 20–23 does not grant a municipal planning board standing to appeal the decision of a board of appeals. Quoting *Commonwealth v. Jones*, the SJC concluded, "If the law is to be changed, the change can only be made by the Legislature." 780 N.E.2d 902, 908, *quoting* Commonwealth v. Jones, 417 Mass. 661, 664 (1994).

concerns regarding the extent of affordable housing already existing within the city,[5] environmental impacts generated by the new development,[6] traffic congestion and emergency access,[7] stormwater runoff,[8] visual impacts and property devaluation,[9] school overcrowding,[10] inconsistency with a locally adopted plan,[11] impact

---

[5] Hadley West Associates v. Haverhill Board of Appeals (Mass. Housing Appeals Committee No.74-02, Sept. 24, 1974). "Nor does...the fact that Haverhill ranks among 'the top ten cities in the Commonwealth with state and federal housing units in occupancy and progress' imply that Haverhill has complied with any of the mathematical criteria for 'consistent with local needs'. *Id.* at 8.

[6] C.S.R. Management, Inc. v. Yarmouth Board of Appeals (Mass. Housing Appeals Committee No.95-01, Sept. 5, 1995).

[7] Dexter Street LLC v. North Attleborough Board of Appeals (Mass. Housing Appeals Committee, No.00-01, July 2000).

[8] Spencer Livingstone Assoc. Ltd. Partnership v. Medfield Zoning Board of Appeals (Mass. Housing Appeals Committee, No.90-01, June 12, 1991).

[9] Cedars Holdings, Inc. v. Dartmouth Board of Appeals (Mass. Housing Appeals Committee, No.98-02, May 24, 1999).

[10] Interfaith Housing Corporation v. Board of Appeals of Gardner, (Mass. Housing Appeals Committee No. 72-05, Feb. 13, 1974). Prior to the decision, the City of Gardner High School had lost its accreditation due to overcrowding and based its denial of the comprehensive permit, in part, on the overcrowding of its public schools. "The unfortunate combination of overcrowded schools, high construction costs to provide more schools and taxes already at the breaking point, is a sad fact of life that presently besets almost every municipality in the country.... Apparently, the legislature felt that existing needs for low and moderate income housing were so overriding as to have priority over the admittedly pressing problem of overcrowded schools." *Id..* at 14.

[11] Planning Office for Urban Affairs v. North Andover Board of Appeals, (Mass. Housing Appeals Committee, No. 74-03, May 5, 1975). 760 CMR 31.07(3)(d) was revised effective December 20, 2002 to include the following: "Municipal Planning. The Committee may receive evidence of and shall consider the following matters: (1) a city or town's master plan, comprehensive plan, or community development plan, and (2) the results of the city or town's efforts to implement such plans." Two years prior to the above noted revision, the Chairman of the Housing Appeals Committee wrote, "What these cases make clear is that if towns take control of their own planning processes and put affordable housing on their agendas, their local autonomy will be respected under the Comprehensive Permit Law." Werner Lohe, *The Massachusetts Comprehensive Permit Law: Collaboration between Affordable Housing Advocates and Environmentalists,"* Land Use Law & Zoning Digest, May 2000. The combination of the regulatory revision and the Chairman's comments should give hope to cities and towns seeking to develop affordable housing in a state with no planning or consistency requirements. The facts prove differently, however. Since the Chairman's article, the Housing Appeals Committee has: (1) overturned a denial by a board of appeals and approved a comprehensive permit in a community where the median sale price of a dwelling unit was less than the sales price of the deed restricted units permitted by the Committee's order (Delphic Associates v. Middleborough Board of Appeals, (Mass. Housing Appeals Committee, No.00-13, July 17, 2002)); (2) reversed a decision by a board of appeals denying a comprehensive permit to build on a parcel of land noted "Not A Buildable" lot, holding that such a notation could be waived in the pursuit of affordable housing (Woodridge Realty Trust v. Ipswich Board of Appeals, (Mass. Housing Appeals Committee, No. 00-04, June 28, 2001)); (3) concluded that the Legislature's definition of satisfying the statutory obligation for the total land area that is

on the municipality's tax base[12] and water supply and water pressure limitations.[13]

Injured, perhaps, by the publicity and attendant local public outrage accompanying the above noted decisions, the Department of Housing and Community Development embarked on an aggressive campaign to "soften" the applicable regulations[14] and thereby, perhaps, avert the groundswell seeking to repeal the statute.[15] Most notably, however, the 2004 revisions did little to balance municipal interests of concern in areas other than housing against the statutory presumption that new affordable housing construction trumps most, if not all, local concerns.[16]

§ 4.08[1]   What is "Uneconomic"?

The statute requires that a decision approving a comprehensive permit with

---

devoted to affordable housing is measured by the land area in which the building occurs and not the total area of the parcel subject to the development. Cloverleaf Apartments, LLC v. Zoning Board of Appeals of the Town of Natick (Mass. Housing Appeals Committee No. 01-21, Mar. 4, 2002).

[12] "It is irrelevant under the statute." Woodcrest Village Associates v. Board of Appeals of the Town of Maynard (Mass. Housing Appeals Committee No. 72-13 Feb. 13, 1974).

[13] Cooperative Alliance of Massachusetts v. Taunton Board of Appeals, (Mass. Housing Appeals Committee, No.90-05, Apr. 2, 1992). "But this cannot mean that any condition which assures adequate water supply is automatically consistent with local needs. If this were the case, any town wishing to block affordable housing could simply identify a legitimate local concern and then require that it be remedied in the most expensive way possible. Thus we believe that also implicit within the definition of consistency with local needs is that any condition be reasonable." Id. at 14–15.

[14] Among the most noteworthy revisions are the following: (1) a limitation on the number of dwelling units that can be developed per application depending upon the size of the community, 760 CMR 31.07(g), (2) a twelve month "cooling off" period between the filing of a market rate development plan and the filing of a comprehensive permit, 760 CMR 31.07(h) and (3) an ability of a city or town to prepare a housing plan and thus deny or condition comprehensive permits if the city or town creates qualified housing units that amount to at least 3/4 of 1% of the community's total housing stock, per year, 760 CMR 31.07(i). Note that in each case, however, the ability to deny or condition a comprehensive permit remains an option for the board of appeals even where the city or town would otherwise be "consistent with local needs" and thus no appeal by the applicant is allowed to the Housing Appeals Committee. The upshot of this permissive language is that the "lawlessness" and unpredictability of the statute remains in full force and effect even where the city or town has met the obligations set forth in the statute.

[15] As of the summer of 2004, sixty bills were pending in the Massachusetts General Court pertaining to reform of the comprehensive permit statute.

[16] The HAC concluded that a board of appeals could not impose as a condition of approval a requirement that the sale of affordable dwellings be subject to resale restrictions that survive bankruptcy or foreclosure by the lender. This conclusion was based on the Committee's belief that, "there is no evidence that foreclosure is a common occurrence. Second…the town has a right of first refusal that permits it to step in and purchase the unit if no affordable purchaser can be located … And even if the unit is lost, the town is compensated, since it receives the windfall generated by the sale, which can [sic] put that to use for other affordable housing purposes." Delphic Associates, LLC v. Hudson Board of Appeals (Mass. Housing Appeals Comm. No. 02-11 Dec. 23, 2002), p.8.

conditions not render the project "uneconomic." The term "uneconomic" is defined, in relevant part, as the imposition of conditions that make it "impossible for a public or non profit organization to proceed…without financial loss" or for a limited dividend organization to proceed and still realize a reasonable return…within the limitations set by the subsidizing agency… ."[17]

Where a board of appeals approves a comprehensive permit project with conditions, the central issue before the Housing Appeals Committee is whether the conditions render the project "uneconomic." "In the case of an approval with conditions, the applicant shall have the burden of proving that the conditions make the building or operation of the housing uneconomic." 760 CMR 31.06

As of this writing, no subsidizing agency has established guidelines on what constitutes a reasonable return such that the determination of "economic" would be rationally determined. While MassHousing's regulatory agreement sets a "cap" on the profits from fee simple and rental projects, neither MassHousing nor the Housing Appeals Committee has set a "floor." This fact poses complications for counsel representing appellants and municipal clients before the HAC. What is the line in the sand that transforms a project from economic to uneconomic? How does a board of appeals know when to impose conditions when the very imposition of these conditions could, unknowingly, create an "uneconomic" project? Without a benchmark against which to measure a conditioned project, boards of appeals have few choices in reviewing comprehensive permit projects. One option is to simply accept the proposed density as submitted and impose conditions gingerly.

A second option is to determine what the subsidizing agency believes is a "reasonable return" and condition the project with that benchmark in mind. HAC decisions historically have upheld this approach.[18] In July 2004, however, DHCD revised both the procedural and substantive regulations governing the HAC and in doing so, provided the Presiding Officer with the power, sua sponte and with no articulated guiding principles, to rule that a decision with too many conditions

---

[17] G.L. c. 40B, § 20.

[18] *See*, for example, Cooperative Alliance of Massachusetts v. Taunton Board of Appeals, No. 90-05 (Mass. Housing Appeals Committee, Apr. 2, 1992).

"Equally obvious (though unstated), is that if the condition does not make the project uneconomic and it is consistent with local needs, it must be upheld… ." Thus, if the condition does not make the project uneconomic, it should be upheld even if the town cannot prove that it is consistent with local needs. (Once again, this is reflected in 760 CMR 31.06(3); the Committee need not actually inquire into consistency with local needs if the developer has not sustained its burden on the economic issues)." *Id.*, p.8.

See also Drumlin Development, LLC v. Sudbury Board of Appeals, (Mass. Housing Appeals Comm. No. 01-03, Sept. 27, 2001),

"But even if the Board's position is ill advised, the burdens of proof set out in the statute and our regulations are designed to ensure that we do not second guess the Board's imposition of local standards unless their effect is to undermine the viability of affordable housing. The Board may insist upon a condition such as the one here if that condition does not render the housing uneconomic." *Id.*, p.3.

could be, a denial.[19] Whether this grant of power will survive challenge remains an open question. The effect of such a ruling dramatically alters the burden of proof and the likely outcome of the litigation. As noted below, a denial of a comprehensive permit in a community that is not consistent with local needs shifts the burden almost entirely on the city or town to prove that the project would so threaten public health, safety or welfare that it outweighs the need for affordable housing. In addition, even though the Commonwealth is losing population,[20] this burden of demonstrating that a particular project's impact will outweigh the regional need for affordable housing is almost insurmountable.

A third and recommended option for boards of appeals is to evaluate other benchmarks for determining when a project becomes "uneconomic," including, but not limited to definitions from the subsidizing agency, local developers, bankers and appraisers. Knowing industry standards and expected returns from developments of similarly sized projects will help the board know where the benchmark of "uneconomic" lies. By understanding the benchmark, the board can then knowingly condition the project such that the conditions do not render the project uneconomic, subject to reversal on appeal.

In a surprising decision, however, a Superior Court held that where a board of appeals conditions a comprehensive permit by reducing the number of dwelling units (e.g. from an application density of 100 dwelling units to an approval of 80 dwelling units), the HAC's review should focus not on the economic impacts, but rather, on the fact that the board's decision is actually a denial of the dwelling units that the applicant applied for, but did not receive.[21] In other words, whereas in takings jurisprudence the Court looks not a what was taken, but what is left, to adjudicate whether government's regulations have gone "too far," at least one Court has concluded that in the world of comprehensive permits, the HAC should look at what was "taken" as opposed to what was approved.

The Superior Court's decision in *Rehoboth* appears to contradict the belief that the Legislature never intended to rob a municipality of its ability to condition comprehensive permit approvals (albeit provide the town with far less authority than it ordinarily was granted pursuant to the Zoning Act (G.L. c. 40A) or even the Subdivision Control Law (G.L. c. 41, § 81-L, et seq.). Until *Rehoboth*, the power to condition a comprehensive permit was well established.[22]

---

[19] *See* 760 CMR 30.07(2)(f) and Settlers Landing Realty Trust v. Barnstable, No. 01-08 (Mass. Housing Appeals Committee, Sept. 22, 2003).

[20] "Census shows Mass. At a Loss," Boston Globe, December 26, 2004, pointing out that in 2004, Massachusetts was the only state in the country to "lose residents."

[21] *See* 9 North Walker Street Development, Inc. v. Commonwealth of Massachusetts and Rehoboth Board of Appeals, (Mass. Super. Ct. Dec. 29, 2004).

[22] "Our construction of c. 774 [G.L. c. 40B, § 20–23] does not mean that he board must

Should this holding stand, comprehensive permit applicants are likely (and advised), to apply for the maximum number of dwelling units permitted just short of triggering the "consistent with local needs provisions" of 760 CMR 31.07(g). Thus, any forced reduction by the board of appeals in the development density will be viewed as a denial, shifting the burden of proof to the municipality.

§ 4.08[2]   What is "Consistent with Local Needs"?

A city or town is "consistent with local needs" if it meets one of the three criteria of G.L. c. 40B, § 20 or one of the four criteria of 760 CMR 31.07(1). These seven criteria are quotas that, if met, deprive the Housing Appeals Committee of jurisdiction to review an appeal brought by a comprehensive permit applicant. However, if a city or town has not satisfied one of these criteria, the statute presumes that the community is not consistent with local needs and is vulnerable to an appeal to the Housing Appeals Committee.[23] Where the appeal was brought due to a denial by the board of appeals, the burden is on the board of appeals to demonstrate that the decision is based upon a valid health, safety, environmental, design, open space or other local concern supporting the denial. Adding to this burden, the board of appeals must then prove that this concern outweighs the regional housing need.[24]

Not surprisingly given the burden requirements of the regulations, there are only a handful of cases where the Housing Appeals Committee has ruled that the board's decision to deny or condition a comprehensive permit application was "consistent with local needs" without analyzing the economics of the project. These cases have generally been egregious abuses of the comprehensive permit statute (see, for example, *Hamlet Development Corporation v. Hopedale Zoning Board of Appeals*[25] where the Housing Appeals Committee upheld the Board's denial of a comprehensive permit project located in part, at the end of the runway of the Hopedale airport).[26]

Counsel should be aware therefore, that sustaining the denial of a comprehensive permit application in a community that is not consistent with local needs (by virtue of compliance with one of the seven criteria) is a very difficult burden where the

---

automatically grant comprehensive permits in all cases where the community has not met its minimum housing obligation as it is specifically defined in § 20. The statute merely prevents the board from relying on local requirements or regulations…as the reason for the board's denial of the permit or its grant with uneconomic conditions." Board of Appeals of Hanover v. Housing Appeals Committee, 363 Mass. 339, 367 (1973).

[23] *See* Board of Appeals v. Housing Appeals Committee et al., 363 Mass. 339, 367 (1973).

[24] *See* 760 CMR 31.06(6).

[25] No. 90-03 (Mass. Housing Appeals Committee, January 23, 1992).

[26] Other notable cases include the proposed development of 50 dwelling units on less than two usable acres in Dennis and the development of housing units at a former ammunitions depot in Hingham.

board of appeals seeks to deny the application or condition its approval without analyzing the economics of the project. Municipal counsel should be wary of outright denials in these communities. Instead, if possible, attempts should be made to fashion a project that respects local concerns, protects abutting neighborhoods and generates a sufficient profit such that the project is sufficiently attractive to the developer.

§ 4.09   Intervention by Abutters at the Housing Appeals Committee

760 CMR 31.04 of the procedural regulations governing the Housing Appeals Committee establish the difficult task of intervening in a Housing Appeals Committee hearing. Prior to the 2004 revisions to the 760 CMR 31.04, and as a general rule, intervenors were granted "amicus" status during Housing Appeals Committee cases. Through counsel, Intervenors were often allowed to put on an independent case, cross-examine witnesses for the applicant and the municipality, make opening and closing arguments and submit post-hearing briefs. While the intervenor's motion to intervene was routinely dismissed, at least the intervenor was able to articulate her concerns.

The 2004 revisions and the current practice of the Committee have dramatically curtailed the role of the intervenor. Now, even where the intervenor can articulate specific and unique harms to her real property interests, her intervention status is decided at the beginning of the hearing process, not at the end and more often than not, her status is narrowly proscribed. Where an intervenor cannot satisfactorily articulate specific and unique harms, she is relegated to the role of "interested person" and allowed to make an opening and closing statement and submit post hearing briefs.

§ 4.10   Appeal to Superior Court

The comprehensive permit statute provides for different routes of appeals for the applicant and an aggrieved party other than the applicant. The applicant's appeal, discussed above, is to the Housing Appeals Committee and must be taken within twenty days after the applicant has received notice of the board's decision.[1] The applicant is provided no avenue for appeal to the trial courts. An aggrieved party other than the applicant, an abutter, for example, has a statutory right of appeal to Superior or Land Court pursuant to the provisions of G.L. c. 40A, § 17.[2] Procedurally, an appeal of a board of appeals' decision approving a comprehensive permit application is identical to an appeal of a board of appeals' decision approving a special permit or a variance, discussed in greater detail in Chapter Five. However, note that while it is common practice for boards of appeals to file their

---

[1] G.L. c. 40B, § 22.

[2] G.L. c. 40B, § 21.

decisions with the city or town clerk, the statute does not require such a filing. Counsel for abutters must be careful to identify when the board's decision is due and ensure that an appeal is taken, following the strict guidelines of G.L. c. 40A, § 17.

§ 4.11   Appeal of Housing Appeals Committee Decisions

G.L. c. 40B, § 23 provides that an appeal of a decision of the Housing Appeals Committee be brought pursuant to the G.L. c. 30A. G.L. c. 30A governs appeals of administrative agencies and should be read in conjunction with Superior Court Standing Order 1-96. Together, the statute and the Standing Order provide strict requirements for appeals of the HAC decisions. Not surprisingly given the general grant of deference afforded administrative agencies, appeals of Housing Appeals Committee decision are rarely successful.

Municipal counsel and counsel for abutters challenging a comprehensive permit decision issued by a board of appeals are advised to acknowledge the above noted discussion well before engaging in a comprehensive permit dispute. Unlike traditional land use disputes, litigation of comprehensive permits is undeniably skewed toward the applicant. This fact should be acknowledged early in the process as it will likely lead to a more acceptable outcome for all parties concerned, including the applicant seeking to construct the proposed project, the municipality seeking to protect, as much as possible, issues of local concern and the abutter, seeking to preserve, as much as possible, the integrity of the land use regulations in place prior to the comprehensive permit application.

§ 4.12   The Comprehensive Permit Statute and the Cape Cod Commission Act

The Cape Cod Commission Act and Cape Cod Commission Regulations, including The Code of Cape Cod Commission Regulations, Barnstable County Ordinance 90-12, as amended, and Cape Cod Commission Administrative Regulations, dated October 10, 1991, as amended, (together the "Regulations") require the Commission to conduct a DRI review for projects of a certain size proposed under Massachusetts General Law, Chapter 40B, Sections 20—23 ("Chapter 40B"). For example, the proposed development of "30 or more residential dwelling units" requires DRI review.

The Commission has interpreted the Act to mean that it does not have jurisdiction to require a DRI permit for development projects under Chapter 40B, regardless of their size.

The Commission presumably bases its interpretation on two, identical sentences in the Act. The first appears in Section 11(k) regarding districts of critical planning concern, and the second in Section 12(j) regarding developments of regional impact. The sentence states: "For the purposes of sections twenty to twenty-three, inclusive, of chapter forty B of the General Laws, the commission shall be considered a local board." The term "local board" is defined in Chapter 40B as "Any town or city board of survey, board of health, board of subdivision control appeals, planning board, building inspector or the officer of board having supervision of the construction of buildings or the power of enforcing municipal building laws, or city council or board of selectmen." Section 21 of Chapter 40B establishes that the board of appeals has the "same power to issue permits or approvals as any board or official who would otherwise act with respect to such application... ." The broad definition of local board was broadened further by the SJC in *Old Kings Highway v. Dennis Housing Corporation*,[1] where the Court concluded that even a regional entity created pursuant to state statute constituted a "local board" pursuant to G.L. c. 40B, § 20 where the entity was enforcing local, as opposed to "state" standards.[2]

Notwithstanding the holding in *Dennis*, nothing in the Cape Cod Commission Act expressly eliminates the Commission's role in the review of DRIs filed under Chapter 40B. Contrary to the Commission's current interpretation, the Act establishes that the Commission will comment to the board of appeals on projects that do not meet or exceed DRI thresholds for Commission review. That is, for projects that do not exceed mandatory DRI review thresholds (i.e. projects proposing less than 30 residential dwelling units), the Act contemplates that the Commission will comment to the board of appeals, together with other local permitting authorities. For projects that exceed mandatory regulatory thresholds for DRI review due to anticipated regional impacts (i.e. developments proposing 30 or more residential dwelling units), the Act requires that each Chapter 40B applicant must obtain a DRI permit under the Act.

In addition, the Commission's interpretation conflicts with Section 16(a) of the Act which requires that "Development in Barnstable county subject to commission review or located within a district of critical planning concern shall be consistent with the regional policy plan, local comprehensive plans, district of critical planning concern guidelines, local implementing regulations and conditions imposed by the commission on developments of regional impact."

This interpretation is true to the intent of the Cape Cod Commission Act, which is to protect natural and cultural resources while balancing the need for economic opportunities and affordable housing. Chapter 40B proposals for 30 or more units are presumed to present regional impacts and should be reviewed by the Commission as a DRI. The Commission may conduct such a DRI review consistent with

---

[1] 439 Mass. 71 (2003).

[2] 439 Mass. 71, at 81–82.

its statutory mandate to promote "fair, affordable housing,"[3] just as it incorporates the statutory mandate to promote "balanced economic growth"[4] in its current DRI reviews. This provides the Commission with the opportunity to apply the requirements of the RPP and local plans, bylaws and regulations, and to modify Chapter 40B development proposals that are not consistent, unless the inconsistency is justified as required by the Act or Commission Regulations.

In the alternative, sitting in place of the Commission, the board of appeals must find that each 40B application on Cape Cod meets the requirements for DRI approval, or that the proponent has demonstrated that application of a particular DRI standard for approval renders the project "uneconomic."

The Act sets forth four standards for DRI approval. In its surrogate capacity, the board of appeals must find: 1) the project benefits outweigh project detriments; 2) the project is in compliance with all applicable Minimum Performance Standards set forth in the RPP and with the local comprehensive plan; 3) the project is consistent with municipal development bylaws, or if inconsistent, the inconsistency is necessary to advance a substantial public benefit; and, 4) when the project lies within a County-designated district of critical planning concern, the project is in compliance with Commission-established guidelines and locally adopted implementing regulations for the district.

The first standard for approval is a broad balancing test. The board of appeals, sitting in place of the Commission, must make a finding that the benefits of the project outweigh the detriments. Presumably, the benefit of a Chapter 40B proposal is the creation of affordable housing. However, this benefit must be weighed against potential detriments such as groundwater and surface water degradation due to high-density on-site wastewater disposal, or inadequate stormwater management. Other potential detriments include degradation of wetlands and other natural resources, traffic congestion, and the ability of public safety vehicles to access the proposed development in a safe and timely manner.

The second standard for approval is that the project be consistent with all applicable Minimum Performance Standards of the RPP and the local comprehensive plan. The board of appeals must find that the application is consistent with each applicable MPS and the provisions of the local comprehensive plan, unless the applicant can demonstrate: 1) that application of any part of the plan will render the project "uneconomic;" or, 2) the development proposal, while inconsistent, is not more detrimental to the protected resource than would be allowable under the applicable Minimum Performance Standard, and will result in the same or better protection of the resource at issue.

---

[3] Act, Section 1(c).
[4] Act, Section 1(c).

The third standard requires that the project be consistent with municipal development bylaws. This includes bylaws, rules and regulations of all of the local boards and officials of the town.[5] A project that is inconsistent with local bylaws may only be approved if the board of appeals, sitting in place of the Cape Cod Commission, determines that, "if not consistent, the inconsistency is necessary to enable a substantial segment of the population to secure adequate opportunities for housing, conservation, environmental protection, education, recreation or balanced economic growth."[6]

The fourth standard requires that the project be consistent with applicable regulations for districts of critical planning concern.

Absent a demonstration by an applicant for a comprehensive permit as to the consistency with the four standards set forth above, or a demonstration that a particular standard will render the project "uneconomic," the board of appeals may not grant a comprehensive permit.

Despite popular belief to the contrary, comprehensive permit projects are not immune from the Cape Cod Commission Act. This conclusion simply requires a plain read of the statutory language as discussed above and a dose of common sense. It is axiomatic that a comprehensive permit development of 60 or 120 or 240 dwelling units will have the same impacts upon natural and built environment resources as will a market rate development of 60 or 120 or 240 dwelling units. To conclude that somehow a comprehensive permit project will have a different impact than a market rate project merely perpetuates the cultural and historical stigma associated with affordable housing developments.

§ 4.13   The Comprehensive Permit Statute in Cities and Towns Consistent with Local Needs

Many cities and towns have aspired to achieve "consistency with local needs" status in the hopes of preventing future comprehensive permit applications. The theory was that without an appeal option to the Housing Appeals Committee, a developer would not file a comprehensive permit application, and instead seek to develop land in accordance with local rules and regulations.

Much to the surprise of these communities, nothing in the statute precludes an applicant from filing a comprehensive permit in a city or town that is consistent with local needs and nothing precludes the board of appeals from approving that

---

[5] "Development bylaw," any bylaw, ordinance, rule or regulation adopted by a municipality or municipal agency for the control or regulation of activities related to development affecting any buildings, land, water area or other resources within the boundaries of said municipality." Act at Section 2(g).

[6] Act at Section 13(d)(3).

permit, including attendant waivers from local rules and regulations. At issue is what standards should the board of appeals apply to the waivers of zoning, for example, where the city has achieved consistency with local needs status? More problematic, what assurance do abutters to a proposed comprehensive permit project have, even in communities that have satisfied their statutory obligations pursuant to G.L. c. 40B, § 20–23, that the adjacent parcel zoned for agriculture, for example, will not be approved for 200 dwelling units? If achieving consistency with local needs does not preclude the board of appeals from waiving all local regulations, one might wonder whether in the face of Chapter 40B traditional land use controls have any practical meaning in the Commonwealth.

CHAPTER 5

ZONING—GENERAL PRINCIPLES OF LAW

Synopsis

§ 5.01   Introduction

§ 5.02   Determining Applicable Zoning

§ 5.03   Zoning Changes

§ 5.04   Board of Appeals: Composition and Powers

§ 5.05   Filing; Public Hearing and Notice Requirements

§ 5.06   Withdrawal of Petitions; Reconsideration by Board

§ 5.07   Variances

    § 5.07[1]   Introduction and the Purposes of Variances

    § 5.07[2]   Required Findings for Granting a Variance

        § 5.07[2][a]   *Required Finding #1:* Soil Conditions, Shape Or Topography

            § 5.07[2][a][i]   Soil Conditions

            § 5.07[2][a][ii]   Shape

            § 5.07[2][a][iii]   Topography

        § 5.07[2][b]   *Required Finding #2:* Hardship

        § 5.07[2][c]   *Required Finding #3:* Public Good

    § 5.07[3]   Use Variances

    § 5.07[4]   Conditional Variances

    § 5.07[5]   Lapsed Variances

    § 5.07[6]   Procedural Issues and Grants of a Variance

        § 5.07[6][a]   Filing Requirements

    § 5.07[7]   Public Notice Requirements

    § 5.07[8]   Public Hearing and Voting Requirements

    § 5.07[9]   Decisions of the Board of Appeals

    § 5.07[10]   Decision Filing and Notification Requirements

    § 5.07[11]   Decision Recording Requirements

§ 5.07[12]   Use of Variances While Awaiting Appeals

§ 5.07[13]   Constructive Grant of Variances

§ 5.07[14]   Board of Appeals Liability

§ 5.08   Special Permits

    § 5.08[1]   Introduction and Purpose

    § 5.08[2]   Special Permits in Practice

§ 5.09   Judicial Appeals

§ 5.10   Commonly Encountered Problems in Zoning Practice

    § 5.10[1]   Protections for Nonconforming Structures and Uses

    § 5.10[2]   Vested Rights ("Grandfathering")

        § 5.10[2][a]   Introduction

        § 5.10[2][b]   The Seven Protections of G.L. c. 40A, § 6

            § 5.10[2][b][i]   Preexisting Structure or Use

            § 5.10[2][b][ii]   Building or Special Permit "In Hand"

            § 5.10[2][b][iii]   Single Lot: 50/5,000

            § 5.10[2][b][iv]   Common Lot: 75/7,500

                § 5.10[2][b][iv][A]   Common Lots and the "Merger Theory"

            § 5.10[2][b][v]   Preliminary Plan

            § 5.10[2][b][vi]   Definitive Plan

            § 5.10[2][b][vii]   Approval Not Required Plan

            § 5.10[2][b][viii]   Vested Rights, the Martha's Vineyard, and the Cape Cod Commission Acts

§ 5.11   Nonconforming Uses and Structures

    § 5.11[1]   Introduction

    § 5.11[2]   What are Nonconforming Uses and Structures?

        § 5.11[2][a]   The Use or Structure is Existing When the First Advertisement Appears

        § 5.11[2][b]   The Lot is Existing and Protected

    § 5.11[3]   The Protections Afforded to Nonconforming Uses and Structures

    § 5.11[4]   Extensions and Alterations to Nonconforming Uses and Structures

    § 5.11[5]   Extensions and Alterations to Nonconforming Uses and Structures: Signs

    § 5.11[6]   Extensions and Alterations to Nonconforming Uses and Structures: The Second "Except" Clause (Single and Two Family Residential)

    § 5.11[7]   Changes to Nonconforming Uses

        § 5.11[7][a]   Does the Use Reflect the Nature and Purpose of the Nonconforming Use Prevailing When the Zoning Took Effect?

        § 5.11[7][b]   Is There a Difference in the Quality, Character and/or Degree of the Resulting Use?

§ 5.11[7][c]   Is The Current Use Different In Kind In Its Effect
                             Upon The Neighborhood?
    § 5.11[8]   Abandonment of Nonconforming Uses and Structures
§ 5.12   Spot Zoning
§ 5.13   Contract Zoning and Development Agreements
§ 5.14   Availability of Declaratory Judgment in Zoning Cases
§ 5.15   Failure of Building Inspector to Act
§ 5.16   When Does a Zoning Hearing End?
§ 5.17   Regulating Form of Ownership as Opposed to Use: Condominium and
           Time Share Conversions
§ 5.18   Access Roadways—Different Zones
§ 5.19   The Site Plan Review Process
§ 5.20   Constructive Grant of Variances, Special Permits and Appeals
§ 5.21   Open Meeting, Quorum Requirements and Voting in Zoning Cases
§ 5.22   Judicial Enforcement of Zoning
§ 5.23   Split Lots (Lots Transected By a Zoning Boundary)
§ 5.24   Perimeter Plans—Entitlement to Approval Not Required Endorsement
§ 5.25   Who is 'Aggrieved' Party for Purposes of Zoning Appeal
§ 5.26   Modification of Board's Decision
§ 5.27   Permit Conditions Requiring Off-Site Improvements
§ 5.28   Earth Removal
§ 5.29   Growth Management
§ 5.30   Inclusionary Zoning
§ 5.31   Regulation of Adult Entertainment Businesses
§ 5.32   Additional Zoning Techniques
§ 5.33   Due Process Claims in Zoning and Subdivision Appeals
§ 5.34   Creation of Conforming Lot Resulting in Zoning Violation by Another
           Lot (Infectious Invalidity)
§ 5.35   What Use Qualifies As Accessory
§ 5.36   Expiration and Extension of Special Permits

§ 5.01 Introduction

Zoning is the lawful segregation of land uses into districts and the regulation of land uses within those districts. Zoning was upheld as constitutional in the landmark case of *Village of Euclid, Ohio v. Ambler Realty* in 1926[1] and is a common form of land use control in every state in the country. The Massachusetts Zoning Act, last revised in a comprehensive manner in 1975, is codified as G.L. c. 40A and applies to all cities and towns in the Commonwealth except the City of Boston. Practitioners in Boston should be familiar with G.L. c. 40A, however, as the Boston Zoning Code is similar in many respects and the Courts often cite to G.L. c. 40A in adjudicating zoning matters in Boston.

The Zoning Act is poorly written and in many instances, incoherent. As discussed in Chapter 2, the Act does not require that local zoning regulations be in accordance with a plan or study as a condition precedent to the adoption or amendment of zoning (or other land use regulations). The result is that cities and towns are constantly revising their regulations in response to issues of the moment and rarely in accordance with a long-range vision for the community's or region's needs or goals. Moreover, the Act provides one of the most generous vesting provisions of any zoning act in the nation. While these provisions are beneficial to landowners seeking to develop their land, the breadth of the vested rights granted make innovative land use tools such as development agreements and transfer of development rights programs of little value in Massachusetts. Ironically, the one area of Massachusetts land use law that is inflexible is the one area that demands flexibility: the variance. The statute makes the grant of a variance, as a legal matter, virtually always unlawful. While this rigidity would be appropriate in a state with a strong planning framework as the basis for the adoption of regulations, it is counterproductive in a state with ad hoc zoning standards, early vesting periods and as discussed in Chapter 4, a statutory provision that eradicates local zoning controls.

§ 5.02 Determining Applicable Zoning

Most town or city clerks maintain copies of zoning compilations containing all bylaws/ordinances that are in effect in the municipality. These are usually paperback bound pamphlets with the compilation date and latest amendment date indicated thereon. It is important, particularly if the latest date on the pamphlet is a few years old, to ascertain if any amendments have been adopted subsequent to the publication of the pamphlet. The clerk's office would have these on file but they are often unaware as to which changes are in the pamphlet and which are not. The best place to check on this is with the building or zoning officer, since he or she will work with the code on a daily basis and will probably be aware of the latest

---

[1] 272 U.S. 365 (1926).

changes. Otherwise, it is necessary to review the town meeting warrants or city council minutes back to the date of publication of the pamphlet. If this is not successful, the Attorney General's office has a Municipal Bureau that is charged with reviewing and approving all zoning bylaws (but not zoning ordinances) and may have helpful information.

Where the zoning ordinance or bylaw or accompanying map is unclear or ambiguous with respect to its application to a particular piece of property the landowner is entitled to the full benefit of the ambiguity.[1] This is perhaps just a way of saying that, zoning being a restriction on the free use of property, any ambiguity will be construed against the drafter of the regulation and in favor of the free use of private property. Likewise, a zoning map (or text of the ordinance or bylaw) that is vague fails to comport with basic due process requirements. (Zoning maps often are unclear or drawn to a scale that makes determination of the applicable zoning for a particular parcel difficult. This is particularly true with overlay districts, discussed more fully in Chapter 5.32.)

Note also that where the use of a lot or structure is begun or changed, or, where a building or special permit is issued, after the first publication of notice of public hearing on a proposed zoning amendment then such use or permit will be subject to the amendment if the same is subsequently adopted.[2] The broad array of vested rights protections afforded landowners is discussed in detail in Chapter 5.10[2] below.

§ 5.03   Zoning Changes[1]

Amendments or changes in zoning bylaws and ordinances may be effected only in strict accordance with statutory procedures. A change may be proposed by a city council, board of selectmen, board of appeals, individual owning land to be affected by the change, by petition of ten registered voters of a town pursuant to G.L. c. 39, § 10, by a planning board or regional planning agency, or by any other method provided by municipal charter.

In towns, a petition to initiate a zoning change requires the signature of one hundred registered voters if the change is to be proposed to a special town meeting. Only ten signatures are required if the change is to be proposed to an annual town meeting.

In a town, the proposed change is first submitted to the board of selectmen, in a city it is submitted to the city council. The selectmen or council must, within 14 days of receipt of the proposal, submit the proposal to the planning board. Within

---

[1] Jenkins v. Pepperell, 18 Mass. App. 265, 465 N.E.2d 268 (1984).

[2] G.L. c. 40A, § 6.

[1] *See generally* G.L. c. 40A, § 5 for material discussed in this section.

65 days of its receipt of the proposal, the planning board must hold a public hearing on the proposal. In a city, the city council or a committee designated or appointed for the purpose by the council, must each hold a hearing, together or separately, within 65 days.

Notice of the hearings must be published once each week for two successive weeks in a newspaper of general circulation in the municipality; the first publication to be at least 14 days before the hearing; and it must be posted in a conspicuous place in the city or town hall for a period of at least 14 days before the hearing. While the statute requires a 14-day notice period, it is good practice for the board submitting the notice to allow 15 days between the first advertisement and the opening of the public hearing. As an example, if the hearing is to be held on the 15th of the month, it is advised that the first advertisement occur on the first of the month, followed by the second advertisement in the following week.

Notice requirements are based on procedural due process considerations; the notice must provide fair warning to the public as to scope, intent and the land area(s) that are subject to a potential zoning amendment.

The notice must contain the time, place, and subject matter of the hearing. It must identify the land involved sufficiently for persons to identify it, and it must refer to the place (usually the clerk's office) where the full text and maps may be examined. As a general rule, there is rarely a fact pattern that would support "less" versus "more" notice.

Notice of the hearing must also be sent by first class mail to the Department of Housing and Community Development, the regional planning agency, if any, and to the planning boards of all abutting cities and towns. The statute provides that these entities may submit waivers or affidavits of actual notice to the city or town clerk prior to the legislative action on the proposed ordinance or bylaw amendment. In practice, few abutting cities or towns and even fewer regional planning agencies provide comments to the host community regarding the proposed zoning change.

G.L. c. 40A permits local bylaws and ordinances to contain provisions whereby non-resident owners may annually request notice of all public hearings conducted under that chapter. If the bylaw contains such a provision it is necessary to ascertain if any non-resident owner has requested such notice and, if so, to be sure the notice is given. Any non-resident owner who has filed such a request must be sent notice of such hearings where the proposed amendment involves changes in boundary, density or use which affects his or her property, regardless of whether the ordinance or bylaw so requires. Note that the notification requirements for a non-resident property owner is the only notification provision the statute provides for a land-owner whose land is, or could be, subject to a rezoning. There is no notification provision other than the required advertisements and posting of notices afforded to a resident property owner. This fact is particularly important for counsel representing land owners in cities and towns concerned about the potential impacts of a rezoning to their or abutting property. Counsel must pay careful attention to the legal advertisements and posting at city or town halls on a frequent basis to ensure they are aware of proposed rezonings that may affect their clients' property. Note again, the landowner whose land is subject to the rezoning is not required to be notified of the petition.

Prior to the adoption of any zoning ordinance or bylaw which seeks to further regulate matters dealt with by the State Wetlands Protection Act or the regulations authorized thereunder relative to agricultural or aquacultural practices the city or town clerk must, no later than seven days prior to the city council or town meeting which will consider adoption of the measure, give notice of it to the Farmland Advisory Board established by that Act.

After the public hearing, the planning board may issue a report with recommendations to the city council or town meeting as to the planning board's support for, opposition to, or recommendations for revision. While the report is strictly advisory and has no binding effect upon the ultimate legislative vote, no action may be taken by the legislative body on the proposed change until at least 21 days have elapsed from the date of the public hearing, unless the planning board issues its report prior to the 21–day expiration. If the 21-day period passes with no report from the planning board, or upon submission of such report, the municipal legislature may adopt, reject, or amend the proposed ordinance or bylaw.

Note that the reporting requirement of the planning board provides a planning board with an opportunity to block a legislative vote on petitioned zoning amendments where the board does not have the full 21-day comment period. This is of enormous consequence to petitioners of zoning changes that do not, or cannot, encourage the planning board to hold a public hearing on their petition sufficiently early in the time line discussed above. Thus counsel for a petitioner must work backwards from the date of the legislative action (of particular importance in towns where town meetings occur infrequently) and ensure that the petition will reach the planning board and a public hearing will be held by the planning board in sufficient time to allow for the 21 day reporting period.

If the city council fails to vote to adopt a proposed ordinance within 90 days of the city council hearing, or, if a town meeting fails to vote to adopt any proposed bylaw within six months of the planning board public hearing, the hearings become "stale" and new public hearings must be held. Similar to the strategy employed by the petitioner with respect to ensuring that the planning board has at least 21 days between the holding of its hearing and the legislative vote, the petitioner should try and ensure that a town meeting will be held within six months of the planning board's hearing (as noted, town meetings are held infrequently, while city councils meet, generally, at least once a month).

In order for a proposed zoning change to be adopted, it must receive a two-thirds affirmative vote of all the members of a city or town council or of a town meeting present and competent to vote. The requirement of a two-thirds majority vote is increased to a three-fourths majority vote where, in cities, and towns with a town council form of government (consisting of fewer than 26 members), the owners of 20% or more of the land area affected by such proposed change, or of the land area adjacent to and within 300 feet of the affected land, file a written protest with the clerk giving reasons for their objection.

No proposed zoning change that has been defeated (often labeled "passed over" in many cities and towns) may be considered again by the municipal legislature for a period of two years from the date of such defeat unless the adoption of the change has been recommended in the report of the planning board.[2] While no case has decided this issue, it appears as if the defeated zoning change could be amended—substantively amended—such that the revised petition would constitute a new zoning petition and therefore not require the approval of the planning board.

All zoning bylaws or amendments thereto must be approved by the attorney general pursuant to G.L. c. 40, § 32 prior to becoming effective. Note that only towns and not cities, are required to obtain the attorney general's approval pursuant to G.L. c. 40, § 32 However, once such approval is given the bylaw is effective as of the date of its adoption, provided proper publication is made in the case of a town or a city which has accepted G.L. c. 40, § 32A. In towns, proper publication consists of publication in a town pamphlet or bulletin copies of which are posted in at least five public places in the town, and, if the town is divided into precincts, copies must be posted in at least one public place in each precinct. Alternatively, copies of the bylaw or change may be published twice, at least one week apart, in a newspaper of general circulation in the town.[3]

Procedural defects in the adoption or amendment of bylaws or ordinances must be raised by suit commenced within the time period specified in sections 32 and 32A of Chapter 40 of the General Law (within 90 days of posting or of the second publication). Notice of suit, giving Court, parties, invalidity claimed, and date of filing, together with a copy of the complaint, must be filed with the city or town clerk within 7 days after the action is commenced. Procedural defects could include defects in the notice and advertising requirements (e.g., the advertisement preceding the public hearing was noticed less than 14 days prior to the first hearing), the advertisement of the hearing was vague (e.g. "the planning board will hold a public hearing to discuss the rezoning of land off of South Street"), or a non-resident land owner who complied with the notice provisions of G.L. c. 40A, § 5 was not properly notified.

---

[2] G.L. c. 40A, § 16.
[3] G.L. c. 40, § 32. Note that a third alternative is provided, i.e., hand delivery of a copy of the bylaw or change to every dwelling in town.

§ 5.04　Board of Appeals: Composition and Powers

Municipal boards of appeals are composed of either three or five members. In cities, the board is appointed by the mayor subject to confirmation by the city council, in towns, board members are appointed by the selectmen. The terms of board members are arranged so that the term of one member shall expire annually. Normally the board will also have one or more associate members who sit in cases of absence, inability to act or conflict of interest on the part of regular members. Boards must adopt rules for the conduct of their business and must file a copy of same with the city or town clerk. Boards of Appeals often overlook the importance of adopting rules for conducting business, particularly where it relates to applications pursuant to the comprehensive permit statute (See Chapter 4 for a discussion of rules pertaining to comprehensive permit applications).

Boards of Appeals have the power to hear and decide:

(a) Appeals taken by persons aggrieved by some action or failure to act on the part of an administrative officer (usually the building inspector) under the authority of G.L. c. 40A.

(b) Applications for special permits as provided by the local ordinance or bylaw.

(c) Petitions for variances.

(d) Petitions for comprehensive permits pursuant to G.L. c. 40B, § 20–23.

With the exception of adjudication over comprehensive permit applications, the board has plenary powers to frame remedies. It may make orders or decisions, reverse or affirm, in whole or in part, or modify any order or decision lawfully appealed to it. The board thus has all the powers of the officer from whom the appeal is taken and may issue or direct the issuance of a permit.[1] The board may not deny an application or petition because the person seeking relief has in the past, or is, violating the municipality's zoning bylaw or ordinance.[2]

The members of a board need not base their decision on a shared reason, but may offer different reasons for arriving at the same conclusion.[3] However, in denying an appeal involving a special permit, a board decision is inadequate if it fails to reflect that the appropriate standards were considered in making its decision. A

---

[1] G.L. c. 40A, §§ 12, 14.

[2] Dowd v. Board of Appeals, 5 Mass. App. 148, 360 N.E.2d 640 (1977).

[3] Oakham Sand & Gravel Corp. v. Town of Oakham, 54 Mass. App. Ct. 80, 763 N.E.2d 529 (2002).

board must state in what specific respects an application is deficient.[4]

§ 5.05   Filing; Public Hearing and Notice Requirements

A public hearing is required before a permit or special permit granting authority may take any action pursuant to the zoning bylaw or ordinance. The notice and procedural requirements for such hearings are laid out in the statute with specificity.[1] But, many cities and towns have their own particular requirements and ways of conducting business that amplifies (or unlawfully) modifies the strict requirements of G.L. c. 40A, § 5. This is particularly true as to the question of what must be filed, and where. Certain sensitivity is needed to be sure that protection of a client's interest is reconciled with the need to respect long-established local custom. In most cases, the particular local requirements differ only slightly from those specified by statute.

Where review by a board is sought of an action or inaction of any administrative official (e.g. building inspector) under the provisions of the zoning ordinance or bylaw, the appeal must be taken within 30 days from the date of the order or decision appealed from. This type of appeal is initiated by filing a notice of appeal, containing the grounds upon which the appeal is based, with the city or town clerk.

Where an application for special permit or variance is involved, the board will have original jurisdiction. These may be filed at any time with the board and simultaneously, with the city or town clerk. Note again, however, that many cities and towns have developed specific forms and filing protocol for special permit and variance applications.

After filing the appeal, application, or petition with the city or town clerk[2] the petitioner must file a copy of the same, including the date and time of filing certified by the clerk, with the board of appeals or other special permit granting authority (e.g., the planning board or city council). The board must give proper notice, as set out below, and must hold a hearing within 65 days from the date that the appeal or petition is transmitted to it. In conducting its hearing, the board may administer oaths, summon witnesses, or call for the production of papers.[3] While few boards of appeals place witnesses under oath, petitioner's counsel (and other counsel) may desire that the board of appeals' hearing take on a more formal tone than is traditional and suggest to the board that witness testimony be given under the pains and penalties of perjury.

---

[4] KCI Management, Inc. v. Board of Appeal of Boston, 54 Mass. App. Ct. 254, 764 N.E.2d 377 (2002).

[1] G.L. c. 40A, § 11.

[2] At least in the case of an application for special permit, the failure to file with the city or town clerk will not be fatal in the absence of prejudice to the complaining party. Roberts v. Southwestern Bell Mobile Systems, Inc., 429 Mass. 478 (1999).

[3] G.L. c. 40A, § 15.

Notice of the hearing must be given by publica
must be in a newspaper of general circulation ;
two successive weeks, the first publication to b/
date. Posting for at least 14 days prior to the h/
to be in a conspicuous place in the city or to
in Section 5.07[7], it is recommended that t/
as opposed to the 14th day to ensure complia/
of the statute.

First class mail notice must be sent to all "parties in ınuı.
are defined as the petitioner, abutters, owners of land directly opposite on any p
or private street or way, and abutters to abutters within three hundred feet of the
property line of the petitioner as they appear on the most recent applicable tax list,
regardless of whether the party's land may be located in another municipality, also
the planning boards of the municipality and every abutting city or town. The tax
list of the assessors is conclusive as to the names and addresses of parties in
interest.[4] The municipality and not the applicant, bears responsibility for obtaining
the "applicable tax list" and for notifying parties in interest. While it is common
practice for the applicant or counsel to prepare the list and mail the notifications,
the municipality is the responsible entity. The applicant runs the risk of waiving
any claim to defect of the tax list or other infirmity if the municipality is absolved
of this ministerial function.[5]

In lieu of mail, notice to a party in interest the board may accept a waiver of notice
or an affidavit of actual notice. Where it appears that mail notice was insufficient,
the board may order special notice to a party in interest, allowing between 5 and
10 days for reply.[6] The notice must contain:

(1)   the name of the petitioner;

(2)   a description of the property involved;

(3)   the date, time, and place of the hearing;

(4)   the subject matter of the hearing; and

(5)   the nature of the action or relief requested.

Local ordinances or bylaws may set out further notice requirements.[7] As discussed previously, more detailed notice is far superior than "less."

---

[4] G.L. c. 40A, § 11

[5] *See* Kane v. Board of Appeals of Medford, 273 Mass. 97, 103 (1930) (responsibility of
mailings of notice cannot be "delegated to the interested petitioner") and Planning Board of Peabody
v. Board of Appeals of Peabody, 358 Mass. 81, 83 (1970) (notice mailed by petitioner's attorney
invalid).

[6] *Id.*

[7] *Id.*

operative not only as to the first day of the hearing but also for any
ites.[8] The establishment of a "one time" notice requirement is impor-
ier the board nor the applicant is under an obligation to "re-notice" the
, despite the fact that very few hearings, especially in complex land use
rs, are concluded in one session. For example, comprehensive permit appli-
ions almost never can be concluded with only the original public hearing. To
avoid potential claims of due process violations (or at minimum to avoid angering
the public that seeks to attend continued hearing sessions), the board may re-notice
the hearing, and many communities do so. The board may permissibly pass the
costs of re-advertised hearings onto the applicant provided that the board's rules
so specify.

The deadline for rendering a decision differs depending on the nature of relief
requested.

Where the petition is for a variance or appeal of an administrative decision (e.g.
an appeal of the building inspector's decision or failure to act), the board must
render and file its decision within 100 days after the filing of the application with
the city of town clerk. Note that the 100-day period includes the time necessary
to advertise and hold a public hearing.

Where the petition is for a special permit, the board must render its decision
within 90 days after the close of the public hearing and the public hearing must
have been held within 65 days of the special permit application.

Where the petition is for a comprehensive permit, the board must render its
decision within 40 days after the close of the public hearing and the public hearing
must have been opened within 30 days of the comprehensive permit application.

Note that as applied to each of the above noted four applications, nothing
prevents the applicant and the board from agreeing to an extension of the time
periods established by statute. These extensions should be obtained prior to the
expiration of the statutory period, be obtained in writing and be filed with the city
or town clerk.

Failure of the board to act within the statutory time periods constitutes a grant
of the permit, variance or other relief requested.[9] In the case of appeals pursuant
to G.L. c. 40A, § 15 or petitions for variance pursuant to G.L. c. 40A, § 10, the
written decision of board must be filed with the city or town clerk within 114 days
from the date of filing of the appeal or petition (100 plus 14). In the case of special
permits, the board's decision must be made and filed, within 90 days of the close

---

[8] Tebo v. Board of Appeals, 22 Mass. App. 618, 495 N.E.2d 892 (1986), *review granted*, 398
Mass. 1105, 498 N.E.2d 1357, *aff'd*, 400 Mass. 464, 510 N.E.2d 267.
[9] G.L. c. 40A, §§ 9, 15.

of the public hearing. If these requirements are not met, the requested relief is constructively granted (a so-called "constructive approval").[10]

The board must keep "detailed records" of its proceedings, indicating the vote of each member on each question and any members abstaining or absent and setting forth clearly the reason for its decision. (The case law, however, suggests that where a variance is denied, very little in the way of reasons is required.)[11]

As noted above, copies of the record and decision must be filed by the board in the office of the city or town clerk within 14 days of the date the decision is made. The minutes and decision of the board need not be signed by the members prior to filing with the clerk.[12] Notice of the decision must be mailed forthwith to the petitioner, the parties in interest, and to every person present at the hearing that provided his or her address and requested that notice be sent to him or her. The notice must state that appeals from the decision must be taken within 20 days from the date the decision was filed in the clerk's office.[13] The official record of the proceedings of the special permit granting authority are not admissible in a subsequent de novo judicial appeal.[14]

With respect to matters of form, in addition to the notice of appeal rights, the decision should contain the name and address of the owner, an identifying description of the land affected, a statement of compliance with the statutory requirements for the relief granted, and a certification that copies of the decision and all plans referred to in the decision have been filed with the planning board and city or town clerk.

A copy of the decision, certified by the permit granting authority must be provided to the applicant and to the owner. No variance or special permit or any extension, modification, or renewal of the same shall take effect until a copy of the decision bearing the certification of the town or city clerk that 20 days have elapsed after the decision was filed in his or her office and no appeal has been filed, or if such appeal has been filed, that it has been denied, has been recorded in the appropriate registry of deeds.[15] Note that the practical application of this requirement is to preclude the applicant from recording a special permit or variance granted by the board of appeals that has been appealed pursuant to G.L. c. 40A, § 17.

---

[10] Building Inspector of Attleboro v. Attleboro Landfill, Inc., 384 Mass. 109, 423 N.E.2d 1009 (1981); Capone v. Zoning Bd. of Appeals, 389 Mass. 617, 451 N.E.2d 1141 (1983).

[11] Cefalo v. Board of Appeals, 332 Mass. 178, 124 N.E.2d 247 (1955); Hunters Brook Realty Corp. v. Zoning Bd. of Appeals, 14 Mass. App. 76, 436 N.E.2d 978 (1982).

[12] Tanner v. Board of Appeals, 27 Mass. App. 1181, 541 N.E.2d 576 (1989).

[13] Tanner v. Board of Appeals, 27 Mass. App. 1181, 541 N.E.2d 576 (1989).

[14] Building Inspector of Chatham v. Kendrick, 17 Mass. App. 928, 456 N.E.2d 1151 (1983).

[15] G.L. c. 40A, § 11 (¶ 4).

Where an application or petition for special permit or variance has been constructively granted, a copy of the application or petition, along with a certification by the city or town clerk testifying to the constructive grant and the fact that it has become final, or that any appeal has been denied, must be recorded in the registry of deeds.[16]

§ 5.06   Withdrawal of Petitions; Reconsideration by Board

Pursuant to G.L. c. 40A, § 16, after a petition or application for variance or special permit has been filed, it may be withdrawn by the petitioner, without prejudice, up to the time of publication of the notice of public hearing as required pursuant to G.L. c. 40A, § 11. Thereafter it may be withdrawn without prejudice only if the board approves such withdrawal.

If an appeal, application or petition is finally and unfavorably acted upon, then the same appeal, petition or application may not be favorably acted upon within two years after the date of such unfavorable action except in the following circumstances:

(a) the permit granting authority must find, by a unanimous vote of a three member board or the vote of four members of a five member board or by a 2/3 vote of a board of more than five members (e.g. where the special permit granting authority is a planning board), specific and material changes in the conditions upon which the previous unfavorable action was based, and describes such changes in the record, and

(b) all but one of the members of the planning board has consented to the favorable action. Note that notice is required to have been given to the parties in interest of the time and place of the proceedings when the question of the planning board's consent will be considered.[1]

In summary, this section of the Zoning Act prevents the board from acting favorably upon a petition within two years from the date it has acted unfavorably upon the same petition unless:

a) four out of five members of the board find specific and material changes in the conditions upon which the previous denial was based, described such changes in the record, and

b) four out of five members of the planning board consent, after hearing, to the favorable action.

The specific and material changes that the board would have to find in order to

---

[16] G.L. c. 40A, § 11 (¶ 4).
[1] G.L. c. 40A, § 16.

reconsider the previous denial would, obviously, have to fall into either or both of two categories:

a) changes in the proposal and/or plans, or

b) changes in the surrounding conditions.

Whether there have been such changes is a matter confided by the courts to the board's sound discretion; and it may give weight to differences that in an absolute sense are minor but which given the totality of the impacts, effect a significant change in the proposal.

To the extent that the board believes that its earlier denial of a petition was based on erroneous information or assumptions, which have been corrected at the time of the new submission, this would be considered a change in circumstances sufficient to allow the petition to be reconsidered during the two-year moratorium period.

However, if what is before the board is the identical petition, presented in the identical circumstances that pertained at the time of the earlier denial, then the petition must be denied. An earlier denial, stated by the board to be "without prejudice" cannot have the effect of rendering inoperative the requirements of § 16. (Note, however, that a petition may be withdrawn without prejudice by the applicant, with the board's permission, at any time before it is decided.)[2]

If reapplication is made during the two-year period, it is not clear which hearing should come first, that of the planning board or that of the special permit granting authority. Under the "old" zoning act, in effect before 1978, permission of the planning board was needed before the special permit granting authority could consider a previously denied application within the two-year period. So the planning board hearing was always held first. The 1978 amendments to the Zoning Act changed the statutory language to require that the planning board consent to favorable action on the reapplication. However, old habits persisted, and the planning board hearing in many municipalities is still commonly held first. There seems no objection to this so long as the planning board consents to favorable action, rather than merely to reconsideration.

Where the planning board is itself the special permit granting authority a further procedural puzzle is presented. Should the board hold two separate hearings, one on specific and material change, and the second on the main question of whether or not to grant the permit? It does not seem that this is either legally required or particularly efficient. The finding of specific and material change can be made by the planning board/special permit granting authority as part of a decision to grant

---

[2] Ranney v. Board of Appeals, 11 Mass. App. 112, 414 N.E.2d 373 (1981).

or deny the special permit. Such decision would be made after a duly noticed public hearing at which the board heard evidence on both the issue of change and the issue of whether or not the permit should be granted. The issue of specific and material change could be considered at the first part of the hearing; and if this is decided adversely to the applicant, there would be no need for the board to proceed further.

§ 5.07   Variances

§ 5.07[1]   Introduction and the Purposes of Variances

"No person has a legal right to a variance and they are to be granted sparingly."[1]

So begins a discussion about variances in Massachusetts.

Since its introduction in the early 1920s, the variance—both area and use—has generated more controversy and debate than any other regulatory tool available to cities and towns across the country.[2] Case law is replete with exhortations to local zoning boards about their misuse and abuse of power and state legislatures have often responded with limitations, prohibitions and a strict narrowing of the op-

---

[1] Damaskos v. Board of Appeal of Boston, 359 Mass. 55, 61 (1971). *See* Broderick v. Board of Appeal of Boston, 361 Mass. 472 (1972) and Bottomley v. Board of Appeals of Yarmouth, 354 Mass. 474 (1968). In Dion v. Board of Appeals of Waltham, 344 Mass. 547 (1962), the Supreme Judicial Court wrote: "Variances are to be granted sparingly and granting them has been surrounded by many statutory safeguards. The legislative policy of avoiding variances, except upon a clear showing that the prerequisites have been satisfied, the circumstance that no evidentiary weight may be given to the board's findings and the provisions for a new hearing, viewed together, show that the burden rests upon the person seeking a variance and the board ordering a variance to produce evidence at the hearing...that the statutory prerequisites have been met and the variance justified." . 344 Mass. 547, at 556. *See also* Whelan v. Zoning Board of Appeals of Norfolk, 430 Mass. 1009, 1010 (2000), It is a "principle of longstanding application in the zoning context: a landowner will not be permitted to create a dimensional nonconformity if he could have used his adjoining land to avoid or diminish the nonconformity." *Citing* Planning Bd. of Norwell v. Serena, 406 Mass. 1008, 1009, (1990). *See* Guimond v. Russell, 2003 Mass. Super. LEXIS 228, 16 Mass. L. Rep. 582 (Mass. Super. Ct. 2003) *and* Roberts v. Natick Planning Board, Nos. 283125, 273910 (Mass. Land Ct. Sept. 24, 2004).

[2] "...The variance procedure really falls short of giving intelligent flexibility within a framework designed to accord equal protection of the law. Planning considerations do not receive careful consideration there. The board does not have the expertise to know what is trivial and can be disposed of quickly and what is substantial and requires close examination. For lack of time it cannot sit down with the applicant and, by patience, suggestions, and persuasion, bring him around to making changes that will make the use compatible with the area. Furthermore, because of the 'strict and severe limitations' courts have imposed on the board's powers, the board is not always prepared to be honest and articulate about its reasons for reaching a particular result. It cannot promulgate the kind of standards we need for administrative decisions, for queerly enough, they would be illegal. An ideal breeding ground for adventitious factors results." Jesse Dukeminier, Jr. and Clyde Stapleton, *Boards of Adjustment: The Problem Re-Examined*, Zoning Digest 14, No. 12 (December 1962); 361–371, at 370–371.

portunities for zoning boards to grant variances.

Over the past 60 years, Massachusetts has responded in a fashion similar to many other states. While variances are recognized as a practical means of varying the rigidity of local zoning, they are analogous to automobiles: a necessary element of everyday life, but inherently dangerous in the wrong hands. Massachusetts however, has gone further than most states by the adoption of a statutory scheme that makes granting a variance that will withstand legal challenge extremely difficult.

As discussed below, the vice of a variance lies not with the tool itself, but rather, with how it has been, and still is, used. Despite recent advances in adoption of flexible zoning techniques, and as discussed in Chapter 2, zoning in Massachusetts remains a rigid and imperfect means of regulating land in an increasingly urbanized state. In addition, while some mechanism is required to provide relief—relaxation—of an ordinance that by its very nature is unreasonably re-strictive, the relaxation of an adopted zoning ordinance through the variance raises numerous problems. These include the variance's effect on the neighborhood, the community at large, and even the overall region when granted outside of the statutes carefully and intentionally narrowed criteria.

Commentators on the subject of variances have consistently held that the purpose of the variance was and remains to provide "a constitutional safety valve."[3] The "constitutional" issue is that but for the grant of a variance, the effect of the zoning ordinance would be tantamount to a regulatory taking.[4]

Given the heavy burden carried by the applicant for a variance, where the board denies the variance, and an appeal is taken, the best approach for the disappointed petitioner is to seek a remand back to the board by the trial court since a judgment ordering the variance to issue is almost certain to be reversed on appeal.

§ 5.07[2]   Required Findings for Granting a Variance

G.L. c. 40A, § 10 requires that the grant of a variance be made only where the board of appeals finds that the following three "Required Findings" have been reached in the affirmative. Note that these requirements are conjunctive, not

---

[3] *See*, for example, Curtin's California Land Use and Planning Law, 24th Edition, Solano Press, 2004, "Variances are, in effect, constitutional safety valves to permit administrative adjustments when application of a general regulation would be confiscatory or produce unique hardship." *Id.* at 54.

[4] *See* Chapter 3 for a discussion of regulatory takings. Massachusetts courts have found that a zoning ordinance resulted in a regulatory taking of private property in only few instances, and almost always where the zoning ordinance or other regulation left the property owner with virtually no economic value.

disjunctive.[5] The board must reach affirmative conclusions for all three findings. To repeat, a finding that two of the three requirements have been met is not sufficient for the grant of a variance.[6]

In addition to requiring that all three findings be made in the affirmative, the courts have reminded boards of appeals that their conclusions must be in the form of statements—analyses—that support the findings set forth in the variance decision. This point is also worth repeating. Simply copying the statutory findings language is insufficient. The board must reach affirmative conclusions on the following three requirements that consist of either analytical or otherwise substantive information.[7]

§ 5.07[2][a]　　*Required Finding #1:* **Soil Conditions, Shape Or Topography**

A key requirement of variance law in Massachusetts is the determination that there is "something wrong" or "something unusual" about the parcel for which a variance is sought. By statute, this peculiarity must be evident in the parcel's soil or geologic formation, the parcel's shape or the parcel's topography.[8] Each of

---

[5] "Since the requirements for the grant of a variance are conjunctive, not disjunctive, a failure to establish any one of them is fatal." Guiragossian v. Board of Appeals of Watertown, 21 Mass. App. Ct. 111, 115 (1986), *referencing* Blackman v. Board of Appeals of Barnstable, 334 Mass. 446, 450 (1956). *See also* Wolfson v. Sun Oil Company, 357 Mass. 87 (1970), "Each requirement of the statute must be satisfied before a variance may be granted." 357 Mass. 87, at 90. *See also* Whelan v. Zoning Board of Appeals of Norfolk, 430 Mass. 1009, 1009–10 (2000) and Perez v. Board of Appeals of Norwood, 54 Mass. App. Ct. 139, 144 (2002). "Vara's desire to maximize his profit, however, does not constitute "substantial" hardship under G.L. c. 40A, § 10." *citing* Bruzzese v. Board of Appeals of Hingham, 343 Mass. 421, 424, (1962).

[6] Other jurisdictions have held similarly. "The failure of a zoning board to consider each requirement of a zoning ordinance prior to granting a variance is an error of law." Larsen v. Zoning Board of Adjustment of City of Pittsburgh, 543 Pa. 415, 418 (1996).

[7] "The specific findings necessary to satisfy the requirements for granting a variance are not met by a 'mere repetition of the statutory words.' " Wolfson v. Sun Oil Co., 357 Mass. 87, 89 (1970), *quoting* Barckett. Board of Appeal of the Building Dep't of Boston, 311 Mass. 52, 54 (1942).

[8] *See*, for example, Planning Board of Watertown v. Board of Appeals of Watertown, 5 Mass. App. Ct. 833 (1977), where the Court noted that the peculiarity—the something wrong—must not affect the district as a whole. "…a condition need not affect all property in a district in order to be regarded as a condition generally affecting the district as a whole." 5 Mass. App. Ct. 833, at 835. *See also* Shacka v. Board of Appeals of Chelmsford, 341 Mass. 593 (1961), where the Court, in overruling the grant of a variance based on the pre-1975 revisions to the variance statute (formerly G.L. c. 40A, § 15) wrote: "The change in character of the neighborhood is not one 'especially affecting such parcel'…The change, as the judge found, affects all the nearby area… Even though the trend to commercial use may not affect all the residence district in which the property is located, its effect is general." 341 Mass. 593, at 595. *See also* Perez v. Board of Appeals of Norwood, 54 Mass. App. Ct. 139, 142 (2002) and Bonfiglioli v. Walsh, 2002 Mass. Super. LEXIS 481, 5 (Mass. Super. 2002), for a review of the standing requirements for challenging the grant of a variance.

these three possible attributes is discussed below.

As important as an affirmative finding that the parcel has peculiar soils, shape or topography is the finding that this peculiarity is *unique to the zoning district* where the parcel is located. For example, an applicant with property in Rockport would have trouble satisfying Required Finding #1 by claiming she could not comply with the town's front yard setback requirement due to the presence of bedrock outcrop on her property. As most of Rockport (and the North Shore) contains significant outcrop of bedrock, the uniqueness requirement of this Required Finding would not be met.[9]

Similarly, a landowner in a floodplain, or one whose property contains significant wetland vegetation or steep slopes must be able to demonstrate and the board of appeals must so determine, that the parcel is unique in this regard insofar as the zoning district is concerned. Note that the finding does not have to be town or citywide, but rather in relation to land within the specific zoning district where the parcel lies.[10] Note also that the required finding is likely to

---

[9] *See*, for example, Kirkwood v. Board of Appeals of Rockport, 17 Mass. App. Ct. 423 (1984), where the Appeals Court upheld a lower court's annulment of a variance. The Court concluded, among other things, that the property and its attendant geologic constraints, simply was not unique relative to the zoning district in which it lies. "Ledge (hard rock), similar to that at the locus, comprises frontage of many houses on the waterfront. Most of the dwellings near the water incur similar exposure to the force of the elements and the ocean. Moreover, there is some other property in the district with topography generally like that of the locus. The only characteristic which really distinguishes Wrightson's land is that it extends further into the ocean than the other waterfront property. The fact that inland property in the zoning district is not precisely identical to the locus in topography or shape is not controlling, however, since 'a condition need not affect all property in a district in order to be regarded as a condition generally affecting the district as a whole." 17 Mass. App. Ct. 423, at 428, *citing* Planning Board of Watertown v. Board of Appeals of Watertown, 5 Mass. App. Ct. 833 (1977).

[10] *See*, for example, Wolfman v. Board of Appeals of Brookline, 15 Mass. App. Ct. 112 (1983), where the Appeals Court upheld a lower court decision supporting the grant of a variance where the parcel "contains an irregular pattern of subsurface soil conditions and materials at varying levels of elevation and a relatively high water table…these soil conditions 'show the locus to be unique as compared to other lots along Beacon Street…" 15 Mass. App. Ct. 112, at 115. *See also* Coolidge v. Zoning Board of Appeals of Framingham, 343 Mass. 742 (1962), where the Supreme Judicial Court overturned the grant of a variance that was based on claims that development of residential property that abutted a business district was impractical. "Nor do we think that the subsidiary facts found by the judge would permit a finding that there was hardship 'owing to conditions especially affecting …the locus… but not affecting generally the zoning district in which it is located.'…there is nothing in the record from which we can infer that the factors giving rise to such a situation are not similarly present in the zoning district generally… A district has to end somewhere. Care should be taken last the boundaries of a residence district be pared down in successive proceedings granting variances to owners who from time to time through such proceedings find their respective properties abutting upon premises newly devoted to business purposes…What the interveners seek in effect and what the board has granted is a change in the zone boundary…It may well be…that due to the

trigger the need for expert testimony beyond the expertise of the applicant and members of the board of appeals. This point is crucial with regard to the requirement that the board rest its decision on factual information—studies reports, and expert testimony—pertaining to the parcel's unique characteristics relative to other parcels in the zoning district.

§ 5.07[2][a][i]   Soil Conditions

A parcel's underlying soil and geology affect the size of the structure that can be built, the opportunity to install a subsurface wastewater disposal system, the use of the land for agricultural purposes and the availability of water for consumption and irrigation.

Consistent with their attitude toward variances in general, the Courts have not shown much sympathy to landowners with poor or limited soil conditions. This is most likely due to the problem inherent in demonstrating the uniqueness of a parcel's soil or geologic conditions when compared to abutting properties.

To make the required finding that a parcel is entitled to a variance due to uniquely poor or inadequate soil conditions, the board of appeals must conclude that: (1) within the zoning district in question, the soil limitations are attributable only to the parcel subject to the application;[11] (2) the soil limitation would effect anyone attempting to use the property as permitted by relevant regulations[12] and (3) testimony or other evidence supports the conclusion that the parcel is truly unique with respect to soil or geologic conditions.[13]

---

conditions of the area, in which the intervener's land is located such a change would be beneficial to the community. This, however, is a matter for consideration by the town under procedures adopted for amendments to its zoning bylaws. The board's 'limited and carefully restricted variance power may not be invoked for this purpose.' " 343 Mass. 742, at 745–746.

The holding in *Coolidge* is an important one and reflects a decision on facts common to many Board of Appeals hearings on variances. The owner of residential property abutting a non-residential zone applies for a variance to more fully comport with the uses allowed on her neighbor's property. The argument is straightforward. The imposition of the restrictive residential zoning precludes uses that have any practical value due to the presence of abutting commercial activity. This fact, the argument goes, constitutes a hardship. As discussed throughout this Chapter, while the argument may have emotional merit, neither the statute nor the courts allow for the grant of a variance in this situation. As the Court notes in *Coolidge*, a zoning district must end—stop—somewhere. Ad hoc issuance of variances to compensate the landowner whose property is at the "end of the line" not only violates the statute, but as discussed in Chapter 2, defeats the purpose of the municipality's comprehensive plan and undercuts the authority of the city or town's legislative body.

[11] Where all the parcels, or many of the parcels within a zoning district are negatively affected by current zoning or natural conditions on real property, the court concluded many years ago that the appropriate action is a rezoning, not parcel-by-parcel variances. See, for example, Brackett v. Board of Appeal of Building Department of City of Boston, 311 Mass. 52 (1942).

[12] Wolfman v. Board of Appeals of Brookline, 15 Mass. App. Ct. 112, 116 (1983).

[13] *See*, for example, O'Brian v. Board of Appeals of Brockton, 3 Mass. App. Ct. 740 (1975),

§ 5.07[2][a][ii]   Shape

The configuration—shape—of land parcels is a result of many factors, including the historical use of the land, its location relative to water, roads and utilities, who owned it, when and how it was regulated by the city or town and its economic value. A review of assessor's maps across the Commonwealth reveals extreme differences in parcel layout and design. Nevertheless, Massachusetts courts have consistently held that a lot's peculiar or unusual shape, is unlikely to support the grant of a variance.[14]

Equally consistent, has been the court's conclusion that a lot lacking sufficient area does not justify the grant of a variance under this Required Finding.[15]

Boards of appeals are in a difficult position when confronted with an applicant for an area variance for a lot that lacks minimum area requirements and has lost or never obtained, grandfather protection.[16] As discussed below, the applicant is likely to present a credible case for "hardship" and may similarly be able to demonstrate that the Required Finding #3 (no detriment to the public good) can

---

where the court upheld the grant of a variance where the lower court judge found that the property would be "economically useless for development of a single family residence under the terms of the zoning code" due in part, to "adverse soil conditions." 3 Mass. App. Ct. 740, at 740. (N.B. The variance provided for the construction of a Registry of Motor Vehicle building).

[14] Although there are many relevant cases, a particularly compelling one involved the request by a gasoline station to expand its operation by constructing service bays. Wolfson v. Sun Oil Company, 357 Mass. 87 (1970). Unfortunately, years earlier the city revised its zoning ordinance placing the property into three zoning districts. The proposed service bay construction could not comply with the rear and side yard setback requirements of one of the new zoning districts. The owner applied for and was granted a dimensional variance. On appeal, a lower court found that "because of the size and irregular shape of the locus, and more particularly because of the re-zoning in 1964 which divided it into three separate zones, the locus was unique." 357 Mass. 87, at 88. On appeal, the Supreme Judicial Court reversed. "The special circumstances found by the judge and the board is based on the premise that the size and irregular shape of the locus, together with its division into three separate zones, would result in violations of the code if any additional construction was attempted. Sunoco's desire to change the operation of the gasoline station after purchasing the locus 'with a zoning law limitation on its use cannot be made a fulcrum to lift those limitations...In the instant case there was no 'substantial hardship'...even if the variance is not granted, Sunoco can continue to make reasonable use of the locus as a gasoline station." 357 Mass. 87, at 90. (emphasis added).

[15] *See* for example, Mitchell v. Board of Appeals of Revere, 27 Mass. App. Ct. 1119 (1989), where the court wrote, "...the hardship arises solely from the fact that the lot is too small to qualify as a buildable lot under the zoning ordinance or to achieve exemption under the grandfather clauses applicable to lots created before zoning. In these circumstances, § 10 gives the board of appeal no authority to grant a variance." 27 Mass. App. Ct. 1119, at 1120. *See also* Shafer v. Board of Appeals of Scituate, 24 Mass. App. Ct. 966, 967 (1987), "The 'shape' of a lot is not to be confused with its "size," *citing* McCabe v. Board of Appeals of Arlington, 10 Mass. App. Ct. 934 (1980).

[16] *See*, for example, G.L. c. 40A, § 6.

be satisfied (e.g. it is the only lot in the zoning district similarly situated; all other lots are developed or built to the maximum allowed by zoning).

The difficulty arises where the lack of sufficient area becomes a compelling argument for a variance simply because the owner may have no other options for use of the land. Boards are often confronted with the argument, as discussed above, that this type of situation is precisely why variances are provided for and that the failure to grant a variance will likely result in a regulatory taking. It is worth repeating however, that Massachusetts courts have repeatedly rejected the lack of sufficient area as grounds for the grant of a variance. In fact, the statute clearly omits from consideration a parcel's "size" when deliberating on grants of a variance.[17]

§ 5.07[2][a][iii]   Topography

A land parcel's topographical features—peaks and valleys—for example, can render a lot hopelessly constrained by zoning regulations governing height and setback requirements.

While there are few cases where a variance was granted due to topographic constraints, this is likely a result of the tendency to lump criteria—soils, shape and topography—more than the absence of situations where topographical problems exist. Moreover, while the statute allows the grant of a variance upon demonstration of a related hardship due to soils, shape *or* topography, most boards of appeals tend to see these three variables as fungible. Ironically, a topographic constraint is more readily demonstrated than is, for example, a limitation to the parcel's geology.

Cases that have been decided on topographical constraints follow the same pattern as those discussed previously. Simply avoiding added costs or reducing difficulties associated with development of property with steep slopes or difficult topography does not provide legal justification for a variance.[18]

---

[17] "Its reference to 'shape' lead us to believe that it confused the 'shape' of the lot with its 'size' which is a different attribute and a consideration which § 10 does not include." McCabe v. Zoning Board of Appeals of Arlington, 10 Mass. App. Ct. 934, 934 (1980). *See also* DiCicco v. Berwick, 27 Mass. App. Ct. 312 (1989), "Variances are not normally available to remedy deficiencies in frontage and area." 27 Mass. App. Ct. 312, at 314.

[18] In Martin v. Board of Appeals of Yarmouth, 20 Mass. App. Ct. 972 (1985), the Appeals Court overturned the grant of a variance for the construction of a garage that otherwise violated a front yard setback. One of the justifications for the grant of the variance, claimed the applicant, was that the variance allowed construction of the garage without removal of large oak trees. Similar to petitions requesting a variance to achieve a better view or reduce the amount of cuts and fills on a steep sloped lot, the court held that these factors do not rise justify a variance. That something may be desirable does not, however, rise to the dignity of a hardship." 20 Mass. App. Ct. 972, at 973. In *Mitchell v. Board of Appeals of Revere*, the Appeals Court held similarly. "The hardship in this case is not 'owing to the topography' of the land. The slope does not prevent the erection of a house. Rather the hardship arises solely from the fact that the lot is too small to qualify as a buildable lot

While there are cases where the Courts have upheld the grant of a variance due to topographical constraints,[19] it is important to note that these constraints have been demonstrated through photographs, plans and expert testimony and then linked to a resulting hardship. The importance of this linkage between land constraint and hardship is discussed below.

§ 5.07[2][b]   *Required Finding #2*: **Hardship**

As anyone who has ever attended a board of appeals hearing knows, where the applicant for a variance demonstrates financial, physical or other personal difficulties—so called hardships—the board of appeals and the public at large is generally sympathetic. Such sympathy very often translates into the grant of the requested variance. Unfortunately, at least from a legal perspective, such sympathies, however well intentioned, are rarely the appropriate basis for the grant of a variance.

While hardships come in many shapes and sizes, Massachusetts courts have been consistent in their insistence that the hardship comply with the strict requirements of the statute: "…a literal enforcement of the provisions of the ordinance or bylaw would involve substantial hardship, financial or otherwise."[20]

Because of the vagaries of the phrase "hardship" and the emotional testimony often presented before a board of appeals, it is important to review carefully Massachusetts case law on this particular Required Finding.

Massachusetts's courts have held that the "hardship" "…must relate to the premises for which the variance was sought."[21] In addition, the "hardship" must be linked, or be caused by, the land's unique or problematic soil conditions, shape or topography. In other words, based on the evidence presented in Required Finding #1, there is a demonstrated hardship. This otherwise straightforward requirement can be confusing and is worth repeating.

The statute requires that the board of appeals connect the unique circumstances of the lot (e.g. its soil conditions, shape or topography) to the hardship that these unique circumstances create. For example, a lot with soils that preclude construc-

---

under the zoning ordinance to achieve exemption under the grandfather clauses applicable to the lots created before zoning." 27 Mass. App. Ct. 1119, 1120 (1989). *See also* Kirkwood v. Board of Appeals of Rockport, 17 Mass. App. Ct. 423 (1984).

[19] *See*, for example, Crosby v. Board of Appeals of Weston, 3 Mass. App. Ct. 713 (1975), "…the terrain and contour is such that construction on the locus requires locating the dwelling in a position as not to comply with the sideline requirements…the hardship did not arise from 'changes and commitments made by the …defendant after purchasing the land with a zoning law limitation on its use…" 3 Mass. App. Ct. 713, at 713.

[20] G.L. c. 40A, § 10.

[21] Hurley v. Kolligian, 333 Mass. 170, 173 (1955).

tion within the zoning building envelope and requires extensive financial expenditures provides a link between poor soils and financial hardship. Similarly, a lot with severe slopes (e.g. greater than 25%) that prohibits the construction of a dwelling in compliance with height or setback requirements establishes the required linkage between topographical problems and hardship.

The Supreme Judicial Court stated: "Unless circumstances relating to the soil conditions of the land, the shape of the land or topography of the land cause the hardship, no variance may be granted lawfully."

Because of this required linkage between soils, shape or topography and the hardship caused therefrom, Massachusetts's courts have routinely rejected personal hardships as meeting the test. As noted previously, petitions for a variance based upon personal hardships are the most difficult for many boards of appeals to rule on, simply because the facts are often compelling from an emotional perspective and the basic fact that the petitioners are often neighbors, friends or at least acquaintances of the board membership. Nevertheless, from the Legislature and Court's perspective, personal hardships (emotional or physical) do not fit the definition of "hardship" under the statute. The "hardship" must be linked to the lot's peculiar soil conditions, shape or topography.

There is a fine line, of course, between statutorily acceptable hardships that result from a lot's uniqueness and statutorily unacceptable "personal" hardships resulting from a lot's particular problem. While this line is often difficult to determine, Massachusetts's courts have ruled on several occasions that where the hardship resulted from local regulatory controls or other government actions, the board of appeals could appropriately conclude that the required connection exists and a variance could be lawfully granted.

In one instance, the Appeals Court upheld the grant of a variance where, due to the unique circumstances of the lot's shape (a so-called "pork-chop" lot) and accompanying hardship relating to the use of the land without a variance, the proper linkage was established. The Court found that without a variance, the lot would be unbuildable.. The interesting aspect of this case however, is that in addition to the shape-hardship connection, the applicant argued that a variance was warranted due to the failing health of his father and the family's financial difficulties. The Court rejected as irrelevant these later claims of hardship, but upheld the grant of the variance on the establishment of the relationship to unique shape and resulting hardship to the land.[22]

A second situation arises where government action is the cause of the hardship.

---

[22] "...any other considerations unrelated to the underlying real estate are irrelevant to the board's inquiry into the question of substantial hardship...Since the hardship relates to the land itself, the finding of substantial hardship was not improper." Paulding v. Bruins, 18 Mass. App. Ct.

In *Adams v. Brolly*,[23] the Court upheld the grant of a variance to a petitioner who lacked requisite frontage due to an eminent domain order by the Metropolitan District Commission (MDC). The Court's support for the variance turned on the fact that the petitioner had neither caused the hardship nor could have anticipated that such hardship would arise.[24] In other words, but for the actions of the MDC, the variance would not have been required.

One oft-repeated situation is where the petitioner has created the hardship from which she now needs relief.[25] Examples include the landowner with 2 acres of land in a zoning district requiring one acre minimum lot sizes who divides her parcel such that one parcel contains 1.2 acres and the other 0.8 acres. While the division can be lawfully accomplished, the landowner is now left with one complying lot and one that does not comply. This self-created hardship has consistently met with hostile review by the courts.[26]

Finally, and consistent with this discussion, Massachusetts courts are not sym-

---

707, 711, (1984), *citing* Huntington v. Zoning Board of Appeals of Hadley, 12 Mass. App. Ct. 710, 715–716 (1981).

[23] 46 Mass. App. Ct. 1 (1998).

[24] "...Brolly's hardship was caused by an extrinsic act of a public authority not within his control... The hardship created by the MDC's acquisition of the McNeil property was not of Brolly's own making." 46 Mass. App. Ct. 1, at 8. The Court quoted a 1978 Connecticut case decided on similar grounds. "...surely there is a clear case of uncommon hardship beyond the control of a property owner when the state seeks to condemn a portion of his or her land and thereby render it nonconforming to a minimum lot area restriction." 46 Mass. App. Ct. 1, at 8, *citing* Smith v. Zoning Board of Appeals of Norwalk, 174 Conn. 323 (1978). *See also* Bateman v. Board of Appeals of Georgetown, 56 Mass. App. Ct. 236, 241 (2002), where the Court upheld the grant of a variance where the alleged hardship resulted from the eminent domain actions of the Commonwealth. "In upholding the grant of the variance, the judge found that the 'shape of the lot resulted wholly from the actions of the Commonwealth through its powers of eminent domain which deprived the locus of any frontage and was created by no fault of the current or previous owners.' "

[25] In Adams v. Brolly, 46 Mass. App. Ct. 1 (1998), a strongly worded dissent argued that even the MDC taking did not provide for the necessary connection between unique lot conditions and hardship. The dissent's position was that "the creation by conveyance of an unusually shaped, nonconforming parcel under then existing zoning regulations does not entitled one to a variance." 46 Mass. App. Ct. 1, at 7, *citing* Gordon v. Zoning Board of Appeals of Lee, 22 Mass. App. Ct. 343, 351 (1986).

[26] "...well-established principle in our cases prohibiting self-imposed hardships as a basis for obtaining a variance. Adams v. Brolly, 46 Mass. App. Ct. 1, 4 (1998), citing a long line of Massachusetts cases. Courts in other jurisdictions have taken a similar position in response to hardships created by the landowner. The Supreme Court of Connecticut put it well over 30 years ago. "We have repeatedly held that the hardship which justifies a board of appeals in granting a variance must be one which originates from the zoning ordinance. When the claimed hardship arises because of the actions of the applicant, the board is without power to grant a variance." 151 Conn. 681 (1964). A sometimes contrary conclusion can be found in New York where applicable municipal law states in part, "In making such determination [to grant a variance] the board shall also consider...(5) whether the alleged difficulty was self-created, which consideration shall be relevant

pathetic to the claim that but for the grant of a variance, the applicant will suffer "economic" or "competitive" hardships. Once again, the fatal flaw generally suffered by this argument is its inability to link the unique circumstances of the lot with the hardship (in this case, financial) that these unique characteristics create.[27]

§ 5.07[2][c]   *Required Finding #3*: **Public Good**

The third Required Finding is the board's conclusion that the variance can be granted "without substantial detriment to the public good and without nullifying or substantially derogating from the intent or purpose of such ordinance or by-law."[28]

This Required Finding, more so than the other two, allows the board of appeals some subjective leeway in their decision making process. Whereas Required Findings #1 and #2 are carefully proscribed and mandate that evidence exists linking a demonstrated hardship to a unique attribute of the property, Required Finding #3 allows the board to deliberate prospectively, rather than retroactively.

For example, in upholding the grant of a use variance, the Appeals Court allowed as justification for the variance the fact that the locus with the variance would be a substantial improvement over the locus constrained by existing zoning. "There is no question that the DiFlumeras' use of the site for a small general store will be aesthetically more attractive than what previously existed at the locus... and that their modest business will be of substantial benefit to the district as a whole.[29]

---

to the decision of the board of appeals, but shall not necessarily preclude the granting of the area variance." New York Town Law s. 267-b(3)(b).

[27] "The possible hardship suffered if the variance is denied does not relate to the locus, but rather to the preclusion of Sunoco's competitive and economic advantage...we stated that 'to hold...a personal hardship as one affecting the locus would treat... declining profit derived from a nonconforming use as in itself a hardship permitting a variance to enlarge and expand that use.' Obviously, the converse situation (granting of a variance to permit the owner of the locus to increase profits) does not qualify as a hardship permitting the granting of a variance." Wolfson v. Sun Oil Company, 357 Mass. 87, 90 (1970), *citing* Sullivan v. Board of Appeals of Belmont, 346 Mass. 81 (1963). *See also* The 39 Joy Street Condominium Association v. Board of Appeal of Boston, 426 Mass. 485 (1998), where the Supreme Judicial Court, in a summarized review of several important variance holdings noted, "We note additionally that financial hardship to the owner alone is not sufficient to establish 'substantial hardship' and thereby justify a variance." 426 Mass. 485, at 490, *citing* McNeely v. Board of Appeal of Boston, 358 Mass. 94 (1970). *See also* 157 Pleasant Street Realty Trust v. Civic Center Associates, L.P, 2002 Mass. Super. LEXIS 298, *9 (Mass. Super. 2002), "...the deprivation of a potential economic advantage to a landowner does not qualify as a "substantial hardship" for the purpose of granting a variance," *citing* Bruzzese v. Bd. of Appeals of Hingham, 343 Mass. 421, 424 (1962).

[28] G.L. c. 40A, § 10.

[29] Cavanaugh v. DiFlumera, 9 Mass. App. Ct. 396, 400 (1980). The Court quoted, in part, the lower court's findings. "In concluding that the variance would not cause any substantial detriment to the public good, the judge specifically found the following: that the improvements to which the

Counsel is urged to read the above-noted case with care, however, as there were several "exceptional circumstances" existing in this case unlikely to appear elsewhere.[30] Moreover, the findings of the Appeals Court, absent these "exceptional circumstances", seem to conflict with case law discussed throughout this section. Most notably was the Court's conclusion that the use variance would allow the petitioners an opportunity to use their property such that a bad situation would get better. As noted below, the proper mechanism for this is a zoning change, not a variance.[31]

Although decided ten years *earlier* than *Cavanaugh*, the Supreme Judicial Court set forth a more reliable holding regarding what Required Finding #3 means. In reviewing the grant of a variance that would have significantly improved vehicular parking and traffic conditions, but negatively impact abutting property values, the Court stated: "The test of the statute is general; the effect of a variance on the intent or purpose of the ordinance must be determined by appraising the effect on the entire neighborhood affected."[32]

The Court went further, and provided this instructive advice, still relevant to boards of appeals today.

"We do not think, however, that it can be concluded that the specific hurt here found to at least five residential properties is not a substantial derogation of purpose. The balancing of public advantage against the hurt to individuals that is inevitable with zoning is appropriately done in connection with the enactment or amendment of the ordinance or bylaws... It is of limited operation in determining whether a

---

DiFlumeras had already accomplished 'are much to be preferred over the derelict and rat-infested conditions existing when they acquired ownership; that their modest business enterprise...is...of substantial benefit to the district as a whole..." 9 Mass. App. Ct. 396, at 399.

[30] "We cannot ignore the important fact that there are exceptional circumstances present, arising form the defendants' long-standing good faith reliance on a series of local zoning decisions which allowed commercial uses on the property and which were retroactively declared invalid a circumstance which has been found in the past to justify relaxation of zoning restrictions [sic]." Cavanaugh v. DiFlumera, 9 Mass. App. Ct. 396, 401 (1980).

[31] For example, the Court noted, "...unless the use significantly detracts from the zoning plan for the district, the local discretionary grant of the variance (all the other statutory elements having been satisfied) must be upheld." 9 Mass. App. Ct. 396, at 400. The problem with this statement, of course, is the Court's deference to the Board of Appeals' judgment regarding consistency with zoning. The power to provide flexibility within a zoning ordinance or bylaw is found within G.L. c. 40A, § 9 (special permits), wherein a special permit granting authority can exercise judgment and flexibility with respect to uses and intensity. The Court's remark of "significantly detracts" is unfortunate as the purpose of a zoning ordinance, absent flexibility provided by special permit uses, is to ensure conformity with zoning and not allow an adjudicatory board opportunities to second guess or end-run the legislative process.

[32] Cary v. Board of Appeals of Worcester, 340 Mass. 748, 753 (1960).

proposed variance meets the rigid statutory conditions."[33]

The value of the remarks noted above cannot be overstated. The variance application, either for dimensional or use variation, accompanied by the claims that it will "improve the neighborhood" or "remedy an eyesore" does not, without more, meet the statutory requirements. The point of the Court's last two sentences above is that the proper forum for determining whether improvements to neighborhood will occur or eyesores will be fixed, lies with the City Council or Town Meeting. The board of appeals is not empowered by statue or case law to make land use decisions outside of the strict requirements of G.L. c. 40A, § 10.[34]

§ 5.07[3]   Use Variances

The required findings discussed above apply to both "area" and "use" variances.

An area variance can generally be labeled as an action by the board of appeals to vary or reduce the requirement of a zoning bylaw or ordinance relative to *dimensional requirements* of zoning. These include variations to setback requirements, frontage, area, width, height and lot coverage ratios prescribed by zoning.

A use variance, however, refers to an action by the board of appeals to allow a use *not otherwise allowed* by the zoning ordinance or bylaw. For example, a request to allow a commercial use on residentially zoned property where the zoning ordinance prohibited commercial activities. Similarly, a use variance would be required to allow a multi-family dwelling on a lot zoned residential, but limited to single family detached dwellings. (In some cases, a petition for a use variance may also include a petition for an area variance). Note that when a use variance is granted, the use for which the petition was made is allowed; however, the zoning designation of the land does not change. In other words, a use variance granted to allow a commercial use on residentially zoned land does not change the zoning designation of the parcel. A review of the city or town zoning maps following the grant of a use variance would still indicate that the parcel is zoned residential. Only Town Meeting, Town Council or City Council can change the zoning designation.[35]

The statute treats area and use variances very differently. Area variances may be granted provided the required findings discussed above are complied with, coupled with the procedural requirements discussed, below. Use variances may be only be granted where the municipality has accepted the enabling provisions of

---

[33] Cary v. Board of Appeals of Worcester, 340 Mass. 748, at 753.

[34] Note that Boards of Appeals can be special permit granting authorities under G.L. c. 40A, § 9.

[35] G.L. c. 40A, § 5.

G.L. c. 40A, § 10 and the board of appeals has complied with the required findings discussed above.[36]

To grant a use variance, therefore, the board of appeals must be authorized to do so by Town Meeting, Town Council or City Council and comply with the Required Findings criteria. It is estimated that one-third of the Commonwealth's cities and towns authorize their boards of appeals to grant use variances in compliance with G.L. c. 40A, § 10.

Use variances are considered to be "difficult to justify legally"[37] and with complete disregard to local comprehensive plans and planning efforts.[38]

Perhaps the most compelling argument in opposition to the grant of a use variance is the grant's likely conflict with a local comprehensive plan as discussed in Chapter 2.

A use variance, precisely because it calls for a use not allowed by zoning, represents a direct threat to the plan or study upon which municipal zoning was based.[39] For example, a city may have adopted a watershed overlay protection district designed to prohibit land uses deemed a threat to drinking water quality. The grant of a use variance that now allows the very use or uses the ordinance was designed to prevent contradicts prior city council actions.

This point raises a second problem with use variances. A city or town's legislative body adopts zoning in accordance with G.L. c. 40A, § 5.[40] The adoption of new zoning (or amendment of an existing bylaw or ordinance) can only be accomplished through compliance with several strict and unforgiving procedural requirements, including notice, advertisements, public hearings, reports and, finally, a two-thirds vote of the legislative body. Moreover, in towns, zoning bylaws are reviewed, for both substantive content and procedural compliance by the Attorney General's office.[41] As a result, the zoning adoption and amendment process is considered both thorough and procedurally fair.

---

[36] "Except where the local ordinances or bylaws shall expressly permit variances for use, no variance may authorize a use or activity not otherwise permitted in the district in which the land or structure is located…" G.L. c. 40A, § 10.

[37] DCA Report at 65.

[38] *See*, for example, early commentaries on Boards of Appeals and the use variance, including: Robert Anderson, *The Boards of Zoning Appeals—Villain or Victim?*, Syracuse Law Review 13 (Spring, 1962), R.M. Shapiro, *The Zoning Variance Power—Constructive in Theory, Destructive in Practice*, Maryland Law Review 29 (1969), and Jesse Dukeminier and Clyde Stapleton, *The Zoning Board of Adjustment: A Case Study in Misrule*, Kentucky Law Journal 50 (1962).

[39] See, for example, Cavanaugh v. DiFlumera, 9 Mass. App. Ct. 396, 400 (1980), "…some derogation from the bylaw's purpose is anticipated by every variance."

[40] These include city councils in cities, and town councils and town meetings in towns.

[41] *See* G.L. c. 40A, § 5.

Contrast the adoption of a zoning ordinance with the grant of a use variance, even though, as noted above, the use variance does not technically change the zoning designation. (For all practical purposes, the zoning has been changed by virtue of the use variance).

A use variance is granted by a three or five member board of appeals following the procedural requirements specified in G.L. c. 40A, § 10 and discussed more fully below. Neither legislative action (e.g. Town Meeting or City Council) nor Attorney General review is required. Stated simply, the complexity and intentionally deliberative process established to alter municipal zoning is absent in the variance process, and noticeable when the variance granted is of the "use" variety.

§ 5.07[4]   Conditional Variances

Where a board of appeals concludes that all the Required Findings discussed above have been met, and that a variance should be granted, the board should next deliberate as to what conditions, if any, should be attached to the variance approval.

The board of appeals is granted clear authority to grant variances subject to conditions and limitations. These include: (1) conditions and limitations on the use of the property (e.g. the property's use can be limited to a specified square footage or a building limited to a certain height or operations limited to daylight hours); (2) conditions that "extract" a public benefit necessitated by the grant of the variance (e.g. roadway improvements, stormwater drainage, exterior lighting) and (3) limitations on the time period(s) within which the variance will be valid (e.g. the variance shall expire in three years from the date of issuance or the variance shall be exercisable only during the months of June, July and August).

A condition of approval *may not* include the continuation of the applicant's ownership of the property (e.g., that the variance will be void if the applicant conveys the property).[42]

Where a variance is to be granted, it is strongly recommended that boards of appeals impose relevant and appropriate conditions. Boards are urged to be mindful of the fact that not only is there is no legal right to a variance but that a grant of a variance, in some fashion, likely harms the integrity of the municipality's zoning ordinance or bylaw. While the imposition of a condition does not negate the harm

---

[42] "The permit granting authority may impose conditions, safeguards and limitations both of time and of use, including the continued existence of any particular structures but excluding any condition, safeguards or limitation based upon the continued ownership of the land or structures to which the variance pertains by the applicant, petitioner or any owner." G.L. c. 40A, § 10. This prohibition makes sense. As discussed throughout this Chapter, the hardship finding, assuming one is found, must relate to the land or structure, not solely the applicant. Simply put, if the hardship exists for one party, it logically will exist for a subsequent purchaser.

caused to zoning regulations, it can often soften the impact, particularly where the conditions are tailored carefully.

§ 5.07[5]   Lapsed Variances

Variances must be used—put into practice—within one year of the date they are granted or else they lapse by operation of statute.[43] The statute provides however, that the board of appeals may, upon written petition from the variance recipient, extend the variance grant for up to six additional months. Requests for an extension must be filed with the board of appeals prior to the lapse of the original grant of the variance (e.g. before the one year period expires).[44] The board of appeals has 30 days from the date requested to grant such an extension or the request is deemed denied. If the variance extension is denied or the board of appeals fails to act, the variance is deemed to have lapsed.

A lapsed variance cannot be re-instated. A new variance must be applied for, all procedural requirements complied with and the variance ultimately approved, for a second time, by the board of appeals.[45]

It is important to note that an application for a new variance subsequent to a lapsed variance must comply, in all respects, with the procedural and substantive requirements for a grant of a variance. In essence, no "credit" is allowed, nor should be given, to an applicant who applies for a variance after a previously issued variance has lapsed. The entire process must begin anew and while the petitioner may choose to emphasize the fact that a previous board, on a previous occasion

---

[43] "If the rights authorized by a variance are not exercised within one year of the date of grant of such variance such rights shall lapse..." G.L. c. 40A, § 10.

[44] "...the permit granting authority in its discretion and upon written application by the grantee of such rights may extend the time for exercise of such rights for a period not to exceed six months; and provided further, that the application for such extension is filed with such permit granting authority prior to the expiration of such one year period." G.L. c. 40A, § 10.

[45] "...variance rights which are not seasonably exercised will automatically become void, that the holder of a lapsed variance who seeks to reestablish his rights must initiate a new proceeding under s10; that he must therefore make a new showing of the requirements set out in the first paragraph of that statute; and that it is for the board, as before, to decide the matter in the exercise of its discretion." Hunters Brook Realty Corporation v. Zoning Board of Appeals of Bourne, 14 Mass. App. Ct. 76, 81 (1982). *See also* Callahan & Sons, Inc. v. Board of Appeals of Lenox, 30 Mass. App. Ct. 36 (1991), where the Appeals Court required the recipient of a variance limited to a five-year period to offer the same levels of proof required by the statute for a renewal of the variance as he was required to demonstrate for the original grant. "Accordingly, the denial of the plaintiff's application for a permanent variance must be reviewed under established principles which dictate that the denial is in excess of the defendant's authority only if it is unreasonable, whimsical, capricious or arbitrary or based solely on legally untenable grounds." 30 Mass. App. Ct. 36, at 40, *citing* Pendergast v. Board of Appeals of Barnstable, 331 Mass. 555 (1954) and DiGiovanni v. Board of Appeals of Rockport, 19 Mass. App. Ct. 339 (1985).

saw fit to grant a variance, this emphasis has no legal significance without adequate findings by the board of appeals.[46]

The statute and case law are silent as to whether deliberations on an extension request require a public hearing as discussed below. Nor is there guidance on whether the Board of appeals could grant an extension contemporaneously with the original grant of the variance, such that the variance could be exercised for a period of up to 18 months. Prudence would suggest however, that a Board of appeals act conservatively with respect to both issues.

It is recommended that all requests for extensions that otherwise comply with the statute be subject to the same notice, hearing and recordation requirements applicable to the original grant of a variance. Similarly, it is recommended that an extension for exercise of a variance not be granted at the same time the original variance is approved, but rather that any requests for an extension be made subsequent to the original grant. This position argues that if the Legislature wanted the original exercise period for variances to be up to 18 months, it would have so specified.

It is important to note that prior to the re-write of the Zoning Act in 1975, the statute did not contain a lapse provision for variances. At issue in many communities is whether these "old" variances are still valid, even if not exercised and despite the revisions to variance law in Massachusetts.

The Appeals Court has hinted that forcing an "old", un-exercised variance into a lapsed status is too harsh and not consistent with the intent of the old or even new provisions of the statute.[47] On the other hand, the Land Court ruled in 1997 that the lapse provisions of the new statute could be applied retroactively to a

---

[46] *See*, for example, Lopes v. Board of Appeals of Fairhaven, 27 Mass. App. Ct. 754 (1989), where the Appeals Court held that a new application for a lapsed variance (referred to by the Court as a "replacement variance") required the applicant to "prove anew the existence of each of the statutory conditions for a variance...Unassisted by the earlier findings, the variance cannot stand...Whatever the grantor's situation might have been, the Sullivans, having purchased less frontage than that called for by the zoning bylaw and less than their grantor could have conveyed, can not now be entitled to a variance. 27 Mass. App. Ct. 754, at 756, 757.

[47] *See* Hogan v. Hayes, 19 Mass. App. Ct. 399 (1985). "The notion that variances more than one year old, and remaining unexercised by the effective date of the new statute, are destroyed wholesale by a retroactive application of s.10, would appear quite drastic, and hardly matches the text of that provision." 19 Mass. App. Ct. 399, at 403. Note however, the Appeals Court's important caveat. "In holding that the variance at bar did not lapse but on the contrary has been sufficiently availed of, we do not mean to reflect in any way upon a possibility that an old variance, long unexercised, may lose its force by reason of radically changed conditions at the locus, including changes brought about by revisions of a zoning ordinance or bylaw." 19 Mass. App. Ct. 399, at 405. *See also* Asack v. Board of Appeals of Westwood, 47 Mass. App. Ct. 733, 734 (1999).

variance that had not been exercised where the variance was not necessary to facilitate its conveyance.[48]

Given the two decisions noted above, it is clear that the law governing "old" lapsed variances remains unsettled. On one hand, the Appeals Court signaled its reluctance to apply retroactively the current lapse provisions to old variances. On the other, the Land Court held, at least in one case, that the lapse provisions could apply to a variance that was neither exercised, nor necessary to fulfill the land-owner's plans.

§ 5.07[6]   Procedural Issues and Grants of a Variance

§ 5.07[6][a]   Filing Requirements

The statute provides no direction to either applicant for a variance or the board of appeals as to what documents, maps, surveys or other materials must be submitted as part of an application for a variance.

As no case law exists providing guidance on how much the Board can require, or in what form such materials must be in, the best advice in this regard is application of common sense.[49] While the Board may appropriately require (and in fact likely must require) the submission of evidence that the underlying soils of a parcel are bedrock or that depth to groundwater is only three feet, cities and towns should take care that their submission requirements are relevant and would not be perceived by a reviewing court as excessive.

On the other hand, many communities fail to require enough information to review appropriately a variance application. At a minimum, the applicant should be required to complete a form identifying their relationship to the land, the location of the land, assessor's reference for the land, size of the land, the relevant zoning district in which the land lies, the current and proposed use of the land and, most important, the section(s) of the zoning ordinance or bylaw from which relief is being requested.

Many communities require the submission of a site plan or other visual depiction of the property relative to its surroundings and/or the unique nature of the site. While this requirement is appropriate, it is recommended as a minimum submission. Notwithstanding the fact that an accompanying claim to many variances is "financial hardship", municipalities should not allow variance applications to be

---

[48] Alroy v. World Realty and Development Co., Massachusetts Land Court, Misc. Case No. 230584 (December 22, 1997).

[49] G.L. c. 40A, § 12 mandates that Boards of Appeals adopt rules for the conducting of business, but the statute is not specific. "The board of appeals shall adopt rules, not inconsistent with the provisions of the zoning ordinance or bylaw for the conduct of its business and for purposes of this chapter and shall file a copy of said rules with the city or town clerk."

reviewed in the absence of detailed, professionally drawn and stamped plans,[50] profiles or other survey and/or design documents.

Some communities require the applicant to articulate how the petition complies with the statutory requirements for a variance. This practice is discouraged, as the required findings must be made independently by the Board. The applicant's (or counsel's) opinion as to why the grant of a variance will comply with the statute is irrelevant.

§ 5.07[7]   Public Notice Requirements

Not surprisingly, a public hearing must precede the grant of variance. The public hearing must be held subsequent to the strict and unyielding notice requirements of Section 11 of the Zoning Act.

Discussion of the purpose of the public notice requirements and public hearing requirements is unnecessary given the audience for this Chapter. The intent is to provide an opportunity for the public to attend and speak relative to the request for a variance. What is important however, is underscoring the complete intolerance of the Courts to the failure of a board of appeals to follow exactly the requirements of Section 11.[51]

The fact is, providing proper notice of a required public hearing is easy. So easy that there is no good excuse for failing to follow these straightforward, explicit steps:

First, the Board must ensure that the notice includes each of the statutory requirements. These are: (1) the name of the petitioner; (2) a description of the area or premises; (3) street address or other means of identifying the location; (4) the date, time and place of the public hearing; (5) the subject matter of the hearing; and (6) the nature of the relief requested.[52] Debate as to what con-

---

[50] For example, a Professional Land Surveyor, Landscape Architect, Architect or Professional Engineer licensed in the Commonwealth.

[51] "A defect in the general notice to the public cannot be overcome by the appearance of some citizens and the absence of objection to the notice. All citizens are entitled to the statutory notice and the opportunity to be heard." Gallagher v. Board of Appeals of Falmouth, 351 Mass. 410, 414 (1966).

[52] A suggested notice is as follows: "On January 3, 2000, the Essex Board of Appeals shall hold a public hearing to discuss the request of John Jones for a variance from Section 200.2 of the Essex Zoning Bylaw as it affects his property on 200 Main Street, Essex, Massachusetts. Section 200.2 establishes front, side and rear yard setbacks within the Town of Essex. Said parcel is identified on the Essex Assessor's Maps as Sheet 20, Section 2, Parcel 15-002 and contains approximately 28,500 square feet of area and 75 feet of frontage on Main Street. Mr. Jones seeks relief from the application of Section 200.2 as it relates to his construction of a two-family dwelling on the above-noted property. The public hearing will be held at 8:00 PM in Hearing Room on the second floor of Town Hall, 50 Main Street, Essex, Massachusetts. Interested parties are invited to attend the hearing and

stitutes "sufficient" notice is beyond the scope of this Chapter. Clearly, a board of appeals should default to the most conservative notice possible—one that provides more, as opposed to less—information. It is understood that a reviewing court will not invalidate a Board's decision on a variance petition if the public hearing notice is too long, rather than too short.

Second, the Board must ensure that the notice be advertised in "a newspaper of general circulation in the city or town once in each of two successive weeks, the first publication to be not less than fourteen days before the day of the hearing... ."[53]

This requirement has caused problems for many Boards, so a quick dissection is in order.

What constitutes a newspaper "of general circulation" was decided almost 40 years ago when Plymouth residents made a challenge to actions by the Plymouth Board of Appeals for a hearing advertised in the Brockton Enterprise. The plaintiffs claimed that the Enterprise was not a Plymouth paper of general circulation.[54] The Court's response: "The statute does not require publication in a newspaper published in the town."[55]

This decision is important for the numerous communities that rely on newspapers published outside of the city or town (typically towns). As long as the newspaper is of "general circulation in the city or town", advertisement within this newspaper will meet the statutory requirements for advertising.

On the opposite side of this problem are communities that have multiple newspapers both printed and circulated within the city or town. Again, a strict read of the statute is warranted. The statue only requires publication in "a" newspaper of general circulation, not "the" newspapers.

The notice must be published "once in each of two successive weeks, the first publication to be not less than fourteen days before the day of the hearing... ."[56] "Two successive weeks" should be interpreted as meaning two successive calendar weeks, and not that there must be seven days between advertisements.[57] The "not

---

be heard on matters relevant to Mr. Jones' request for a variance. Copies of Mr. Jones's variance application are on file with the Board of Appeals and may be reviewed in Town Hall during normal business hours."

[53] G.L. c. 40A, § 11.

[54] Smith v. Board of Appeals of Plymouth, 340 Mass. 230 (1960).

[55] Smith v. Board of Appeals of Plymouth, 340 Mass. 230, 232 (1960).

[56] G.L. c. 40A, § 11.

[57] This was the holding in Crall v. City of Leominster, 362 Mass. 95 (1972). However, a more conservative approach would be to treat the statute literally and place the first advertisement on, for

less than fourteen days before the hearing" requirement should be interpreted literally. Conservative advice is to hold the hearing no earlier than the fifteenth day following the first advertisement. For example, if the public hearing is to be held on June 22, the first advertisement should appear before June 8.[58] The statute does not prohibit advertising more than fourteen days in advance of the hearing, only less than fourteen days in advance.

Third, the Board must ensure that the notice is posted "in a conspicuous place in the city or town hall for a period of not less than fourteen days before the hearing."[59] Most city and town halls have public notice posting boards, generally near or in front of the city or town clerk's office. It is recommended that the board of appeals request the city or town clerk post the notice, indicating the clerk's receipt of the notice with an official "Received" date stamp.

Fourth, the board must ensure that the notice is mailed to all parties entitled to receive the notice.

Parties entitled to receive notice are "parties in interest." These individuals are clearly identified in the statute. They are: (1) the petitioner, (2) abutters, (3) owners of land directly opposite on any public or private street or way, and (4) abutters to the abutters within three hundred feet of the property line of the petitioner.

As noted below, *it is the job of the assessor's office* to ascertain the correct parties in interest relative to notice requirements for a variance hearing. The Board does not (and should not) get involved in this process beyond a timely submission of the variance application to the assessor's with a request for a timely development of the list of those entitled to notice.

At issue in many communities is whether the Board can require the applicant, or even consent to the applicant's offer, to mail the required notice. The statute is far from clear on this point, although case law is: the Board cannot delegate the mailing of notice required by the Zoning Act, Section 11.[60] The Board must complete the mailing of the notice.

---

example, Tuesday, June 15 and the second advertisement on Tuesday, June 22.

[58] There are few cases that help clarify this matter. As a result, a conservative recommendation is to ensure that the first advertisement is placed at least fifteen days prior to the hearing. If the hearing date is the fourteenth day following the first advertisement, an argument could be made that the statute's requirement of "not less than fourteen days before the day of the hearing" has not been met. Thus if the hearing is to be held on the 16th, the first advertisement should appear no later than the 1st of the month.

[59] G.L. c. 40A, § 11.

[60] In a Supreme Judicial Court decision from 1930, the Court, ruling on compliance with a predecessor section regarding variances to the current Zoning Act, stated: "The petition is to be addressed to the board. Plainly the hearing must be held and the decision be rendered by the board. It is equally plain that the notice of the hearing which 'shall be mailed to the petitioner' must be mailed to the petitioner by the board of appeals…It would be vain to require that the petitioner mail

While practice varies among cities and towns, it is strongly recommended that the notice be mailed certified, return receipt requested. This practice has the obvious advantage of protecting both applicant and the Board against claims that notices were not received. In addition, while the notice must be mailed by the Board, the statute does not preclude the Board (read: Town or City) from recouping the costs of the certified mailing.

Equally problematic, although no case law exists to help clarify the issue, is whether the Board can allow the applicant (or her agent) to prepare the list for the party to whom the notice shall be mailed (the so-called "abutter's list"). It is common practice for the applicant to prepare the abutter's list and request its certification by the assessor. This practice likely violates the statute however, in light of the Court's holdings regarding mailing of the notice.[61] It is recommended therefore, that the board of appeals recruit the assessor to prepare and certify the abutter list. These actions should be completed without the applicant's assistance or involvement.

Another commonly faced problem is whether the notice to the parties in interest occurred in sufficient time for the recipient to have fair warning of the variance petition and time and date of the hearing. This problem, similar to difficulties encountered by some communities regarding timely advertisement of the hearing, has not found sympathy with the Courts. While case law holds that "what constitutes reasonable notice depends upon the facts and circumstances of each case,"[62] the truth is that no board of appeals should ever find itself on the losing end of a "notice case."

---

notice to himself..." Kane v. Board of Appeals of Medford, 273 Mass. 97, 102 (1930). In a more recent case, this one involving the grant of a special permit, the Supreme Judicial Court, *citing Kane, supra,* held that notice must be mailed by the board of appeals. "The notice to affected property owners and to the planning board must be mailed by the board of appeals. The board cannot delegate that duty to the petitioner or his attorney." Planning Board of Peabody v. Board of Appeals of Peabody, 358 Mass. 81, 83 (1970).

[61] The statute is clear: "The assessors maintaining any applicable tax list shall certify to the permit granting authority...the names and addressees of parties in interest... G.L. c. 40A, § 11. (emphasis added).

[62] Kasper v. Board of Appeals of Watertown, 3 Mass. App. Ct. 251, 257 (1975), *quoting* Rousseau v. Building Inspector of Framingham, 349 Mass. 31, 37 (1965). In *Kasper,* the plaintiffs complained that they received notice of a public hearing regarding a special permit only twelve days prior, not sufficient time to prepare their arguments in opposition. The Appeals Court found otherwise. "There was nothing in the evidence to suggest that the plaintiff was prejudiced in any way by the board's failure to send him written notice, and it is implicit in the judge's confirmation of the board's decision that no such prejudice was present." 3 Mass. App. Ct. 251, at 257–258. The plaintiff's case was clearly weakened by the fact that he and his son attended the hearing, were recorded in opposition to the special permit and presented photographs supporting their argument. The Court concluded that these facts were equivalent to a waiver of their objection to failure of proper notice. 3 Mass. App. Ct. 251, at 258.

However, note that cures exist to a notice mistake. First, the statue allows boards to obtain waivers from parties to whom a notice should have been sent[63] Second, upon discovering a notice problem, the board can generally fix the error by moving quickly to send out a new round of notices, even if the notices must be delivered by overnight courier. Third, note that claims of notice defects will usually be rendered moot if the objecting party or her representative attends the public hearing and presents materials in opposition.[64]

When the Board receives the variance application, its clerk or staff should immediately (e.g. within the next three to five days) submit a copy to the assessor's office, together with a request for the abutter's list. At the same time, the Board's clerk or staff should prepare the public hearing notice. Once the assessor's forward the certified list, the clerk or staff should mail out the public hearing notice. There is nothing wrong or inappropriate with mailing the notice prior to the newspaper advertisement. The important issue is to have all the notice requirements completed more or less at the same time, and always earlier than required by statute.

§ 5.07[8]   Public Hearing and Voting Requirements

The purpose of the public hearing is to allow for an open discussion of the variance application. The words "public" and "hearing" have important meanings. By "public," the Board must hold the hearing in a room accessible to the public and large enough to accommodate all those interested in attending. Note that the Board, not the applicant, has an affirmative duty to ensure that those wishing to attend the hearing, at the time and place advertised, are accommodated.

By "hearing," the statute requires that the Board conduct a formal discussion, debate and review of all the relevant facts pertaining to the variance petition. While Boards are free to conduct the hearing as they choose (e.g. the petitioner presents her case, followed by questions from the Board, followed by questions from the audience), it is important to emphasize that the Board must afford the public an

---

[63] G.L. c. 40A, § 11 provides, "the permit granting authority…may accept a waiver of notice from, or an affidavit of actual notice to any party in interest or, in his stead, any successor owner of record who may not have received a notice by mail… ." The above-noted portion of Section 11 continues, "…and may order special notice to any such person, giving not less than five nor more than ten additional days to reply." G.L. c. 40A, § 11.

[64] For example, in *Kasper*, discussed *supra*, the Court found that the plaintiff's attendance and presentation at the public hearing constituted a waiver of their right to object to a defect in notice. In *Gamache*, discussed below for other reasons, the Court found that the attendance and presentation at the public hearing by the plaintiff's attorney provided proof that the sufficiency of notice of the public hearing was not inadequate. "It is enough to say that they learned of the hearing because of a published newspaper notice; one of them appeared at the hearing with counsel; and counsel at the hearing represented that he managed to file an action with Superior Court protesting the rehearing before it began. There was a defect in notice, but it caused no prejudice… The plaintiffs found time to prepare for the hearing." Gamache v. Town of Acushent, 14 Mass. App. Ct. 215, 218 (1982).

opportunity to ask questions of the applicant and the Board and the applicant must be afforded an opportunity to make her case. To that end, even though many Boards have extremely full agendas on their typical weeknight-hearing schedule, adequate time must be afforded all hearings on the request for a variance.

The Board, as always, cannot conduct official business without a quorum. However, because the grant of a variance requires an affirmative vote of all 3 members of a 3 member Board or 4 out of 5 members of a 5 member Board, the required quorum as far as a variance hearing goes is 3 members of a 3 member Board and 4 members of a 5 members Board.

A common problem arises when a member of Board is not able to attend the advertised public hearing for a variance. This is clearly a problem with a three member Board (as a necessary quorum would not be present) unless the Board has alternate members who can replace the absent member. The relevant question is this: can the absentee member, upon joining the Board during its next meeting, cast his or her vote? Alternatively, as was the case in Acushnet, can the Board re-orient itself into a smaller Board if one or two members are absent or should resign? (This may be a critical vote given the super majority requirement of a five member Board and the unanimous requirement of a three member Board). Case law is clear: No. The member(s) that missed the hearing are ineligible to vote on the variance.[65]

As discussed below, the board of appeals has 100 days, from the day the application is filed with the city or town clerk, unless an extension has been granted, to render its decision. Prior to reaching a decision, of course, the Board must hold a public hearing and that hearing must be preceded by at least 14 days to comply with the notice requirements. As a result, the typical Board of Appeals, especially those that only meet once a month, is under extreme time pressure to rule on variance applications.[66]

Regardless of this fact, however, it is strongly urged that except for extremely

---

[65] In Gamache v. Town of Acushnet, 14 Mass. App. Ct. 215 (1982), the five member Board of Appeals had only four members in attendance at the public hearing for the plaintiff's variance petition. Soon thereafter, one of the four members who attended the hearing resigned, leaving only three members of the Board who were present at the public hearing. The Board believed they could not act on the matter and required a new hearing before at least four members of the Board. On appeal, the Court found, "It continued to be a board of five members and a decision by the board required the concurring vote at least four members. Accordingly, the board act properly in reserving action until at least four members could rehear the case." 14 Mass. App. Ct. 215, at 219.

[66] For example, the greatest amount of time available to the Board to reach a decision after the public hearing, unless an extension is requested and granted, is 85 days (100 – 15). More commonly however, the public hearing is not held until at least 30 days after the application has been filed, leaving a Board that meets infrequently only one or two meetings after the hearing to discuss the issues involved. This fact coupled with the likelihood that the Board has several other pending matters makes the post-public hearing analysis by the Board limited and often diluted.

obvious cases, the Board not render its decision on the variance the same night of the pubic hearing. This is especially true where the Board believes that an applicant is entitled to the variance being requested. The fact is, as noted throughout this Chapter, the grant of a variance requires specific, independent and relatively detailed findings. It seems unlikely that a Board, even a Board with professional staff, could render a decision that comports with the statutory rigor on the same evening of the applicant's presentation. While many Boards feel pressure to free up busy and burdened agendas, neither the statute nor the Courts allow the grant of a variance without compliance with the Required Findings noted above. Arriving at these Findings takes time.

§ 5.07[9]   Decisions of the Board of Appeals

The Board must render a decision regarding the variance petition within 100 days of the application's filing with the city or town clerk.[67] As discussed below, the Board must file its decision with the city or town within fourteen days of making—rendering—it.[68] It is important to note that both of these requirements must be met, it is not sufficient that the Board reaches a decision but fails to file.

It is clear that the Board's decision must be reduced to writing: a written decision that can be filed with the City or Town Clerk.[69]

As noted above, this requirement argues that a Board not render a final decision on a variance application on the same day (evening) as the public hearing discussed

---

[67] "The decision of the board shall be made within one hundred days after the date of the filing of an appeal, application or petition..." G.L. c. 40A, § 15.

[68] "...copies of all of which shall be filed within fourteen days in the office of the city or town clerk and shall be a public record..." G.L. c. 40A, § 15.

[69] In an interesting twist to the procedural filing requirements for special permits, and likely variances, the Supreme Judicial Court ruled in 1999 that the filing requirements to constitute "final action" do not include the requirement that the Board file their reasons for denying a special permit. The Court held that the mere filing of its decision to deny, as opposed to the denial language itself, was all that is required by G.L. c. 40A, § 9. In a strongly worded dissent, however, three Justices argued that the failure to require the decision and the grounds for the decision invites abuse. "The cure proposed by the court is no cure at all and, in fact, invites abuse. The court states that the proper procedure for an applicant to follow is to request a remand to the SPGA so that the SPGA may file the statutorily required statement of reasons. No time limitation applies, and so the result is that the applicant may have to wait a further many months before having the statement of reasons the Legislature wanted the applicant to have." Board of Aldermen of Newton v. Maniace, 429 Mass. 726, 733 (1999). Although the majority opinion represents the law, it still follows that the full decision of the Board be filed with the city or town clerk. *See also* Cardwell v. Board of Appeals of Woburn, 61 Mass. App. Ct. 118, 122 (2004), where the Court held that while the board of appeals must act "timely" in its review of a comprehensive permit application, the board's failure to file a written decision, provided a decision was reached during a public meeting, should not impose the "heavy penalty of a constructive grant," *citing* Alderman of Newton v. Maniace, 429 Mass. 726, 730 (1999).

above. Rather, it is recommended that a, or some, Board member(s) prepare a draft decision subsequent to the public hearing, but within the 100-day time frame for rendering a decision, reflective of the Board's opinion in the matter. In this way, the Board can deliberate the draft decision in public, make changes to the draft, and render a final decision that can then be recorded.

§ 5.07[10]   Decision Filing and Notification Requirements

The decision rendered by the board of appeals must be filed with the city or town clerk within fourteen days of the decision and within 100 days following submission of the application for a variance. In addition, the board of appeals is required to forward a copy of the decision "and all plans referred to in the decision" with the planning board.[70]

The purpose and importance of recording the decision with the city or town clerk needs to be underscored. Unless and until the decision is recorded with the clerk's office, it is as if a decision on the application was never reached.[71] As official custodian of decisions made by the Board of Appeals, the clerk's office serves as a reliable and official keeper of municipal zoning decisions. As such, it is the clerk's receipt of a rendered decision that commences the statutory period for appealing the grant of a variance.[72]

------

[70] G.L. c. 40A, § 11. This interesting requirement, one that seems to elevate the planning board to what other states suggest are true "planning" agencies, is believed to be frequently overlooked by many Boards of Appeals.

[71] Although case law states that failure to file the variance decision within the fourteen-day period will not result in constructive approval, Boards are nevertheless urged to file their rendered decision within this two-week period. As noted in selected quotations from the Supreme Judicial Court's holding on this matter, a future Court could decide very differently. "…no remedy is specified for failure to file a decision 'within fourteen days'. The omission is significant. Even if the Legislature did intend to require that a decision be filed within fourteen days after it is made, we conclude that it did not intend to remedy the type of violation committed by the board in the case before us. We note that this result is consistent with our interpretation of similar statutes where no remedy is specified. 'As to a statute imperative in phrase, it has often been held that where it relates only to the time of performance of a duty by a public officer and does not go to the essence of the thing to be done, it is only a regulation for the orderly and convenient conduct of public business and not a condition precedent to the validity of the act done." Zuckerman v. Zoning Board of Appeals of Greenfield, 394 Mass. 663, 666–667 (1985).

There are other reasons to ensure the decision is filed soon after its rendering, but certainly within fourteen days of its rendering and absolutely within 100 days of the variance filing. First, and discussed below, delays in filing a decision denying an application for a variance likely places the applicant in difficult position in terms of other options. In other words, until the rendered decision is reduced to a written decision, the applicant only knows her application was denied, but not necessarily why. Second, delays in filing an approved variance puts potentially aggrieved abutters in a similar position. Unless and until the variance is filed, they cannot analyze their options regarding an appeal or other remedies.

[72] "Under a strict reading of § 17, a person aggrieved by a denial by the board of appeals of

The Board is also required to send by mail a "notice of the decision" to (1) the applicant,[73] (2) the parties in interest as described above and to (3) "every person present at the hearing who requested that notice be sent."[74]

Because an approved variance must be recorded before it becomes effective,[75] the Zoning Act requires that only applicants who have obtained variance approval are entitled to the actual Board of appeals decision.[76] This requirement has led many Boards to send only an abbreviated notice of their decision to the three groups listed above. While this complies with the statute, recommended practice is to send a copy of the full decision, not just "notice", to all parties noted above. Moreover, it is recommended that all correspondence with the applicant regarding the final variance decision be completed via certified, return receipt mail.

§ 5.07[11]   Decision Recording Requirements

As noted above, the approved variance must be recorded at the registry of deeds for the county in which the land is located.[77] It is the responsibility of the Board of appeals to prepare a written decision that can be recorded by the registry. It is the responsibility of the city or town clerk to comply with the statute's certification requirements such that the registry can accept the Board's decision.

§ 5.07[12]   Use of Variances While Awaiting Appeals

A frequently occurring question with regard to grants of a variance (as well as

---

his petition could be prevented from filing an appeal if the board never filed its decision. Conversely, if the board granted a petition but failed to file its decision, any person aggrieved, such as an abutter, would have 'what may be an unlimited period of time...to cloud the rights of a landowner to use his land,' as the person aggrieved would have twenty days in which to file his appeal after the board finally filed its decision." Capone v. Zoning Board of Appeals of Fitchburg, 389 Mass. 617, 623 (1983), *citing* Noe v. Board of Appeals of Hingham, 13 Mass. App. Ct. 103, 111 (1982).

[73] G.L. c. 40A, § 15 states, "petitioner, applicant or appellant."

[74] G.L. c. 40A, § 15.

[75] "No variance...or any extension, modification or renewal thereof shall take effect until a copy of the decision bearing the certification of the city or town clerk that twenty days have elapsed after the decision has been filed in the office of the city or town clerk and no appeal has been filed...is recorded in the registry of deeds...." G.L. c. 40A, § 11.

[76] G.L. c. 40A, § 11.

[77] The decision must have affixed to it a certification by the city or town clerk that "twenty days have elapsed after the decision has been filed in the office of the city or town clerk and no appeal has been filed or that if such appeal has been filed, that it has been dismissed or denied, and if it is a variance...which has been approved by reason of the failure of the permit granting authority...to act thereon within the time prescribed, a copy of the...petition for the variance accompanied by the certification of the city or town clerk stating the fact that the permit granting authority...failed to act within the time prescribed and no appeal has been filed and that the grant of the ...petition resulting from such failure to act has become final or that if an appeal has been filed, that it has been dismissed or denied, is recorded in the registry of deeds... ." G.L. c. 40A, § 11.

special permits) is whether the applicant to whom a variance is granted, but granted with conditions, can accept portions of the variance while appealing others. For example, a variance is granted providing relief from a 35-foot front yard setback requirement but is conditioned on the requirement that the structure be limited to 25 feet in height. The applicant obtained the variance she wanted, but a new and arguably unforeseeable condition has been added. The question is whether she can accept the portion of the variance she needs and appeal the added condition.

The answer is yes; the applicant can challenge the condition (but as noted below, not use the variance) without running the risk of losing the entire variance. However, note that the applicant cannot appeal the condition while exercising the relief granted by the variance. In the above-noted example, if the applicant chose to appeal the condition regarding building height as arbitrary and irrelevant to the variance petition, she would be required to wait for resolution of that appeal prior to using the front yard setback variance.[78]

§ 5.07[13]   Constructive Grant of Variances

To no surprise of anyone involved in the local permitting process, the Courts and the Legislature have been unsympathetic to boards of appeals that fail to comply with the strict procedural guidelines discussed, above. Failure to comply triggers the opportunity for the applicant to take advantage of a liberal constructive grant process.

The statute establishes clear requirements for applicants seeking to enforce a constructive grant.[79] In addition, while this information is relevant to boards of appeals in general, the purpose of this Chapter is to set forth the procedural and substantive requirements of variance law from the board of appeals' perspective. Discussion of appeals procedure by an aggrieved party is left to other documents.

To that end, the message that Boards of Appeals should receive, both from the statute and case law, is that failure to comply with the advertising, notice, public hearing and timely filing requirements will likely lead to a constructive—default—grant of the variance application.

To repeat advice given throughout this Chapter, boards of appeals should interpret procedural rules conservatively. For example, as discussed above, notices of public hearings should be more, not less inclusive of information. The uncertainty of the 14 day in advance requirement can be resolved by advertising at least 15 days in advance of the public hearing. The filing requirement uncertainty can

---

[78] As noted previously, no variance can take effect until it is recorded at the registry of deeds, and the city or town clerk cannot provide the needed certification until it has been confirmed that no appeal has been taken or if one has, that it has been resolved. *See* G.L. c. 40A, § 11.

[79] *See*, for example, G.L. c. 40A, §§ 9, 11 and 15

be resolved by filing the board's full decision with the city or town clerk.

§ 5.07[14]   Board of Appeals Liability

Members of a Board of Appeals are not personally liable for negligence, including gross negligence. They are liable for intentional torts only if a court finds that they acted "in bad faith, maliciously or corruptly."[80] Costs of suit are not allowed against the Board of Appeals "unless it shall appear to the court that the board...acted with gross negligence, in bad faith or with malice."[81] Discussion of what constitutes "bad faith" or "malice" is beyond the scope of this Chapter. However, it is strongly advised that Board members or the Board in total seek advice from town or city counsel if any doubt exists on these points as to their contemplated actions on a pending zoning application.

§ 5.08   Special Permits

§ 5.08[1]   Introduction and Purpose

The purpose of special permits is to provide flexibility to the zoning ordinance or bylaw. A special permit is based on the conception that the same use can be either beneficial or noxious depending on its location in the district and on other circumstances surrounding the use. The special permit process allows each case to be examined on its own merits and allows the use to be permitted, denied, or allowed on conditions, based on a determination by the local board. The bylaw or ordinance must contain standards sufficient to guide and regulate the discretion of the board in the issuance of permits.[1] The board then takes evidence, finds facts, and applies the guidelines in the ordinance or bylaw to the facts to develop a decision on whether the permit shall issue. It is important to note that a fundamental distinction between a special permit and a "use by right" is that the former empowers the special permit granting authority with significant discretion while the latter provides no discretionary authority at all.

As discussed in Chapter 3, it is the use or abuse of this discretion that often gives rise to regulatory takings claims. Moreover, the discretion found within a special permit adjudication empowers the special permit granting authority to condition the project such that the authority may, in its judgment, approve the project. Thus a characteristic of an adjudicative permit such as a special permit is that the permit would be otherwise denied but for the adjudicative authority's imposition of conditions.

---

[80] Middlesex & Boston Street Railway Co. v. Board of Aldermen of Newton, 371 Mass. 849, 861 (1977), *citing* Gildea v. Ellershaw, 363 Mass. 800, 820 (1973).

[81] *See* G.L. c. 40A, § 17.

[1] Duteau v. Zoning Board of Appeals, 47 Mass. App. 664 (1999).

§ 5.08[2]   Special Permits in Practice

G.L. c. 40A, § 9 provides that zoning ordinances or bylaws "shall" provide for specific types of uses which shall only be permitted in specified districts upon the issuance of a special permit. Special permits govern that class of uses that lie between those that are prohibited and those allowed as of right.[2]

There is not the same bias against special permits that exists in the case of variances.

Counsel for the applicant should read the local zoning ordinance or bylaw with the goal of determining the "level of difficulty" of obtaining a special permit. Some ordinances, for example, provide that the "special permit shall be granted provided that the applicant comply with… ." These types of special permits—those that require their grant if—have a much lower level of difficulty than special permits that leave open the range of the authority's discretion. For example, an ordinance that read, "Special permits for the uses noted below may be granted only if the special permit granting authority, in its sole and exclusive judgment, determines that… ."

This latter example has a high level of difficulty; the reviewing board has broad discretion. A simple way of explaining the level of difficulty concept to your client is that a use by right (for example obtaining a building permit for a single family residential structure that complies with zoning) is a "one" on the scale of difficulty. Uses by right allow for no discretion. The application for a building permit in the above example, one that otherwise complies with zoning, cannot be negotiated, no conditions can be imposed and the outcome is certain: the use or structure is allowed by right and permit must be issued. This type of non-negotiable, non-discretionary permit is a "one" on the difficulty scale.

A use or structure by variance, on the other extreme, is a use or structure that is simply not allowed except under the most unusual fact patterns. Thus, a variance would be a "ten" on the scale of difficulty. As there is no lawful right to a variance, a variance is the scale's polar opposite. Whereas a use by right is "easy to obtain", a use by variance is "impossible."

Uses by special permit can be anywhere in between a "one" and a "ten." As noted above, the determination of where on this scale your client's project lies is best determined by first reading the ordinance's language carefully, researching similar applications for special permits and discussing your particular application, prior to filing, with city or town hall staff.

Of course, as is traditional in zoning law, the courts give great weight to the

---

[2] Clark v. Board of Appeals, 348 Mass. 407, 204 N.E.2d 434 (1965).

discretion of local boards in deciding whether a special permit should issue. However, where the board's denial of a permit is challenged, the applicant has a much easier task in establishing error and securing a reversal in a special permit dispute than in the case of a variance.[3]

Where the permit is granted by the board but the grant is challenged in court the deference given to the local board's decision and the fact that there is no legal bias against special permits combine to make the permit difficult to overturn.[4] Therefore it is most important to obtain a favorable decision from the local board.

The presentation to the board should address generally the reasons the particular use or structure was made subject to special permit and how these concerns are addressed by the applicant's proposal. More importantly, counsel should be sure to provide the board with specific and detailed evidence as to how the application complies with the general or specific condition precedent requirements of the ordinance or bylaw pertaining to the grant of a special permit.

Local bylaws or ordinances sometimes provide that special permits shall be granted in certain cases by boards other than the board of appeals, for example by the planning board, board of selectmen or city council. Special permit granting boards must adopt and file with the city or town clerk rules relative to the issuance of such permits. Such rules must prescribe in detail the submissions required and the procedures applicable to the special permit process.

Special permits may only be granted upon unanimous vote of a three member board, four out of five of a five member board and a two-thirds vote of a board with more than five members (e.g., a planning board consisting of seven members requires an affirmative vote of five members and a planning board consisting of nine members requires an affirmative vote of six members).[5]

In proper cases, a board may require that the applicant post a bond to assure compliance with the conditions of a special permit.[6]

While the cases prohibit the conditioning of a variance on the ownership, or continued ownership of the parcel involved by a specific person or persons (precisely because the three conjunctive requirements of G.L. c. 40A, § 10 must relate to the land, not an individual),[7] special permits, the benefits of which are limited

---

[3] Murphy v. Zoning Board of Appeals, 2 Mass. App. 876, 317 N.E.2d 90 (1974); Malcomb v. Board of Appeals, 361 Mass. 887, 282 N.E.2d 681 (1972); MacGibbon v. Board of Appeals, 356 Mass. 635, 255 N.E.2d 347 (1970).

[4] Boyajian v. Board of Appeals, 6 Mass. App. 283, 374 N.E.2d 1237 (1978); S. Volpe & Co. v. Board of Appeals, 4 Mass. App. 357, 348 N.E.2d 807 (1976).

[5] G.L. c. 40A, § 9.

[6] Lovaco, Inc. v. Zoning Bd. of Appeals, 23 Mass. App. 239, 500 N.E.2d 843 (1986).

[7] Huntington v. Zoning Bd. of Appeals, 12 Mass. App. 710, 428 N.E.2d 826 (1981).

to a particular applicant have been upheld by the Massachusetts courts.[8] But the considerations on which the grant of the special permit is based must still relate to the land rather than the applicant in order for the permit to be lawful. That is, the special permit granting authority must base its decision as to whether or not to grant a special permit on considerations related to the land or relevant structures. Once it is decided that such considerations justify the issuance of a permit, it may then be limited to the particular applicant.[9]

As authorized by town meeting or city council, special permits may not be required for all uses in any one zoning district. At least one use must be allowed as of right. The logic of this requirement is that the uniformity provision of G.L. c. 40A, § 4 would be jeopardized if special permit granting authorities were empowered with "roving and virtually unlimited power to discriminate as to uses between landowners similarly situated."[10]

While a permit may not be "warehoused" indefinitely where a developer anticipates completing work in stages, begins construction within two years, and a "substantial use" has started, permission to complete the project may continue unless there is express language to the contrary in the permit.[11]

§ 5.09   Judicial Appeals

The judicial review of zoning cases has many unique features. First, such cases are procedurally unusual and contain pitfalls for the unwary. Extreme caution and careful reading of the statute are mandatory.[1]

Review may be sought in the superior court, land court or in the district court within whose jurisdiction the land lies. In regions or areas served by a housing court, appeal may also be taken to that court. If appeal is taken in the district court, any party may remove the case to the superior court within 25 days after service of the appeal is completed. In practice, nearly all zoning appeals go to the superior court or land court.

---

[8] Hopengarten v. Board of Appeals, 17 Mass. App. 1006, 459 N.E.2d 1271 (1984).

[9] Hopengarten v. Board of Appeals, 17 Mass. App. 1006, 459 N.E.2d 1271 (1984). However, *see* Solar v. Zoning Bd. of Appeals, 33 Mass. App. 398, 600 N.E.2d 1001 (1992), which suggests that the personal condition must also be related to the land or at least to the purposes of the bylaw.

[10] *See* SCIT, Inc. v. Planning Board of Braintree, 19 Mass. App. Ct. 101, 108 (1984) and Gage v. Town of Egremont, 409 Mass. 345 (1991). "...the statutory provisions (G.L. c. 40A, § 9) that special permits are to be 'granted only for uses specifically authorized' would not justify a bylaw in which not even one use was generally authorized in a zoning district and all uses required a special permit." 409 Mass. 345, at 348.

[11] Bernstein v. Chief Building Inspector and Building Commissioner of Falmouth, 52 Mass. App. Ct. 422, 754 N.E.2d 133 (2001) (noting that G.L. c. 40A, § 9, ¶ 13 allows extensions where substantial use has commenced or for "good cause").

[1] G.L. c. 40A, § 17.

The complaint must have attached to it a copy of the decision appealed from, bearing the date of filing thereof, certified (a true attested copy) by the city or town clerk. The complaint must allege that the decision exceeds the authority of the board, and any facts pertinent to the issue, and must contain a prayer that the decision be annulled. It must be filed in court and received by the city or town clerk within 20 days after the decision is filed in the office of the clerk,[2] except that suits alleging defects in publication or notice may be brought in 90 days.

The 90–day appeal period applies only to defects of procedure or notice by publication or posting for public hearings required by the first paragraph of G.L. c. 40A, § 11, and not to defects in notice in the mailing of the decision required by c. 40A, § 15.[3] However, appeals from a constructive grant of relief by board inaction must be filed with the court and city or town clerk (the filing with the clerk should contain a cover letter clearly marked "Notice of Complaint Pursuant to G.L. c. 40A, § 17 and have attached the board's decision) within 20 days after the statutory notice of constructive grant has been given to the clerk by the petitioner.[4] Failure to meet the filing time requirements will result in the case being dismissed.[5] The courts apply these requirements strictly.[6]

The 90-day appeal period applies only to defects in publication, mailing or posting, not to other defects in procedure.[7] These defects can be divided into two categories based on the case law: failures of publication notice and failures of mail notice to parties in interest.

In the case of deficiencies in publication, (and presumably posting although there are no reported cases), the cases have uniformly held that the board never obtains jurisdiction and its decision is void.[8] In the case of deficiencies in mailing notice,

---

[2] G.L. c. 40A, § 17.

[3] Cappuccio v. Zoning Bd. of Appeals, 398 Mass. 304, 496 N.E.2d 646 (1986); Bingham v. City Council of Fitchburg, 52 Mass. App. Ct. 566, 754 N.E.2d 1078 (2001) (failures to meet deadline not forgiven; notice of action and complaint given mayor only fifteen minutes after clerk's office closed, but neither clerk nor anyone in office aware appeal had been commenced until, at best, following morning; where permit applicant provided certification that no appeal had been filed within twenty-day period, intended purpose of providing third persons notice of appeal had not been accomplished within time limit).

[4] G.L. c. 40A, §§ 9, 15; see also § 2:10.11, infra.

[5] Brady v. Board of Appeals, 348 Mass. 515, 204 N.E.2d 513 (1965); Nightingale v. Board of Appeals, 7 Mass. App. 887, 386 N.E.2d 1064 (1979).

[6] But see Konover Management Corp. v. Planning Bd. of Auburn, 32 Mass. App. 319, 588 N.E.2d 1365 (1992), for a case where the court bent over backward to avoid a dismissal on this type of procedural ground.

[7] G.L. c. 40A, § 17.

[8] Gallagher v. Board of Appeals, 351 Mass. 410 (1966); Planning Board of Peabody v. Board of Appeals of Peabody, 358 Mass. 81 (1970); Roman Catholic Archbishop of Boston v. Board of Appeal, 268 Mass. 416, 167 N.E. 672 (1929).

the board will obtain jurisdiction in spite of the deficiency but its decision may be declared invalid if attacked by the party entitled to mail notice. Individual parties in interest are entitled only to "reasonable notice" of the hearing.[9] What constitutes reasonable notice depends on the facts and circumstances of each case. However, the party attacking the decision must be able to show that he/she suffered some prejudice as a result of late mail notice or absence of mail notice.[10] In summary, the courts have taken a jurisdictional approach to publication notice, but only a procedural due process (fairness in the procedure) approach to mail notice.[11]

Where the appeal is taken by the person who applied to the board, the members of the board must all be made parties to the suit. For example, a disgruntled applicant appealing the board's denial of her special permit must name all the board members in her appeal. Where zoning relief was granted by the board and a person other than the applicant has appealed, then service must also be made upon the person or entity who was the applicant before the board and all the members of the board. For example, a disgruntled abutter to the locus subject to the grant of a special permit must name all the board members *and* the recipient of the special permit in her appeal.

The statute's requirement that "all the members of the board of appeals" be named and served poses a problem where a board has several alternate members and where some members of the duly constituted board did not attend or participate in the hearing and deliberative process. While no case exists clarifying the question as to whether all members of the board need to be named and served, caution suggests naming and serving each board member, regardless of their participation.

Where the plaintiff has failed to name the applicant before the board as a party, the trial court may in its discretion allow late joinder, provided the appeal has been timely filed and there is no showing of prejudice.[12] Service is made upon the defendants by delivery or by certified mail within 14 days after filing the suit in court. It is recommended that service include the complaint, the notice of complaint filed with the city or town clerk and the tracking order issued by the Court. (As of 2005, the Land Court will be issuing tracking orders similar to those issued by the Superior Court). Note that the service requirement of G.L. c. 40A, § 17 is very different than the "traditional" service requirements of the Massachusetts Rules of Civil Procedure.

---

[9] Rousseau v. Building Inspector of Framingham, 349 Mass. 31, 206 N.E.2d 399 (1965). It has been held that there is no statutory entitlement to notice of the decision.

[10] Chiuccariello v. Building Comm'r of Boston, 29 Mass. App. 482, 562 N.E.2d 96 (1990); Ranney v. Board of Appeals, 11 Mass. App. 112, 414 N.E.2d 373 (1981); Kasper v. Board of Appeals, 3 Mass. App. 251 (1975).

[11] Cappuccio v. Zoning Board of Appeals, 398 Mass. 304, 496 N.E.2d 646 (1986); Co-Ray Realty v. Board of Zoning Adjustment, 328 Mass. 103, 101 N.E.2d 888 (1951).

[12] Cox v. Board of Appeals, 42 Mass. App. 422 (1997).

Within 21 days after commencing suit, an affidavit of service must be filed. As a matter of practice, it is recommended that the affidavit be sent to the Court and opposing counsel (if known) upon completion of service of process. Although the statute says that failure to timely file an affidavit of service will result in dismissal, the courts have refused to give that language effect. The usual result of raising such failure in recent years is that additional time is given to file the affidavit.[13] No answer is required to be filed in zoning appeals, although counsel representing a defendant board or the applicant for the permit should weigh the advantages and disadvantages of filing an answer. There is no right to a jury trial.

The case law that gave persons aggrieved by the constructive grant of an appeal, application or petition the right to seek complete judicial review has been codified into the statute.[14]

The problem of a potentially unlimited time for appeal in the case of claimed constructive grant, which previously existed under the case law,[15] has been eliminated. Under the statute the petitioner who claims that zoning relief has been constructively granted must, within 14 days from the date of the constructive grant, begin the process of establishing his or her rights as a matter of record by notifying the city or town clerk and all parties in interest.[16] This notice in turn begins the running of the 20-day appeal period.

The failure by the petitioner to send the required notice within 14 days will foreclose his right to claim a constructive grant.[17]

Just as the rules of civil procedure are unusual in zoning cases, so is the nature of review. Where the appeal is from a local board decision granting relief the decision must contain all the facts necessary to support the board's decision or it will be void on its face.[18] However the decision has no evidentiary value in and of itself.[19]

The court hears all the evidence and finds all the facts de novo. It then applies the facts found to the decision of the board. If the board's decision is incorrect as

---

[13] Pierce v. Board of Appeals, 369 Mass. 804, 343 N.E.2d 412 (1976); City Council of Waltham v. Board of Appeals, 5 Mass. App. 773, 359 N.E.2d 651 (1977). Indeed, with the exception of failure to make timely filing of the appeal and notice with the court and town clerk, it is unlikely that other procedural lapses by the plaintiff will result in dismissal. Carr v. Board of Appeals, 361 Mass. 361, 280 N.E.2d 199 (1972).

[14] G.L. c. 40A, § 17, as amended by St. 1987, c. 498.

[15] See Noe v. Board of Appeals, 13 Mass. App. 103, 430 N.E.2d 853 (1982); Girard v. Board of Appeals, 14 Mass. App. 334, 439 N.E.2d 308 (1982).

[16] See G.L. c. 40A, §§ 9, 15.

[17] Uglietta v. Somerville, 32 Mass. App. 742, 594 N.E.2d 887 (1992).

[18] Barnhart v. Board of Appeals, 343 Mass. 455, 179 N.E.2d 251 (1962).

[19] Devine v. Zoning Board of Appeals, 332 Mass. 319, 125 N.E.2d 131 (1955).

a matter of law it will be annulled, otherwise it must be affirmed.[20] If the court annuls the board's decision, it may also remand it to the board for further action in light of the Court's decision.[21] The case law repeatedly admonishes that the court is not to invade the field of adjudicative discretion and substitute its judgment for that of the board.[22] The decisions of local boards, with their unique knowledge of local conditions are entitled to judicial deference and the presumption of validity. This is true not only as to matters of fact but also, perhaps to a lesser extent, as to the interpretation of the local ordinance or bylaw itself.[23]

This standard of judicial review was recently framed by the appeals court as follows: "Even when a zoning board cites no particularized reasons or and specific evidence for its denial decision, its action will be upheld, as will that of a judge affirming that action under G.L. c. 40A, § 17, if a rational basis for the denial exists which is supported by the record. So long as 'any reason on which the board can fairly be said to have relied has a basis in the trial judge's findings and is within the standards of the zoning bylaw and The Zoning Enabling Act, the board's action must be sustained regardless of other reasons which the board may have advanced.'" [citations omitted][24] This statement may, as a practical matter, be most applicable to cases that have been affirmed by the trial court and are being reviewed by an appellate court rather than cases that are being reviewed by the trial court.

Note however that this discretion is not limitless. In practice, the trial court will be hearing all the evidence again, perhaps more evidence than the Board heard during the hearings on the application. If the trial judge's sympathies lie with the applicant at the end of the trial, only a discretionary decision solidly grounded in fact will be liable to survive.[25]

Nevertheless, if after finding the facts, the judge determines that the board's decision is not incorrect as a matter of law it must be upheld. The judge may not order a special permit or variance granted whenever on the facts found the board could have granted it.[26] And the board's decision must be upheld if it reaches a correct result on the actual facts found by the judge even if the reasons given by

---

[20] *See* Britton v. Zoning Board of Appeals of Gloucester, 59 Mass. App. Ct. 68 (2003).

[21] Roberts-Haverhill Associates v. City Council of Haverhill, 2 Mass. App. 715, 319 N.E.2d 916 (1974).

[22] Pendergast v. Board of Appeals, 331 Mass. 555, 120 N.E.2d 916 (1952); Kemble Fischer Realty Trust v. Board of Appeals, 9 Mass. App. 477, 402 N.E.2d 100 (1980), *cert. denied*, 449 U.S. 1011, 66 L. Ed. 2d 468, 101 S. Ct. 566, *rehearing denied*, 449 U.S. 1134, 67 L. Ed. 2d 121, 101 S. Ct. 957; Board of Appeals v. Boyle, 4 Mass. App. 824, 349 N.E.2d 373 (1976).

[23] Duteau v. Zoning Board of Appeals, 47 Mass. App. 664 (1999).

[24] Davis v. Zoning Board of Chatham, 52 Mass. App. 349, 356 (2001).

[25] *See, e.g.*, Colangelo v. Board of Appeals, 407 Mass. 242, 552 N.E.2d 541 (1990).

[26] Subaru of New England, Inc. v. Board of Appeals, 8 Mass. App. 483, 395 N.E.2d 880 (1979).

the board for making its decision are incorrect.[27] However, where the improper action by the board is clear on the record, and the plaintiff's entitlement to the relief sought is equally clear, the court may order the permit to issue.[28] The court may not grant the plaintiff relief that she could have, but did not, seek from the board.[29]

If the applicant is granted a special permit or variance but is unhappy with the conditions the board has attached to it he or she must appeal pursuant to the same rules governing appeals discussed above. As in the case of subdivision approvals, the recording of the plan or decision with the conditions is construed to be an acceptance of them, whether they are legally imposed or not. The applicant may not later attempt to attack the conditions by applying for a modification of the special permit or variance and then appeal the denial of such application.[30] Moreover, note that a special permit or variance cannot be recorded and therefore cannot be used, unless the town or city clerk certifies that twenty days have elapsed without appeal or that where an appeal has been taken, the matter has been resolved.

The form of decision that the court may make is also carefully circumscribed. If the decision of the board is to be upheld, the Supreme Judicial Court requires that the wording of the judgment be "…that the decision of the board did not exceed its authority, that no modification of it is required, and that the clerk of the court within thirty days after entry of the decree send an attested copy thereof to…" the defendants.[31]

Because the Superior Court conducts a limited de novo hearing, the Court's decision results in a limited judgment. Counsel trying a zoning case should, therefore, be aware of the Court's powers—and its limits—prior to embarking on an appeal and ideally, advising the client of these powers and limits well in advance of the decision being appealed. . The normally broad discretion, which a court of equity has to frame a remedy to fit the case, is not present in a zoning case.[32]

In essence, the court is limited to affirming the board's decision, annulling it, or remanding the matter to the board for reconsideration based on the legal guidance contained in the court's decision. A remand order, which allows the board no

---

[27] Parrish v. Board of Appeal, 351 Mass. 561, 223 N.E.2d 81 (1967).

[28] Crittenton Hastings House of the Florence Crittenton League v. Board of Appeal, 25 Mass. App. 704, 521 N.E.2d 1374 (1988); Newbury Junior College v. Brookline, 19 Mass. App. 197, 472 N.E.2d 1373 (1985), *review denied*, 394 Mass. 1102, 475 N.E.2d 401.

[29] Di Giovanni v. Board of Appeals, 19 Mass. App. 339, 474 N.E.2d 198 (1985), *review denied*, 394 Mass. 1103, 477 N.E.2d 595.

[30] Klein v. Board of Appeals, 31 Mass. App. 777 (1992); Bonfatti v. Board of Appeals, 48 Mass. App. 46 (1999).

[31] Lambert v. Board of Appeals, 295 Mass. 224, 3 N.E.2d 784 (1936). *See also* Waldron v. Board of Appeals, 1974 Mass. App. Ct. Adv. Sh. 687, for form of judgment of remand.

[32] Board of Selectmen v. Monument Inn, Inc., 8 Mass. App. 158, 391 N.E.2d 1265 (1979), *later appeal*, 14 Mass. App. 957, 438 N.E2.d 365.

significant discretion upon reconsideration, will be subject to appeal. If the board has such discretion, the trial court decision may not be appealed until the board has acted and the trial court has thereafter acted on the second decision.[33]

§ 5.10   Commonly Encountered Problems in Zoning Practice

§ 5.10[1]   Protections for Nonconforming Structures and Uses

Without exception, the most complicated area of land use law in Massachusetts is reserved for counsel representing an applicant seeking to expand, alter or change a pre-existing non-conforming use or structure, or counsel representing an abutter opposed to an application seeking to expand, alter or change a pre-existing non-conforming use or structure.

Portions of the controlling statute have been referred to by the Courts as "difficult and infelicitous,"[1] and planning boards, boards of appeals and building departments have struggled with the complexities of the statute for years. This Section seeks to demystify this complicated but critically important section of the Zoning Act.

This Section addresses two substantive issues that landowners and virtually every municipal board and agency confront on a frequent basis.

First, which land parcels and uses are "protected' from amendments to zoning ordinances or bylaws petitioned and ratified by town meeting, town council or city council votes? These issues—vested rights—are discussed in Section 5.10.2.

Second, to what extent can pre-existing, nonconforming structures and uses expand, alter or change without losing their protected status? Section 5.10.3 reviews the ability and mechanisms for expansions, alterations and changes to nonconforming structures and uses.

§ 5.10[2]   Vested Rights ("Grandfathering")

§ 5.10[2][a]   Introduction

The concept that some land uses or vacant land should be protected, sometimes indefinitely, from a zoning change, dates back to the earliest days of zoning and land use law.[2]

---

[33] Federman v. Board of Appeals, 35 Mass. App. 727, 626 N.E.2d 8 (1994), summary op at 22 M.L.W. 949 (Mass. App.).

[1] Fitzsimonds v. Board of Appeals of Chatham, 21 Mass. App. Ct. 53, 55–56 (1985).

[2] "This scenario sets off a "race of diligence" between the municipality seeking to change the law and the developer seeking to build... Determining the point in time when a project is far enough along to acquire immunity from changing laws is the subject of the law of vested rights and estoppel." Juergensmeyer, J. and Roberts, T., "Land Use Planning and Control Law," West Pub. Co., 1998, p.227.

The very definition of the word "vested" and the phrase "vested right"[3] implies that the landowner has more than a mere "expectancy" to use or develop real property, but rather that one holds an "entitlement" to some use of the property, most likely being that use allowed by local regulations in effect at the point in time that the right vested. Thus, in most states, a key issue in establishing whether a vested right exists (and if so, the extent of a landowner's vested rights) is determining the date that the property right transformed from an "expectancy" to an "entitlement."

As the United States and all state Constitutions protect deprivations of, or substantial interference with, entitlements to use real property, a zoning regulation that unreasonably interferes with a property owner's protected (vested) rights, may trigger a regulatory "taking."[4]

Fortunately, the Zoning Act, specifically G.L. c. 40A, § 6, makes determining this date of transformation relatively simple. Section 6 contains a clear (although not clearly written) accounting of when and how a landowner obtains vested rights

---

[3] Although complex, the following definition of "vested rights" from Blacks Law Dictionary is helpful. "In constitutional law, rights which have so completely and definitively accrued to or settled in a person that they are not subject to be defeated or canceled by the act of any other private person, and which it is right and equitable that the government should recognize and protect, as being lawful in themselves, and settled according to the then current rules of law, and of which the individual could not be deprived arbitrarily without injustice, or of which he could not justly be deprived otherwise than by the established methods of procedure and for the public welfare...A right complete and consummated, and of such character that it cannot be divested without the consent of the person to whom it belongs..." Blacks Law Dictionary, West Pub. Co., Sixth Ed., 1990.

[4] A discussion of regulatory takings is found in Chapter 3. A regulatory taking has been defined as where government regulation goes "too far" such that the regulation, when applied to private property, leaves a landowner with no economic value, and/or where the regulation serves no valid public purpose. Thus when the legislature (either federal, state or local) enacts and enforces a regulation that deprives a landowner of all (or most) economic value, the courts have ruled that government has affected a taking. While the land is not literally taken (as in an eminent domain action), the courts have equated unbearable regulation with eminent domain action. The difference, of course, is that when government exerts its eminent domain authority, compensation must always be given. Thus courts are extremely skeptical when government seeks to regulate private property in a manner that resembles eminent domain, but where no compensation is made. A second form of regulatory taking arises during the issuance of an "adjudicative permit." In Massachusetts, G.L. c. 40A, § 9 governs the issuance of adjudicative or special permits. However, as discussed below, G.L. c. 40A, § 6 also provides for the issuance of special permits. A regulatory taking can occur during the issuance of a special permit where the special permit granting authority imposes conditions upon the issuance of a special permit that do not have a relationship—nexus—to the permit being sought and the harm the issuance of the permit will cause. Thus a special permit to expand or alter a preexisting nonconforming structure could not be conditioned on the applicant's donation of $300,000 to the town's library. There simply is no logical connection between the building expansion and the town's library needs. See, for example, Nollan v. California Coastal Commission, 483 U.S. 825 (1987).

under zoning. A detailed discussion of the opportunities to establish vested rights is discussed in detail below.

Each state defines vested rights differently and each state places different limitations on local government's ability to "interfere" with real property and associated entitlements. For example, in California, a so-called "late vesting" state, a landowner's vested right does not mature until she has received a building permit for a use or particular structure.[5]

To the contrary, Massachusetts is an early vesting state. This fact has a policy background well beyond the scope of this Chapter. However, it is important to understand the state's philosophical views regarding vested rights and property ownership as these views provide the foundation upon which Section 6 rests.

A 1971 Supreme Judicial Court opinion reflects the past and current judicial and legislative attitude toward vested rights protections:

> "Purchasers of real estate are entitled to rely on the applicable zoning ordinances or bylaws in determining the uses which may be made of the parcel they are buying…For many persons, particularly those purchasing houses, this is the largest single investment of their lives. It is important that such purchasers be able to determine with reasonable accuracy, before making that investment, just what the applicable zoning ordinances and bylaws are, and what uses they permit or prohibit."[6]

§ 5.10[2][b]   The Seven Protections of G.L. c. 40A, § 6

G.L. c. 40A, § 6 provides seven (7) independent protections from zoning

---

[5] *See*, for example, Avco Community Developers, Inc. v. South Coastal Regional Commission, 17 Cal. 3d 785 (1976), where the California Supreme Court articulated this late vesting rule. "If we were to accept the premise that the construction of subdivision improvements or the zoning of the land … are sufficient to afford a developer a vested right to construct buildings on the land in accordance with the laws in effect at the time the improvements are made or the zoning enacted, there could be serious impairment of the government's right to control land use policy… ." 17 Cal. 3d 785, at 797. California and many other late vesting states offered land owners threatened with the loss of previously allowable land uses an interesting tool: development agreements. Allowed in Massachusetts only through the Cape Cod Commission Act (development agreements elsewhere in Massachusetts would likely be labeled as illegal "contract zoning"), a development agreement is a contract between the landowner/developer and the municipality. The agreement embodies elements of both contract and regulatory law and when used effectively, can be a powerful tool for local governments. In exchange for vested rights protection from the local government, the landowner is required to offer public benefits that, but for the contract, is more extensive than would be allowed under traditional subdivision or special permit review.

[6] Vazza v. Board of Appeals of Brockton, 359 Mass. 256, 263 (1971). *See also* Junior v. Wiley, 2004 Mass. Super. LEXIS 278, at *20, 18 Mass. L. Rep. 125 (Mass. Super. Ct. 2004).

changes for real property owners in the Commonwealth. Despite several instances of confusing verbiage and unbearable run-on sentences, the statutory protections can be clearly flushed out of the text. The following discussion presents these seven protections, together with examples. Please note that the discussion that follows corresponds to the order in which the protections appear in the statute.

§ 5.10[2][b][i]   Preexisting Structure or Use

Discussed in detail below, G.L. c. 40A, § 6 protects a structure or use, lawfully in existence or lawfully begun, prior to the first advertisement for the zoning change that makes (or will make) the structure or use nonconforming. Please refer to the discussion below for a detailed review of the status of preexisting structures and uses and their ability to expand, alter or change.

§ 5.10[2][b][ii]   Building or Special Permit "In Hand"

The second protection insulates from the impact of a new zoning change, a structure or use for which a building or special permit has been issued—and is literally in the hand of the applicant—prior to the first advertisement for the zoning change that makes (or will make) the structure or use nonconforming.

Note that the "in hand" requirement is different than "applied for" and the time period between application and receipt can be extensive.

An "applied for" building permit is often not issued, and thus not "in hand", until several days or weeks following the submission of a completed application. The Massachusetts Building Code provides the building official up to thirty (30) days to issue a building permit following the submission of a completed application.[7]

An "applied for" special permit is rarely issued quickly. The special permit granting authority has up to sixty-five (65) days to hold a public hearing on the petition and is allowed ninety-days (90) within which to issue a decision.[8] The ninety (90) day period commences at the close of the public hearing. Assuming the special permit is approved, the permit cannot be issued until the statutory appeal period has expired. This period is twenty (20) days.[9] Thus, the maximum time period, without extensions, for a special permit to be issued is 175 days (sixty-five, plus ninety plus twenty). Practice indicates that few special permits are approved and issued sooner than seventy to one hundred days after application has been made and most are not issued until the statutory periods have been exhausted.

---

[7] 780 CMR 114.1

[8] G.L. c. 40A, § 9.

[9] The term "issued" in this context is confusing. For the purposes of G.L. c. 40A, § 6 vested rights (grandfathering) protection, the special permit granting authority's approval of the special permit commences the protection period. However, the special permit cannot be "issued"—given or handed to the applicant—until the twenty-day appeal period has expired.

§ 5.10[2][b][iii]   Single Lot: 50/5,000

"Any increase in area, frontage, width, yard, or depth requirements of a zoning ordinance or bylaw shall not apply to a lot for single and two-family residential use which at the time of recording or endorsement, which ever occurs sooner was not held in common ownership with any adjoining land, conformed to then existing requirements and had less than the proposed requirement but at least five thousand square feet of area and fifty feet of frontage."[10]

The third protection of G.L. c. 40A, § 6 is the "single lot" exemption and should be contrasted with the exemption discussed in Section 5.10[2][b][iv] (common lots) below.

The single lot[11] exemption protects a vacant[12] lot in existence when the new zoning regulations become effective[13] from any increase in area,[14] frontage,[15]

---

[10] G.L. c. 40A, § 6.

[11] A single lot is one that does not abut property owned by the same party. *See* Sturges v. Chilmark, 380 Mass. 246 (1980). "The judge was …correct in ruling that the plaintiffs may treat as buildable lots each of two nonconforming lots which 'come together at only one point,' that is…two lots whose 'relationship to each other is like that of similarly colored squares on a checkerboard." 380 Mass. 246, at 260. *See also* Clarke v. Board of Appeals of Nahant, 338 Mass. 473 (1959), where the Court upheld the conclusion that lots that adjoined each other for "about thirteen feet" were in common ownership. 338 Mass. 473, at 477.

[12] The single and common lot exemptions do not apply to structures and uses, but rather only to vacant land. This is consistent with the legislative intent of the statute: to protect landowners of one to three lots from a zoning change that could render their land valueless or greatly diminished in value. "There is nothing on the face of the fourth paragraph to suggest that it was intended to apply to anything but vacant land." Willard v. Board of Appeals of Orleans, 25 Mass. App. Ct. 15, 18 (1987).

[13] Discussed more fully below, the effective date of a zoning ordinance or bylaw amendment is the date the legislature (city council, town council or town meeting) votes to approve the amendment. The effective date of a zoning ordinance or bylaw should not be confused with the date of the first advertisement for the public hearing at which the zoning amendment will be discussed. While this advertised date has an affect upon certain categories of uses or structures, it is not the effective date of the zoning amendment. This semantic distinction is very important.

[14] "Area" has traditionally been defined by minimum lot size (e.g. 20,000 or 60,000 square feet required per dwelling unit). However, at least one case stated that an increase in the buildable portion of a lot (protected as a single or common lot) was an increase in area requirements and was therefore not effective. Schofield v. Tolosko, Misc. No. 153570 (Land Court 1992). This reading of the statute would, therefore, protect a single or common lot from increases in maximum upland requirements and all requirements that are linked to minimum or maximum requirements with any ratio requirements for area and building. This interpretation may be too broad however. A strict construction of the statute would interpret "any increase in area…shall not apply" literally. Left unanswered, however are regulations that link number of bedrooms per square footage of land area or size of structures per square footage of land area. Neither of these regulations would preclude construction of a single or two-family dwelling, they merely limit the size of the eventual structure.

width,[16] yard,[17] or depth[18] requirements if the lot has at least 50 feet of frontage and 5,000 square feet of land area.[19] As there is no time limit on this protection (as distinguished from the discussion in Section 5.10[2][b][iv] below), the single lot protection lasts literally forever.[20]

While the single lot exemption is extremely broad, it is important to note that

---

See also Cotty v. Parks, Misc. No. 219911 (Land Court, 1999), where the Court held that a change in the definition of "frontage" within the zoning bylaw would not be applicable against a lot held in single ownership. Note that the bylaw in question did not change the numerical frontage requirements, but rather the definition of the word "frontage" within the bylaw. *Id.* at page 4. Much welcome clarification, at least as it relates to a maximum building coverage bylaw, was provided by the Superior Court in Tietjen v. Wells, 2003 Mass. Super. LEXIS 87, 16 Mass. L. Rep. 65 (Mass. Super. Ct. 2003). In *Tietjen*, the plaintiffs claimed that their single, but undersized, lot was protected from all zoning changes pursuant to the single lot protection of G.L. c. 40A, § 6. Relying on the principals of statutory construction, the Court concluded that G.L. c. 40A, § 6 does not specifically include protections from changes to maximum building coverage requirements and therefore, the Town of Chatham could reasonably establish maximum building coverage requirements even for those lots historically thought of as protected from all amendments to zoning.

[15] Frontage is generally defined by most zoning ordinances and bylaws as that portion of the lot that is parallel to the road or way providing access to the lot.

[16] Width is generally defined as the minimum distance permitted between a lot's sidelines.

[17] The yard requirements of a lot typically include front, rear and side. The requirements are expressed as minimum setbacks; such that a twenty-five foot front yard requires that no structure be placed within twenty-five feet of the lot's front lot line.

[18] A lot's depth requirement is generally presented as the minimum distance permitted between front and rear lot lines.

[19] The following language is found immediately below the language establishing the single and common lot protections with G.L. c. 40A, § 6: "The provisions of this paragraph shall not be construed to prohibit a lot being built upon, if at the time of the building, building upon such lot is not prohibited by the zoning ordinances or bylaws in effect in a city or town." This enabling authority has been interpreted as the means by which local government can grant greater protections than those afforded by Section 6. *See*, for example, Seltzer v. Board of Appeals of Orleans, 24 Mass. App. Ct. 521 (1987), where the Court upheld application of the Orleans zoning bylaw treating certain common lots as if they were single ownership lots for the purposes of zoning compliance. *See also* Lee v. Board of Appeals of Harwich, 11 Mass. App. Ct. 148 (1981). "While it is generally the policy of zoning bylaws to freeze and minimize substandard lots...this policy does not vitiate the authority of municipalities to preserve legislatively certain substandard lots for building purposes." 11 Mass. App. Ct. 148, at 154. *See also* Junior v. Wiley, 18 Mass. L. Rep. 125, 2004 Mass. Super. LEXIS 278, at *23, 18 Mass. L. Rep. 125 (Mass. Super. Ct. 2004), where in reference to the Town of Marshfield's zoning bylaw, the Court noted, "The Town is permitted to adopt the provisions of Section 9.03 on the basis that paragraph four of G.L. c. 40A, § 6 'provides only a floor' and that a municipality is free to grant more liberal treatment to the owner of a nonconforming lot." *Citing* DeSalvo v. Chatis, Misc. Case No. 149615, at 7 (Land Ct. 1991), Baldiga v. Bd. of Appeals of Uxbridge, 395 Mass. 829, 834 (1985), Seltzer v. Bd. of Appeals of Orleans, 24 Mass. App. Ct. 521 (1987), and Lee v. Bd. of Appeals of Harwich, 11 Mass. App. Ct. 148 (1981).

[20] "This amounts to perpetual exemption from restrictive zoning for the single-lot owner and leaves the lot to that extent open to building." Ferzoco v. Board of Appeals of Falmouth, 29 Mass. App. Ct. 986 (1990).

the statute does not provide "blanket" protection from all zoning changes. For example, the statute specifically omits vested rights protection from increases in requirements pertaining to the maximum height of single or two family residential structures or requirements relating to how a structure's height is measured.[21] Similarly, the statute is silent as to when the protected lot is entitled to receive a building permit. While it is clear that the lot is protected from most dimensional changes, the statute does not protect the lot from an ordinance or bylaw instituting growth timing regulations, building permit caps or other phased development regulations.[22]

Finally, note that the protections afforded by G.L. c. 40A, § 6 apply only to amendments to the municipal *zoning* bylaw or ordinance. The statute provides no protection from changes to the local board of health regulations,[23] local wetlands bylaws or other regulations that may directly or indirectly affect the development of the lot.

§ 5.10[2][b][iv]   Common Lot: 75/7,500

"Any increase in area, frontage, width, yard or depth requirement of a zoning ordinance or bylaw shall not apply for a period of five years from its effective date or for five years after January first, nineteen hundred and seventy-six, whichever is later, to a lot for single and two-family residential use, provided the plan for such lot was recorded or endorsed and such lot was held in common ownership with any adjoining land and conformed to the existing zoning requirements as of January first, nineteen hundred and seventy-six, and had less area, frontage, width, yard or depth requirements than the newly effective zoning requirements but contained at least seven thousand five hundred square feet of area and seventy-five feet of frontage, and provided that said five year

---

[21] For example, a zoning ordinance that redefines the definition of building height from the current definition of "measured from the mean height of the finished grade" to "measure from the mean height of the grade prior to site work or grading" could have a significant impact on the completed height of a new structure. The single lot exemption would not protect a lot from such a definitional change.

[22] G.L. c. 40A, § 6 contains language extending the vested rights protection period for definitive subdivision plans during the period that "a city or town imposes or has imposed upon it by a state, a federal agency or a court, a moratorium on construction, the issuance of permits or utility connections." Applying the principles set forth by this clause to single and common lots, it seems reasonable to conclude that while the vested rights of a single or common lot cannot be disturbed, the exact point in time at which the lot is entitled to a building permit has not been guaranteed. *But see* Zuckerman v. Hadley, 442 Mass. 511 (2004), where the SJC held invalid a seemingly perpetual growth management regulation.

[23] *See*, for example, G.L. c. 111, § 127P, which provides limited protection from new health regulations upon the timely filing of a preliminary, definitive or approval not required plan. *See also* for example, Independence Park, Inc. v. Board of Health of Barnstable, 25 Mass. App. Ct. 133 (1987). The statute does not, however, provide similar protection for single or common lots.

period does not commence prior to January first, nineteen hundred and seventy-six, and provided further that the provisions of this sentence shall not apply to more than three of such adjoining lots held in common ownership."[24]

The common lot protection is a variation of the single lot protection discussed in Section 5.10[2][b][iii] above, except that it protects up to three adjoining and commonly held lots. The common lot protection is far more limited than the single lot protection, however.

First, the protection is afforded for five years from the date the lots became nonconforming.[25] Recall that the single lot protection is unlimited as to time.

Second, the protection is afforded to two or three contiguous and commonly held lots. Thus, four abutting and commonly held lots would not receive the protection. Interestingly enough, no reported case law exists as to what happens to the fourth lot. Strict statutory construction urges the conclusion that the fourth lot, on its own, does not receive the five-year zoning protection afforded the other three lots. While the fourth lot could be divided and annexed to abutting property, the statute clearly offers no zoning protection to it once it becomes nonconforming.

Finally, and perhaps the most confusing aspect of this vested rights protection, is determining the status of the lots after a zoning change where the lots are then conveyed to a single or multiple purchasers. The following example should help.

James owns three lots abutting lots, each containing 100 feet of frontage and 10,000 square of feet of area (thus complying with the 75/7,500 requirement). On January 1, the minimum lot size for the zoning district in which James' land lies is increased to 20,000 square feet. Clearly, James' lots are protected from the effective date of the downzoning (January 1) for five years. However, on February 1, James sells Lot 1 to Sandra, Lot 2 to Annie and Lot 3 to Caleb. At issue is the protections acquired by Sandra, Annie and Caleb.

---

[24] G.L. c. 40A, § 6.

[25] Recall that this date will always be the date that the local legislative body adopted the new zoning regulation and not the date of the first advertisement required by G.L. c. 40A, § 5. The Supreme Judicial Court reviewed the question of what happens if the five-year period commences after January 1, 1976. The Town of Uxbridge argued that the language within Section 6 governing common lot protection applied only to those lots shown on a plan that was recorded or endorsed prior to January 1, 1976. The Court disagreed. "We reject the town's contention that the statute's use of the word 'conformed" rather than "conforms" to precede the phrase "to the existing zoning requirements as of January [1, 1976]" suggests that the plan and the lot must not only conform at some date to the zoning requirements in effect on January 1, 1976, but also must have been in existence in 1976 and conformed to the zoning requirements at that time. The town's argument ignores the fact that the statutory language consistently uses the past tense to describe all of the conditions needed for a lot to qualify for "grandfather" protection." Baldiga v. Board of Appeals of Uxbridge, 395 Mass. 829, 833–834 (1985).

The answer to the question is straightforward: the subsequent purchaser of lots that are nonconforming at the time of the purchase is entitled to no greater protection than owner of the land when the land became nonconforming. Therefore, because the land was nonconforming on January 1 and James owned all three parcels on January 1, he cannot convey protections to Sandra, Annie and Caleb greater than he had. As he had common lot protection and as this protection is only viable for five years, Sandra, Annie and Caleb's protections are only valid for five years. In addition, note that the five years commences not at the time of purchase, but of course, at the time the lots became nonconforming (January 1).

Thus, the key question to ask when reviewing the protected status of nonconforming lots is: "What was the status of the lots' ownership when the lot became nonconforming?"

If the lot was in single ownership and complied with the minimum requirements (50/5,000) at the time it became nonconforming, the owner can transfer the lot to a new buyer and the zoning protections run with the land. In this case, the new buyer receives indefinite protection from zoning changes affecting area, frontage, width, yard or depth requirements.[26] (*See* Section 5.[10][2][b][iii] *supra*).

But if the lots were in common ownership at the time they became nonconforming, the owner's transfer of the two or three lots does not serve to transform—piggyback—common lot protection into single lot protection.[27] The subsequent purchasers of the two or three lots will have the same amount of protection the original owner had to obtain building permits; five years from the date the lots became nonconforming. The nonconforming date is always the effective date of the zoning change. The effective date is always the date of town meeting, town council or city council vote.

§ 5.10[2][b][iv][A] Common Lots and the "Merger Theory"

Given the harsh distinction between the single and common lot protections, it is not surprising that many landowners whose common lot protection has expired seek to define their lots as in "single ownership" and not in "common ownership" when the zoning changed rendering the lots nonconforming.

This result has given rise to several related issues, each discussed below.

First, as the status of the ownership of multiple lots when the zoning changed is the determinative issue as to whether single or common lot protection applies,

---

[26] *But see* the discussion below, regarding the occasion where one individual acquires title to two previously protected, undersized single ownership lots.

[27] "There was no intention, we think, to pile on one grandfathered period upon another: the five year exemption added to the plaintiffs' grandfather status as of 1976." Ferzoco v. Board of Appeals of Falmouth, 29 Mass. App. Ct. 986 (1990).

landowners with multiple lots caught by surprise by a zoning change often attempt to "checkerboard" the ownership pattern. This practice has been the subject of interesting judicial discussion.

The consensus of recent case law is that the validity of a landowner's claim that adjoining lots are not hers and thus can avail themselves of single or common lot protections turns on the control the landowner had/has over the lots in question.[28] The conclusion has routinely been single ownership protection will not be granted where one party exercises or could exercise control over the lots and their future, regardless of the individuals whose names are listed as the title owner.

A second problem occurs in one of two variations.

The first variation is exemplified by a fact pattern where commonly held lots have lost their five year or definitive plan protections afforded by statute. In these situations, one individual or corporate entity could own multiple adjoining lots, none of which comply with current zoning requirements.

The second fact pattern is where the owner of a nonconforming lot, protected by the single lot exemption discussed above, acquires title to an abutting nonconforming lot. The individual then owns two adjacent nonconforming lots.[29]

---

[28] "The crux, thus, was not the form of ownership, but control: did the landowner have it "within his power," i.e., within his legal control, to use the adjoining land so as to avoid or reduce the nonconformity?" Planning Board of Norwell v. Serena, 27 Mass. App. Ct. 689 (1989), aff'd, 406 Mass. 1008 (1990). See also Lee v. Board of Appeals of Harwich, 11 Mass. App. Ct. 148 (1981), which involved the transfer of lot ownership between husband and wife to obtain single lot protection. The Court upheld the conveyance due to the town of Harwich's zoning bylaw protection of an otherwise nonconforming lot, but noted, "Checkerboarding" is a device whereby an owner conveys title to lots in a subdivision to related persons in such a manner so that no adjoining lots are owned by the same person. The purpose of this conveyancing maneuver is to retain for all lots in a subdivision certain immunities...It is highly doubtful that sham conveyances to related parties accomplish the desired result...We view the 1968 "checkerboarding" as a transparently ineffective attempt to defeat the lot combination provisions." 11 Mass. App. Ct. 148, at 151, 153. Finally, see Distefano v. Town of Stoughton, 36 Mass. App. Ct. 642 (1994). In Distefano, the Court reviewed a complicated series of transactions set in motion by the plaintiff immediately before the definitive plan protections on his subdivision were about to expire. The transactions involved conveyance of individual lots to the plaintiff as trustee of a trust, the plaintiff individually, the plaintiff's spouse and the plaintiff's corporation, of which he was the sole officer and director. "It is a familiar principle that a landowner may not claim rights from the nonconformity of a lot if that same person owns adjoining land that would avoid the nonconformity..... We may disregard the shell of purportedly discrete legal persons engaged in business when there is active and pervasive control of those legal persons by the same controlling person and there is a confusing intermingling of activity among the purportedly separate legal persons while engaging in a common enterprise...the judge rightly disregarded the checkerboard conveyances, a device whose utility we have previously had occasion to question." 36 Mass. App. Ct. 642, at 645, referencing Lee v. Board of Appeals of Harwich, Mass. App. Ct. 148 (1981).

[29] A third, but rare possibility is where the owner of a protected nonconforming parcel acquires

These recurring fact patterns have resulted in the judicially created "merger doctrine."

Relying upon the "general purpose of the zoning law—to foster the creation of conforming lots,"[30] a long line of cases has held that nonconforming parcels held in common ownership merge by operation of law.[31] (The overriding purpose being to minimize nonconformities with current zoning regulations).

These cases have held that commonly held and nonconforming lots, not protected by the common lot protections discussed above or the definitive plan protections discussed below, merge automatically, unless the individual lot status is preserved by the provisions of the local zoning ordinance or bylaw.[32]

---

title to an abutting and not protected nonconforming parcel. At issue is whether the protected parcel somehow loses its protected status. Consistent with the merger theory discussed herein, the Court ruled that the protection cannot be lost be such an annexation. "...there appears no authority supporting the proposition that when an owner of a nonconforming lot entitled to grandfathered status acquires an adjacent nonconforming lot not entitled to such protection, and then merges the two lots, this merger somehow voids the protected status of the first lot. On the contrary, the Massachusetts decisions interpreting the former Section 5A, the present section 6 and other similar grandfather clauses suggest the opposite conclusion—that such protection is preserved upon the merger of two or more nonconforming lots." Learoyd v. Thurston, Misc. No. 125271 (Essex Superior Ct. 1990).

[30] Murphy v. Kotlik, 34 Mass. App. Ct. 410, 414 n.7 (1993).

[31] In an interesting review of the legislative history of G.L. c. 40A, § 6 regarding single and common lot protections, the Appeals Court upheld several lower court interpretations of the merger theory (including the lower court's decision in this case, Preston v. Duffy, No. 97-1087-B (Plymouth Superior Ct. 1997). "In Massachusetts, the merger doctrine is undeniably favored. The merger doctrine has been held to apply in nearly every circumstance where a landowner has it within his or her power to extinguish or diminish a zoning non-conformity by combining two contiguous lots." Id at 4, citing Planning Board of Norwell v. Serena, 27 Mass. App. Ct. 689 (1989)) and ruled that nonconforming lots previously afforded the single lot protections, when purchased by one owner, merge automatically, even though as single lots, they were protected by statute. "Because the zoning changes had already taken place at the time the plaintiff bought her lots, there is no equitable basis for her claim that she is entitled to a building permit for one of her lots without the other." Preston v. Board of Appeals of Hull, 51 Mass. App. Ct. 236 (2001), citing Asack v. Board of Appeals of Westwood, 47 Mass. App. Ct. 733 (1999). See also Heavey v. Board of Appeals of Chatham, 58 Mass. App. Ct. 401, 404 (2003). "Several decisions point out that a landowner has an obligation to avoid or minimize the creation of a nonconformity," citing Planning Bd. of Norwell v. Serena, 27 Mass. App. Ct. 689, 691 (1989).

[32] Thus, in referring to the protective aspects of the Orleans zoning bylaw preserving the buildability of common lots even where their zoning protections under the Zoning Act had expired, the Court wrote, "Provisions of this type are obviously intended to avoid the application of the general principle that adjacent lots in common ownership will normally be treated as a single lot for zoning purposes so as to minimize nonconformities with the dimensional requirements of the zoning bylaw or ordinance." Seltzer v. Board of Appeals of Orleans, 24 Mass. App. Ct. 521, 523 (1987), citing over ten similarly decided cases. See also Soucy v. Movalli, No. 00-1138-B (Essex Superior Ct. 2000), where the Court noted, "Because lots E and F are adjoining parcels which are held in

§ 5.10[2][b][v] Preliminary Plan

"If a definitive plan, or a preliminary plan followed within seven months by a definitive plan, is submitted to a planning board for approval under the subdivision control law, and written notice of such submission has been given to the city or town clerk before the effective date of the ordinance or bylaw, the land shown on such plan shall be governed by the applicable provisions of the zoning ordinance or bylaw, if any, in effect at the time of the first such submission while such plan or plans are being processed under the subdivision control law, and, if such definitive plan or amendment thereof is finally approved, for eight years from the date of the endorsement of such approval..."[33]

The preliminary plan and definitive plan protections should be reviewed together, as the benefits of the preliminary plan protections are limited to seven months if the preliminary plan is not followed by a properly submitted definitive plan. The details of the definitive plan protections are discussed below.

As discussed previously, the effective date of a zoning change is the date that the legislature votes the zoning change and not the date the change was first advertised for a public hearing. Thus the freeze protections afforded a preliminary plan filing accrue when the plan is first filed[34] and the filing need only occur prior to the effective date of the zoning change.[35]

---

common ownership, they are considered one lot for the purposes of zoning." *Id.* at 7, *citing* Heald v. Zoning Board of Appeals of Greenfield, 7 Mass. App. Ct. 286 (1979).

The Appeals Court applied the merger theory where the owner of four contiguous, undersized and unprotected lots sought to combine the four lots into two, each with less area than the minimum required by the current zoning bylaw. The Court rejected the combination, citing the intent and purpose of the Zoning Act to minimize nonconformities. "Their attempt to create two undersized lots, however, runs contrary to a long line of cases standing for the principle that landowners may not create dimensional nonconformity if the use of adjoining land they own avoid or diminish the nonconformity." Burke v. Zoning Board of Appeals of Harwich, 38 Mass. App. Ct. 957, 958–960 (1995), *citing* Vetter v. Zoning Board of Appeals of Attleboro, 330 Mass. 628 (1953) and others. The Court stated that the statute would allow, however, the combination of all four of the lots into one undersized, but protected lot. *Citing* Vassalotti v. Board of Appeals of Sudbury, 348 Mass. 658 (1965), the Court wrote: "...it is open to the Toppis to combine their four lots and to produce one nonconforming grandfathered lot..." Burke, 38 Mass. App. Ct. 957, at 958.

[33] G.L. c. 40A, § 6.

[34] "The proposed bylaw was not in effect when the plaintiff's preliminary plan was submitted since it had not been adopted by the town meeting... It was therefore error to disapprove the plan on the ground that it did not conform to the provisions of that bylaw. The plaintiff was entitled to a decision governed by the zoning bylaw then in force." Ward & Johnson, Inc. v. Planning Board of Whitman, 343 Mass. 466, 467 (1962).

[35] *See*, for example, Chira v. Planning Board of Tisbury, 3 Mass. App. Ct. 433 (1975), decided under the predecessor to the current Zoning Act. "The trial judge ruled that the...plans were

There is no provision for appealing the denial of a preliminary plan, nor does an appellate right accrue if the planning board fails to act on a preliminary plan within the time period specified by statute.[36]

The definition of a preliminary plan and the requirements a city or town may impose upon a preliminary plan submission are specified in the Subdivision Control Law, G.L. c. 41, § 81-L. These requirements are specific and narrow[37] and it is clear that the legislature intended to limit the number of obstacles that can be imposed on the filing of a preliminary plan.[38]

§ 5.10[2][b][vi]　Definitive Plan

"If a definitive plan, or a preliminary plan followed within seven months by a definitive plan, is submitted to a planning board for approval under the subdivision control law, and written notice of such submission has been given to the city or town clerk before the effective date of the ordinance or bylaw, the land shown on such plan shall be governed by the applicable provisions of the zoning ordinance or bylaw, if any, in effect at the time of the first such submission while such plan or plans are being processed under the subdivision control law, and, if such definitive plan or amendment thereof is finally approved, for eight years from the date of the endorsement of such approval..."[39]

The definitive plan protection provides the most comprehensive vested rights protection afforded landowners by the Zoning Act. A properly filed definitive plan

---

governed by the zoning bylaw as in effect before its 1973 amendment...He was correct in so ruling." 3 Mass. App. Ct. 433, at 436–437.

[36] *See* Livoli v. Planning Board of Marlborough, 347 Mass. 330 (1963). "The purpose of these provisions is plain. They are designed to give an applicant who has filed a preliminary plan the benefit of subdivision control regulations and zoning ordinances that were in effect at the time the preliminary plan was filed, and he was not to lose these rights by a disapproval of the preliminary plan. The power to disapprove a preliminary plan was to have no effect on such rights..." 347 Mass. 330, at 335.

[37] "Preliminary plan' shall mean a plan of a proposed subdivision or resubdivision of land drawn on tracing paper...showing (a) the subdivision name, boundaries, north point, date, scale, legend and title "Preliminary Plan;"...(e) the proposed system of drainage, including adjacent existing natural waterways, in a general manner; (f) the approximate boundary lines of proposed lots, with approximate areas and dimensions;..(h) and the topography of the land in a general manner." G.L. c. 41, § 81-L.

[38] "There is no right to refuse to receive a definitive plan submitted properly...merely because a preliminary plan...is disapproved...None of the defects mentioned in the board's disapproval of the plan is sufficient to place that plan outside the definition set forth in Section 81-L, and most of them do not merit discussion." Livoli, Inc. v. Planning Board of Marlborough, 347 Mass. 330, 336 (1964).

[39] G.L. c. 40A, § 6.

provides protection from all zoning changes affecting the land for eight years from the date the definitive plan was endorsed by the planning board. The protection accrues when the plan is properly filed with the planning board and city or town clerk.[40]

A key issue relating to definitive plan protection is the meaning of the words "the land shown on the plan" contained within the statute. The Supreme Judicial Court recently resolved this often-debated phrase previously a source of conflicting court decisions and application at the local level.[41]

The meaning of the words "land shown on the plan" the Court concluded, are exact.[42]

The statute protects the land delineated on the plan, not the plan itself. Thus a definitive plan filed prior to the effective date of the zoning change (or a preliminary plan filed prior to the effective date of the zoning change if the definitive plan is filed within seven months) that illustrates a fourteen lot subdivision protects the land shown on the four corners of the plan, regardless of the number or configuration of the lots shown on the filed plan. The plan can be altered, amended, revised and reconfigured without jeopardizing the landowner's protections afforded by statute.[43]

---

[40] "[the statute] operates prospectively in that it directs planning boards thereafter to approve or disapprove subdivision plans in the light of the zoning bylaw in effect at the time of filing the plan rather than the bylaw in effect when the planning board makes its decision." Doliner v. Planning Board of Millis, 349 Mass. 691, 697 (1965). Note however, that if the applicant's definitive plan is disapproved and an appeal not taken, the zoning freeze established by the filing of a preliminary plan will expire if the amended definitive plan is not submitted within seven months of the filing of the preliminary plan. Quoting Green v. Board of Appeals of Norwood, 358 Mass. 253, 257 n.4 (1970), the Appeals Court noted "Any definitive plan, filed more than seven months after a preceding preliminary plan, is to be treated as a new plan, which gains protection under [G.L. c. 40A]...only from the date when it is filed and not as of the date of the filing of the preliminary plan." Arenstam v. Planning Board of Tyngsborough, 29 Mass. App. Ct. 314, 317 (1990).

[41] Massachusetts Broken Stone Company v. Town of Weston, 430 Mass. 637 (2000). The case has a fascinating history. The initial Land Court decision held that the correct interpretation of the definitive plan exemption was to protect the land, not the plan. The Appeals Court reversed, concluding that the freeze applied only to the original plan and not an amended plan. (45 Mass. App. Ct. 738 (1998)). The Supreme Judicial Court reversed the Appeals Court, concluding that the Land Court was correct in its read of the statute. "We therefore, conclude that G.L. c. 40A, § 6, ¶ 5 applies to the land." Massachusetts Broken Stone, 430 Mass. at 642. *See also* Cicatelli v. Board of Appeals of Wakefield, 57 Mass. App. Ct. 799, 803 (2003). *But see* DiCarlo v. Ellsworth, 2002 Mass. Super. LEXIS 389, 15 Mass. L. Rep. 295 (Mass. Super. Ct. 2002), where the Court held that notwithstanding *Broken Stone*, the land sought for protection must be the same land as shown on the previously submitted plan. *Id*. at ¶ 5.

[42] "Here the words, 'the land shown' are clear and unambiguous. While the Legislature could have, written "subdivision shown" or "lot shown", it wrote "land shown." 430 Mass. 637, at 640.

[43] "G.L. c. 40A, § 6, ¶ 9, provides that a landowner may submit an amended plan or a further

The eight-year vested rights protection does not commence until the planning board has endorsed the plan. Note that "endorsed" is defined as the act of signing the definitive plan such that the plan can be recorded at the registry of deeds.[44]

Thus, "endorsed" must be distinguished from "approved." The plan is "approved" by the planning board, typically with conditions, upon a vote by the planning board within the statutory period. The plan cannot be endorsed, however, until the twenty-day appeal period has expired.[45]

The relevance of this distinction is that the eight-year protection, particularly if the definitive plan was preceded by a preliminary plan, is far greater than eight years. As the eight years does not commence until the plan is endorsed, and the actual endorsement often occurs well after the expiration of the twenty-day appeal period,[46] the land shown on the definitive plan filed prior to the zoning change will be protected for an extremely long period of time.[47]

---

subdivision of all or part of the land at any time after an initial filing, and that the later submission will not constitute a waiver of a zoning freeze secured when a plan was filed initially, nor will it extend the freeze." Heritage Park Development Corporation v. Town of Southbridge, 424 Mass. 71, 75 n.6 (1997).

[44] The Subdivision Control Law, G.L. c. 41, § 81-X establishes the requirements for recording a subdivision plan at the registry of deeds. The statute provides for two alternatives to recording subdivision plans, the first requiring the planning board's endorsement and the second requiring a certificate from the city or town clerk that the planning board failed to act within the statutory time period, resulting in the constructive approval of the plan.

[45] "In case of approval of a plan by action of the planning board, after expiration of twenty days without notice of appeal to the superior court, or if appeal has been taken after the entry of a final decree of the court sustaining the approval of such plan, the planning board shall cause to be made upon the plan a written endorsement of its approval." G.L. c. 41, § 81-V.

[46] In practice, once the plan has been approved and the appeal period expired, the successful applicant has the luxury of not pressuring the planning board for its endorsement. As the planning board may not endorse the plan until the applicant has provided one of the four surety guarantees required by G.L. c. 41, § 81-U, the applicant is under no pressure (other than market considerations) to move the process forward. Once endorsed, however, the plan must be filed with the registry of deeds within six months. G.L. c. 41, § 81-X. Note, however, that the planning board could include within its rules and regulations and as a condition of definitive plan approval, the requirement that the plan be submitted for endorsement no later than a specified number of days (e.g., 30) following the expiration of the appeal period.

[47] An interesting question is whether the eight-year protection can ever be removed—taken away—by a subsequent action of the planning board. Not surprisingly, the Court has said "no." In Heritage Park Development Corporation v. Town of Southbridge, 424 Mass. 71 (1997), the Supreme Judicial Court reviewed a fact pattern where the definitive plan approval was rescinded due to the failure of the applicant to complete specific road and infrastructure improvements by a specific date. The Court ruled that this type of automatic rescission or a rescission voted by a planning board under G.L. c. 41, § 81-W, does not serve to terminate grandfather protections authorized by zoning. "We caution against confusing the rights and obligations of a planning board under the subdivision control law and its rights and obligations under the zoning laws. Whatever subdivision control the

Despite the broad and extended protections afforded to definitive and preliminary plan filings, there are a handful of cases discussing the disposition of lots within a definitive plan that did not obtain building permits within the freeze period.

Not surprisingly and consistent with the discussion in Section 5.10[2][b][iv], above, the Courts have not allowed the "piggybacking" of one protection onto another.[48] Thus, a lot contained within a subdivision that was filed before the effective date of a zoning change will have eight years from the date of the endorsement of the plan to obtain a building permit under the zoning rules in effective at the time of plan submission. The lot will not benefit from, however, single or common lot protections subsequent to the expiration of the definitive plan protections.[49]

§ 5.10[2][b][vii]   Approval Not Required Plan

"When a plan referred to in section eighty-one-P of chapter forty-one has been submitted to a planning board and written notice of such submission has been given to the city or town clerk, the use of the land shown on such plan shall be governed by applicable provisions of the zoning ordinance or bylaw in effect at the time of the submission of such plan while such plan is being processed under the subdivision control law including the time required to pursue or await the determination of an appeal referred to in said section, and for a period of

---

board may exercise cannot operate to deprive Heritage of the zoning protection it secured in 1989." 424 Mass. 71, at 75.

[48] The fact pattern of Wright v. Board of Appeals of Falmouth, 24 Mass. App. Ct. 409 (1987), provides an excellent example of a landowner who failed to take advantage of the definitive plan protection and whose attempt at checkerboarding the lots into a single ownership pattern was rejected. The issue in *Wright*, as well as in all the fact patterns presented above and below, is the status of the lot prior to the zoning change making it nonconforming. If the lot was in single ownership at the date of the zoning change, it will be entitled to the protections discussed in Section 5.10[2][b][iv] above. So too with common lots; they will be entitled to the protection discussed in Section 5.10[2][b][iii] above. Lots shown on definitive and preliminary plans are similarly treated. Thus in *Wright*, the Court looked to the status of the lots when they became nonconforming by virtue of the town's downzoning. As the lots were all held in common ownership, the Court refused to extend the definitive plan protection any further (the protections in effect when the plan was submitted was seven years, revised to eight years by the Legislature in 1982). "As of the date of each of these lot size increases, all the lots shown on the subdivision plan were still owned by W&J...The new c. 40A, § 6 thus affords each of the plaintiffs no protection from the present zoning bylaw lot size requirements." 24 Mass. App. Ct. 409, at 415. *See also* Tsagronis v. Board of Appeals of Wareham, 415 Mass. 329 (1992), where the Supreme Judicial Court concluded that the zoning freeze protections afforded a plan approved in the 1970s were no longer applicable to a lot that had not obtained a building permit during the freeze period.

[49] Note that the zoning ordinance or bylaw could provide "piggy-back" protection if the city or town choose to authorize such protection. *See* Lee v. Board of Appeals of Harwich, 11 Mass. App. Ct. 148 (1981).

three years from the date of endorsement by the planning board that approval under the subdivision control law is not required, or words of similar import."[50]

While the filing of a definitive plan provides broad and comprehensive protections against changes to zoning affecting both use and dimension, the approval not required plan provides protection against changes to *use* only, and for a period limited to three years from the date of endorsement of the plan.

This so-called "ANR use freeze" raises several issues.

First, defining ANR plans, or defining what is not an ANR plan, remain the "secret" province of planning boards. Few individuals outside of planning boards understand the nuances of ANR plans and the mechanics of plan filing. The fact that only planning boards may endorse the plan, but the board of appeals and building department often has ultimate review authority over the land shown on the plan, argues for a more comprehensive discussion regarding the impact of ANR endorsement throughout the community.

An approval not required plan is the statutory opposite of a subdivision plan. As the statute does not define ANR plans, we are left to assume, that a plan that does not constitute a subdivision, must therefore, be an ANR.

While the ANR plan is entitled to use protection only, the subdivision plan is entitled to the broad protections discussed above.

Second, while the statute clearly protects the use of the land from a zoning change for three years, at issue is whether cities and towns can impose a dimensional change upon the land?

Not surprisingly, the courts have ruled that a de facto denial of a use protected by an ANR plan through increased dimensional requirements violates the spirit and intent of the use protection. Thus if a use is protected (e.g. a commercial use in a newly adopted residential district), the city cannot prohibit the use through increasing dimensional requirements (e.g. setbacks) such that development of the use is impossible.[51]

---

[50] G.L. c. 40A, § 6.

[51] An interesting and unsettled question is whether the ANR endorsement protects a use previously allowed by right from a requirement to obtain a special permit. In Samson v. San-Land Development Corporation, 17 Mass. App. Ct. 977 (1984), the Appeals Court ruled that the use was protected from a special permit requirement. "...the statutory protection extends to San-Land, and it is not required to seek a special permit." 17 Mass. App. Ct. 977, at 979. *See also* Miller v. Board of Appeals of Canton, 8 Mass. App. Ct. 923 (1979). "The plaintiffs' sole contention is that [G.L. c. 40A, § 6] gives its three-year use protection only to uses which were permitted as of right before a zoning change and not to those which were subject to a special permit. That contention finds no support in the language [of the statute]." 8 Mass. App. Ct. 923, at 923. However, in Cape Ann

Third, can a planning board refuse to endorse an approval not required plan if the plan does not depict new lots or ways?

The answer to this question remains unsettled. On one hand, a planning board must endorse a plan "approval not required" if the plan does not constitute a subdivision.

However, is the board required to endorse the plan if it shows neither a subdivision nor an ANR?

This latter possibility is often referred to as a "surveyor's certificate;" the Subdivision Control Law's provision for the recording of a plan of land that does not show "new lot lines or ways." Thus, a plan of land that constitutes neither an ANR nor a subdivision can be recorded at the Registry of Deeds without granting the three year use freeze afforded to ANR plans. At issue is whether the planning board must endorse a plan as "approval not required" where no subdivision of land is shown.

Many have argued that planning board endorsement of a surveyor's certificate plan (often referred to as a "perimeter plan") cannot be withheld. This argument holds that the planning board must determine if the plan is a subdivision and if it is not, the plan must receive ANR endorsement.

This position cites cases wherein the Appeals and Supreme Judicial Court have upheld the endorsement of perimeter plans and concludes that the freeze protection of G.L. c. 40A, § 6 must therefore apply.[52] However, each of these cases involves

---

Development Corp. v. City of Gloucester, 371 Mass. 19 (1976), the Supreme Judicial Court held that the ANR use freeze did not protect the landowner from the requirement that a special permit be obtained for the protected use. The Court warned however, that the City could not vitiate the use protection by denying the special permit. "But, the city council may not decline to grant a special permit for the reason, in whole or in part, that the locus will be used for center purposes. Section 7A protects that use, and the protection of Section 7A may not be eroded by the denial of a special permit for that use when the reason for that denial is the proposed protected use." 371 Mass. 19, at 24. Another difficult question is, "what dimensional rules should apply to an ANR plan that protects a use for which no dimensional requirements are included within the zoning ordinance or bylaw?" was discussed in Perry v. Building Inspector of Nantucket, 4 Mass. App. Ct. 467 (1976). The Appeals Court's answer leaves room for interpretation. "We hold…that…a reasonable accommodation must be made, applying either the intensity regulations applicable to a related use within the zone, or, alternatively, applying the intensity regulations which would apply to the protected use in a zone where that use is permitted. No hard and fast rule can be laid down. The reasonableness of the accommodation will depend on the facts of each case. "Zoning bylaws must be construed reasonably." 4 Mass. App. Ct. 467, at 472, *quoting* Green v. Board of Appeals of Norwood, 358 Mass. 253, 258 (1970).

[52] There are three cases relied upon by those claiming that planning boards must endorse perimeter plans. *See*, for example, Cape Ann Development Corp. v. City of Gloucester, 371 Mass. 19 (1976), Wolk v. Planning Board of Stoughton, 4 Mass. App. Ct. 812 (1976), and Samson v.

the planning board's voluntary action to endorse the plan (or have the city clerk endorse the plan for the planning board's failure to act in the required time period).

The issue is not whether a planning board *may* endorse a perimeter plan and thus provide use protection, but rather whether the board *must* endorse the plan.[53] Some have taken the position, therefore, that the planning board may properly refuse to endorse a perimeter plan if the plan does not show any new lot lines or ways.[54]

Finally, the Courts have rejected "piggybacking" of the ANR protection with the protections discussed above. Thus, the filing of an ANR will serve to freeze the use of the land allowed by the zoning in effect when the plan was filed, but that freeze cannot later be extended or expanded by the filing of either another ANR plan[55] or a definitive plan.[56]

San-Land Development Corporation, 17 Mass. App. Ct. 977 (1984). In each case, the applicant received the use protections of the statute by filing a perimeter plan. In none of these three cases was the Court confronted with the issue of planning board refusal to endorse the plan as a statutorily-provided alternative (G.L. c. 41, § 81-X) existed.

[53] A 1991 Land Court decision was explicit. "Nothing in the statute requires the conclusion that only divisions of land which are deemed by virtue of the provisions of G.L. c. 41, § 81-L not to constitute a subdivision were entitled to such an endorsement. The plain language says otherwise and as it presently reads, a perimeter plan must be endorsed by the Board. Costello v. Preston, Misc. No. 152765, p.2 (Land Court 1991).

A related issue, addressed by the Appeals Court, is whether the purpose of the ANR application is relevant. In other words, can an applicant file for ANR endorsement simply to obtain the use freeze offered by the statute? The Court said "yes." In addition, the Court reads the ANR protections as afforded to the land shown on the plan regardless of whether the plan is ever recorded at the Registry of Deeds. "...nothing in G.L. c. 40A, § 6, ¶ 6, requires recording of the plan as a prerequisite for a freeze. Only submission to the planning board and endorsement are referred to in the statute as prerequisites. Moreover, if a purpose such as Price's would disqualify one from receiving ANR endorsement, the planning board would frequently be called upon to consider evidence of the intent of the person submitting a plan." Long v. Board of Appeals of Falmouth, 32 Mass. App. Ct. 232, 235 (1992). *See also* Kelly v. Planning Board of Weston, Misc. No. 162655 (Massachusetts Land Court 1993), where the Court, *citing Long*, and referring to ANR plans noted, "Subsequent recording of the endorsed plan is not required, however, for the landowner to benefit by the three year freeze...Thus a plan meeting the basic requirements...is entitled to Board endorsement even if the sole motivation behind its submission is to obtain the limited three year freeze..." *Id.* at ¶ 6.

[54] As there is no explicit appellate case law on this issue, it is recommended that planning boards seek the advice of counsel before acting on a perimeter plan. Also, the ability to transform a perimeter plan parcel into a qualifying ANR requires merely the creation of a new lot line, regardless of the size. Thus a landowner motivated to obtain the ANR use freeze can readily create a plan requiring endorsement. However, where the applicant has filed a plan that could otherwise be recorded without benefit of the three-year use freeze, the board should at least discuss whether it wants to provide the plan with ANR endorsement and the accompanying use protections.

[55] "...I find and rule that the Board was not required to endorse a plan otherwise entitled to an ANR endorsement where the identical plan previously had been similarly endorsed. If the Board had so elected to endorse the plan, it would not have extended the then existing three year freeze for an

§ 5.10[2][b][viii]   Vested Rights, the Martha's Vineyard, and the Cape Cod Commission Acts

For the 21 communities on Martha's Vineyard and Cape Cod, the vested rights protections of G.L. c. 40A, § 6 may be modified and even potentially eliminated through the provisions of the Martha's Vineyard Commission Act[57] and the Cape Cod Commission Act.[58]

The Martha's Vineyard Commission and the Cape Cod Commission administer these statutes, respectively. These two regional planning agencies are unique in the Commonwealth because in addition to their planning responsibilities, each agency has regulatory authority to review and permit land developments of various sizes and impacts.

Their regulatory authority includes both the review of individual projects, known as Developments of Regional Impact ("DRIs") and regulation on a district-wide basis, through Districts of Critical Planning Concern ("DCPCs"). Through both DRI review and the creation of DCPCs, grandfathering may be reduced or eliminated if necessary to advance regional planning goals.

The Supreme Judicial Court addressed the impact of the regional statutes on the protections provided by the predecessor to G.L. c. 40A, § 6 in the decision of *Island Properties Inc., Trustee v. Martha's Vineyard Commission.*[59]

In *Island Properties*, the property owner obtained definitive subdivision approval in June of 1974. During the seven-year protection period provided under G.L. c. 40A, § 6, the Martha's Vineyard Commission approved a DCPC with DCPC implementing regulations that were more stringent than the regulations that led to the 1974 subdivision approval. As a result, the property owner brought suit seeking to assert its rights to construct under the 1974 approved plan.

Simply stated, the Court found that:

> "approval of the plan, while satisfying c. 41, does not obviate the need for compliance with regulations and procedures under [the Martha's Vineyard

---

additional three year period." Kelly v. Planning Board of Weston, Misc. No 162655, 7 (Land Court 1993).

  56 "There is no merit in the plaintiff's contention that the zoning bylaw amendment was rendered inapplicable to his subdivision plans…as we can discern no basis in the language or history…for permitting the two zoning "freeze" provisions in its first and second paragraphs to be combined in the "piggy-back" fashion attempted by the plaintiff." Wolk v. Planning Board of Stoughton, 4 Mass. App. Ct. 812 (1976).

  57 *See* Martha's Vineyard Commission Act, 1975 Mass. Acts Chapter 808, as amended.

  58 *See* Cape Cod Commission Act, 1989 Mass. Acts Chapter 716, as amended.

  59 372 Mass. 216 (1974).

Commission Act]."[60]

In reaching this holding, the court noted that the Martha's Vineyard Commission is entrusted with protection of regional resources

> "which, the Legislature could believe, the town themselves had not and would not severally bring to bear."[61]

The court further stated that the Martha's Vineyard Commission Act "is a polar opposite" from subsequent local enactments contemplated by section 6 and went on to state

> "it might be thought a perverse anomaly if ... regional purposes could be thwarted, as to undeveloped resources requiring CPC or DRI status, by freezing and preserving for seven years preexisting local bylaws with narrow orientation."[62]

The Cape Cod Commission Act contains similar, and often duplicate, language and although the Cape Cod Commission Act has not been court tested in this regard, a similar outcome seems likely.

Because of the two Acts, vested rights protection on Martha's Vineyard and Cape Cod can be very different from vested rights protection elsewhere in the Commonwealth. On the Vineyard and Cape Cod, by virtue of both DCPC and DRI designation, the protections afforded by G.L. c. 40A, § 6 may not be available.

For example, and as discussed above, a new DCPC designation allows for the development of rules and regulations to govern land development within the District. These rules—implementing regulations—once adopted may limit or even remove development rights that predated the designation. Under the traditional scheme in Massachusetts, a landowner would likely be protected from these new regulations through one of the seven protections discussed above. Under the Commission Act's, however, the protections of G.L. c. 40A, § 6 do not necessarily apply and the landowner may be required to adhere to the newly adopted regulations.

For a complete discussion of the Martha's Vineyard and Cape Cod Commission Acts, or the applicability of G.L. c. 40A, § 6 on the Vineyard or Cape Cod, contact the respective Commissions.

---

[60] Island Properties Inc., Trustee v. Martha's Vineyard Commission, 372 Mass. 216, at 232.

[61] 372 Mass. 216, at 229.

[62] 372 Mass. 216, at 229.

§ 5.11   Nonconforming Uses and Structures

§ 5.11[1]   Introduction

The existence of uses or structures that are "nonconforming" to current zoning requirements raises three important questions. First, can the municipality require the use or structure to become "conforming" to current requirements? Second, can the municipality "freeze" the current use or structure such that the nonconformity does not increase? Third, what controls—constraints—can be placed on the use or structure to ensure that permissible extensions or alterations are consistent with the city or town's comprehensive plan and/or in concert with neighborhood trends and the desires of community residents?

The presence of nonconforming uses and structures has concerned cities and towns throughout the nation since zoning was first adopted. The simple fact is that every time a local government alters its zoning code, it likely creates a nonconforming use or structure or both.

Early case law suggested that local governments could "eradicate" noncon-forming uses and structures by applying newly adopted zoning regulations retro-actively.[1] This position slowly eroded, however. Today, virtually all preexisting nonconforming uses and structures have a protected, vested right to continue and cannot be the subject to retroactive zoning provisions.

Most states, Massachusetts included, have taken the position that nonconforming uses and structures, despite their protected status, are to be "tolerated" and proposed expansions, alterations or changes should be carefully reviewed and monitored. The theoretical support for this position is that the nonconforming use or structure does not comport with the city or town comprehensive plan.[2] As it is inconsistent

---

[1] *See*, for example, Hadacheck v. Sebastian, 239 U.S. 394 (1915), where the U.S Supreme Court held that a preexisting brickyard could be required to cease operation. Many early zoning cases equated preexisting nonconforming uses and structures with nuisances, thus allowing the munici-pality to remove the use without having to pay compensation. (One of the few examples of where government can destroy private property and not be required to compensate the landowner is where government seeks to preclude a public nuisance. *See* Lucas v. South Carolina Coastal Council, 505 U.S. 1003 (1992)). Similar attempts to regulate preexisting uses and structures took place in New Orleans in 1900 and Nevada in 1980 (regulation of prostitution) and Des Moines in 1916 (regulation of smoke stack emissions).

[2] Although a full discussion is beyond the scope of this Chapter, it is interesting to note that comprehensive planning in Massachusetts has a checkered history. While G.L. c. 41, § 81-D requires a planning board to prepare a "master plan", the statute neither requires nor encourages the plan to be consistent with local rules and regulations such as zoning, subdivision control, health or wetlands protection regulations. This failure to require consistency between planning and zoning puts Massachusetts in the dubious category of a "non-plan" state, a classification shared by only one other New England state (Connecticut). Thus states that have had far less progressive political

with the comprehensive plan, any change creating a further inconsistency should be discouraged.[3]

Given their protected status, the issue facing landowners and local governments alike is the future of these preexisting uses and structures. Determining the disposition of these uses and structures is complicated by an extremely confusing and awkwardly drafted section of G.L. c. 40A, § 6. This lengthy garbling of words has, however, been unraveled by the courts, particularly the Appeals Court over the past 25 years. We now have, fortunately, several clear rules and tests with which landowners and reviewing boards and agencies can intelligibly discuss the future of nonconforming uses and structures. These rules and tests are discussed in detail below.

§ 5.11[2]   What are Nonconforming Uses and Structures?

"Except as hereinafter provided, a zoning ordinance or bylaw shall not apply to structures or uses lawfully begun, or to a building or special permit issued before the first publication of notice of the public hearing on such ordinance or bylaw required by section five…"[4]

Despite the precise language of the statute, several threshold questions haunt landowners and regulatory boards alike. These questions include:

1. Can a use or structure commenced or built "unlawfully" ever achieve nonconforming status?
2. Can a use or structure that has received a variance achieve nonconforming status?
3. Can land that has been partially subject to an eminent domain taking become lawfully nonconforming?
4. Given questions 1 and 2, above, exactly when does a preexisting use or structure become lawfully nonconforming?

Question 1: Can a use or structure commenced or built "unlawfully" ever achieve nonconforming status?

No. The commencement of an unlawful use or construction transforms what might have otherwise been a lawful use or structure into an unlawful use or

---

history are well ahead of Massachusetts in terms of planning and land use visioning; a sad fact given the enormous rate at which undeveloped land is being consumed in the Commonwealth.

[3] "The view that has been followed is that a few nonconforming buildings and uses if allowed to continue will not be a substantial injury to a community if only such nonconforming buildings are not allowed to multiply where they are harmful or improper. Zoning has sought to safeguard the future, in the expectation that time will repair the mistakes of the past." Edward M. Basset, Zoning, p.115–116 (1936).

[4]   G.L. c. 40A, § 6.

structure. More importantly for the present discussion however, the opportunities to expand or alter the use or structure provided by G.L. c. 40A, § 6 (discussed below) are not available to these *unlawful* uses or structures.[5]

Question 2: Does a use or structure that has been granted a variance achieve nonconforming status?

No. The use or structure must be lawfully preexisting as a nonconforming use or structure. The Appeals Court held that where a series of variances had been granted for specific uses and structures, the uses and structures were not entitled to nonconforming status.[6] This holding is consistent with the strict interpretation of G.L. c. 40A, § 10 (*See* Section 5.7 regarding variances) set forth by the Massachusetts courts.[7]

Question 3: Can land that has been partially subject to an eminent domain taking become lawfully nonconforming?

The question raises a rare, but possible third means[8] by which a use or structure can become nonconforming: a governmental action such as an eminent domain taking.

Interestingly, despite decades of the use of eminent domain in Massachusetts,

---

[5] "The plaintiffs have the burden of showing that they are entitled to the protection of the statute...They must show, first, that the prior use was lawful." Hall v. Zoning Board of Appeals of Edgartown, 28 Mass. App. Ct. 249 (1990), *citing* Cape Resort Hotels, Inc. v. Alcoholic Licensing Bd. of Falmouth, 385 Mass. 205, 223 n.11 and Selectmen of Wrentham v. Monson, 355 Mass. 715, 716 (1969).

Note, however, that a use can be a valid nonconforming use (or structure) even though it may not have all required licenses or permits for operation. "A valid nonconforming use is not unlawful by failure to possess requisite government approval, provided that such approval can be easily obtained. Derby Refining Company v. City of Chelsea, 407 Mass. 703, 711(1990). *But see* Whitten v. Board of Appeals of Woburn, 38 Mass. App. Ct. 949 (1995), where the Appeals Court stated that the possession of a license or permit does not necessarily mean that the use or structure is a lawful nonconforming use or structure. "A licensed use of property is not axiomatically a lawful use of property for zoning purposes." 38 Mass. App. Ct. 949, at 950.

[6] "...a use achieves the status of nonconformity conformity for statutory purposes if it precedes the coming into being of the regulation which prohibits it...It came about, not through preexisting right, deprivation of which might raise constitutional questions, but through the after-the-fact dispensation of a variance...the question is not merely whether the use is lawful but how and when its became lawful." Mendes v. Board of Appeals of Barnstable, 28 Mass. App. Ct. 527, 529–531 (1990). *See also* Barron Chevrolet, Inc. v. Danvers, 419 Mass. 404 (1995). "Such a use cannot be a prior nonconforming use because, by definition, a variance was required and it therefore was not allowed by right." 419 Mass. 404, at 408.

[7] See Chapter 5 for a detailed discussion of the law of variances in the Commonwealth.

[8] The first possibility is the most common: the use or structure predates a zoning amendment. The second possibility is that the use or structure was made nonconforming through an unlawful means.

there is only one reported case regarding whether a nonconforming "remnant" parcel could be classified as a lawful nonconforming use or structure.[9]

In a related matter, the Court upheld the grant of a variance to a petitioner who lacked requisite frontage due to an eminent domain order by the Metropolitan District Commission. The Court's support for the variance was based upon the fact that the petitioner had neither caused the hardship nor could have anticipated that such hardship would arise.[10]

Question 4: Given questions 1 and 2, above, exactly when does a preexisting use or structure become lawfully nonconforming?

A preexisting use or structure becomes lawfully nonconforming by one of two possible methods.

First, a use or structure becomes a "nonconforming use" or a "nonconforming structure" if it is in existence or lawfully begun, when the first notice of publication for a public hearing on a zoning change, as required by G.L. c. 40A, § 5, has appeared in the local newspaper.[11] (This presumes, of course, that town

---

[9] *See* Helmer v. Town of Billerica, Misc. No. 228924 (Land Court 1997). "...counsel suggested that locus should nonetheless receive protection under § 6 because it was rendered nonconforming by the eminent domain action by the Commonwealth, and not by any voluntary conveyance...However, plaintiff cited no authority for this suggestion, and s.6 provides no such protection." *Id.* at p.2. *See also* Bateman v. Board of Appeals of Georgetown, 56 Mass. App. Ct. 236, 241 (2004). In upholding the grant of a variance, the Appeals Court acknowledged that the Commonwealth's taking of a portion of the plaintiff's land rendered it of an unusual shape, providing grounds for variance pursuant to G.L. c. 40A, § 10.

[10] *See* Adams v. Brolly, 46 Mass. App. Ct. 1 (1998). The Appeals Court quoted a 1978 Connecticut case decided on similar grounds. "...surely there is a clear case of uncommon hardship beyond the control of a property owner when the state seeks to condemn a portion of his or her land and thereby render it nonconforming to a minimum area restriction." 46 Mass. App. Ct. 1, at 8, *citing* Smith v. Zoning Board of Appeals of Norwalk, 174 Conn. 323 (1978). Note though, that even the extreme fact pattern of the case—the petitioner land was left in its condition by action of the MDC—failed to find sympathy with the dissenting justice. The dissent's position was that the "creation by conveyance of an unusually shaped, nonconforming parcel under then existing zoning regulations does not entitle one to a variance." 46 Mass. App. Ct. 1, at 7. Thus even an eminent domain action rendering a land parcel or use nonconforming to current standards may not rise to the status of a lawful nonconforming use or structure.

[11] In Tamerlane Realty Trust v. Board of Appeals of Provincetown, 23 Mass. App. Ct. 450 (1987), the Appeals Court concluded: "The nature of the use prevailing when the zoning bylaw took effect is clearly material to the outcome of the case, as it is a key element in the judicial test for determining whether a special permit should be granted in these circumstances." 23 Mass. App. Ct. 450, at 455. At issue are the words "took effect" in the Court's decision. As discussed in detail above, the date of "effectiveness" differs depending upon the breadth of protection afforded the use or structure by the statute. Thus in *Tamerlane*, where the Court was reviewing the protections afforded an existing structure and use that sought to expand, the Court referred to the critical date for determining nonconforming status as the "advertised date", not the date of legislative action (e.g.

meeting, town council or city council adopts the advertised zoning change).

Second, a use or structure becomes nonconforming if the use or structure is (was) in existence or lawfully begun, when the legislature of the city or town adopts the zoning amendment making the use or structure nonconforming.

The distinction between these two possibilities is discussed below.

§ 5.11[2][a]   The Use or Structure is Existing When the First Advertisement Appears

A pre-existing use or structure (one that is either in existence, under construction according to the terms of a validly issued building permit,[12] or permitted to proceed with construction under the terms of a validly issued building or special permit issued before the first advertisement appears[13]) becomes a non-conforming use or structure if it does not conform to the newly advertised zoning amendment and that amendment is ultimately approved[14] by town meeting, town council or city council vote.

§ 5.11[2][b]   The Lot is Existing and Protected *or* an Appropriate Plan has Been Filed Prior to the Legislative Vote on the Zoning Change

As discussed previously, a single lot, common lot, land shown on a preliminary or definitive subdivision plan or land shown on an approval not required plan have each been granted specific protection—vested rights—by G.L. c. 40A, § 6. The statute protects the land from certain zoning changes voted on, and made effective

---

Provincetown town meeting). This should be differentiated from the critical date for determining nonconforming status for several of the other uses or categories of use afforded by G.L. c. 40A, § 6. For example, a lot of record, zoned for single-family use, that complies with the dimensional minimums discussed in Part One, does not become a nonconforming parcel unless and until the legislature votes the zoning change. The first advertised date required by G.L. c. 40A, § 5 does not alter the lot's status, unlike its effect upon a pre-existing structure or use. The explanation requires another look at the "second" protection of G.L. c. 40A, § 6, more fully discussed above.

[12] In this instance, the permit is "in-hand" prior to the first advisement. Note that the permit must have been issued and not merely "applied for."

[13] Note that the building or special permit must be used—activated— within six months of its issuance to obtain the protections under the "old" zoning regulation. G.L. c. 40A, § 6 requires that zoning bylaws and ordinances contain a provision with the following language or effect. "...construction or operations under a building or special permit shall conform to any subsequent amendment of the ordinance or bylaw unless the use or construction is commenced within a period of not more than six months after the issuance of the permit and in cases involving construction, unless such construction is continued through to completion as continuously and expeditiously as is reasonable." G.L. c. 40A, § 6.

[14] Note that the advertisement is only valid for six months. G.L. c. 40A, § 6.

by, legislative action.[15] However, note that in these instances and for these specific protections, it is the legislative action—the city council, town council or town meeting vote—that establishes the effective date of the new zoning ordinance or bylaw. Unlike the discussion above, the first advertisement date has no effect on the lot or the land's conforming status.

For example, an advertised downzoning[16] from 2 units per acre to 1 unit per acre would not make a 30,000 square foot lot, in existence at the time of the advertisement, nonconforming to the advertised bylaw. The 30,000 square foot lot would only become nonconforming upon the bylaw's adoption by town meeting.

Although the time differential between advertisement and legislative vote is often not extensive,[17] the distinction between conforming and nonconforming status is extremely important. As discussed below, a land use or structure only obtains the potential benefits of the G.L. c. 40A, § 6 protections if it is a lawfully existing, nonconforming use or structure.

§ 5.11[3]   The Protections Afforded to Nonconforming Uses and Structures

As noted previously, nonconforming uses and structures must be lawfully in existence as of the first advertised date making them nonconforming to obtain the protections of G.L. c. 40A, § 6. Note also that the protections afforded a nonconforming use or structure "run with the land (or structure)" and not with the owner of the land or structure.[18]

---

[15] Recall that the effective date of a zoning change is the date that the legislature approves the zoning change (e.g. city council, town council or town meeting vote).

[16] "Downzoning" refers to the increase in minimum lot size or other requirements of the zoning bylaw and is used to refer to a rezoning of land from non-residential to residential use. "Upzoning" is the opposite; the reference to a relaxation of minimum requirements or an allowance of more intensive use of land than previously permitted by the zoning ordinance.

[17] While there must be at least 14 days between the advertised date and the public hearing held by the planning board on the zoning change (G.L. c. 40A, §§ 5 and 11), there is no minimum separation between the public hearing and legislative action. Thus it is possible and quite common, for a planning board to advertise for a public hearing to be held only several days prior to the legislative vote. This practice raises other problems however. For example, the planning board is provided 21 days to issue a report to the legislature following the public hearing on the proposed zoning amendment. If there are not twenty-one days between the public hearing and the legislative vote, however, and the planning board chooses not to issue a report, the legislature is precluded from acting on the amendment. This Machiavellian inclusion in G.L. c. 40A, § 5 was held valid by the Supreme Judicial Court in Whittemore v. Town Clerk of Falmouth, 299 Mass. 64 (1937) and can be effectively used, on occasion, by planning boards that seek to preclude legislative action on a petitioned zoning change.

[18] "The right to continue a nonconforming use after adoption of zoning regulations is not personal to the particular owner or occupant on the effective date of the regulation." Revere v. Rowe Contracting Co., 362 Mass. 884, 885 (1972).

A frequent question, however, is whether an unlawfully developed use or structure can obtain the Section 6 protections.

The answer lies in G.L. c. 40A, § 7 and *Lord v. Board of Appeals of Somerset*.[19]

G.L. c. 40A, § 7 provides "amnesty" for two categories of "zoning misbehavior."[20] The first category is a six-year statute of limitations against enforcement of a building permit that was issued, but misused. In this category, for example, a recipient of a lawfully issued building permit constructs a structure in compliance with the permit but such construction is not authorized by the zoning ordinance or bylaw. Construction of a 35-foot structure where the zoning regulations authorized construction of a 30-foot structure is an example.[21]

A second example covered by this category is the abuse of the authorized use granted by the permit. For example, the permit authorizes use or construction of a two family dwelling, but the owner converts the structure into a three family dwelling.

In both examples, enforcement against the misuse (abuse) of the permit is limited to a six-year period, said period commencing at the date of the violation.[22] However, note that in neither case does the use or structure that resulted from the misused (or abused) building permit obtain the status of a nonconforming use or structure. While the statute protects the landowner from enforcement action, it *does not* elevate the status of the use or structure to one of a lawfully pre-existing nonconforming use or structure.

The second category is discussed by G.L. c. 40A, § 7 and *Lord v. Board of Appeals of Somerset*.[23] They involve those instances where a landowner builds a structure not in accordance with the terms of a building permit and/or simply ignores the building permit process and constructs a structure or adds an addition to an existing structure without obtaining a building permit at all. These examples, not surprisingly, are treated far more harshly than the first category discussed previously.

The statute provides protection from enforcement only for *structural* violations

---

[19] 30 Mass. App. Ct. 226 (1991).

[20] *See* Murphy v. Kotlik, 34 Mass. App. Ct. 410, 414 (1993).

[21] "...under the association's view of Section 7, no alteration of or additions to, existing buildings, even those undertaken in accordance with properly issued building permits, would be protected by the Section 7 statute of limitations. This result conflicts with the obvious intent of the Legislature to limit the time within which building permits could be attacked as issued in violation of a zoning regulation." Cape Resort Hotels, Inc. v. Alcoholic Licensing Board of Falmouth, 385 Mass. 205, 218 (1982).

[22] Lord v. Board of Appeals of Somerset, 30 Mass. App. Ct. 226, 227 (1991).

[23] 30 Mass. App. Ct. 226 (1991).

that occurred in the absence of a building permit and only if enforcement is not commenced within ten years from the violation. Clearly absent from the statutory protections is amnesty from any use violations occurring in the absence of a building permit.[24]

§ 5.11[4]   Extensions and Alterations to Nonconforming Uses and Structures

"Preexisting nonconforming structures or uses may be extended or altered, provided, that no such extension or alteration shall be permitted unless there is a finding by the permit granting authority or by the special permit granting authority designated by ordinance or bylaw that such change, extension or alteration shall not be substantially more detrimental than the existing nonconforming use to the neighborhood."[25]

Arguably, the most difficult clause to interpret in the Zoning Act,[26] the above noted sentence raises significant issues of construction and application. The clause is important because the extent to which a preexisting nonconforming use or structure[27] can be extended or altered is a recurring challenge to Boards of Appeals across the state. However, it is rarely addressed in a consistent fashion.

The problem is this. On one hand, the statute specifies that changes or extensions to nonconforming uses and structures be allowed only if they comply with the then current zoning regulations. On the other hand, the statute appears to allow such change or extension provided that the change or extension not be substantially more detrimental to the neighborhood.

---

[24] "The omission of protection for use violations not sanctioned by permit is plain on the face of the statute." Lord v. Board of Appeals of Somerset, 30 Mass. App. Ct. 226, at 227. *See also* Moreis v. Oak Bluffs Board of Appeals, 62 Mass. App. Ct. 53 (2004), "The six-year limitations period in s.7 applies to both structural and use violations authorized by a building permit. However, unlike structural violations for which no permit was obtained (which enjoy a ten-year limitations period), no such protection is afforded use violations unsanctioned by any permit." 62 Mass. App. Ct. 53, at 60, *citing Lord.*

[25] G.L. c. 40A, § 6.

[26] In referring to this portion of Section 6, the Appeals Court wrote, "These are as difficult and infelicitous as other language of the act recently reviewed…" Fitzsimonds v. Board of Appeals of Chatham, 21 Mass. App. Ct. 53, 55–56 (1985).

[27] Note that the statute states that the test governing extension or alteration is whether it will be substantially more detrimental than the existing nonconforming use to the neighborhood. Faced with the question as to what to do about extensions or alterations to nonconforming structures, the Court in Willard v. Board of Appeals of Orleans, 25 Mass. App. Ct. 15 (1987), wrote, "we read the concluding portion of the second sentence of the first paragraph of the present G.L. c. 40A, § 6, as follows: 'shall not be substantially more detrimental than the existing nonconforming structure or use to the neighborhood." 25 Mass. App. Ct. 15, at 21. *See also* Rogel v. Collinson, 54 Mass. App. Ct. 304, 316 (2002).

This ambiguity has been addressed by several relatively recent court decisions, but was most clearly explained by the Appeals Court in 1991.[28] The resulting explanation is straightforward.

The statute creates enabling—permissive—authority with respect to the change or extension of a preexisting nonconforming use or structure. As such, a local government may choose to allow for such changes or extensions by providing specific authority to do so in its zoning ordinance or bylaw.[29] However, the statute does not compel this allowance. A local government may prohibit the change or extension of preexisting nonconforming structures and uses and essentially "freeze" in place these structures and uses for all time.

The Appeals Court left unanswered the question as to an expansion or change to a preexisting nonconforming use or structure where the expansion is conforming to current regulations. For example, a structure may be nonconforming as to sideline setbacks (the building is within ten feet of the sideline, yet the current zoning ordinance requires a twenty five foot setback), but conforming to all other dimensional requirements. At issue is whether the structure can be expanded in size such that the nonconforming setback is not exacerbated and all other setbacks are complied with following the expansion. In other words, can the structure be expanded such that the existing nonconformity is not made worse and no new nonconformities are created?

The answer to this question first requires a review of the previous discussion. As noted above, a municipality can prohibit the expansion or change of a preexisting nonconforming structure or use, period. However, where the local zoning ordinance or bylaw provides for the expansion or change, the expansion or change must comply with the current zoning ordinance or bylaw. Then, the Supreme Judicial Court added, the expansion or change is subject to the "not substantially more detrimental" test of Section 6.[30]

This multi-pronged requirement bears repeating.

---

[28] Blasco v. Board of Appeals of Winchendon, 31 Mass. App. Ct. 32 (1991). *See also* Saffie v. Audy, 13 Mass. L. Rep. 35, 2001 Mass. Super. LEXIS 84, at *10 (Mass. Super. 2001), upholding the City of Lawrence's prohibition on used car lots within the relevant zoning district and the ordinance's impact on a pre-existing commercial use seeking to sell used cars.

[29] "If the law were such that any property owner had the right to change a nonconforming use to any other use so long as the new use was not substantially more detrimental to the neighborhood, nonconforming uses would tend to exist in perpetuity, and any comprehensive municipal plan for regulating uses in particular districts would never fully take effect... .Based on both the legislative history... and the policies underlying it, we resolve the ambiguity in the statue by recognizing the continuing right of a municipality...to regulate or forbid changes in nonconforming uses." Blasco v. Board of Appeals of Winchendon, 31 Mass. App. Ct. 32, at 39.

[30] Rockwood v. Snow Inn Corporation, 409 Mass. 361 (1990).

First, local governments can prohibit the expansion or change of preexisting nonconforming uses and structures.[31] Second, where local zoning allows for expansion or change of preexisting nonconforming uses or structures, the expansion or change must comply with current zoning requirements.[32] Third, if local zoning allows for expansion or change, the newly expanded structure or changed use must be subjected to the test requiring that the expansion or change not be substantially more detrimental than the existing nonconforming use or structure to the neighborhood.[33]

§ 5.11[5]   Extensions and Alterations to Nonconforming Uses and Structures: Signs

Cities and towns may regulate the placement and dimensions of signs and other advertising devices through zoning control, through a general bylaw or ordinance[34]

---

[31] A variation on this prohibition is where the zoning ordinance or bylaw require a Section 6 finding for any change of use to a nonconforming use or structure, even if the new use is one that is allowed by right under the zoning ordinance or bylaw. In Nichols v. Board of Zoning Appeal of Cambridge, 26 Mass. App. Ct. 631 (1988), the Court upheld the City's requirement for a Section 6 finding even though "the footprint of the building has not changed, and there has been no increase in its nonconformity." 26 Mass. App. Ct. 631, at 634.

[32] *See*, for example, Wrona v. Board of Appeals of Pittsfield, 338 Mass. 87 (1958), where the Court ruled that a special permit provision allowing for the expansion of preexisting nonconforming structures could not be used as a substitute for a variance, where the board of appeals sought to grant permission to an extension beyond the minimum zoning setback. "The board could properly have allowed an extension to the nonconforming use up to the setback lines under the exception. However, when it permitted the extension beyond the very precise setback requirements contained in the ordinance it exceeded its authority." 338 Mass. 87, at 89. *See also* Cox v. Board of Appeals of Carver, 42 Mass. App. Ct. 422 (1996), where the Court, similar to the holding in *Wrona*, found that the Section 6 finding of "not substantially more detrimental" is an incorrect test for approving a use or structure that requires a variance. "… absent a variance, Commercial's use of this land for a mobile home park did not meet the 100-acre requirement for a mobile home park under the Carver zoning bylaw. A finding that the extension of the nonconforming use would not be substantially more detrimental to the neighborhood is simply not enough." 42 Mass. App. Ct. 422, at 426.

[33] *See*, for example, McLaughlin v. City of Brockton, 32 Mass. App. Ct. 930 (1992), where the Court ruled that a board of appeals must make a finding as to the impact of a proposed expansion of a preexisting nonconforming use, upon the neighborhood. "An ordinance that permitted an alteration of a nonconforming use in the absence of such a finding would be in violation of the literal mandate of Section 6…We conclude that the board should have an opportunity to reconsider its decision and to make findings…including a specific finding as to whether the plaintiff's altered use is more detrimental to the neighborhood than the protected nonconforming uses of his predecessor." 32 Mass. App. Ct. 930, at 932. The board's decision may permissibly include an analysis of the impact of the requested use but a board may "…not deny a permit simply by conjuring a parade of horribles, particularly when it has the power to prevent them." Britton v. Zoning Board of Appeals of Gloucester, 59 Mass. App. Ct. 68, 75 (2003).

[34] Adopted under the Home Rule Amendment, Mass. Const. Amendment. Art. 2 § 6.

and/or in accordance with G.L. c. 93, § 29.[35] The provisions of G.L. c. 40A, § 6 relating to signs regulated through a zoning ordinance or bylaw was deleted by the Legislature in February 2000.[36]

However, where a local government regulates signs in the zoning ordinance or bylaw, the signs benefit from the protections afforded by G.L. c. 40A, § 6, specifically those discussed in Section 4.0, above. Therefore, and consistent with the prior discussion, a local government may regulate preexisting nonconforming signs such that no alteration, expansion or change to the sign or advertising device would be permissible. Alternatively, the zoning ordinance or bylaw could specify the extent to which preexisting nonconforming signs and advertising devices could be altered or changed.[37] As discussed previously, this type of guidance should prove extremely useful to both an applicant for a sign modification and the board of appeals reviewing the application request.

§ 5.11[6]   Extensions and Alterations to Nonconforming Uses and Structures: The Second "Except" Clause (Single– and Two–Family Residential)

The difficult language of Section 6 with respect to extensions and alterations to nonconforming uses and structures have, unfortunately, been repeated with respect to extensions and alterations to single and two family residential structures—with a twist. The twist lies in the statute's use of the so-called second "except" clause.

> "except where alteration, reconstruction, extension or structural change to a single or two family residential structure does not increase the nonconforming nature of said structure."[38]

Recall that local governments need not authorize the extension or change to nonconforming structures and uses (not applying to single and two family

---

[35] G.L. c. 93, § 29 establishes the "outdoor advertising board" for the Commonwealth and enables cities and towns to regulate signs and billboards not inconsistent with the statute. Note again that regulation of signs and billboards through this statute does not provide the protections afforded G.L. c. 40A, § 6.

[36] St.2000, c. 29, approved February 17, 2000.

[37] *See*, for example, Baron Chevrolet, Inc. v. Town of Danvers, 419 Mass. 404 (1995). In *Baron*, the Court ruled that the town could not prohibit the modification of signs, as the zoning bylaw did not include such a prohibition. As a result, the town was required to apply a Section 6 finding to the sign modifications; an application that the Court ruled did not constitute a "change, extension, reconstructions or alteration…" 419 Mass. 404, at 413. *See also* Strazzulla v. Building Inspector of Wellesley, 357 Mass. 694 (1970). "…we are convinced that Wellesley has the power to specify the conditions necessary for or limitations on changes in a nonconforming sign." 357 Mass. 694, at 697.

[38] G.L. c. 40A, § 6.

structures). However, the ability of local governments to preclude the extension or structural change to nonconforming single and two family residential structures is not clear. At issue is: (1) whether zoning can prohibit the extension or structural change to a nonconforming single and two family residential structure and/or (2) whether zoning can "contain" or "limit" an approved extension or structural change.

Each of these questions is discussed below.

Question 1: Can zoning regulate the extension or structural change to a nonconforming single and two family residential structure?

Yes, but likely only to a limited extent. Whereas the Appeals Court has held that local zoning regulations can prohibit the expansion or alterations of preexisting nonconforming uses,[39] case law over the past 30 years appears to hold that the owner of a preexisting nonconforming single or two family residential structure has, at a minimum, at least the opportunity to make a case before the permit or special permit granting authority[40] that the expansion or alteration will not increase the nonconforming nature of said structure.[41]

In 1991, the Appeals Court, after reviewing prior decisions by the Supreme Judicial Court[42] and its own earlier decisions,[43] established a logical process for reviewing proposed expansions and structural alterations to preexisting nonconforming single and two family residential structures.[44] The Court's decision, although logical, caught many local officials by surprise as it established a procedure that had not been common practice.

At the outset, it is important to stress that the ability to expand or structurally change a nonconforming single or two family residential structure is based on the determination, made by either the permit granting authority or the special permit granting authority, as to the extent of the increase, if any, in the nonconforming

---

[39] Blasco v. Board of Appeals of Winchendon, 31 Mass. App. Ct. 32 (1991).

[40] Note that either the permit granting authority or the special permit granting authority can make a Section 6 finding. "General Laws c. 40A, Section 1A, differentiates between the permit granting authority and the special permit granting authority under the zoning bylaw, the principal distinction being that the latter is the authority that issues special permits...We conclude that G.L. c. 40A, § 6, authorizes, but does not require, a municipality to choose a special permit application as the procedure for extension or alteration of a nonconforming use." Shrewsbury Edgemere Associates, Limited Partnership v. Board of Appeals of Shrewsbury, 409 Mass. 317, 321–322 (1990).

[41] Extensions or structural changes could occur in an endless variety of ways including increasing the height or width of the structure, and adding extensions that protrude from the structure (e.g. a greenhouse or a deck).

[42] Rockwood v. Snow Inn Corp., 409 Mass. 361 (1991).

[43] See especially Willard v. Board of Appeals of Orleans, 25 Mass. App. Ct. 15 (1987).

[44] Goldhirsh v. McNear, 32 Mass. App. Ct. 455 (1991).

nature of the single or two family residential structure.[45]

A nonconforming single or two family residential structure can expand or be structurally changed according to the following rules:

First, an application must be made to the *board of appeals*[46] to expand or change the structure. While many jurisdictions require that applications first be made to the building inspector or building department, both the statute and resulting case law require the application to be made to the board of appeals.

Second, the board of appeals must make a determination as to "the particular respect or respects in which the existing structure does not conform to the requirements of the present bylaw."[47] Note again, that the board of appeals must make this determination. While the board may certainly rely on advice and counsel from the building department and officials, the determination has been delegated to the board.[48]

Third, "should the board conclude that there will be no intensification or addition, the applicant will be entitled to the issuance of a special permit."[49] This determination is a critically important step in the evolution of nonconforming single and two family residential structures. If at this step in the process, the board determines that the proposed alteration will not intensify the preexisting nonconformity, the court has ruled that the permit (or special permit) should be granted. Thus as a threshold determination, the board holds the power to allow expansions of single and two family nonconforming structures without subjecting these expansions to the test discussed in step four and five, below.[50]

---

[45] "...the question is whether the proposed changes to the nonconforming residential structure will increase its nonconforming nature. 32 Mass. App. Ct. 455, at 459.

[46] Acting either as the permit granting authority or the special permit granting authority.

[47] Willard v. Board of Appeals of Orleans, 25 Mass. App. Ct. 15, 21 (1987).

[48] "After Goldhirsh v. McNear, 32 Mass. App. Ct. 455 (1992), if proposed alterations affect the nonconforming aspect of a lawfully nonconforming single or two family structure, the determination that the alterations 'do not increase the nonconforming nature of said structure' can no longer be left to the zoning enforcement officer even if the alterations are entirely confined within the existing building envelope." Serieka v. Town of Winchester Board of Zoning Appeals, Misc. Case No. 183095 (Land Court 1993).

[49] *See* Serieka v. Town of Winchester Board of Zoning Appeals, Misc. Case No. 183095 (Land Court 1993. An interesting question is why, where the board is acting as a special permit granting authority, is a special permit required? An alternative would be for the applicant, once receiving notice that the board finds that the increase does not intensify the nonconformity, to obtain a building permit. As the grant of a special permit triggers significant paperwork, creates an appeal period and appellate rights far greater than the issuance of a building permit, requiring the issuance of a special permit appears unduly burdensome.

[50] One of the most important results of the Goldhirsh decision was the reversal of decades of practice at the local level regarding what was affectionately called the "footprint theory" of expansions and changes to single and two family residential structures. Prior to *Goldhirsh* and

Fourth, if the board determines, based upon its analysis of the proposed extension or change, that the proposal will intensify the nonconforming structure, "the applicant will be required to show that the change will not be 'substantially more detrimental than the existing nonconforming structure or use to the neighborhood."[51]

Fifth, unless previously satisfied, the board must determine the extent to which the proposal will be substantially more detrimental than the existing nonconforming structure or use to the neighborhood. This is the second threshold determination. If the board determines that the proposal will be more substantially detrimental to the neighborhood, the permit (or special permit) should be denied or approved with conditions mitigating the impact.

Question 2: Can zoning prescribe limits to the extent a single or two family residential structure can be extended or structurally changed?

A common problem encountered by boards of appeals applying the five-part test discussed above is how to measure, either quantitatively or qualitatively, the proposed expansion's impact on the neighborhood. Left unexamined by case law, however, is whether it is permissible for a city or town to articulate what is meant by the phrase "substantially more detrimental to the neighborhood" in its zoning ordinance or bylaw.

---

consistent with Appeals Court decisions in *Fitzsimonds* and *Willard*, *supra*, the practice of boards of appeals (and building officials) was to reach the automatic conclusion that if the structure's footprint was not being altered, there would not be—could not be—an intensification of the existing nonconforming structure. Thus, the theory went, a single-family dwelling, nonconforming as to side line setbacks or area requirements, could expand by adding a second or third story without an intensification of the preexisting use or nonconformity. The expansion would thus be allowable by right. This practice was supported by several Land Court cases, most notably Theodosopouios v. Ipswich Board of Appeals, Misc. Case No. 156280 (Land Court, 1992), Goldmuntz v. Hulsizer, Misc. Case No. 139026 (Land Court, 1990) and Harrison v. Demers, Misc. Case No. 134666 (Land Court, 1990). In *Theodosopouios*, the Court noted, "In a recent line of cases, this Court has adopted the position that a vertical extension of the walls of a nonconforming structure do not increase the nonconforming nature, as long as the extension is within the bylaw limits...Moreover, if the footprint of the structure is not changed by the alterations, the Town must issue a building permit." *Id.* at 4. *Goldhirsh* reversed this practice. "The fact that there will be no enlargement of the foundational footprint is but one factor to be considered in making the necessary determination or findings. Goldhirsh v. McNear, 32 Mass. App. Ct. 455, at 461, *citing* Willard v. Board of Appeals of Orleans, 25 Mass. App. Ct. 15, 21 (1987), Fitzsimonds v. Board of Appeals of Chatham, 21 Mass. App. Ct. 53 (1985) and Nichols v. Board of Zoning Appeal of Cambridge, 26 Mass. App. Ct. 631 (1988). Today, and consistent with the realization that expansions of single and two family structures can substantially impact abutting properties and the neighborhood, even where the expansion is "up" and not "out," all expansions or structural changes are subject to the five part *Goldhirsh* test.

[51] Goldhirsh v. McNear, 32 Mass. App. Ct. 455, at 460, *quoting* Willard v. Board of Appeals of Orleans, 25 Mass. App. Ct. 15, 21 (1987) and *citing* Fitzsimonds v. Board of Appeals of Chatham, 21 Mass. App. Ct. 53 (1985).

The position taken in this Chapter is that it is permissible for cities and towns to define what they believe constitute the "substantially more detrimental" test. Moreover, it is a recommended approach.

Many of the subjective difficulties of the current statute are resolved if the board of appeals is provided with objective guidance as to what expansions or structural changes the city or town believes will constitute a "substantially more detrimental" structure to the neighborhood.[52] For example, the zoning ordinance or bylaw could be explicit about limitations on expansions or structural changes. This could be accomplished by specifying standards, either explicitly or implicitly that would define what constitutes "substantially more detrimental to the neighborhood."

Explicit standards could include maximum increases in height, width, bulk or floor area ratio. Implicit standards could include detailed qualitative language to assist the board in determining what constitutes "substantially more detrimental to the neighborhood." For example, "any increase in height, width, bulk or extension of a preexisting, nonconforming single or two family residential structure that impairs views or vistas from a public way" would provide subjective guidance to the board.

Finally, in reviewing a petition that the board determines requires a "substantially more detrimental" analysis, an open question remains as to what provisions of the local zoning ordinance or bylaw the board should apply. This is particularly important where local governments adhere to the explicit or implicit advice noted above. Logic would point the petitioner and the board to the section of the ordinance or bylaw governing special permits. But as the Appeals and Land Courts have stated, albeit indirectly, reliance on the "traditional" special permit criteria[53] for Section 6 special permit decisions may be incorrect.[54]

Although the issue is far from settled, communities that elaborate on the local

---

[52] "There is no question that whether the plaintiff could build a new house outside the footprint of the demolished house under the town's zoning bylaw and G.L. c. 40A, § 6, presented complex and confusing issues for the town officials to solve." Murphy v. Town of Duxbury, 40 Mass. App. Ct. 513, 519 (1996).

[53] G.L. c. 40A, § 9 and locally adopted special permit requirements.

[54] See Murray v. Board of Appeals of Barnstable, 22 Mass. App. Ct. 473 (1986), where the Court found that the criteria applicable to special permits in general was not applicable to the review of a proposed expansion of a nonconforming inn into apartments. See also Harrison v. Zoning Board of Appeals of Chilmark, Misc. No. 134666 (Land Court, 1990), where the Court wrote, "…I find and rule that the plaintiff was entitled under the provision of G.L. c. 40A, § 6 to the issuance of a special permit to make the alterations…I further note that the general case law relative to special permits does not apply to a section 6 finding which is entirely different from other provisions of Chapter 40A relative to special permits. Id. at 6. But see Willard v. Board of Appeals of Orleans, 25 Mass. App. Ct. 15, where the Appeals Court held that the board of appeals could look to various sections of the zoning bylaw in reaching a decision as to what constitutes "substantially more detrimental."

requirements for a special permit to expand or structurally change a nonconforming single or two family dwelling are urged to include specific "Section 6" criteria in their ordinance or bylaw. This inclusion should clearly specify that the criteria are intended to apply to the review process of the board of appeals under G.L. c. 40A, § 6 as well as distinguish the "Section 6" criteria from the "Section 9" criteria that applies to other special permit uses. While in many cases the criteria for a Section 6 finding will be the same as the criteria for a Section 9 finding, the duplication appears warranted.

§ 5.11[7]   Changes to Nonconforming Uses

"...a zoning ordinance or bylaw shall not apply to structures or uses lawfully in existence or lawfully begun...but shall apply to any change or substantial extension of such use... ."[55]

A significant body of case law has evolved defining the permissible limits that a nonconforming use or structure can change or expand without municipal approval. Note that the discussion that follows should be distinguished from the previous discussion where the question presented was the extent that the Board of Appeals could permit an expansion, alteration or change to a preexisting nonconforming structure or use.

This Section presents the extent that a preexisting nonconforming use or structure can be changed or extended *without* approval and retain its protected status.

The extent to which a preexisting nonconforming use or structure can be changed or expanded is limited by a three part test, first articulated by the Supreme Judicial Court in 1966[56] and repeated many times since.

The three-part test, phrased below as questions, is often referred to as the "*Powers*"[57] tests.

1. Does the use reflect the nature and purpose of the nonconforming use prevailing when the zoning took effect?
2. Is there a difference in the quality or character and/or degree, of the resulting use?
3. Is the current use different in kind in its effect upon the neighborhood?

A negative answer to the first question or an affirmative answer to question two

---

[55] G.L. c. 40A, § 6.

[56] Bridgewater v. Chuckran, 351 Mass. 20 (1966).

[57] So-called, based upon the decision in Powers v. Building Inspector of Barnstable, 363 Mass. 648 (1973).

or three results in the loss of the nonconforming protections previously enjoyed by the use.[58] This point is extremely important as once the protections are lost, they may be impossible to restore.

Note again that this three-part test applies to nonconforming uses that change, expand or increase their size or activity *without* complying with the provisions of G.L. c. 40A, § 6. The protections are lost not because of an affirmative action taken by the city or town, but rather through the deliberate actions taken by the landowner without benefit of board of appeals approval.

A brief review of the *Powers* test questions are presented below.

§ 5.11[7][a]   Does the Use Reflect the Nature and Purpose of the Nonconforming Use Prevailing When the Zoning Took Effect?

There are numerous cases in which the Appeals and Supreme Judicial Court ruled on the "nature and purpose" of an expanded use. The cases generally have turned on the definition first set forth by the Supreme Judicial Court in *Powers*.

> "it is not different in kind...simply because it is bigger... a nonconforming use of the same premises may be not only continued but also increased in volume...The distinction is between an increase in the amount of business, even a great increase, which does not work a change in use, and an enlargement of a nonconforming business so as to be different in kind in its effect on the neighborhood."[59]

---

[58] Note that a failure to answer "no" to any one of the three questions fails the *Powers* test. *See* Green v. Board of Appeals of Provincetown, 26 Mass. App. Ct. 469 (1988), *reversed on other grounds*, 401 Mass. 571 (1989). "While all three tests were satisfied in *Chuckran* [Bridgewater v. Chuckran, 351 Mass. 20 (1966), the predecessor to *Powers*], we have found no case, and the defendants cite none, holding all three to be requisite to a finding that change or extension has taken place." 26 Mass. App. Ct. 469, at 472. *See also* Oakham Sand & Gravel Corp. v. Town of Oakham, 54 Mass. App. Ct. 80, 84 (2002). "Once there is a change or substantial extension to a nonconforming use, the resulting use must comply with the current zoning bylaws to avoid becoming an illegal use. Although '[t]he character of a [nonconforming] use does not change solely by reason of an increase in its volume ..., or because the hours of operation have expanded ..., or because improved equipment is used," *citing* Board of Selectmen of Blackstone v. Tellestone, 4 Mass. App. Ct. 311, 315 (1976).

[59] Powers v. Building Inspector of Barnstable, 363 Mass. 648, 653 (1973). *See also* Cape Resort Hotels, Inc. v. Alcoholic Licensing Board of Falmouth, 385 Mass. 205 (1982). In this case, the Supreme Judicial Court reviewed the legitimacy of the expansion of a hotel into a controversial nightclub, relying on the "nature and purpose" test to rule that the expansion/conversion was beyond the permissible scope of the statute. "This enterprise is much less a hotel with entertainment facilities present for its guests and the public, than it is an entertainment complex with some guest

Note that the "nature and purpose" test does not mean that a building or use cannot be updated or modernized to insure structural integrity or improved interior or exterior functions.[60]

"We have accepted the principle that improved and more efficient means of a nonconforming use are permissible if they are ordinarily and reasonably adapted to the original use and do not constitute a change in the original nature and purpose of the undertaking."[61]

§ 5.11[7][b]   Is There a Difference in the Quality, Character and/or Degree of the Resulting Use?

The second *Powers* test is difficult to distinguish from the first as the "nature and purpose" of a use is often synonymous with its "quality or character." One approach for distinguishing the two is to use physical indicators to evaluate the second test,[62] whereas the first test seems to be more reliant upon an impact analysis—the measurable impact before the use or structure was expanded or altered and after the expansion or alteration.[63]

---

rooms...The facts found by the judge...indicate that the expansion and updating of the hotel's activities were not adapted to the original nonconforming use. Thus the shift from hotel to 'entertainment complex' constitutes a change in the nature and purpose of the undertaking." 385 Mass. 205, at 213, 216.

[60] *See* Boston and Albany Railroad Company v. Department of Utilities, 314 Mass. 634 (1943), where the Supreme Judicial Court provided a useful distinction between a "repair" and an "alteration" regarding improvements to a bridge overlying a railroad bed. "A structural change or renewal for the purpose of extending or improving the bridge is different from a restoration of the structure to its original sound condition...It is thus apparent that the Legislature... intended to treat as an alteration structural changes that strengthened or improved a bridge and to treat as repairs work done for the purpose of restoring a bridge to proper condition. The substitution of a sound part for a decayed or worn out part of a structure ordinarily increases its strength, but the work on that account does not become more than an ordinary repair." 314 Mass. 634, at 641.

[61] Berliner v. Feldman, 363 Mass. 767, 775 (1973), *citing* Wayland v. Lee, 325 Mass. 637, 643 (1950). "Consistent with this view, we have approved the installation of heat and electricity in a nonconforming structure (Morin v. Board of Appeals of Leominster, 352 Mass. 620, 622 (1967)) and interior remodeling, including the enclosure of porches (Paul v. Selectmen of Scituate, 301 Mass. 365, 368, 370 (1938))...Although each circumstance must be assessed on its facts, and in relation to the applicable bylaw, interior changes not amounting to reconstruction or structure change...generally may be made in a nonconforming building." Berliner v. Feldman, 363 Mass. 767, at 775.

[62] For example, in Green v. Board of Appeals of Provincetown, 26 Mass. App. Ct. 469 (1988), the Court noted that a change from an existing restaurant to a Burger King failed the second test. "The number of customers was expected to double to treble that of Cicero's. The manner of operation was to be substantially different, changing from a primarily sit-down, full-service restaurant, with a secondary commerce in take-out sandwiches, pizzas and bakery items, to a fast food, counter service operation... ." 26 Mass. App. Ct. 469, at 472.

[63] Thus in *Powers*, the Court wrote: "(the Warehouse) is different in quality and character from

§ 5.11[7][c]   Is The Current Use Different in Kind in Its Effect Upon The Neighborhood?

This third test relies on both objective and subjective evidence and is similar to the "not substantially more detrimental to the neighborhood" test discussed in Sections 4.0 and 5.0, above.

Increased traffic, noise and overall impacts to property values are relevant indicators to determine whether the expanded use has a greater or different impact upon the neighborhood. Note that impact must be greater or different (and worse) than the prior impact.[64]

§ 5.11[8]   Abandonment of Nonconforming Uses and Structures

"A zoning ordinance or bylaw may define and regulate nonconforming uses and structures abandoned or not used for a period of two years or more."[65]

The above-noted clause raises several interesting issues.

First, note that the regulation of abandoned or "not used" uses and structures is permissive. The applicable zoning ordinance or bylaw must include this provision of the Zoning Act for the provision to be enforceable.

Second, the statute and resulting case law create two independent and alternative ways that a use or structure loses its nonconforming protection. First, the owner (or lessee) has indicated intent to abandon, regardless of how long the use or structure had been unused.[66] Second, the owner (or lessee) has not used the

---

that use prevailing before 1957, the difference being that what was a warehouse and distribution facility used for the purpose of serving customers within physical reach of one day delivery by truck is now such a facility for serving customers nationwide." Powers v. Building Inspector of Barnstable, 363 Mass. 648, 662 (1973).

[64] In Derby Refining Company v. City of Chelsea, 407 Mass. 703 (1990), the Supreme Judicial Court ruled that the continuation of offensive fumes from a liquid asphalt facility, if no worse than before the use changed, would not constitute a failure of the third test and thus was protected by G.L. c. 40A, § 6.

[65] G.L. c. 40A, § 6.

[66] "Under Massachusetts law, the right to continue a nonconforming use is not confined to the existing user, but runs with the land...However, that right can be lost if a predecessor in title has abandoned the use. To constitute an abandonment, the discontinuance of a nonconforming use (structure or lot) must result from 'the concurrence of two factors, (1) the intent to abandon and (2) voluntary conduct, whether affirmative or negative, which carries the implication of abandonment." Derby Refining Company v. City of Chelsea, 407 Mass. 703, 708 (1990), *quoting* Pioneer Insulation & Modernizing Corp. v. Lynn, 331 Mass. 560, 565 (1954). In *Pioneer*, the Court was faced with the question of whether an involuntary abandonment would constitute abandonment under the statute, where the property owner was barred from intervening in the decision ruling his property had lost nonconforming protection. "Thus nonoccupancy of the premises and suspension or cessation of

structure or use two years or more without regard to the reasons or intentions for the nonuse.

Note that these categories are independent. The Appeals and Supreme Judicial Court have held that local governments can regulate nonconforming uses and structures under either category or both.[67]

Finally, the Appeals Court held that the rules of abandonment and nonuse apply to all land uses and structures, not solely to commercial property.[68] "Nothing in par. 3 [G.L. c. 40A, § 6] suggests that it does not apply to single and two-family residences, and we assume it is applicable to such dwellings."[69]

§ 5.12   Spot Zoning

When a zoning change is proposed by a property owner to a municipal legislative body, counsel almost invariably faces, as a threshold issue, the problem of spot

---

business due to causes over which the owner has no control do not of themselves constitute a discontinuance; and lapse of time is not the controlling factor, although it is evidential, especially in connection with facts showing an intent to discontinue use." 331 Mass. 560, at 565. "Mere nonuse or sale of property does not, by itself, constitute an abandonment." Derby, 407 Mass. at 709. Note also that the "act of abandonment" can exist "as a matter of law", even if the local zoning regulations do not define what constitutes abandonment. "Nevertheless, we consider this a case where the lapse of time following the demolition— twenty three years—is so significant that abandonment exists as a matter of law." Dial Away Co., Inc. v. Zoning Board of Appeals of Auburn, 41 Mass. App. Ct. 165, 172 (1996). See also Wells v. Zoning Board of Billerica, 2003 Mass. Super. LEXIS 191, at * 25, 16 Mass. L. Rep. 568 (Mass. Super. Ct. 2003) (2003), "This section, [of the Billerica Zoning Bylaw] must mean that a structure that was torn down more than two years ago cannot be "reconstructed" without conforming with current requirements (or at least with the requirements for grandfathered lots, if applicable... Were it otherwise, every nonconforming lot containing a cellarhole would be a buildable lot, a result that the two-year abandonment provision was evidently drafted to avoid." See also Bransford v. Tomassian, Nos. 272521, 278436, (Mass.Land Ct. May 27, 2004), where the Land Court concluded that G.L. c. 40A, § 6 does not distinguish between "voluntary and involuntary" demolition of an existing structure as it relates to determination of abandonment.

[67] Davis v. Zoning Board of Chatham, 52 Mass. App. Ct. 349, 356–357. "A zoning policy inimical to such enlargement is consistent with the statutory mandate of G.L. c. 40A, § 6, which disfavors extensions of existing nonconformities and places the burden on parties seeking them to persuade the local authorities of the lack of substantially increased detriment resulting therefrom." See also Bartlett v. Board of Appeals of Lakeville, 23 Mass. App. Ct. 664 (1987) and Ka-Hur Enterprises, Inc. v. Board of Appeals of Provincetown, 424 Mass. 404 (1997). In Ka-Hur, the Court, referring to Bartlett, noted, "In that case we concluded that a municipality now has two choices for terminating nonconforming uses, one being abandonment and the other a simple cessation of a nonconforming use for a period of at least two years." 424 Mass. 404, at 406.

[68] This holding is important as the great majority of cases involving abandonment and nonuse focus on non-residential properties and land uses.

[69] Dial Away Co., Inc. v. Zoning Board of Appeals of Auburn, 41 Mass. App. Ct. 165, 171 (1996).

zoning. This is because the property owner rarely proposes to include more than one or two parcels in the area subject to the zoning change. Even where more than two parcels are included they are almost always contiguous, under the same beneficial ownership, and therefore liable to be treated as a single parcel for zoning purposes. While this dilemma is predictable (why would a private landowner seeking a more beneficial zoning designation for her land simultaneously petition to rezone the land of another?), it must be addressed carefully.

Given the delicate nature of the zoning legislative process and the generally unpredictable nature of municipal legislatures, the proponent of the zoning change is very often reluctant to include in the area subject to the zoning change property other than his own. The reasons for this can vary according to the particular case, but two reasons are very often a consideration: The owners of the other property to be included are local residents who oppose the change because it would prevent them from making a planned or potential future use of unimproved property; or, the owners of the other property to be included are local residents who oppose the change because it would make uses or structures currently existing on their property nonconforming. Opposition by such persons can foredoom any proposed zoning change.

When these factors pertain, the proponent of the zoning change must restrict the proposal to his own property if he is to have any chance at all. However, when he does so he is invariably met with the objection that the proposal constitutes illegal spot zoning.

The basis of a spot zoning attack is the claim that a particular parcel or parcels within a zoning district have been singled out for treatment more favorable than other parcels with similar characteristics.[1] Such a result is held to violate the so-called principle of uniformity that is fundamental to Euclidean Zoning and the requirements of G.L. c. 40A, § 4.[2]

An additional argument against spot zoning is that the singling out of one parcel, to the exclusion of all other parcels is de facto arbitrary. The claim that the action is arbitrary is far easier to argue where the rezoning is not in compliance with a plan or analysis supporting the rezoning. Thus in plan states (see Chapter 2), a rezoning that is not in accordance with a plan, is generally void or voidable. In *National Amusements v. City of Boston*, the Appeals Court, in upholding the Land Court's determination that the City's rezoning efforts constituted spot zoning and was based on "fig leaves of rationalization" is as close as the Courts have come

---

[1] McHugh v. Board of Zoning Adjustment, 336 Mass. 682, 147 N.E.2d 761 (1958).

[2] *See* G.L. c. 40A, § 4 and prior c. 40A, § 2; *see also* Hines v. Attleboro, 355 Mass. 336, 244 N.E.2d 316 (1969).

to support the premise that any rezoning in the absence of a plan is vulnerable to a spot zoning or arbitrary attack.[3]

In evaluating whether spot zoning is involved the size of the "spot" is no criterion, and the reported cases have run the gamut.[4] The decisive element is not whether a parcel has been singled out for less restrictive treatment than land of a similar character, but whether this has been done solely for the economic benefit of the owner and not to serve the public interest.[5]

A review of the cases shows that the courts have had little difficulty finding a public purpose in the zoning change and upholding the challenged amendment.[6]

§ 5.13   Contract Zoning and Development Agreements[1]

Contract zoning is related to spot zoning and may indeed be described as a form of spot zoning. Contract zoning occurs when a property owner agrees with a municipality to make certain concessions, which can include monetary payments or restrictions on the affected land, in exchange for a vote by the municipality rezoning that land.[2] As discussed below, attacks on zoning amendments arising out of these kinds of arrangements have not been successful in Massachusetts. The proponent of the amendment need only show that the legislative body was motivated by its view of the public interest rather than "extraneous considerations." Even outright monetary payments to the municipality to induce the favorable vote are not fatal, as long as the payments are reasonably intended to meet public needs

---

[3] National Amusements v. City of Boston, 29 Mass. App. Ct. 305, 311 (1990).

[4] Vagts v. Superintendent & Inspector of Bldgs., 355 Mass. 711, 247 N.E.2d 366 (1969) (230 sq. feet); Peters v. City of Westfield, 353 Mass. 635, 234 N.E.2d 295 (1968) (19,000 sq. feet); Sullivan v. Board of Selectmen, 346 Mass. 784, 196 N.E.2d 185 (1964) (80,230 sq. feet); Raymond v. Building Inspector of Brimfield, 3 Mass. App. 38, 322 N.E.2d 197 (1975) (5 acres).

[5] Lamarre v. Commissioner of Public Works, 324 Mass. 542, 87 N.E.2d 211 (1949); Board of Appeals v. Housing Appeals Committee in Dept. of Community Affairs, 363 Mass. 339, 294 N.E.2d 393 (1973).

[6] For extreme cases, see Raymond v. Building Inspector of Brimfield, 3 Mass. App. 38, 322 N.E.2d 197 (1975) and Peters v. City of Westfield, 353 Mass. 635, 234 N.E.2d 295 (1968).

[1] See David L. Callies, Daniel J. Curtin, Jr. and Julie A. Tappendorf, Bargaining for Development: A Handbook on Development Agreements, Annexation Agreements, Land Development Conditions, Vested Rights and the Provision of Public Facilities (Environmental Law Institute, Wash. D.C. 2003); Daniel J. Curtin, Jr., Exactions, Dedications & Development Agreements Nationwide and in California: When and How Do Nollan/Dolan Apply, Chapter 2.33 Annual Institute of Planning, Zoning and Eminent Domain, Matthew Bender, 2003; Daniel J. Curtin, Jr., Effectively Using Development Agreements to Protect Land Use Entitlements: Lessons from California, 25 Zoning and Planning Law Report, no. 5 (West Group, May 2002); Development Agreement Manual: Collaboration in Pursuit of Community Interest (Institute for Local Self Government, 2002). See also Development Agreements: Contracting for Vested Rights, 28 Boston College Envtl. Affairs L. Rev., ch. 9 (Summer 2001).

[2] Sylvania Electric Products, Inc. v. Newton, 344 Mass. 428, 183 N.E.2d 118 (1962).

arising out of the zoning change.[3] Of course the usual evaluation standards applicable to claims of spot zoning would apply as well to contract zoning cases. The practical watchwords for counsel who wish to see a contract zoning agreement sustained are

- identify the public interest served by the zoning change and be sure it appears clearly in the record of meetings up to and including the one that include the vote on the zoning change; and

- relate any monetary payment as closely to the impacts of the proposed development as the circumstances allow.

In a case remarkable for the Court's willingness to sanction an overt trade of zoning for cash,[4] the Massachusetts Supreme Judicial Court upheld a rezoning that was directly and indisputably linked to the payment of an eight million dollar gift. The Court upheld the payment-for-rezoning scheme citing the rational basis test. "In general, there is no reason to invalidate a legislative act on the basis of an 'extraneous consideration' because we defer to legislative findings and choices without regard to motive. We see no reason to make an exception for legislative acts that are in the nature of zoning enactments... ."[5] Only the dissenting Justices seemed concerned about issues of enforceability (what happens if the beneficiary of the rezoning breaches?) and the public policy issues raised where "needy" cities and towns see their zoning powers as for sale to the highest bidder.[6]

In *McLean Hospital Corporation v. Belmont*,[7] the Appeals Court upheld a re-zoning linked to options benefiting the Town and off-site improvements to be made by the landowner. The Court concluded that if the zoning action by itself is a valid exercise of the police powers, this validity is not negated by bargaining, provided that the bargaining is related to the property subject to the rezoning.[8]

In both cases, the Courts conclude that a promise by a petitioner is different from a requirement imposed as a condition precedent by the municipality. The Courts

---

[3] Rando v. Town of North Attleborough, 44 Mass. App. 603 (1998).

[4] Durand v. IDC Bellingham, LLC, 440 Mass. 45 (2003).

[5] Durand v. IDC Bellingham, L.L.C., 440 Mass. 45, 793 N.E.2d 359, 369 (2003). Three Justices filed a partial dissenting opinion. "It was a sale of the police power because there is nothing in the record to legitimize the $8 million offer as 'intended to mitigate the impact of the development upon the town... .'" The dissent suggests however, that if the $8 million offer was directly linked to the impacts caused by the proposed power plant (as opposed to a cash gift of $8 million unconnected to any specific impact), the zoning contingent upon payment deal would have been appropriate.

[6] "Sadly, these circumstances demonstrate government and private interests at their shameful worst, and are most likely to involve the most needy towns." Durand v. IDC Bellingham, L.L.C., 440 Mass. 45, 57, 793 N.E.2d 359, 371.

[7] 56 Mass. App. Ct. 540 (2002).

[8] "...ancillary agreements not involving consideration extraneous to the property being rezoned." McLean Hospital Corporation v. Belmont, 56 Mass. App. Ct. 540, at 546.

also seem to conclude that if the re-zoning would have been permissible without the promise, then the promise did not induce or influence the legislative action. Finally, while the Appeals Court appears to require some nexus between the re-zoning and the extracted (or proffered) promise, the Supreme Judicial Court appears to conclude that the rational basis test allows cities and towns to bargain freely whether or not the extraction or offer is related to the re-zoning. Neither the Appeals Court nor the Supreme Judicial Court considered the issue of "permissive contract zoning" pursuant to a development agreement statute.

The development agreement has successfully bridged the gap between unfettered bargaining and rigid, inflexible zoning.[9] As employed in several other states and Cape Cod pursuant to the Cape Cod Commission Act, development agreements are a valuable and vital tool to overcoming the problems inherent with the latter and the dangers associated with the former.

Many states have authorized use of development agreements mainly for the purpose of giving the developer some assurance that its project can be completed once all land use and discretionary approvals have been obtained. However, as development agreements have come into more use, more and more local agencies have been using them to obtain benefits for the public that normally could not be obtained using the normal land use process (e.g. development agreements are not constrained by the nexus and proportionality limitations of *Nollan* and *Dolan. See* Chapter 3). Thirteen states so far have adopted legislation enabling local governments to enter into development agreements with property owners/developers.[10]

---

[9] Not infrequently, those who challenge projects governed by development agreements will argue that such agreements are invalid because the local agency is "contracting away" its police power. While no Massachusetts decision is available, the courts have not been persuaded by this argument. For example, a California neighborhood association contended that because San Luis Obispo County had entered into a development agreement freezing zoning for a five-year period for a project before the project was ready for construction, the county improperly contracted away its zoning authority. SMART v. San Luis Obispo County, 84 Cal. App. 4th 221, 232–233 (2000). In holding for the county, the court noted that land use regulation is an established function of local government, providing the authority for a locality to enter into contracts to carry out the function. The county's development agreement required that the project be developed in accordance with the county's general plan, did not permit construction until the county had approved detailed building plans, retained the county's discretionary authority in the future, and allowed a zoning freeze of limited duration only. The court found that the zoning freeze in the county's development agreement was not a surrender of the police power but instead "advance[d] the public interest by preserving future options."

[10] *See* Ariz. Rev. Stat. Ann. § 9-500.05 (West 1996 & Supp. 2000) (amended 1997); Cal. Gov't Code § 65864 (West 1997); Colo. Rev. Stat. § 24-68-101–106 (2000); Fla. Stat. Ann. § 163.3220 (West 2000); Haw. Rev. Stat. § 46-123 (1993); Idaho Code § 67-6511A (1995 & Supp. 2000) (amended 1999); La. Rev. Stat. Ann. § 33:4780.22 (West 1988 & Supp. 2000); Nev. Rev. Stat. § 278.0201 (1997); N.J. Stat. Ann. § 40:55D-45.2 (West 1991); Or. Rev. Stat. § 94.504 (1999) (enacted into law in 1993 by the Legislative Authority but not made a part of the Oregon Revised

However, some states such as Texas, use development agreements without the need for state legislation.

§ 5.14   Availability of Declaratory Judgment in Zoning Cases

There is a longstanding rule in Massachusetts jurisprudence that excludes "premature review of administrative activity."[1] In *Clark & Clark Hotel Corp. v. Building Inspector of Falmouth*, 20 Mass. App. 206, 479 N.E.2d 699, 702 (1985), the Appeals Court set out the rule as follows:

> "'In recent years [the Supreme Judicial Court] has frequently emphasized the importance of judicial application of exhaustion principles ...' *Murphy v. Administrator of the Div. of Personnel Admin.*, 377 Mass. 217, 220, 386 N.E.2d 211 (1979), and cases cited. The general rule, even where there is an alternate judicial or statutory remedy providing access to the courts, is that, if administrative action 'may afford the plaintiffs some relief, or may affect the scope or character of judicial relief, exhaustion of the possibilities [of such administrative action] should ordinarily precede independent action in the court'." [citation omitted].

The policy behind this rule is the desire to "preserve the integrity of the administrative process while sparing the judiciary the burden of reviewing administrative proceedings in piecemeal fashion." Murphy v. Administrator, 386 N.E.2d 211, at 214. "The rationale against interlocutory review, furthermore is 'particularly cogent' when, a proceeding is still in 'its earliest stages', [citation omitted] and the party seeking declaratory relief has access to additional administrative procedures which may correct or render moot any alleged error." McKenney v. Commission on Judicial Conduct, 402 N.E.2d 1356, at 1359.

While the general policy requiring exhaustion of administrative remedies is a very strong one indeed and not one to be lightly dispensed with, Clark & Clark Hotel Corp, 479 N.E.2d 699. at 703, in areas of law other than zoning it is still a rule to be exercised in the discretion of the court. However, the situation is different in zoning law. The Appeals Court in a series of cases decided since 1981 has held that the present Zoning Act (G.L. c. 40A, § 7) actually deprives the court of subject matter jurisdiction to review administrative actions under local zoning bylaws

---

Statutes until much later); S.C. Code Ann. § 6-31-10 (Law. Co-op. Supp. 2000); Va. Code Ann. § 15.2-2303.1 (Michie 1997) (applies only to counties with a population between 10,300 and 11,000 and developments consisting of more than 1000 acres); Wash. Rev. Code Ann. § 36.70B.170 (West 1991 & Supp. 2000).

[1] McKenney v. Commission on Judicial Conduct, 380 Mass. 263, 402 N.E.2d 1356, 1358 (1980).

where the plaintiff has not exhausted his administrative remedies pursuant to G.L. c. 40A, §§ 7, 8, and 17.[2]

Although the breadth of the rulings in these cases has probably been somewhat narrowed by the SJC,[3] it remains the law in Massachusetts that where suit is brought to compel enforcement of a zoning ordinance or bylaw against an offending property owner, the court has no subject matter jurisdiction where the plaintiff has failed to exhaust his administrative remedies.[4]

This is not to say that a declaratory judgment action will never lie in a zoning case. For example, an attack on the validity of a zoning ordinance or bylaw may be made in this manner[5] and it would appear that one may seek an interpretation of rights under a bylaw.[6] But it must not appear that the plaintiff is employing declaratory judgment only as a way of sidestepping or superseding the administrative remedy.[7]

§ 5.15   Failure of Building Inspector to Act

Under the State Zoning Act,[1] any person may request that the building inspector enforce the zoning ordinance or bylaw, and may, if aggrieved, appeal any adverse decision by the inspector to the board of appeals and thereafter, to the courts.[2]

The question of what rights such persons may have if the building inspector simply fails to act, (leaving the case in administrative limbo), has evaded judicial determination. The two cases which considered, without deciding, the problem[3] suggest two possible ways out of the dilemma. Either appeal the failure to act to the board of appeals, or bring a complaint for mandamus. An interesting question arises as to whether a person who is not "aggrieved" as defined in the Green case by the failure of the building inspector to act may still bring a mandamus pro-

---

[2] Neuhaus v. Building Inspector of Marlborough, 11 Mass. App. 230, 415 N.E.2d 235 (1981); William C. Bearce Corp. v. Building Inspector of Brockton, 11 Mass. App. 930, 416 N.E.2d 509 (1981); McDonald's Corp. v. Seekonk, 12 Mass. App. 351, 424 N.E.2d 1136 (1981); Board of Selectmen v. Granfield, 17 Mass. App. 1011, 460 N.E.2d 199 (1984); Woburn v. McNutt Bros. Equipment Corp., 16 Mass. App. 236, 451 N.E.2d 437 (1983).

[3] Banquer Realty Co. v. Acting Bldg. Comr., 389 Mass. 565, 451 N.E.2d 422 (1983).

[4] Clark & Clark Hotel Corp. v. Building Inspector of Falmouth , 479 N.E.2d 702, n.4.

[5] Whitinsville Retirement Soc. v. Northbridge, 394 Mass. 757, 477 N.E.2d 407 (1985).

[6] Whitinsville Retirement Soc. v. Northbridge, 394 Mass. 757, 477 N.E.2d 407 (1985). *See also* Woods v. Newton, 349 Mass. 373, 208 N.E.2d 508 (1965).

[7] Iodice v. Newton, 397 Mass. 329, 491 N.E.2d 618 (1986).

[1] G.L. c. 40A, § 7.

[2] G.L. c. 40A, §§ 8, 17; Green v. Board of Appeals, 404 Mass. 571, 536 N.E.2d 584 (1989).

[3] Vokes v. Avery W. Lovell, Inc., 18 Mass. App. 471, 468 N.E.2d 271 (1984), *review denied*, 393 Mass. 1103, 470 N.E.2d 798; Worcester County Christian Communications, Inc. v. Board of Appeals, 22 Mass. App. 83, 491 N.E.2d 634 (1986).

ceeding, even though he is foreclosed from appealing the nonaction to the board of appeals. The case law suggests that any citizen has standing to bring an action to require a public officer to perform a nondiscretionary duty.[4]

A similar situation pertains when a building permit is applied for and the inspector simply fails to act, and the same two remedies are probably also available; certainly mandamus would be.[5] However, there is also an additional remedy in such cases. One may send a written request to act to the building inspector. If there is no response for 45 days an appeal may be taken to the State Building Code Appeals Board.[6] This is usually effective in getting action (often adverse) from the building inspector, which action may then be appealed in the usual fashion.

It is important to realize that the appeal taken to the Building Code Appeals Board from the failure of the building inspector to act gives that Board jurisdiction only to review the failure to act within 30 days of submission of the application as required by 780 CMR 114.1; it does not give the Board jurisdiction to review zoning issues raised by the application.[7] In practice the Board has been known to pay lip service to this principle while discussing and purporting to resolve the zoning issues.

Where a request for enforcement is denied by the building inspector and appealed to the board of appeals it may be constructively granted by the board's failure to act during the statutory period. In such cases the court must issue an order requiring the building inspector to act in accordance with the Request for Enforcement, provided the Request is sufficiently definite and specific. In any litigation brought by the building inspector to enforce the Request the substantive issues precluded from consideration in the zoning appeal by the constructive grant would be open to full judicial inquiry.[8]

§ 5.16   When Does a Zoning Hearing End?

Certain provisions of the Zoning Act provide that the failure of the board of appeals to decide, and file its decision, within certain time limits results in a constructive grant of the relief sought by the applicant.[1]

In the case of special permits the board must take final action "within 90 days following" the public hearing. It therefore becomes important on occasion to

---

[4] Pilgrim Real Estate v. Superintendent of Police, 330 Mass. 250, 112 N.E.2d 796 (1953).

[5] Gricus v. Superintendent & Inspector of Bldgs., 345 Mass. 687, 189 N.E.2d 209 (1963).

[6] G.L. c. 23B, §§ 16, 23: 780 CMR 126.

[7] Balcam v. Town of Hingham, 41 Mass. App. 260, 669 N.E.2d 461 (1996), *review denied*, 423 Mass. 1111, 672 N.E.2d 539 (1996), Carstensen v. Cambridge Zoning Bd. of Appeals, 11 Mass. App. 348, 416 N.E.2d 522 (1981).

[8] Cameron v. Board of Appeals, 23 Mass. App. 144, 499 N.E.2d 847 (1986).

[1] G.L. c. 40A, §§ 9, 15.

determine when the public hearing has ended and the 90-day period begun.

The 90-day decision period does not begin to run until after the first noticed hearing date if the board continues the hearing to a subsequent date. It begins to run at the close of the last continued hearing date at which information is received.[2] The Appeals Court has held that "public hearings end when the right of interested parties to present information and argue is cut off."[3] Therefore, even if the board continues to meet to discuss the application, once it stops taking evidence and/or hearing arguments the 90-day period begins to run.

The board must schedule continued hearing dates at reasonable intervals consistent with the statutory objective of timely decisions. The courts have implied that in cases of abuse of the continuance process a constructive grant may be held to have occurred.[4]

§ 5.17 Regulating Form of Ownership as Opposed to Use: Condominium and Time Share Conversions

In recent years there has been a rather dramatic increase in the conversion of multi unit residential properties to the condominium form of ownership, and to a form of condominium ownership known as "time-sharing." A time-sharing residential property is one where persons own the legal right to occupy a particular dwelling unit during a certain period or periods of the calendar year. This right is evidenced by a legal instrument and is transferable in the same fashion as any other condominium interest.[1]

So-called condo conversions began in the large cities and then moved into the suburbs. Time-sharing has tended to be concentrated in the resort areas of the state, particularly coastal and mountain areas. As these trends accelerated municipalities began to attempt to regulate, (or perhaps prevent is a more accurate word), the conversions.

This area of the law is still evolving rapidly and it is difficult to state general rules, but it seems clear that the reach of municipal ordinances or bylaws into this area will be narrowly circumscribed by the courts. The leading case on this point[2] makes

---

[2] Kenrick v. Board of Appeals, 27 Mass. App. 774, 543 N.E.2d 437 (1989), *review denied*, 406 Mass. 1101, 546 N.E.2d 375.

[3] Milton Commons Associates v. Board of Appeals, 14 Mass. App. 111, 436 N.E.2d 1236 (1982), *appeal denied*, 387 Mass. 1101, 440 N.E.2d 21.

[4] Pheasant Ridge Associates Ltd. Partnership v. Burlington, 399 Mass. 771, 506 N.E.2d 1152 (1987).

[1] G.L. c. 183B, added by St. 1987, c. 760, extensively regulates time-share properties. Section 3 of the new statute makes it clear that time-share estates of five years or more have the character and incidents of ownership estates in realty at common law.

[2] CHR General, Inc. v. Newton, 387 Mass. 351, 439 N.E.2d 788 (1982).

it clear that "a municipality's zoning power is confined to regulating the use of a property rather than its form of ownership."

However, where a form of ownership necessarily implies a significant change in the nature of the use of the property a bylaw or ordinance may regulate the form of ownership.[3] The apparent rationale for this is that even though such a bylaw is phrased in terms of type of ownership, it is in essence an attempt to regulate the use of property and therefore valid.[4]

Where a nonconforming use is attempted to be converted to a condominium, municipalities sometime have attempted to require a special permit on the ground that the use is being "changed, extended, or altered."[5] These attempts are likely to be turned aside by the courts,[6] but in some circumstances may prevail.[7]

§ 5.18   Access Roadways—Different Zones

Where a zoning district boundary line divides a lot leaving different parts of the lot subject to different regulations as to use there is sometimes a problem with access roadways. For example, assume that a large lot is divided by a zoning boundary line between industrial and residential zones. Assume also that the owner of a lot wishes to make a legal industrial use of the lot on the portion that is industrially zoned but wishes to access that use by crossing the portion of the lot that is residentially zoned. Unless specifically permitted by the ordinance or bylaw, such a use of the residential property would be prohibited.[1] However, and notwithstanding the warnings provided in Section 5.7, where the denial of such access would prevent all access for any legal use it may be that the property owner is entitled to a variance.[2]

§ 5.19   The Site Plan Review Process

More and more municipalities in recent years have adopted site plan review provisions as part of their zoning ordinances and bylaws. There is no authorization

---

[3] Goldman v. Dennis, 375 Mass. 197, 375 N.E.2d 1212 (1978).

[4] Goldman v. Dennis, 375 Mass. 197, 375 N.E.2d 1212 (1978); Gamsey v. Building Inspector of Chatham, 28 Mass. App. 614, 553 N.E.2d 1311 (1990), *review denied*, 408 Mass. 1101, 557 N.E.2d 1385.

[5] G.L. c. 40A, § 6.

[6] Sullivan v. Board of Appeals, 15 Mass. App. 286, 445 N.E.2d 174 (1983), *appeal denied*, 388 Mass. 1105, 448 N.E.2d 766.

[7] *See* Stonegate, Inc. v. Great Barrington, Land Court Case Misc. 117553.

[1] Harrison v. Building Inspector of Braintree, 350 Mass. 559, 215 N.E.2d 773 (1966); Richardson v. Zoning Board of Appeals, 351 Mass. 375, 221 N.E.2d 396 (1966); Building Inspector of Dennis v. Harney, 2 Mass. App. 584, 317 N.E.2d 81 (1974).

[2] Lapenas v. Zoning Board of Appeals, 352 Mass. 530, 226 N.E.2d 361 (1967); Chelmsford v. Byrne, 6 Mass. App. 848, 372 N.E.2d 1307 (1978).

for, or even mention of, site plan review in the State Zoning Act, so the process is entirely local in origin.[1] Not unexpectedly, the substance and procedure of site plan review varies widely among municipalities. Accordingly, consultation with local officials about their particular process is essential prior to application. Some ordinances and bylaws have thresholds relating to the intensity of development before site plan review applies. Others require a site plan review special permit for large-scale non-residential developments. Others require site plan review for all but single or two family residential uses.

The usual reviewing body is the board of appeals or planning board. Site plan review is concerned with specific site or development related issues such as drainage, building location, parking, lighting, pedestrian and vehicular traffic flow, landscaping and other "details" of land development. The purpose of site plan review is to provide for an overall administrative review of certain otherwise permitted uses prior to the issuance of a building permit. In some municipalities it may be an informal review by a board or official. In others site plan review triggers the need for a special permit, with all of the attendant procedures.

In *SCIT, Inc. v. Planning Bd. of Braintree*,[2] the Appeals Court invalidated a zoning bylaw provision which required a special permit for all uses in the business zone. This has led some lawyers to question the validity of the site plan review processes in the various cities and towns. It is suggested that the *SCIT* case does not present any peril to properly drafted site plan review bylaws, as SCIT, referring to G.L. c. 40A, § 4, stated that the requirement of a special permit for all uses would violate the uniformity (or predictability) clause of the statute.

Therefore, according to the Court, at least one use must be available by right in each zoning district. A special permit requirement for site plan review does not run afoul of the *SCIT* requirement precisely because of the limitations of site plan review. The purpose of the adjudicative review is not to pass judgment on the use of the locus, but rather the relevant site or development related issues that are raised by the proposed use.

Therefore, site plan review ordinances and bylaws should create a narrowly circumscribed process, directed not to the question of whether a use should be allowed, but rather to questions of the manner in which it will be allowed. The

---

[1] "Although site plan review is a permissible regulatory tool for the imposition of reasonable terms and conditions on uses permitted as of right, it is well settled that the Zoning Act…does not expressly recognize the site plan review "as an independent method of regulation." American Retirement Corporation v. Barrell, Nos. 276776, 288051 (Mass. Land Ct. Jan. 19, 2005) *citing* Osberg v. Planning Board of Sturbridge, 44 Mass. App. Ct. 56, 57 (1997) and Y.D. Dugout, Inc. v. Board of Appeals of Canton, 357 Mass. 25 (1970).

[2] SCIT, Inc. v. Planning Bd. of Braintree, 19 Mass. App. 101, 472 N.E.2d 269 (1984). *See also* Biotti v. Board of Selectmen of Manchester, 25 Mass. App. 637 (1988).

standards guiding the reviewing board must be definite and its discretion limited.[3] Ordinances or bylaws that meet these standards should withstand any challenge based on the *SCIT* case.[4]

There appears to be some uncertainty in the case law as to just what kind of a procedure site plan approval is. The tendency of the recent decisions has been to look to the nature of the procedural process created by the local ordinance or bylaw to determine whether the site plan review process is a special permit process.[5] This question is more than academic, since the way it is answered determines issues such as the scope of the board's review, the formality attending its review, the need for a super majority for approval, and the availability, timing and scope of judicial review.[6] A fair reading of the decisions suggests that unless the local ordinance or bylaw explicitly makes site plan review a special permit process, it will not be so treated by the courts. Counsel representing applicants in circumstances where a special permit is not otherwise required should seek common ground with the board at the outset on the nature of the site plan review process.

The standard of judicial review of the action of a board in denying or conditioning site plan approval is substantially different than is the case with an ordinary form of special permit. The reviewing court hears the evidence and finds the facts de novo but is not required to give the deference to the decision of the board that it must give in the ordinary special permit review.[7] Since the site plan review process looks to allowance of a use with conditions rather than its denial, where site plan approval is denied the reviewing court after finding the facts, examines the reasons given by the board only to see if the problems are "so intractable" as to "admit of no reasonable solution."

The court may uphold the denial of site plan approval only where both it and the board have independently concluded that no form of reasonable conditions could be devised to satisfy the problems with the plan.[8]

---

[3] Y. D. Dugout, Inc. v. Board of Appeals, 357 Mass. 25, 255 N.E.2d 732 (1970).

[4] Auburn v. Planning Bd. of Dover, 12 Mass. App. 998, 429 N.E.2d 71 (1981), *appeal denied*, 385 Mass. 1102, 440 N.E.2d 1174.

[5] St. Botolph Citizens Comm., Inc. v. Boston Redevelopment Authority, 429 Mass. 1, n.9 (1999); Osberg v. Planning Board, 44 Mass. App. 56 (1997); Berkshire Power Dev., Inc. v. Zoning Board of Appeals, 43 Mass. App. 828 (1997); Quincy v. Planning Board, 39 Mass. App. 17, 652 N.E.2d 901 (1995).

[6] *See* Osberg v. Planning Board and St. Botolph Citizens Comm., Inc., *supra*. The latter case holds that the decision of a municipal board granting site plan approval, where the bylaw does not create such review as a special permit process, may not be appealed until the resulting building permit is issued.

[7] Prudential Ins. Co. v. Board of Appeals, 23 Mass. App. 278, 502 N.E.2d 137 (1986).

[8] Prudential Ins. Co. v. Board of Appeals, 23 Mass. App. 278, at 284, n.9, 502 N.E.2d 137, at 141, n.9 (1986).

Further, it has now been made explicitly clear that where a use is allowed as of right, subject to site plan review, no appeal will lie from the grant or denial of site plan approval where the reviewing board is not acting as a special permit granting authority. In such cases an aggrieved party must await the issuance, or denial, of the building permit, which latter action is subject to appeal. The review of the building permit decision will include a review of the site plan action upon which it is predicated.[9]

§ 5.20   Constructive Grant of Variances, Special Permits and Appeals

As pointed out previously,[1] the statute[2] provides that petitions for variance, applications for special permit, comprehensive permits and appeals from the building inspector must be decided by the local board within specified time limits or the requested relief is deemed constructively granted. The phrase "constructive grant" is often used incorrectly. As discussed below, the party claiming approval of a permit due to the inaction of a municipal board must take affirmative steps to perfect the "grant" and the "grant" cannot be perfected unless and until the time period afforded the permit granting authority has been exhausted.

With respect to variances, special permits and appeals pursuant to action or inaction of the building inspector, the statute also provides that the decision of the board must be filed with the city or town clerk within 14 days after it is made.[3] And it is provided that any appeal from a decision of the local board must be taken within 20 days after the decision is filed with the city of town clerk.[4]

The appellate courts have had considerable difficulty applying these various requirements in a coherent way to many of the specific factual circumstances that have arisen in practice.

Although the case law is still evolving in this area, it is now established that a variance, or appeal under § 8, is constructively granted if the board does not make its decision within 100 days from the date of filing and file its decision with the city or town clerk within 114 days from the date of filing (100 days in which to render the decision plus 14 days to file the decision with the city or town clerk).[5]

---

[9] "In cases where the site plan is related to a use as of right, the local board has no discretionary power to deny the use, and may only impose reasonable terms and conditions on the proposed use. American Retirement Corporation v. Barrell, Nos. 276776, 288051 (Mass. Land Ct., Jan. 19, 2005), *citing* Osberg v. Planning Board of Sturbridge, 44 Mass. App. Ct. 56, 59 (1997) and Dufault v. Millenium Power Partners, L.P., 49 Mass. App. 137, 139 (2000).

[1] *See* § 5.07[13].

[2] G.L. c. 40A, §§ 9 and 15.

[3] G.L. c. 40A, § 15.

[4] G.L. c. 40A, § 17.

[5] Burnham v. Town of Hadley, 58 Mass. App. Ct. 479, 481 (2003). "We conclude that § 15 allows the board to file its decision within fourteen days following the one hundred day period in

It is also established that a special permit is constructively granted if the board does not make and file its decision within 90 days after the public hearing is closed.[6] And it is established that where the board decides in less than 100 days but does not file its decision within 14 days of deciding, there is no constructive grant of relief as long as the decision is filed with the town clerk by the 114th day.[7] The 14 day requirement having been held directory in the case of variances where the overall time limits are met,[8] it may be expected that the same result will occur when the question is presented with respect to special permits. That is, where the board decides and files its decision within the 90-day period, there will be no constructive grant where more than 14 days intervene between the decision and the filing of the same with the town clerk.

Where the board files an incomplete decision and a constructive grant is claimed the results have also been unpredictable. In a case where the applicant applied for a variance from two provisions of the zoning bylaw and the board's denial only referred to one provision, the Appeals Court found a constructive grant as to the omitted provision. The board's attempt to correct what was apparently an inadvertent error by filing an amended decision some 22 days after the statutory deadline for action had passed was deemed ineffective.[9] On the other hand, the Supreme Judicial Court, reversing the Appeals Court, held that a timely filed decision denying a special permit that contained no reasons for the decision, and in fact contained reasons supporting the issuance of the permit, did not result in a constructive grant.[10]

The person who claims that an appeal, petition for variance, or application for special permit has been constructively granted must take certain statutorily prescribed steps to establish this claim.

Within 14 days from the expiration of the time within which the board was required to act (or any agreed extension thereof), the person claiming a constructive grant of relief must send mail notice of such grant to all parties in interest. Within the same 14 days such person must also notify the city or town clerk in writing of the claimed constructive grant and that notice of the same has been sent to all parties in interest.

---

which it must act. If the board fails to act within the one hundred day period (which was not the case here), a constructive grant has already occurred, regardless when the board files a written decision with the clerk, and the petitioner may upon expiration of the one hundred days send out notice of this circumstance."

[6] Burnham v. Town of Hadley, 58 Mass. App. Ct. 479, 481 (2003).
[7] O'Kane v. Bd. of Appeals, 20 Mass. App. 162, 478 N.E.2d 962 (1985).
[8] O'Kane v. Bd. of Appeals, 20 Mass. App. 162, 478 N.E.2d 962 (1985).
[9] Board of Appeals of Westwood v. Lambergs, 42 Mass. App. 411 (1997).
[10] Board of Aldermen of Newton v. Maniace, 429 Mass. 726 (1999).

The notice sent to parties in interest must notify them of the constructive grant and that appeals from such grant, if any, must be taken pursuant to G.L. c. 40A, § 17 within 20 days after the date the city or town clerk received written notice from the petitioner of the constructive grant.

After the expiration of 20 days without notice of appeal, or, if an appeal is taken, after receipt of notice from the court that such appeal has been dismissed or denied, the city or town clerk must forward to the petitioner a certificate. This certificate must state the date of the constructive grant, the fact that the board failed to take final action, and that the approval resulting from such failure has become final.[11]

Constructively granted variances or special permits will not take effect until the petitioner or applicant records in the proper registry of deeds a copy of the application for special permit or petition for variance along with the above-described certificate from the city or town clerk.[12]

The statutory time period leading to a constructive grant begins with the filing of the petition/application with the city or town clerk. Many cities and towns have an internal policy or rule that zoning applications must be reviewed by a particular board or officer for form or completeness prior to acceptance by the town clerk. The filing with such board or officer will not start the constructive grant clock running; only filing with the city or town clerk will do this. The applicant has a right to insist that the clerk accept its petition for filing.[13]

The constructive grant provisions do not apply to petitions for reconsiderations made within two years of an earlier denial, pursuant to G.L. c. 40A, § 16,[14] nor to matters remanded to the permit granting authority by judicial order.[15]

§ 5.21 Open Meeting, Quorum Requirements and Voting in Zoning Cases

The Zoning Act requires more than a simple majority vote in order for a permit granting authority or special permit granting authority to grant a variance or special permit, or to overturn a decision of the building inspector.[1]

Given the fact that by definition, local zoning boards are composed of citizen volunteers, there are frequently occasions where less than the full complement of board members appears for a scheduled hearing. At a later meeting the absent

---

[11] G.L. c. 40A, §§ 9, 15.

[12] G.L. c. 40A, § 11 (¶ 4).

[13] Racette v. Zoning Bd. of Appeals, 27 Mass. App. 617, 541 N.E.2d 369 (1989).

[14] Paquin v. Board of Appeals, 27 Mass. App. 577, 541 N.E.2d 352 (1989).

[15] Nasca v. Board of Appeals, 27 Mass. App. 47, 534 N.E.2d 792 (1989), *review granted*, 404 Mass. 1105, 537 N.E.2d 1248.

[1] G.L. c. 40A, §§ 9 and 15.

members may be present and attempt to vote on a petition after having read the minutes or listened to tapes of the meeting or meetings missed.

Counsel for an applicant will on such occasions be faced with a decision whether to go forward with less than a full board and/or to agree to allow members absent from the hearing to vote on the decision of the case. The following summary of the pertinent rules should be of assistance in such cases.

In order for a board of appeals to grant a variance or special permit there must be an affirmative vote of all three members of a three-member board and four out of five members of a five-member board.[2] In order for a special permit granting authority other than the board of appeals to grant a special permit there must be an affirmative vote of four members of a five-member board and two-thirds of the members of a board consisting of more than five members.[3] Thus, a nine–member planning board acting as a special permit granting authority is required to cast 6 affirmative votes to approve a special permit.

As indicated, the vote of the board granting a variance or special permit must be by a so-called super majority. However, the Zoning Act also requires that the board "make a detailed record of its proceedings, indicating the vote of each member upon each question... and setting forth the reasons for its decision."[4] It sometimes happens that the necessary super majority will agree on the issuance of the variance or special permit but disagree on the reasons of granting such relief. Is the variance or permit valid in such circumstances? It has been held that a super majority of the board must agree on the required findings supporting its decision, but that each member can arrive at those findings through a different reasoning process.[5]

A "quorum" of the board, which is hearing such an application or petition, is, for purposes of the Zoning Act, the same number as would be necessary to make a favorable decision on the application or petition.[6] All members of the board who vote on the decision must have been present at the public hearing.[7] These requirements are jurisdictional and cannot be waived, even with the assent of all interested parties.[8]

---

[2] G.L. c. 40A, §§ 9 and 15.

[3] G.L. c. 40A, § 9.

[4] G.L. c. 40A, §§ 9, 15.

[5] Security Mills Ltd. Partnership v. Board of Appeals, 413 Mass. 562 (1992).

[6] Sesnovich v. Board of Appeal, 313 Mass. 393, 47 N.E.2d 943 (1943).

[7] Sesnovich v. Board of Appeal, 313 Mass. 393, 47 N.E.2d 943 (1943); Mullin v. Planning Bd. of Brewster, 17 Mass. App. 139, 456 N.E.2d 780 (1983). Presumably this means all public hearings held on the issue.

[8] Sesnovich v. Board of Appeal, 313 Mass. 393, 47 N.E.2d 943 (1943); Mullin v. Planning Bd. of Brewster, 17 Mass. App. 139, 456 N.E.2d 780 (1983).

Thus, even with a favorably disposed board of less than the statutory "quorum," counsel should decline to go forward, since his client may otherwise end up with a defective permit. Similarly at continued public hearings on subsequent nights counsel should be alert to the presence of a statutory quorum composed of members who were present at earlier meetings. In addition, counsel should review any decision to be sure the members who participated in the public hearing make up a quorum of members voting on the decision. The Open Meeting Law[9] governs all permit granting authorities, special permit granting authorities, and any sub-committees of the same.[10] One can conceive of few situations where any of the statutory exceptions to the open meeting requirements would apply to zoning proceedings. Therefore, counsel for applicants are well-advised to be sure that the board is complying with open meeting requirements in order to prevent any subsequently issued permit from being vulnerable. This often takes a certain degree of delicacy where one is not certain how the board is disposed.

§ 5.22   Judicial Enforcement of Zoning

G.L. c. 40A, § 7 allows municipalities to provide in their bylaws for fines of up to $300 per day for violations of such ordinance or bylaw. The ordinance or bylaw may also be enforced by injunction. For purposes of enforcement, conditions of variances and special permits are deemed to be part of the ordinance or bylaw pursuant to which they were issued. They are enforced in the same manner and to the same extent as the bylaws themselves.[1] Both the District Court and the Superior Court have jurisdiction over criminal complaints seeking fines for violations of zoning bylaws.[2] However, there is no right in the municipality to seek fines in a civil action brought to enforce the ordinance or bylaw through injunction.[3] The inspector of buildings is designated by the statute as the municipal official charged with enforcing the ordinance or bylaw. (Contrary to popular belief, only the building inspector is empowered to enforce the zoning ordinance or bylaw). Unlike others who seek enforcement of the bylaw, the inspector need not first pursue the administrative process set out in G.L. c. 40A, § 8, 15, and 17 before filing suit in court.[4]

With respect to uses that violate the zoning ordinance or bylaw, there is a six-year

---

[9] G.L. c. 39, §§ 23A-24.

[10] Yaro v. Board of Appeals, 10 Mass. App. 587, 410 N.E.2d 725 (1980); Nigro v. Conservation Com of Canton, 17 Mass. App. 433, 458 N.E.2d 1219 (1984); J. & C. Homes, Inc. v. Planning Board of Groton, 8 Mass. App. 123, 391 N.E.2d 1232 (1979).

[1] Wyman v. Board of Appeals, 47 Mass. App. 635 (1999).

[2] Commonwealth v. Porrazzo, 25 Mass. App. 169, 516 N.E.2d 1182 (1987), *review denied*, 401 Mass. 1104, 519 N.E.2d 595.

[3] Burlington Sand & Gravel, Inc. v. Harvard, 31 Mass. App. 261 (1991).

[4] Commonwealth v. A. Graziano, Inc., 35 Mass. App. 69, 616 N.E.2d 825 (1993), summary op at (Mass. App) 21 M.L.W. 3223, *review denied*, 416 Mass. 1103, 621 N.E.2d 380, 22 M.L.W. 9.

statute of limitations on the prosecution of such violations if the use was commenced in accordance with the terms of a building permit issued by a person duly
authorized to issue such permits. Otherwise, for example, where the use was
commenced in violation of zoning and without obtaining a building permit, the
violation may be prosecuted indefinitely.[5]

With respect to structures that violate the bylaw, or the conditions of any variance
or special permit, no action may be brought to compel the removal, alteration, or
relocation of any such structure more than ten years after the commencement of
the violation, regardless of whether or not the structure was erected in accordance
with a duly issued permit.[6]

Note that where an unlawful use is commenced without permit in a structure that
was unlawfully erected or altered, the ten-year statute of limitations on enforcement
action will prevent judicial action to remove the structure but not to terminate the
use. For example, where a single-family structure is converted to a multifamily
structure in violation of the bylaw the conversion cannot be judicially undone after
the passage of ten years. However, judicial action can be taken to prevent the
unlawful multifamily use commenced without permit even after the passage of ten
years.[7]

Where the Inspector of Buildings fails to take action to enforce the ordinance
or bylaw, the statute provides that he may be requested to do so by any person,
and he must respond to the request for enforcement in writing, within fourteen (14)
days, if he declines to act.[8] In an unfortunate case, the Appeals Court held that the
enforcement request provided by G.L. c. 40A, § 7 confers a "directory" and not
a "mandatory" duty upon the building inspector or building official named in the
local bylaw or ordinance.[9] The Court held that although the fourteen-day period
is designed to encourage enforcement—or at least an investigation—the enforcing
agent may need more than the fourteen days allotted by statute. The unfortunate
aspect of the Court's decision is that, of course, without a mandatory duty, it is
possible that the enforcing authority will be under little pressure to respond to the
complaints of aggrieved parties. As G.L. c. 40A, § 7 provides the aggrieved party
with no other form of relief an absent an expensive claim in equity, the Court's
holding eviscerated the purpose and intent of allowing aggrieved abutters or
community residents to rely on the building department and/or zoning enforcement
officials to ensure zoning compliance.

---

[5] G.L. c. 40A, § 7; Ferrante v. Board of Appeals, 345 Mass. 158, 186 N.E.2d 471 (1962).

[6] G.L. c. 40A, § 7.

[7] Lord v. Board of Appeals, 30 Mass. App. 226 (1991).

[8] G.L. c. 40A, § 7.

[9] Vokes v. Avery W. Lovell, Inc., 18 Mass. App. Ct. 471 (1984), *review denied*, 393 Mass.
1103.

Once the building official has acted, either by refusing to enforce the request or denying the relief sought, a party aggrieved by such action may appeal to the board of appeals pursuant to G.L. c. 40A, § 15, and from there to the courts pursuant to G.L. c. 40A, § 17. Parties who are not aggrieved as that term is defined in the case law may not appeal and must rest content with the response of the building inspector.[10]

Municipal boards, but not the individual members of such boards, and municipal officials with duties to perform in relation to the building code or zoning, also have standing to appeal the building inspectors refusal of a request for enforcement.[11]

§ 5.23   Split Lots (Lots Transected By a Zoning Boundary)

Difficult problems often arise where a single lot is within two or more zoning districts, particularly where the lot lies partially in a residential zone and partially in a business or industrial zone. Very few ordinances or bylaws deal in any detail with how such lots are to be treated. Often, local zoning officials and boards of appeals will treat the zoning boundary as a lot line, particularly where the owner proposes to make a use allowed in the less restricted zone but prohibited in the more restricted zone. However, it is the lot line and not the zoning boundary line that controls.

The Appeals Court has ruled that, in the absence of a specific prohibition in the ordinance or bylaw, the lot owner may use the entire lot, including the more restricted portion, to make up dimensional and density requirements, such as setback requirements. Nevertheless, the use restrictions of each district will continue to apply to that portion of the lot that is within such district.[1] So the factory built in the industrial zone of a split lot could not have its loading or parking facility in the residential zone on the same lot. This rule applies whether the different zoning districts are in the same municipality or in different municipalities.[2]

Note however, that the language of the ordinance or bylaw itself can make the zone boundary, rather than the lot boundary, the operative parameter for calculating compliance with dimensional and density requirements.[3]

Where a use crosses zoning districts and is conforming in one and lawfully nonconforming in the other, non-use of the nonconforming portion of the lot can result in extinguishment of the right to make the use on that portion, even where

---

[10] G.L. c. 40, §§ 8, 17; Green v. Board of Appeals, 404 Mass. 571, 536 N.E.2d 584 (1989).

[11] Harvard Square Defense Fund, Inc. v. Planning Bd. of Cambridge, 27 Mass. App. 491, 540 N.E.2d 182 (1989), *review denied*, 405 Mass. 1204; Green, *supra* at 404 Mass. 572, n.5.

[1] Tofias v. Butler, 26 Mass. App. 89, 523 N.E.2d 796 (1988), and cases cited therein.

[2] Dupont v. Town of Dracut, 41 Mass. App. 293, 670 N.E.2d 183 (1996).

[3] Goldlust v. Board of Appeals, 27 Mass. App. 1183, 541 N.E.2d 1019 (1989).

the use continues uninterrupted on the conforming portion.[4]

§ 5.24 Perimeter Plans—Entitlement to Approval Not Required Endorsement

Many property owners when faced with a proposed use amendment to the zoning bylaw will attempt to secure the three–year zoning use freeze provided by G.L. c. 40A, § 6 by filing so-called perimeter plans with the planning board pursuant to G.L. c. 41, § 81P. Such plans do not divide the property at all but merely show its boundaries. They would be entitled to be recorded under G.L. c. 41, § 81X without planning board endorsement, if they bear a certification from a registered land surveyor that the property and way lines shown on the plan are not newly created.

However plans with a surveyor's certificate receive no grandfathering, while ANR plans endorsed by the planning board are entitled to the three–year use freeze. Therefore, property owners naturally prefer the latter.

Read literally, G.L. c. 41, § 81P suggests that perimeter plans are entitled to ANR endorsement. And the Appeals Court has construed the statute literally, holding that the property owner may submit a perimeter plan for ANR endorsement even if he intends no division or conveyance of the property and merely seeks to secure the zoning freeze. It is not even necessary for the plan to be recorded.[1] *But see* the discussion regarding a contra opinion as to a perimeter plan's entitlement to ANR endorsement in Section 5.10[2][b][vii].

§ 5.25 Who is 'Aggrieved' Party for Purposes of Zoning Appeal

The right to seek judicial review of the decision, or failure to act, of a special permit granting authority is limited to (1) "any municipal officer or board"[1] and (2) "any person aggrieved by such decision or nonaction."[2]

---

[4] Burlington Sand & Gravel, Inc. v. Harvard, 26 Mass. App. 436, 528 N.E.2d 889 (1988). For other cases involving split lots, *see* Brookline v. Co-Ray Realty Co., 326 Mass. 206, 93 N.E.2d 581 (1950); Harrison v. Building Inspector of Braintree, 350 Mass. 559, 215 N.E.2d 773 (1966); Richardson v. Zoning Board of Appeals, 351 Mass. 375, 221 N.E.2d 396 (1966); Building Inspector of Dennis v. Harney, 2 Mass. App. 584, 317 N.E.2d 81 (1974); Chelmsford v. Byrne, 6 Mass. App. 848, 372 N.E.2d 1307 (1978); Lapenas v. Zoning Board of Appeals, 352 Mass. 530, 226 N.E.2d 361 (1967); Tambone v. Board of Appeal, 348 Mass. 359, 203 N.E.2d 802 (1965); Moore v. Swampscott, 26 Mass. App. 1008, 530 N.E.2d 808 (1988).

[1] Long v. Board of Appeals, 32 Mass. App. 232, 588 N.E.2d 692 (1992), *review denied*, 412 Mass. 1104, 592 N.E.2d 751.

[1] Only municipal officers or boards within the same municipality have standing under this provision. Planning Bd. of Marshfield v. Zoning Board of Appeals of Pembroke, 427 Mass. 699 (1998).

[2] G.L. c. 40A, § 17.

Whether or not a party is aggrieved for purposes of the Zoning Act is a matter of degree, and calls for the exercise of discretion by the court, rather than the imposition of an inflexible rule.[3]. As discussed in Chapter 4, the standing requirements of the Zoning Act apply to claims by parties seeking to challenge the issuance of a comprehensive permit pursuant to G.L. c. 40B, § 21.

The fact that a person is or is not a "party in interest" under G.L. c. 40A, § 11 is not dispositive of the issue, but there is a rebuttable presumption that persons "entitled to receive notice of the pubic hearing [are] persons aggrieved."[4] It is important to remember that the statute defines persons entitled to receive notice and persons aggrieved in a different manner in two different sections,[5] so the presumption is indeed rebuttable, being of the class of presumptions often called "disappearing" by writers on the law of evidence.[6]

To determine whether a plaintiff is a person aggrieved under G.L. c. 40A, § 17, the trial court must first decide whether he or she has suffered significant—and particularized—harm as a proximate result of a deviation from the statute or bylaw or the project as approved by the permit granting authority.[7] The harm must be real, substantial, and directly caused by the zoning decision or nonaction that is being challenged.[8] And the harm must be of a type greater than that suffered by members of the public and others with only a general interest in the preservation of the values protected by the ordinance or bylaw.[9]

Where the harm alleged is the loss of integrity of the zoning district, the plaintiff's property and the use of that property must be among the class of property and the class of uses that the zoning scheme was intended to protect. Thus an owner of business property has no right to complain when a variance or special permit is granted in a residence district to allow another business use.[10] Similarly, property within a materially different type of zoning district than the district to which the challenged zoning decision relates may be outside the scope of concern of the zoning provision at issue.

In sum, to be aggrieved, a plaintiff must always be able to demonstrate a direct,

---

[3] Rafferty v. Santa Maria Hospital, 5 Mass. App. 624, 629, 367 N.E.2d 856 (1977).

[4] Paulding v. Bruins, 18 Mass. App. 707, 470 N.E.2d 398 (1984).

[5] G.L. c. 40A, §§ 11, 17.

[6] Redstone v. Board of Appeals, 11 Mass. App. 383, 416 N.E.2d 543 (1981); Marotta v. Board of Appeals, 336 Mass. 199, 143 N.E.2d 270 (1957).

[7] Monks v. Zoning Bd. of Appeals of Plymouth, 37 Mass. App. Ct. 685, 688 (1994). *See also* Butler v. City of Waltham, 63 Mass. App. Ct. 435 (2005), where the Court introduced both "qualitative" and "quantitative" tests to establish standing.

[8] Waltham Motor Inn, Inc. v. La Cava, 3 Mass. App. 210, 326 N.E.2d 348 (1975).

[9] *See* Green v. Board of Appeals, 404 Mass. 571, 536 N.E.2d 584 (1989).

[10] Circle Lounge & Grille, Inc. v. Board of Appeals, 324 Mass. 427, 86 N.E.2d 920 (1949); Redstone v. Board of Appeals, 11 Mass. App. 383, 416 N.E.2d 543 (1981).

tangible harm to a private property right or private interest. The harm must be particularized and not be that suffered by general members of the community.[11] The zoning ordinance or bylaw itself may create such a private property right or interest sufficient to create standing where it would not otherwise exist.[12] However, it has also been held, at least in cases where the proposed use is not permitted, or is otherwise alien to the zoning scheme of the district, the claim of tangible harm may be posited solely on the abutter's right to have the integrity of the zoning district preserved, provided his property is located in the same zoning district.[13]

The Supreme Judicial Court has at least partially overturned what had been a growing stream of cases from the Appeals Court imposing greater standing requirements on abutter-plaintiffs in zoning appeals.[14] In view of the recently unsettled state of the law on what it means for an abutter to be "aggrieved" for purposes of taking an appeal the Court's most recent summing up on this point follows: "Only a 'person aggrieved' may challenge a decision of a zoning board of appeals. As noted, a plaintiff is a 'person aggrieved' if he suffers some infringement of his legal rights. The injury must be more than speculative, but the term 'person aggrieved' should not be read narrowly. Abutters entitled to notice of zoning board of appeals hearings enjoy a rebuttable presumption that they are 'persons aggrieved'.

If standing is challenged, the jurisdictional question is decided on 'all the evidence with no benefit to the plaintiffs from the presumption.' A review of standing based on 'all the evidence' does not require that the fact finder ultimately find a plaintiff's allegations meritorious. To do so would be to deny standing, after the fact, to any unsuccessful plaintiff. Rather, the plaintiff must put forth credible evidence to substantiate his allegations. In this context, standing becomes, then, essentially a question of fact for the trial judge."[15]

The concerns in *Marashlian* that the Court found to be sufficient 'aggrievement' were that the proposed development would diminish the amount of public parking

---

[11] Denney v. Board of Appeals of Seekonk, 59 Mass. App. Ct. 208 (2003). A generalized, nonspecific interest in enforcement of the zoning law is not the same as an assertion that a private interest has been affected. A plaintiff does not satisfy this requirement by asserting "a claim that involves a matter of general public interest." *Citing* Nickerson v. Zoning Bd. of Appeals of Raynham, 53 Mass. App. Ct. 680, 683 (2002).

[12] Monks v. Zoning Bd. of Appeals, 37 Mass. App. 685, 642 N.E.2d 314 (1994).

[13] Jaffe v. Zoning Bd. of Appeals, 34 Mass. App. 929, 612 N.E.2d 693 (1993); Cohen v. Zoning Bd. of Appeals, 35 Mass. App. 619, 624 N.E.2d 119 (1993), summary op at Cohen v. Zoning Bd. of Appeals, 22 M.L.W. 742 (1993, Mass. App.).

[14] *See* Watros v. Greater Lynn Mental Health & Retardation Ass'n, 421 Mass. 106, 653 N.E.2d 589 (1995); Harvard Square Defense Fund, Inc. v. Planning Bd. of Cambridge, 27 Mass. App. 491, 540 N.E.2d 182 (1989), *review denied*, 405 Mass. 1204, 542 N.E.2d 602.

[15] Marashlian v. Zoning Bd. of Appeals, 421 Mass. 719, 721, 660 N.E.2d 369 (1996).

available, and increase traffic, in the central business district of the City of New-buryport.[16]

Yet in a footnote to the case, the Court went out of its way to state its approval of an Appeals Court case that had denied standing on similar grounds.[17] It seems fair to say that the Appeals Court, however haltingly, was moving toward more objective standards by which trial courts could determine aggrievement. The Supreme Judicial Court has now made it clear that such a determination is 'one of degree calling for discretion rather than inflexible rule' and that the term 'person aggrieved' is not to be construed narrowly.[18]

In *Rinaldi v. Board of Appeal of Boston*,[19] a next-door abutter in a densely built up city neighborhood was held not to have standing to challenge a variance, thus showing that summary judgment on the aggrievement issue may be the only practical way of making a variance stand up on appeal.

To survive a motion to dismiss for lack of standing, counsel representing a plaintiff challenging a permit pursuant to G.L. c. 40A, § 17 must do more than simply allege injury. As obvious as it may seem, the plaintiff needs more than simple allegations. Affidavits from engineers, appraisers, land use planners and/or other experts averring to the specific injury the permit (and project) will cause is critical to support her claim of injury.[20] Counsel representing the defendant board or permit grantee is advised to do the same: produce expert witness testimony, only

---

[16] *See also* Braccia v. Mountain, No. 289072 (Mass. Land Ct. Jan. 20, 2005), "With regard to alleged drainage impacts, the Braccias have again only brought forward very generalized and unsubstantiated claims that the Scotland Woods plan will, when built, cause more drainage to flow onto their property."

[17] Riley v. Janco Cent., 38 Mass. App. 984, 652 N.E.2d 631 (1995), *review denied*, 421 Mass. 1108, 659 N.E.2d 287. *See also* Nickerson v. Zoning Board of Appeals of Raynham, 53 Mass. App. Ct. 680, 761 N.E.2d 544 (2002), where the plaintiff argued he had standing, although he lived one mile from the site at issue. The trial court determined there was standing under *Marashlian* because the plaintiff used a particular intersection "on a regular basis" and there was credible evidence the proposed development would result in at least some increase in traffic. The appeals court said the lower court failed to address a separate and "essential element" of standing: whether the plaintiff's injury was particularized. In the context of the facts in *Nickerson*, the question was whether the plaintiff's traffic concerns were special and different from those of the rest of the community. The appellate court found no standing, concluding that while the plaintiff undoubtedly was inconvenienced by the existing traffic, those concerns were an insufficient predicate for finding that he was a "person aggrieved." His interest was not substantially different from that of all other members of the community frustrated and inconvenienced by heavy traffic.

[18] Marashlian v. Zoning Bd. of Appeals, 421 Mass. 719, 721, 660 N.E.2d 369 (1996).

[19] 50 Mass. App. 657 (2001).

[20] *See*, for example, Braccia v. Mountain, No. 289072 (Mass. Land Ct., Jan. 20, 2005); "With regard to alleged drainage impacts, the Braccias have again only brought forward very generalized and unsubstantiated claims that the Scotland Woods plan will, when built, cause more drainage to flow onto their property."

that this testimony must demonstrate that the particularized harm claimed by the plaintiff is precisely that harm shared by the general public. In addition or in the alternative, the defendant board or permit grantee can attempt to show that the project as approved will not impact the plaintiff as alleged. Once again, this is best accomplished through expert testimony.

§ 5.26   Modification of Board's Decision

The decision of a permit granting or special permit granting authority is final once it is filed with the municipal clerk. At least during the 20–day appeal period the board may correct "inadvertent or clerical errors" in its decision. However, it may not make a "substantive amendment which changes the result of an original deliberate decision" without a new hearing duly noticed in accordance with the statute.[1]

It seems clear that the Board can, after proper notice and hearing, modify a special permit or variance granted months or even years earlier, if the owner of the affected land so requests.[2] It is less clear whether such a modification can occur against the wishes of the owner of the benefited land after he or she has materially changed position in reliance upon the permit.[3]

§ 5.27   Permit Conditions Requiring Off-Site Improvements

It is not at all uncommon for a special permit granting authority to impose conditions on the grant of a special permit that require the applicant to construct improvements on property other than that which is the subject of the permit. The most common example of this is to require improvements in off-site roadways, construction or extension of water or sewer lines, set aside of open space and other exactions rationally connected to the special permit and in proportion to the impacts caused by the special permit use or structure.

Not unusual is the requirement that applicants secure easements or other rights from abutters in order to "loop" utility mains or connect roadways for secondary access. The legality of such conditions has been frequently questioned by counsel for developers. This question is at least partially answered by an Appeals Court decision that invalidated a special permit condition that required the developer to make improvements in an adjacent state highway. In so holding the Court stated, "It is unreasonable to impose a condition the performance of which lies entirely

---

[1] Tenneco Oil Co. v. Springfield, 406 Mass. 658, 549 N.E.2d 1135 (1990).

[2] Huntington v. Zoning Bd. of Appeals, 12 Mass. App. 710, 428 N.E.2d 826 (1981); Board of Selectmen v. Monument Inn, Inc., 8 Mass. App. 158, 391 N.E.2d 1265 (1979), *later appeal*, 14 Mass. App. 957, 438 N.E.2d 365.

[3] *See* Hogan v. Hayes, 19 Mass. App. 399, 474 N.E.2d 1158 (1985).

beyond the applicant's power."[1] It remains to be seen just what "entirely beyond the applicant's power" really means. Would for example, the applicant be required to approach the legal entity that controls the off-site property or utility and offer money or other consideration for the rights necessary to fulfill the condition?

As a general rule, however, adjudicative boards may extract, as a condition of approval of a special permit, off-site improvements if, but for the improvements, the special permit could be denied. See Chapter 3 for a discussion of regulatory takings relating to adjudicative permits.

§ 5.28   Earth Removal

Gravel is a very valuable construction commodity, and is found frequently in Massachusetts in large deposits left by the last glacial age, most notably south of Boston, on Cape Cod and the islands of Martha's Vineyard and Nantucket. (In addition, lands that contain large amounts of sand and gravel deposits, precisely because of their geologic composition, can typically accommodate wastewater disposal systems).

Unfortunately for the owners of these deposits the mining of them entails a great deal of noise, dust and heavy truck traffic. Many communities regulate (in practice prohibit) this activity through their zoning ordinances and bylaws. Many others regulate it through a general bylaw enacted under the authority of G.L. c. 40, § 21(17) or the Home Rule Amendment to the State Constitution. Some regulate it in both zoning and general bylaws. Where the regulation is solely through zoning, there are occasional attempts to incorporate the disfavored gravel removal use into a, nearly sanctified, agricultural type of use. A common example is the "need" to remove a large hill of gravel in order that the parcel can be leveled for successful farming, or even excavated below the sub-surface to create a cranberry bog. As the "agricultural use" is likely protected from aggressive zoning regulation pursuant to G.L. c. 40A, § 3 (see Chapter 6), disguising an earth removal operation as an "agricultural activity" may evade effective local review.

On the other hand, where the community or abutters successfully resist, it is usually because they can demonstrate that the incidental use clearly dominates over the agricultural use. The word "incidental" in zoning bylaws or ordinances incorporates two concepts: It means that the use must not be the primary use of the property but rather one that is subordinate and minor in significance. When used to define an accessory use, the word incidental must also incorporate the concept of reasonable relationship with the primary use. It is not enough that the use be subordinate; it must also be attendant or concomitant.[1]

---

[1] V.S.H. Realty, Inc. v. Zoning Board of Appeals, 30 Mass. App. 530 (1991).
[1] Henry v. Board of Appeals, 418 Mass. 841, 641 N.E.2d 1334 (1994); Old Colony Council-Boy

Where earth removal is regulated by both zoning and general bylaws the applicant must obtain two separate and independent approvals. Lawful denial of either permit will prevent the use even if one of the permits has already been obtained.[2] But where earth removal is not mentioned as an allowed use in the zoning bylaw, while being permitted subject to permit under an earth removal general bylaw, the zoning bylaw will not be interpreted as prohibiting the earth removal use.[3]

Note that in considering an application for an earth removal permit under a general bylaw the permit granting authority may not properly consider the increase in truck traffic over municipal roadways, but can properly consider noise and dust caused by the extraction and transport of the gravel.[4] Traffic is of course a proper zoning concern where removal is governed by the zoning ordinance or bylaw.

Finally, the removal of large amounts of gravel often has a negative impact on surface and ground water supplies and thus the activity may be regulated by one or more state (or federal) statutes or regulations. Of greatest concern is that the removal of sand and gravel leaves the subsurface more vulnerable to contamination, simply because there will be less surface materials to assimilate contamination that falls on the land surface.

§ 5.29   Growth Management

Massachusetts cities and towns have long engaged in "growth management" or the intentional and planned interfering with the private sector timing of new residential, commercial and industrial development. The Supreme Judicial Court has historically upheld moratoria on new growth,[1] limitations on the timing of new growth,[2] minimum lot sizes as it related to new growth[3] and the phasing of new growth. In *Zuckerman v. Town of Hadley*,[4] the Court reversed its long held position that cities and towns may permissibly places limits on the number of building permits an individual may receive within a specified period of time. The *Zuckerman* holding is of great importance to municipal and private counsel alike.

There is no doubt that the Court's holding in *Zuckerman* was correct as a matter

---

Scouts of America v. Zoning Board of Appeals, 31 Mass. App. 46 (1991).

[2] McIntyre v. Board of Selectmen of Ashby, 31 Mass. App. 735 (1992).

[3] Jaworski v. Earth Removal Bd., 35 Mass. App. 795, 626 N.E.2d 19 (1994), summary op at 22 M.L.W. 1043 (Mass. App.), *review denied*, 417 Mass. 1102, 631 N.E.2d 57, 22 M.L.W. 1358.

[4] Jaworski v. Earth Removal Bd., 35 Mass. App. 795, 626 N.E.2d 19 (1994), summary op at 22 M.L.W. 1043 (Mass. App.), *review denied*, 417 Mass. 1102, 631 N.E.2d 57, 22 M.L.W. 1358., and cases cited therein.

[1] Collura v. Arlington, 367 Mass. 881 (1975).

[2] *See*, for example, Sturges v. Chilmark, 380 Mass. 246 (1980).

[3] *See*, for example, Simon v. Needham, 311 Mass. 560 (1942).

[4] 442 Mass. 511 (2004).

of law.[5] It is axiomatic that growth management regulations—in this case an annual cap on the issuance of building permits—must be linked to an identified deficiency in municipal infrastructure, financial crises or other concern relating to public health or safety that the regulation seeks to address. The Town of Hadley's perpetual limitation on building permits ran contrary to the underlying purpose of growth management regulations: guiding and managing growth to provide time to develop plans, construct needed infrastructure and raise revenues to enable municipal government to function. Thus the holding in *Zuckerman* is unremarkable. Growth management regulations, unlimited as to time, raise substantive due process issues. The rational basis for the regulation—limiting growth to coincide with the planning for growth—is not supported by the regulation itself.

As discussed in Chapter 2 however, what is remarkable is the fact that Massachusetts remains without any comprehensive planning legislation requiring (or even encouraging) cities and towns to plan. The state's Zoning Act has not been revised in 30 years. The Act is not linked to plans or planning. The word "planning" as a verb or "plan" as a noun do not appear once in the Zoning Act. Cities and towns routinely revise their zoning ordinances and bylaws without reference to or in accordance with, a plan.

Whereas a zoning change that is not in accordance with a plan in true plan states is deemed void ab initio, Massachusetts cities and towns are held to a simple "rational basis" standard. Given the maxim that a reviewing Court will not substitute its judgment for that of the local legislature, when coupled with the fairly debatable test,[6] it is exceedingly difficult for a municipality to "fail" the rational basis test.

Yet the *Zuckerman* Court concluded that growth management regulations cannot be employed in the absence of a planning study. "Restraining the rate of growth for a period of unlimited duration, and not for the purpose of conducting studies or planning for future growth is inherently and unavoidably detrimental to the public welfare, and therefore not a legitimate zoning purpose."[7]

How would municipal counsel know what this study should contain? Upon what regional or statewide policy or goal should it be based? How should municipal growth management concerns be linked to those of abutting communities in the absence of state or regional guide? How should this planning study prioritize competing public policy issues such as the need for affordable housing, open space

---

[5] Portions of this discussion are based upon an article by Jonathan D. Witten, *Linking Planning and Zoning* Planning & Environmental Law, October 2004, Vol. 56.

[6] "If its reasonableness is fairly debatable, [a zoning bylaw] will be sustained." Zuckerman v. Town of Hadley, 442 Mass. at 516, *citing* Sturges v. Chilmark, 380 Mass. 246 (1980).

[7] Zuckerman v Town of Hadley, 442 Mass. 511, at 518.

and agricultural preservation, protection of surface and ground water supplies and so on?

As almost any land use regulation can be justified as furthering the public health, safety or welfare, the rational basis standard of land use regulation, in the absence of a planning requirement, creates chaos. Without Court adjudication, it is impossible to determine whether a local land use regulation is permissible. No wonder that the Town of Hadley believed its growth management regulation was permissible. Rather than require municipalities to adopt a plan and regulations consistent with that plan, Massachusetts simply enables cities and towns to adopt regulations, regardless of any link to a plan or planning policy.

On one hand, the Court has reminded us that zoning in the absence of planning violates due process. On the other hand, however, Massachusetts has failed to create any framework for comprehensive planning legislation such that cities and towns could adopt plans and regulations that comport with the substantive due process requirements that the Court (and the Constitution) demands.

Without planning legislation that demands consistency between planning policy and land use regulations, cities and towns do the best they can but are guided not by long term state or regional interests, but rather by the issues of the day. They struggle with numerous issues, but have no means for coordinating these often contradictory challenges. Undoubtedly, this is what the New York Court of Appeals meant when it stated that the comprehensive plan "…is the insurance that the public welfare is being served and that zoning does not become nothing more than just a Gallup poll." *Udell v. Haas*, 21 N.Y.2d 463, 469 (1968).

The cynic often remarks that nothing is stopping a Massachusetts city or town from adopting a comprehensive plan and "living by it." Nevertheless, without a legal basis for the plan and planning consistency, a municipality's plan is meaningless. "Neither the master plan itself nor the law requires that zoning be in strict accordance with a master plan." *Rando v. Town of North Attleborough*, 44 Mass. App. Ct. 603, 612 (1998).

The irony is that non-plan states are perceived as granting their cities and towns broad discretion while plan states are viewed as too paternalistic and controlling. The truth is just the opposite. As highlighted by *Zuckerman*, without a mandatory link between planning and zoning, cities and towns may be free to adopt any controls they wish, but once challenged, all bets are off as to the outcome.

All land use regulations in Massachusetts are theoretically vulnerable to attack and the outcome of *Zuckerman*. As Massachusetts does not require regulations to be based upon a plan and very, very few municipal ordinances or bylaws are the result of a planning study such as the one demanded by the Court in *Zuckerman*. It is not unreasonable to think that all local zoning regulations in a city or town that are defended on a growth management basis are vulnerable, including but not limited to: minimum lot sizes, height and dimensional controls, use restrictions and use prohibitions.

If Massachusetts were a plan state and Hadley's growth management regulations were in accordance with its plan, *Zuckerman* would have (or should have) been decided differently. The regulation in question would have been tailored to meet the Town's long-term growth management goals as embodied in the Town's plan. The fact that the Zuckermans could only obtain four building permits per year for their land would have been consistent with the plan and logically undisturbed by the Court.

§ 5.30 Inclusionary Zoning

As discussed in Chapter 4 and given the controversy attendant with the comprehensive permit statute, it would seem that a solution to the Massachusetts affordable housing problem that avoided such controversies would be embraced by all concerned.

Inclusionary zoning represents one such a solution.[1] Mandatory inclusionary zoning is not currently authorized in Massachusetts, however.[2] It is important to note, though, that as of this writing, no less than three communities (Marion, Stow

---

[1] An additional solution is the use of impact fees. Unfortunately, impact fees are not authorized in the Commonwealth of Massachusetts with the exception of towns on Cape Cod. *See*, for example, Emerson College v. City of Boston, 462 N.E.2d 1098 (1984) and Greater Franklin Developers Association, Inc. v. Town of Franklin, 730 N.E.2d 900 (Mass. App. Ct. 2000). By virtue of the Cape Cod Commission Act (Ch. 716 of the Acts of 1989 and Ch. 2 of the Acts of 1990, s.12–13), towns on Cape Cod that have a comprehensive plan, certified by the Cape Cod Commission, are able to impose impact fees on new development. The grant of authority to Cape Cod towns to impose impact fees (as well as enter into development agreements that would otherwise be deemed illegal contract zoning) coincides with the Cape Cod Commission Act's requirement of comprehensive plan development and consistency with the Regional Policy Plan for Cape Cod. While towns are not required to prepare and have certified a comprehensive plan, nine of the 15 towns have certified plans and the remaining six are presumed to have plans in place by the end of 2004.

[2] Ironically, the same state that has pioneered a bludgeon to force cities and towns to "accept" affordable housing (G.L. c. 40B, § 20–23) has prohibited those same cities and towns from developing affordable housing in a manner successfully used elsewhere. G.L. c. 40A, § 9 authorizes increases in density above that allowed by the underlying zoning upon the set aside of, among other things, affordable housing units. The limitation to this enabling authority is that a special (adjudicative) permit is required from a local board, thus increasing the odds that the local board will extract additional public benefits from the developer and decreasing the odds that the developer will be able to challenge the extraction upon appeal. Simply put, the special permit requirement creates an option that few developers will choose given the other option available to them—a comprehensive permit under G.L. c. 40B, § 20–23. As a result, inclusionary zoning in Massachusetts will never achieve successful results and as long as the comprehensive permit option is available, is unlikely to be an option selected by a developer.

and Duxbury) have each adopted—and have had approved by the Attorney General's office—mandatory inclusionary zoning bylaws. In each case, a division of land greater than the thresholds established in the bylaw trigger the need for a special permit. In exchange for the grant of a special permit, the applicant must comply with the set aside of no less than 10% of the proposed number of dwelling units at a sales price of no less than 80% of median income. While no challenge has yet been made to these bylaws, each are logically defensible.

First, they do not run afoul of the uniformity requirements of G.L. c. 40A, § 4 and *SCIT v. Braintree*. Whereas the *SCIT* Court concluded that a special permit could not be required for all uses in any one zoning district, in the present case, a special permit is only required if the applicant exceeds the thresholds established in the bylaw. Second, the very nature of the special permit process is one of extraction of public benefits commensurate with impacts of the proposed development, subject to the framework of *Nollan* and *Dolan*, discussed in Chapter 3. There is hardly any doubt that below market housing units is rationally related to the development of market rate housing. Third, each of the three bylaws have established the same percentage requirement (10%) for inclusion as does the comprehensive permit statute. It is suggested that it would be difficult to argue that the comprehensive permit statute's requirement of 10% is rational but the requirements of Marion, Stow and Duxbury are not.

Common sense dictates that if inclusionary zoning were in place in every suburban and rural community in the state, the stated purpose of the comprehensive permit statute, to reduce the barriers of restrictive zoning in the suburbs, would be unnecessary.[3]

The requirement that a developer of land or a petitioner for an adjudicative permit set aside land, money or "things" is a traditional and common practice. The validity of municipal extractions of land, money or "things" as required by legislation and adjudicative permits is well settled.[4]

It should be no surprise, therefore, that cities and towns seeking to increase the number of dwelling units sold or rented at below market rates would be attracted

---

[3] "It is nonsense to single out inclusionary zoning…and label it "socio-economic" if that is meant to imply that other aspects of zoning are not…It would be ironic if inclusionary zoning to encourage the construction of lower income housing were ruled beyond the power of a municipality because it is "socio-economic" when the need has arisen from the socio-economic zoning of the past that excluded it." Southern Burlington County, NAACP v. Township of Mt. Laurel, 456 A.2d 390, 449 (1983). (*Mt. Laurel II*).

[4] Referring to the decisions in *Nollan* and *Dolan*, *supra*, the California Supreme Court noted "scholarly comment on the cases is almost unmanageably large. Ehrlich v. City of Culver City, 12 Cal. 4th 854, 868 (1996). The Court proceeded to cite seventeen references to *Nollan* and *Dolan* and the issue of adjudicative extractions of land, money and "things."

to the time tested practice of extractions—quid pro quos—in exchange for the grant of a development permit.[5]

Inclusionary zoning—the method of extracting on or off-site dwelling units or fees in lieu of the extraction—in exchange for subdivision approval, approval of an adjudicative permit or a variance is a logical tool for increasing the stock of below market rate housing within a particular development or the community at large.[6]

Inclusionary zoning requirements are highly effective within rapidly growing suburban and rural communities in Massachusetts, but can be tailored to work effectively in the state's urban areas as well.[7]

-----

[5] A study completed in 1992 revealed that over 20,000 affordable dwelling units were created as a result of the use of inclusionary zoning regulations by local governments in California. *See*, for example, San Diego Housing Commission, 1992; California Inclusionary Housing Survey, San Diego, CA, San Diego Housing Commission. A study completed in 2002 concluded that over 50,000 affordable dwelling units had been created in California via inclusionary regulations. *See* Barbara Kaurtz, *"In Defense of Inclusionary Zoning: Successfully Creating Affordable Housing"*, 36 U.S.F.L. Rev. 971 (2002). Montgomery County, Maryland's inclusionary housing ordinance has produced over 11,000 affordable dwelling units. Karen D. Brown, *"Expanding Affordable Housing Through Inclusionary Zoning: Lessons From the Washington Metropolitan Area,"* The Brookings Institution Center on Urban and Metropolitan Policy, October 2001. "Many jurisdictions throughout the country have implemented inclusionary zoning ordinances, from Burlington, VT to Santa Fe, NM to dozens of communities in California. Nationwide, Montgomery County, MD has been the most successful. *Id.* at p.2. "If cities in the metro area [Minneapolis/St. Paul] were to adopt this approach [inclusionary zoning], up to $15,000 per housing unit could be saved and nearly 40,000 affordable units could be built within twenty-five years." Justin D. Cummins, *"Housing Matters: Why Our Communities Must Have Affordable Housing,"* 28 Wm. Mitchell L. Rev. 197, 216 (2001).

[6] The National Association of Homebuilders, while not overtly opposed to inclusionary zoning requirements, raise an interesting question of equity. "Do programs impose a cost, and if so, who bears that cost-the builder or the purchaser of the market rate homes? If there is a cost to the builder (even if only in more work or regulatory complications), is it fair for the builder to shoulder the cost of providing a needed social good?" C. Kent Conine, Vice President, National Association of Home Builders, in "New Century Housing", The Center for Housing Policy, Washington, D.C., Vol. 1, Issue 2, October 2000, p.27. Of interest is applying Mr. Conine's comments to the Massachusetts comprehensive permit statute. In that case, there is no cost to the builder for building affordable dwellings. Rather, as discussed previously, there is an unearned and unpaid for gift. But note that Mr. Conine questions who should bear the public burden of providing affordable housing. Mr. Conine and presumably most land developers would argue that the cost should be born by the community at large and not by a private developer alone. It is equally likely that anyone could reasonably argue that the burden should be born solely by those abutting a comprehensive permit development. In fact, that is the net result of the Massachusetts comprehensive permit statute. Those abutting the proposed project, individuals who could not have predicted the development's scale or impact are left shouldering the burden of the Commonwealth's mandate. In essence, the abutters to a comprehensive permit project are held accountable for their municipality's "failure" to achieve the statute mandate of affordable housing.

[7] As noted, inclusionary zoning has a proven track record of success and is particularly well

Inclusionary zoning requirements could extract affordable dwellings, lots, fees in lieu of, or a combination of the three within every new subdivision created throughout the Commonwealth.

Within a plan state's suburban and rural communities, inclusionary zoning can ensure that the housing element and attendant goals are met by requiring that all new developments—residential and non-residential—extract a percentage of dwelling units or fees in lieu of dwelling units. A percentage extraction ensures that new development does not continually force the municipality below the target goal. For example, if the housing plan calls for no less than 15% of the total housing stock to meet affordable criteria, an inclusionary regulation would need to ensure that no less than 15% of the dwelling units within a new subdivision meet the established affordability criteria.[8]

For example, a zoning ordinance could require that every subdivision plan containing 5 lots or more set one lot aside for sale to a moderate income purchaser.

In the alternative, the ordinance could allow the applicant to pay an equivalency

---

suited for adoption by Massachusetts cities and towns given the case-by-case, ad hoc adjudication that accompanies Massachusetts land use regulation. But as noted by others, there are several other techniques that have proven useful in the creation of low and moderate-income housing units. "However, Inclusionary zoning is not an end in itself; it is only one example…Consider some of the other market regulation techniques that might easily be required as part of a Mount Laurel compliance program: rent control laws, anti-gentrification laws, restrictions on condominium conversions and zoning for 'mobile' homes." John M. Payne, *Fairly Sharing Affordable Housing Obligations: The Mount Laurel Matrix*, 22 W. New. Eng. L. Rev. 365, 374 (2001).

[8] This requirement points out yet another irony of the Massachusetts comprehensive permit statute. Not formally enabled to adopt inclusionary zoning requirements, Massachusetts cities and towns could hardly be expected to keep pace with the 10% requirement sufficient to keep an applicant from an entitlement to, and approval from, the Housing Appeals Committee. Simply put, for every market rate building permit issued in Massachusetts, the city or town falls one-tenth of a percentage point behind the Sisyphean quota. Perhaps it is no wonder that less than 30 of the state's 351 cities and towns have met this target in the 34 years since the statute was enacted.

of the lot set aside requirement[9] into a fund established for the purposes of developing affordable housing.[10]

In urban and mostly developed cities and towns, inclusionary zoning requirements could extract affordable dwellings units or fees in lieu of the construction of the dwelling units as redevelopment or urban infill or occurs. There are numerous examples of successful inclusionary zoning programs in the nation's urban centers. While many of these programs are often referred to as "linkage" or "impact fee" regulations, the end result—requiring the development community to pay a fair share cost for affordable housing—remains the same.[11]

§ 5.31   Regulation of Adult Entertainment Businesses

Since 1982, the State Zoning Act (G.L. 40A) has contained a section (§ 9A) specifically authorizing local bylaws or ordinances which "provide for special permits authorizing the establishment of adult bookstores, adult motion picture theaters, adult paraphernalia stores, adult video stores or establishments which display live nudity for their patrons ..." as those terms are defined in the statute. The statute further provides that the ordinance or bylaw adopted pursuant to it may prescribe specific improvements, amenities or locations of such uses and may require that they be a specific distance from residential zones, other adult book-

---

[9] An example of a fees-in-lieu of provision from the Town of Duxbury, Massachusetts follows:

As an alternative to the requirements of Section 560.5, and as allowed by law, an applicant may contribute to the Duxbury Housing Trust Fund to be used for the development of affordable housing in lieu of constructing and offering affordable units within the locus of the proposed development or off-site.
Calculation of fees-in-lieu of units. The applicant for development subject to this Bylaw may pay fees in lieu of the construction of affordable units. For the purposes of this Bylaw, the fee in lieu of the construction or provision of affordable units is determined to be $200,000 per unit. For example, if the applicant is required to construct two affordable income units, they may opt to pay $400,000 in lieu of constructing or providing the units. Unless and until adjusted by Town Meeting, the fee in lieu of the construction of affordable units shall increase three (3%) percent every twelve months from the effective date of this Bylaw. Zoning Bylaw, Duxbury, Massachusetts, Section 560 (2003).

[10] While it is clear that adjudicative permitting is subject to judicial review based upon the tests enunciated in *Nollan* and *Dolan, infra,* at issue is whether extractions such as fees-in-lieu-of the set aside of affordable dwelling units is also measured against the "nexus" and "proportionality" standards. In City of Monterey v. Del Monte Dunes at Monterey, Ltd., 526 U.S. 687 (1999) and Eastern Enterprises v. Apfel, 524 U.S. 498 (1998), the Supreme Court narrowed the applicability of *Nollan* and *Dolan* to instances where real property—and not money—is the subject of the exaction. *See also* Ehrlich v. City of Culver City, 12 Cal. 4th 854 (1996). A more conservative approach, however, is to assume that the nexus and proportionality tests apply to all extractions, including the acceptance of fees in lieu of the set-aside of affordable dwelling units.

[11] Successful "urban" inclusionary zoning and linkage programs are numerous. *See,* for example, Seattle (Seattle Municipal Code, § 22.210, 1985), San Francisco (San Francisco Planning Code § 313(d)(1), 1985), Miami (City of Miami Ordinance § 1556.2.2, 1983) and Boston (Boston Zoning Code, Article 26A and 26B, 1986). For a discussion of the Boston "linkage" program, *see* Cynthia M. Barr, "Boston Zoning", Massachusetts Continuing Legal Education, 1997, p.93.

stores or motion picture theaters and from establishments serving alcoholic beverages.

Since the current Zoning Act is not an enabling act, local zoning being an exercise of powers granted under the Home Rule Amendment to the state constitution, it is not clear what zoning powers the 1982 version of § 9A gave to municipalities that they did not already possess. All that changed with the passage of St. 1994, c. 60, §§ 69–71, (and a later technical amendment, St. 1996, c. 345), which amended both § 6 and § 9A of c. 40A.

As amended, § 9A requires that any existing adult bookstore, adult motion picture theater, adult paraphernalia store, or adult video store apply for a special permit to continue operating, within ninety days following the adoption of a bylaw or ordinance regulating such uses. A provision was added to § 6 eliminating the protection given by that section to nonconforming uses where the use in question is an adult motion picture theater, adult paraphernalia store, adult video store or establishment which displays live nudity for its patrons.

Now, when a municipality adopts a bylaw or ordinance under § 9A regulating the kinds of adult entertainment specified therein either one or two sets of issues arise, depending on whether the bylaw is being applied to a proposed or an existing use. In the case of a proposed use, heavy conditioning or outright denial of the use will raise First Amendment issues. In the case of an existing use conditioning or denial will raise takings issues as well as First Amendment issues.

There is a good deal of judicial guidance on the First Amendment issues raised by this kind of zoning. In summary, the analysis of the bylaw and/or special permit action should proceed as follows.

- Is the bylaw content neutral?
- If so, is it designed to serve a substantial governmental interest? For example, is it intended to address deleterious so-called "secondary effects" of the adult entertainment, which effects were researched and identified prior to enactment of the bylaw.
- If so, does it allow for reasonable alternative avenues of communication?

Only if the answer to all three of these questions is in the affirmative will the bylaw withstand First Amendment challenge.[1] Note the importance of providing some avenue for adult entertainment speech—reasonable alternative avenues of communication—that are not illusory. *See*, for example, *T&D Video, Inc. v. City of Revere* (Mass. Super. CA No. 94-6216A, 2002), where the Superior Court,

---

[1] Renton v. Playtime Theatres, Inc., 475 U.S. 41, 89 L. Ed. 2d 29, 106 S. Ct. 925, 12 Media L. R. 1721 (1986), *rehearing denied*, 475 U.S. 1132, 90 L. Ed. 2d 205, 106 S. Ct. 1663 (1986); T & D Video v. City of Revere, 423 Mass. 577, 670 N.E.2d 162 (1996).

concluded that the City's relegation of adult entertainment video stores to land that was impractical, was tantamount to an effective ban. The Superior Court's review of the Revere ordinance followed the Supreme Judicial Court's grant of a preliminary injunction against the enforcement of a previous Revere "adult entertainment" ordinance. *See T&D Video, Inc. v. City of Revere*, 423 Mass. 577 (1996).

There is nothing like the same degree of clear judicial guidance on the question of the extent to which the application of a zoning amendment to substantially diminish or eliminate an existing business will result in a taking for which compensation must be paid. Since grandfathering of existing uses has been a part of Massachusetts zoning law since its inception, our courts have not had to address this question. The courts of most other states have upheld the application of zoning amendments to existing businesses, at least where a reasonable amortization period is allowed.[2] But some courts have held otherwise.[3] Federal takings cases have usually involved a claimed denial of all economically viable use. Even then no compensation need be paid if the use prevented would be a nuisance under state law. (*See* Chapter 3 for a discussion of the takings issue).[4] In the usual case where a § 9A bylaw is applied to an existing business, one supposes that the purveyor of adult entertainment will continue to have some economic use of his property, most obviously by changing to general entertainment. When a case finally reaches the Supreme Judicial Court, the Commonwealth's tradition of deference to pre-existing uses will have to be balanced against the Court's traditional reluctance to find that a regulatory taking has occurred.[5]

§ 5.32 Additional Zoning Techniques

- Overlay Districts

An overlay district is as the title suggests: an additional layer of regulation overlaying the underlying zoning district. Overlay districts are common and found throughout cities and towns in Massachusetts. They are employed to protect groundwater and surface water resources, historic districts,[1] roadways, floodplains,

---

[2] *See, e.g.,* Northend Cinema, Inc. v. Seattle, 90 Wash. 2d 709, 585 P.2d 1153, 4 Media L. R. 1732, 1 A.L.R.4th 1284 (1978), *cert. denied*, 441 U.S. 946, 60 L. Ed. 2d 1048, 99 S. Ct. 2166 (1979).

[3] Pennsylvania Northwestern Distribs. v. Zoning Hearing Bd., 526 Pa. 186, 584 A.2d 1372, 8 A.L.R.5th 970 (1991).

[4] Lucas v. South Carolina Coastal Council, 505 U.S. 1003, 120 L. Ed. 2d 798, 112 S. Ct. 2886, 92 Daily Journal DAR 9030, 34 Envt. Rep Cas. 1897, 22 E.L.R. 21104, 6 F.L.W. Fed S. 715 (1992), *on remand*, 309 S. Ct. 424, 424 S.E.2d 484, 23 E.L.R 20297 (1992); Lopes v. City of Peabody, 417 Mass. 299, 629 N.E.2d 1312 (1994), summary op at 22 M.L.W 1423 (Mass. 1994); Reinman v. Little Rock, 237 U.S. 171, 59 L. Ed. 900, 35 S. Ct. 511 (1915).

[5] Turnpike Realty Co. v. Dedham, 362 Mass. 221, 284 N.E.2d 891, 4 Envt. Rep. Cas. 1344, 3 E.L.R. 20221 (1972), *cert. denied*, 409 U.S. 1108, 34 L. Ed. 2d 689, 93 S. Ct. 908, 4 Envt. Rep. Cas. 1912 (1973) is a notable example.

[1] *See* Britton v. Zoning Bd. of Appeals of Gloucester, 59 Mass. App. Ct. 68, 794 N.E.2d 1198

coastal embayment and in one community "deer corridors."[2] While the resource subject to the regulation varies, the purpose and intent of the overlay district is typically the same: the strengthening of underlying zoning by the addition of the overlay regulations. As a zoning ordinance or bylaw, the regulation is adopted pursuant to G.L. c. 40A, § 5 and is subject to the procedural and substantive rules governing zoning in Massachusetts.

- Prohibition of Various Uses

The prohibition of various uses is a common element of zoning regulations today. The ordinance or bylaw specifies those uses that are prohibited by listing within specific zoning districts the offending use. Some cities and towns go further and specify those uses that are "specifically prohibited." While it is tempting to underscore the uses that the community "really, really does not desire", the practice of specifically articulating uses (and structures) that are undesirable is not recommended.

Rather, a zoning ordinance or bylaw should specify those uses (and structures) that the community desires, categorized by zoning district and identified as to whether the use or structures is allowed "by right" or "by special permit." The ordinance or bylaw should simultaneously contain a clause to the effect that "only those uses and structures specifically permitted by right or special permit are allowed." Further, "any use or structure not specifically permitted by right or special permit shall be prohibited."

- Large lot requirements

Massachusetts is an urbanized state. Little of the state's historic agricultural landscape remains and east of Route 495 the state continues to develop as a commuting suburb of Boston. With these facts as backdrop, the Courts have had little patience with cities and towns—mostly towns—that sought to adopt "large lot" minimum zoning requirements. The most recent case testing how far a municipality could go in adopting large lot minimums was decided by the Supreme Judicial Court in favor of the Town of Edgartown. However, the holding came with a clear message: large lot zoning is frowned upon in areas not concerned unique. "Unique areas" appear to include Martha's Vineyard, Nantucket and perhaps Cape Cod. The other question left unanswered by the Court is, "what minimum lot size is "too large."

Among the many allegations raised by the plaintiffs in *Johnson v. Edgartown*,[3] the Court considered whether the three-acre minimum lot size required by zoning

---

(2003), where the Court concluded that "aesthetic" protection is a legitimate basis upon which an adjudicating permit may be denied or conditioned.

[2] *See* Falmouth, Massachusetts zoning bylaw.

[3] 425 Mass. 117, 680 N.E.2d 37 (1997).

district in the relevant portions of Edgartown was devoid of a rational basis and therefore, unconstitutional. Relying on testimony that three-acre minimum lot sizes were required to maintain the health of a series of coastal ponds (by limiting the amount of nitrogen entering the groundwater discharging to the ponds), the Court upheld Edgartown's minimum lot size. Referencing prior "large lot" cases, the Court concluded that the underlying public purpose of the minimum lot size requirement was met and the bylaw therefore valid.

Edgartown is important for the issues not discussed by the Court. For example, if the town had produced credible evidence that minimum lot sizes of seven or ten acres were needed to avoid euthrophication of the coastal ponds or to protect drinking water supplies, would the Court similarly have concluded that the rational basis test was met? Would a community in the Berkshires or central Massachusetts likewise be able to produce scientific evidence that endangered species habitat will be irreparably harmed without minimum lot sizes of ten or fifteen acres? The answers to these questions are not clear, but the Court did not hesitate to caution cities and towns against the use of large lot zoning.

- Cluster and planned unit developments

G.L. c. 40A, § 9 provide for "cluster developments and "planned unit developments" as development options cities and towns may allow upon receipt of a special permit, or, if the municipality consents, by right. Cluster and planned unit developments are alternatives to traditional "grid" or Euclidean subdivisions common throughout Massachusetts.

Cluster-type developments have been successfully used across the state to preserve open space, minimize site alteration and protect portions of a site less conducive to development. Cluster development:

- Provides landowners with design flexibility
- Preserves open spaces
- Reduces impervious surfaces and the need for extensive stormwater treatment areas
- Promotes groundwater recharge
- Reduces the costs of road and utility construction.

Cluster bylaws and ordinances must specify the minimum parcel size for eligibility, establish guidelines for the use of the resulting open spaces and define allowable density bonuses, if any.

Where the city or town allows a cluster by right, the rules and regulations of the planning board pursuant to the Subdivision Control Law govern the development. The allowance of cluster developments by right poses an interesting challenge to cities and towns. Often avoided by land developers due to the requirement that a special permit be obtained (and the attendant risks of excessive exactions, time delays and discretion permitted the special permit granting authority), cluster development by right provides the applicant with the benefits of clustering without the risks associated with a special permit.

From the municipality's perspective however, clustering by right requires the adoption of detailed rules and regulations and a clear articulation of the minimum and maximum open spaces, setbacks, density and related development factors tolerated by the community. While cluster developments are generally a better alternative to land development than traditional grid subdivisions, a cluster sub-division by right leaves the planning board with little discretion and limited powers. The limitations of the planning board's powers pursuant to the Subdivision Control Law is discussed in detail in Chapter 10.

- G.L. c. 40R

G.L. c. 40R, entitled "Smart Growth and Housing Production" was adopted by the General Court in 2004. The statute creates the Department of Housing and Community Development as an ¨uber planning agency,[4] without any of the at-tendant consistency requirements established in plan states. (As discussed in Chapter 2, plan states require consistency among the competing interests and issues cities and towns face, including but not limited to, housing development, open space preservation, transportation networks and economic development).

40R is enabling authority, permitting willing cities and towns to create dense development districts (minimum density is 20 units per acre for multi-family housing and 8 units per acre for single family dwellings) with inclusive affordable housing units (no less than 20 percent of the dwelling must be "affordable" as defined),[5] in exchange for payments from DHCD.[6] The purported purpose of the statute is to encourage "smart growth" but the statute's clear purpose is to produce housing.

- Impact Fees

Impact fees are the fees associated with the impacts of new development as passed onto the developer by the host community. Impact fees are widely used in fifteen states across the country, including California, Rhode Island, Hawaii and Georgia. With the exception of the fifteen towns on Cape Cod and the City of Boston,[7] impact fees are illegal in Massachusetts.

Impact fees are distinguished from on-site improvements typically associated

---

[4] G.L. c. 40R, § 4.

[5] G.L. c. 40R, §§ 2 and 6.

[6] G.L. c. 40R, § 9. The wisdom of DHCD enticing cities and towns to rezone land for cash payments as opposed to enticing cities and towns to adopt meaningful land use plans is left for other commentators.

[7] Boston's enabling authority permits the imposition of "linkage payments."

with subdivision approvals . For example, and as discussed in greater detail in Chapter 10, the Subdivision Control Law allows cities and towns to require a subdivider to install improvements intended to benefit the specific subdivision, including but not limited to underground utilities, road widening, landscaping and stormwater management related improvements.[8] The subdivider can also be required, although to a lesser extent, to improve roads and related infrastructure off-site.[9]

Massachusetts cities and towns may impose fees in the exercise of their police powers; the authority to impose user and regulatory fees is clearly established. However, where the imposed payment is categorized as a tax, regardless of what it is called, the mandated payment will be invalidated.

The critical distinction between fees and taxes was highlighted by the SJC in *Emerson College v. City of Boston*[10] and restated by the Appeals Court in *Greater Franklin Developer's Association v. Town of Franklin*.[11] The SJC applied three criteria to distinguish fees from taxes. The *Emerson College* tests have been since modified by the Courts of other states, most notably Hawaii.[12]

1. Particularly: If the sum paid is a requirement for the provision of a specific governmental service that benefits only the payor, the payment is likely to be upheld; the Court will conclude that the payment is a fee and not a tax.

2. Reimbursement: If the sum collected is intended to compensate the city or town for the provision of a service such as water or sewer—and not to raise general revenue—the fee will likely be upheld. Again, the Court will be able to conclude that the payment is a fee and not a tax.

3. Choice: If the party charged the fee is utilizing a municipal service and has an option of avoiding that service, the Court is likely to conclude that the charge is a fee and not a tax. Residents may permissibly avoid the payments of fees by avoiding the service offered. Taxes, however, are "unavoidable." Note that in some situations, the criteria of "choice" is illusory. For example, it would be disingenuous to claim that a resident of Chelsea could avoid the payment of sewer use fees charged by the Metropolitan Water

---

[8] G.L. c. 41, § 81Q.

[9] *See*, for example, North Landers Corp. v. Planning Board of Falmouth, 382 Mass. 432 (1981) and Castle Estates, Inc. v. Park and Planning Board, 344 Mass. 329 (1962), where, as discussed in Chapter XXX, the Court made clear that had the town required the installation of on and off site requirements within the local subdivision rules and regulations, improvements to specific infrastructural needs could be permissibly be tied to subdivision approval.

[10] 391 Mass. 415 (1984).

[11] 49 Mass. App. Ct. 500 (2000).

[12] *See* State v. Medeiros, 89 Hawaii 361 (1999).

Resource Authority (MWRA) as she could install an on-site septic system.[13]

• Carrying Capacity (Performance Standards)

A carrying capacity analysis is an assessment of the ability of a built (roadway, wastewater treatment plant, municipal swimming pool) or natural (aquifer, surface water body, coastal estuary) resource to absorb population growth and related physical development without degradation such that the system fails to perform as designed,[14] or, in the case of a natural resource, diminishes in health or productivity.[15]

Understanding the carrying capacity or constraints of a built or natural resource provides governments with an effective method for identifying which portions of the community are suitable for new or expanded development. Moreover, the converse is also true. By identifying the carrying capacity of a resource, plans, policies and regulations can be revised to ensure that carrying capacities are not exceeded. Simply put, knowledge of carrying capacity limitations allows municipal residents and officials to make more rational and defensible decisions regarding where and at what density development can occur.[16]

While many cities and towns have adopted carrying capacity regulations and they

---

[13] The SJC acknowledged the tenuous nature of the "choice prong" in Nuclear Metals, Inc. v. Radioactive Waste Management Board, 421 Mass. 196 (1995).

[14] Built resources such as bridges, roads, water distribution systems and wastewater treatment facilities, for example, each have design carrying capacities. *See*, for example, *Standard Handbook for Civil Engineers*, Third Ed., F. Merritt, Ed., McGraw-Hill Book Co., 1983.

[15] It is presumed that all natural resources have a carrying capacity, although the carrying capacity for many natural resources has not been quantified. For example, underlying many federal laws designed to protect wildlife is the assumption that wildlife habitat must be protected to ensure the protection of the species. (*See*, for example, Northern Spotted Owl v. Lujan, 758 F. Supp. 621 (W.D. Wash. 1991)).

[16] In his famous work *The City of To-Morrow and its Planning*, Payson & Clarke, Ltd., 1929, Le Corbusier criticized the cities of Europe for their poor design, inadequate infrastructure and absence of planning logic as unable to support the growing population, a growth that would only be possible by rebuilding the infrastructure and the urban center. Le Corbusier also noted, however, that the lack of adequate infrastructure was only half of the problem. The other half, as discussed in this article, is that built systems have a tolerance level—a limit—that once exceeded, render the system inoperable or unsafe, at least until repaired or expanded. This tolerance level is exceeded by land development and its coincident population growth. "If we study the curve of growth in a district or suburb, it will be seen that it is of precisely the same nature as that of a great city; it is a simultaneous phenomenon. Nonetheless, in the case of a district there occurs a "stop;" i.e. the moment where the capacity of the district is definitively limited by its superficial area...At this point, we have super-saturation, a population in excess of the district's normal capacity, overcrowding and a crisis in housing; and finally, as the pendulum swings first one way and then another, we reach a settled condition of full saturation. This will continue until some new external event intervenes... ." *Id*. at 112.

are a common feature in state regulations, performance based regulations had not been squarely before the courts until *Johnson v. Edgartown*,[17] first brought in Land Court in 1995. As discussed above, in *Johnson*, at issue, among many, was the permissible reliance of the Town of Edgartown's three-acre minimum lot size on the protection of the water quality of a series of coastal ponds along the Town's southern shoreline. Edgartown argued that a minimum of three acres was needed per dwelling unit to protect the ponds from excessive nutrient loading. If the loadings exceeded a specified amount, the Town claimed, the ponds' ability to support shellfish would diminish, declining oxygen in the ponds would cause noxious odors and unsightly weed growth: the carrying capacity would be exceeded. In upholding the validity of the three-acre zoning requirement, former Chief Justice Cauchon (Land Court) sustained the legitimacy of the carrying capacity analysis.[18] The SJC affirmed, citing to testimony regarding the risks of "eutrophication" without the acreage minimum in place.

Establishing the carrying capacity of a built or natural resource is often a rigorous quantitative analysis and is likely avoided due to the perception that the scientific investigations required are beyond the financial or technical abilities of many governmental agencies.[19]

---

[17] 425 Mass. 117, 680 N.E.2d 37, 1997 Mass. LEXIS 120 (1997).

[18] Johnson v. Town of Edgartown, Misc. Case No. 198373 (Land Ct. 1996).

[19] An additional dilemma is the degree of certainty of the science or engineering upon which the regulation is based. While "more" science is generally better than "less," local governments should adopt carrying capacity regulations even though the science is incomplete. This fact is underscored by case law dating back to Euclid v. Ambler Realty, 272 U.S. 365 (1926). "Before (a zoning) ordinance can be declared unconstitutional, (it must be shown to be) clearly arbitrary and unreasonable, having no substantial relation to the public health, safety, morals or general welfare." 272 U.S. 365, at 395. *See also* Johnson v. Town of Edgartown, 425 Mass. 117 (1997)." The general rule is that a zoning bylaw whose reasonableness is fairly debatable will be sustained...the challenger must prove by a preponderance of the evidence that the zoning regulation is arbitrary and unreasonable, or substantially unrelated to the public health, safety, morals or general welfare." 425 Mass. 117, at 121. The U.S. Supreme Court framed the breadth of local government regulatory powers in Berman v. Parker, 348 U.S. 26 (1954). "Public safety, public health, morality, peace and quiet, law and order—these are some of the more conspicuous examples of the traditional application of the police power to municipal affairs. Yet they merely illustrate the scope of the power and do not delimit it...the concept of the public welfare is broad and inclusive. The values it represents are spiritual as well as physical, aesthetic as well as monetary. It is within the power of the legislature to determine that the community should be beautiful as well as healthy, spacious as well as clean, well-balanced as well as carefully patrolled." 348 U.S. 26, at 32–33. Finally, in a case challenging restrictions placed upon the shrimping industry due to the collateral impacts to sea turtles, the United States Court of Appeals, Fifth Circuit noted, "Although we believe appellants' challenge is not totally without merit, we are mindful that under the arbitrary-and-capricious standard, our deference to the agency is greatest when reviewing technical matters within its area of expertise, particularly its choice of scientific data and statistical methodology. In reviewing such technical choices, 'we must look at the decision not as the chemist, biologist or statistician that we

Nevertheless, and as discussed further below, completing a carrying capacity analysis provides Massachusetts cities and towns with a powerful and legally defensible tool for making decisions and choices about how to resolve conflicts between development and preservation goals.[20]

It is important to remember that all built and natural resources have a carrying capacity.[21] When that capacity is exceeded, the resource fails to function as intended or hoped. For example, residents of eastern Massachusetts have experienced carrying capacity failures on roadways leading into and out of Boston for decades.[22] The failure is the fact that the system cannot accommodate the numbers seeking to use the facility at the same time.

Solutions to carrying capacity failures for built resources are plentiful. In the example noted above, Massachusetts chose to construct the "Big Dig," in part to

---

are qualified neither by training nor experience to be, but as a reviewing court exercising our narrowly defined duty of holding agencies to certain minimal standards of rationality." State of Louisiana v. Verity, 853 F.2d 322, 328 (1988), *quoting* Avoyeelles Sportsmen's League, Inc. v. Marsh, 715 F.2d 897, 905 (1983).

[20] "Development" is part of the concept of sustainable development. Most environmentalists do not propose rolling society back to the natural conditions of the frontier. But human actions that cause continuing net losses overall, deplete critical resource bases, or foreclose other future necessities, are a shortsighted endgame that long has been the target of environmental law's protective efforts." Zygmunt J.B. Plater, Robert H. Abrams, William Goldfarb and Robert L. Graham, *Environmental Law and Policy: Nature, Law and Society,* Teacher's Manual, West Group, 1998, p.21.

[21] Numerous commentators have written extensively on the fact that natural systems are not inexhaustible and that few natural resources can withstand indefinite impacts without undergoing fundamental change. See for example, The World Commission on Environment and Development, *Our Common Future,* Oxford University Press, 1987, *Managing Planet Earth: Readings from Scientific America Magazine,* Scientific America, Inc., 1989, Timberlake, L., *Only One Earth,* Sterling Publishing, 1987. Contrary opinions are plentiful. Professor Pipes' recent work provides a good example. "Environmental hysteria—the primeval fear that the planet is about to be destroyed, previously linked to nuclear weapons—provides a powerful emotional rationale for encroachments on property rights. For just as during the Cold War it was often said that any concession to the Soviet Union was justified if it prevented a putative nuclear holocaust, so today it is maintained—often by the same people—that property rights must be sacrificed for the sake of survival of life on earth. In both cases, the driving force is a deep seated human propensity for doomsday scenarios." Richard Pipes, *Property and Freedom,* Vintage Books, p. 250–251, 1999.

[22] Carrying capacity analyses for road and highway systems is accomplished through an alphabetic (A to F) rating system entitled "level of service." Level of service is defined as a qualitative measure describing operational conditions within a traffic stream and perceptions by motorists as to mobility and safety. A level of service definition provides a determination as to quality of traffic flow in terms of factors such as speed, freedom to maneuver, comfort, safety, and travel time. Six levels of service are defined for each roadway, with level of service "A" defined as little or no delay, and level of service "F" indicates significant delays with volume exceeding roadway capacity. See Highway Capacity Manual, Special Report 209, Third Edition, Transportation Research Board, Washington, D.C., 1994.

improve the carrying capacity of the Central Artery and roads leading to and from Boston. There may be financial limitations to such improvements in service and expansions of facilities, but for the most part, built resources can be re-built, larger, better and perhaps more accommodating.

Natural resource carrying capacities are not so readily improved, however, and once exceeded, they may be impossible to restore.

Consider the following examples.

Example 1:

Water used for human consumption has public health related carrying capacities. Consumption of water in excess of these capacities poses risks to human health. Unlike roads, bridges or schools, "fixing" the carrying capacity of a water supply once it has been reached is impractical. For example, the carrying capacity for nitrogen in drinking water is established at 10 parts per million.[23] Once a drinking water supply has exceeded this capacity, the supply no longer meets federal and state health regulations and no longer constitutes potable water. At issue is the "fix."

No practicable remediation of the increased nitrogen levels exists, with the exception of reduction of the sources of nitrogen. In other words, the water at the well cannot be effectively treated to remove nitrogen.[24] Thus the only effective means of re-establishing potability for the well is to reduce nitrogen levels over time by slowing or ceasing nitrogen inputs to groundwater. Ironically, of course, this requirement could have been avoided by simply limiting nitrogen inputs to the carrying capacity of the well in the first place.

Example 2:

Coastal waters have been the subject of intensive investigation with respect to their ability to assimilate nutrients such as nitrogen and phosphorus. While little doubt remains that coastal systems have carrying capacities,[25] an oft-debated issue is whether coastal waters have the same carrying capacity in Massachusetts as they

---

[23] A maximum contaminant level (MCL) for nitrate, as "N," in drinking water supplies was established at 10 mg/l by the Public Health Service in 1962 and subsequently adopted by the U.S. Environmental Protection Agency under the Safe Drinking Water Act of 1986.

[24] The difficulty of removing nitrogen lies in the fact that nitrogen dissolves inground water; it does not float on or sink in, ground water. Thus excessive nitrogen loading to the ground water through non-point sources such as septic systems, agricultural runoff or a host of other diffuse contributors removes practical options for "capturing" the contaminant.

[25] For example, in nitrogen limited coastal systems, excessive nitrogen loadings increase the growth of aquatic plants, which leads to diminished water clarity, loss of shellfish habitat, depressed dissolved oxygen levels, build up of bottom sediments and fish kills. Long-term exposure of certain coastal waters to excessive nitrogen levels alters the ecosystem, causing indigenous species to be replaced with an overpopulation of nuisance species, a process commonly referred to as

do in Hawaii or even the same carrying capacities within Boston Harbor as Vineyard Sound. Given their variations in water temperature, flushing, salinity and depth, coastal water bodies are believed to have unique carrying capacities that do not lend themselves to generalities.

Nevertheless, individual water body carrying capacities can be determined, and regulations imposed, that will ensure that the capacity will not be exceeded. Several towns on Cape Cod have adopted coastal water carrying capacity regulations as has the Cape Cod Commission. As discussed in Example 1, above, preventing the carrying capacity from being exceeded requires virtually the same effort as the necessary "fix" required after the carrying capacity has been reached.

Example 3:

As discussed in Chapter 8, wetlands "replication"—the art and science of creating new or expanded wetlands habitat as a quid pro quo for permission to fill an existing wetland— is often seen as a tool for protecting wetlands while simultaneously allowing development.

At first glance, wetlands replication appears to challenge the proposition that all resources have a carrying capacity. If a resource can be "re-created" on the same or different locus than the one being developed, there has been no true loss of the resource.

However, replication and re-creation of a natural resource, even where feasible, does not diminish the importance of understanding carrying capacity thresholds. For example, a developer of land seeks to comply with local subdivision regulations that require two means of egress from her development. To satisfy this requirement, she proposes to fill several acres of wetlands but replicate the filled wetland elsewhere on her property. While the proposal clearly complies with the "no net loss" policy for wetland protection, the replication of the resource requires application of the principles of carrying capacity. Where will the replication occur and what impacts will surrounding land uses have on the resource? What is the threshold for the newly created resource relative to nitrogen, phosphorus, metals and other contaminants? How will the newly created resource survive in the proposed location?[26]

---

eutrophication. *See*, for example, Valiela, I. and J.M. Teal. 1979. The nitrogen budget of a salt marsh ecosystem. Nature. 780 (5724): 652–656.

[26] *See*, for example, a 1989 study prepared by the US Army Corps of Engineers (US Army Corps of Engineers, New England Division, "Evaluation of Freshwater Wetland Replacement Projects in Massachusetts", December 1989) and a 1998 study by the University of Massachusetts (S. Brown and P. Veneman, "Compensatory Wetland Mitigation in Massachusetts, Massachusetts Agricultural Experiment Station, University of Massachusetts, Amherst, September 1998), wherein the success of wetland mitigation and replication projects were analyzed. The findings of both studies demonstrate that replication does not always work and the values of the original wetland

Wetlands replication, similar to transfer of development rights programs,[27] assumes that one portion of a resource or region has a greater carrying capacity than another. This determination cannot occur, however, unless and until the carrying capacity of each affected resource—built or natural—has been established.

§ 5.33   Due Process Claims in Zoning and Subdivision Appeals

Often an applicant, disappointed in his quest for a special permit or variance believes that he or she has been the victim of improper discrimination by the local board. This belief may arise out of the perception by the applicant of personal animosity toward him by the board. It may arise out of the perception that other applicants in substantially similar circumstances have received permits. Alternatively, it may arise out of what the applicant perceives as undue delays by the board in processing the decision, while they make him "jump through hoops." Sometimes these perceptions are real; sometimes they are illusion. In either case the unsuccessful, and bitter, applicant will want his counsel to seek redress against the board and/or its individual members, and/or the municipality. When such claim is brought it is usually couched in terms of a denial of constitutional due process. In general, the courts have not been sympathetic to this kind of claim in the land use context. In *Pruneyard Shopping Center v. Robins*, the United States Supreme Court held that "that the guaranty of due process... demands only that the law shall not be unreasonable, arbitrary or capricious, and that the means selected shall have a real and substantial relation to the objective sought to be obtained."[1] In *PFZ Properties, Inc. v. Rodriguez*, the First Circuit Court of Appeals identifies the high standard a landowner must meet to be successful in a due process challenge.[2] The court found that "except in egregious circumstances "erroneous land use decisions do not give rise to a claim that the agency has violated the owner's constitutional right to due process. The First Circuit has concluded that constitutional protection does not extend to the "conventional planning dispute—at least when not tainted with fundamental procedural irregularity, racial animus, or similar issues."[3] The government's conduct must be "stunning, evidencing more than humdrum legal error."[4] Even a "bad faith refusal to follow state law in local administrative matters simply does not amount to a deprivation of due process where the state courts are available to correct the error."[5]

---

resource (e.g., plant community diversity and wildlife habitat) were generally not replicated.

[27] *See*, for example, Transfer of Development Rights Revisited, February 9, 2000 Audio Program by the American Planning Association, Chicago, IL.

[1] 447 U.S. 74, 84–85 (1980).

[2] 928 F.2d 28 (1st Cir. 1991). *See also* Chiplin Enters. Inc. v. Lebanon, 712 F.2d 1524 (1st Cir. 1983).

[3] Creative Environments, Inc. v. Estabrook, 680 F.2d 822, 833 (1st Cir. 1982).

[4] Licari v. Ferruzzi, 22 F.3d 344 (1st Cir. 1994).

[5] Chiplin Enterprises v. City of Lebanon, 712 F.2d 1524, 1528 (1st Cir. 1983).

State courts have echoed the First Circuit's approach to due process challenges. In *Freeman v. Planning Board of West Boylston*, a landowner brought suit under § 1983 of the Civil Rights Act to recover damages incurred when a planning board, acting in excess of its authority, placed unlawful conditions on a subdivision plan.[6] The Supreme Judicial Court found that although the board had acted inappropriately, the property owner had not shown that the board's decision was a product of "personal animus that other developers were treated more favorably than the plaintiff, or that board members stood to profit personally from the actions."[7] The court determined that a property owner, in order to succeed on a due process claim in such a case would have to show a "truly horrendous" situation or "egregious" behavior.[8] Absent such a rule the court said, "virtually every alleged legal or procedural error of a local planning authority ... could be brought to federal court on the theory that the erroneous application of state law amounted to a taking of property without due process; neither Congress nor the courts have, to date, indicated that section 1983 should have such reach."[9]

Constitutional due process claims, based on the Fourteenth Amendment to the federal constitution fall into two generic categories, denial of substantive due process and denial of procedural due process.

A viable substantive due process claim requires proof that the governmental action was, in and of itself, egregious, outrageous or shocking to the conscience.[10] As pointed out above, both the First Circuit and the state appellate courts, following the federal precedent, have been extremely unreceptive to these claims. The threshold for establishing the requisite abuse of government power is extremely high in practice.[11]

A viable procedural due process claim requires proof that the claimant (1) had a property right under state law in the permit denied, and (2) was deprived of that interest under color of state law without adequate process.[12] In practice these claims have fared no better than substantive due process claims. Given the wide discretion land use permitting authorities have under Massachusetts law a claimant can rarely establish that it had a property interest in the denied permit. Even if the requisite property interest can be established, state law provides full, de novo judicial review of the action of the zoning officials.

---

[6] 419 Mass. 548 (1995)

[7] 419 Mass. 548, at 563.

[8] 419 Mass. 548, at 563.

[9] Creative Environments, Inc. v. Estabrook, 680 F.2d 822, at 831.

[10] Amsden v. Moran, 904 F.2d 748, 754 (1st Cir. 1990).

[11] *See* Steele Hill Development v. Town of Sanbornton, 469 F.2d 956 (1st Cir. 1972); Chongris v. Board of Appeals, 811 F.2d 36 (1st Cir. 1987); Nestor Colon Medina & Sucesores, Inc., 964 F.2d 32 (1st Cir. 1991).

[12] Logan v. Zimmerman Brush Co., 455 U.S. 422, 428 (1982).

Claims that the denial of a permit violated the applicant's constitutional right to equal protection of the laws have received an equally cold response from both federal and state courts. The most frequently cited federal case sets out the prevailing standard, and atmosphere, as follows, "Every appeal by a disappointed developer from an adverse ruling by a local Massachusetts planning board necessarily involves some claim that the board exceeded abused or 'distorted' its legal authority in some manner, often for some allegedly perverse (from the developer's point of view) reason. it is not enough simply to give these state law claims constitutional labels such as 'due process' or 'equal protection' in order to raise a substantial federal question..."[13] In order to prevail on an equal protection claim the plaintiff must demonstrate that, (1) compared with other similarly situated persons, he/she was selectively treated; and (2) that such selective treatment was based on impermissible considerations such as race, religion, intent to inhibit or punish the exercise of constitutional rights, or malicious or bad faith intent to injure him/her.[14] Again, Massachusetts appellate courts have followed the federal case law. "The allegation that others similarly situated obtained permits is not, without more, a denial of the equal protection of the laws. Allegations of clear and intentional discrimination are required."[15]

There is some question as to whether the above-described requirement that the plaintiff show some subjective bad faith or ill will on the part of the permitting authority comports with the controlling case law as laid down by the United States Supreme Court. In a brief, per curiam, decision handed down in October of 2000, that Court held that selective treatment of an applicant for a local permit that was without rational basis was enough to form the basis of an equal protection claim. In that decision it described the "subjective ill will" theory upon which the Seventh Circuit Court of Appeals had relied as an "alternative theory" which was not necessary to make out the claim.[16] The court seemed to treat this as a not very notable point of settled law, citing cases going back to 1918. The court also held that one person could make up a class for equal protection purposes (the so-called "class of one"), this being the ostensible point of its allowing certiorari in the case. It may be that *Olech* is not implicitly overruling the law in the First Circuit but rather saying the same thing in a different way. A per curiam opinion of a few paragraphs is not the usual way to reconcile conflicting law in the circuits or to overrule a long line of cases in one particular circuit. At any rate the earth has not yet moved in this area of law and at least one district court judge has issued an opinion, after

---

[13] Creative Environments, Inc. v. Estabrook, 680 F.2d 822, 833 (1st Cir. 1982), *cert. denied*, 459 U.S. 989 (1982).

[14] Rubinovitz v. Rogato, 60 F.3d 906, 910 (1st Cir. 1995).

[15] Rosenfeld v. Board of Health of Chilmark, 27 Mass. App. 621, 628–629 (1989).

[16] Village of Willowbrook v. Olech, 528 U.S. 562 (2000).

Olech, that the plaintiff must show "bad motive" or animus on the part of the permitting authority.[17]

That being said, and judges being human, the presence of bad behavior, not quite reaching the denial of due process standard, may dispose them to find against the board on the facts underlying the zoning appeal itself. It is probably this type of consideration that is at least partly responsible for the increase in the use of monetary counts in zoning appeals.

§ 5.34   Creation of Conforming Lot Resulting in Zoning Violation by Another Lot (Infectious Invalidity)

When the creation of a lot that conforms to the zoning ordinance or bylaw in all respects results in a zoning violation on another lot, the newly created lot may be denied a building permit.[1] The usual circumstance where this so-called "infectious invalidity" occurs is the separation of land from an existing lot that needs the separated land to meet zoning requirements. Zoning bylaws typically contain provisions prohibiting such conveyances, but the Alley case stands for the proposition that a local bylaw prohibition is not necessary for infectious invalidity to occur. The local zoning officials may treat the lots for zoning purposes as if the illegal conveyance had not occurred.[2]

Note however, that the doctrine of "infectious invalidity" does not permit a planning board to withhold approval not required endorsement where the plan does not constitute a subdivision, even if the lots to be created contain zoning violations. While the planning board may permissibly require the applicant to include a notation on the plan calling attention to the zoning violations, the planning board must nevertheless endorse the plan

§ 5.35   What Use Qualifies As Accessory

Where a particular principal use is allowed by a zoning ordinance or bylaw, uses that are accessory or incidental to that principal use are usually either implicitly or explicitly allowed.[1] While this is a simple enough concept to grasp in the abstract, as the claimed accessory use moves to the penumbra of uses that have a logical relation to the principal use it can become difficult to apply in practice. The

---

[17] Rubin v. Town of Norton, *supra*.

[1] Alley v. Building Inspector of Danvers, 354 Mass. 6, 234 N.E.2d 879 (1968).

[2] *Cf.* Murphy v. Kotlik, 34 Mass. App. 410, 611 N.E.2d 741 (1993). *See also* Norton v. Duxbury Board of Appeals, Nos. 256473, 283993 (Mass. Land Ct., May 10, 2004).

[1] "Uses which are 'incidental' to a permissible activity on zoned property are permitted as long as the incidental use does not undercut the plain intent of the zoning bylaw. Simmons v. Board of Appeals of Newburyport, 60 Mass. App. Ct. 5, 11 (2003), *citing* 2 E.C. Yokley, Zoning Law and Practice § 8-1 (4th ed.1978).

seminal definition of accessory use is contained in the case of *Harvard v. Maxant*.[2] In that case the supreme judicial court, construing a bylaw allowing "customarily incidental" uses to allowed principal uses, said that an accessory use must be subordinate and minor in significance compared to the principal use, as well as being attendant or concomitant to it.[3]

As might be expected given this definition, the case law has proven to be very fact-driven.[4] The bylaw permitting the use of the greenhouse or nursery did not allow sale of cut Christmas trees or wreaths, or garden tools and equipment as accessory uses. However, sale of fungicides, insecticides, chemicals, and peat moss to maintain live trees sold as part of principal use was allowed as accessory use.[5] The sale of ice cream cones and packages, frappes and sundaes was allowed as accessory to permitted farm use if milk used in products was produced on site. Nevertheless, sale of fruit punch was not allowed.[6]

In some more recent cases property owners have put a new twist on this old problem by claiming that a use not allowed as a principal use, and wholly different in nature and effect from a particular allowed principal use, is in fact allowed as incidental to the principal use. The agricultural earth removal cases provide a good example. In these cases, the applicant proposed to remove huge amounts of gravel, which it claimed to be necessary in order to prepare its land for allowed agricultural cultivation. In denying the appeals from local permit denial both the supreme judicial court and the appeals court added a new corollary to the above stated conceptual definition of a use incidental to an allowed use. Even if a proposed use satisfies the general definition, the court must "compare the net effect of the incidental use to that of the primary use and evaluate the reasonableness of the relationship" between them. In short, the incidental portion of the use may not, in its effect, swallow up the principal use of which it is a part.[7]

§ 5.36 Expiration and Extension of Special Permits

Local zoning ordinances and bylaws must require that a use or construction authorized by special permit must be commenced within a specified period of time, not to exceed two years, from the date the special permit is granted, "except for good cause." G.L. c. 40A, § 9, ¶ 13. If substantial use has not commenced, or construction has not been begun, within such time the special permit lapses. Most

---

[2] 360 Mass. 432 (1971).

[3] 360 Mass. 432, at 438.

[4] Gallagher v. Board of Appeals, 44 Mass. App. 906, and cases cited therein.

[5] Town of Needham v. Winslow Nurseries, Inc., 330 Mass. 95 (1953).

[6] Parrish v. Board of Appeals, 351 Mass. 561 (1967).

[7] Henry v. Board of Appeals, 418 Mass. 841, 641 N.E.2d 1334 (1994); Old Colony Council-Boy Scouts of America v. Board of Appeals, 31 Mass. App. 46, 574 N.E.2d 1014 (1991).

ordinances and bylaws provide the full two years, although a significant minority allow only one year. Counsel are well advised to check this carefully and inform their clients in writing of the expiration date of any unexercised special permit. Once a substantial use has commenced the permit is exercised and, absent express language in the permit to the contrary, the project may be completed over a period of time that extends beyond the lapse date.[1] The good cause exception in the statute appears to authorize the special permit granting authority to extend the lapse date of an unexercised special permit. There is no case law giving guidance as to what kinds of factual situations constitute sufficient cause upon which the authority can base an extension. Given the broad discretion given to the authority in deciding whether or not to issue the permit in the first place, one may assume that the courts will give great deference to a decision to extend an existing permit for periods reasonable in the circumstances. The *Bernstein* case says the purpose of the statutory lapse provisions is to prevent the "warehousing" of special permits indefinitely. It may be that an extension will be upheld as long as it does not compromise this purpose. However it has been held that an extension must be requested prior to the expiration of the original statutory period, not after the special permit has expired.[2]

Similar logic has not necessarily been applied to the expiration of project eligibility letters issued pursuant to a comprehensive permit application. See Chapter 4.

---

[1] Bernstein v. Chief Building Inspector of Falmouth, 52 Mass. App. 422, 427 (2001). There is some ambiguity in the language of this case. It states that where use or construction has commenced within the two-year period the project may be completed. But then implies that an extension from the permit granting authority is necessary for such completion. It bases this latter suggestion on an incorrect reading of the statute as allowing for extensions "where a substantial use has commenced," when in fact the extension language refers to the situation where substantial use or construction has not commenced.

[2] Hutner v. Cape Codder Condominium Board of Trustees, 52 Mass. App. 429, 434 (2001).

CHAPTER 6

ZONING—EXEMPTIONS FROM LOCAL REGULATION

Synopsis

§ 6.01   **Introduction**

§ 6.02   **Exemptions under the State Building Code**

§ 6.03   **Exemptions for Agricultural, Religious and Educational Uses**

     § 6.03[1]   **Exemptions for Agricultural Uses**

         § 6.03[1][a]   **Definition of Agriculture**

         § 6.03[1][b]   **"Primarily for Agriculture"**

            § 6.03[1][b][i]   **"Majority of Such Products:" The 50 Percent Rule**

            § 6.03[1][b][ii]   **Parcels Less than Five Acres**

     § 6.03[2]   **Exemptions for Religious Uses and Educational Uses**

         § 6.03[2][a]   **Definition of Religious and Educational Use**

         § 6.03[2][b]   **To What Extent Can the Protected Activity Be Regulated?**

     § 6.03[3]   **Exemptions for Governmental Uses**

     § 6.03[4]   **Exemptions for Public Service Uses**

     § 6.03[5]   **Exemptions for Child Care Facilities and Family Day Care Homes**

     § 6.03[6]   **Exemptions for Hazardous Waste, Refuse Treatment and Disposal Facilities**

     § 6.03[7]   **Exemptions for Scientific Research Facilities**

     § 6.03[8]   **Exemptions for Amateur Radio Operators**

     § 6.03[9]   **Telecommunications Act**

     § 6.03[10]   **Exemptions for Solar Energy Systems**

     § 6.03[11]   **Exemptions for Handicapped Access Ramps**

§ 6.03[12]   **Exemptions for Temporary Mobile Homes**
§ 6.03[13]   **Conclusion**

§ 6.01   Introduction

This Chapter reviews several land uses and activities where the Legislature, through its Constitutional powers, has chosen to limit the reach of local government regulation.[1] Unlike many aspects of zoning law in Massachusetts, in the discussion that follows, local authority—autonomy—has been clearly removed or limited.[2]

Massachusetts is considered a "Home Rule" state, as distinguished from a "Dillon's Rule" jurisdiction.[3] The distinction is important, as cities and towns in the Commonwealth are free to adopt any[4] zoning ordinance or bylaw that protects the health, safety and welfare of local residents with two exceptions. The first exception is that a local government can not *conflict* with state or federal law.

---

[1] This Chapter reviews many of the exemptions contained in the Zoning Act, General Laws Chapter 40A, Sections 3 and 9. Where reference is made to Section 3 or Section 9, the reference is to the Zoning Act. Also, please note that the Zoning Act (G.L. c. 40A) applies to 350 of the Commonwealth's 351 municipalities. The City of Boston has been subject to special zoning legislation since 1904 and the requirements and conditions of G.L. c. 40A do not apply within the City's corporate boundaries.

[2] The limitations on local powers must be made clear by the Legislature to have the desired effect. "In deciding whether under § 6 of the Home Rule Amendment a municipal ordinance or bylaw is 'not inconsistent with the constitution or laws enacted by the general court in conformity with powers reserved to the general court by' by § 8 of the Home Rule Amendment, we have said that 'the legislative intent to preclude local action must be clear.'…The task is, of course, relatively easy if the Legislature has made an explicit indication of its intention in this respect." Wendell v. Attorney General, 394 Mass. 518, 589 (1985), *citing* Bloom v. Worcester, 363 Mass. 136, 155 (1973).

[3] Judge Dillon of Iowa formulated "Dillon's Rule" in 1911. "It is a general and undisputed proposition of law that a municipal corporation possesses and can exercise the following powers, and no others: First those granted in express words; second those necessarily or fairly implied in or incident to the powers expressly granted; third, those essential to the accomplishment of the declared objectives and purposes of the corporation—not simply convenient but indispensable. Any fair, reasonable, substantial doubt concerning the existence of power is resolved by the courts against the corporation, and the power is denied…" Dillon, Municipal Corporations, § 237(89), 5th ed. 1911.

[4] The use of the term "any" raises several questions beyond the scope of this Chapter. For example, the Zoning Act does not specifically authorize, for example, the use of transfer of development rights, yet such a planning technique neither conflicts with nor is precluded by the statute. This statement is supported by the Legislature's establishment in 1975 of today's Zoning Act (1975 Mass. Acts 808), specifically Section 2A of the Act. "The purposes of this act are to facilitate, encourage and foster the adoption and modernization of zoning ordinances and bylaw by municipal governments…to achieve greater implementation of the powers granted to municipalities thereunder…This section is designed to suggest objectives for which zoning might be established which include, but are not limited to, the following:… to conserve health, to secure safety from fire, flood, panic…to conserve the value of land and buildings, including the conservation of natural resources…Said regulations may include but are not limited to restricting, prohibiting, permitting or regulating: 1. use of land, including wetlands…2. size, height, bulk, location and use of structures…"

"Municipalities may not adopt bylaws or ordinances that are inconsistent with State law."[5]

An example of such a conflict includes the requirement that a petition for a zoning bylaw change must be followed by a public hearing, which must be advertised at least twice, the first advertisement occurring at least 14 days prior to the public hearing.[6] It would be a conflict with state law for a town to hold the public hearing on the zoning change 12 days prior to the public hearing.

The second exception, and the focus of this Chapter, is where the Commonwealth or the federal government explicitly or by implication prohibit a local government's action or interference in a particular field or area. This prohibition is commonly referred to as *pre-emption*.[7] Where the state or federal government has precluded local involvement, the city or town has been pre-empted—blocked—from regulating or otherwise becoming involved in that particular area.

The Legislature has prepared and enacted a straightforward list of activities that it has determined should be removed from local control or local action; areas where local involvement has been more or less pre-empted. Several of these activities have little or no associated appellate case law and discussion in this Chapter is limited to identifying the pre-empted activity. Other activities have generated significant debate and litigation and are presented with greater detail and discussion.

An additional introductory note is important. As discussed below, the list of exempted areas comes in two varieties. First, activities that local governments are precluded—barred—from regulating. These include, for example, activities regulated by the State Building Code. The second variety, and the more difficult area in terms of differentiating how far is "too far", are limitations, as opposed to outright

---

[5] Boston Gas Company v. Somerville, 420 Mass 702, 703 (1995). "To determine whether a local ordinance is inconsistent with a statute, this court has looked to see whether there was either an express legislative intent to forbid local activity on the same subject or whether the local regulation would somehow frustrate the purpose of the statute so as to warrant an inference that the Legislature intended to preempt the subject." 420 Mass 702, at 704. *See also* Fafard v. Conservation Commission of Barnstable, 432 Mass. 194 (2000).

[6] *See* G.L. c. 40A, § 5

[7] "...in some circumstances we can infer that the Legislature intended to preempt the field because legislation on the subject is so comprehensive that any local enactment would frustrate the statute's purpose." Boston Gas, 420 Mass. at 702. *See* Roberts v. Southwestern Bell Mobile Systems, 429 Mass. 478 (1999), "State law, including municipal regulations, can be preempted by an act of Congress if the State law 'conflicts with federal law or would frustrate the federal scheme, or if the courts discern from the totality of the circumstances that Congress sought to occupy the field to the exclusion of the States.' " 429 Mass. 478, at 486, *citing* Arthur D. Little, Inc. v. Commissioner of Health & Hosps. of Cambridge, 395 Mass. 535, 548 (1985). *See also* Bremer v. Planning Board of Wellfleet, 238 F.3d 117 (1st Cir. Mass. 2001).

prohibitions on regulation at the local level. The Legislature uses language to "prohibit or unreasonably regulate" to signal that some (but not too much) regulation through zoning is permissible. These activities include, for example, agricultural uses; land used for religious or educational uses and lands used for day care centers.

Although discussed in greater detail below, the formula to be used in determining how far local zoning can go where, within Section 3, the Legislature has allowed local regulation, was defined in *Trustees of Tufts College v. City of Medford.*[8]

Although the Court was resolving a challenge regarding the educational exemption (discussed in Section 6.03[2], below), their holding regarding the breadth of allowable local regulation under the Zoning Act's Section 3 is instructive.[9]

As the material below is reviewed, please keep in mind the Court's admonition that Section 3 exemptions, where not absolute, permit local regulations, provided these regulations do not result in the unreasonable frustration—de facto prohibition—of the protected activity.

§ 6.02 Exemptions under the State Building Code

Section 3 precludes a local zoning ordinance or bylaw from regulating or restricting the use of materials or methods of construction of structures regulated by the state building code.[1]

---

[8] 415 Mass. 753 (1993). *See also* Martin v. Corporation of Presiding Bishop of Church of Jesus Christ of Latter-Day Saints, 434 Mass 141, 148 (2001), Rogers v. Town of Norfolk, 432 Mass. 374, 378 (2000), Trustees of Boston College v. Board of Aldermen of Newton, 58 Mass. App. Ct. 794, 796 (2003), and Lorden v. Town of Pepperell, No. 276791 (Mass. Land Ct., June 30, 2003), among many others.

[9] "Local zoning requirements adopted under the proviso to the Dover Amendment which serve legitimate municipal purposes sought to be achieved by local zoning, such as promoting public health or safety, preserving the character of an adjacent neighborhood, or one of the other purposes sought to be achieved by local zoning...may be permissibly enforced." 415 Mass. 753, at 758–759, (1993). The Court continued: "What we have said thus far suggests that the question of reasonableness of a local zoning requirement, as applied to a proposed education use, will depend on the particular facts of each case. Because local zoning laws are intended to be uniformly applied, an educational institution making challenges similar to those made by Tufts will bear the burden of proving that the local requirements are unreasonable as applied to it proposed project. The educational institution might do so by demonstrating that compliance would substantially diminish or detract from the usefulness of a proposed structure, or impair the character of the institution's campus, without appreciably advancing the municipality's legitimate concerns. Excessive cost of compliance with a requirement imposed on an education institution, without significant gain in terms of municipal concerns, might also qualify as unreasonable regulation of an educational use... ." 415 Mass. 753, at 759–760.

[1] The State Building Code, 780 Code Mass. Regs. S202 (1997) defines the word "building" as follows: "A structure enclosed within exterior walls or firewalls, built, erected and framed of a

At first glance, this pre-emption seems clear. Local zoning cannot allow, for example, 2x4's where the state building code require 2x6's. Nor could a zoning ordinance alter the building code's requirements for window access or emergency door placement. Some communities have raised questions, however, about potential conflicts with local zoning and the building code preemption insofar as the zoning ordinance establishes, for example, the maximum number of bedrooms allowed within a dwelling or the maximum footprint of the dwelling.[2]

It is important to note that these requirements, and ones of similar design and intent, do not run afoul of the Section 3 preemption. The purpose of the preemption is to establish a uniform set of rules and regulations governing the health and safety aspects of building construction in the Commonwealth. While local zoning may not interfere with the use of materials or methods of construction standards, local zoning may regulate and reasonably restrict the size, shape and location of structures.[3]

"It should be borne in mind that the purposes and operation of zoning laws and building codes are somewhat divergent…Whereas the main purpose of zoning is to stabilize the use of property and to protect an area from deleterious uses… a building code 'relates to the safety and structure of buildings.'"[4]

---

combination of any materials, whether portable or fixed, having a roof, to form a structure for the shelter of persons, animals or property."

[2] An interesting question was asked and answered in a 1976 case involving a an order by the Housing Appeals Committee to the Town of North Andover regarding construction of housing units under G.L. c. 40B, § 20–23 While the Housing Appeals Committee clearly has jurisdiction to override locally adopted rules and regulations that impede development of affordable housing, does the Committee have jurisdiction to override encumbering regulations passed by the Legislature? The answer is no. "We find nothing in those sections [referring to the State Building Code] or in the *Hanover* case which suggest that the Housing Appeals Committee has been empowered with authority to override or ignore laws passed by the Legislature or regulations validly promulgated by the Commonwealth's various boards, departments, agencies or commissions." Board of Appeals of North Andover v. Housing Appeals Committee, 4 Mass. App. Ct. 676, 680 (1976), referring to Board of Appeals of Hanover v. Housing Appeals Committee, 363 Mass. 339 (1973). *But see* Dennis Housing Corporation v. Zoning Board of Appeals of Dennis, 439 Mass. 71, 80 (2003), where the SJC determined that the Old King's Highway District, an historic district governing large portions of Route 6A on Cape Cod was subject to being overridden by the Dennis Board of Appeals. The Court concluded that while the District was created by the Legislature, it nonetheless was enforced by local, not state entities and thus was subject to board of appeals discretion pursuant to G.L. c. 40B, § 20–23. *See* Chapter 4 for further discussion regarding G.L. c. 40B, § 20–23.

[3] "We perceive nothing beyond the limits of proper zoning objectives in a provision of the amendment restricting apartments to three rooms, a kitchen and a bath. This, as the judge ruled, is a size description which cannot be said, as a matter of law, to be unreasonable. If that provision has any effect upon the 'density of population' in, or the 'use' of, apartment buildings, those matters

§ 6.03   Exemptions for Agricultural, Religious and Educational Uses

§ 6.03[1]   Exemptions for Agricultural Uses

General Laws Chapter 40A Section 3 provides broad, but somewhat confusing language establishing protection from local zoning for uses generally referred to as "agricultural."[1] It is important to note at the outset that whether a land use is entitled to the statutory protection of Section 3 does not turn on whether the use was commercial—involving retail sales—or not. An agricultural use or activity that has no retail or wholesale distribution is nevertheless protected by Section 3. "All agriculture conducted for profit is commercial in some degree."[2]

Confusion has centered on several areas of the statute; notably the definition of "agriculture" and the statute's intent regarding "majority of such products" when referring to products raised on the property being regulated. These issues are discussed in detail below.

§ 6.03[1][a]   Definition of Agriculture[3]

Faced with whether the Town of Mansfield could lawfully exclude the raising

---

constitute appropriate consideration in the framing of zoning bylaw." Hallenborg v. Town Clerk of Billerica, 360 Mass. 513, 521 (1973).

   4 Enos v. City of Brockton, 354 Mass. 278, 280–281 (1968), *citing* Norcross v. Board of Appeal of the Bldg. Dept. of Boston, 255 Mass. 177, 182. *See also* Van Rensellar v. City of Springfield, 58 Mass. App. Ct. 104, 108 (2003) and Rinaldi v. City of Boston, 50 Mass. App. Ct. 657, 660 (2001).

   1 "...nor shall any such ordinance or bylaw prohibit, unreasonably regulate or require a special permit for the use of land for the primary purpose of agriculture, horticulture, floriculture or viticulture; nor prohibit, or unreasonably regulate, or require a special permit for the use, expansion or reconstruction of existing structures thereon for the primary purpose of agriculture, horticulture, floriculture or viticulture, including those facilities for the sale of produce, and wine and dairy products, provided that during the months of June, July, August and September or every year during the harvest season of the primary crop raised on the land of the owner or lessee, the majority of such products for sale, based on either gross sales dollars or volume, have been produced by the owner or lessee of the land on which the facility is located, except that all such activities may be limited to parcels of more than five acres in area not zoned for agriculture, horticulture, floriculture or viticulture. For such purposes, land divided by a public or private way or a waterway shall be construed as one parcel." G.L. c. 40A, § 3

   2 Cumberland Farms of Conn. Inc. v. Zoning Board of Appeals of North Attleborough, 359 Mass. 68, 74–75. *See also* Prime v. Zoning Board of Appeals of Norwell, 42 Mass. App. Ct. 796 (1997), "We reject the abutters' first argument. Their suggestion is that a 'retail' operation is inconsistent with the agricultural use of the land and therefore not within § 3." 42 Mass. App. Ct. 796, at 800. *See also* Town of Natick v. Modern Continental Construction, 1998 Mass. Super. LEXIS 103 (Mass. Super. Ct. Mar. 6, 1998), where the Superior Court, quoting *Cumberland* and *Prime* noted, "The exemption operates even where the agricultural use in question is retail or commercial in nature." 1998 Mass. Super. LEXIS 103, at *10.

   3 Note that the statute refers to agriculture, horticulture, floriculture and viticulture. Only the phrase horticulture is further defined within the statute. "For the purpose of this section, the term

and keeping of pigs within town boundaries, the Appeals Court concluded that the plain and ordinary meaning of the phrase "agriculture" included "piggeries." "When a statute does not define its words we give them their usual and accepted meanings, as long as those meanings are consistent with the statutory purpose."[4]

The importance of the Court's holding in the *Mansfield* case, coupled with a subsequent Appeals Court decision originating in *Tisbury*,[5] is that the Court's definition of the Legislature's intentionally undefined phrase "agriculture" is very broad.[6]

---

horticulture shall include the growing and keeping of nursery stock and the sale thereof. Said nursery stock shall be considered to be produced by the owner or lessee of the land if it is nourished, maintained and managed while on the premises." G.L. c. 40A, § 3.

[4] Building Inspector of Mansfield v. Curvin, 22 Mass. App. Ct. 401, 402, *citing* Commonwealth v. Zone Book, Inc., 372 Mass 366, 369 (1977) and others. In an interesting concurring opinion however, Justice Cutter noted: "Thus I am less certain than the majority...that...the Legislature had in mind...to include in the term "agriculture" the keeping of swine...It may be that the legislative intention was to confine the regulation of piggeries to the prevention and prohibition of nuisances by local boards of health...rather than by zoning legislation. Mansfield, 22 Mass. App. Ct. 401, at 406.

[5] Tisbury v. Martha's Vineyard Commission, 27 Mass. App. Ct. 1204 (1989).

[6] "The agricultural use exemption embodied in § 3 is interpreted broadly in order to promote the economic viability of agricultural enterprises in Massachusetts." Minty v. Arena, 1998 Mass. Super. LEXIS 109, at * 7 (1998), *citing* Tisbury v. Martha's Vineyard Commission, 27 Mass. App. Ct. 1204 (1989). *See also* Town of Sturbridge v. McDowell, 35 Mass. App. Ct. 924 (1993), where the Appeals Court, faced with a challenge to the raising and boarding of dogs, wrote: "We fail to see how the raising and training of dogs for sale is distinguishable from the raising and training of other domestic animals such as ponies or horses which we concluded in *Steege* amounted to an agricultural pursuit. Consequently, we conclude that the breeding, raising, and training of dogs owed by defendant on the land is an agricultural pursuit under G.L. c. 40A, § 3." 35 Mass. App. Ct. 924, at 926.

Compare the holding in *Sturbridge with* a 1958 Supreme Judicial Court decision stating that the raising of greyhounds for racing purposes was outside of the statutory protection afforded by § 3. "Pigs are farm animals and raising them could much more reasonably be regarded as farming than the maintenance of dogs intended for use solely for commercial racing connected with a pari-mutuel (sic) system of wagering rather than with any agricultural pursuit." Mioduszewski v. Town of Saugus, 337 Mass. 140, 144 (1958), citing several cases from other jurisdictions. (Note that *Mioduszewski* was decided prior to applicable revisions to G.L. c. 40A, § 3). *See also* Modern Continental Construction v. Building Inspector of Natick, 42 Mass. App. Ct. 901 (1997), where the Court upheld the use of land for the slaughtering of livestock as consistent with agricultural activities. "We think it reasonable to regard the slaughter of animals as a normal and customary part of preparing them for market. It then follows from the acceptably broad definitions of the word 'agriculture' that a slaughterhouse used for the butchery of animals raised on the premises is primarily agricultural in purpose." 42 Mass. App. Ct. 901, at 902. *See also* Deutschmann v. Board of Appeals of Canton, 325 Mass. 297 (1950). "The fact that the products are not in their natural state does not mean that they cease to be products raised on the farm of their owner, who seeks there to sell them...We do not believe that one who on his premises processes milk and cream from cows on his premises thereby ceases to be a farmer, selling on his farm products they raise." 325 Mass.

This broad interpretation requires that cities and towns seeking to regulate agricultural land uses and activities do so only within the narrow options provided by the statute.

These options include local regulations that help clarify, as discussed below, the meaning of the statutory requirement that the land be used primarily for agriculture, that the majority of the agricultural products be produced on the land subject to the zoning regulation and that the parcel being regulated is less than five acres and is not zoned for agricultural use.

To obtain protection from the statute, the land in question must: (1) be used primarily for agriculture, (2) the majority of the products sold (if any) must have been produced by the owner or lessee and (3) the parcel of land must either be greater than five acres *or* zoned for agricultural uses. These three criteria are discussed more fully below.

§ 6.03[1][b]   "Primarily for Agriculture"

The statutory protection afforded to agricultural activities under Section 3 is limited in several ways, including the requirement that the land be used for the "primary purpose of agriculture, horticulture, floriculture or viticulture." At issue is the limiting phrase, "primary purpose." The "primary purpose" limitation is distinguishable from the "majority of such products" and "five acre requirement" as discussed below.

The statute precludes local prohibition of agricultural use where the parcel is greater than five acres or in an area-zoned agriculture if, the primary—principle—use of the land is agricultural.

"Section 3 does not include a definition of the word 'primary' in the context of the use of land, and thus we give the word its usual and accepted meaning from 'other legal contexts and dictionary definitions...Contrast the use of the word 'incidental' in the zoning context: "not...the primary use of the property but rather one which is subordinate and minor in significance."[7]

The above-noted comments provide a recent and consistent example of the Courts' differentiation between "primary" and "accessory" or "incidental" as these phrases relate to agricultural land use.

The distinction is important. If the use of the land is primarily for agricultural purposes, and the other relevant criteria are met, local zoning cannot "unreasonably

---

297, at 301, *cited in* Minty v. Arena, 1998 Mass. Super. LEXIS 109, at *7.

[7] Town of Eastham v. Clancy, 44 Mass. App. Ct. 901, 902 (1997), *citing* Building Inspector of Mansfield v. Curvin, 22 Mass. App. Ct. 401, 402 (1986). *See also* Simmons v. Board of Appeals of Newburyport, 60 Mass. App. Ct. 5 (2003).

regulate or require a special permit" for its use.[8]

If the use of the land *is not* primarily for agricultural purposes, the ordinance or bylaw may regulate the use, either through special permit criteria and constraints or outright prohibition.

A problem arises, however, where a landowner is engaging in a protected activity (e.g. cultivating cranberries) and an accessory activity at the same time (e.g. gravel extraction). At issue is whether the accessory activity, perhaps related to the protected activity, is likewise protected by statute.

Resolution of this commonly occurring issue generally turns on the matter of degree. "Uses which are 'incidental' to a permissible activity on zoned property are permitted as long as the incidental use does not undercut the plain intent of the zoning bylaw."[9]

The distinction between "primary" and "incidental" is further amplified—and clarified—by the Court's "50 Percent Rule" discussed below.

§ 6.03[1][b][i]   "Majority of Such Products:" The 50 Percent Rule

The agriculture statutory exemption provides protection for two types of agricultural activities. First, as discussed above, protection is given to a broad range

---

[8] Note that cities and towns may require a special permit for structures associated with a protected agricultural use(s). Citing Cumberland Farms of Conn., Inc. v. Zoning Board of Appeals of North Attleborough, 359 Mass. 68 (1971), the Appeals Court held in Prime v. Zoning Board of Appeals of Norwell, 42 Mass. App. Ct. 796 (1997), that a special permit may be required for structures that are associated with agricultural uses, unless the requirement is a "sham." "In other words, the application of the bylaw [may not] nullify a protected use." 42 Mass. App. Ct. 796, at 802, *citing* Trustees of Tufts College v. Medford, 415 Mass. 753, 763 (1993). "Local regulation of a new structure must take into account the factors mentioned in *Cumberland*." (The court stated that the local regulation 'must bear a reasonably direct relation to significant considerations of public health... ." 42 Mass. App. Ct. 796, at 802, *citing* Cumberland, 359 Mass. at 75. Finally, and as discussed throughout this Chapter, note the court's admonition regarding the use of special permits for otherwise protected activities. "But the special permit may not be imposed unreasonably and in a manner designed to prohibit the operation of the farm stand, nor may the permit be denied merely because the board would prefer a different use of the locus, or no use." 42 Mass. App. Ct. 796, at 802–803.

[9] Henry v. Board of Appeals of Dunstable, 418 Mass. 841, 844 (1994). "The word incidental in zoning bylaws or ordinances incorporates two concepts: "It means that the use must not be the primary use of the property but rather one which is subordinate and minor in significance...But incidental' when used to define an accessory use, must also incorporate the concept of reasonable relationship with the primary use. It is not enough that the use is subordinate; it must also be attendant or concomitant. To ignore this latter aspect of 'incidental' would be to permit any use which is not primary, no matter how unrelated it is to the primary use." 418 Mass. 841, at 845. (emphasis added). *See also* Simmons v. Zoning Bd. of Appeals of Newburyport, 60 Mass. App. Ct. 5 (2003).

of agricultural land uses, regardless of the final destination point of the crops or end product of the activity. The statute protects the activity—the process—of growing crops, raising animals and other agricultural processes.

The second type of activity protected by statute, and the more commonly challenged use, is the sale of products claimed to be agricultural and thus exempt from unreasonable regulation and the requirement of obtaining a special permit.

The reach of this protection is extremely broad and in many cases, a significant problem for local communities. The reasons are simple. Those activities protected by Section 3 become those land uses a city or town can not prohibit or be forced to go through the special permit process. For example, the sale of agricultural products grown on the property via the traditional "farm stand" is clearly protected. At issue though is the sale of diary products not grown or raised on the farm. At what point does the "farm stand" become a "convenience store" typically not allowed in agricultural or residential zoning districts?

The answer to this commonly asked question has been phrased by the Courts as the "50 percent rule." "…just because the locus is subject to an agricultural use exemption does not mean every facility or activity on that locus also may benefit from the exemption."[10]

The statute and case law are clear. To achieve the protective benefits of Section 3, at least half of the products sold on the locus must be or have been produced by the owner of the land *on the land in question.*[11] In other words, protection is not afforded to a landowner who "imports" more than fifty percent of the products for sale.[12]

---

[10] Minty v. Arena, 1998 Mass. Super. LEXIS 109, at *12 (Mass. Super. 1998). *See also* Town of Eastham v. Clancy, 44 Mass. App. Ct. 901, 902 (1997), "The inquiry is whether Barnes used his property 'primarily' for agriculture. 'Primarily' means 'chiefly, mainly.' American Heritage Dictionary 1438 (3d ed. 1992). Contrast the use of the word "incidental" in the zoning context: "not … the primary use of the property but rather one which is subordinate and minor in significance," *citing* Henry v. Board of Appeals of Dunstable, 418 Mass. 841, 845, 641 N.E.2d 1334 (1994).

[11] In *Town of Eastham v. Clancy*, the Appeals Court upheld a lower court denial of Section 3 protection to a farm stand used for the sale of produce where only one-third of the landowner's 5.5 acres were used for agricultural production. "While Barnes did testify as to which vegetables and fruits were grown on the premises and which were bought elsewhere to be sold, we agree with the trial judge that he did not sustain his burden of proof that a majority of products for sale were produced by him." 44 Mass. App. Ct. 901, at 902. *But see* Steege v. Board of Appeals of Stow, 26 Mass. App. Ct. 970 (1988), where the Court wrote: "the plaintiffs purchase and raising of horses, their stabling, training through the operation of the riding school, and their participation in horse shows are all part of the one whole and constitute agriculture as that phrase is used in c. 40A, § 3." 26 Mass. App. Ct. 970, at 972.

[12] Note the Legislature's response in 1994 to the obvious problem encountered with the raising of trees, plants and other nursery items. "Said nursery stock shall be considered to be produced by

§ 6.03[1][b][ii]   Parcels Less than Five Acres

"The obvious purpose of the Act...is to promote agricultural use within all zoning districts in a municipality. Such use may not be prohibited or unduly restricted even in an area not specifically zoned for the purpose as long as the parcel being used is one of more than five acres."[13] (emphasis added).

Stated simply, a property owner with greater than five acres of land who uses her property for agricultural purposes, in keeping with the discussion above, benefits from the protections of the statute regardless of the land's zoning designation.[14]

§ 6.03[2]   Exemptions for Religious Uses and Educational Uses

It is important to note at the outset that Massachusetts's courts have consistently granted great deference to interpretations of the Legislature's exemption from local zoning for religious and educational uses. "...we do not believe it irrational for the Legislature to determine that educational and religious institutions, because of their unique locational requirements and because of their importance to society generally, may be exempted from the application of zoning laws...We deem it significant that courts of other jurisdictions have reached the same conclusion even in the absence of a statutory basis therefor."[15]

The statutory basis found within Section 3 and reprinted below[16] is referred to as the "Dover Amendment." The Dover Amendment was adopted in 1950 as a response to the Town of Dover's regulation of educational land uses; regulations that were ruled invalid by the Supreme Judicial Court in 1951.[17] Although

---

the owner or lessee of the land if it is nourished, maintained and managed while on the premises." G.L. c. 40A, § 3.

[13] Building Inspector of Mansfield v. Curvin, 22 Mass. App. Ct. 401, 402–403 (1986).

[14] Counsel should be aware that local governments have means, other than zoning, to regulate against the sometimes-negative impacts associated with agricultural land uses. These techniques include health regulations under G.L. c. 111, § 31 and others. But note, as discussed in the introduction to this Chapter, local governments are pre-empted from certain activities, including those involving certain regulation of pesticides, fertilizers and herbicides. Advice from counsel should be obtained prior to developing regulations in these areas. *See*, for example, Town of Wendell v. Attorney General, 394 Mass. 518 (1985).

[15] Sisters of the Holy Cross of Massachusetts v. Town of Brookline, 347 Mass. 486, 496, (1964), referencing case decisions from New York, Texas, Ohio, and Missouri.

[16] G.L. c. 40A, § 3 reads, in part: "No zoning ordinance or bylaw shall regulate or restrict...the use of land or structures for religious purposes or for educational purposes on land owned or leased by the commonwealth or its agencies, subdivisions or bodies politic or by a religious sect or denomination or by a nonprofit educational corporation; provided however, that such land or structures may be subject to reasonable regulations concerning the bulk and height of structures and determining yard sizes, lot area, setbacks, open space, parking and building coverage requirements."

[17] Attorney General v. Dover, 327 Mass. 601 (1951).

revised several times, the intent of the Dover Amendment remains unchanged: local zoning is limited in its ability to control or otherwise regulate the use of land for religious and/or educational purposes. "Section 3 codifies the case law interpreting its statutory predecessor, the so-called Dover amendment...The amendment insures that a municipality will not express 'preferences as to what kind of...religious denominations it will welcome.'"[18]

Relative to other sections of the Zoning Act, the exemption provisions for religious and educational uses are straightforward. Case law reflects two general concerns regarding religious and educational use exemptions. First, what defines a "religious or educational purpose"? Second, how far can local zoning controls go in their "reasonable regulations" before these regulations are tantamount to an outright, and unlawful, use prohibition?

§ 6.03[2][a]   Definition of Religious and Educational Use

The protections afforded religious and educational uses derive from the Court's broad definition of what constitutes these activities.[19]

Exemptions from local zoning have been applied to religious and educational programs where the students were adults,[20] where the institution furnished resi-

---

[18] Southern New England Conference Association of Seventh Day Adventists v. Town of Burlington, 21 Mass. App. Ct. 701, 705–706 (1986).

[19] *See*, for example, Mount Hermon Boys' School v. Gill, 145 Mass. 139 (1887). "...the process of developing and training the powers and capabilities of human beings...Education may be particularly directed to either the mental, moral or physical powers and faculties, but in its broadest and best sense it relates to them all." 145 Mass. 139, at 146. *See also* Fitchburg Housing Authority v. Board of Appeals of Fitchburg, 380 Mass. 869 (1980), "This court has long recognized 'education' as 'a broad and comprehensive term.' " 380 Mass. 869, at 875, *citing* Mount Hermon, 145 Mass. 139 (1887). *See also* Brockton Coalition for Homeless v. Tonis, 2004 Mass. Super. LEXIS 124, at *4, 17 Mass. L. Rep. 554 (Mass. Super. Ct. 2004), where the Court concluded that the provision of shelter housing, where coupled with education, qualifies as educational activities pursuant to G.L. c. 40A, § 3. *But see* City of Medford v. McDonald, 12 Mass. L. Rep. 734, 2000 Mass. Super. LEXIS 582 (Mass. Super. 2000), where the Court held that the renting of rooms to visiting scholars studying at Tufts University did not invoke the protections granted by G.L. c. 40A, § 3 where the University itself was not a party to the litigation.

Not surprisingly, the Courts have had a more difficult time defining "religious" activities. "It is all very heady business and defies precision, but we emerge with the understanding that what is religious requires a system of belief, concerning more than the earthly and temporal, to which the adherent is faithful. Fortunately, the subject at hand is land use, not philosophy, and, in the more prosaic context of the former, the puzzle begins to unravel." Needham Pastoral Counseling Center, Inc. v. Board of Appeals of Needham, 29 Mass. App. Ct. 31, 34 (1990).

[20] *See* Fitchburg Housing Authority v. Board of Zoning Appeals of Fitchburg, 380 Mass. 869 (1980). "The proposed facility would fulfill a significant educational goal in preparing its residents to live by themselves...Inculcating a basic understanding of how to cope with everyday problems and to maintain oneself in society is incontestably an educational purpose. 380 Mass. 869, at 875.

dential housing[21] and where the students were considered "emotionally disturbed."[22] Precisely because of the Court's broad interpretation of religious and educational use and strict guidelines as to the extent these activities can be regulated, counsel for petitioners and municipalities alike could reasonably predict the outcome of applications for new or expanded religious and educational activities.

This relative certainty has been upset by the Court's 2001 decision in *Martin v. Corporation of the Presiding Bishop*, 747 N.E.2d 131 (Mass. 2001). The question in *Martin* was whether the Church of Jesus Christ of Latter-day Saints could construct a new temple with a steeple that was 139 feet in height, far taller than that permitted by the Belmont zoning bylaw. Citing to the Dover amendment (as well as the Notre Dame Cathedral and St. Peter's Basilica), the Court concluded that the Church, and not the Town nor the Court has the right to determine whether the architectural elements of the temple (in this case height) are "necessary" to the "faith served by those buildings." 747 N.E.2d 131, at 138.

Prior to *Martin*, not all claims of religious or educational use were entitled to the statutory or judicial protection afforded by G.L. c. 40A, § 3. Query with the *Martin* holding in place, whether the Court might today hold differently than as noted below.

In *Needham Pastoral Counseling Center, Inc. v. Board of Appeals of Needham*,[23] the Appeals Court denied zoning protection where a nonprofit counseling agency sought to offer counseling services within a church. "The activity concerned is not an enterprise of the landlord church and is not designed primarily for the parishioners of that church. Specific religious doctrine is subordinated... ."[24]

In *Worcester County Christian Communications, Inc. v. Board of Appeals of Spencer*, the Appeals Court declined to decide whether the use of a radio station ostensibly for religious broadcasting was entitled to Section 3 protection. Relying

---

[21] *See* President and Fellows of Harvard College v. Assessors of Cambridge, 175 Mass. 145 (1900) and The Bible Speaks v. Board of Appeals of Lenox, 8 Mass. App. Ct. 19, 31 (1979), *citing* Radcliffe College v. Cambridge, 350 Mass. 613, 618 (1966), "...holding that parking and the feeding and housing of college personnel is 'within the broad scope of the educational powers... .'"

[22] *See* Harbor Schools, Inc. v. Board of Appeals of Haverhill, 5 Mass. App. Ct. 600 (1977). At issue in *Harbor Schools* was whether a dwelling used for the treatment and care of emotionally disturbed children qualified for protections from local zoning under the predecessor to Section 3. "But 'education' and 'rehabilitation' do not denote functions so distinct that the master could be required to quantify them relative to each other. They are not mutually exclusive." . 5 Mass. App. Ct. 600, at 604.

[23] 29 Mass. App. Ct. 31 (1990).

[24] Needham Pastoral Counseling Center, Inc. v. Board of Appeals of Needham, 29 Mass. App. Ct. 31, 37 (1990).

on an earlier decision regarding a purported educational exemption,[25] the Court concluded that the claimant for the exemption must demonstrate that religious or educational content will be conveyed. "For all that appears in the record...the plaintiff's intended use of the radio station is to provide a listening audience with programs which the plaintiff perceives to be of greater intellectual and inspirational value than those currently available. Although that purpose is laudable, it is neither religious nor educational..."[26]

As the discussion above points out, prior to *Martin*, the definition of religious and educational activities entitled to statutory protection are broad, but not complete. Following *Martin*, it is unclear as to whether any claim of religious use or activity can be subject to local regulation and judicial review.[27] The next logical question, assuming that the activity is entitled to protection, is the extent to which local zoning can alter or otherwise regulate the eventual development footprint of the protected activity.

§ 6.03[2][b]   To What Extent Can the Protected Activity Be Regulated?

Prior to *Martin*, it was well accepted that Massachusetts cities and towns could regulate, albeit not prohibit, structures and uses operated for religious and educational purposes, provided that the regulation did not amount to a de facto prohibition.

For example, while a zoning ordinance could not lawfully limit impervious lot coverage to two percent for churches or synagogues (and thus run afoul of a de facto prohibition), it could, at least prior to *Martin*, regulate traditional dimensional aspects of structures, including bulk and height.

Martin challenges this long-standing belief that cities and towns can regulate aspects of religious structures-in this case the height of a steeple—even though the statute clearly allows such regulation. "The judge should have considered whether compliance with Belmont's height restriction would have impaired the character of the temple...The character of the temple with its steeple surely encompasses both

---

[25] "Merely an 'element of education', however, provided not by a formal program or trained professionals, but only informally gleaned from the interplay among residents of the nursing home community, is not within the meaning of 'educational purpose' pursuant to G.L. c. 40A, § 3." Whitinsville Retirement Society, Inc. v. Town of Northbridge, 394 Mass. 757, 761 (1985).

[26] Worcester County Christian Communications, Inc. v. Board of Appeals of Spencer, 22 Mass. App. Ct. 83, 89 (1986).

[27] *See also* the Religious Land Use and Institutionalized Persons Act (RILUIPA), 42 U.S.C. §§ 2000cc-200cc-5(2000). RILUPA narrows the authority of states and local governments with respect to land use regulations that impose a substantial burden on religious exercise and regulations that impose a substantial burden on the religious activities of individuals residing in or confined to, a state owned or operated institution (e.g. penal institution or institution for the disabled or handicapped).

its architectural beauty, as well as its religious symbolism." 747 N.E.2d 131, at 139.

The most complicated aspect of *Martin* is that the Court held that the statutory pre-emption against unreasonable regulation relates to the "land" or "structure" and not the "use of an element or part of a structure." Id. at 137. Thus under *Martin*, it is not for the adjudicatory body (e.g. the planning board or board of appeals) or even the local legislature to challenge a religious institution's assertion that the proposed height, width or bulk of a religious structure is necessary. "We agree with the board that a rigid application of Belmont's height restrictions for uninhabited 'projections' would impair the character of the temple without advancing any municipal concerns." 747 N.E.2d 131, at 140.

Left unanswered by the Court is what those municipal concerns might be. The steeple height approved by the board of appeals was 70 feet greater than that allowed by right. One plaintiff's complaint alleged that the steeple, illuminated at night, would be visible, day and night, from virtually all of her property.

Prior to *Martin*, it was appropriate advice to suggest that while local zoning can regulate and restrict religious and educational uses, these restrictions can not result in the de facto prohibition of the use. Post *Martin*, cities and towns must be more circumspect. The adjudicative body must explore whether the claimed exemption applies to the religious activities proposed for the land or structure. To the extent that the applicant can demonstrate that the religious use is directly linked to the land or structure and that the element of concern is integral to the religious practice (e.g. the steeple), the pre-emption language of G.L. c. 40A, § 3 is likely to overcome the municipal concerns identified by the *Martin* Court.

Finally, the Appeals Court held in 1979, that a special permit *cannot* be required for religious or educational uses or development related activities.[28] While bulk, dimensional and parking regulations may be regulated, they may not be made subject to a special permit. This point is important for those cities and towns that have established site plan review procedures that require a special permit under certain circumstances.[29] Application of these requirements to educational and religious uses violates Section 3.

---

[28] "Any such restrictions imposed under the authority of the bylaw may well have the effect of nullifying, or seriously diminishing the educational institutions entitlement to reasonable growth. It also, as a practical matter, enables the town to exercise its preferences as to what kind of educational or religious denominations it will welcome...In our opinion, the provisions of the bylaw taken together invest the board with a considerable measure of discretionary authority over an educational institution's use of it facilities and create a scheme of land use regulation for such institutions which is antithetical to the limitations on municipal zoning power in this area prescribed by G.L. c. 40A, § 3...The Legislature did not intend to impose special permit requirements, designed under c. 40A, § 9 to accommodate uses not permitted as of right in a particular zoning district, on legitimate educational uses which have been expressly authorized to exists as of right in any zone. The Bible Speaks v. Board of Appeals of Lenox, 8 Mass. App. Ct. 19, 33 (1979).

[29] For example, some municipalities require a site plan review special permit for uses that

§ 6.03[3]   Exemptions for Governmental Uses

A detailed review of governmental immunity from zoning regulations is beyond the scope of this Chapter. However a quick summary should prove helpful.

First, absent a waiver of immunity, the federal government is immune from municipal zoning regulations (as well as many analogous state regulations). "The Supremacy Clause establishes federal law as the supreme law of the land...'A corollary to this principle is that the activities of the Federal Government are free from regulation by any state."[30]

Second, absent a waiver of immunity, the state government is immune from local zoning ordinances or bylaws. "As a general proposition, the State and State instrumentalities are immune from municipal zoning regulations, unless a statute expressly provides the contrary."[31]

For example, in *Freetown v. Zoning Board of Appeals of Dartmouth*, the Appeals

---

require more than a specified number of parking spaces (e.g. greater than 10).

[30] United States of America v. Alaska Public Utilities Commission, 23 F.3d 257, 260–261 (1994), *citing* Mayo v. United States, 319 U.S. 441, 445 (1943).

[31] Inspector of Buildings of Salem v. Salem State College, 28 Mass. App. Ct. 92, 95 (1989). Note that this immunity includes the state, its instrumentalities and its agencies. For example, in an action against the Bristol County Commissioners regarding the construction of a new jail in Dartmouth, the Supreme Judicial Court held that county governments are immune from local zoning: "...an entity or agency created by the Massachusetts Legislature is immune from municipal zoning regulations (absent statutory provisions to the contrary) at least insofar as that entity or agency is performing an essential government function. Like the Massachusetts Turnpike Authority...counties also are organized by the General Court for the convenient administration of some parts of government. They are bodies politic and corporate. They exist solely for the public welfare." County Commissioners of Bristol v. Conservation Commission of Dartmouth, 380 Mass. 706, 710–711 (1980).

Finally, in a decision consistent with the discussion above, the Supreme Judicial Court held that the Martha's Vineyard and Nantucket Steamship Authority was exempt from the Bourne zoning bylaw insofar as the bylaw would preclude the use of real property for commuter (e.g. ferry) parking. "There is no question that the Legislature has entrusted exclusive management of the boat line to the Authority...As a consequence, the Authority can lawfully execute the lease in issue without complying with requirements of the Bourne zoning bylaw." Town of Bourne v. Plante, 429 Mass. 329, 334 (1999). The Court went to great lengths explaining the Authority's need for the "off-site" parking, including the well-publicized fact that during the July 4th weekend in 1995, traffic in Woods Hole, and Falmouth in general, created extremely dangerous vehicular and pedestrian conditions. The Court's analysis implies that the Authority's need for the extra parking was an emergency situation (although it is not clear whether their holding would differ if exigent circumstances did not exist). Absent from the Court's analysis, unfortunately, was the fact that the Authority exacerbated a decades old traffic problem in the summer by allowing ferry passengers to travel standby, and thus encouraged travelers to queue along Falmouth's roadways, on the July 4th weekend. Note again, all state agencies and state instrumentalities are exempt from local zoning requirements and prohibitions.

Court was faced with a challenge to a regional landfill, authorized by statute to provide landfill services to several communities in southeastern Massachusetts.[32]

At issue was whether the Town could deny approval of the landfill, claiming that provisions of the Zoning Act authorize review and imposition of conditions on solid waste facility construction at the local level.[33] Despite the clear language in the Zoning Act authorizing such review, the Court wrote: "Case law extending from *Teasdale v. Newell & Snowling Construction Co.*, 192 Mass. 440 (1906) to *Inspector of Buildings of Salem v. Salem State College*, 28 Mass. App. Ct. 92 (1989), 'assert the supremacy of the State over local land use regulations in connection with State construction projects, unless the Legislature has made express provision to the contrary.' "[34]

Note however, that the Court has upheld local regulation of otherwise immune activities where the city or town is enforcing against a "nuisance" and the enforcement does not otherwise negate the supremacy clause. "This does not mean, however, that the legislatively created entity has absolute immunity from all local regulation. It remains subject to regulations, including anti-nuisance regulations, that do not interfere with its ability to fulfill its essential governmental purposes and have only a negligible effect on its operations."[35]

Third, local governments are not immune from their own zoning,[36] unless, of course, city council or town meeting chooses to exempt the respective government from compliance.[37]

§ 6.03[4]　Exemptions for Public Service Uses

The public service preemption in Section 3 is broad[38] and has been the subject

---

[32] New Bedford, Acushnet, Dartmouth and Fairhaven.

[33] *See* G.L. c. 40A, § 9.

[34] Town of Freetown v. Zoning Board of Appeals of Dartmouth, 33 Mass. App. Ct. 415, 419 (1992).

[35] Greater Lawrence Sanitary District v. Town of North Andover, 439 Mass. 16, 22 (2003), *citing* Village on the Hill, Inc. v. Massachusetts Turnpike Auth., 348 Mass. 107, 118 (1964). *See also* Martha's Vineyard Land Bank Commission v. Board of Assessor's of West Tisbury, 62 Mass. App. Ct. 25, 31 (2004).

[36] "… the town was bound to comply with any general provision of its zoning bylaw applicable to it… ." Pierce v. Wellesley, 336 Mass. 517 (1957).

[37] For example, in *Rose v. Commissioner of Public Health*, the Supreme Judicial Court held as valid a Northampton ordinance that exempted the city from compliance with certain requirements pertaining to new landfills. 361 Mass. 625 (1972). "It more closely resembles Pierce v. Wellesley, 336 Mass. 517 (1957), where the town was permitted by its zoning bylaw to maintain parking lots in residence areas and it was held that 'the town reserved to itself…the privilege of carrying on town functions in any zone in the town." 361 Mass. 625, at 631.

[38] "Lands or structures uses, or to be used by a public service corporation may be exempted in particular respects from the operation of a zoning ordinance or bylaw if, upon petition of the

of many appellate cases since its inclusion in the statue in 1952. The preemption grants authority to the state to determine which services and service providers are offering a "necessity or convenience" that the public could not otherwise readily obtain.[39]

The Courts have broadly interpreted the definition of which entities qualify for the Section 3 preemption.[40] Past cases included determinations that the pre-emption for public service utilities differs in a significant respect from the pre-emptions discussed throughout this Chapter. This preemption is only triggered if the Department of Telecommunications and Energy (DTE) determines that certain aspects or provisions of local zoning impede the development of the public service utility.[41] When such a determination is made, the DTE must then conclude that the public would not be injured if the zoning regulation(s) were set aside.[42]

In other words, local zoning can only be set aside if the DTE concludes that "but for" the local regulations the public service utility could proceed, and proceeding would not injure public health or safety.

§ 6.03[5]   Exemptions for Child Care Facilities and Family Day Care Homes

The Section 3 protections afforded family daycare homes and childcare facilities differ. In addition, note that the only statutory distinction between the two types of facilities is one of size.[43] Nevertheless, the statutory protections afforded the two uses are very different.

---

corporation, the department of telecommunications and energy shall, after notice given pursuant to section eleven and public hearing in the town or city, determine the exemptions required and find that the present or proposed use of the land or structure is reasonably necessary for the convenience or welfare of the public... ." G.L. c. 40A, § 3.

[39] *See*, for example, Save the Bay, Inc. v. Department of Public Utilities, 366 Mass. 667 (1975).

[40] "..."public service corporation' is a term of art which is not limited to corporations...The zoning exemption available under G.L. c. 40A, § 3 is intended to assure utilities ability to carry out their obligation to serve the public when this duty conflicts with local interests...This concern for public service applies to all utilities, not just those operated by corporations." Planning Board of Braintree v. Department of Public Utilities, 420 Mass. 22, 26–27 (1995).

[41] "The department has the power to exempt land or structures in all respects. The exemption is based on the fact that the use is 'reasonably necessary for the convenience or welfare of the public.'...The department can exempt specified uses of specified property from bylaws and ordinances to the extent applicable..." 420 Mass. 22, at 29.

[42] "The issue before us is whether the proposed use is reasonably necessary for the convenience or welfare of the public....We may not ignore the fact that...Framingham has zoned the locus as a general residence district, and an exemption should be granted only on the basis of a preponderance of evidence that the public convenience or welfare would be better served if the zoning bylaw were not enforced... ." New York Central Railroad Company v. Department of Public Utilities, 347 Mass. 586, 590 (1964).

[43] G.L. c. 28A, § 9 defines a "family day care home" as "any private residence which on a regular basis, receives for temporary custody and care... children under seven years of age or

A family day care home is protected as a permitted use, unless prohibited or otherwise regulated (e.g. by special permit).[44]

The protections afforded childcare facilities by Section 3 are broader. The statute states that no special permits may be required and no prohibitions may be enforced regarding the use of land or structures for the primary, accessory or incidental purposes of operating a child care facility.[45] While cities and towns are allowed to establish dimensional standards, such as bulk, lot coverage, parking requirements, height and setbacks, these standards must be "reasonable." The "reasonable" test, as established by *Tufts* (discussed in Section 6.01), requires a careful balancing of the municipality's goals with the protections afforded by Section 3.

However, as noted below, the Courts will be suspicious of regulations that impede childcare facilities.

In applying the principles from *Tufts*, the Appeals Court determined, for example, that local zoning requirements that would have forced the relocation of an historic barn, that was to be used as a child care facility, violated the intent of Section 3.

"All of that compliance work not only would destroy the barn's unique Italianate cupola and Palladian window, but also would adversely change the massing of the structure, disturb the sense of the building's continuity, and ruin both its historical character and architectural integrity... . In light of this evidence, the judge determined that imposition of the town's dimensional requirements on the project would

---

children under sixteen years of age...provided, however, in either case, that the total number of children under sixteen ...shall not exceed six." A "child care facility" includes a "day care center" or a "school age child care program." There are no enrollment limitations set by statute for these uses for the purposes of Section 3.

[44] "Family day care home, as defined in section nine of chapter twenty eight A, shall be an allowable use unless a city or town prohibits or specifically regulates such use in its zoning ordinance or bylaw." G.L. c. 40A, § 3.

[45] In an interesting 1998 decision, the Land Court analogized the Appeals Court's holding in Prime v. Zoning Board of Appeals of Norwell, 42 Mass. App. Ct. 796 (1997) to childcare facilities. The Court stated that the requirement of a special permit for a child care facility could be within the municipality's power, provided that the special permit requirement and attached conditions did not result in a preclusion of the protected use. "...I conclude that a zoning bylaw may require a special permit for the construction of a new structure to be used as a child care facility just as, under *Prime*, it may require a special permit for the construction of a new structure to be used for agricultural purposes. However, as in *Prime*, "the special permit may not be imposed unreasonably and in a manner designed to prohibit the operation of the farm stand, nor may the permit be denied merely because the Board would prefer a different use of the locus, or no use." Campbell v. Town of Weymouth, Misc. Case No. 237269 (September 23, 1998), *quoting* Prime, 42 Mass. App. Ct. 796, at 802–803.

levy excessive costs of compliance…and effectively deny the use of the premises for a childcare facility… ."[46]

Section 9C of the Zoning Act provides interesting language pertaining to child-care facilities and imposes limits on the extent that a zoning ordinance or bylaw can regulate these facilities as an accessory use.[47] General Laws, Chapter 40A, Section 9 should be read in conjunction with Section 3.

§ 6.03[6]   Exemptions for Hazardous Waste, Refuse Treatment and Disposal Facilities

The preemption for hazardous waste, refuse treatment and disposal facilities is not contained with Section 3, but rather within Section 9 of the Zoning Act.[48] While Section 9 identifies pre-emptions for "hazardous waste facility" independently from "a facility" (read: solid waste facility), the pre-emptions are similar and limited case law regarding either "facility" exists.

These pre-emptions are extremely broad in their application, but are clearly limited to lands zoned for industrial use.[49]

---

[46] Petrucci v. Board of Appeals of Westwood, 45 Mass. App. Ct. 818, 827 (1998), *cert. denied*, 707 N.E.2d 1079 (1999). *See also* Rogers v. Town of Norfolk, 432 Mass. 374, 386 (2000). In keeping with the purpose of the statute, a municipality should not be able to discriminate against child care uses of property unless there is a reasonable basis for the discriminatory treatment. Thus, a bylaw that is specific to child care uses and subjects the use to more restrictive regulation than other uses permitted in the zone, without a reasonable justification for that discriminatory treatment, should be invalidated."

[47] "When any zoning ordinance or bylaw in any city or town limits the floor of any structure, such floor area shall be measured exclusive of any portion of such structure in which a child care facility is to be operated as an accessory or incidental use, and the otherwise allowable floor area of such structure shall be increased by an amount equal to the floor area of such child care facility up to a maximum increase of ten percent." No case law exists interpreting this clause. It appears to allow, for accessory day care uses only, an exclusion of up to 10 percent above the maximum floor area established by local zoning.

[48] The preemption for hazardous waste facilities reads in part: "A hazardous waste facility as defined in section two of chapter twenty-one D shall be permitted to be constructed as of right on any locus presently zoned for industrial use pursuant to the ordinances and bylaws of any city or town provided that all permits and licenses required by law have been issued to the developer and a siting agreement has been established…following the submission of a notice of intent…a city or town may not adopt any zoning change which would exclude the facility from the locus specified in the notice of intent." The pre-emption for solid waste facilities reads, in part, "A facility, as defined in section one hundred and fifty A of chapter one hundred and eleven, which has received a site assignment…shall be permitted to be constructed or expanded on any locus zoned for industrial use unless specifically prohibited by the ordinances or bylaws of the city or town…" G.L. c. 40A, § 9.

[49] In the most comprehensive case on this issue to date, the Supreme Judicial Court held that "zoned for industrial use" is to be liberally interpreted. Thus, a municipality that seeks to avoid the preemption of Section 9 could not do so, for example, by labeling what would otherwise be

Hazardous waste facilities can take advantage of the preemption only insofar as the land is zoned industrial or used in a manner that could otherwise be categorized as industrially used. Further, the preemption only applies where the applicant files a "notice of intent" and all other statutory requirements have been met.[50]

For solid waste (refuse) facilities, the preemption applies *only* to those facilities that require a site assignment from the local Board of Health.[51]

Put a different way, a facility that does not require site assignment is ineligible for the protections afforded by Section 9 and local zoning regulations, including use prohibitions, will control. The types of facilities that require a site assignment are somewhat counterintuitive. For example, a hazardous waste facility, as discussed above, does not require a site assignment. Nor do most industrial or manufacturing operations.[52] To repeat, if a site assignment is not required, the pre-emption of Section 9 does not apply.

For facilities that require a site assignment, Section 9 precludes the adoption of an ordinance or bylaw that prohibits such facility, or the expansion of an existing facility, unless the prohibition or other restriction was in effect as of July 1, 1987.

Note, however, that Section 9 allows the imposition of special permit controls on a facility requiring a site assignment. Consistent with previous discussions regarding "reasonable regulations", these controls can be used to mitigate potential impacts, but they cannot be tantamount to prohibiting the use allowed under an approved site assignment.

---

classified as "industrial use" as "heavy commercial." At issue of course is the distinction between "industrial" and "commercial" as it relates to this preemption. "We construe the words 'zoned for industrial use' as referring to land on which industrial uses are permitted, because they are not prohibited, by the town's bylaws. We hold, therefore, that the town's bylaw...which would exclude from the town any hazardous waste facility that would store, treat or dispose of wastes generated outside the town is inconsistent with G.L. c. 40A, § 9 and is, therefore, unenforceable." Warren v. The Hazardous Waste Facility Site Safety Council, 392 Mass. 107, 122 (1984).

[50] These include compliance with G.L. c. 21 D, 990 CMR § 1.00–16.00 and G.L. c. 111, § 150B. "The filing of the notice of intent and the site specification had the effect of establishing the right of IT Corporation to build and operate the proposed facility if the other statutory requirements are met...To the extent that the town's powers have been affected by reasons of the action of IT Corporation, that is the result of a determination by the Legislature that the siting procedure be initiated by the developer's act." Warren v. The Hazardous Waste Facility Site Safety Council, 392 Mass. 107, 123 (1984).

[51] G.L. c. 111, § 150A and 310 CMR § 16.20 (12) establish the standards for site assignment approval.

[52] For a complete list of those facilities and uses that require a site assignment, *see* 310 CMR 16.05. "310 CMR 16.00 shall govern the process of application, review, public hearing and decision for a site assignment to expand a solid waste management facility or establish a new solid waste management facility at an unassigned site." 310 CMR 16.05 (1).

Finally, the Section 9 preemption does not apply to lands identified as "zones of contribution of existing or potential public supply wells" or "recharge areas of surface drinking water supplies."[53] This fact provides a strong inducement for cities and towns to ensure that these resource areas, whether in current use or for future use, are delineated in compliance with procedures established by the Department of Environmental Protection.

§ 6.03[7]   Exemptions for Scientific Research Facilities

There is no case law clarifying the purpose or intent of this portion of Section 9.[54] The point of this clause is to ensure that cities and towns allow, either by right or by special permit, uses that are accessory to scientific research or scientific development, whether or not the principle use is on the same parcel. The statute clearly provides local governments with options.

First, zoning could allow by right, accessory uses for scientific development or research provided the accessory use is on the same parcel as the principle use or activity.[55]

In the alternative, and following the provisions of this portion of Section 9, zoning must allow by special permit an accessory use for scientific development or research on a *different* parcel than the principle use, provided that the "activities are necessary in connection with scientific research or scientific development" *if* the principle use is "permitted as a matter of right."

It is important to consider what scientific research or scientific development uses are generally permitted as of right. Clearly, as discussed in Section 6.03[2] of this Chapter, Section 3 precludes the imposition of special permit requirements on educational and religious institutions.[56] Thus for example, the Marine Biological Laboratory in Woods Hole, or the University of Massachusetts in Amherst or Tufts

---

[53] G.L. c. 40A, § 9. The reference to "recharge areas of surface drinking water supplies" likely refers to the watershed of the surface water body.

[54] "Zoning ordinances or bylaws shall also provide that uses, whether or not on the same parcel as activities permitted as a matter of right, accessory to activities permitted as a matter of right[, which activities are necessary in connection with scientific research or scientific development or related production, may be permitted upon the issuance of a special permit provided the granting authority finds that the proposed accessory use does not substantially derogate from the public good." G.L. c. 40A, § 9.

[55] In most instances where uses are allowed only by special permit, it is the principle use so constrained. Accessory uses are typically allowed by right.

[56] As noted previously, special permits are not permissibly imposed upon religious or educational uses, "The Legislature did not intend to impose special permit requirements, designed under c. 40A, § 9 to accommodate uses not permitted as of right in a particular zoning district, on legitimate educational uses which have been expressly authorized to exist as of right in any zone." The Bible Speaks v. Board of Appeals of Lenox, 8 Mass. App. Ct. 19, 33 (1979).

University in Medford could qualify for the scientific research protections afforded by Section 9. Similarly, hospitals, veterinary clinics and other institutions classified as educational or religious conducting scientific research qualify for this narrow exemption.

Note also that the special permit granting authority must find that the accessory use "does not substantially derogate from the public good." This language is in addition to Section 9's more comprehensive requirement that "special permits may be issued only for uses which are in harmony with the general purpose and intent of the ordinance or bylaw."

At issue is whether the special permit must meet the lesser "does not substantially derogate" test, or the greater "in harmony" test. Conservative advice is to follow the lesser standards set by the language "does not substantially derogate from the public good," although as noted, no case law exists helping clarify this issue.

§ 6.03[8]   Exemptions for Amateur Radio Operators

While the 1996 Telecommunications Act has caused a significant stir among local governments throughout the state (and nation), the pre-emption clause included within Section 3 is targeted solely at "federally licensed amateur radio operators." While there are few cases on point regarding amateur radio operators, there is likely to be many in the next several years regarding the Telecommunications Act. A discussion of both follows.

The Section 3 exemption regarding amateur radio operators is confusing. Although, there are no reported decisions since this exemption was codified by the Legislature in 1995, in 2003, the United States District Court remanded a matter to state court for clarification as to the breadth of exemptions provided for amateur radio operators pursuant to G.L. c. 40A, § 3.[57]

On one hand, and consistent with language governing other topics in this Chapter where case law does exist, the statute allows limited local regulation of radio towers used for amateur radio operations. For example, while a zoning ordinance cannot prohibit the construction or use of an antenna structure for an amateur radio operator, the ordinance may regulate the antenna's height and/or location. (As discussed below, this is consistent with interpretations of the Telecommunications Act.)

On the other hand, however, is the statute's concluding phrase that the regulation

---

[57] Chedester v. Town of Whately, 279 F. Supp. 2d 53, 57 (D. Mass. 2003). In short, given that the FCC has left the regulation of amateur radio antenna structures, in the first instance, to state and local authorities, albeit within certain general limits, this court believes it best to have the state court, in the first instance, determine whether the Town's bylaw comports with the state statute." 279 F. Supp. 2d 53, at 58.

be the "minimum practicable regulation necessary to accomplish the legitimate purposes of the city or town enacting such ordinance or bylaw." The problem, of course, is whether limiting radio towers to specified districts and within those districts, limiting towers to specified heights, complies with the spirit and intent of the statute. A quick answer is "yes", but it is accompanied by the same warnings that have been discussed previously.

A reviewing court is likely to rule invalid any regulation that purports to allow a use but in practice, amounts to a de facto prohibition. For example, an ordinance that allows radio towers in specified districts, but limits those towers to 25 feet, will likely be ruled in conflict with the Section 3 pre-emption. At best, the reviewing court would require the municipality to demonstrate how such a height limitation was the minimum practicable regulation necessary to accomplish local planning goals. At worst, the reviewing court would see the height limitation as a crude way of avoiding the protection afforded by Section 3 and strike down the ordinance and its application.

In a case that preceded the pre-emption language within Section 3, the Appeals Court ruled that Federal law did not preempt local regulation of radio towers.[58] Interestingly, such regulation is similarly not pre-empted under the new Telecommunications Act.

§ 6.03[9]   Telecommunications Act

The explosion in the use of mobile telephones has generated a growing need to site the structures that hold the equipment that supports those devices. Most controversial have been telecommunications towers. These structures often reach as much as one hundred feet in height and, even allowing for differences in esthetic tastes, are quite unattractive. Frequently the locations for these towers that are dictated by the technology run afoul of local zoning requirements, or simply local preferences. Many municipalities are only a little more receptive to communications towers than they are to adult entertainment businesses. The zoning issues presented by the siting of these structures are made unique by Federal statutory intervention into the process by means of the Telecommunications Act of 1996 (TCA).

---

[58] In Sleeper v. Old King's Highway Regional Historic District Commission, 11 Mass. App. Ct. 571 (1981), the Appeals Court held that the Regional Historic District Commission's (Cape Cod) denial of a 68–foot amateur radio tower based on aesthetic concerns was a legitimate action, and that the tower was not protected by federal or state law. "Although the Federal Communications Act of 1934…preempts "local regulation of radio transmission…it does not purport to regulate the manner in which physical structures involved in radio transmission have an impact upon local land use considerations. The regulation, for example, of antenna height is a matter of local concern, not national interest." 11 Mass. App. Ct. 571, at 575.

The Telecommunications Act was designed to "accelerate private sector deployment of new telecommunications technologies."[59] In less formal language, the Act was intended to allow for unimpeded mobile telecommunications (e.g. mobile telephones) on a national level. Despite local concerns to the contrary, the Act does not prohibit local regulation of telecommunication towers. While local governments may not prohibit, either directly or indirectly telecommunication towers, the Act allows significant latitude in local government planning and regulation of telecommunication towers and related devices.[60]

This fact, read in conjunction with the previous discussion regarding G.L. c. 40A, § 3, in general, provides broad opportunities to local governments to develop a plan for the most appropriate locations for telecommunications towers and their accessories.[61] Neither G.L. c. 40A, § 3 nor the Telecommunications Act preclude local regulations governing where these towers are located, at what height they can be built, what they must look like, or whether they must be "co-located" such that one tower accommodates several carriers.[62]

---

[59] Roberts v. Southwestern Bell Mobile Systems, Inc., 429 Mass. 478, 487 (1999); Building Commissioner of Franklin v. Dispatch Communications of New England, Inc., 48 Mass. App. Ct. 709, 711 (2000). *See also* Brehmer v. Planning Board of Wellfleet, 238 F.3d 117, 122 (1st Cir. Mass. 2001). *Brehmer* is an important case for counsel representing abutters to proposed telecommunication facilities and a good reminder as to the importance of abutter counsel intervening in litigation between permit applicants and cities and towns. "Appellants make a final equitable argument that this method of awarding special permits, which they describe as being 'worked out by the adepts in secret away from the gaze of the citizens of Wellfleet to protect the mystery,' is fundamentally unfair in that it effectively shuts them out of the permitting process. We cannot agree with this characterization of the process followed, as appellants had the opportunity to intervene, and fully assert their rights, in the suit brought by Omnipoint against the Planning Board that ultimately led to the settlement agreement. Appellants failed, however, to avail themselves of that opportunity." 238 F.3d 117, at 122.

[60] While much litigation has focused on local moratoria on new towers, the Act nevertheless does not preclude short-term, temporary moratoria on new towers while the municipality develops a plan to accommodate towers in the future. For an interesting discussion from the carrier's perspective, *see* David Hughes, "*When NIMBYS Attack: The Heights to Which Communities Will Climb To*," 23 J. Corp. L. 469 (1998).

[61] *See*, for example, a report prepared by the Cape Cod Commission entitled "Siting Criteria for Personal Wireless Service Facilities, 1997," as well as a model regulation also prepared by the Commission, for the siting of telecommunication towers.

[62] "…except as provided in this paragraph, nothing in this chapter shall limit or affect the authority of a State or local government over siting decisions of PWS facilities…The legislative history is equally clear: 'The conference agreement creates a new section 704 which prevents [FCC] preemption of local and State land use decisions and preserves the authority of State and local governments over zoning and land use matters except in limited circumstances set forth in the conference agreement…Particularly where the subject of the Federal provisions at issue, here zoning and local land use regulation, is one traditionally within the purview of State and local government. Federal law will not preempt unless that is the clear and manifest intent of Congress.' " Roberts v. Southwestern Bell Mobile Systems, Inc., 429 Mass. 478, at 487.

Substantively, local regulation may not unreasonably discriminate among mobile telephone service providers, nor may it prohibit or have the effect of prohibiting the provision of such service. There may be no regulation on the basis of the environmental effects of radio frequency emissions other than as required by the Federal Communications Commission.

Procedurally, a local zoning authority must act within a reasonable period of time on any request regarding a telecommunication tower (or other telecommunications facility), taking into account the nature and scope of the application. Any decision to deny a request to site a tower must be in writing and supported by substantial evidence contained in a written record. The TCA further provides for expedited review, in either Federal or State court, to any person adversely affected by the act of a local zoning authority that is inconsistent with the limitations imposed by the TCA. To the extent consistent with these standards, local zoning control over telecommunications facility siting is preserved by the TCA.

From the practice standpoint one may expect the Federal courts to be more hospitable to mobile telephone service providers who have been denied permits by local zoning authorities, since they are liable to weigh the Federal policy to encourage a vital and deregulated communications industry more heavily than traditional local zoning objectives. Review in the Federal courts will be on the administrative record, which in the case of the volunteer local boards characteristic of Massachusetts will often be inadequate to sustain the decision. The State courts, which have concurrent jurisdiction, may be expected to be more sympathetic to state and local concerns. In addition, the trial court finds the facts de novo, so the board has a new opportunity to create an adequate record in support of its decision. It would seem that where an applicant faces opposition that could result in litigation it is better to have its application denied and to appeal the denial in the Federal courts. If the application is granted it will almost certainly be appealed by any aggrieved party to the State courts. The wrongful denial of a permit for a tele-communications tower has been held to be a basis for a suit for damages and attorneys' fees under 42 U.S.C. § 1983. Such a suit can of course be brought in either Federal of State court, but once again the Federal forum would seem to be preferential for the applicant.

There has been a good deal of divergence among the various Federal district courts and courts of appeal in interpreting the Telecommunications Act (TCA). However some general principles may be safely stated. The act contains grants of both procedural and substantive protections to personal wireless service providers. The two main procedural safeguards are (1) the requirement that the local board's decision be in writing, and (2) the requirement that the decision be based on substantial evidence. The two main substantive protections are that the local regulation, or decision thereunder, must not (1) prohibit or have the effect of prohibiting personal wireless services, or (2) unreasonably discriminate among providers of functionally equivalent services.

The substantial evidence standard is essentially the same under Massachusetts and Federal law. It is a familiar standard. Substantial evidence is "such relevant evidence as a reasonable mind might accept as adequate to support a conclusion. Under this definition, a court may not displace an agency's choice between two fairly conflicting views, even though the court would justifiably have made a different choice had the matter been before it de novo." But "the reviewing court must take into account contradictory evidence in the record." Given this standard the written decision requirement probably means a reasoned decision with subsidiary findings of fact leading to factual conclusions, against which conclusions the local law is applied. The local bylaw still provides the standard against which the properly supported factual findings are to be measured. Although some reviewing courts have required a good deal less formality in the local board's decision, the Massachusetts federal district courts have been among the very strictest interpreters of the TCA. Most federal courts (and certainly those in Massachusetts), have been willing to evaluate the quality of the evidence in the record made before the local board in deciding whether the substantial evidence test has been met. A record that contains only generalized statements of opposition by neighbors or conclusory fact finding by the board, to be weighed against the scientific or engineering evidence produced by the applicant, will not be adequate to sustain a denial.

As to the substantive protections of the TCA, a municipality could prohibit or have the effect of prohibiting personal wireless service by the terms of its bylaw, either by an outright ban or by permit limitations that have the effect of a ban. Judging by the reported cases this does not seem to have been a problem. Instead, it is denials of individual applications that have been challenged as effective prohibitions on personal wireless service. Again the case law is not consistent. Some courts have held that an individual denial can never have the effect of prohibiting personal wireless service, that there must be a general ban to run afoul of the TCA. The better formulation, although it is much more difficult to apply in practice, is that of the First and Second Circuits, "Individual denial is not automatically a forbidden prohibition, but disallowing the only feasible plan... might amount to prohibiting personal wireless service." With respect the prohibition against unreasonable discrimination among providers, it seems that the operative word is "unreasonable." The act explicitly contemplates that some discrimination among providers of functionally equivalent services is allowed. Any discrimination need only be reasonable. The local permit granting authority may thus take into account differences in circumstances such as proposed sites or types of proposed structures, and other traditional zoning concerns, in denying a permit to one provider while granting a permit to another. Given a proper basis in the administrative record, the local authority's conclusions on these points would be entitled to judicial deference.

§ 6.03[10]   Exemptions for Solar Energy Systems

No case law exists on this pre-emption, although the preemptive language is consistent with that used throughout the statute. "No zoning ordinance or bylaw shall prohibit or unreasonably regulate the installation of solar energy systems or the building or structures that facilitate the collection of solar energy, except where necessary to protect the public health, safety or welfare."

This preemption allows local governments to regulate solar energy systems and their appurtenances[63] provided the regulation is not tantamount to a prohibition of the system. As noted previously, the phrase "unreasonably regulate" should be construed as liberal language allowing local government control over aspects of height, bulk, setback and visual quality, provided that the control does not lead to a de facto prohibition. Note also that the operative language does not preclude requiring a special permit for solar energy systems.

Note that the Zoning Act contains several mechanisms for local governments to encourage and to some extent, guarantee solar access, including establishing a special permitting process to ensure that solar access is protected.[64]

§ 6.03[11]   Exemptions for Handicapped Access Ramps

Section 3 provides broad preemption against local zoning regulation of handicapped access ramps "used solely for the purpose of facilitating ingress or egress of a physically handicapped person... ."[65] The preemption prohibits zoning regulations that would preclude or influence the placement of access ramps including, but not limited to front, rear or side yard setbacks or open space requirements often contained in local zoning. By implication, this likely includes restrictions on lot coverage as well. No case law exists interpreting this preemption.

§ 6.03[12]   Exemptions for Temporary Mobile Homes

The exemption language for temporary mobile homes is clear and no case law exists in Massachusetts on this provision.[66] Zoning may not prohibit the placement

---

[63] G.L. c. 40A, § 1A defines "solar access" as "the access of a solar energy system to direct sunlight." "Solar energy system" is defined as "a device or structural design feature, a substantial purpose of which is to provide daylight for interior lighting or provide for the collection, storage and distribution of solar energy for space heating or cooling, electricity generating or water heating."

[64] *See* G.L. c. 40A, § 9B.

[65] "Physically handicapped person" is defined by G.L. c. 22, § 13A, in part, as "any person who has a disability that substantially limits one or more major life activities, including but not limited to, such functions as performing manual tasks, walking, seeing, hearing, speaking, breathing, learning and working."

[66] "No zoning ordinance or bylaw shall prohibit the owner and occupier of a residence which has been destroyed by fire or other natural holocaust from placing a manufactured home on the site

of a mobile home for a period of up to twelve months, where fire or other disaster destroyed the owner's original dwelling. Note that the statute requires that there existed a dwelling that was destroyed, prior to the allowance that a mobile home be placed on the lot. Note also that the mobile home must be on the same lot as the dwelling that was destroyed, and is now in the process of being rebuilt.

§ 6.03[13]   Conclusion

The Commonwealth and its instrumentalities, by statute and case law, are as a general proposition immune from municipal zoning regulation unless a statute expressly provides to the contrary. The scope of immunity is broad and applies not only to property and facilities owned by the entity or agency, but also to leased property and facilities. The immunity extends to all activities reasonably related to the essential governmental function of the agency. Such instrumentalities include regional solid waste disposal districts and transportation authorities.

As discussed above and with the above noted limitations in mind, attempts by municipalities to apply zoning regulations to otherwise exempt religious, educational or child care uses under the authority granted by the provisos contained in the second paragraph of G.L. c. 40A, § 3 are subject to attack as either facially invalid or invalid as applied. In either kind of attack, the property owner bears the burden of overcoming the presumptive validity of the zoning bylaw. Although, the case law seems to pay lip service to this principle while in effect imposing the burden of proof on the municipality.

A bylaw is facially valid if can be shown to be, as a general proposition, rationally related to the furtherance of a legitimate municipal zoning interest. But a bylaw valid on its face may still be struck down if it is found to be unreasonably restrictive as applied to a particular property. The question of reasonableness will depend on the facts of each case. The factual analysis involves the court balancing the degree of detriment to the applicant's property caused by the enforcement of the bylaw against the degree of advancement of the municipal zoning objectives.

---

of such residence and residing in such home for a period not to exceed twelve months while the residence is being rebuilt. Any such manufactured home shall be subject to the provisions of the state sanitary code." G.L. c. 40A, § 3.

CHAPTER 7

ZONING—THE PRACTICE

Synopsis

§ 7.01   Obtaining Building and Use Permits, Comprehensive
          Permits, Zoning Variances and Zoning Changes
          § 7.01[1]   Preliminary Information Gathering
          § 7.01[2]   Determine Applicable Zoning
          § 7.01[3]   Decide Whether a Variance, Special Per-
                         mit or Zoning Change is Necessary
                § 7.01[3][a]   To Obtain a Variance
                § 7.01[3][b]   To Obtain Special Permit
                § 7.01[3][c]   To Obtain a Zoning Change in a
                                Town
                § 7.01[3][d]   To Obtain a Zoning Change in a
                                City
                § 7.01[3][e]   Obtain Board of Health Ap-
                                proval Where Necessary
                § 7.01[3][f]   Obtain Additional Planning
                                Board or Appeals Board Ap-
                                proval Where Necessary
                § 7.01[3][g]   Obtain Conservation Commis-
                                sion Approval Where Necessary
                § 7.01[3][h]   Obtain A Comprehensive Permit
                § 7.01[3][i]   Obtain Building Permit
                § 7.01[3][j]   Advise Client of Period of Valid-
                                ity of Permit
                § 7.01[3][k]   Flow Charts

§ 7.01   Obtaining Building and Use Permits, Comprehensive Permits, Zoning Variances and Zoning Changes

§ 7.01[1]   Preliminary Information Gathering

Step 1. Obtain the basic initial information from the client which is necessary to complete the Information Lists—Obtaining Building and Use Permits Zoning Variances and Special Permits, Volume 6, Chapter 7.

Step 2. Discuss in general terms with the client the circumstances surrounding his or her proposal: what exists on the site, what is adjacent to it, what the client plans to do and when, how the client's proposal relates to the present use of surrounding property, the client's past relations with abutters, the client's estimate of the nature, and the intensity of opposition to the client's plans. Consult the flow charts contained within this chapter, to familiarize yourself with the municipal land use regulation scheme.

Step 3. Obtain a compilation of the municipal plan, if there is one, and the zoning bylaws or ordinances from the town clerk. Try to obtain all amendments to the regulations adopted since publication of the booklet.

To be certain you have picked up all amendments, talk to the building inspector or zoning officer. These officials sometimes put out bad information so the only way to be completely certain is to review all town meeting warrants or city council minutes back to the date of publication of the compilation. The Municipal Bureau of the Attorney General's office may also be helpful with this.

§ 7.01[2]   Determine Applicable Zoning

Step 4. Locate your client's property by zone location on the map and read the bylaw to determine use, dimension, and density requirements for the zone.

Step 5. Where circumstances make it desirable and feasible have a surveyor make a plot plan. An instrument survey is best if the expense can be justified. Whenever possible, take a view of the property.

§ 7.01[3]   Decide Whether a Variance, Special Permit or Zoning Change is Necessary

Step 6. Be sure you understand thoroughly all proposed present and future uses your client intends to make of the land and structures involved. If necessary talk to him again on this point.

Step 7. Decide whether your client has a right to make the proposed use or whether he will need a variance, special permit or zoning change.

Step 8. If your client's proposal is not permitted as of right, decide whether a special permit, variance, or zoning change is appropriate in the circumstances.

Discuss the "level of difficulty" if a special permit is needed and the presumption that a variance is practically unobtainable.

§ 7.01[3][a]   To Obtain a Variance

(a) Be sure your client has standing to apply, and check if there has been an application within the past two years for the same variance. If the same variance has been turned down in the past two years you must get the consent of all but one member of the planning board before the appeals board can rule favorably on your petition.

(b) Read the rules promulgated by the board of appeals.

(c) Understand thoroughly and in detail the circumstances surrounding your client's land and any structures as they presently exist, and the nature and effect of your client's proposed changes.

(d) Know the history of the property where at all relevant.

(e) If opposition is anticipated know as much as you can about the opponents and their position.

(f) If your client can afford it, have an artist's or architect's drawing of any proposed structure or improvement prepared, not overly fancy, but nicely done.

(g) Include a succinct well-organized factual statement favorable to your position as part of your application. Be specific as to what you want. Be sure the notice published in the paper, posted, and mailed, satisfies all statutory requirements and accurately states the relief you are requesting.

Contact the abutters and neighbors well in advance of the hearing and do what you can to smooth out any objections; exercise diplomacy, and avoid confrontation. A hearing must be held by the board within 65 days from the filing of the petition.

(h) If difficult questions of law are involved, prepare a concise memo of law and submit it at the hearing.

(i) You must deal with the issues of soil conditions, topography, or shape of land or structures and hardship relating thereto. Since the requisite conditions as a matter of law only rarely exist, you just have to pay lip service to these points and get by them as quickly as you can.

(j) Touch on the main points you must prove under the statute and local bylaw to be entitled to a variance, but emphasize the lack of detriment to the neighborhood and the overall positive effect that your proposal will have. Concentrate on your strongest points.

(k) If the board indicates it is favorably disposed to your position offer to write a draft opinion for its consideration. The board must decide within 100 days of the filing of the petition or any extension agreed upon by the petitioner and the board in writing, or the variance is deemed allowed. Diary this date. Note also that the decision of the board must be filed with the town clerk within 114 days of the date of filing of the petition or it is deemed allowed. Check to see if this has been done.

(l) If the variance is granted, wait until the 20 day appeal period runs, obtain a certificate from the town clerk that no appeal has been taken, and record the variance with the certificate in the registry of deeds. Note that proceedings to question the validity of board action based on alleged defects in publication, mailing, or posting can be brought within 90 days of the filing of the decision.

If an appeal is taken and later denied or dismissed, get a certificate of the clerk to this effect and record it with the variance.

(m) If the variance is denied, you have 20 days from the date the decision is filed with town clerk to file in the office of the town clerk a notice of appeal along with a copy of the complaint. (Volume 6, Chapter 7, Forms 35, 37.1). Be sure to attach to the complaint a certified copy of the decision appealed from, showing the date such decision was filed with the town clerk. Be sure you can prove timely filing with the clerk.

(n) Diary all filing deadlines, some of them are jurisdictional in nature.

(o) You have 14 days from the date the complaint is filed in court to serve it on all defendants by certified mail, return receipt requested. Diary this date.

(p) You have 21 days after filing the complaint to file in court an affidavit certifying that proper notice has been given. (Volume 6, Chapter 7, Form 36). Diary this date.

(q) If the board fails to decide, or to file its decision within the statutory periods, you have 14 days from the expiration of such period to file with the city or town clerk a notice of approval by inaction and a statement that such notice has been sent by mail to all parties in interest. (Volume 6, Chapter 7, Form 37.2). In addition to informing them of the constructive grant, the notice to parties in interest should inform them that appeals, if any, must be filed within 20 days after the date the city or town clerk received notice from the applicant of the approval by inaction. (Volume 6, Chapter 7, Form 37.3).

§ 7.01[3][b]   To Obtain Special Permit

(a) Be sure your client has standing to apply, best to be the owner of affected property. Check if there has been an application in the past two years for the same permit. If same special permit was turned down in the past two years you must get the consent of all but one member of the planning board before favorable action can be taken by the permit granting authority. Misguided local practice may require that you apply for a building or use permit and be denied prior to applying to the board of appeals, since this procedure was required by prior law in the case of variances and local officials are often confused on these points.

(b) Obtain and read the rules of the permit granting authority to which you must apply.

(c) Examine carefully the provisions of the local ordinance or bylaw to see what you must show to be entitled to a permit.

(d) Understand thoroughly and in detail the circumstances surrounding your client's land and any structures thereon as they presently exist, and the nature and effect of the proposed changes.

(e) Know the history of the property where at all relevant.

(f) If opposition is anticipated know as much as you can about the opponents and their position.

(g) If your client can afford it have an artist's or architect's drawing of any proposed structure or improvement prepared, not an overly elaborate one.

(h) Include a succinct, well-organized factual statement with your application. Be specific as to what exactly you want the board to do.

Be sure the notice published in the paper, posted, and mailed, satisfies all statutory requirements and accurately states the relief you are requesting.

Contact the abutters and neighbors well in advance of the hearing and do what you can to smooth out any objections where possible; exercise diplomacy and avoid confrontation. Hearing must be held within 65 days of filing of the application. Diary this date.

(i) If difficult questions of law are involved prepare a concise memo of law and submit it at the hearing.

(j) The local ordinance or bylaw must set out standards for the granting of special permits, which are specific and definite enough to guide applicants, and the permit granting authority in deciding when a permit should be issued.

You will want to deal with each of these requirements at the hearing, concentrating on your strong points. All the while emphasize the great improvement that will be wrought in the neighborhood in either beauty, tax revenue, or economic well-being, and how the changes will harmonize with the general purpose of the bylaw.

(k) If the board indicates it is favorably disposed to your position offer to write a draft opinion for its consideration. The board must decide the case within 90 days after the close of the hearing or the permit is deemed to be granted. Diary this date. Note that the board must both decide the case and file its decision with the town clerk within 90 days after the hearing date or the permit is deemed granted. Check to see if this has been done.

(l) If the special permit is granted, wait until the 20–day appeal period has expired, having previously diaried this date. Then obtain a certificate from the clerk that no appeal has been taken and record the permit with certificate in the registry of deeds. Note that proceedings to question the validity of board action based on alleged defects in publication, mailing, or posting can be brought within 90 days of filing of the decision.

If an appeal is taken and is later denied or dismissed get a certificate of the clerk to this effect and record with the permit.

(m) If special permit is denied, you have 20 days from the date the decision is filed with the town clerk to file in the office of the town clerk a notice of appeal along with a copy of the complaint. (Volume 6, Chapter 7, Forms 37, 37.1). Be sure to attach to the complaint a certified copy of the decision appealed from, showing the date the decision was filed with the town clerk. Be sure you can prove timely filing with the clerk.

(n) Be sure to diary all filing deadlines, some of them are jurisdictional in nature.

(o) You have 14 days from the date the complaint is filed in court to serve a copy of it on all defendants by certified mail, return receipt requested. Diary this date.

(p) You have 21 days after filing the complaint to file in court an affidavit certifying that proper notice has been given. (Volume 6, Chapter 7, Form 36). Diary this date.

(q) If the board fails to decide, or to file its decision within the statutory periods, you have 14 days from the expiration of such period to file with the city or town clerk a notice of approval by inaction and a statement that such notice has been sent by mail to all parties in interest. (Volume 6, Chapter 7, Form 37.2). In addition to informing them of the constructive grant, the notice to parties in interest should inform them that appeals, if any, must be filed within 20 days after the date the city or town clerk received notice from the applicant of the approval by inaction. (Volume 6, Chapter 7, Form 37.3).

§ 7.01[3][c] To Obtain a Zoning Change in a Town

(a) Begin preparations at least 6 months before the annual town meeting. Find out the requirements and deadlines to get an article on the next town meeting warrant. Diary relevant dates. Do not underestimate how difficult this process will be.

(b) Draft the proposed new bylaw or amendment. (Volume 6, Chapter 7, Form 38).

(c) Have a professionally prepared plan created which shows in detail the area to be affected by the zoning change and the areas adjacent thereto.

(d) Ask to meet with the planning board before submitting the proposed bylaw to the selectmen. (Volume 6, Chapter 7, Form 39).

(e) Contact the municipal attorney early on; provide him or her with a copy of your proposed bylaw; deal with any technical or drafting changes required to satisfy this person whose opinion on these issues will be so influential among municipal officials.

(f) Explain the effect of the proposed bylaw thoroughly to the planning board. Explain also why your client wants this change and why it is desirable for the town.

Wherever possible, allay their fears and incorporate any suggestions for changes that they may have.

(g) Submit the proposed amendment to the selectmen or city council. (Volume 6, Chapter 7, Form 40)

(h) Begin missionary work in the community in support of the proposal. Particularly you should make contact with everyone whose property will be affected by the change and if you cannot win them to your side at least try to neutralize them. Also contact leading citizens.

If you are not well known in the community much of this lobbying will have to be done by your client or your client's friends, preferably the latter. (Volume 6, Chapter 7, Form 41).

(i) Diary the date 14 days after submission of the proposal. The selectman must have transmitted it to the planning board by this date. Call to see if this has been done.

(j) A properly noticed public hearing must be held by the planning board within

65 days of the transmittal of the proposal to them by the selectmen. Diary this date. Now diary a date three weeks prior to this date and make a note at that time to call and gently remind the planning board secretary that the meeting notice should be published as soon as possible to make the 65-day deadline.

(k) Be sure that the notice as published, posted, and mailed is timely and complies with other statutory requirements.

(l) Get people favorable to the proposal to appear at the public hearing or at least to write letters to the planning board.

(m) Diary the date 21 days after the planning board hearing. If no report has been issued by this date the proposal can be brought before town meeting for approval. If a report has been issued the proposal can be brought to town meeting at the time of such issuance. Check to be sure there are arrangements to get the article on the town meeting warrant.

(m) If necessary, diary the date 6 months from the date of the planning board hearing; if the town meeting has not acted on the proposal by this date it cannot thereafter be acted upon without a new planning board hearing.

(n) On the floor of town meeting or before the city council, try to get as many well-respected citizens to speak in favor of the proposal as you can. Unless a lawyer is well known and liked in the community it may be best to have the client present the proposal if he or she is reasonably articulate. Alternatively, the lawyer may present the proposal and have the presentation close with an appeal by the client. Liberal use should be made of attractive visual aids.

(o) If the zoning change is approved, diary the date 15 days after final adjournment of the town meeting or the city council's hearing. Check on that day to see if the town clerk has sent a copy of the bylaw with supporting documentation to the Attorney General (AG) for approval. (Note that the requirements for submission to the Attorney General pertain to towns, not cities).

(p) Next, diary the date 90 days after the date on which the bylaw was sent to the AG for approval. If the AG has taken no action by this date then the bylaw is effective, as of the date it was adopted, without approval. Usually the AG will act on the bylaw within the 90-day period.

(q) If the AG has failed to act within the 90-day period, check to see if the town clerk has entered in his records a statement that the bylaw has become effective for the reason that the AG has failed to act.

(r) Follow-up with the clerk's office to see that proper publication is made pursuant to statute.

(s) Advise client that the zoning change is not effective until these procedures are completed so he or she is not entitled to a building or use permit until then.

§ 7.01[3][d]   To Obtain a Zoning Change in a City

(a) Begin preparations at least six months before date you hope to get city council approval.

(b) Draft the proposed new ordinance or amendment. (Volume 6, Chapter 7, Form 42).

(c) Have a professionally prepared plan created which shows in detail the area to be affected by the zoning change and the area adjacent thereto.

(d) If there is a planning board in the city, ask to meet with them before submitting the proposed ordinance to the city council. (Volume 6, Chapter 7, Form 43).

(e) Explain the effect of the proposed ordinance thoroughly to the board. Explain why your client needs the change and why it is desirable for the city.

(f) Wherever possible allay their fears and incorporate any suggestions for changes that they may have.

(g) Submit the proposed amendment to the city council or committee thereof. (Volume 6, Chapter 7, Form 44).

(h) In smaller cities, begin missionary work in the community in support of the proposal. Contact should be made with each member of the city council and with the mayor's office to try to enlist support and to determine the location and extent of any opposition. Particularly you should make contact with everyone whose property will be affected by the change and if you cannot win them over to your side at least try to neutralize them. Also contact any prominent citizen whom you believe may be willing to voice support for the proposal.

If you are not well known in the city, much of this lobbying will have to be done by your client or your client's friends, preferably the latter. (Volume 6, Chapter 7, Form 41). In the larger cities, this activity is not so useful and it is best to try and impact leading politicians while defusing any opposition.

(i) Diary the date 14 days after submission of the proposal. The council must have transmitted it to the planning board, if any, by this date. Call to see if this has been done.

(j) The planning board and the city council, or designated committee thereof, each must hold a properly noticed public hearing together or separately, on the proposal within 65 days of the transmittal of the proposal by the council. If there is no planning board the hearing must be held within 65 days of filing of the proposal with the council. Diary the appropriate date.

(k) Now diary a date 3 weeks prior to this date and make a note at that time to call the planning board and city council officers to gently remind them that the meeting notice should be published as soon as possible to make the 65-day deadline.

(l) Be sure that the notice as published, posted, and mailed is timely and complies with other statutory requirements.

(m) Get well-respected local people favorable to the proposal to speak at the public hearings or to write letters to the council and board. Note that the council cannot vote to adopt the proposal at this point unless the planning board has made its report and recommendation or unless 21 days has elapsed after the planning board hearing without submission of a report. This requirement will not often have been satisfied at the time of the council hearing.

(n) Diary the date 21 days after the planning board hearing. If no report has been issued by the board by this date, the proposal can be brought up to the council for a vote. If a report is issued prior to the 21-day deadline, the proposal can be brought to vote at the time of such issuance. Make arrangements to have the matter placed on the council agenda.

(o) If necessary, diary the date 90 days from the date of the planning board hearing; if the council has not acted on the proposal by this date it cannot thereafter be acted upon without a new planning board hearing.

(p) Check prior to the final hearing to see if a written protest has been filed by the owners of at least 20% of the affected land or of adjacent land within 300 feet.

(q) If so, check the legal standing of the signers of the protest and be prepared to challenge where appropriate. Also since you will now need a 3/4 vote of the council you may wish to consider trying to postpone a vote on the proposal to give you time to negotiate with the protestors, unless you are positive that you have the votes. Remember, if the proposal is voted down it cannot be considered again for 2 years unless it is recommended for passage by the planning board.

(r) Examine the city charter. If it requires that zoning ordinances be published to be effective, you must then find out whether the council has adopted G.L. c. 40, § 32A. Now follow up to see if legally sufficient publication is made.

§ 7.01[3][e]   Obtain Board of Health Approval Where Necessary

Step 9. If the client is building in an area served by public sewer then be sure he or she will be allowed to connect before he or she begins construction.

Step 10. If new construction is involved in a non-sewered area, the client must apply for a disposal works construction permit. Local practice varies, but this should usually be done at the same time or even before an application for building permit is completed. The building permit will not issue without evidence that an approved on-site sewage system can be installed on the property. (Volume 6, Chapter 7, Forms 54.1, 54.2, 54.3.)

If an alteration or expansion of an existing structure is involved which will increase the actual or design flow of sewage to an on-site septic system it may be necessary to upgrade the system to current Title 5 standards. Some municipalities have even more stringent local upgrade requirements. Check the local practice on this.

Step 11. If health board approval is necessary, percolation and water table determination tests should be made on the site. Test data and a plan of the proposed system should be submitted to the board. Call the health board to arrange an appointment for a test or have your engineer or sanitarian do so. Most boards only allow water table testing during certain months of the year.

Step 12. Diary the date 45 days after submission of the completed application to the board. In the case of residential buildings with four or fewer units, the application must be acted upon by this date or the permit is deemed to have been granted.

§ 7.01[3][f]   Obtain Additional Planning Board or Appeals Board Approval Where Necessary

Step 13. If the local bylaw requires site plan approval, (usually required for nonresidential uses), obtain board regulations and submit the required information and plan. For many municipalities the procedure generally is that of an application for special permit. However, check the local practice.

Step 14. Many municipalities have superimposed districts that regulate or limit building otherwise permitted as of right in certain zones. An example would be the Wetland or Flood Plain zoning overlayments common in many communities. More recently, cities and towns have adopted the Department of Environmental Protection's (DEP) wellhead protection or "Zone II" delineations. These areas (including those land areas identified as "Zone I" and "Zone III") represent land areas that provide recharge to public drinking water supplies. Pursuant to the federal Safe Drinking Water Act, DEP has established regulations governing the land uses and densities allowed within the above noted zones. The regulations are found at 310

CMR 22.00 *et seq.* Moreover, correlate with the density restrictions imposed by Title 5 (310 CMR 15.00) governing on-site wastewater disposal systems.

Related to the discussion above and given the relationship between wetland resources and drinking water supplies, if your client's property is anywhere near a wetland resource area, you should check the local zoning ordinance or bylaw to see if he or she requires a special permit pursuant to what the city or town may have adopted as a local variation of DEP's wellhead protection program.

§ 7.01[3][g]   Obtain Conservation Commission Approval Where Necessary

Step 15. Determine whether your client's property is coastal or inland wetlands subject to the jurisdiction of the local Conservation Commission. (*See* Chapter 9 for applicable law, practice and forms.)

§ 7.01[3][h]   Obtain A Comprehensive Permit

Step 1. Discuss in general terms with the client the circumstances surrounding his or her plans. What exists on the site, what is adjacent to it, what the client plans to do and when, how the client's proposal relates to the present use of surrounding property, any past relations with abutters, the client's estimate of the nature and intensity of opposition, and so on. Decide what other permits, in addition to the comprehensive permit, are required.

Step 2. Meet with city or town officials, staff and relevant boards and commissions prior to filing a formal application. These very same officials, staff, boards and commissions will be asked to comment on the application later. Note that a prerequisite for MassHousing's issuance of a project eligibility letter is a meeting with the city or town's chief elected officials or the city or town manager.

Step 3. Obtain a current copy of rules and regulations of the board of appeals from the clerk of the board or the city or town clerk.

Step 4. Confirm that the rules contain (or do not contain) specific rules and requirements pertaining to comprehensive permit projects.

Step 5. Coincident with Steps 3 and 4, prepare an application to the intended subsidy agency (e.g. MassHousing, MassDevelopment or DHCD) for the specific program desired (e.g. rental or fee simple). While the subsidy agency will likely require less than is required for the filing with the board of appeals pursuant to 760 CMR 31.02(2), the applicant should file as detailed an application as possible, including more than that required by 760 CMR 31.02(2). This is especially true where the application is for land constrained by wetlands or other limitations.

Step 6. Follow the procedural rules of 760 CMR 31.01(2) regarding notification of DHCD of application to the intended subsidy agency.

Step 7. Continue dialogue with city or town officials while awaiting project eligibility approval from the subsidy agency. This is particularly important as the city or town will have an opportunity to comment on the application between the filing with the subsidy agency and its issuance of a project eligibility letter.

Step 8. Once the project eligibility letter has been received, file a complete comprehensive permit application with the board of appeals and the city or town clerk. While 760 CMR 31.02(2) establishes the minimum filing requirements, the applicant is encouraged to file as much pertinent information as practical to assist the board render the desired decision. Note that the board of appeals is required to notify relevant boards, commissions and departments with city or town government of the application. Note also the specific terms and conditions imposed by the project eligibility letter (if any) and be prepared to address each at the opening board of appeals hearing.

Step 9. Continue dialogue with abutters and concerned residents. It is possible that their concerns can be readily addressed and both the applicant and the abutters can represent an agreed upon project to the board of appeals.

Step 10. Diary the date 30 days after submission of the completed application to the board of appeals. Absent an extension from the applicant, the board must open the public hearing within this period and comply with the advertisement and notice provisions of G.L. c.40A, § 11.

Step 12. If the city or town has professional staff in the planning department, conservation commission or department of public works, for example, meet with the appropriate representatives to continue a dialogue.

Step 13. Monitor the advertisement and notification process within the 30-day period to ensure compliance with the due process requirements of G.L. c.40A, § 11.

Step 14. Prepare for the public hearing by querying staff or the chair of the board of appeals as to procedure. How much time will be allotted to this application? To what date (approximately) will the hearing be continued? Would the board prefer to discuss substantive issues together or reserve various hearing sessions for distinct issues (e.g. traffic, wastewater disposal, project economics, environmental issues and so on)?

Step 15. Prepare for the public hearing. Determine who on the applicant's team is best qualified to make the initial presentation. Depending on the results of Step 14 and if the project is complicated, all relevant consultants should be present and be prepared to address their particular area of expertise.

Step 16. Prepare for each continued hearing session by responding to the concerns raised in the prior session. Address those concerns if they can be addressed by revised plans or documents, testimony or supplemental information. Saying "no" to requests for information is unlikely to yield a desired permit from the board of appeals.

Step 17. Diary the date 40 days from the close of the public hearing. The board must render its decision within this period unless extended by the applicant. If a decision has not been rendered within this 40 day period, and if the city or town is not consistent with local needs, the applicant may take an appeal to the Housing Appeals Committee pursuant to 760 CMR 30.06(8).

Step 18. Diary the date 20 days from the date the board is required to render its decision. An appeal to the Housing Appeals Committee (if the city or town is not consistent with local needs) will need to have been filed within this period.

§ 7.01[3][i]   Obtain Building Permit

Step 19. Once all the necessary special permits, variances, site plan approvals, etc., have been obtained, take them to the building inspector to obtain the needed building, use, or occupancy permit.

§ 7.01[3][j]   Advise Client of Period of Validity of Permit

Step 20. Advise your client that most zoning ordinances and bylaws require that work under a building permit must be commenced within a certain period of time after issuance and actively prosecuted to completion within a further time, usually 1 year. The building inspector may have the power to grant extensions in certain circumstances. Check the bylaw and the State Building Code.

Special permits must be used within two years unless a shorter time is provided in the local bylaws.

Variances must be used within 1 year from granting.

Where a use or construction is commenced within 6 months after the issuance of a permit therefor the owner need not comply with subsequent amendments to the zoning bylaw, provided that, in the case of construction, it is completed continuously and expeditiously.

Your client should be aware of all of these time limits and it is recommended that your client be informed in writing. (Volume 6, Chapter 7, Form 48).

§ 7.01[3][k]   Flow Charts
a. Building Permit Process

[SEE CHART IN ORIGINAL]
b. Building Permit Process Where Construction Will Not Occur In or Near Wetlands or Where Wetlands Proceedings are Concluded

[SEE CHART IN ORIGINAL]
c. Permitted Use

[SEE CHART IN ORIGINAL]
d. Use by Special Permit

[SEE CHART IN ORIGINAL]
e. Use Prohibited

[SEE CHART IN ORIGINAL]
f. Special Procedures Required for Construction in or Near Wetlands

[SEE CHART IN ORIGINAL]
g. Process of Obtaining Approval of On-Site Septic System

[SEE CHART IN ORIGINAL]
h. Typical Path of Application for Building Permit Through Town Regulatory Process

[SEE CHART IN ORIGINAL]

CHAPTER 8

REGULATIONS PROTECTING NATURAL RESOURCES—IN GENERAL

Synopsis

§ 8.01   Introduction

§ 8.02   Regulations Protecting Natural Resources in Massachusetts

    § 8.02[1]   National Pollution Discharge Elimination System

    § 8.02[2]   Massachusetts Endangered Species Act

    § 8.02[3]   Massachusetts Environmental Policy Act

    § 8.02[4]   Historic Resources

    § 8.02[5]   State Environmental Code

§ 8.03   Wetland Resources

    § 8.03[1]   The Scientific Framework for Wetland Protection

    § 8.03[2]   Types of Wetland Protection Regulation

§ 8.04   Wetland Protection—Zoning Ordinances and Bylaws

§ 8.05   State Inland and Coastal Wetland Protection Statutes

§ 8.06   Wetland Protection—General Bylaws

§ 8.07   "Chapter 91 License Requirements"—Filled or Flowed Tidelands and the Public Trust Doctrine

§ 8.08   Federal Wetlands Regulation

§ 8.01   Introduction

Real estate law and the laws protecting real property are semantically—and legally—intertwined. Counsel with a predominately-transactional practice is concerned with laws governing the development potential of her client's real property just as counsel with a municipal practice needs to be familiar with the rules governing the recording of plans at the Registry of Deeds. Both counsel need a working familiarity with the numerous "environmental" regulations in play throughout the state.

As discussed in previous Chapters, because Massachusetts is a "non-plan" state, there is little coordination of land use activities at the state or local level. Virtually all development projects of any significant size, density or intensity require numerous permits, obtained from boards, commissions and departments that have little authority over other boards, commissions and departments. The fact that the permitting matrix in Massachusetts is complicated is not by itself a problem, as few states have adopted true "streamlined" procedures. Rather, the complication lies in the fact that the permitting of development projects—big and small—is accomplished without any guiding principles other than those adopted by cities and towns, their respective legislatures, boards, departments and commissions. Making matters worse, even where a city or town has attempted to coordinate real estate development projects according to a plan, as discussed in Chapter 4, the comprehensive permit statute overrides the plan and the regulations adopted pursuant to the plan.

While numerous state regulations addressing land and land development exist in Massachusetts, the Wetlands Protection Act (and regulations adopted pursuant to "local" wetlands ordinances and bylaws) is the regulation most likely encountered by private and public counsel. A discussion of the Act and the effect of local wetland regulations begins at Section 8.03, below.

Provided below is the statutory reference and a brief description of other, but not all, relevant natural resource regulations governing land development in the Commonwealth.

§ 8.02   Regulations Protecting Natural Resources in Massachusetts

§ 8.02[1]   National Pollution Discharge Elimination System

The NPDES program, as part of the federal Clean Water Act, is designed to regulate point source discharges of contaminants to water resources. A point source discharge is distinguished from a "non-point" source discharge. Whereas the former is likely traced to a single "point" (e.g. a pipe or other conveyance), non-point sources are diffuse (e.g. sheet flow from a roadway or parking lot). Obtaining permits under the program is complicated given that while the US

Environmental Protection Agency administers the program, DEP issues permits for point source discharges. The permits are enforceable by both EPA and DEP. To be effective, an NPDES permit also requires approval from DEP and the Massachusetts Office of Coastal Zone Management pursuant to the Water Quality Certification Program (G.L. c. 21, § 26–53, 314 CMR 4.00 and 314 CMR 9.00). This later program is linked to the NPDES program and is required where an NPDES permit is required. (Note that projects that trigger federal review due to filling in or dredging of, waters or wetlands, will also require a Water Quality Certification pursuant to the same authorities as noted above).

§ 8.02[2]   Massachusetts Endangered Species Act

The Massachusetts Endangered Species Act (MESA) is codified at G.L. c. 131A and administered by the Department of Fish and Wildlife's Natural Heritage and Endangered Species Program in 321 CMR 8.00 and 321 CMR 10.00. MESA is linked to MEPA (discussed below) and the Wetlands Protection Act (discussed in Section 8.04, *infra*). The purpose of the statute and its regulations, similar to the federal Endangered Species Act, is to protect certain identified living species from avoidable disruption to their habitat or survival. Where a project is proposed in an area that contains a species that is listed as endangered, threatened or "special concern," the regulations empower the Department to ensure that the proposed project will not result in a "take" of the species or the disruption of its habitat. Counsel for applicants proposing a development project in or near an endangered species habitat should contact Natural Heritage to confirm whether known endangered species exist at this location and the protocol for moving forward.

§ 8.02[3]   Massachusetts Environmental Policy Act

The Massachusetts Environmental Policy Act (MEPA) establishes a procedure for the review of certain projects by state agencies that "trigger" articulated thresholds. The statute is codified at G.L. c. 30, § 61-62H. The regulations governing MEPA review are 301 CMR 11.00. Projects that trigger MEPA review are those that need both state financing, state permitting or use state resources (e.g., land) and are of a certain size or impact. For example, while large shopping center may trip the threshold trigger of size (e.g. creation of greater than 10 acres of impervious surface and creation of more than 300 parking spaces), the project may not necessarily require state financing or a state permit. Thus even though the project will be large and arguably raise environmental concerns, the project is not automatically subject to MEPA review.

Projects reviewed pursuant to MEPA are reviewed either by the submission of an Environmental Notification Form (ENF) and then, if required an Environmental Impact Report (EIR). The later is far more costly and time consuming. The regulations differentiate between those projects that require an ENF filing and may require an EIR and those that categorically require an EIR. As these thresholds are identifiable, they are also avoidable and counsel should be aware of the significant distinction between being "scoped" by MEPA for an EIR (either categorically or as required by MEPA on a case by case basis) as opposed to the requirements for the preparation of an ENF.

§ 8.02[4]   Historic Resources

The Massachusetts Historic Commission (MHC), located in the Secretary of State's office is charged with the administration of the Massachusetts Historic District Act (G.L. c. 40C) and the protection of properties located on the State Register of Historic Places (950 CMR 71.00). Projects that may threaten what could be an historic resource need approval from MHC. While these projects are often reviewed by MHC during the MEPA process, many smaller projects, those that do not trigger MEPA review, are often not submitted to MHC, at the applicant's peril. As MHC does not maintain a public database for proponents to review, applicants should notify MHC of their intentions using MHC's Project Notification Form.

§ 8.02[5]   State Environmental Code

The State Environmental Code (310 CMR 15.00, often referred to as Title 5) governs all aspects of the location and construction of on-site wastewater disposal systems (septic systems). Where an on-site wastewater disposal system is proposed and the wastewater generated by the project is less than 10,000 gallons of wastewater per day, permitting is the responsibility of the municipal board of health pursuant to 310 CMR 15.00 and local board of health regulations adopted pursuant to G.L. c. 111, § 31. Where the project will generate flows of 10,000 gallons per day or greater, permitting for the project is the responsibility of DEP, pursuant to 314 CMR 5.00 and 314 CMR 6.00.

§ 8.03   Wetland Resources

§ 8.03[1]   The Scientific Framework for Wetland Protection

Unlike many aspects of land use control that often rely on opinion as support for regulations, the protection of wetland resources has a well documented scientific foundation. It is recommended that counsel involved in wetland applications before state and local agencies understand, at least in general terms, this foundation as discussed below.

A wetland is a complex ecosystem distinguished by features such as the presence of water either at the surface or within the root zone, hydric soils and vegetation adapted to or tolerant of saturated soils.

Wetlands are defined differently according to federal, state and, as discussed below, specific city or town regulation. This poses a complicated problem for counsel. Not only do you need to ensure that all levels of wetland regulations are being considered, you also need to determine the impact of each jurisdictional regulation will have on the proposed project.

The Clean Water Act defines a wetland as including those areas that are inundated or saturated by surface or groundwater a prevalence of vegetation. (33 CFR § 328.3(b) 1984). The Massachusetts Wetlands Protection Act and its implementing regulations (310 CMR 10.00, et seq.) do not provide a specific definition of a wetland. Rather, the regulations provide a definition for the resource areas protected under the act. For example, the resource area referred to as a "bordering vegetated wetland" is defined, as is the resource area identified as "land under water" and so on.

This seemingly insignificant issue of semantics poses many traps for the unwary. First, precisely because each level of government defines wetland resources very differently, a project that triggers review of a local wetland bylaw, for example, does not necessarily trigger the Massachusetts Wetlands Protection Act. Second, a project that requires review by the local municipal bylaw may similarly require review by state and federal agencies, even though the physical areas subject to review are very different. Third, application and submission procedures, adjudicative criteria and appellate procedures differ greatly among the respective levels of government review.

Contrary to popular belief, a wetland resource does not need to contain standing water to constitute a wetland. While the presence of water is critical at the wetland vegetation's root zones, the fact that the resource area is "dry" is not relevant to its classification as a wetland.

Wetlands play numerous roles in the ecological balance of watersheds. Wetlands are some of the most biologically productive ecosystems in the world. Wetland resource areas provide food, shelter and spawning/nesting sites for numerous birds, fish, mammals, amphibians and invertebrates. Wetlands provide flood control by acting like a sponge, intercepting runoff, temporarily storing floodwaters and then releasing the captured water slowly. Wetlands minimize storm damage and control erosion by forming a natural buffer against wind, rain and wave actions. Wetlands function as filters by removing contamination from waters flowing through them. Wetlands often store water and serve as a regulator of stream flows, essential in maintaining water quality and quantity flows to groundwater, rivers, lakes and streams.

Federal, state and many local wetland bylaws allow for "wetland mitigation," essentially allowing wetland areas on a portion of a parcel to be filled in exchange for a greater amount of "wetland creation" elsewhere. The concept of wetland mitigation or wetland replication has been criticized.

§ 8.03[2]   Types of Wetland Protection Regulation

Wetland protection regulations fall generally into four classes: local zoning ordinances or bylaws, local general bylaws, state inland/coastal wetland statutes and regulations, and federal statutes and regulations.

The courts usually hold that where local and state regulations affect the same wetland protection concern the stricter regulation will apply.[1]

§ 8.04 Wetland Protection—Zoning Ordinances and Bylaws

Local zoning ordinances and bylaws frequently contain wetland protection provisions which are administered and enforced pursuant to G.L. c. 40A, § 7 (by the zoning enforcement officer or building official), often with the assistance of the Conservation Commission. The most frequent approach taken is to create overlay districts (discussed in Section 5.32) that are superimposed on the underlying zoning districts (i.e., residential, commercial, industrial) and create supplemental regulation of those parts of such districts that fall within the overlay. In the present case, overlay districts are normally labeled "wetland" or "floodplain" districts. Wetlands typically identified as land areas containing water or vegetated land areas defined as wetland resources, while floodplain frequently refers to normally dry land within the water elevation map line for the 100-year storm shown on maps prepared by the Federal Environmental Management Agency (FEMA).

The zoning ordinance or bylaw with wetland or floodplain provisions will normally utilize a special permit, site plan, or design review mechanism to implement those provisions. The applicant for a development permit is usually required to submit site plans, contour maps, soil borings, and indications as to depth to ground water, and must meet certain criteria outlined in the regulation before a permit will be issued. Note that floodplain regulations have routinely been upheld by the Courts, even where the regulation deprives the landowner of significant economic value.[1]

The local ordinance or bylaw must be reviewed carefully and coordinated with requirements established by the regulations implementing the Wetlands Protection Act (310 CMR 10.00), as well as other land use controls enforced locally. In many cases, and due to the imprecision of zoning to regulate natural resources with imperfect boundaries such as wetlands, wetland resource regulations often conflict with one another. For example, it is common to find a zoning ordinance intending to regulate wetlands that includes significant non-wetland areas. While this same upland area is absolved from compliance pursuant to the Wetlands Protection Act or the local wetlands bylaw, the locus may be subject to stringent regulations pursuant to zoning.

---

[1] Golden v. Board of Selectmen, 358 Mass. 519, 265 N.E.2d 536 (1970); Lovequist v. Conservation Com. of Dennis, 379 Mass. 7, 393 N.E.2d 858 (1979).

[1] Turnpike Realty Co. v. Dedham, 362 Mass. 221 (1972), *cert. denied,* 409 U.S. 1108 (1973), *citing* Turner v. Walpole, 10 Mass. App. Ct. 515 (1980).

Municipal counsel are advised against using zoning as a means of regulating wetland resources (as opposed to regulating floodplains). First, as noted above, zoning regulations rarely comport with non-zoning regulations (a predictable result given the lack of a requirement for planning and regulatory consistency). Second, wetland resources expand and contract, a result of numerous factors including urbanization and stormwater runoff. As zoning regulations (and maps) can only be revised pursuant to the due process requirements of G.L. c. 40A, § 5, it simply is not practical to rely on zoning as a means of protecting wetland resources. Third, and consistent with the previous comment, relying on zoning to regulate wetland resources will likely result in incorrect identification of wetland areas, subjecting the regulations to facial and as applied attacks under both void for vagueness and substantive due process theories.

§ 8.05 State Inland and Coastal Wetland Protection Statutes

Although there are about a dozen state statutes which in some way deal with wetlands protection, the three most likely to affect the local landowner or real estate developer are the Coastal Wetlands Act,[1] the Inland Wetlands Act,[2] and the Act[3] regulating removal, dredging, alteration, and filling of wetlands.

Several substantive amendments were made to the regulations governing the Wetlands Protection Act in early 2005.

The foregoing statutes create schemes whereby the state Department of Environmental Protection may restrict development and other activities in certain areas it designates as Inland or Coastal Wetlands. More importantly for the person who seeks a local building or development permit, the statutes create a local wetlands protection review process administered by local conservation commissions, subject to appeal to the state Department of Environmental Protection (DEP).

The Act and the Regulations issued by the DEP identify the following interests as subject to regulatory protection in the form of pre-construction project review:

1. public or private water supply,
2. groundwater supply,
3. flood control,
4. storm damage prevention,
5. prevention of pollution,
6. protection of land containing shellfish,
7. protection of fisheries,

---

[1] G.L. c. 130, § 105.
[2] G.L. c. 131, § 40A.
[3] G.L. c. 131, § 40.

8.   protection of wildlife habitat,

9.   protection of the riverfront area, consistent with the foregoing purposes 1–8.

Wildlife habitat and riverfront area are the only two of the nine interests subject to protection under the Act that are defined in the statute itself. Wildlife habitats are "areas subject to [the Act] which due to their plant community composition and structure, hydrologic regime or other characteristics provide important food, shelter, migratory or over wintering areas, or breeding areas for wildlife." The definition of "riverfront area" is rather lengthy and complex. Nevertheless, in substance, it is that area of land situated between a river's mean annual high-water line and a parallel line located two hundred feet away, except in certain densely developed areas defined in the statute where the parallel line is twenty-five feet away. (The statute itself should of course be carefully consulted on this point).

The following natural areas are subject to protection under the Act:

a) Any bank, riverfront area, wetland, beach, dune, flat, marsh, or swamp bordering on the ocean, or on any estuary, creek, river, stream, pond or lake;

b) Land under any of the water bodies listed in subparagraph a) above;

c) Land subject to tidal action;

d) Land subject to coastal storm flowage;

e) Land subject to flooding.

There is a rebuttable presumption that each of the areas subject to protection under the Act is significant to one or more of the interests subject to protection. These presumptions are set forth in each of the so-called Preambles to the Coastal and Inland Wetlands Regulations dealing with the specific natural areas subject to protection. Each preamble is followed by a set of Performance Standards. Performance standards establish threshold criteria to adjudicate whether a specific project or projects will threaten or exceed the carrying capacity of the resource; in this case, wetland resource.

Determination of the proposed project's relationship to the established performance standards is the intended basis of the Order of Conditions issued by the Commission. The Order of Conditions is designed to protect the characteristics of the particular natural resource that are significant to the interests protected by the Act.

The statute and regulations provide specific additional protections to riverfront areas. In addition to meeting the otherwise applicable requirements of the Act, the applicant must prove to the Commission or DEP, by a preponderance of the evidence, that:

1. the proposed work, with mitigation, will have no significant adverse impact

on the riverfront area with respect to the above enumerated interests subject to protection under the Act, and

2. there is no practicable and substantially equivalent economic alternative to the proposed project with less adverse effects on such purposes.

The statute and regulations go on at some length in an attempt to guide regulators in deciding when an alternative is a "practicable and substantially economically equivalent." This attempt, after a good deal of thrashing about, reaches the predictable result.

In determining the applicability of the statute, the person proposing the project or applying for permit must decide if his activity will involve removal, filling, dredging, or alteration of protected land. Under the standards set by regulations issued by DEP and effective until April 1, 1983 almost any activity in or near wetlands would invoke the provisions of the statute. Most conservation commissioners applied the so-called 100-foot rule that held that any alteration, removal or disturbance within 100 feet of wetlands as defined by the statute would require compliance with the notice and hearing provisions. This rule, of dubious legality, caused tremendous inconsistency from municipality to municipality in the application of the regulations because of the difficulty in defining the proper zones of regulation. Many local commissions regularly exceeded their authority.

In an attempt to bring some order to the process, the DEP issued revised regulations, effective April 1, 1983. These regulations require that a Notice of Intent must be filed where the proposed work is actually in defined wetlands. A new, more precise regulatory definition of "wetlands" was promulgated, which requires, inter alia, that regulated wetlands must contain 50% or more of indigenous wetland plants. The old 100-foot rule that made all persons proposing work within 100 feet of wetlands apply for and receive an Order of Conditions has been modified. Prior to 2005, the regulations created a so-called "buffer zone" which covers all land within 100 feet of defined wetlands. Persons who propose to work in this buffer zone could first submit a Request for Determination of Applicability (RDA) to the Conservation Commission. (Volume 6, Chapter 7, Form 45). This allowed the commission to review the proposed project and to determine whether any alteration of the neighboring wetlands will occur. If the commission determines that such an alteration will occur then it will notify the applicant that a Notice of Intent must be filed and an Order of Conditions must be obtained. Otherwise the project may proceed as if no wetlands were involved. In the alternative, the applicant could simply skip the RDA process and file a Notice of Intent. This is of course the better way to go if the impact on wetlands is clear or if other factors indicate that filing a Request for Determination of Applicability would be a waste of time.

As of 2005, DEP amended the standards for work within a defined buffer zone on the asserted basis that buffer zone reviews constituted an "administrative burden." The new regulations exempt "minor activities" from regulation and provide for a "simplified review"[4] of activities outside of and more than fifty (50) feet from, a defined resource area (e.g. bank, wetland, land subject to flooding, etc.).[5] The "simplified review" is accomplished by the issuance of an Order for Resource Area Delineation and a certification from the applicant that, among other things, the development will not occur within 50 feet of the resource area.[6] Orders for Resource Area Delineation are valid for three years, although may be extended for up to an additional three years upon certification that the delineations have not changed.[7] Note that, as under the prior procedure, the applicant may still proceed directly with the filing of a Notice of Intent.

Finally, the regulations make it clear that work that is outside the wetlands and the 100-foot buffer area can proceed without pre-construction review. Jurisdiction over such work can be asserted by the commission only where it can be shown that it has actually altered a protected area (Often referred to as "unless and until," DEP effectively ended the practice of some commissions that asserted jurisdiction over projects far from wetlands were it was claimed that upgradient activities would affect downgradient wetlands. While this practice was frustrating for applicants, the logic of asserting that a development 101 feet from a wetland would not have an impact on a wetland resource while a development 99 feet from a wetland would, is questionable. While the regulations allow jurisdiction "if" the project 101 feet from the resource impacted the resource, in most cases, the impact cannot be regulated, "unless and until" the damage has been done).

After the Request for Determination, if any, has been filed, with notice to the landowner and the DEP, the Conservation Commission has 21 days to hold a hearing and to issue its decision. Notice of such hearing must be given, at least 5 days before the meeting, by publication in a newspaper of general circulation in the city or town in which the land is located, and by mailing notice to the applicant, the owner of the land, the board of health and the planning board. The commission's determination must be mailed to the DEP, the applicant and to the owner, and the determination is valid for 3 years.

The Notice of Intent must be filed on one of two forms, a long form (Form 3) and an abbreviated form (Form 4). See Volume 6, Chapter 9, Forms 45.2 and 45.3. The abbreviated form may only be used where the proposed work is in the buffer or flood plain zone, the work will disturb less than 1000 square feet of surface area within the buffer or flood plain zone, and the work will not require Army Corps

---

[4] *See* Commentary to 310 CMR 10.02.
[5] 310 CMR 10.02 (2)(b)(i), (ii).
[6] 310 CMR 10.02(2)(b)(ii), 310 CMR 10.05(3)(a), and 310 CMR 10.05(4)(b)(3).
[7] 310 CMR 10.06(d).

of Engineers section 10 or section 404 permits, see regulations at 40 C.F.R. § 230, or a license from the State Division of Waterways under G.L. c. 91. Along with the Notice should be filed all required plans and maps and the filing fee, two copies of all submissions should be sent, certified mail, to the DEP regional office. (Note that the statute requires that the plans submitted shall be such as are necessary to describe the activity and its effect on the environment. All plans and other submissions should be addressed to the interests that the statute is designed to protect, as outlined below. The regulations of the DEP should be consulted on this point.)

The Notice of Intent cannot be sent until the applicant has also applied for or obtained all permits, variances, and approvals required by local bylaw with respect to the proposed activity. The submittal to the Commission must also include any information submitted to other local agencies that is necessary to describe the effect of the proposed activity on the environment.

The Commission must hold a hearing on the Notice of Intent within 21 days after it is filed, unless the applicant consents to a further delay. Public notice of the hearing must be given by mailing to the planning board and board of health and by publication in a newspaper of general circulation in the city or town at least five days before the hearing. The 2005 revisions require notification of abutters within 100 feet of the property subject to the Notice of Intent.[8]

After holding the hearing, the Commission has another 21 days to issue its decision, in the form of a Notification of Nonsignificance or an Order of Conditions. (Volume 6, Chapter 9, Forms 45.6 and 45.7).

The Regulations give the Commissioner of DEP the power to grant variances from the Performance Standards in certain very limited cases, but such variances are rarely granted.

If the area is significant to one of the protected interests then the Commission must impose such conditions on the activity as will contribute to the protection of such interests and all work must be done in accordance with the Order.

The Order of Conditions must be signed by a majority of the Commission members and must be recorded in the appropriate registry of deeds before any work is undertaken.

If the final order, determination or notification requires the recording of a plan which:

(1)   shows the location of the work,

(2)   is prepared by a registered professional engineer or land surveyor, and

(3)   is in recordable form,

---

[8]   310 CMR 10.05(4)(a).

then no work may be undertaken until such plan is recorded in the registry of deeds.

If the Commission fails to hold a hearing within 21 days of the filing of the Notice of Intent, fails to issue an Order within 21 days after the public hearing, or issues an Order unsatisfactory to the applicant, then such Order or inaction may be appealed. The appeal must be taken in 10 days, except that where the commission has failed to act, the appeal may be within 70 days after the last day for action.[9] The persons entitled to appeal are

1) the applicant;

2) the owner, if not the applicant;

3) any person aggrieved by a Determination or Order;

4) an owner of land abutting the land on which the work is to be done;

3) any ten residents of the city or town where the land is located; and

4) the Department of Environmental Protection.

The appeal is taken by mailing notice of the same by certified mail to the DEP regional office, the Conservation Commission, and to the applicant if applicable.

The appeal is usually in the form of a letter. It should specify the action appealed from and the basis for the claim that the action is incorrect. The DEP investigates the situation, consults with the parties and, makes its own determination of the issues decided by the Commission. Within 70 days the DEP is required to issue its own Superseding Order of Conditions, which thereafter controls the case.

It frequently happens that after an appeal to the DEP Regional office is taken the parties to the appeal and the conservation commission will undertake negotiations to resolve the appeal. When such negotiations are successful the Commission often issues an "Amended Order of Conditions." The applicant then records the Amended Order and commences construction of the project. Sometimes the parties will even fail to withdraw the pending DEP appeal.

The position of the DEP is that such Amended Orders are of no effect, since the local Commission loses jurisdiction of the project once the Notice of Appeal is filed with the DEP, and cannot act on it further.

According to the Department, the legally correct way to effectuate the settlement at the local level is for the applicant to submit an entirely new application, with the agreed upon changes, obtain a new file number and go through the entire process at the local level once again. The Commission can then issue its new Order of Conditions, after which the appealing party can withdraw its appeal.

However, it will often be possible to negotiate at the regional or central DEP level

---

[9] 310 CMR 10.05(7)(c).

a Superseding Order that reflects the agreement of the parties. This will avoid the procedural difficulties outlined above. Of course, once the DEP is involved it is not bound in its wetland protection duties by any agreement of the parties.

Where, as is more and more often the case, there is a local wetlands protection bylaw administered by the conservation commission, there can be additional procedural complications. If the applicant accepts amended orders of condition under both state and local regulations, and the state amended orders are invalid for the reasons stated above, the project may be found by lender's or buyer's counsel to be in a kind of regulatory limbo. The commission could not issue a valid Certificate of Compliance on the invalid amended order of conditions.

Where a settlement of an appeal is reached with the local commission in this type of two-tier regulatory situation it will be best to draft a provisional agreement for judgment resolving the appeal in superior court under the local bylaw. Then the parties can advise the Department of the settlement and see if a State order can be obtained on the same terms. This is necessary because of the DEP policy staying all state wetland appeals proceedings until the local bylaw dispute is resolved.

Within 10 days after the Superseding Order of Conditions is issued any party may request a full adjudicatory hearing before the DEP hearings officer. The 2005 amendments specify that the request may only be made by a party other than the applicant, landowner or conservation commission if they are "previously a participant in the permit proceedings."[10] The revisions further require that an individual seeking an adjudicatory hearing must include "sufficient written facts to demonstrate status as a person aggrieved."[11] In order to preserve their rights to a full adjudicatory hearing, abutters and ten resident petitions pursuant to G.L. c. 30A, § 10A must participate either: (1) during the original conservation commission hearings through written testimony, or (2) by timely request of a Superseding Order or Determination or (3) by providing written testimony to DEP prior to the issuance of a Superseding Order or Determination.

There is a limited right of judicial review, under the substantial evidence standard, of final decisions after a DEP adjudicatory hearing pursuant to G.L. c. 30A, § 14. During such review the Supreme Judicial Court has made it quite clear that

---

[10]   310 CMR 10.05(7)(j).

[11]   310 CMR 10.05(7)(j). Whether the requirement that an abutter plead issues of aggrievement as a condition precedent to an adjudicatory hearing is "putting the cart before the horse" remains an open question. Whether an abutter is entitled to an adjudicatory hearing is dependant upon whether they can allege that the Superseding Order or Determination is inconsistent with the Regulations or the Act and not upon the substantive merits of their argument. The 2005 Revisions Requirement for Pleading "Sufficient Written Facts" should not be, unless contradicted, a requirement that the aggrieved party prove his or her case through the initial pleadings.

great deference is to be given by the courts to DEP's expertise in wetlands matters.[12]

A review of the applicable regulations should be made prior to taking a DEP appeal to determine whether the issuance of a superseding order by the agency will invoke the provisions of the Massachusetts Environmental Policy Act.[13] If it will, the developer may wish to revise the plan and have another go at convincing the conservation commission.

Orders of Condition are valid for three years and in certain special cases five years, but will usually be extended if application for extension is made prior to expiration. Extensions should be recorded. (*See* Form 45.8).

When the work is completed the applicant should obtain a Certificate of Compliance and record it in the registry of deeds, since otherwise the title may be clouded.[14] (Volume 6, Chapter 9, Form 45.10).

The issuance of an Enforcement Order (Volume 6, Chapter 9, Form 45.11) is the usual first step in the enforcement process.

The Supreme Judicial Court has ruled that conservation commissions have no enforcement duties under the Act, the responsibility for enforcement being placed on "natural resource officers, deputy natural resource officers, and any officer having police powers.[15]

This surprising ruling, which was made in the context of a criminal prosecution for unauthorized and un-permitted filling of wetlands, raises questions as to the authority of conservation commissions to make inspections of property to ascertain compliance with Orders of Condition issued by the commission, absent the permission of the property owner. Regulations issued under local wetland protection bylaws often grant access rights to the commission.

§ 8.06   Wetland Protection—General Bylaws

Many cities and towns have passed local wetland protection ordinances and bylaws, which are administered separately from the State Acts and local zoning. These general bylaws usually parallel the state wetlands acts, except that they are frequently stricter and almost always authorize prohibition of activities upon a general finding of environmental detriment. These stricter local bylaws, adopted

---

[12] Citizens for Responsible Environmental Management v. Attleboro Mall, Inc., 400 Mass. 658, 511 N.E.2d 562, 18 ELR 20118 (1987).

[13] G.L. c. 30, § 67-62H; 301 CMR 11.00 *et seq.*

[14] *See* 310 CMR 10.05(9)(f).

[15] Commonwealth v. John G. Grant & Sons Co., 403 Mass. 151, 526 N.E.2d 768 (1988).

under Home Rule powers, have been upheld by the Courts.[1] The state law authorizes prohibition only where an Order of Conditions cannot be framed to protect the Act's eight protected environmental interests.[2] It has become increasingly common for conservation commissions to adopt regulations implementing the local ordinance or bylaw. Sometimes the adoption of such regulations has been explicitly authorized, sometimes not. The regulations typically expand the reach of the Commission's authority. The Appeals Court seems to have assumed without deciding that Conservation Commissions have authority to adopt such regulations.[3] However, that Court has refused to uphold a permit denial under a local bylaw based on a "policy" of the Conservation Commission not lawfully adopted as a regulation.[4]

Often these ordinances and bylaws have no provisions respecting procedure or appeal. Judicial review must be sought by way of a complaint in the nature of certiorari.[5] (*See* Volume 6, Chapter 9, Form 47.1). Only a person "aggrieved" has standing to take such an appeal. A potential litigant is not aggrieved solely by virtue of being an abutter to the project, but must show that she has suffered an injury different in nature or magnitude from that of the general public.[6] This is similar to the standing requirement to take zoning appeals.

It has been common in the past for conservation commissions to issue identical Orders of Conditions under both the State Wetlands Act and the local municipal wetlands bylaw. If the applicant succeeded in obtaining a more favorable Superseding Order from the DEP, as was often the case, the commission could still insist on its original Order under the local bylaw.

However, it has now been held that this option is only available to the commission where its local Order of Conditions is issued under a bylaw "which is

---

[1] *See* Lovequist v. Conservation Com. of Dennis, 379 Mass. 7, 393 N.E.2d 858 (1979).

[2] 310 CMR 10.05(6)(b).

[3] Fafard v. Conservation Comm'n, 41 Mass. App. 565, 672 N.E.2d 21 (1996).

[4] Fieldstone Meadows Development Corp. v. Cons. Comm. of Andover, 62 Mass. App. Ct. 265 (2004).

[5] *See* for example, Hargreaves-Heald, et al. v. Town of Lincoln Conservation Commission, 16 Mass. L. Rptr. 798, (Mass. Super. 2002). "Pursuant to G.L. c. 249, § 4, the Court has jurisdiction to review, in the nature of certiorari, decisions of local conservation commissions made under a wetland bylaw," *citing* F.I.C. Homes of Blackstone v. Conservation Commission, 41 Mass. App. Ct. 681, 684 (1996). "Judicial review under G.L. c. 249, § 4 is limited to correcting substantial errors of law apparent on the record adversely affecting material rights," *citing* Carney v. City of Springfield, 403 Mass. 604, 605 (1995), *quoting* Murray v. Second District Court of E. Middlesex, 389 Mass. 508, 511 (1983). "The standard of review varies according to the nature of the action for which review is sought," *citing* F.I.C. Homes of Blackstone, Inc., 41 Mass. App. Ct. 681, at 684, *quoting* Forsyth School for Dental Hygienists v. Board of Registration in Dentistry, 404 Mass. 211, 217 (1989). *See also* Fafard v. Conservation Commission of Barnstable, 432 Mass. 194 (2000).

[6] Friedman v. Conservation Commission of Edgartown, 62 Mass. App. Ct. 539, 543 (2004).

consistent with the [state] act, but which permissibly imposes 'more stringent controls' than the minimum statewide standards set by the Legislature."[7] Where the local bylaw, as is often the case, adopts by reference portions of the State Act, or the DEP Regulations implementing the Act, (e.g. the definitions of protected areas), then the Superseding Order issued by the DEP will supersede the Order issued by the Conservation Commission under the local bylaw as well. This is the rule at least with respect to areas of dispute where the two regulatory schemes are congruent.

In addition to this explicit holding, the *DeGrace* case is susceptible to being interpreted as holding that whatever part of the local Order is based on a local bylaw provision that is not more stringent that the analogous State regulations will be superseded by the DEP Superseding Order. Certiorari review of local conditions that survive the *DeGrace* test is under the arbitrary and capricious standard,[8] a difficult, but not impossible, standard to meet.[9]

It is important for a disappointed applicant to perfect her right to judicial review of adverse actions of the DEP or the local Conservation Commission. The procedural requirements are specific and the time limits short.[10]

A failure to meet these requirements spells doom and no alternative form of pleading will revive a lost appeal.[11]

§ 8.07 "Chapter 91 License Requirements"—Filled or Flowed Tidelands and the Public Trust Doctrine

The commonwealth has issued comprehensive and complex regulations, which control construction and other activities in or near the ocean, great ponds, all waterways, all filled or flowed tidelands and what is commonly referred to as lands held for in trust for the public.[1] The regulations define tidelands in terms of the historic high water mark, as it existed before any alteration by humans, no matter how long ago such alteration occurred. This definition is extremely important

---

[7] DeGrace v. Conservation Commission of Harwich, 31 Mass. App. 132 (1991).

[8] T.D.J. Dev. Corp. v. Conservation Comm'n, 36 Mass. App. 124, 629 N.E.2d 328 (1994), summary op at 22 M.L.W. 1323 (Mass. App.) and *review denied*, 418 Mass. 1103, 636 N.E.2d 279, 22 M.L.W. 1996.

[9] FIC Homes v. Conservation Comm'n, 41 Mass. App. 681, 673 N.E.2d 61 (1996), *review denied*, 424 Mass. 1104, 676 N.E.2d 55 (1997); Fafard v. Conservation Comm. of Reading, 432 Mass. 194 (2000).

[10] Note that the Land Court does not have subject matter jurisdiction to hear disputes brought pursuant to a local wetlands protection bylaw. *See* Sayle v. Town of Nantucket Conservation Commission, No. 301051 (Mass. Land Court, Oct. 26, 2004).

[11] *See* Conservation Commission of Falmouth v. Pacheco, 49 Mass. App. 737, 733 N.E.2d 127 (2000).

[1] 310 CMR 9:00 *et seq.*

because of the onerous requirements for a license to conduct so-called "nonwater-dependent" activities or construction.

In response to considerable outcry from the development community after draft regulations were issued in 1987, the jurisdiction over filled tidelands was, at least for the time being, limited so as to exclude so-called "landlocked" tidelands. Landlocked tidelands are those that on January 1, 1984 were entirely separated by a public way or interconnected public ways from any flowed tideland, unless located within 250 feet of the present high water mark or within a Designated Port Area.

Anyone preparing to fill, dredge, build, or alter structures in tidelands or other areas subject to Chapter 91 jurisdiction must obtain a license from the Division of Wetlands and Waterways of the Department of Environmental Protection (DEP). Any existing use of fill or structures not previously authorized under Chapter 91, or for which a previously granted license is no longer valid, which is within the jurisdictional areas, requires a new license. (There has been an amnesty program for certain types of unlicensed uses.)

The most notable features of the new regulations from the point of view of the lawyer are probably the provisions of 310 CMR 9.51–9.55, which impose zoning-like requirements and public access requirements on nonwater-dependent uses and structures.

A full discussion of the Chapter 91 regulations is beyond the scope of this work. Suffice to say that counsel should be aware of the jurisdictional extent of the regulations and should consult them most carefully before advising a client to embark upon a project that is subject to them.

The SJC has upheld the power of municipalities to enact local wetlands bylaws regulating pier construction in so-called "Commonwealth tidelands," (land lying seaward of mean low water), against a challenge that such regulation was pre-empted by Chapter 91 and its regulations.[2] The court adopted reasoning substantially similar to that which it had used in upholding challenges to the power of municipalities to adopt local wetlands ordinances or bylaws more stringent than the DEP wetlands regulations.[3]

---

[2] Fafard v. Conservation Commission of Barnstable, 432 Mass. 194, 198–199 (2000). "When the original thirteen States became a nation, trusteeship of these interests on behalf of the public passed to the Commonwealth, which continues to act as trustee of the public's right to fishing, fowling, and navigation on the flats"... "The Commonwealth, as successor to the colonial authorities, owns and controls lands seaward of the flats," *citing* Michaelson v. Silver Beach Improvement Ass'n, Inc., 342 Mass. 251, 253–254 (1961). "These lands are held in trust by the Commonwealth to preserve the general rights of the public." 342 Mass. 251, at 253, *quoting* Home for Aged Women v. Commonwealth, 202 Mass. 422, 427 (1909).

[3] *See* Golden v. Board of Selectmen, 358 Mass. 519, 265 N.E.2d 536 (1970); Lovequist v.

§ 8.08   Federal Wetlands Regulation

Federal jurisdiction over wetlands is in most cases co-extensive with state jurisdiction, and in some cases more extensive. Rather than requiring a dual regulatory procedure of applicants in all cases, the U.S. Corps of Engineers, which administers the Federal program, issues a Programmatic General Permit (PGP) applicable to all wetland projects in Massachusetts.[1] The PGP divides projects into three categories, mainly based on the size or nature of wetlands degradation caused by the project. Category I projects require no review or reporting to the Corps. Category II projects are required to submit an application to the Corps for screening to determine if an individual permit under the Federal program will be required. Category III projects are required to obtain an individual permit from the Corps, requiring full review by Federal regulatory authorities.

A discussion of federal regulations and programs governing wetland resources, including, but not limited to, the National Environmental Policy Act, the Clean Water, the Safe Drinking Water Act and others are beyond the scope of this text. Counsel is advised to research the multitude of applicable federal laws applicable to the specific project of concern.

Conservation Com. of Dennis, 379 Mass. 7, 393 N.E.2d 858 (1979).

[1] *See generally* 33 CFR 320–331.

CHAPTER 9

WETLANDS PROTECTION—THE PRACTICE

Synopsis

§ 9.01   Applying for State and Local Wetland Permits

§ 9.01   Applying for State and Local Wetland Permits

Step 1. File a Notice of Intent along with the Environmental Data Form, maps, plans and filing fee with the commission. Send complete copies at same time to DEP regional office. (Volume 6, Chapter 9, Forms 45.2 and 45.3).

Where the site contains a resource area identified on the most recent Estimated Habitat Map (if any) of state-listed vertebrate and invertebrate animal species occurrences in resource areas, as prepared by the Massachusetts Heritage and Endangered Species Program (Program), an additional filing must be made. Contact the Program office in Westboro if you are unsure as to the presence of state-listed species on the subject property.

At least ninety days prior to the filing of the Notice of Intent, the applicant must notify the Program, by certified mail or in-hand delivery (so that the Program will have received its notice prior to the filing of the Notice of Intent), of any proposed work which would alter such a resource area.

Notification to the Program must include a copy of Appendix A to the Notice of Intent along with a copy of an 8 1/2 x 11 section of the USGS quadrangle map of the area with enough information to enable the Program to locate the precise boundaries of the portions of the wetland area(s) to be altered. (*See* Volume 6, Chapter 9, Forms 46.1 and 46.2). Proof of receipt of Appendix A by the Program must be submitted with the Notice of Intent.

Where time is a great factor to your client the Notice should be filed prior to receiving, but after applying for, any other necessary variances or permits. All filings and service on abutters, the DEP, and other parties in interest, should always be sent certified mail, return receipt requested.

Step 15. If you are not sure as to the applicability of the Wetlands Law, and you have plenty of time, submit a Request to Determine Applicability of the Wetland Protection Act. (Form 45, *infra*).

Send copies to DEP, and all abutters, including those across streets or waterways.

Step 16. Diary a date 21 days after submission of the Request. If the commission has still not acted you may submit the same Request to the DEP within 10 days.

Step 17. If you must file a Notice of Intent diary the date 21 days after it is filed. A public hearing must be held by this date. Obtain a copy of the commission rules and regulations.

Step 18. Be sure the published notice of hearing satisfies the statutory requirements and accurately describes what your client intends to do.

Step 19. At the hearing be well informed, with your engineer or wetland scientist present to explain and answer questions. Try to keep the commission's inquiry confined to its statutorily defined areas of concern; it is not a planning board. Always appear courteous and forthcoming.

Step 20. Diary the date 21 days after the public hearing. The commission must issue an Order of Conditions by this date.

Step 21. If the Commission issues its Order in a timely fashion, diary the date 10 days after the Order is issued. If the Commission does not issue its Order in a timely fashion, diary the date 70 days after the time for issuance has expired. (Any appeal to the DEP from such Order or failure to act must be taken by this date. Such appeals can be lengthy. If your client can accommodate himself or herself to the requirements of the local commission, this should be done.)

Step 22. Where necessary draft a Letter of Appeal to the appropriate regional office of DEP. The letter should state clearly and concisely the objections of the appellant to the local commission's action. Where, as is usually the case, a Superseding Order is being sought, the letter should also state how the Order of conditions being appealed is inconsistent with applicable regulations and does not contribute to the protection of the interests identified in the Act. If the Commission has allowed the time for issuing an Order to expire, and then issued its Order late, the appeal to DEP should raise the failure to act as well as appealing the late Order on its merits. (*See* Volume 6, Chapter 9, Form 46.3).

Step 23. Diary the date 10 days after the Superseding Order is issued. (Any request for an adjudicatory hearing before a DEP hearing officer in Boston must be filed by this date.)

Step 24. Where necessary draft the request for adjudicatory hearing. This must state clearly and concisely the facts of the proceeding, the reasons that the Superseding Order is alleged to be inconsistent with the regulations and not to contribute to the protections of the interests identified in the Act, and the specific relief sought by the appellant. (*See* Volume 6, Chapter 9, Form 46.4).

Step 25. Once a satisfactory Order has been obtained, record the Order of the Commission or DEP in the Registry of Deeds and provide the commission or DEP with proof you have done so. Where the Order requires the recording of a plan that shows the location of the work, is prepared by a registered professional engineer or land surveyor, and is in recordable form, the plan must be recorded in the appropriate registry of deeds before work can begin.

Step 26. After work has been completed, obtain a Certificate of Completion from the Commission or DEP, as appropriate, and record it in the registry of deeds.

CHAPTER 10

SUBDIVISION CONTROL—GENERAL PRINCIPLES OF LAW

Synopsis

§ 10.01   Determining Applicability of Subdivision Control
           Law
           § 10.01[1]   G.L. c. 41, § 81-L: What Is a Subdivision?
§ 10.02   Approval Not Required Plans
§ 10.03.   Subdivision Plans; Preliminary
§ 10.04.   Subdivision Plans; Definitive
§ 10.05.   Modification, Amendment, or Recission of Previously Approved Plan (G.L. c. 41, § 81-W)
§ 10.06.   Judicial Review Under Subdivision Control Law
§ 10.07   Commonly Encountered Problems in Subdivision
           Control Law
           § 10.07[1]   Approval Not Required Plans (§ 81P)
                         Which Show Zoning Violations
           § 10.07[2]   Entitlement to Approval Not Required
                         Endorsement—Judicial Guidelines
           § 10.07[3]   Creation of Lots With Inadequate
                         Frontage By Means of a Plan
           § 10.07[4]   Refusal of Planning Board to Accept
                         Plan
           § 10.07[5]   Disapproval of Preliminary Plan—Effect
           § 10.07[6]   Consideration By Planning Board of
                         Matters Outside the Proposed Subdivision
           § 10.07[7]   Dead End Streets—The Double Bubble
                         and Issues Related to G.L. c. 41, § 81-R
           § 10.07[8]   The Practical Role of the Board of
                         Health in Subdivision Approval Process
           § 10.07[9]   Adequacy of Statement of Reasons for
                         Planning Board's Disapproval of Plan
           § 10.07[10]   Conditional Approval of Plan Limited
                         as to Time

§ 10.07[11]   **Amendments to Previously Approved, or Disapproved, Plans After an Intervening Zoning Change**

§ 10.07[12]   **Constructive Approval of Plans**

§ 10.07[13]   **Effect of Restrictive Notes**

§ 10.07[14]   **Effect of Pre-existing Easements on Approvals of Plan**

§ 10.07[15]   **Problems Relative to Long-Term Maintenance of Engineering Structures**

§ 10.07[16]   **Development In or Near Historically or Archeologically Significant Sites**

§ 10.07[17]   **Requirement of Connection to Abutting Land**

§ 10.07[18]   **Resubmission of Disapproved Plans**

§ 10.07[19]   **Plan Approval Conditioned on Subsequent Compliance with Rules and Regulations**

§ 10.07[20]   **Subdivision of Single Lot Containing Two or More Buildings**

§ 10.01   Determining Applicability of Subdivision Control Law

Although the Subdivision Control Law[1] is complex in practice and generates a good deal of litigation it is conceptually quite simple. An underlying explanation is found in the purpose section of the statute (G.L. c. 41, § 81-M). The purpose of the Subdivision Control Law is clear: to facilitate the division of land into two or more parcels. Of course, the statute adds complexity to this basic premise, but it is good practice for counsel to remember that land is not best regulated, nor intended to be vigorously regulated, at the subdivision stage of development in Massachusetts.

The law is designed to ensure that concerns such as road width, road construction, and utility placement and related engineering—not planning and density—issues are addressed. The law is clearly intended to preclude cities and towns from extracting too many public benefits from a subdivider of land or impose planning considerations at this stage of the development process.

This point bears repeating. The statute presumes that a subdivision plan will be submitted in accordance with the city or town's zoning regulations and, therefore, the intent of those regulations are reflected in the submitted plan. It is not for the planning board in its review of a submitted plan to impose restrictions that should have otherwise been established by zoning ordinance or bylaw.

Planning boards are often frustrated by this lack of enabling authority and abutters to proposed land divisions even more frustrated by the planning board's apparent callous response to the proposed division of the undeveloped woods in the neighborhood or the division of a seemingly undividable parcel into several small lots. Again, the purpose of the statute is not to impose planning requirements on dividers of land, but rather, often minimal, engineering standards. "A planning board has no discretion to disapprove a subdivision plan which has been approved by the board of health and is in conformance with the reasonable rules and regulations of the planning board."[2] Municipal counsel are advised to remind their planning board members of this fact before the last remaining open space in the community is proposed for division. It is simply "too late" to protect and preserve land from development at the subdivision control level.

The Subdivision Control Law provides very few opportunities for cities and towns to gain a second chance at regulating land from a planning perspective once a plan for division has been filed. As a result, counsel for the applicant and the municipality should be familiar with these "second chance" options. As discussed below, these include the provisions contained in G.L. c. 41, § 81-L (Section

---

[1] G.L. c. 41, § 81K *et seq.*

[2] MP Corpo v. Planning Board of Leominster, 27 Mass. App. Ct. 821, 819–820 (1989), *quoting* Patelle v. Planning Board of Woburn, 6 Mass. App. Ct. 951, 951 (1978).

10.01[1]), § 81-R (Section 10.07[7]), 81-U (Section 10.07[8]) and 81-W (Section 10.05).

The statute is enforced by the local planning board, but a secondary control mechanism lies with the registry of deeds. The Register may accept no plan for recording unless:

1) The plan bears the endorsement of the planning board that the plan has been approved in accordance with the Subdivision Control Law, and a certificate of the city or town clerk that no appeal was received during the 20 days next after receipt and recording of notice from the planning board of approval of the plan, or, if an appeal was taken a final judgment has entered sustaining the approval of the plan. In this case, a definitive plan has been approved and endorsed and no appeal has been taken or the appeal has been resolved, or

2) The plan bears the endorsement of the planning board that approval under the Subdivision Control Law is not required. In this case, an approval not required plan has been endorsed, or

3) The plan is accompanied by a certificate of the city or town clerk that the plan has been approved by operation of law because of the failure of the planning board to act within the statutory time limit. In this case, the planning board has failed to act on the submitted plan in time and the clerk has endorsed the plan in accordance with the statutory powers granted that office.[3]

Thus, in order for a plan to be entitled to be recorded it must bear evidence on its face of some compliance with subdivision control. (There is a sole exception for plans bearing a certificate by a registered land surveyor that the property lines shown on the plan are lines dividing existing ownerships and the lines of streets and ways shown are those of streets or ways already established, and that no new lines for division of existing ownership or for new ways are shown. *See* G.L. c. 41, § 81-X).

Because of the increased marketability, and hence value, of land shown on recorded plans, and because development of land almost invariably necessitates the recording of a plan, the foregoing restrictions on recording are quite effective in securing compliance with subdivision control. Nevertheless, there is a further control mechanism in the office of the building inspector.

The building inspector is prohibited from issuing any permit for the erection of a building unless first satisfied that the lot upon which the building is to be erected is not within a subdivision, or that a way furnishing access to such lots as required

---

[3] *Id.*, § 81X.

by subdivision control is shown on a plan recorded or entitled to be recorded under the provisions of G.L. c. 41, § 81X.[4]

The net effect of the foregoing, then, is that a permit cannot be obtained to build on a lot unless it is not in a "subdivision" as defined by the statute, or unless it is served by a way shown on a plan entitled to be recorded under the terms of the statute.

§ 10.01[1]   G.L. c. 41, § 81-L: What Is a Subdivision?

The threshold question then becomes, is the lot part of a subdivision for purposes of subdivision control? A subdivision is defined by the statute[5] as "the division of a tract of land into two or more lots, [including] resubdivision." The word "lot" is defined as "an area of land in one ownership, with definite boundaries, used, or available for use, as the site of one or more buildings."

Therefore, whenever a single parcel of land is divided into two or more parcels available for use as building sites, it is a subdivision, unless it can meet one of the exemptions in the statute. Such a division of land will not be deemed a subdivision for purposes of the statute if at the time the division is made every lot has frontage on:

1) a public way or a way which the city or town clerk certifies is used or maintained as a public way, or

2) a way shown on a plan previously approved and endorsed in accordance with the subdivision control law, or

3) a way in existence when the subdivision control law became effective in the city or town in which the land lies, having, in the opinion of the planning board, sufficient width, suitable grades and adequate construction to provide for the needs of vehicular traffic in relation to the proposed use of the land abutting thereon or served thereby, and for the installation of municipal services to serve such land and the buildings erected or to be erected thereon. See additional discussion on this third definition of "not a subdivision" in Section 10.07[2], below.

Such frontage must be at least equal to that required by the zoning ordinance or bylaw at the time the division is made, or 20 feet if there are no such frontage requirements.

Conveyances changing the size and/or shape of lots are not considered subdivisions if all lots, as changed, have adequate frontage as described above. In

---

[4] *Id.,* § 81Y.
[5] *Id.,* § 81L.

addition, where two or more buildings stand on a single lot when subdivision control goes into effect in the city or town, the lot may be divided such that each building stands alone on a separate lot without such division being subject to subdivision control.

Where a subdivision plan of unregistered land is recorded prior to the effective date of subdivision control in the city or town the land on such plan is not exempt from the statute, except with respect to lots which had been sold and were held in ownership separate from that of the remainder of the subdivision when subdivision control went into effect.[6] Where the portion of the subdivision held in separate ownership is comprised of a cluster of contiguous undersized lots the owner can be required to combine the lots into a single lot, unless he is willing to comply with subdivision control.[7] In the case of registered land, if it was registered or confirmed prior to February 1, 1952, the plan so registered or confirmed is deemed to be approved for purposes of subdivision control.

In the case of both registered and unregistered land, it would appear that the municipality can require some kind of bond, covenant or other assurance that the ways will be constructed, as a condition to the issuance of building permits.[8]

§ 10.02   Approval Not Required Plans

Massachusetts remains one of the last states that allow the division of land without approval (or at least without much approval) from the municipality. An approval not required (ANR) plan has a logical historical basis, but one that is now outdated. As the purpose of subdivision control was to ensure adequate access to the subject parcel, the historical theory argued that if a landowner already had access to the parcel, why should municipal approval be necessary to divide the land into smaller parcels? This theory may have worked in the days with little knowledge regarding storm water management or little concern regarding a motorist's ability to make a left turn into the new Wal-Mart shopping center.

However, today, the landscape is permanently scarred by land divisions that simply had sufficient frontage on a way such that planning board approval was not required. Approval not required meant and means, no jurisdiction to impose any requirements regarding infrastructure, traffic or pedestrian safety, or other require-ment as a condition of endorsement (as the plan is not "approved", the planning board's action is to "endorse" the plan, "approval not required", thus enabling the

---

[6] *Id.*, § 81FF. *See* Toothaker v. Planning Bd. of Billerica, 346 Mass. 436, 193 N.E.2d 582 (1963); Clows v. Planning Bd. of Middleton, 1981 Adv. Sheets 1213, 422 N.E.2d 457 (Mass. App. 1981), *appeal denied*, 440 N.E.2d 1172 (Mass.).

[7] Clows v. Planning Bd. of Middleton, 1981 Adv. Sheets 1213, 422 N.E.2d 457 (Mass. App. 1981), *appeal denied*, 440 N.E.2d 1172 (Mass.).

[8] *See* Richard v. Planning Bd. of Acushnet, 10 Mass. App. 216, 406 N.E.2d 728 (1980).

register of deeds to accept the plan for recording.

If a landowner believes that the division of property as proposed does not constitute a subdivision or is otherwise exempt from the statute, he should submit his or her plan to the planning board and request that it be endorsed with the words "approval under the subdivision control law not required." (ANR Plan).

The submission must be made in accordance with the requirements of the statute and local regulations governing submission of ANR plans. Written notice of the submission of the plan must be given to the clerk of the city or town by delivery or by certified mail. The notice must describe the land to which the plan relates sufficiently for identification, and must state the date when the plan was submitted and the name and address of the owner of the land. The notice must be filed with the town clerk simultaneously or, at least, very promptly after submission to the board. The failure to make such a reasonably prompt filing with the city or town clerk will prevent the applicant from obtaining a constructive grant of plan endorsement if the board fails to act within the statutory period.[1]

If the planning board determines that the plan does not require subdivision approval, it must forthwith, without public hearing, endorse the plan as an approval not required plan. Unlike the approval of a definitive plan,[2] an ANR may be endorsed by a majority of the planning board members present, even if the voting majority is not the majority of the full planning board.[3] In other words, whereas approval of a definitive plan before a five member planning board will require at least three affirmative votes regardless of the quorum present, endorsement of an ANR plan requires only a majority of the quorum present at the planning board's meeting. Thus even though the board consists of five members, an ANR could be endorsed by affirmative vote of two members where the quorum consisted of three out of the five member board.

Not infrequently, a property owner will submit an ANR plan a few days before a zoning change is to be considered by the municipal legislative body, in order to secure the three year zoning use freeze provided by G.L. c. 40A, § 6. These plans must be acted on as promptly as those submitted at other times must. The planning

---

[1] Korkuch v. Planning Bd. of Eastham, 26 Mass. App. 307, 526 N.E.2d 1301 (1988).

[2] McElderry v. Planning Board of Nantucket, 431 Mass. 722 (2000). "We conclude that action by a planning board to approve a definitive subdivision plan requires the affirmative vote of a majority of the members of the board." 431 Mass. 722, at 727.

[3] *See* Poulos, Trustee v. Mahoney et al., (cite), December, 2004. Note that the Superior Court reached this conclusion given the absence of specific requirements to the contrary in either state or local (Framingham) regulation. Without further guidance from an appellate court, cities and towns may wish to clarify the voting requirements for ANR endorsements within their subdivision rules and regulations pursuant to G.L. c. 41, § 81-Q.

board may not "pocket veto" the zoning freeze by delaying action on the plan until after the vote on the zoning change.[4]

If the board determines that the plan requires approval it must, within 21 days of the date of submittal, give notice of this determination to the city or town clerk and to the person submitting the plan. The applicant may then either submit the plan for subdivision approval, or appeal the decision of the board to court.

If the board fails to act upon the plan or notify the clerk of its action within 21 days, the plan is deemed to be entitled to an approval not required endorsement. In such an event, the board is required to supply such endorsement forthwith, and failing this, the applicant is entitled to a certificate to the same effect from the city or town clerk recordable with the plan to show approved status.[5]

§ 10.03. Subdivision Plans; Preliminary

Where the plan requires subdivision approval and it shows lots in a residential zone, the applicant "may submit" to the planning board and board of health a preliminary plan followed by a definitive plan, or may file only a definitive plan. In the case of a nonresidential subdivision the applicant "shall submit" a preliminary plan before submitting a definitive plan. The preliminary plan, as the name suggests, may be less formal than the definitive plan, although in practice they tend to be very similar and to contain much the same information. The usual function of a preliminary plan is to "test the waters" to see at an early stage of the project what the attitude of the planning board will be toward the project and to appear to be working with the board toward an acceptable definitive plan. Developer's counsel are urged to advise their clients to submit preliminary plans. The requirement for the contents of preliminary plans is laid out in the statute, but is often amplified by local regulation.[1]

The person submitting the preliminary plan gives notice of such submission to the city or town clerk by delivery or certified mail. Within 45 days after submission of the plan, each board must notify the applicant and the city or town clerk that the plan has been approved, or has been approved with modifications suggested by the board or agreed to by the applicant, or that the plan has been disapproved. Where the plan is disapproved, the notice should contain detailed reasons for the disapproval. There is no remedy in the statute if the board simply fails to act on the plan.[2]

---

[4] Bisson v. Planning Board, 43 Mass. App. 504 (1997).

[5] G.L. c. 41, § 81 P. Schafer v. Zoning Agent of Bellingham, 351 Mass. 651, 223 N.E.2d 398 (1967).

[1] G.L. c. 41, § 81L.

[2] G.L. c. 41, § 81S.

Note that the submission of a preliminary plan will freeze zoning as of that date, provided a definitive plan is submitted within seven months.[3] Such filing also freezes the subdivision rules and regulations as of the filing date.[4]

§ 10.04. Subdivision Plans; Definitive

A subdivision plan is considered submitted for purposes of the statute when delivered at a meeting of the planning board or sent to the board by registered or certified mail. If the plan is mailed the date of submission is the date it is received by the planning board.[1]

The person submitting a definitive subdivision plan to the planning board must give written notice of such submission to the city or town clerk, by certified mail or by delivery. The notice must describe the land to which the plan relates sufficiently for identification, and must state the date when the plan was submitted and the name and address of the owner of the land.[2] The applicant for approval of a definitive plan must be the owner of the land or his/her agent. This statutory requirement may not be waived by the planning board. The board may by regulation require that only the owner may be the applicant.[3]

A copy of the definitive plan must be filed with the board of health at the time it is filed with the planning board. The board of health has 45 days to report to the planning board in writing its approval or disapproval of the plan. If the board of health disapproves, it must make specific findings as to which areas shown on the plan cannot be used for building sites without injury to the public health, and it must include those findings and the reasons therefore in the report. Where possible the health board must make recommendations for correction of the health-related defects in the plan.

The planning board must hold a public hearing before final action on the plan. Notice of the hearing must be given by the board by publishing in a newspaper of general circulation in the city or town once each week for two successive weeks, the first publication being not less than 14 days before the hearing. (If there is no newspaper then posting in the city or town hall may be substituted). A copy of the advertisement must be mailed to the applicant and to all owners of land abutting on the land included in the plan.[4]

After the hearing the planning board must approve, modify and approve, or

---

[3] G.L. c. 40A, § 6.

[4] G.L. c. 41, § 81Q.

[1] G.L. c. 41, § 81O.

[2] G.L. c. 41, § 81T.

[3] G.L. c. 41, § 81L; Batchelder v. Planning Board of Yarmouth, 31 Mass. App. 104 (1991).

[4] G.L. c. 41, § 81L; Batchelder v. Planning Board of Yarmouth, 31 Mass. App. 104 (1991).

disapprove the plan. The key to approval is compliance with all applicable zoning requirements affecting the lots and ways shown on the plan, and compliance with the board's Subdivision Rules and Regulations. The latter are regulations adopted by each municipal planning board pursuant to statutory authority, which must be recorded in the appropriate registry of deeds to be effective.[5] If the plan complies with applicable zoning and with the Rules and Regulations it is entitled to approval.[6] A plan may be denied for failure to comply with applicable zoning even if a requirement for such compliance is not included in the Rules and Regulations.[7]

A plan is governed throughout the approval process by the Rules and Regulations in effect on the date the definitive plan is filed, or on the date any preliminary plan is filed if it is followed within seven months by a definitive plan.[8]

If the board disapproves the plan it must state in detail where the plan does not conform to the Rules and Regulations or recommendations of the health board, and must approve the plan if it is amended to conform to the Rules and the recommendation.[9]

Under G.L. c. 41, § 81R, a planning board "may in any particular case, where such action is in the public interest and not inconsistent with the intent and purpose of the subdivision control law, waive strict compliance with its rules and regulations... ." The decision as to whether or not to waive some of its rules and regulations is largely left by reviewing courts to the discretion of the board.[10] Except in truly egregious cases judicial attack on a waiver or refusal to waive rules and regulations will have little chance of success.

There is no requirement that a planning board give reasons for its decision to waive its regulations. Indeed the board is not even required in its decision to state precisely which regulations it is waiving, as long as the record demonstrates that the board "purposefully consented to deviations from the regulations."[11] See further discussion in Section 10.07[7], however, for suggested approaches to the grant of waivers pursuant to § 81-R.

The board must file a certificate of its action with the city or town clerk and send

---

[5] G.L. c. 41, § 81L; Batchelder v. Planning Board of Yarmouth, 31 Mass. App. 104 (1991); G.L. c. 41, § 81Q.

[6] G.L.c. 41, § 81U; Canter v. Planning Bd. of Westborough, 4 Mass. App. 306, 347 N.E.2d 691 (1976). *But see* Campanelli, Inc. v. Planning Bd. of Ipswich, 358 Mass. 798, 261 N.E.2d 65 (1970).

[7] Beale v. Planning Bd., 423 Mass. 690, 671 N.E.2d 1233 (1996).

[8] G.L. c. 41, § 81Q.

[9] G.L. c. 41, § 81U.

[10] Arrigo v. Planning Bd. of Franklin, 12 Mass. App. 802, 429 N.E.2d 355 (1981), *appeal denied*, 385 Mass. 1101, 440 N.E.2d 1173.

[11] Meyer v. Planning Bd. of Westport, 29 Mass. App. 167, 558 N.E.2d 994 (1990), *review denied*, 408 Mass. 1104.

a copy of the same to the applicant by certified mail. Minor irregularities in the form or filing of the board's decision with the town clerk will not invalidate the decision.[12]

In the case of a nonresidential subdivision, where a preliminary plan has been filed and acted upon, or where 45 days have elapsed from filing, and a definitive plan is then submitted, the planning board must act on the definitive plan, and file a certificate of its action within 90 days after submission of the definitive plan. Failure to take action or file a certificate of action within the required time constitutes constructive approval of the plan.

In the case of a subdivision showing lots in a residential zone, where a preliminary plan has been filed and acted upon, or where 45 days has elapsed from filing, and a definitive plan is submitted, the planning board must also act and file its certificate within 90 days of the date of submission.

But, where a definitive plan showing lots in a residential zone is filed without being preceded by a preliminary plan, or where the definitive plan is filed before the expiration of 45 days from the date of submission of a preliminary plan, then the board has 135 days to act on the plan and file its certificate with the city or town clerk, although the board may at the written request of the applicant extend the statutory time limit, with failure to act by the end of any extension also being deemed approval.[13] Note however that the board has the power, after hearing, to rescind approval of a constructively approved plan if it has a "good reason" for doing so.[14] Action by a planning board to approve a definitive subdivision plan requires the affirmative vote of the majority of all members of the board. A majority of a quorum is not sufficient for plan approval.[15] Prior to actually signing the plan the board will require that the construction of ways and the installation of municipal services be secured by one, or in part by one and in part by another, of the following methods, which method or combination of methods may be selected and from time to time varied by the applicant:

1) by performance bond,

2) by deposit of money or negotiable securities,

3) by recorded covenant running with the land,

4) by delivery to the board of a security agreement to the board signed by the

---

[12] Miles v. Planning Bd. of Millbury, 29 Mass. App. 951, 558 N.E.2d 1150 (1990), *review denied*, 408 Mass. 1104.

[13] G.L. c. 41, § 81U (¶ 4).

[14] Zaltman v. Town Clerk of Stoneham, 5 Mass. App. 248, 362 N.E.2d 215 (1977); Young v. Planning Board of Chilmark, 402 Mass. 841, 525 N.E.2d 654 (1988).

[15] McElderry v. Planning Board of Nantucket, 431 Mass. 722 (2000).

applicant and the lender under any first mortgage given to secure future advances, whereby the lender agrees to withhold funds from the proceeds of such mortgage to secure the construction of ways and utilities.

Where methods 1, 2, or 4 are chosen the board may require that the applicant specify time within which such construction shall be completed. The amount posted or withheld must be sufficient in the opinion of the planning board to secure the construction of ways and utilities shown on the plan. In making this determination, the board shall require amounts that bear a direct and reasonable relationship to the expected cost, including the effects of inflation, necessary to complete the project. Such amounts must, from time to time, be reduced as work progresses so that the amount bonded or held continues to reflect the actual expected cost of work remaining to be completed.[16] There is no explicit provision allowing the board to increase the amount of the bond or retainage as time passes, but planning boards often have sufficient practical power over the developer to require such increases where construction of ways and utilities has been delayed.

Upon completion of the ways and utilities, the applicant must send notice of this fact to the city or town clerk and to the planning board by certified mail. This notice must contain the name and address of the applicant.

Upon receipt of this notice, the board must either release the bond, deposit, or covenant or specify in a notice sent by certified mail to the applicant and to the city or town clerk, the details wherein the said construction or installation fails to comply with its rules and regulations.

The board must send its notice within 45 days after receipt by the clerk of the applicant's notice of completion. Failure by the board to make timely response results in the bond or covenant becoming void, and in the deposit or retainage being immediately due the applicant. Upon the failure of the board to make timely response, the applicant is entitled to a recordable certificate to this effect.[17]

After the approval of the plan by the planning board, aggrieved persons may appeal the board's decision to superior court or land court during a 20-day appeal period. When the appeal period has expired the board will sign the plan and the city or town clerk will certify on the plan that no appeal of the board's decision was received during the 20-day period or that if such appeal was filed it has been dismissed. Where the approval is constructive due to the board's failure to act the clerk will issue a certificate to this effect. The plan should then be recorded with the planning board's endorsement or with the clerk's certificate dated within thirty

---

[16] G.L. c. 41, § 81U, (¶¶ 5, 6, 7).
[17] G.L. c. 41, § 81U, (¶ 8).

days of recording the plan.[18] The plan must also be accompanied by a municipal lien certificate indicating that all taxes, assessments and charges applicable to the land shown on the plan have been paid in full.[19]

§ 10.05. Modification, Amendment, or Recission of Previously Approved Plan (G.L. c. 41, § 81-W)

Approved plans may subsequently be modified, amended, or rescinded by the board on its own motion or upon petition of any interested person. The rules applicable to original approval apply to plans amended, modified, or changed under threat of recission.

No amendment, modification, or recission of a plan shall affect the lots in the subdivision that have been sold or mortgaged to bona fide purchasers for value subsequent to approval, except where the entire subdivision or all lots not previously released are sold to a single grantee.

Any of the previously mentioned changes may take effect for unregistered land only upon recordation of:

1) The plan as originally approved and a certified copy of the vote of the planning board making the change, along with any additional plan referred to in such vote;

2) An endorsement made on the original approved plan referring to the vote changing the plan;

3) A copy of the vote indexed in grantor index under the names of the owners of record of the land affected.[1]

This right to rescind exists even where the plan has been constructively approved through inaction by the board.[2] But the board may not rescind approval of either an actively approved or constructively approved plan without a "good reason" for doing so.[3]

An abutter to a plan subject to modification may lose her right to appeal the modified plan if she failed to appeal the board's decision approving the original plan.[4]

---

[18] G.L. c. 41, § 81X.

[19] G.L. c. 60, § 23.

[1] G.L. c. 41, § 81W.

[2] Zaltman v. Town Clerk of Stoneham, 5 Mass. App. 248, 362 N.E.2d 215 (1977).

[3] Young v. Planning Bd. of Chilmark, 402 Mass. 841, 525 N.E.2d 654 (1988).

[4] "While the statute provides that even if a person does not challenge the action at the planning board level…the provision does not permit an appeal of a modification plan to revive matters

The planning board has no authority to rescind an approval not required endorsement given under § 81P.[5] Presumably, this rule would also apply where the approval not required endorsement was constructively given through board inaction. Action by a planning board to approve a definitive subdivision plan requires the affirmative vote of the majority of all members of the board. A majority of a quorum is not sufficient for plan approval.[6]

§ 10.06. Judicial Review Under Subdivision Control Law

Any person aggrieved by the decision or failure to act of the planning board may appeal to superior court for the county in which the land is situated or to the land court.[1] Although there is very little judicial gloss on the word "aggrieved" used in G.L. c. 41, § 81BB, the Appeals Court has effectively incorporated the extensive decisional law defining the same term as used in G.L. c. 40A, § 17. In sum, a person is aggrieved if he suffers some infringement of his legal rights that is more than speculative and can be shown to be "particularized."

Abutters are presumed to be aggrieved, but once that presumption is challenged, it recedes. The abutter then has the burden of proving his aggrieved status. Appeals under § 81BB must be taken within 20 days after the decision is recorded in the office of the city or town clerk or within 20 days after the expiration of the time within which the board had to act.

Thus, for example, if the plan is approved as the result of the board's failure to act for 90 days after submittal, the appeal period begins on the 91st day. Where the board fails to act in a timely fashion, but later files its certificate of action, the appeal, if any, is from the constructive grant, not from the late filed certificate of action, which is a nullity.[2] It has been held that a judicial appeal from the action of a planning board is not within the scope of the lis pendens statute (G.L. c. 184, § 15).[3]

The nature of review in an appeal under the Subdivision Control Law is virtually identical to that in an appeal of a board of appeals decision under the Zoning Act (G.L. c. 40A, § 17).[4] The court hears all the evidence and finds all the facts de novo.

---

unchanged by the modification and not reconsidered by the board. This is so even if the original decision of the board was invalid." (emphasis added), Sergi v. Planning Board of Kingston, 60 Mass. App. Ct. 918, 919 (2004), *citing* Campanelli v. Planning Board of Ipswich, 358 Mass. 798 (1970) and Marino v. Board of Appeals of Beverly, 2 Mass. App. Ct. 859 (1974).

[5] Cassani v. Planning Board of Hull, 1 Mass. App. 451, 300 N.E.2d 746 (1973).

[6] McElderry v. Planning Board of Nantucket, 431 Mass. 722 (2000).

[1] McElderry v. Planning Board of Nantucket, 431 Mass. 722 (2000); G.L. c. 41, § 81BB.

[2] Windsor v. Planning Bd. of Wayland, 26 Mass. App. 650, 531 N.E.2d 272 (1988).

[3] McCarthy v. Hurley, 24 Mass. App. 533, 510 N.E.2d 779 (1987) (text cited by court).

[4] Strand v. Planning Bd. of Sudbury, 5 Mass. App. 18, 358 N.E.2d 842 (1977), *later appeal*, 7 Mass. App. 935, 390 N.E.2d 1141.

It then applies the law to the facts so found. The decision of the planning board is then either affirmed, annulled and the case remanded, or simply annulled. The Court does not substitute its discretion for that of the board and where reasonable minds may differ the judgment of the board should control. As the court said in *Strand v Planning Bd. of Sudbury,*[5]

> "the judge's proper role was to determine whether, on the facts found by him, the board had exceeded its authority in approving the plan aired at the public hearing. In the course of that process, he should have determined whether that plan conformed to the rules and regulations of the planning board and to the recommendations of the board of health. [citation omitted]. If such rules and regulations had been complied with and the plan comported with the recommendations of the board of health, he should have determined that the planning board did not exceed its authority in approving the plan. [citation omitted]. The judge should not have arrogated to himself the functions of the board of health or those of the planning board, or attempted to improve upon the work of either board."

The Appeals Court has set out in detail the method and standard which the trial courts are to use in deciding appeals under G.L. c. 41, § 81BB.[6] The trial court is to conduct "a hearing de novo, find the relevant facts, and, confining its review to the reasons stated by the planning board for its disapproval of the subdivision plan, determine the validity of the board's decision." [citations omitted].

The Supreme Judicial Court has held that the decision of the board of health under G.L. c. 41, § 81U should be reviewed in the same proceeding with the review of the planning board decision and that "the scope of review of the decision of the board of health should be the same as the scope of review of the planning board decision."[7]

In conjunction with its de novo review of the facts and its application of the facts so found to the decision of the boards, the trial court must determine whether each reason given by the planning board for its denial is supported by a duly adopted regulation of the board, in existence at the time the plan was filed.[8] For example, "absent a regulation regarding traffic on adjacent ways, the board may not disapprove plan on grounds of increased traffic congestion."[9] And the regulation relied

---

[5] Strand v. Planning Bd. of Sudbury, 5 Mass. App. 18, 358 N.E.2d 842 (1977), *later appeal*, 7 Mass. App. 935, 390 N.E.2d 1141.

[6] Fairbairn v. Planning Board of Barnstable, 5 Mass. App. 171, 360 N.E.2d 668 (1977).

[7] Loring Hills Developers Trust v. Planning Board of Salem, 374 Mass. 343, 372 N.E.2d 775 (1978).

[8] North Landers Corp. v. Planning Bd. of Falmouth, 382 Mass. 432, 416 N.E.2d 934 (1981).

[9] Canter v. Planning Bd. of Westborough, 4 Mass. App. 306, 347 N.E.2d 691 (1976), *appeal*

on must be "comprehensive, reasonably definite, and carefully drafted, so that owners may know in advance what is or may be required of them."[10]

Consistent with the requirement of definiteness in the planning board's regulations under the Castle Estates doctrine, the appeals court has held that a board may not rely on the kind of broad purpose language included at the beginning of the regulations promulgated by most planning boards to deny approval of a subdivision plan. This language typically is framed in terms of protection of public safety, insuring sanitary conditions, reducing danger to life and limb, and the like.

Oftentimes the introductory language mirrors the purpose section of the Subdivision Control Law itself. G.L. c. 41, § 81M. So a planning board could not deny approval of a subdivision the construction of which would involve significant blasting of rock based upon the introductory language of its regulations referring to "protecting the safety, convenience and welfare" of residents. A more precisely drawn regulation was required.[11]

Taken together, the cases hold that the proper method for the trial court to review a subdivision disapproval is to consider each reason for denial given by the board, determining in each case, (1) if there is a reasonably definite regulation upon which the reason may be based, and (2) if there is factual support for the reason, based on the facts as found de novo by the Court.

§ 10.07   Commonly Encountered Problems in Subdivision Control Law

The purpose of the following sections is to describe a few of the problems most commonly encountered in practicing subdivision control law and to set out the law that applies to them. Naturally, given the enormous variety of real estate development and the often-unique nature of individual parcels no attempt at comprehensiveness is possible.

§ 10.07[1]   Approval Not Required Plans (§ 81P) Which Show Zoning Violations.

As pointed out above,[1] in certain cases a plan showing a division of land into two or more parcels may be presented to a planning board for endorsement without the necessity of complying with the subdivision approval process.

There is a great deal of misunderstanding among landowners, planning boards, and building inspectors as to the effect of these so-called ANR endorsements,

---

after remand, remanded, 7 Mass. App. 805, 390 N.E.2d 1128.

[10] Castle Estates, Inc. v. Park & Planning Bd., 344 Mass. 329, 182 N.E.2d 540 (1962).

[11] Sealund Sisters, Inc. v. Planning Board of Weymouth, 50 Mass. App. 346, 348–349 (2000).

[1] *See* §§ 10.01[1] and 10.02 *supra.*

specifically with respect to whether the lots shown on the plan are made buildable by the endorsement. There is no doubt that the endorsement of a planning board on a plan pursuant to § 81P of the Subdivision Control Law does not give the lots shown on that plan any status with respect to the local zoning bylaw.[2] In order to be entitled to an ANR endorsement on his or her plan the applicant need only demonstrate to the planning board that: a) all the lots shown on the plan have at least the minimum required frontage on one of the three types of ways described in G.L. c. 41, § 81L, and b) there is adequate access to such lots as required by G.L. c. 41, § 81M.[3]

This being the case, it follows that the endorsement, in and of itself, cannot make the lots shown on the plan buildable. Since the planning board may not consider zoning questions, other than frontage, in acting on the plan, the applicant cannot logically claim that the ANR endorsement makes the lots buildable under the zoning ordinance or bylaw. Note however that, notwithstanding the foregoing, where the lot access criteria of the zoning regulation parrot the language of § 81L of the Subdivision Control Law, a determination of adequacy under the latter may be held to bind the planning board under the former.[4]

Corollary to this principle is the rule that the planning board may not refuse an ANR endorsement solely for the reason that one or more of the lots shown on the plan violates the zoning bylaw in a respect other than frontage.[5]

§ 10.07[2]   Entitlement to Approval Not Required Endorsement—Judicial Guidelines

There are a number of cases which, taken together with the statutory language, set out fairly definite parameters for planning boards to use in considering applications for ANR endorsements. The basic rule is that the endorsement of such a plan is a routine act, ministerial in character, and constitutes an attestation of compliance with neither zoning nor subdivision control regulations.[6]

Even though the planning board has very little discretion when it is presented

---

[2] Smalley v. Planning Board of Harwich, 10 Mass. App. 599, 410 N.E.2d 1219 (1980); Lee v. Board of Appeals, 11 Mass. App. 148, 414 N.E.2d 619 (1981); Duhaime v. Planning Bd. of Medway, 12 Mass. App. 907, 422 N.E.2d 790 (1981).

[3] Smalley v. Planning Board of Harwich, 10 Mass. App. 599, 410 N.E.2d 1219, 1222.

[4] Shea v. Board of Appeals, 35 Mass. App. 519, 622 N.E.2d 1382 (1993), summary op at (Mass. App.) 22 M.L.W. 576; Corrigan v. Board of Appeals, 35 Mass. App. 514, 622 N.E.2d 1379 (1993), summary op at (Mass. App.) 22 M.L.W. 574.

[5] Shea v. Board of Appeals, 35 Mass. App. 519, 622 N.E.2d 1382 (1993), summary op at (Mass. App.) 22 M.L.W. 576; Corrigan v. Board of Appeals, 35 Mass. App. 514, 622 N.E.2d 1379 (1993), summary op at (Mass. App.) 22 M.L.W. 574; Bloom v. Planning Bd. of Brookline, 346 Mass. 278, 191 N.E.2d 684 (1963).

[6] Hamilton v. Planning Board, 35 Mass. App. 386 (1993).

with a plan which on its face meets the statutory criteria for an ANR endorsement, its function is not entirely as ministerial as the statutory language suggests. The frontage relied on by the applicant to support the claimed exemption from subdivision control must be on a way which provides "adequate access ... safe and convenient for travel," as contemplated by § 81M of c. 41.[7] Therefore proposed plans which relied for the required frontage on an expressway,[8] a town road which had never been laid out and built,[9] on unbuilt streets of an old subdivision where there was no assurance that the streets would be constructed,[10] or on a way shown on a prior ANR plan,[11] were held properly denied ANR endorsements. Moreover, for the same reasons, the denial of an ANR endorsement to a plan, which showed lots fronting on a public way by means of narrow, sharply angled necks, was upheld.[12]

However, the appellate courts have taken pains to point out that the range of discretion of the planning board to deny exemption to plans that meet the technical requirements of the statute is very narrow indeed. Such plans may be denied only where the access proffered by the applicant is illusory in fact.[13] Further some cases suggest that the impediments to access must be physical and not regulatory in order to form the basis for denial.[14] It is perhaps more accurate to say that if the regulatory impediment to access is absolute, then endorsement may be denied. Whereas if the regulation merely requires an application for approval and possible submission to conditions of approval, then endorsement may not be denied.[15] Also, in the case of physical impediments to access, partial obstruction of the frontage is not

---

[7] Perry v. Planning Bd. of Nantucket, 15 Mass. App. 144, 444 N.E.2d 389 (1983), *appeal denied*, 388 Mass. 1103, 447 N.E.2d 670.

[8] Hrenchuk v. Planning Board of Walpole, 8 Mass. App. 949, 397 N.E.2d 1292 (1979).

[9] Perry v. Planning Bd. of Nantucket, 15 Mass. App. 144, 444 N.E.2d 389 (1983), *appeal denied*, 388 Mass. 1103, 447 N.E.2d 670; G.L. c. 41, § 81U (¶¶ 5, 6, 7).

[10] Richard v. Planning Bd. of Acushnet, 10 Mass. App. 216, 406 N.E.2d 728 (1980).

[11] Goldman v. Planning Board of Burlington, 347 Mass. 320, 197 N.E.2d 789 (1964).

[12] Gifford v. Planning Board of Nantucket, 376 Mass. 801, 383 N.E.2d 1123 (1978).

[13] Gallitano v. Board of Survey and Planning, 10 Mass. App. 269, 407 N.E.2d 359 (1980); Hutchinson v. Planning Bd. of Hingham, 23 Mass. App. 416, 502 N.E.2d 572 (1987). *See also* Fox v. Planning Bd. of Milton, 24 Mass. App. 572, 511 N.E.2d 30 (1987), where lots with frontage on MDC Parkway but separated from paved portion by 175-foot greenbelt were held entitled to an ANR endorsement.

[14] Corcoran v. Planning Bd. of Sudbury, 406 Mass. 248, 547 N.E.2d 911 (1989). The fact that wetlands on the lot prevented access without further regulatory approval was not basis for denial. Long Pond Estates, Ltd. v. Planning Bd. of Sturbridge, 406 Mass. 253, 547 N.E.2d 914 (1989). The fact that the public way frequently flooded was not grounds for denial. Poulos v. Planning Bd. of Braintree, 413 Mass. 359, 597 N.E.2d 417 (1992). Where the state highway guardrail prevented access but would be removed if land rendered access illusory until guardrail actually removed.

[15] McCarthy v. Planning Board of Edgartown, 381 Mass. 86 (1980); Hobbs Brook Farm Property Co. Limited Partnership v. Planning Board of Lincoln, 48 Mass. App. 403 (2000).

necessarily a sufficient basis for denial if the unobstructed portion is adequate for vehicular access.[16] At least in close cases the entitlement to ANR endorsement will be very much fact driven, something not usually expected when an agency is acting in its ministerial role.[17]

Where the land fronts on a public way, the planning board has even less flexibility. Deficiencies in a public way are insufficient grounds for denying the ANR endorsement unless they are so severe as to render access illusory.[18] More recently the Appeals Court has formulated this dichotomy by describing all public ways as falling into one of two categories for purposes of § 81P, "[t]here is the 'could be better but manageable' category and the 'illusory' category. The first category warrants a § 81P endorsement; the second does not."[19]

While there is a very narrow range of discretion in the planning board to examine the adequacy of the way itself, (as opposed to access to the way), in the case of public ways and approved subdivision ways, there still remains some uncertainty about the range of planning board discretion where the applicant relies for frontage on "… a way in existence when the subdivision control law became effective in the city or town in which the land lies, having, in the opinion of the planning board, sufficient width, suitable grades and adequate construction…" (G.L. c. 41, § 81L, subsec. (c) in definition of "Subdivision"). What width, grade and construction is "sufficient" to secure entitlement to an ANR endorsement; and how much deference is to be given by the court to the "opinion" of the planning board? It is clear that the board has "broader powers … to determine the adequacy of the ways described in subsection (c) …" than it does in the case of public or subdivision ways.[20] But its inquiry and discretion is surely not as broad as what would pertain if it were considering the road as part of an application for full subdivision approval. Because if the way is "of sufficient width and suitable to accommodate motor vehicle traffic and to provide access for fire-fighting equipment and other emergency vehicles … an 81P endorsement is required."[21] However the use of the word "opinion" in the statute suggests that at least some deference should be paid by the court to the

---

[16] Hobbs Brook Farm Property Co. Limited Partnership v. Planning Board of Lincoln, 48 Mass. App. 403 (2000).

[17] Gates v. Planning Board, 48 Mass. App. 394 (2000). This case contains a very useful summary of the case law on the standards for ANR review. It is also interesting to note that the locus subject to the litigation in *Gates* was granted a comprehensive permit by the Dighton Board of Appeals in 2004 for 88 dwelling units.

[18] Sturdy v. Planning Bd. of Hingham, 32 Mass. App. 72, 586 N.E.2d 11 (1992). Note that refusal of mandamus to require the town to repair the inadequate public way upheld on appeal. Long Pond Estates, Ltd. v. Planning Bd. of Sturbridge, 406 Mass. 253, 547 N.E.2d 914 (1989).

[19] Ball v. Planning Board of Leverett, 58 Mass. App. Ct. 513, 517 (2003).

[20] Hutchinson v. Planning Bd. of Hingham, 23 Mass. App. 416, 502 N.E.2d 572 (1987).

[21] Hutchinson v. Planning Bd. of Hingham, 23 Mass. App. 416, 502 N.E.2d 572 (1987).

determination of the administrative body in the case of a subsection (c) way.[22]

Municipal counsel are encouraged to assist their planning boards clarify the local meaning of subsection (c). For example, a city or town planning board could define within its subdivision rules and regulations its interpretation of "sufficient width" and "suitable grades" thus guiding the board's decision making pursuant to applications under subsection (c). As the Court will use the distinction between "deficient" and "illusory" as its guide,[23] the planning board is advised to help a reviewing Court with that determination. For example, if the board includes in its subdivision rules and regulations that frontage for the purposes of an ANR cannot include that portion of the lot along the frontage that contains wetland resources, the regulations would be strengthened by a cross reference to the city or town's local wetland regulations that preclude filling of wetland areas. Similarly, if the city or town does not have fire fighting apparatus that can orchestrate tight turns on narrow roads, the regulations would be improved by commentary that state that ANR frontage that requires turn radii greater than the fire truck can safely handle is deemed illusory.

Where a zoning boundary transects the lot, leaving frontage in a less restricted zone with the main body of the lot in a more restricted zone, a question can arise as to the minimum frontage required for a lot to be entitled to ANR endorsement. There is no case law specifically on point.

The statute[24] provides that "such frontage shall be of at least such distance as is then required by zoning or other ordinance or bylaw, if any, … for erection of a building on such lot…"

It would thus appear that the frontage necessary to secure an ANR endorsement in split lot cases must somehow be referable to the structures proposed for such lot.

It might plausibly be argued that if the lot contained enough area in the less restrictive zone to allow for the construction of a building under applicable zoning then the property owner is entitled to endorsement if the lot frontage meets the requirements of that zone.

Split lot zoning decisions in other types of cases seem to make it clear that dimensional and density requirements are ancillary and referable to the use being

---

[22] Jaxtimer v. Planning Bd., 38 Mass. App. 23, 643 N.E.2d 1064 (1995).

[23] "We must determine whether the portion of January Road that fronts upon Lot 1 is merely 'deficient' (i.e. could be better but manageable) or whether it fails to provide acceptable physical access according to the goals of § 81M (i.e. access is "illusory"). Ball v. Planning Board of Leverett, 58 Mass. App. Ct. 513, 517 (2003).

[24] G.L. c. 41, § 81L.

made of the property.[25] This is especially true of frontage, which has adequate access to the lot as its main objective. The adequacy of access to a lot is in turn very much related to the use to be made of it.

The planning board has little to fear in granting such an endorsement since the property owner could not secure a permit under the zoning bylaw to erect a structure in the more restrictive zone because the newly created lot would have inadequate frontage. This is yet another example of why an attempt at regulating land use is best accomplished through zoning, and not via subdivision control. The planning board's role under the Subdivision Control Law, especially as it pertains to plans seeking ANR approval, is extremely limited.

A person who records a plan that contains restrictive notations, after obtaining an ANR endorsement of the plan from the planning board based thereon, is deemed to have agreed to submit the land to such restrictions, whether or not they could have been lawfully imposed. It would take further planning board or judicial action to modify the restrictions.[26] So the applicant who obtains a legally flawed or overly restrictive ANR endorsement may very well be doing him or herself more harm than good.

Of interest in this regard is a holding by the Appeals Court that a plan showing three parcels, two of which had restrictive notes indicating that they were not building lots, was not a plan showing a "subdivision" as defined under § 81L. Therefore, the Court reasoned, the plan was entitled to an ANR endorsement under § 81P, without regard to whether the planning board deemed the way furnishing access to the one building lot was adequate.[27]

The time within which the propriety of an ANR endorsement may be reviewed at the behest of a person other than the applicant is not limited to the 20 day period set out in G.L. c. 41, § 81BB. Neither does the language contained in § 81P to the effect that the endorsement "shall be conclusive on all persons" insulate the planning board action from judicial review.[28] A suit challenging the grant of an ANR endorsement by a planning board is one in the nature of certiorari under G.L. c. 249, § 4 and must be brought within sixty days after the date upon which the endorsement is made.[29]

---

[25] Tofias v. Butler, 26 Mass. App. 89, 523 N.E.2d 796 (1988); Moore v Swampscott, 26 Mass. App. 1008, 530 N.E.2d 808 (1988).

[26] Tofias v. Butler, 26 Mass. App. 89, 523 N.E.2d 796 (1988); Moore v Swampscott, 26 Mass. App. 1008, 530 N.E.2d 808 (1988).

[27] Cricones v. Planning Bd., 39 Mass. App. 264, 654 N.E.2d 1204 (1995), *review denied*, 421 Mass. 1106, 657 N.E.2d 1273.

[28] *See* Lee v. Board of Appeals, 11 Mass. App. 148, 414 N.E.2d 619 (1981).

[29] Stefanick v Planning Bd., 39 Mass. App. 418, 657 N.E.2d 475 (1995), *review denied*, 422 Mass. 1104.

The requirement that a parcel of land be subject to a note "Not a Building Lot" or words of similar import has little lasting value. If the land is not subject to a deed or conservation restriction (pursuant to G.L. c. 184, § 32), the fact that the note was required to be placed or placed voluntarily on an ANR plan, does not preclude the parcel from becoming a building lot at a later date, nor does the notation appear to have any meaning under the comprehensive permit statute.[30]

§ 10.07[3]   Creation of Lots With Inadequate Frontage By Means of a Plan.

On occasion a property owner desires to subdivide a parcel of land fronting on an existing street in such a manner that one or more of the lots created will have less than the then required minimum frontage under the local zoning ordinance or bylaw. A common misconception in such cases is the belief that once the plans, and necessary waivers, have been approved by the planning board under the Subdivision Control Law the substandard lot or lots are buildable. In fact, in this type of situation two separate approvals, from two separate boards, using two different sets of standards, are required.[31] The planning board must grant waivers from the minimum frontage requirements under the Subdivision Control Law pursuant to G.L. c. 41, § 81-R[32] and the board of appeals must grant a variance from the frontage requirements of the zoning ordinance or by-law[33] before a building permit can issue.

§ 10.07[4]   Refusal of Planning Board to Accept Plan.

For varying reasons, idiosyncratic or otherwise, some planning boards will refuse to accept a definitive plan from an applicant. This is not something the board has power to do. A simple refusal to accept and act on a plan, properly filed, according to the statute, will ripen into a constructive approval of the plan.[34] Notwithstanding, counsel for an applicant seeking planning board approval or endorsement should be aware of and comply with, the board's filing requirements for plan submission. Planning boards should always "accept" a proffered filing, advertise for the public

---

[30] *See*, for example, Woodridge Realty Trust v. Ipswich Board of Appeals, 00-04, (Mass. Housing Appeals Comm. June 28, 2001), where the Housing Appeals Committee ruled that the Board of Appeals (and the Housing Appeals Committee) is empowered to rescind or waive restrictions imposed by a planning board during the review of plans pursuant to the Subdivision Control Law.

[31] Arrigo v. Planning Bd. of Franklin, 12 Mass. App. 802, 429 N.E.2d 355 (1981), *appeal denied*, 385 Mass. 1101, 440 N.E.2d 1173.

[32] G.L. c. 41, § 81 R; Seguin v. Planning Bd. of Upton, 33 Mass. App. 374, 600 N.E.2d 185 (1992).

[33] G.L. c. 40A, § 10.

[34] Pierce v. Town Clerk of Rochester, 3 Mass. App. 728, 325 N.E.2d 300 (1975). *See* Racette v. Zoning Bd. of Appeals, 27 Mass. App. 617, 541 N.E.2d 369 (1989).

hearing in accordance with the statute and open the public hearing. Prior to that time, the board's agent should contact the applicant and inform her that the filing is defective and that this issue, if not cured, may result in the board voting to disapprove the plan. If not cured prior to the public hearing, the board should open the public hearing and read into the record the filing deficiencies that it believes are present. If the board believes the deficiencies are substantive, it may then close the hearing and vote to deny the application.

At risk for the board, however, is that pursuant to the Subdivision Control Law, a plan that is denied may become "approved", by virtue of the applicant's addressing the grounds for denial. Therefore, in the unusual situation where an applicant simply will not comply with the board's filing requirements and the board seeks to deny the project accordingly, the board is advised to include all the reasons for denial of the project, not just those relating to the filing deficiency.

§ 10.07[5] Disapproval of Preliminary Plan—Effect.

Some planning boards tend to treat the preliminary plan as if it were of the same status as a definitive plan. The applicant is required to modify and resubmit the preliminary plan until it meets the board's approval, then a definitive plan is created, identical to the last preliminary, and immediately approved.

Not only is this procedure contrary to that contemplated by the statute, but the applicant who indulges a board in this manner must be very cautious that the definitive plan is filed within 7 months of the first preliminary, or the zoning[35] and subdivision rules[36] freeze will be lost.

While the filing of a preliminary plan is required for non-residential land divisions,[37] a preliminary plan is not required for the division of land zoned residential. The disapproval of a preliminary plan is not appealable and has no final effect on the applicant's rights under the Subdivision Control Law.[38]

§ 10.07[6] Consideration By Planning Board of Matters Outside the Proposed Subdivision.

It frequently happens that a planning board in evaluating a proposed subdivision plan wishes to consider factors outside the confines of the subdivision itself, such as municipal water supplies, traffic conditions and public safety services. This is particularly true in communities that are experiencing rapid growth and where the proposed subdivision is large.

---

[35] G.L. c. 40A, § 6.
[36] G.L. c. 41, § 81Q.
[37] G.L. c. 41, § 81-S.
[38] Paul Livoli, Inc. v. Planning Bd. of Marlborough, 347 Mass. 330, 197 N.E.2d 785 (1964).

There was language in some of the earlier[39] (and indeed some of the later),[40] cases that suggested that a planning board must look only to matters within the subdivision in making its decision; or at least could not deny approval based on circumstances existing outside the subdivision. However, in recent years this rule, to the extent it was a rule, has been substantially refined and limited. It is argued that this recent refinement is appropriate in a state that does not allow cities and towns to extract impact fees as a condition of development approval. See further discussion regarding impact fees in Section 5.32.

In 1976, the Appeals Court suggested,[41] and in 1981 the Supreme Judicial Court confirmed,[42] that the planning board could adopt and implement rules and regulations which looked to conditions outside the confines of the subdivision. However, it does still appear that there must be some fairly intimate connection—nexus—between the subdivision itself and the condition outside the subdivision which is the basis of the denial or conditional approval.[43] And the SJC has specifically refrained from ruling that conditions outside the subdivision, standing alone, are sufficient to justify disapproval of a plan.[44] It seems quite certain at least that general community conditions, (i.e.) water supply, fire and police, traffic congestion, rapid growth, and so on, are not in and of themselves sufficient bases for the denial of a subdivision plan.[45]

However, the board will never be within its rights in considering matters outside the subdivision unless those matters are relevant to some requirement set forth in its rules and regulations.[46] This is the so-called *Castle Estates* standard, named after the early case that established the general principle that a planning board may not require anything of an applicant that is not set out in its rules and regulations.[47]

---

[39] Daley Constr. Co. v. Planning Bd. of Randolph, 340 Mass. 149, 163 N.E.2d 27 (1959); Pieper v. Planning Board of Southborough, 340 Mass. 157, 163 N.E.2d 14 (1959).

[40] Mac-Rich Realty Constr., Inc. v. Planning Board of Southborough, 4 Mass. App. 79, 341 N.E.2d 916 (1976).

[41] Canter v Planning Bd. of Westborough, 4 Mass. App. 306, 347 N.E.2d 691 (1976).

[42] North Landers Corp. v. Planning Bd. of Falmouth, 382 Mass. 432, 416 N.E.2d 934 (1981).

[43] North Landers Corp. v. Planning Bd. of Falmouth, 382 Mass. 432, 416 N.E.2d 934 (1981), and cases cited therein. Miles v. Planning Bd. of Millbury, 29 Mass. App. 951, 558 N.E.2d 1150 (1990), *review denied*, 408 Mass. 1104.

[44] North Landers Corp. v. Planning Bd. of Falmouth, 416 N.E.2d 934, at 938.

[45] Mac-Rich Realty Constr., Inc. v. Planning Board of Southborough, 4 Mass. App. 79, 341 N.E.2d 916, 920 (1976).

[46] North Landers Corp. v. Planning Bd. of Falmouth, 416 N.E.2d 934, at 938. *But see* Rattner v. Planning Board, 45 Mass. App. 8 (1998), which holds that the planning board has an obligation under § 81M to consider the adequacy of ways outside the subdivision. The Court also relied on "indications" in the subdivision rules and regulations of an intent to lessen congestion on adjacent roadways.

[47] Castle Estates, Inc. v. Park & Planning Bd., 344 Mass. 329, 182 N.E.2d 540 (1962).

Castle Estates and its progeny also make it clear that, except with respect to zoning compliance and access rights, the board cannot deny a plan or impose conditions based on the broad language of G.L. c. 41, § 81M unless it has adopted proper regulations to implement the powers granted by that section.[48]

The *Castle Estates* standard satisfies traditional due process considerations. First, by requiring a sufficient nexus between the proposed project's impact and the requirements imposed to ameliorate those impacts, the planning board will be complying with the basic notion that a city or town can reasonably impose conditions of approval on new development that are rationally related to the development's impacts. Second, by requiring that the exactions to be required be set forth in the planning board's rules and regulations, the applicant is on notice as to what may be expected from her and the board will be estopped from extracting improvements otherwise unforeseeable.

The board may not as a condition of approving the plan require improvements to public ways adjacent to the subdivision, or impose any other condition the performance of which lies beyond the control of the applicant. However, assuming a proper supporting regulation, the board may require the applicant to dedicate a portion of its property for use in improving adjacent public ways.[49]

Finally, it should be noted that even where an area of concern is outside the regulatory authority of the board it may inquire into that matter, and may, as a corollary to this principle, require the applicant to provide it with information relevant to such area of concern.[50] But here again the *Castle Estates* standard applies and such information may only be required if the board has a regulation permitting it to make such inquiries.[51]

§ 10.07[7]   Dead End Streets—The Double Bubble and Issues Related to G.L. c. 41, § 81-R

Nearly all planning boards have adopted a regulation limiting the length of dead

---

[48] *But see contra* suggestions, at least with respect to zoning compliance, in Arrigo v. Planning Bd. of Franklin, 12 Mass. App. 802, 429 N.E.2d 355 (1981), *appeal denied*, 385 Mass. 1101, 440 N.E.2d 1173 and Canter v. Planning Bd. of Westborough, 4 Mass. App. 306, 347 N.E.2d 691 (1976), *appeal after remand, remanded*, 7 Mass. App. 805, 390 N.E.2d 1128, culminating in the holding that compliance with zoning need not be included in the rules and regulations to form the basis of a plan denial. Beale v. Planning Board, 423 Mass. 690 (1996). Also, a requirement that the applicant demonstrate a legal right to use an access road outside the subdivision necessary to the plan as proposed may be imposed in the absence of a rule to that effect. Parker v. Black Brook Realty Corp., 61 Mass. App. Ct. 308 (2004).

[49] Sullivan v. Planning Board of Acton, 38 Mass. App. 918 (1995), 1995 Mass. App. LEXIS 28.

[50] Loring Hills Developers Trust v. Planning Board of Salem, 374 Mass. 343, 372 N.E.2d 775 (1978).

[51] Loring Hills Developers Trust v. Planning Board of Salem, 374 Mass. 343, 372 N.E.2d 775 (1978).

end streets in subdivisions. It very frequently happens that in order to maximize the potential of his or her land the applicant will wish to make use of a longer dead end street than allowed by the regulations. One solution of course is to seek a waiver from the planning board. However, a case decided in 1974 by the Appeals Court[52] will, depending circumstances, provide an alternative to the applicant. If instead of using a single straight road off of an existing way the subdivision engineer lays the road out in the form of a "T" with turnarounds at each end of the crossbar of the "T", and gives the two bars of the "T" different street names, it may be possible to avoid a violation of the maximum dead end street length regulation.

In the *Sparks* case, the town's subdivision rules and regulations did not contain a definition of 'dead end street' and the Court was forced to supply one. It concluded that as long as a street is open at both ends it is not a dead end street. This definition leaves a certain amount of leeway for the creative subdivision designer. However, as the *Sparks* court suggests, subdivision rules and regulations can be drafted in such a way as to prevent an undesirable judicial interpretation.[53]

While applicable to the general discussion of planning boards and the Subdivision Control Law, the traditional enforcement of a "maximum length of dead end street requirement" presents a particularly appropriate opportunity to mention the causal connection between the local subdivision rules and regulations and the comprehensive permit statute.

It is frequently the case that a comprehensive permit applicant is an applicant who previously sought subdivision approval but was denied due to the local dead end road requirements, intersection offset requirements or other specifically local regulation that renders a parcel of land difficult to develop as the landowner wishes it developed. In addition, while the planning board has broad authority to waive strict compliance with its own subdivision rules and regulations pursuant to G.L. c. 41, § 81-R, many planning boards have difficulty finding the "public interest" in such a waiver as required by § 81-R.

The public interest may be, however, that without a grant of a waiver from, for example, a maximum dead end road length, the applicant will simply file for a comprehensive permit with the board of appeals. Not only will the board of appeals have plenary power to determine whether it will waive the dead end requirement, thus leaving the planning board left to wonder why it was so rigid and dogmatic, the overall density of the comprehensive permit project is likely to be many, many

---

[52] Sparks v. Planning Board of Westborough, 2 Mass. App. 745, 321 N.E.2d 666 (1974).

[53] Sparks v. Planning Board of Westborough, 2 Mass. App. 745, 321 N.E.2d 666 (1974); Federline v. Planning Bd. of Beverly, 33 Mass. App. 65, 596 N.E.2d 1028 (1992), *review denied*, 413 Mass. 1105, 600 N.E.2d 171; Carbone v. Planning Bd. of Beverly, 33 Mass. App. 909, 596 N.E.2d 1031 (1992), *review denied*, 413 Mass. 1104, 600 N.E.2d 171.

times greater than that sought before the planning board.

The point is that planning boards are advised to use their limited powers in the review of subdivision and approval not required plans cautiously and with a dose of reality. As long as the comprehensive permit statute remains a viable alternative to land development in the Commonwealth, an unsatisfied applicant before the planning board will always have an alternative. If the planning board does not use its waiver powers where and when appropriate, the very same parcel of land may be the subject of a much larger development with many more attendant problems, but without the need to comply with the board's rules and regulations. While it is true that planning boards are not required to grant a waiver, it is suggested that this discretionary power to grant a waiver is an extremely powerful tool.[54]

Planning boards may wish to include in their subdivision rules and regulations under what scenarios a waiver pursuant to § 81-R may be warranted. For example, the regulations may list the minimum conditions necessary for a waiver to be granted, examples of what the planning board considers "in the public interest" or related examples of when and how a waiver might be granted.

An additional problem that arises with respect to § 81-R waivers is the claim by an applicant that the very same waiver she requests today, was granted previously by the board under a similar situation. The intimation is that an equal protection claim is at hand if the board is not consistent with its grant of the desired waiver(s) pursuant to § 81-R.

The irony, of course, is that the Subdivision Control Law provides no guidance as to when waivers should or should not be granted, the grant or denial of a waiver is not tied to a comprehensive plan and the entire land development process is subject to unconstrained bargaining.[55] At issue is how a board would know when a potential equal protection problem was to arise without some standards within which to issue or deny waivers pursuant to § 81-R. While the unsuccessful plaintiff may argue an equal protection violation, the Courts, to date, have not been sympathetic.[56]

§ 10.07[8]   The Practical Role of the Board of Health in Subdivision Approval Process

G.L. c. 111, § 31 provides broad authority to boards of health to adopt and

---

[54] *See* Musto v. Planning Board of Medfield, 54 Mass. App. Ct. 831, 837 (2002), *citing* Miles v. Planning Board of Millbury, 404 Mass. 489, 490 (1989) and Mac-Rich Realty Construction, Inc. v. Planning Board of Southborough, 4 Mass. App. Ct. 79 (1976).

[55] See discussion in Chapters 2 and 5.

[56] *See* Lakeside Builders, Inc. v. Planning Board of Franklin, 56 Mass. App. Ct. 842, 847 (2002).

enforce health regulations designed to protect public health through a variety of controls. In 1959, the Supreme Judicial Court interpreted G.L. c. 111, § 31 as providing for "comprehensive, separate, additional source of authority for health regulations...The legislative history...shows no purpose to limit its scope."[57]

Comparatively, the role of the local board of health in the subdivision approval process is rather limited in scope. However, the health board has great power within its narrow range of authority. For example, the determination of all health questions respecting the disposal of sewerage in a subdivision that will not be connected to a municipal sewer is vested exclusively in the board of health, and any attempt by the planning board to address these concerns through its own rules will be invalid. The standard to be applied by the board of health in deciding whether to approve or disapprove a plan in whole or in part (or to require the imposition of conditions) is that found in § 81U, namely, whether "the lots shown on such plan [can] be used for building sites without injury to the public health."[58]

Further, the statutory language itself[59] suggests that the board's oversight in health matters is broader than simply sewerage disposal, and very possibly encompasses the broad range of health concerns entrusted to the board under G.L. c. 111. For example the Appeals Court has upheld a regulation of the Board of Health of Edgartown that, was directed at limiting nitrate pollution of drinking water wells. The method chosen to limit such pollution was to limit the size of dwellings and to prohibit guesthouses and multifamily dwellings.[60] The growing concern over nitrate pollution of ground and surface waters may prompt more boards of health to deny approval of subdivisions based on such concerns. In any case, boards of health as a matter of practice rarely concern themselves with matters other than proposed septic systems to serve the subdivision, and proposed wells if there is no municipal water supply. There is a form of grandfathering of subdivisions with respect to board of health regulations that is similar to the grandfathering with respect to zoning bylaws.[61] In essence, the land shown on the subdivision plan is governed by the board of health regulations in effect on the date the definitive plan was submitted, or on the date the preliminary plan was submitted if it is followed within seven months by a definitive plan. The grandfathering period extends through the approval process, during the pendency of any judicial appeal, and for three years after endorsement.

The Supreme Judicial Court, reversing the Appeals Court, has held that the

---

[57] Board of Health v. Sousa, 338 Mass. 547, 550–552 (1959).

[58] Fairbairn v. Planning Board of Barnstable, 5 Mass. App. 171, 360 N.E.2d 668 (1977).

[59] G.L. c. 41, § 81U. *See also* United Reis Homes, Inc. v. Planning Board of Natick, 359 Mass. 621, 270 N.E.2d 402 (1971).

[60] Hamel v.Board of Health, 40 Mass. App. 420, 664 N.E.2d 1199 (1996), *review denied*, 423 Mass. 1102, 667 N.E.2d 1158 (1996).

[61] G.L. c. 111, § 127P.

recommendations made by the board of health to the planning board under § 81U may impose more stringent requirements on the developer than would be required under the board of health's own regulations, without violating the developer's rights under the grandfathering provisions of G.L. c. 111, § 127P. But such recommendations may not actually "contradict" the board of health regulations applicable to the project under 127P.[62]

The Court states this somewhat elusive distinction as follows: "A recommendation by the board of health may supplement the regulations when they are silent on a given matter, but its recommendations may not contradict an existing regulation."[63]

Where the board of health disapproves a plan it must make specific findings as to which, if any, areas shown on the plan cannot be used for building sites without injury to the public health, and must include such findings and the reasons therefore in its report to the planning board. Where possible, the board of health must also make recommendations as to how such health problems can be corrected.[64]

Faced with an adverse report from the board of health, the planning board has no choice but to disapprove the plan[65] or to amend it according to the recommendations of the health board and to approve it as amended.[66] Therefore it is important to sound out the board of health shortly after the plan has been submitted to see if it has any serious concerns. In appropriate cases, a hearing should be requested before the health board in order to address its concerns prior to the planning board hearing and certainly well within the board of health's forty-five day comment period.

In the usual case, the health board will simply require that planning board approval be on condition that no building shall be built in the subdivision without prior approval of the health board or will refer to its regulations respecting the construction and installation of private drinking water wells on the use of on-site septic systems.

Municipal counsel should be aware, however, that the board of health is missing an important opportunity to review the cumulative public health impacts of new subdivisions where the board of health fails to provide commentary within the forty-five day period or relies on lot-by-lot reviews of wells or septic systems. For example, the board of health's review of a subdivision plan provides one of the

---

[62] Independence Park, Inc. v. Board of Health, 403 Mass. 477, 530 N.E.2d 1235 (1988).

[63] Independence Park, Inc. v. Board of Health, 403 Mass. 477, 481, 530 N.E.2d 1235 (1988).

[64] Independence Park, Inc. v. Board of Health, 403 Mass. 477, 481, 530 N.E.2d 1235 (1988).

[65] Fairbairn v. Planning Board of Barnstable, 5 Mass. App. 171, 360 N.E.2d 668 (1977).

[66] K. Hovnanian v. Planning Board of Taunton, 32 Mass. App. 480 (1992), *review denied*, 413 Mass. 1103.

few opportunities for a municipal agency to analyze a development's overall impact on public water supplies, downgradient natural resources or even nearby private drinking water wells. In many cases, these are issues identified as important concerns of the community, yet the only opportunity to review—and regulate—for these concerns is often during the board of health's review pursuant to G.L. c. 41, § 81-U.

Where the board of health does actually disapprove the subdivision, the propriety of its actions may now be tested by means of appeal under G.L. c. 41, § 81BB. The reviewing court may inquire into the legal and factual basis for the disapproval of the board of health.[67] This is of course a de novo proceeding and consequently one need not be as concerned as in the past to make a proper record before the health board.

§ 10.07[9]   Adequacy of Statement of Reasons for Planning Board's Disapproval of Plan.

The Subdivision Control Law implicitly assumes that the subdivision will, wherever possible, eventually be allowed. In furtherance of this goal § 81U requires that whenever a plan is disapproved the board shall "state in detail wherein the plan does not conform to the rules and regulations of the planning board ... and shall revoke its disapproval and approve a plan which as amended conforms to such rules and regulations... ."

In *North Landers Corp. v. Planning Bd. of Falmouth*,[68] the Supreme Judicial Court emphasized that the words "in detail" mean exactly that. The disapproval statement must apprise the applicant of the deficiencies in his plan with sufficient definiteness and detail to allow him or her to correct the disapproved plan and resubmit it for approval. The *North Landers* Court refers to "a legislative intent to maximize the dialogue between board and developer and thus to ensure the developer's right to approval of plans which are brought into compliance with the statutory and regulatory requirements applicable to the locus."[69] In a well-drafted decision the board's findings and conclusions will be keyed to specific sections of its rules and regulations. If a basis for denial exists in the rules and regulations but is not set out in the decision, it may not later be relied on in court to support that decision.[70]

---

[67] Loring Hills Developers Trust v. Planning Board of Salem, 374 Mass. 343, 372 N.E.2d 775 (1978), *overruling in part* the holding in Fairbairn v. Planning Board of Barnstable, 5 Mass. App. 171, 360 N.E.2d 668 (1977).

[68] 382 Mass. 432, 416 N.E.2d 934, at 942–943.

[69] North Landers Corp. v. Planning Bd. of Falmouth, 382 Mass. 432, 416 N.E.2d 934, at 942–943.

[70] Massachusetts Broken Stone Co. v. Planning Board, 45 Mass. App. 738 (1998).

Where the developer corrects the deficiencies set out by the board in its denial and resubmits it for approval, there must be another duly noticed public hearing before the board may approve the plan.[71] And where the changes in the plan involve matters within the purview of the board of health, such as drainage or on-site wastewater disposal, the plan must be resubmitted to that board.[72]

§ 10.07[10]   Conditional Approval of Plan Limited as to Time

It is settled that a planning board may, as a condition of approval, require that the roads and utilities shown on the plan be completed within a specified time.[73] This rule grew as an offshoot of the earlier rule that where a conditional approval is not challenged within the statutory period it becomes binding on the applicant and successors in interest even where the conditions are beyond the power of the board.[74] The earlier cases upholding the right of a planning board to limit the time of the validity of its approval dealt with condition language that explicitly provided for automatic recission if improvements were not completed within the designated time. However, in 1978[75] the Appeals Court held, "It is clear that when a plan has been approved upon conditions, the failure of any of the conditions will result in automatic recission of the approval." [citations omitted]. This statement is dicta, and is not the holding of the authorities cited in support of it, so each may make his or her own judgment of its effect.

§ 10.07[11]   Amendments to Previously Approved, or Disapproved, Plans After an Intervening Zoning Change.

Where a plan is submitted, approved, and later modified or amended by the planning board, on the motion of an interested person or on its own motion,[76] and there has been an intervening zoning change, the zoning change will not apply to the subdivision if the modification or amendment occurs within the freeze period provided by G.L. c. 40A, § 6 (¶ 6).[77] This rule also applies where a plan is submitted, disapproved, resubmitted and eventually approved.[78] Nor will the intervening zoning change apply to land shown on a plan the approval of which has

---

[71] Patelle v. Planning Bd. of Woburn, 6 Mass. App. 951, 383 N.E.2d 94 (1978), *later appeal*, 20 Mass. App. 279, 480 N.E.2d 35.

[72] Doeblin v. Tinkham Development Corp., 7 Mass. App. 720, 389 N.E.2d 1044 (1979).

[73] Campanelli, Inc. v. Planning Bd. of Ipswich, 358 Mass. 798, 261 N.E.2d 65 (1970); Costanza & Bertolino, Inc. v. Planning Board of North Reading, 360 Mass. 677, 277 N.E.2d 511 (1971). *See* G.L. c. 41, § 81U (¶ 5) as amended by St. 1981, c. 421.

[74] Campanelli, Inc. v. Planning Bd. of Ipswich, 358 Mass. 798, 261 N.E.2d 65 (1970).

[75] Patelle v. Planning Bd. of Woburn, 6 Mass. App. 951, 383 N.E.2d 94 (1978), *later appeal*, 20 Mass. App. 279, 480 N.E.2d 35.

[76] *See* G.L. c. 41, § 81W.

[77] Patelle v. Planning Bd. of Woburn, 20 Mass. App. 279, 480 N.E.2d 35 (1985).

[78] *See* Doliner v. Planning Board of Millis, 349 Mass. 691, 212 N.E.2d 460 (1965).

been rescinded by the board, either through an automatic recission provision in the Certificate of Action or by affirmative action of the board.[79] However, the statute suggests that the resubmitted plan will be governed by the subdivision rules and regulations as in effect on the date of its submission..[80]

§ 10.07[12]　Constructive Approval of Plans.

The statute[81] provides that failure of the planning board to take final action or to file with the city or town clerk a certificate of such action within either 90 or 135 days (depending on whether a preliminary plan was filed), after submission of the definitive plan, (or such further time as may be agreed upon at the written request of the applicant), results in a constructive approval of the plan. Thus the decision must be made and a written statement of that decision must be filed with the clerk, both within the statutory period. Where the board fails to act in a timely fashion, but later files its certificate of action, the late-filed certificate is a nullity.[82]

The formal requirements of the certificate of action are not great, but there must at least be a clear and unequivocal statement that final action on the plan of a specific type was taken by the board.[83] Otherwise a constructive approval will result.[84]

§ 10.07[13]　Effect of Restrictive Notes.

The planning board will very frequently, as a part of the subdivision approval process, endorse upon the plan as approved certain restrictive conditions. Somewhat less frequently the board will require such conditions to be endorsed upon a plan as a condition to an endorsement under G.L. c. 41, § 81P.

In either case, if the applicant does not take a statutory appeal under § 81BB at the time the restriction is imposed, but instead records the plan, he or she and any successors in interest will be bound by the restrictions.[85] No subsequent relief may be obtained from the effect of such restrictions from either the building inspector, the board of appeals,[86] or the planning board of appeals[87] (if one has been established). Relief may only be obtained through the planning board by means of a new plan submission or a release of the restriction.[88] In the case of conditions imposed as a part of subdivision approval under G.L. c. 41, § 81U, this is true even

---

[79] Heritage Park Dev. Corp. v. Town of Southbridge, 424 Mass. 71, 674 N.E.2d 233 (1997).

[80] G.L. c. 41, § 81U; Antonelli v. Planning Board of N. Andover, 4 LCR 67 (1996).

[81] G.L. c. 41, § 81U.

[82] Windsor v. Planning Bd. of Wayland, 26 Mass. App. 650, 531 N.E.2d 272 (1988).

[83] Kay-Vee Realty Co. v. Town Clerk of Ludlow, 355 Mass. 165, 243 N.E.2d 813 (1969).

[84] Zaltman v. Town Clerk of Stoneham, 5 Mass. App. 248, 362 N.E.2d 215 (1977).

[85] Bloom v. Planning Board of Brookline, 346 Mass. 278, 191 N.E.2d 684 (1963).

[86] G.L. c. 40A, § 12.

[87] G.L. c. 41, § 81Z.

[88] Marino v. Board of Appeal, 2 Mass. App. 859, 311 N.E.2d 580 (1974).

if the planning board has endorsed a later plan under § 81P which plan does not contain the restriction.[89]

§ 10.07[14]   Effect of Pre-existing Easements on Approvals of Plan

It frequently happens that land submitted for approval under the Subdivision Control Law is alleged to be burdened by various easements or restrictions. Often times these issues are raised by persons opposing approval of the plan. Unless the existence or non-existence of the easement or restriction directly affects the ability of the applicant to comply with the Subdivision Rules and Regulations, the board should not consider it.[90] In general, the existence of easements will not prevent land from being subdivided, nor will the subdivision of land affect the validity of any pre-existing easements or restrictions.

§ 10.07[15]   Problems Relative to Long-Term Maintenance of Engineering Structures

The increasing stringency of wetlands and groundwater protection regulations in the 1980's, along with the fact that most of the so-called "easy" sites have already been developed, has resulted in increased development of sites that present difficult regulatory problems. Consequently, more and more developments contain engineering structures that are sufficiently complex to require long-term maintenance, or even replacement, e.g., drainage retention facilities.

Local public works departments will very often strenuously object to assuming the maintenance of such structures, and planning boards will often respond by demanding assurances from the applicant that there are means in place to assure private maintenance of the facility. There can be formidable problems in creating workable and enforceable legal documents that will achieve this end. Form 53.5 in Volume 6, Chapter 11, is an example of one approach to solving this problem. It creates an association of subdivision homeowners that is responsible for proper maintenance and repair of subdivision infrastructure. See also G.L. c. 40A, § 9 regarding options available for the ownership of open spaces within "cluster" subdivisions.

§ 10.07[16]   Development In or Near Historically or Archeologically Significant Sites

Sections 26C and 27C of chapter 9 of the General Laws have been amended[91]

---

[89] Hamilton v. Planning Bd., 35 Mass. App. 386, 620 N.E.2d 44 (1993), summary op at (Mass. App.) 22 M.L.W. 127.

[90] Hahn v. Planning Bd. of Stoughton, 24 Mass. App. 553, 511 N.E.2d 20 (1987), *review denied*, 400 Mass. 1106, 513 N.E.2d 1289.

[91] St. 1988, c. 254.

to grant the Massachusetts Historical Commission significant jurisdiction over projects, including subdivisions, where (1) the project will have an adverse impact, direct or indirect, on properties or sites which were included in the Inventory of Historic Assets of the Commonwealth prior to the thirtieth day following the submission of the application for approval of the project; and (2) the project is undertaken, financed, or licensed by a state body, as defined in the statute.[92] (See Regulations of State Historical Commission in Appendix F.)

This potential regulatory exposure should be considered when seeking a superseding order on appeal to the DEP from a local conservation commission, for example, because the issuance of a permit from a state agency will invoke the provisions of G.L. c. 9, § 27C, just as it may invoke the Massachusetts Environmental Policy Act (G.L. c. 30, §§ 61–62H). See discussion in Section 8.02[3].

§ 10.07[17]   Requirement of Connection to Abutting Land

Where the subdivision abuts upon a tract of undeveloped land, belonging either to the developer or another person, the planning board will frequently require that a strip of land be reserved for use as a street to connect the subdivision to the streets in the abutting land once it is developed. It will also be required that the developer establish easement rights in the reserved strip running to the owner of the adjacent land. Although developers will sometime resist this requirement it is within the board's power.[93] Experience has shown that planning boards frequently fail to effectuate their intentions in this area by failing to require anything more than a designated easement area on the plan, or failing to follow up to see that necessary deed work is recorded. The historic intent of this provision was to ensure that newly developing cities and towns provided for through-ways and the opportunity to loop water and sewer mains, among other infrastructure. Today, at least in eastern Massachusetts, this common requirement with subdivision regulations seems outdated and in many cases, neither desirable by the developer, the abutting landowners or the local planning board.

§ 10.07[18]   Resubmission of Disapproved Plans

G.L. c. 41, § 81U provides, in part:

"In the event of disapproval the planning board shall state in detail wherein the plan does not conform to the rules and regulations of the planning board or the recommendation of the health board or officer and shall revoke its disapproval and approve a plan which, as amended, conforms to such rules and regulations or recommendations."

---

[92] *See* 950 CMR 71.00 *et seq.*
[93] Patel v Planning Bd. of North Andover, 27 Mass. App. 477, 539 N.E.2d 544 (1989).

This language on its face suggests, and many applicants have asserted, that a planning board must ministerially, and without further ceremony, approve a previously disapproved plan that has been corrected by the applicant and resubmitted. This is not the law. Resubmission of the plan requires the entire notice and hearing process to be begun anew.[94]

The applicant's attorney should be alert to the risk that a zoning freeze applicable to the subdivision may be lost if a zoning change has occurred between the time of submission of the preliminary plan or original definitive plan. It may be necessary to take an appeal of the planning board's disapproval—to freeze the rights in place when the plan was submitted—rather than or in addition to, submitting an amended plan for approval. The plan amendments requested by the planning board would then be made in the context of settlement of the litigation.[95] (See § 5.10 *supra*.)

A much-noted decision by the supreme judicial court, reversing the appeals court, holding that appeal of the denial of a definitive plan extends any zoning freeze applicable to the land shown on the plan (as opposed to the plan itself) points up the prudence of appealing the denial, even where a resubmission is intended.[96]

Logic suggests that where a plan is denied, and the applicant simply corrects the identified deficiencies and resubmits it, the zoning freeze should still apply, without the necessity of an appeal. However, the case law suggests otherwise. There is also a practical problem in trying to resubmit a revised plan after taking an appeal. The average planning board will be confused as to its role since the case is in litigation. It may even refuse to receive the amended plan.

§ 10.07[19]   Plan Approval Conditioned on Subsequent Compliance with Rules and Regulations

Subdivision rules and regulations frequently require that applicants demonstrate, as a prerequisite to plan approval, that they have the right to access public utilities, roadways or other infrastructure. Often such access rights may only be obtained through a separate regulatory process, which may itself be costly and time consuming.

Since the applicant usually will not pursue such access if the subdivision is not otherwise approved, he or she will often request that the board approve the plan conditioned on the later acquisition of necessary permits or access rights. Planning

---

[94] Doeblin v. Tinkham Development Corp., 7 Mass. App. 720, 389 N.E.2d 1044 (1979); Patelle v. Planning Bd. of Woburn, 6 Mass. App. 951, 383 N.E.2d 94 (1978), *later appeal*, 20 Mass. App. 279, 480 N.E.2d 35.

[95] Arenstam v. Planning Bd. of Tyngsborough, 29 Mass. App. 314, 560 N.E.2d 142 (1990).

[96] Massachusetts Broken Stone Co. v. Town of Weston, 430 Mass. 637 (2000).

boards commonly grant such conditional approvals, usually requiring that the other rights be acquired prior to endorsement of the plan, or prior to the issuance of building permits. Although not usually framed as such in board decisions, these conditions seem in legal effect to be partial waivers of the subdivision rules and regulations, of the type authorized under G.L. c. 41, § 81R.

Yet as common as such conditional approvals may be, and as unfair as the denial of such an approval may be in particular cases, it seems that the grant of such approvals is, as in the case of other rule waivers, very much in the discretion of the board. The applicant can be made by the board to take the time and incur the expense of obtaining other permits or rights prior to seeking subdivision approval, even where they will be unnecessary if the plan is not otherwise approved.[97]

§ 10.07[20]   Subdivision of Single Lot Containing Two or More Buildings

A lot that contains two or more buildings, which were standing when the Subdivision Control Law took effect in the city or town, may be subdivided without the need to file a subdivision plan, provided only one building remains standing on each newly created lot.[98] There is only one reported case construing this provision.[99] That case makes it clear that the division of the lot under § 81L does not make the resulting lots buildable under local zoning.

Indeed the lot division itself may create zoning violations that might require a variances or special permit to construct or re-construct a dwelling or other structure on the lot. The case also makes clear that each building to be left on its own lot must be substantial, that a detached garage, chicken coop or woodshed might not qualify. Just how substantial is a question the court left to be resolved later. Also unresolved is whether a local definition of "substantial" (contained within the zoning ordinance or bylaw and the subdivision rules and regulations) would allow a reviewing Court to grant deference to the planning board reviewing an ANR under this provision of G.L. c. 41, § 81-L.

This provision of G.L. c. 41, § 81-L, similar to the approval not required rules in general, are frequently met with disdain by planning boards and if they are aware of the petition, individuals abutting the petitioned lot. (Note that approval not required filings do not implicate the public hearing requirements of the Subdivision Control Law). It hardly seems logical to allow the division of land, without any municipal review, simply because a structure or structures of dubious quality were

---

[97]   K. Hovnanian at Taunton, Inc. v. Planning Bd. of Taunton, 32 Mass. App. 480, 590 N.E.2d 1172 (1992), *review denied*, 413 Mass. 1103, 597 N.E.2d 1371.

[98]   G.L. c. 41, § 81L.

[99]   Citgo Petroleum Corp. v. Planning Board of Braintree, 24 Mass. App. 425, 509 N.E.2d 284 (1987).

constructed on the lot fifty or three hundred years earlier.

But the concerns of the planning board and the abutters are overstated. While the Subdivision Control Law strips planning boards of substantive review authority as to the creation of the lots, Citgo does not preclude revisions to the zoning bylaw or ordinance that subjects substandard lots and the structures on those lots, to a rigorous review by the board of health and board of appeals pursuant to G.L. c. 40A, § 6

CHAPTER 11

SUBDIVISION CONTROL—THE PRACTICE

Synopsis

§ 11.01   Applying for Subdivision Approval
      § 11.01[1]   Preliminary Information
      § 11.01[2]   Approval Not Required Plans
      § 11.01[3]   Decide Whether to Submit a Preliminary Plan
      § 11.01[4]   Submit Definitive Plan
      § 11.01[5]   Prepare for Public Hearing
      § 11.01[6]   After the Hearing, Follow-up
      § 11.01[7]   Flow Chart—The Process of Securing Approval of Subdivision
      § 11.01[8]   Controlling Subdivision Appearance and Amenities-Restrictive Covenants

§ 11.01 Applying for Subdivision Approval

§ 11.01[1] Preliminary Information

Step 1. Obtain basic initial information from the client which is necessary to complete the Information List—Obtaining Approvals of Subdivisions, Volume 6, Chapter 11.

Step 2. Discuss in general terms with the client the circumstances surrounding his or her plans. What exists on the site, what is adjacent to it, what the client plans to do and when, how the client's proposal relates to the present use of surrounding property, any past relations with abutters, the client's estimate of the nature and intensity of opposition, and so on. Decide whether the client's plan needs approval as a subdivision. (See § 10.01, *supra*).

Step 3. Obtain a current copy of rules and regulations of the planning board from the clerk of the board or the city or town clerk.

Step 4. Confirm that the rules you have obtained are identical with those recorded at the Registry of deeds. Only rules that have been transmitted to the registry are effective.

Step 5. Obtain compilation of zoning bylaw or ordinances. Try to obtain all amendments to the bylaw adopted since publication of the booklet. To be certain you have picked up all amendments talk to the building inspector or zoning officer. These officials sometimes put out bad information so the only way to be completely sure is to review all town meeting warrants or city council minutes back to the date of the booklet you are using.

§ 11.01[2] Approval Not Required Plans

Step 6. Where you believe that your client can accomplish his or her purposes by a division of the parcel which leaves each lot with adequate frontage on a public or previously approved way or on a way likely to be satisfactory to the planning board (see discussion in Section 10.02), have the proper plan drawn and submit the plan to the board (with a copy to the City or Town Clerk along with proper statutory notice) with the request that it be stamped "approval not required." (*See* § 10.02, *supra*). (*See* Volume 6, Chapter 11, Form 49).

Step 7. Diary a date 21 days from the date of submission. If the board takes no action for this period, it is deemed to have determined that approval was not required. Obtain endorsement of the board on the plan or certificate of the city or town clerk that approval under the subdivision control law is not required and record at the registry of deeds.

If the board finds that the plan constitutes a subdivision and notifies you with 21 days, you have 20 days to appeal this decision to the courts or you must seek approval pursuant to the Subdivision Control Law.

§ 11.01[3]   Decide Whether to Submit a Preliminary Plan

Step 8. If the land proposed for subdivision is residentially zoned, decide with the client and engineer whether to submit a preliminary plan, which is a kind of rough draft of the proposal. In the case of a nonresidential subdivision a preliminary plan must be submitted. (*See* § 10.03, *supra*.) As a general rule, it is advisable to prepare and file a preliminary plan.

Step 9. Have the preliminary plan, if any, prepared by a qualified engineer who is familiar with the requirements of statute and local board rules.

Step 10. Notify the town clerk by certified mail that the preliminary plan has been submitted. (Volume 6, Chapter 11, Forms 50 and 51).

Step 11. Diary the date 45 days after submission of the preliminary plan. The board must notify the applicant of its approval or disapproval within this period. (*See* § 10.03, *supra*).

Step 12. Use the time after submission to contact officials and make accommodations where possible to their objections or suggestions.

Step 13. After a decision on the preliminary plan is issued, or after the 45-day period has run with no decision, prepare to submit the definitive plan. Note carefully the reasons given for any disapproval of the preliminary plan to see if these problems are correctable.

§ 11.01[4]   Submit Definitive Plan

Step 14. Diary the date 7 months from the date of filing preliminary plan. The definitive plan must be filed by this date in order to retain the freeze on zoning and subdivision rules and regulations. (*See* § 10:3, *supra*).

Step 15. Have definitive plan prepared by a qualified engineer in accordance with the requirements of statute and board rules. If a preliminary plan has been submitted, where possible incorporate suggested modifications of the planning board and other officials into the definitive plan.

Step 16. Prepare notice of submission of definitive plan. (Volume 6, Chapter 11, Form 52).

Step 17. Obtain from the Assessors' office a certified copy of the names and addresses of the owners of all land abutting the subject property as appearing in the most recent tax list.

Step 18. Submit the definitive plan, along with the list of abutters, to the planning board. If the subdivision contains or borders wetlands file a Notice of Intent with the conservation commission. (Volume 6, Chapter 11, Forms 45.2, 45.3 and 53.)

Step 19. Submit plan to the board of health. Frequently percolation and water table determination tests are taken at or even before the preliminary plan stage; if this has not been done, arrange to have it done unless the subdivision will be served by a public sewer. (Volume 6, Chapter 11, Form 54) The health board must report to the planning board its approval or disapproval within 45 days of submission to it; failure to report is deemed to be approval.

Note that boards of health have very different requirements as to percolation testing requirements. While a methodology exists to calculate high water tables throughout the Commonwealth (the so-called "Frimpter method"), many jurisdictions require water table measurements to be taken only allowed during certain months (usually in the spring). Determine the local requirements well in advance of your application.

Step 20. At the same time the plan is submitted to the planning board send the notice of submission to the town or city clerk, certified mail, return receipt requested.

§ 11.01[5] Prepare for Public Hearing

Step 21. If no preliminary plan has been submitted, prior to the hearing try to meet with the planning board, town engineer, board of health, and any other town officials who may have expressed concerns. If a preliminary plan has been submitted and modified it will usually be enough to contact the relevant officials by phone to see if the definitive plan is acceptable as modified. Contact the conservation commission to see if they will be asking for major changes in the plan.

Step 22. Be sure that the proper publication and mail notice of the public hearing has been given by the planning board. (*See* § 10.04, *supra*).

Step 23. Prior to the hearing, if serious objection to the plan is expected, try to ascertain the source and nature of the objection and prepare to meet it as well as you can. Have your engineer with you to answer questions. Do not be argumentative, irascible, or condescending. Make your points firmly but courteously.

Remind the board that compliance with published regulations entitles your client to have his or her plan approved. (*See* § 10.04, *supra*).

Step 24. Be prepared to resist as much as possible the imposition of onerous "conditions" of approval that may be beyond the power of the board.

If such illegal conditions are imposed you must either appeal or they will become binding. (*See* § 10.04, *supra*). But it may be better to live with the conditions than put up with the delays of litigation.

§ 11.01[6] After the Hearing, Follow-up

Step 25. Diary the date 90 days after the date of submission of the definitive plan, if you filed a preliminary plan, or 135 days if no preliminary plan was filed. If the board has not acted by this date and filed its certificate of Action with the town clerk, the plan is deemed approved, unless you consent to a delay in writing. Often you will be offered a choice between consenting to a delay and being denied. If you feel the requested extension is sincerely sought and is not a mere delaying tactic you should agree.

Step 26. If the board fails to act, diary the date 20 days after the date of deemed approval. If no appeal is taken request a certificate to this effect from the clerk, obtain the plan and record both at the registry. (*See* § 10.04, *supra*).

Step 27. If the plan is disapproved, diary the date 20 days after the date the notice of the disapproval was filed with the town clerk. Any appeal must be filed within this time. (*See* § 10.04, *supra*).

Step 28. Examine the reasons given by the board for disapproval to evaluate their legal sufficiency. Discuss possibilities of appeal with client.

Step 29. If an appeal is taken, notice of appeal must be filed with the city or town clerk within the same 20-day period as in Step 27, *supra*. Note filing here means actual receipt by the clerk. (Volume 6, Chapter 11, Form 55).

Step 30. If plan is approved, before endorsement of the plan the board will require that restrictive covenants or a performance bond be filed to assure proper installation of streets and utilities. Obtain the standard form agreements from the board secretary. Diary the date 20 days after notice of approval filed with town clerk.

Step 31. If negotiation is necessary respecting the bond or restrictions make an appointment with the board.

Step 32. File the agreed upon bond and/or restrictions. (Volume 6, Chapter 11, Forms 53.4 and 53.5).

Step 33. After the 20-day appeal period has expired secure the signatures (endorsement) of a majority of the planning board on the plan indicating approval, and obtain a certificate of the municipal clerk that no notice of appeal was received during the appeal period.

Step 34. Diary the date 6 months from the date of the endorsement or certificate of the clerk. Record the plan in the registry of deeds on or before this date.

§ 11.01[7]   Flow Chart—The Process of Securing Approval of Subdivision

[SEE CHART IN ORIGINAL]

§ 11.01[8]   Controlling Subdivision Appearance and Amenities-Restrictive Covenants

If the developer intends the subdivision to be the site of more expensive homes, or otherwise wishes to impose uniform standards on its development, it may be necessary to impose restrictive covenants on the lots prior to sale. The specific restrictions on site development can be varied to fit the particular development, but the kinds of things that are regulated by the various forms of restrictions in use tend to be the same. Probably the major difference in these types of restrictions is whether or not site development and building alteration continues to be regulated after the developer has sold out of the project. Form 53.6 in Volume 6, Chapter 11, is a form of subdivision restrictive covenants that creates a Planning Committee of lot owners to control site and building development after the developer has sold a certain number of lots. The use of this form can sometimes create marketing problems because certain prospective purchasers will resent this limitation on the future use of their property. These forms are most commonly used in very upscale developments. Form 53.7 in Volume 6, Chapter 11, is a form of subdivision restrictive covenants that allows the developer to control site development, but imposes no controls after the lot is built upon and sold to the individual lot owner who will live there.

CHAPTER 12

FORECLOSURE OF REAL ESTATE MORTGAGES—LAW AND PRACTICE

Synopsis

§ 12.01   Matters Preliminary to Instituting Foreclosure

§ 12.02   Prerequisites to Instituting Foreclosure Proceedings

§ 12.03   Court Proceedings

§ 12.04   The Foreclosure—Notice and Sale
            § 12.04[1]   Deeds In Lieu of Foreclosure

§ 12.05   Redemption

§ 12.06   Bankruptcy

§ 12.07   Default and Foreclosure
            § 12.07[1]   Actions Prior to Foreclosure Sale
            § 12.07[2]   Actions Taken at Foreclosure Sale
            § 12.07[3]   Actions Taken After Foreclosure Sale

§ 12.01   Matters Preliminary to Instituting Foreclosure

Prior to instituting foreclosure proceedings it is wise to examine the note and mortgage. As a rule the note will be one of a number of standard pre-printed forms which are widely available from legal stationers. The provisions of the note and mortgage should be checked to be sure there is an acceleration clause and to assure compliance with all the conditions precedent to the right to accelerate.

Similarly the mortgage will usually be of a standard form containing statutory conditions and power of sale.[1] Nonetheless the mortgage terms should be checked carefully to be sure there are no surprises and that all terms of the mortgage are strictly complied with during foreclosure.

Where a second mortgage is involved and the property consists of a dwelling house with six or less separate households which is occupied in whole or in part at the time the loan is made as a home by any mortgagor or obligor the papers should be examined for compliance with G.L. c. 140, § 90B. This statute requires that the note and mortgage must specify as separate items the principal sum, the rate of interest or its equivalent in money, the period of the loan, and the periodic due dates, if any, of principal and interest. A lender who fails to comply with this provision has no right to collect interest.

The mortgagee's attorney should also check with the assessors' office to ascertain whether the property is being taxed as agricultural/horticultural land under G.L. c. 61A, or as recreational land under G.L. c. 61B. Where such land is involved the mortgagee must give written notice of the foreclosure sale, 90 days before the sale date, to the Mayor and City Council or Board of Selectmen, to the Assessors, Planning Board, and Conservation Commission. The notice must identify the land and state the time and place of sale. Such notice must be sent certified mail.

§ 12.02   Prerequisites to Instituting Foreclosure Proceedings

Where a second mortgage on owner-occupied residential real estate containing six or fewer units and assessed for forty thousand dollars or less is involved the mortgagee must give "at least 15 days prior to the commencement of foreclosure proceedings, by certified mail, a statement of intention to foreclose which shall specify the amount of principal, interest, and other indebtedness, if any, owing and accruing under the note and mortgage." Failure by the mortgagee to comply with this requirement suspends his or her rights until he or she complies.

In order to have the right to bring an action for a deficiency in the event the amount realized at the foreclosure sale is not sufficient to satisfy the debt, the mortgagee must send a notice of intention to foreclose together with a warning of

---

[1] G.L. c. 183, § 20, 21.

liability for the deficiency to the person sought to be charged with the deficiency at his or her last known address, by certified mail, not less than 21 days before the date of sale, and an affidavit must be signed and sworn to, within 30 days after the foreclosure sale, of the mailing of such notice. The notice must be in substantially the form set forth in the statute.[1] These statutory requirements are strictly enforced and any substantial deviation from them will defeat a later suit against the mortgagor for a deficiency. Even actual notice by the mortgagor will not cure the failure to comply with the requirements of § 17B.[2] The deficiency notice need not be sent where the mortgage is foreclosed by entry and possession.[3]

Since § 17B is directed to deficiency after foreclosure of a mortgage securing the note, it does not require holders of multiple mortgages exercising rights under a senior instrument to give notice regarding rights they were not exercising under junior instruments. Thus, where a bank held first and third mortgages and did not foreclose on the third, there could be no deficiency after foreclosure of that mortgage and no notice was required under the statute.[4]

Although the two most recent cases construing § 17B are not congruent in certain minor respects on these points, prudence dictates that if there is any possibility that a foreclosing mortgagee intends to seek to recover any deficiency which may result, the notice should be given to anyone whose name appears on the note in any capacity.[5] Likewise, makers or guarantors who intend to seek contribution from their co-makers or co-guarantors should pass along to them any § 17B notice they receive.[6] The bringing of proceedings seeking authorization to foreclose under the Soldiers and Sailors Civil Relief Act constitutes the "commencement of foreclosure proceedings,"[7] and probably brings this statute into play. Consequently the sending of this notice, where required, should be the first step in the foreclosure proceeding.

The statutory language of both § 14 and § 17B is phrased in terms of the sending of notice, and not its receipt. They do not explicitly, or implicitly, state that such notice must be received, only that it must be sent. The Appeals Court has resolved some earlier confusion on the question of whether the notice must actually have been received by the mortgage debtor. The rule now is that when a mortgagee has adhered to the statutory prescription for notice it will not be required to demonstrate

---

[1] G.L. c. 244, § 17 B. Framingham Sav. Bank v. Turk, 40 Mass. App. 384, 664 N.E.2d 472 (1996), *review denied*, 422 Mass. 1110, 665 N.E.2d 1003 (1996).

[2] Bead Portfolio, LLC v. Follayttar, 47 Mass. App. 533 (1999).

[3] Wornat Dev. Corp. v. Vakalis, 403 Mass. 340, 529 N.E.2d 1329 (1988).

[4] BankBoston, N.A. v. Yodice, 54 Mass. App. Ct. 901, 763 N.E.2d 80 (2002).

[5] *But see* SKW Real Estate Limited Partnership v. Gold, 428 Mass. 520 (1998).

[6] G.L. c. 140, § 90B; Federal Credit Union v. Laterman, 40 Mass. App. 116 (1996).

[7] *See* Petti v. Putignano, 8 Mass. App. 293, 393 N.E.2d 935 (1979).

actual receipt. Conversely, where the statutory notice requirements are not followed it will not help the mortgagee to show that the debtor had actual notice of the foreclosure sale.[8]

The mortgagee need notify only those persons (including mortgagors), liable on obligations secured by the mortgage, whom the mortgagee chooses to make targets of a potential deficiency claim. There is no statutory obligation to notify guarantors, because the liability of a guarantor does not flow from "an obligation secured by a mortgage of real estate" but is independent of that obligation.[9] An action to recover a deficiency judgment must be brought within two years after the date of the foreclosure sale, or two years after the maturity date of the principal, whichever is later.[10]

§ 12.03   Court Proceedings

In Massachusetts, court proceedings are not required to effect the foreclosure itself. Instead, such proceedings are merely an inquiry into whether the owner(s) of the equity of redemption are entitled to the benefit of the Soldiers and Sailors Civil Relief Act.[1] This is the only issue in the case. If the court answers the question in the negative it must enter a judgment authorizing the foreclosure.[2]

For foreclosures after December 31, 1990, no proceeding under the Act need be brought if the record owner of the equity of redemption on the 30th day next preceding the foreclosure sale is one or more of the following entities, whether domestic or foreign:

a) a corporation,

b) a limited partnership,

c) a Massachusetts business trust under G.L. c. 182,

d) a general partnership limited liability company or joint venture of which all the general partners of record appear to be one or more of the foregoing types of entities.

Recording a copy of the judgment authorizing foreclosure in the appropriate

---

[8] Carmel Credit Union v. Bondeson, 55 Mass. App. Ct. 557, 561 (2002); Framingham Savings Bank v. Turk, 40 Mass. App. Ct. 384, 386 (1996).

[9] Seronick v. Levy, 26 Mass. App. 367, 527 N.E.2d 746 (1988), *review denied*, 403 Mass. 1104, 530 N.E.2d 797.

[10] G.L. c. 244, § 17A.

[1] St. 1943, c. 57, St. 1945, c. 120, St. 1951, c. 25, St. 1959, c. 105.

[2] Beaton v. Land Court, 367 Mass. 385, 326 N.E.2d 302 (1975), *appeal dismissed*, 423 U.S. 806, 46 L, Ed, 2d 27, 96 S. Ct. 16; Guleserian v. Pilgrim Trust Co., 331 Mass. 431, 120 N.E.2d 193 (1954).

registry of deeds and city or town clerk's office constitutes conclusive evidence of compliance with the Act, to the extent the Court has power to determine the same, as against all persons whose interests appeared of record prior to the recording of the Order of Notice, if they were named as defendants or otherwise had notice of the proceedings.[3]

The usual procedure is to obtain a judgment under the Soldiers and Sailors Act before beginning the steps leading to the actual sale of the property. Occasionally these steps are initiated while the court proceedings are pending, although delays in the court system can make this risky. In emergency situations foreclosure is sometimes undertaken without court proceedings with appropriate legal proceedings later being taken to clear up the title. Naturally the latter course should only be taken where the mortgagee's attorney is confident that no party in interest has the benefit of the Act. These last mentioned so-called "fast track" foreclosures are controversial among the conveyancing bar. It seems fair to say that the majority of current opinion is that they present unacceptable risk and should rarely be used.

§ 12.04 The Foreclosure—Notice and Sale

Once the court authorization to foreclose is obtained and the date for the foreclosure sale is chosen the mortgagee must begin the actual statutory foreclosure proceedings. The requirements for foreclosure are carefully laid out and must be strictly observed.[1]

For foreclosures after June 28, 1998, no proceeding under the act need be brought if the record owner of the equity of redemption on the 30th day next preceding the foreclosure sale is either a limited liability company or a limited liability partnership, or one of the entities referred to in the main text. It should be noted that there is no statutory or decisional authority for this 30-day period. It is generally accepted and has its roots in the requirement of notice of sale to equity owners and holders of junior encumbrances as of thirty days prior to sale which is found in G.L. c. 244, § 14. Where the foreclosing mortgagee becomes aware of a transfer of title to a person who is not exempt from the provisions of the Act in the thirty-day period before the foreclosure sale. Conservative practice may dictate postponement of the sale pending compliance with the act.

These proceedings are begun by sending the statutory notice of sale to all parties in interest by certified mail. Notice must also be published in a newspaper which:

a) is published in the town where the land lies, or

b) has a general circulation in such town, or

---

[3] St. 1990, c. 496, § 1.
[1] G.L. c. 244, § 14.

c) if neither of these is available, then is published in the county where the land lies. A newspaper which by its title page purports to be printed or published in the appropriate town or county is sufficient for the purpose.

The notice should be strictly in accordance with the form set out in the statute. It should set out all encumbrances prior to the mortgage being foreclosed whether or not listed in the mortgage. Note that "no purchaser at the sale shall be bound to complete the purchase if there are encumbrances other than those named in the mortgage and included in the notice of sale which are not stated at the sale and included in the auctioneer's contract with the purchaser."[2]

Notice must be sent on or before the 14th day prior to sale by certified mail to the owners of the equity of redemption and to the owners of the junior encumbrances as of 30 days prior to the date of sale.[3]

The auctioneer is not, however, bound to sell the property in accordance with the terms of sale advertised in the notice. Such terms may be changed by the auctioneer as long as the changed terms are announced prior to the commencement of the auction sale and are included in the auctioneer's contract with the eventual purchaser.[4]

In the case of the owners of the equity of redemption, the notice goes to the address set forth in G.L. c. 185, § 61 where registered land is involved. If the land is unregistered notice goes to:

a) the last address of the owner or owners of the equity of redemption appearing on the records of the holder of the mortgage, or

b) if none, to the address of the owners as given on the deed or probate petition by which title was acquired, if any, or

c) if in either case no address appears, to the address to which the tax collector last sent the tax bill for the premises, or

d) if no tax bill has been sent for the last three years, to the address of any of the parcels in the name of the owner.

Notice sent to holders of junior interests must be mailed to the address of such persons set forth in any document evidencing their interest or to the last address of such person known to the mortgagee.

If a Federal tax lien has been recorded on or before the 31st day before the

---

[2] G.L. c. 244, § 14.

[3] *See* § 12.02, *infra* for discussion of question of necessity for receipt of notice.

[4] Dundas Corp. v Chemical Bank, 400 Mass. 588, 511 N.E.2d 520 (1987).

foreclosure sale, the sale will be subject to the lien unless on or before 25 days prior to the sale, a written notice of sale is given by certified mail or personal service to the District Director for the district in which the sale is to be conducted, marked attention of "Chief, Special Procedures Staff." The notice must contain:

a) the name and address of the person submitting the notice of sale;

b) a copy of each Notice of Federal Tax Lien (Form 668) relating to the property, or if a copy of the lien is not provided, then, the Internal Revenue District named in the lien the name and address of the taxpayer and the date and place of filing of the notice of lien;

c) a detailed description of the property including address, city, state, legal description and, if available, copy of the abstract of title;

d) the date, time, place and terms of the sale; and

e) the approximate amount of the principal obligation, plus interest secured by the mortgage, and a description of the other expenses which may be charged against the sale proceeds.[5]

Where the notice of sale is properly given to the IRS the sale at foreclosure will not be subject to the Federal tax lien. However, the government has the right to redeem the property from the purchaser at foreclosure by tendering the amount paid within 120 days from the date of the foreclosure auction. The purchaser at the foreclosure sale may apply to the IRS requesting that it release its redemption rights prior to the expiration of the 120 day period. Such application is made to the District Director.

Obviously where a foreclosing mortgagee bids in the property he or she must be sure to bid an amount sufficient to cover the debt and costs owed if there is an outstanding Federal tax lien on the property.

Where there is an outstanding junior Massachusetts tax lien the Commonwealth should be given the same notice as other junior lienholders.

In exercising a power of sale in a mortgage the mortgagee is required to act in good faith and to use reasonable diligence to protect the interests of the mortgagor.[6] However this duty does not preclude the mortgagee from bidding at the foreclosure sale and buying in at the lowest price possible.[7]

If the title examination of the property reveals that the property is subject to an agricultural restriction under G.L. c. 61A, § 9, is recreational land under G.L. c.

---

[5] 26 U.S.C.S. § 7425(b), (c) and Regs. thereunder.

[6] Seppala & Aho Constr. Co. v. Petersen, 373 Mass. 316, 367 N.E.2d 613 (1977).

[7] G.L. c. 183, § 25; Cambridge Sav. Bank v. Cronin, 289 Mass. 379, 194 N.E. 289 (1935).

61B, § 6, or is forest land as defined in G.L. c. 61, § 2, then more stringent notice requirements must be met before a sale may take place. For instance, notice by certified mail must be provided to the mayor and council or board of selectmen, assessors, planning board, and conservation commission ninety days prior to the foreclosure sale. G.L. c. 61A, § 14; G.L. c. 61B, § 9, G.L. c. 61, § 8. Proof of notice to the city or town can be demonstrated by recording an affidavit attesting to such notice.

Mere inadequacy of price will not invalidate a foreclosure sale unless it is so gross as to indicate bad faith or lack of reasonable diligence. And the mere fact that the mortgagee was the only bidder at the sale does not establish that the price received was so grossly inadequate as to invalidate the sale.[8]

The mortgagee may get a bargain at the foreclosure sale, but a nominal bid followed by a suit to recover a deficiency on the underlying instrument will not likely survive judicial challenge.[9]

The most important thing is for the mortgagee to avoid conduct that could be construed as "chilling" the sale. Chilling of the sale is conduct inconsistent with the mortgagee's duty of good faith and due diligence, which has arguably resulted in a diminished price being paid for the property at foreclosure. The mortgagee must use reasonable diligence to get the best price and must avoid setting conditions or conducting the sale in a manner such as to reduce either the supply of viable bidders or the price.

In determining whether this duty has been met the courts use a rule of reason test. The standard is what a man of ordinary prudence would do in an effort to ensure that he received the best possible price at a forced sale of his or her own property.[10]

The foreclosure sale must take place on or near the mortgaged premises, or if more than one parcel is being sold then on or near one of the parcels, or at such place as may be designated for the purpose in the mortgage.[11]

If there is a voluntary, or forced, postponement of an advertised foreclosure sale the attorney or auctioneer should appear at the date, time and place of the sale to announce the postponement and to obtain the names, addresses and telephone numbers of potential bidders who appear. No re-advertisement or written notice

---

[8] Chartrand v. Newton Trust Co., 296 Mass. 317, 5 N.E.2d 421 (1936).

[9] *See* Danvers Sav. Bank v. Hammer, 122 N.H. 1, 440 A.2d 435 (1982) (applying Massachusetts law); *See* Victorine v. Gudmand, 25 Mass. App. 992, 522 N.E.2d 7 (1988), for discussion of mortgagors' rights in such cases.

[10] Manoog v. Miele, 350 Mass. 204, 213 N.E.2d 917 (1966); Cambridge Sav. Bank v. Cronin, 289 Mass. 379, 194 N.E. 289 (1935).

[11] G.L. c. 183, § 21.

of the continued foreclosure sale date are required under State law.[12]

If the sale produces a surplus over the amount owed to the foreclosing mortgagee it goes to junior creditors in order of priority, and finally to the mortgagor. Junior lienholders have an equitable lien in the surplus proceeds.[13] The foreclosing mortgagee can either pay the surplus over to the parties he or she deems entitled, with an indemnity agreement, or, as is more commonly done, file an interpleader action and pay the surplus into court. An insurer foreclosing a first mortgage it holds by assignment and subrogation may not through the foreclosure process wipe out junior mortgagees that were named as loss payees in its policy.[14]

Where a contract is entered into at the foreclosure sale and a deposit received, and where the successful bidder fails to complete the sale, the deposit may be applied to the expenses of sale with any surplus being applied to the mortgage debt.[15]

§ 12.04[1]   Deeds In Lieu of Foreclosure

Because of delays in obtaining court approval of foreclosure, and occasionally for other reasons as well, mortgagees will sometimes seek deeds in lieu of fore-closure from defaulting mortgagors. The use of this technique presents a number of problems:

a) The mortgagee will take subject to encumbrances intervening between the recording of the mortgage and the deed.[16]

b) In the case of condominiums, depending on the condominium documents, a first mortgagee may end up holding a unit subject to claims for fee arrearages which would otherwise be cut off by the foreclosure.

c) The mortgagor/grantor or those claiming under him or her may try to defeat the conveyance by asserting that it was intended to be a mortgage subject to later redemption upon payment of the debt.

d) In the event of a bankruptcy filing by the mortgagor the creditors may try to set the conveyance aside as a preference or fraudulent conveyance. Where a deed in lieu is used it will customarily contain language intended to forestall any later claim that it is really a new mortgage. It is also customary to obtain an estoppel statement or affidavit from the mortgagor/grantor again asserting

---

[12] Fitzgerald v. First National Bank of Boston, 46 Mass. App. 98 (1999).

[13] First Colonial Bank for Sav. v. Bergeron, 38 Mass. App. 136, 646 N.E.2d 758 (1995).

[14] The Money Store/Massachusetts, Inc. v. Hingham Mutual Fire Insurance Co., 46 Mass. App. 636 (1999).

[15] G.L. c. 183, § 27.

[16] See J & W Wall Systems, Inc. v. Shawmut First Bank & Trust Co., 413 Mass. 42, 594 N.E.2d 859 (1992).

the absolute nature of the conveyance, the consideration for the conveyance, the non-fraudulent nature of the conveyance, and anything else the mortgagee's attorney thinks may be useful later on. (*See*Volume 6, Chapter 13, Form 87.2). The Appeals Court has held that a deed in lieu of foreclosure is the functional equivalent of a formal foreclosure, at least for purposes of consumer protection statutes such as G.L. c. 183A, § 22.[17]

e) Determination of who pays the deed stamps. The Department of Revenue requires that documentary stamps be paid as part of a deed-in-lieu of foreclosure transaction. No deed stamps would be required if the mortgage remains in place and the property is conveyed subject to the mortgage, even if the borrower is freed from liability. While in some cases a deed-in-lieu of foreclosure benefits both parties, it may also create problems with the title. Since it is considered to be a voluntary conveyance, encumbrances placed on the property after the mortgage remain on the property. The same is not true if a lender proceeds with a mortgage foreclosure.

§ 12.05   Redemption

By statute[1] a mortgagor is entitled to redeem the mortgaged premises after breach of a mortgage condition in accordance with carefully prescribed rules. Redemption must be commenced before the three-year period after entry for purposes of foreclosure has expired or before the property has been sold pursuant to a power of sale.[2]

The person seeking to redeem must pay or tender the whole amount due under the mortgage and must perform any other condition of the same. If the mortgagee refuses the tender, the mortgagor can commence suit to redeem within one year from the date of tender. Upon filing suit, the mortgagor must pay the amount tendered into court if he or she wishes to be sure of stopping any scheduled foreclosure sale.

The right to redeem can spring back to life if the successful bidder fails to close on the property. Between the time of the auction sale and the time of delivery of the deed, the owner has the right to an accounting for rents and profits,[3] carries responsibility for casualty.[4]

§ 12.06   Bankruptcy

The filing of a petition in bankruptcy, whether voluntary or involuntary, will

---

[17] Moloney v. Boston Five Cents Sav. Bank FSB, 422 Mass. 431, 663 N.E.2d 811 (1996).

[1] G.L. c. 244, § 18–35.

[2] Outpost Cafe, Inc. v. Fairhaven Sav. Bank, 3 Mass. App. 1, 322 N.E.2d 183 (1975).

[3] Beal v. Attleborough Savings Bank, 248 Mass. 342 (1924).

[4] Schanberg v. Automobile Ins. Co. of Hartford, 285 Mass. 316 (1934).

automatically stay any foreclosure proceedings. The mortgagee may file with the Bankruptcy Court a request for relief from the stay; and the stay is terminated as of 30 days from the date of filing of such request, unless the Court, after notice and hearing, continues the stay in effect. In spite of the provisions in the Code for expedited treatment of requests for relief from foreclosure stays, the filing of a bankruptcy petition will usually result in many weeks of delay before the fore-closure sale can be held.[1]

During the 1980s, two federal bankruptcy judges sitting in the District of Massachusetts held that a foreclosure sale, conducted strictly in accordance with Massachusetts law, could still be set aside as a fraudulent conveyance under 11 U.S.C.S. § 548, where such sale was conducted

1) within a year of the bankruptcy petition,

2) the mortgagor was insolvent or was rendered insolvent by the sale, and

3) the property was sold for less than "reasonably equivalent value."[2]

Assuming the one-year and insolvency tests were met, the validity of the sale was held to depend on the bankruptcy court's conclusion as to whether "equivalent value" was paid.

While each of the two judges took a different approach to the standards to be used in determining whether equivalent value was paid at the sale, they each, in effect, took a wide disparity between market value and foreclosure sale price as the catalyst for further analysis of the circumstances of the sale. Once the disparity was established, the proponents of the sale had to show to the court's satisfaction some sort of aggressive advertising of the sale to prospective purchasers, along with the absence of any so-called "chilling" activities in the terms or conduct of the sale.[3]

The so-called *Ruebeck* line of cases resulted in the establishment of certain standard methods and procedures in the conduct of mortgage foreclosures in Massachusetts. More aggressive advertising of foreclosure sales became com-monplace, as did pre-foreclosure appraisals, and the so-called 70% rule, which held that the mortgagee should bid at least 70% of the appraised value. All of this was well beyond the requirements imposed upon foreclosing mortgagees by Massa-chusetts case law, which required only compliance with applicable statutes, good

---

[1] 11 U.S.C.S. § 362(a), (d), (e).

[2] *In re* Ruebeck , 55 B.R. 163, 13 Bankr. Ct. Dec. 1106, Bankr. L. Rptr. (CCH) ¶ 70876 (1985, Bankr.D. Mass. 1985); *In re* General Industries, Inc., 79 B.R. 124, 16 Bankr. Ct. Dec. 775, 17 CBC2d 1042, Bankr. L. Rptr. (CCH) ¶ 72103 (Bankr. D. Mass. 1987); Durrett v Washington Nat. Ins. Co., 621 F.2d 201, 6 Bankr. Ct. Dec. 954, 23 CBC 95 (1980, CA5 Tex).

[3] *Id.*

faith and reasonable diligence in the foreclosure sale process.[4] Nevertheless it quickly became the rule.

However, in 1994, the United States Supreme Court overruled *Ruebeck*, its bretheren and progeny. The Court held that "reasonably equivalent value" for bankruptcy law purposes with respect to real estate sold at foreclosure is "the price in fact received at foreclosure sale so long as all the requirements of the State's foreclosure law have been complied with."[5]

It might be seem that the *Ruebeck* procedures were but a momentary aberration and that foreclosing mortgagees can now return to the old days of certified mail notice to parties and publication of the legal notice at the back of a local newspaper. However, a Supreme Judicial Court case, also decided in 1994, has given some pause. In that case, the Court held that, "the mortgagee must act in good faith and must use reasonable diligence to protect the interests of the mortgagor. The mortgagee's duty is more exacting when it becomes the buyer of the property. 'When a party who is entrusted with a power to sell attempts also to become the purchaser, he will be held to the strictest good faith and the utmost diligence for the protection of the rights of his principal.' Consistent with these requirements, the mortgagee has a duty to 'obtain for the property as large a price as possible.'"[6]

It is difficult to know what to make of this language in the *Williams* case. Some have interpreted it as reading the *Ruebeck* requirements, or some modified version of them, back into Massachusetts foreclosure law where the mortgagee buys in at the sale. Since one will rarely know beforehand whether or not the mortgagee will buy in, the reasoning goes, one should utilize the *Ruebeck* procedures in all cases. The problem with this interpretation of the *Williams* case is that, having announced the above quoted standards of conduct for purchasing mortgagees, the Court proceeded to uphold against attack under G.L. c. 93A actions of such a mortgagee which were well short of those standards.

Just when a sense of stability and certainty was returning to this area of law the Federal and State courts have joined together to bring back the former uncertainty and confusion. Presumably financial institutions, being conservative by nature, will retain at least some form of the *Ruebeck* procedures, at least with larger commercial properties.

---

[4] Pemstein v. Stimpson, 36 Mass. App. 283, 630 N.E.2d 608, 23 UCCRS 2d 877 (1994), summary op at 22 M.L.W. 1531 (Mass. App.) and *review denied*, 418 Mass. 1103, 636 N.E.2d 279, 22 M.L.W. 1996, and cases cited therein.

[5] BFP v. Resolution Trust Corp., 511 U.S. 531, 128 L. Ed. 2d 556, 114 S. Ct. 1757 (1994), *rehearing denied*, 512 U.S. 1247, 129 L. Ed. 2d 884, 114 S. Ct. 2771 (1994).

[6] Williams v. Resolution GGF Oy, 417 Mass. 377, 630 N.E.2d 581 (1994), summary op at 22 M.L.W. 1530 (Mass.).

§ 12.07 Default and Foreclosure

Step 1. Where default occurs, read all loan documents, including the note and mortgage, carefully. Send a certified, return receipt letter to the mortgagor with a warning of intention to foreclose. If the mortgage or mortgage note has an acceleration provision, find out whether the client has sent a legally sufficient notice of acceleration. If not, do so yourself. (Volume 6, Chapter 13, Form 84.1 is an example). This letter is not part of formal foreclosure proceeding except where a second mortgage subject to G.L. c. 140, § 90B is involved, in which case it must be sent out 15 days before taking any action to foreclose. (Volume 6, Chapter 13, Form 85).

§ 12.07[1] Actions Prior to Foreclosure Sale

Step 2. The mortgagor or a person claiming under him has a right to redeem the property from foreclosure prior to sale. If a timely tender of all amounts due plus costs of any legal action is made the mortgage should be discharged. (§ 12.05, *supra*).

Step 3. Order a municipal lien certificate from the tax collector of the town where the property is located. (Volume 6, Chapter 13, Form 86).

Step 4. Have the title run from the date of the mortgage being foreclosed. Check with assessors to see if property is subject to G.L. c. 61A or 61B, if so you must send out notices pursuant to those statutes 90 days before the sale date.

Step 5. Determine if any holders of encumbrances prior to your mortgage have subordinated their interests to it, since they will not show up on the title run, but may be entitled to notice.

Step 6. Send Notice of Intention and Liability for Deficiency by registered or certified mail at least 21 days before the date of sale. (Volume 6, Chapter 13, Form 87). This notice should be sent to any person or entity liable on the obligation(s) secured by the mortgage that the mortgagee may wish to pursue for any deficiency between the proceeds of the mortgage sale and the balance owed on the obligation(s). Prudence dictates sending the notice to entities that may not be entitled to it rather than omitting one which is entitled and thereby losing the right to recover the deficiency. Affidavit of mailing of Notice must be completed within 30 days of sale. (Volume 6, Chapter 13, Form 88).

Step 7. Draw and file in Land Court or Superior Court a Complaint for permission and approval of foreclosure under Soldiers' and Sailors' Civil Relief Act. (Volume 6, Chapter 13, Forms 89, 90)

Step 8. Record the Order of Notice in the Registry of Deeds as soon as it is received from the Court.

Step 9. Run the title again to see if the defendant is still the record owner.

Step 10. File a motion to add a party defendant where necessary. (Volume 6, Chapter 13, Form 91).

Step 11. Publish Order of Notice in accordance with court instructions. First publication must be at least 21 days before the return day.

Step 12. Mail Order of Notice to each party defendant by certified or registered mail, return receipt requested, at least 14 days before the return day. If you are not successful in obtaining certified mail service fairly quickly have the defendant(s) served by a deputy sheriff.

Step 13. On the day following the return day make return of service to the court, which includes: (a) order of notice with return of service and newspaper publication attached thereto, (b) registered mail receipts, (c) military affidavit, (d) completed form of judgment if in superior court, (e) motion to take the Bill *pro confesso* if in land court, motion for or request for default if in superior court. Call to find out local practice. (Volume 6, Chapter 13, Forms 92, 93, 94, and 95).

Step 14. After obtaining judgment from the court, choose the sale day. Then 29 days before the sale have the title run to pick up any Federal tax liens and to be sure that the mortgagor is still the owner.

Step 15. If a Federal tax lien is on record send the required notice to the District Director, Internal Revenue Service, at least 25 days prior to sale, by registered or certified mail, return receipt requested. (Volume 6, Chapter 13, Form 96).

Step 16. Publish statutory advertisement of sale once each week for three successive weeks in a newspaper published or having general circulation or purporting on its masthead to be published in the town where the land lies and having a circulation therein, or, if there is none, in a paper published in the same county and having circulation in the town. The first publication must be at least 21 days prior to date of sale.

Step 17. Mail copy of the statutory advertisement of sale to the owners of record of the equity of redemption and holders of junior encumbrances as of 30 days prior to sale. This notice must be mailed fourteen days prior to the date of sale, certified or registered mail, return receipt requested.

Step 18. Run junior encumbrances to see if any have been assigned. Remember that if there is an outstanding junior Massachusetts tax lien on the record as of 30 days prior to sale, the Commonwealth should be given the same notice as other junior lienholders.

Step 19. If you are extra cautious you can have the title run the day before the sale to pick up any last minute Federal tax liens.

Step 20. If the mortgagee may bid in the property at the foreclosure sale and acquire outright title, some more aggressive advertising of the sale may be in order so that you can demonstrate that commercially reasonable actions were taken to assure the best possible price at the foreclosure sale.

Consider the following:

(a) obtain an appraisal of the property,

(b) advertise in a well circulated newspaper in the area,

(c) mail notice to local real estate brokers and anyone who has expressed interest in the property or whose name has been submitted by the mortgagor, and

(d) run new advertisements and issue new notices in the event the foreclosure sale is continued.

Discuss the pros and cons of this step with your client before deciding on it. (*See* § 12.06, *supra*.).

Step 21. Obtain a written Power of Attorney to make Entry. (Volume 6, Chapter 13, Form 97).

§ 12.07[2]   Actions Taken at Foreclosure Sale

Step 22. Make entry for purpose of foreclosure.

Step 23. Have the Certificate of Entry executed by two witnesses. (Volume 6, Chapter 13, Form 98).

Step 24. Have the auctioneer display his or her flag, and require that prospective bidders register and show that they have the required deposit in cash or bank funds.

Step 25. Auctioneer reads the newspaper notice, and announces any additional terms of sale. Auctioneer should also announce any encumbrances on the property which are not named in the mortgage and included in the notice of sale. Auctioneer then produces and reads a Municipal Lien Certificate indicating he or she makes no representation of its accuracy.

Step 26. Auctioneer reads memorandum of sale, including therein any encumbrances on the property not named in the mortgage and included in the notice of sale. It is important to err on the side of inclusion when it comes to announcing encumbrances at the sale and listing them in the memorandum of sale. Failure to do so may result in the purchaser at the foreclosure sale being able to later avoid the sale. (Volume 6, Chapter 13, Form 99).

Step 27. Hold the sale. Be sure that the mortgagee bids the full amount due if there is a Federal tax lien on the property. (§ 12:04, *supra*)

Step 28. Complete and execute the memorandum of sale. Execute affidavit of mailing deficiency notice. (Volume 6, Chapter 13, Form 87). Prepare and have executed the so-called *Ruebeck* Affidavit reciting the actions taken to ensure proper notice of the auction sale to the real estate community and the absence of chilling activity at the sale itself.

§ 12.07[3]   Actions Taken After Foreclosure Sale

Step 29. Prepare the foreclosure deed and affidavit of sale. Statute form of affidavit should be modified by adding recital of mailing notice to the mortgagor and holders of junior encumbrances with date and manner of mailing per G.L. c. 244-14. (Volume 6, Chapter 13, Forms 100, 101).

Step 30. Hold Closing.

Step 31. If your mortgagee bought the property, run the title to date and record the deed, notice and affidavit of sale, power of attorney, certificate of entry, and judgment authorizing foreclosure under the Soldiers' and Sailors' Civil Relief Act. There is no longer any time limit for recording these documents.

Step 32. Within 30 days of taking possession prior to foreclosure, or of conveying title by foreclosure deed, notify by mail all residential tenants of the premises, and the municipal assessor or tax collector, and any entities which provide water or sewer service to the premises of the taking possession or conveyance by the mortgagee.

CHAPTER 13

SUMMARY PROCESS—GENERAL PRINCIPLES OF LAW

Synopsis

§ 13.01   Generally

§ 13.02   Plaintiffs in Summary Process Action

§ 13.03   Defendants in Summary Process Action

§ 13.04   Grounds

§ 13.05   Notice

§ 13.06   Defenses to Summary Process

§ 13.07   Procedure
    § 13.07[1]   Execution.

§ 13.08   Stay of Execution

§ 13.09   Appeals

§ 13.10   Security Deposits
    § 13.10[1]   Statutory Security Deposit and Advance Rental Requirements Respecting Residential Real Estate

387

§ 13.01   Generally

Summary process has historically been an action very limited in nature and in many aspects, particularly procedurally, unique. It was for hundreds of years merely an expeditious method to determine the right to the possession of land. The plaintiff had to plead and prove only that his or her right to possession was superior to the defendant who was holding the land against that right.[1] The only fruit of such an action was an execution allowing a sheriff to evict the defendant, forcibly if necessary.

In 1960, the statute was amended to allow an action for rent to be joined to a summary process action.[2] Later amendments, beginning in 1965 and continuing through the 1970's, dramatically expanded the summary process action by creating statutory defenses and counterclaims based on sanitary code and other violations.[3] The Supreme Judicial Court, in 1973, dramatically changed the common law by creating an implied warranty, in the case of residential property, that the premises are fit for human habitation and will remain so throughout the term of the lease. It was held that the duty to pay rent was conditioned on the maintenance of the premises in habitable condition.[4] The Court has held that "a dwelling afflicted with a substantial Sanitary Code violation is not habitable."[5] And, the court has further created a common law right to rent abatement, in whole or in part, during the period that the premises remain uninhabitable after the landlord has notice of the defects. This right to abatement exists without regard to whether the defects are the landlord's fault or whether he or she is making reasonable efforts to correct the defects.[6]

All these new statutory and common law causes of action may be pleaded and litigated by a defendant in a summary process action.

§ 13.02   Plaintiffs in Summary Process Action

A summary process action is a creature of statute and the statute defines the persons who are entitled to be plaintiffs.[1] The action may be brought by (1) an owner or lessor, (2) his or her legal representative, assignee, heirs or devisees, (3) a grantee of the owner, (4) a lessee who has in turn become a sublessor, (5) any joint tenant or tenant in common, (6) a foreclosing mortgagee, (7) the holder of a foreclosed tax title, and (8) a buyer where the seller wrongfully holds over.

---

[1] Davis & O'Connor Co. v. Shell Oil Co., 311 Mass. 401, 41 N.E.2d 287 (1942).

[2] St. 1960, c. 463.

[3] G.L. c. 239, § 8A; c. 186, §§ 14, 15B, 18.

[4] Boston Housing Authority v. Hemingway, 363 Mass. 184, 293 N.E.2d 831 (1973).

[5] Berman & Sons, Inc. v. Jefferson, 379 Mass. 196, 396 N.E.2d 981 (1979).

[6] Berman & Sons, Inc. v. Jefferson, 379 Mass. 196, 396 N.E.2d 981 (1979).

[1] G.L. c. 239, § 1.

§ 13.03   Defendants in Summary Process Action

The legal status which defines the summary process defendant is, in essence, that he or she hold possession or claim the right to possession of the premises against the claimed right of the plaintiff. The defendant may be a tenant holding over after termination of a lease, a mortgagor whose equity of redemption has been foreclosed, a seller who has given a deed but failed to vacate the premises, and so on.

§ 13.04   Grounds

The usual summary process action of course involves a landlord trying to obtain possession from a tenant who holds over after the tenancy has terminated either by its own terms, by operation of law, upon default in payment of rent, or upon other material breach of the terms of the lease.

We may thus summarize the most common grounds for a summary process action as:

- holding over after the expiration of the lease term and after notice to quit;
- default in the payment of rent, followed by a proper statutory notice to quit for nonpayment;
- breach of an express covenant of the lease, if the lease terms provide that such a breach shall terminate the lease;
- use of the premises for an illegal purpose.

§ 13.05   Notice

Except in the case of a tenant at sufferance,[1] there are strict notice requirements which are conditions precedent to the bringing of a summary process action.

Tenancies may for these purposes be divided into two types, those subject to a written lease, and those which are oral. Usually the written lease creates a tenancy for a term of years and the oral agreement creates a tenancy at will.

Where there is a written lease, default in the payment of rent requires fourteen (14) days notice to quit, in writing, from landlord to tenant before a summary process action may be instituted.[2] For defaults other than non-payment, the lease will usually specify the required notice period. Most leases will give the tenant a period to cure his or her breach where it is other than a nonpayment situation.

Where there is an oral tenancy at will, and the tenant defaults in payment of rent the notice requirements are the same as in the case of a written lease, 14 days notice to quit, in writing. Where the tenancy at will is sought to be terminated for reasons

---

[1] Staples v. Collins, 321 Mass. 449, 73 N.E.2d 729 (1947).

[2] G.L. c. 186, § 11.

other than nonpayment, then notice to terminate must be three months' notice in writing, or, if the rental payment period is less than three months, then notice equal to the rental payment period or 30 days, whichever is longer. So, if payments are made every three months then three months' notice is required. If payments are made every two months then two months' notice is required. If payments are made every two weeks, then 30 days' notice is required. The statute has been construed to mean that the notice must fix the time for termination as a day upon which the rent is payable.[3] In the absence of a contrary agreement the rent day is the last day of the monthly period.[4]

The notice to quit may not be served by leaving the same at the defendant's last and usual address. Service of the notice must be either in hand to the tenant, his or her agent, spouse, or other responsible occupant of the leased premises, or, must be by certified mail, return receipt requested with evidence that the defendant has received it.[5] If counsel suspects that the defendant will attempt to evade service of the notice, it may be sent certified mail with no return receipt and the plaintiff may rely on the usual presumption of receipt. In the case of a fault termination the notice should contain all the grounds for termination of the tenancy of which the landlord is aware, since many judges will limit any later summary process hearing founded on the notice to these grounds. Certainly the hearing will be so limited if the grounds alleged in the complaint were "curable" by the tenant under applicable law.

A tenant at sufferance is entitled to no notice of termination of that status before the landlord begins an action to obtain possession. However, under G.L. c. 186, § 13, if a tenancy at will of premises occupied for dwelling purposes is terminated by operation of law, then the tenant is entitled to notice of termination, not of the tenancy at sufferance but of the preceding tenancy at will. The notice given must be "equal to the interval between the days on which the rent reserved is payable or thirty days, whichever is longer…"[6] Thus a foreclosing mortgagee would have to give notice of termination to tenants at will of the mortgagor, even though they would only be tenants at sufferance as to the mortgagee.

§ 13.06   Defenses to Summary Process

As indicated above,[1] he defenses available to residential tenants in summary process actions have been dramatically expanded by both court and legislature over the past thirty years. Lack of money and/or sophistication has kept most tenants

---

[3] U-Dryvit Auto Rental Co. v. Shaw, 319 Mass. 684, 67 N.E.2d 225 (1946).
[4] Connors v. Wick, 317 Mass. 628, 59 N.E.2d 277 (1945).
[5] Ryan v. Sylvester, 358 Mass. 18, 260 N.E.2d 148 (1970).
[6] Rubin, Trustee v. Prescott, 362 Mass. 281, 284 N.E.2d 902 (1972).
[1] See § 13.01, supra.

from taking advantage of these, but the well-represented tenant can give a landlord no end of trouble in a simple summary process case.

The first, and perhaps most obvious, defense to summary process is available to all tenants whether residential or not. This is the defense of rebutting the elements of the plaintiff's case in chief. In other words, the tenant may show that he or she has not breached the lease, or that he or she has cured the breach, or that no proper notice to quit was given, or that his or her right to possession is equal or superior to that of the plaintiff.

Secondly, the tenant under a written lease may defend by showing that he or she paid or tendered all unpaid rent due, with interest and costs of suit, on or before the day the Answer is due in court. In the case of a tenancy at will, the tenant may show that, within 10 days after the receipt of notice to quit, he or she paid or tendered the full amount of rent due. This defense is not available if the tenant has received a prior notice to quit for nonpayment within the 12 months next preceding the date of receipt of the second notice. The notice must contain a disclosure of this right to redeem by full payment. If it does not then the time to redeem by payment or tender of rent due is extended to the day the Answer is due in court.[2]

It is specifically provided by statute[3] that in the case of premises used for dwelling purposes the tenant or occupant shall be entitled to raise in the summary process action, "by defense or counterclaim, any claim against the plaintiff relating to or arising out of such property, rental, tenancy or occupancy for breach of warranty, for breach of any material provision of the rental agreement, or for a violation of any other law."[4] To the extent that there was any doubt before, the Supreme Judicial Court has now made it clear that commercial tenants cannot bring counterclaims against landlords within the summary process action.[5]

The implied warranty which would be raised would likely be the implied warranty of habitability created by the Supreme Judicial Court in the *Hemingway* and *Berman* cases.[6] These cases hold that where the landlord has failed to maintain the premises in habitable condition, free from substantial Sanitary Code violations, the tenant has a right to a full or partial rent abatement, from the time of notice to the landlord to the time the defects are corrected. A similar right is given by statute whereby the tenant may claim a reduction of rent equal to the difference between the contract rent and the fair value of the use and occupancy of the

---

[2] G.L. c. 186, §§ 11, 12.

[3] G.L. c. 239, § 8A.

[4] G.L. c. 239, § 8A. These defenses are also available to tenants at sufferance. Hodge v. Klug, 33 Mass. App. 746, 604 N.E.2d 1329 (1992).

[5] Fafard v. Lincoln Pharmacy of Milford, Inc., 439 Mass. 512 (2003).

[6] *See* Boston Housing Authority v. Hemingway, 363 Mass. 184, 293 N.E.2d 831 (1973); Berman & Sons, Inc. v. Jefferson, 379 Mass. 196, 396 N.E.2d 981 (1979).

premises in their defective condition.[7] However, the statutory abatement right has more conditions attached to it than does the common law right. Before any rights arise under the statute the following conditions must be satisfied:

(1) The tenant must show that the owner or his agents, servants, or employees, or other person to whom the tenant or occupant customarily paid his rent knew of such conditions before the tenant or occupant was in arrears in his rent;

(2) The landlord does not show that such conditions were caused by the tenant or occupant or any other person acting under his control; except that the tenant shall have the burden of proving that any violation appearing solely within that portion of the premises under his control and not by its nature reasonably attributable to any action or failure to act of the landlord was not caused by the tenant or person for whom he is responsible;

(3) The tenant shows that the premises are not situated in a hotel or motel, nor in a lodging house or rooming house wherein the occupant has maintained such occupancy for less than three consecutive months; and

(4) The landlord does not show that the conditions complained of cannot be remedied without the premises being vacated; but this condition is not satisfied where the premises must be vacated for lead paint removal under the so-called Lead Paint Law. It does not appear that this kind of showing is necessary to make out a *Hemingway*-type abatement claim.

The most likely violation of law claim which might be raised by defense or counterclaim to a summary process action would be a claim under G.L. c. 93A. It should be noted that the Attorney General has pursuant to G.L. c. 93A, § 2(e) issued a set of regulations defining unfair and deceptive acts or practices in the rental of dwelling units.

If the court finds that the amount due the landlord equals or is less than the amount due the tenant by reason of any counterclaim or defense raised under the statute, there shall be no recovery of possession. If the amount found to be due the landlord exceeds the amount due the tenant, there shall be no recovery of possession if the tenant, within one week after having received written notice from the court of the balance due, pays to the clerk the balance due the landlord, together with interest and costs of suit.[8]

A residential tenant may not be evicted in reprisal or retaliation for exercising his or her rights under any federal, state, or local law, regulation, bylaw, or ordinance, which has as its objective the regulation of residential premises, nor may the tenant be evicted for reporting actual or suspected violations of any law or

---

[7] G.L. c. 239, § 8A. *See* State Sanitary Code at 105 CMR 4.00 *et seq.*
[8] G.L. c. 239, § 8A (¶ 5).

regulation having such objective. And, the tenant may not be evicted for organizing or joining a tenants' union or similar organization or for making a payment of rent directly to the unit owners' organization of a condominium pursuant to G.L. c. 183A, § 6(c).

Any action taken by the landlord to evict the tenant or to materially alter the terms of the tenancy within six months after the tenant has exercised any of the aforesaid rights shall create a rebuttable presumption that such action is retaliatory which presumption may only be rebutted by clear and convincing evidence to the contrary. The establishment of retaliatory eviction is a complete defense to a summary process action.[9]

Acceptance by the landlord of rental payments subsequent to the sending of a notice of termination may constitute a waiver by the landlord and revive the tenancy. Whether or not a waiver will be found depends largely on the factual circumstances in each case. But in any case there will be no waiver if the landlord expressly and unequivocally reserves his or her rights when he or she accepts the payments.[10]

Where the failure to pay rent was caused by a failure or delay of the federal government, the commonwealth, or any municipality, department, or agency in the mailing or delivery of any subsistence or rental payment, other than a salary payment, to either the tenant or the landlord, the court must continue the hearing for at least seven days and furnish notice of the action to the appropriate agency. If, within the period of such continuance, all rent due together with interest and costs of suit is tendered to the landlord the court must treat the tenancy as not having been terminated.[11]

A tenant can also raise by way of counterclaim in a summary process action the willful failure of the landlord to provide water, hot water, heat, light, power, gas, elevator service, telephone service, janitor service or refrigeration service, if the landlord was obliged to provide such services. Also, any claim for interference with quiet enjoyment of any residential premises may be raised by counterclaim.[12] The measure of damages is defined in the statute as three month's rent or the actual and consequential damages suffered by the tenant, whichever is greater. Where the tenant has remained in possession of the premises, which would be the usual situation, actual damages for interference with quiet enjoyment are measured by the difference between the value of what the tenant should have received and the

---

[9] G.L. c. 239, § 2A, c. 186, § 18.
[10] Slater v. Krinsky, 1981 Adv. Sheets. 386, 416 N.E.2d 983 (Mass. App. 1981).
[11] G.L. c. 186, § 12.
[12] G.L. c. 186, § 14.

value of what he did receive. The statute also provides for reasonable attorneys fees if the tenant prevails.[13]

The landlord cannot charge a residential tenant a late payment penalty or interest on a late rental payment until thirty days after the payment was due.[14] It has been held that a lease provision requiring the tenant to pay the constable fee incurred by the landlord in sending out a notice to quit, which notice could be served as soon as one day after the rent was due, violated this prohibition and G.L. c. 93A as well.[15]

§ 13.07   Procedure

With the abolition of the two-trial procedure for civil cases seeking money damages and summary process cases throughout the Commonwealth, effective August 9, 2004, the plaintiff contemplating bringing a summary process action must make a threshold decision not previously required. If money damages are sought, and it is reasonably believed that the recovery will be greater than $25,000, plaintiff must decide whether to bring the case in the district, housing or Boston municipal court, or whether to bring it in the superior court. There is no longer an appeal de novo to the superior court in summary process cases decided in the district court. If the case is brought in district court it will be tried jury-waived or before a jury of six in that court, regardless of the amount sought as money damages. However the case cannot be brought in superior court unless money damages as well as possession are sought and there is no reasonable likelihood that recovery will be $25,000 or less. A case brought in superior court in violation of this requirement is subject to dismissal by the court without prejudice. Although not dealt with explicitly, reading the amendments together, it seems that if the case is brought in district court the defendant must litigate any counterclaim or cross claim brought in the action in the district court as well, regardless of the amount in controversy.[1] To the extent the defendant's claims are permissive a tactical choice will have to be made as to whether or not to bring a separate action based upon them.

The Uniform Summary Process Rules, which became effective on September 1, 1980, brought a measure of order to an area which had been characterized by procedural idiosyncrasies from court to court. However, they reflect the old two-tier trial system rather than the new procedure. To the extent they conflict with the

---

[13] Curtis v. Surrette, 49 Mass. App. 99 (2000).

[14] G.L. c. 186, § 15B(1)(c).

[15] Commonwealth v. Chatham Development Co., Inc., 49 Mass. App. 525, 731 N.E.2d 89 (2000).

[1] St. 2004, c. 252, amending multiple procedural statutes, including most notably, G.L. c. 218, §§ 19, 19A and 19B; G.L. c. 212, §§ 3 & 3A; G.L. c. 231, § 97; G.L. c. 239, §§ 2 & 5.

statutory amendments they will not control.[2]

Under the uniform rules the plaintiff first obtains from the clerk of the proper court a blank form Summary Process Summons and Complaint. This form is the same for all courts. Next the plaintiff must choose an Entry Day. In choosing this day the plaintiff considers that the hearing date will automatically be assigned based on the date selected as the Entry Day. The rules provide that the hearing date will be the second Thursday after the Entry Day, but the First Justice of any particular court may designate Friday, Monday, Tuesday and Wednesday as summary process trial dates, either as alternatives or in addition to Thursday. The option is frequently exercised by the various courts and it is necessary to verify the local practice before filing. Where Thursdays or Fridays are the summary process hearing day the case is assigned for hearing on the second such day following the Entry Day, without further notice to the parties. Where Tuesday or Wednesday is the summary process hearing day the case is automatically assigned for hearing on the third such day after the Entry Day. The plaintiff also considers that service on the defendant must be made not later than the seventh day nor earlier than the thirtieth day before the Entry Day chosen. Entry Days are always Mondays.

Service may not be made prior to the termination date of the tenancy except as provided by law.[3]

After having the defendant served, the plaintiff files, on or before the close of business on the Entry Day, the Complaint and Summons with return of service, the filing fee, a copy of the notice of termination along with proof of delivery of the same, and where appropriate a copy of the certificate of eviction from the rent control agency and an affidavit of compliance with any local condominium conversion eviction laws.[4] The failure of the plaintiff to file any of the foregoing documents with the complaint on or before the Entry Day will not automatically result in dismissal of the case. Rather the trial judge must determine whether the lack of timely filing had interfered with the "purposes implicit in the statutory scheme" and if the defendant has been prejudiced, before deciding what, if any, consequences will flow from the lack of timely filing.[5] Any certificate of eviction must have been issued prior to the commencement of the action. Commencement occurs when proper service is made on the defendant.[6]

The defendant must file his or her Answer on or before the first Monday after the Entry Day. The Answer is filed with the clerk and served on the plaintiff by delivery pursuant to Rule 5(b) Mass. R. Civ. P. or by mailing first-class mail. Filing

---

[2] ROPT Ltd. Partnership v. Katin, 431 Mass. 601 (2000).
[3] G.L. c. 186, § 11, 12; c. 239, § 1A.
[4] Rule 2(d), Uniform Summary Process Rules.
[5] Weston Assocs. Management Co. v. McWilliam, 35 Mass. App. 933 (1993).
[6] District Court Administrative Regulation No. 3-73.

is complete upon receipt. The Answer must contain the hearing date just below the caption and must deny every allegation in the Complaint which is in dispute. It must also assert any affirmative defense which may be available. The Uniform Rules also allow Counterclaims to be asserted as provided in G.L. c. 239, § 8A. However, all Counterclaims, except possibly those arising under G.L. c. 239, § 8A, are permissive and not mandatory in a Summary Process action.[7] Where Counterclaims are pleaded they must be expressly designated as such. No responsive pleading to a Counterclaim is required.[8] The Clerk's office will provide official blank Answer forms on request.

Motion practice in Summary Process cases is in accordance with usual civil motion practice except that all pre-trial motions must be filed and served no later than the Monday next proceeding the hearing date. Service is by first class mail or delivery. Unless the court otherwise orders, the hearing on any properly filed pretrial motion is automatically marked for hearing on the date originally set for trial of the case in chief. However, a motion to dismiss filed on or before the Entry Day may, upon request of the defendant, be heard on the Thursday following the Entry Day.

All other motion are filed and heard as the court may permit or direct.[9]

The Uniform Rules allow a limited and expedited form of discovery in Summary Process cases. Discovery is obtained by filing with the court and serving on the opposing party a demand for discovery. Such demand must be filed and served no later than the first Monday after the Entry Day.

Discovery may be in the form of written interrogatories, requests for admissions, or requests for production of documents. When a demand for discovery is properly filed and served the hearing in the case is automatically postponed for two weeks. When serving the demand the party seeking discovery must also notify the other party of the postponement, the new trial date, and the requirement that answers be served in 10 days after receiving the demand. The usual sanctions are available for failure to answer.[10]

Where a jury trial is desired, a demand must be filed on or before the date on which the defendant's answer is due..[11]

If the defendant fails to appear at the trial date, whether or not the defendant has filed an Answer, and the plaintiff does appear, then the defendant shall be defaulted. If neither party appears the case will be dismissed seven days after the trial date

---

[7] Rules 3, 5, Uniform Summary Process Rules.
[8] Rule 5, Uniform Summary Process Rules.
[9] Rule 6, Uniform Summary Process Rules.
[10] Rule 7, Uniform Summary Process Rules.
[11] Rule 8, Uniform Summary Process Rules.

unless either party requests a new trial date within the seven day period. If the defendant appears but has not previously filed an Answer the court shall postpone the hearing for one week, unless the plaintiff agrees in writing to go forward immediately. If the defendant appears but has failed to file a timely answer and the plaintiff appears, the court will postpone the trial date one week from the original trial date and notice shall be sent to the plaintiff. If the plaintiff fails to appear after being so notified the case shall be dismissed.

If the defendant files a timely Answer and appears for trial, and plaintiff fails to appear, the case will be dismissed.

A default or dismissal may be removed on motion of either party at any time prior to the entry of judgment.[12] All judgments are entered at 10:00 A.M. on the next business day following the court's decision after hearing or the entry of default or dismissal. Where a default is pending no judgment may enter until:

1) a military affidavit has been filed,

2) where a claim for rent is made, plaintiff files an affidavit stating the aggregate amount of payments which have been made by defendant subsequent to the commencement of the action, and

3) the clerk reviews the file to be sure the Summons and Complaint were properly completed, served and returned, and any other documents required by Rule 2(d) have been filed.[13]

§ 13.07[1]   Execution.

In the case of residential property there are detailed statutory requirements relating to the service or levying upon executions for possession. They are as follows:

- The officer must at least 48 hours prior to serving or levying give the defendant written notice that at a specific date and time the execution will be served or levied, and that at such time he will physically remove the defendant and his possessions from the premises if the defendant has not left voluntarily prior to that time.

- The notice must contain (1) the signature, full name, full business address and business telephone number of the officer, (2) the name of the court and docket number of the case, (3) a statement that the officer will place any personal property remaining on the premises at the time the execution is levied in storage at a licensed public warehouse, and the full name, full

---

[12] Rule 10, Uniform Summary Process Rules.
[13] Rule 10(d), Uniform Summary Process Rules.

business address and the business telephone number of the warehouse to be used, (4) a statement that the warehouser's storage rates may be ascertained by contacting the commissioner of public safety, and the address and phone number of such agency, (5) a statement that the warehouser may sell at auction any property that is unclaimed after 6 months and may retain that portion of the proceeds necessary to compensate him for any unpaid storage fees accrued as of the date of the auction, subject to the limitations of G.L. c. 239,§ 4, (6) a statement that the defendant should notify the warehouser in writing at the business address listed in the notice of any change in the defendant's mailing address. This notice must be served in the same manner as the summary process summons and complaint and must be filed in court, presumably with return of service endorsed thereon.. The officer must select the public warehouser identified in the notice in a manner calculated to ensure that the defendant's property will be stored within a reasonable distance from the premises from which it was removed. The officer may not select a warehouser whom the officer knows or reasonably believes to be in violation of any provision of G.L. c. 239, § 4.[14] It should be noted that as of November 7, 2004, substantial new statutory obligations and potential liability is imposed on warehousers that accept the personal property of evicted tenants for storage.

- If the officer serving the execution does in fact remove personal property from the premises he must store it at the facility listed in the notice described above, or in the facility designated by the defendant in writing. The officer must provide to the defendant in hand, or by receipted mail if he is not present at the eviction, a receipt containing a description of the goods removed or of the packages containing them, as well as the name and signature of the officer. This receipt must also be filed with the court. The plaintiff must pay the costs of removing the defendant's property to the storage facility, but is entitled to reimbursement from the defendant for such costs.[15] In practice the landlord will end up guaranteeing storage costs before any storage facility will accept the tenant's property.

- No execution for possession of residential premises may be served or levied upon after 5:00 P.M. or before 9:00 A.M., nor on Saturdays, Sundays, or legal holidays. Where in the case of residential property the underlying money judgment has been satisfied, together with any charges for use and

---

[14] G.L. c. 239, § 4 has been extensively rewritten to impose significant regulation of the storage of the property of evicted tenants. Such regulations fall primarily on the warehouser. The officer's duty appears to be satisfied if he chooses a properly licensed and bonded warehouser, or a warehouser of the defendant's choosing if he notifies the officer before the time of removal of the property.

[15] G.L. c. 239, § 3.

occupancy accruing since the judgment, the plaintiff is barred from levying for possession and must return the execution to court as fully satisfied. Where no execution has issued, the plaintiff in such cases must notify the court that the judgment is satisfied, and thereafter no execution may issue. The tenant at this point is once again considered lawfully in possession. So far so good, but there is a rather puzzling final coda in the part of the statute dealing with satisfied underlying judgments. It provides that the landlord is not required to accept full satisfaction of the money judgment, and that such refusal will not "ban enforcement of said judgment in any lawful manner." Taken together, this language seems to give the landlord the right to accept satisfaction of the money judgment and restore the tenancy, or to refuse satisfaction of the judgment, evict the tenant, and thereafter to seek to collect the judgment

§ 13.08   Stay of Execution

Upon application of the tenant, or his or her surviving spouse, parent, or child, (provided the latter occupied the premises for dwelling purposes, and not in violation of the terms of the tenancy, at the time the tenancy was terminated), the court may in its discretion grant a stay of execution for up to six months, or, if the tenant is a handicapped person as defined in the statute, the stay may be for up to twelve months. However where the tenancy is terminated for nonpayment of rent, no such stay may be granted.[1]

Although stays of execution are discretionary, the statute provides guidelines for the court in applying that discretion. The court will grant a stay if after hearing it appears that:

1) the premises are used for dwelling purposes;

2) the defendant cannot secure suitable premises for himself or herself and his or her family elsewhere within the city or town in a neighborhood similar to that in which the premises are located;

3) defendant has used reasonable efforts to secure such other premises;

4) that his or her request is made in good faith and that he or she will abide by and comply with such terms and provisions as the court may prescribe;

5) or that by reason of other facts a stay is warranted.[2]

Once a stay has been granted, either by a court or through the agreement of the parties, no execution may issue prior to the expiration of such stay, except after

---

[1] G.L. c. 239, § 9.
[2] G.L. c. 239, § 10.

hearing on motion by the plaintiff where the court finds that the defendant is in substantial violation of a material term or condition of the stay or agreement.

§ 13.09 Appeals

Either party may appeal the judgment in a Summary Process case by filing a notice of appeal with the court entering the judgment within 10 days after entry of such judgment. However, the timely filing of a motion to alter or amend judgment pursuant to Mass. R. Civ. P. Rule 59(e). will toll the running of the ten day period until the court acts on the motion.[1] No execution may issue until after the expiration of the appeal period.

Where the defendant seeks to appeal from a judgment of the superior court, housing court, or district court granting the plaintiff possession the defendant must give a bond in such sum as the court orders payable to the plaintiff, with sufficient sureties approved by the court, or secured by cash or equivalent deposited with the clerk, in a reasonable amount to be fixed by the court. The bond must be conditioned to enter the case in the proper court and to pay the plaintiff, if final judgment is in plaintiff's favor, all rent accrued at the date of the bond, all intervening rent, and all damage or loss which the plaintiff may sustain by the withholding of possession of the premises and by any injury done thereto during such withholding, with all costs, until possession is given to the plaintiff. All other appeals require only a $100 bond conditioned to pay any judgment for costs which may be entered against the appellant.[2]

A party may move for waiver of the appeal bond if he or she is indigent as defined in § 27A of G.L. c. 261. The motion together with supporting affidavits and notice of appeal must be filed within the 10-day appeal period. The court is required to waive the appeal bond or security if it is satisfied that the party is indigent and has a defense that is not frivolous.

The court must decide the motion "forthwith," and in the case of a defendant appealing a judgment for possession if the court waives the bond it must require that "all or any portion of any rent which shall become due after such waiver" be paid in installments as they become due.

A party aggrieved by the court's decision on the motion may seek review of such decision by filing a request for review in the trial court within the time limit for filing an appeal or within six days after receiving notice of the decision on the motion, whichever is later. The request for review is heard on an expedited basis. No execution may issue until five days after the defendant receives notice of the decision of the reviewing court. During such five-day period the defendant must

---

[1] Manzaro v. McCann, 401 Mass. 880, 519 N.E.2d 1337 (1988).
[2] G.L. c. 239, § 5(a), (b), (c).

comply fully with the decision or his or her appeal will be dismissed.

Where the case is first heard in the district court review of all actions by the trial court is in the appropriate appellate division of the district court. Where the case is entered originally in the superior court or housing court review of the decision on the appeal bond or conditions is by the single justice of the Appeals Court.[3] Review of final judgments of the superior court or housing court is by the full bench of the Appeals Court.

§ 13.10   Security Deposits

The requirements with respect to security deposits are laid out in excruciating detail in G.L. c. 186, § 15B and counsel for landlords, in particular, should read this statute.

Of special interest here is clause 7 of § 15B which provides that if the landlord fails to comply with certain requirements respecting security deposits the tenant shall be awarded damages equal to three times the amount of such security deposit or balance thereof to which the tenant is entitled plus interest at 5% from the date the deposit was required to have been returned, plus court costs and reasonable attorneys' fees. One may logically expect that a claim under this section if it exists will be raised as a counterclaim in a Summary Process action and counsel for both sides should be sensitive to this. Note also that under G.L. c. 239, § 8A if the amount due the landlord is less than the amount found to be due the tenant under any counterclaim there shall be no recovery of possession.

The acts or omissions by a landlord which give rise to this cause of action are:

1) failure to keep the security deposit in a separate, interest bearing account in a bank located within the commonwealth under such terms as will place such deposit beyond the claims of creditors of the lessor, including a foreclosing mortgagee or a trustee in bankruptcy; and to give the tenant within 30 days after such deposit is received a receipt indicating the name and location of the bank in which the security deposit has been deposited and the amount and account number of such deposit;

2) failure to transfer the security deposit to his successor in interest upon conveyance of the property, or, where landlord is a grantee, failure to notify the tenant, within 45 days of transfer of the security deposit, that the deposit has been transferred to him or her and he or she is holding the same; such notice to be in writing and to contain the transferee's name, business address and business telephone number and the name, business address and telephone number of his or her agent, if any;

---

[3] G.L. c. 239, § 5.

3) failure to return the security deposit to the tenant, or any balance thereof to which he or she is entitled after deductions allowed by statute, together with any interest due, within 30 days after termination of the tenancy.[1]

The security deposit statute does not apply to any lease, rental, occupancy, or tenancy of one hundred days or less duration which lease or rental is for a vacation or recreational purpose.[2]

For those who have landlord clients not yet involved in summary process litigation involving security deposits, or, who have landlord clients who wish to avoid future losses arising out of violations of G.L. c. 186, § 15B, there are included in this volume procedures and forms[3] to be used to insure compliance with this intricate statute. There follows a more detailed breakdown of the statutory requirements imposed on landlords who require security deposits and or advance rent. This breakdown may be easily adapted to an advisory letter to landlord clients for use by them as a reference and reminder of their obligations under the statute.

§ 13.10[1]　Statutory Security Deposit and Advance Rental Requirements Respecting Residential Real Estate

I. Maximum amounts that may be required of a tenant at or prior to commencement of tenancy:

　a. a security deposit equal to the first month's rent, plus

　b. the purchase and installation cost for a key and lock, plus

　c. first month's rent, plus

　d. last month's rent at same rate as first month.

A Security Deposit:

　a. continues to be the property of tenant even after the landlord receives and banks it;

　b. may not be commingled with other funds of the landlord;

　c. must be held in a separate, interest-bearing account in Massachusetts bank under terms that will place it beyond the reach of landlord's creditors and will provide for its transfer to subsequent owners of the leased property;

　d. if held for one year or longer bears interest at the rate of 5% per year, or such lesser amount of interest as has been received from the bank where the

---

[1] G.L. c. 186, § 15B(7).
[2] G.L. c. 186, § 15B(9).
[3] *See* § 14.01, *infra*; Volume 6, Chapter 15, Forms 117–123.

deposit has been held, payable by landlord to tenant within 30 days after the end of each year of the tenancy or within 30 days after termination of the tenancy if such termination occurs prior to the anniversary date of the lease;

e. at the end of each year of tenancy landlord must send tenant the interest due on the security deposit or a notification that tenant may deduct the interest from the next rental payment.

f. must be returned to tenant within 30 days after termination of occupancy in case of tenancy at will or 30 days after termination of tenancy in case of written lease, less lawful deductions.

1. Landlord may, if he or she has fully complied with law governing security deposits, deduct from the security deposit, at the end of the tenancy, the following items:

a. any unpaid rent or water charges not validly withheld of deducted pursuant to law;

b. any unpaid increase in real estate taxes lawfully charged to the tenant under the terms of written lease;

c. reasonable amounts necessary to repair damage caused by the tenant, provided that

(i) landlord provides to tenant within 30 days a precise, detailed and itemized list of the nature and extent of damages and the repairs needed to correct the same, and

(ii) the said list is sworn to by the landlord under the pains and penalties of perjury, and

(iii) the said list is accompanied by written evidence such as bills, estimates, invoices or receipts indicating the actual or estimated cost of such repairs.

B. Advance Rent:

a. is binding on all successors in interest to the original landlord accepting the same;

b. if paid for last month of tenancy carries interest at the rate of 5% per year, or such lesser amount of interest as has been received from the bank where the deposit has been held (but interest does not accrue during the last month of the tenancy), payable by landlord to tenant within 30 days after the end of each year of the tenancy or within 30 days after termination of the tenancy if such termination occurs prior to the anniversary date of the lease;

c. if paid for last month of tenancy must be credited by landlord who transfers property ownership to successor in interest for benefit of tenant.

Any provision of a lease which conflicts with the above statutory requirements relative to security deposits or rental advances, and any attempted waiver by a tenant or prospective tenant of such requirements are void and unenforceable as against public policy.

CHAPTER 14

SUMMARY PROCESS—THE PRACTICE

Synopsis

§ 14.01 Insuring Compliance with Security Deposit and Advance Rent Requirements Imposed on Residential Landlords
  § 14.01[1] Obtain Required Information
  § 14.01[2] Send Proper Notices to Tenant
  § 14.01[3] Maintain Proper Documentation
  § 14.01[4] Transfer Security Deposit and Accrued Interest to New Owner

§ 14.02 Summary Process/Evictions Representing the Landlord
  § 14.02[1] Prior to Hearing in Court
  § 14.02[2] At the Court Hearing
  § 14.02[3] After the Hearing

§ 14.03 Summary Process/Evictions Representing the Tenant
  § 14.03[1] Prior to Court Hearing
  § 14.03[2] At the Court Hearing
  § 14.03[3] After the Court Hearing

(Rel. 0-0/1960 Pub.68860)

§ 14.01   Insuring Compliance with Security Deposit and Advance Rent Requirements Imposed on Residential Landlords

The following are the steps that should be taken by landlord to ensure compliance with the security deposit and advance rent requirements:

§ 14.01[1]   Obtain Required Information

Step 1. Obtain the information required to enable you to complete the Information List. Insuring Compliance With Security Deposit and Advance Rental Requirements, Volume 6, Chapter 14.

§ 14.01[2]   Send Proper Notices to Tenant

Step 2. Send tenant a receipt for the security deposit and/or Advance Rent. At the time he receives a security deposit landlord must give tenant a signed receipt indicating the amount of the security deposit, the name of the person receiving it, the name of the landlord, the date it was received, and a description of the premises leased. (*See* Volume 6, Chapter 14, Form 117.) At the time the rental advance is received the landlord must give the tenant a receipt indicating the amount of the advance, the date on which it was received, its intended application as rent for the last month of the tenancy, the name of the landlord and of the agent receiving the advance for the landlord, a description of the leased premises, a statement indicating that the tenant is entitled to interest payable at the rate of 5% per year or such other lesser amount of interest as has been received from the bank where the deposit has been held, and that the tenant should provide the landlord with a forwarding address at the end of the tenancy where the tenant wishes the interest to be sent. (*See* Volume 6, Chapter 14, Form 122.)

Step 3. Send tenant a statement of present condition of premises.

Upon receipt of the security deposit, or within 10 days after commencement of the tenancy, whichever is later, landlord must give tenant a separate written statement of the present condition of the leased premises in the proper statutory form. (*See* Volume 6, Chapter 14, Form 118.) If tenant submits to landlord a separate list of damages, landlord must, within 15 days, return a signed copy of the list to tenant with a statement clearly agreeing or disagreeing with the contents of the tenant's list. (*See* Volume 6, Chapter 14, Form 119.)

Step 4. Send tenant statement showing locations of security deposit.

Within 30 days after the deposit is received landlord must give tenant a receipt which indicates the name and address of the bank where the security deposit is held, and the amount and account number of the deposit. (*See* Volume 6, Chapter 14, Form 120.)

Step 5. Send tenant statement of interest due.

At the end of each year of the tenancy the landlord must send the tenant a statement indicating the name and address of the bank in which the security deposit has been placed, the amount of the deposit, the account number, and the amount of interest payable by the landlord on the deposit. (*See* Volume 6, Chapter 14, Form 121.)

At the end of each year of the tenancy the landlord must give or send to the tenant a statement indicating the amount of interest due the tenant from the landlord. This statement should also advise the tenant that either the amount due is enclosed, or, that the tenant may deduct such amount from the next rental payment. (*See* Volume 6, Chapter 14, Form 123.)

§ 14.01[3]   Maintain Proper Documentation

Step 6. Be sure records are kept for statutory period after end of tenancy.

During the period of the tenancy, and for 2 years after its termination, landlord must maintain the following records for all security deposits received:

     (i) a detailed description of any damage done to the dwelling unit by any tenant;

     (ii) the date upon which the occupancy of the tenant or tenants charged with such damage was terminated;

     (iii) whether repairs were performed to remedy such damage, the dates and cost of such repairs, with receipts for the same;

     (iv) copies of any receipt or statement of condition given to a tenant or prospective tenant.

The foregoing records must be available to be inspected by the tenant at the office of the landlord during normal business hours.

§ 14.01[4]   Transfer Security Deposit and Accrued Interest to New Owner

Step 7. Be sure security deposit and interest are transferred to new owner upon sale of property.

When the landlord transfers his/her interest in the dwelling unit to which the security deposit applies, he must transfer the security deposit, and any interest accrued, to the new owner.

§ 14.02   Summary Process/Evictions Representing the Landlord

§ 14.02[1]   Prior to Hearing in Court

Step 1. Get the basic information from the client which is necessary to complete the Information List—Summary Process, Volume 6, Chapter 14.

Step 2. Send Notice to Quit for Nonpayment or Notice of Termination of Tenancy, whichever is appropriate. (Volume 6, Chapter 14, Forms 102, 103.) Where you anticipate seeking money damages in excess of $25,000 or anticipate a possible counterclaim in excess of such amount, consider whether you wish to bring the case in district court, housing court or superior court.

Step 3. When the time fixed in notice has expired obtain form of Summary Process Summons and Complaint from the clerk of court where the action is to be brought. (Volume 6, Chapter 14, Form 104.) If you have received a notice of sanitary code violations from the local health officials (see Volume 6, Chapter 14, Form 103), it is a good idea to have the code violations corrected before proceeding further with Summary Process. *See* § 13.06, *supra.*

Step 4. Complete the form, choosing a hearing date which is convenient to you and your client. The reason for eviction must be stated on the form in clear, non-technical language.

Step 5. Send the form to the process server with instructions that it must be served not less than seven (7) nor more than thirty (30) days before the entry day. (Volume 6, Chapter 14, Form 105.) Diary the entry day. (Note the other requirements of Rule 2 of the Summary Process Rules.)

Step 6. Enter the case on the proper entry day (two Mondays before the hearing date if the summary process day is a Thursday or Friday, three Mondays if hearing day is Tuesday or Wednesday), by filing with the clerk the following documents:

(a) the original Summons with return of service endorsed thereon;

(b) a copy of any notice of termination of tenancy upon which you intend to rely and proof of delivery of such notice;

(c) where applicable, a copy of the certificate of eviction from the appropriate rent control agency, or affidavit of exemption;

(d) where applicable, a copy of any affidavit of compliance with local con-dominium conversion eviction laws;

(e) the entry fee, unless waived; and

(f) jury claim if deemed desirable.

Step 7. If an Answer is filed by the defendant, review it to see if any affirmative defenses or counterclaims are asserted. If a jury claim has not been filed and a counterclaim has been filed with no jury claim, consider whether to file a demand for jury trial as to the counterclaim. The Rules read together with the statute creating the one trial system, (G.L. c. 218, § 19B), are not clear on this point. The statute provides that any party may demand a jury trial by filing a demand in writing "after the commencement of the action." But it also refers to a "timely demand for jury trial." The Uniform Summary Process Rules provide that a jury demand must be filed no later than the date upon which the defendant's answer is due.[1] They also provide that no responsive pleading to a counterclaim is necessary.[2] The Rules further provide that where the Summary Process Rules then the Rules of Civil Procedure do not cover a matter shall govern.[3] Rule 38 of the Rules of Civil Procedure provide that a jury trial of any issue triable of right by a jury may be demanded no later than 10 days after service of the last pleading directed to that issue. Reading all this together it is submitted that the plaintiff could file an answer to any counterclaim along with a jury claim within 10 days after service of the counterclaim.

Step 8. Determine if you need discovery, and if so move for postponements to allow for discovery. Remember that discovery requests by either side always mean delay. (Summary Process Rule 7) Since the defendant may have sent you a set of burdensome discovery papers which will often go somewhat afield of the issue in the case, i.e., did he pay his rent, you may consider sending interrogatories of your own. Note however that if you receive a discovery request from defendant on the Monday before the hearing the Rule read literally seems to require that you file your own discovery requests on the same day.

Step 9. If a request for discovery is filed by the defendant, the hearing date is automatically postponed and you must respond to the request within 10 days of receipt. Diary this day and the new hearing date, which is two weeks after the original hearing date.

§ 14.02[2]　At the Court Hearing

Step 10. If an Answer is timely filed by the defendant, appear with witnesses on the scheduled hearing date ready for trial.

Step 11. If no Answer is filed you have the option of appearing on the original hearing date without your witnesses. If the defendant appears at the hearing you are entitled to an automatic one week postponement. This can save your client the trouble and expense of appearing ready for trial where there will be no opposition. However, if the defendant does appear and you are not ready to go forward there will be an additional one week delay that could have been avoided if you were ready to go forward. Most landlords are very sensitive to delays if they have stopped receiving rent. You may want to discuss this issue with your client before making a decision. Given the enormous potential for delay inherent in the legal process,

---

[1] Rule 8.
[2] Rule 5.
[3] Rule 1.

if your client has stopped receiving rent it is very much in his interest to negotiate an agreement giving the tenant a period of time, e.g. 30 days, to vacate the premises. This agreement, if it can be worked out, should be put in the form of an Agreement for Judgment with a waiver of all rights of appeal. This way if the tenant reneges on the agreement at the end of 30 days and refuses to leave you still have eliminated the delay potential of appeal and the exposure from any counterclaims which may have been filed.

Step 12. Put on your case in chief separately from rebuttal where counterclaims are alleged. Be sure the judge knows you wish to do this.

You may use the following checklist for entering the landlord's case into evidence:
General
— Show ownership or superior right to possession
— Establish nature of tenancy: lease, oral or written tenant at will
— Introduce notice to quit
— Show actual receipt of notice to quit
— Show notice to quit expired before service date of complaint
Non Payment Case
— Show correct notice period
— Rent records and testimony by landlord
Other Fault Cases
— Show correct notice period and rent day
— Point out facts alleged in the notice to quit
— Same facts alleged in the complaint
— Prove said facts constituting cause
— Show that facts constituting cause are violation of lease terms
Non Fault Cases
— Show correct notice period and rent day

Step 13. If the defendant is defaulted have with you, completed, signed, and ready for filing with the clerk the following:

(a) military affidavit (signed by a competent person on his own knowledge); (Volume 6, Chapter 14, Form 106.)

(b) where a claim for rent is made, an affidavit stating the total of any payments on account of rent made subsequent to the commencement of the action. (Volume 6, Chapter 14, Form 107.) (*See also* Volume 6, Chapter 14, Form 108, widely used prior to adoption of Uniform Rules and probably still acceptable to most courts.)

§ 14.02[3]   After the Hearing

Step 14. If you obtain judgment, wait for the 10-day appeal period to run and request execution from the clerk. When execution is in hand, arrange with a process server for eviction, if defendant will not leave voluntarily. (*See* Volume 6, Chapter 14, Form 109.) Advise the officer as to the statutory limitations on service of and levying upon executions for possession of residential property, where appropriate. It is suggested that a copy of the statute (G.L. c. 239, § 3) be sent along with the execution.

If the defendant appeals then execution will not issue. The court will set an appeal bond which must be posted as a condition to the right to appeal. This bond according to the statute (G.L. c. 239, § 5) is to cover all rent accrued at the date of the bond, all intervening rent, any loss suffered by the landlord from the withholding of possession, including any injury to the premises, and all costs. However district court judges do not in practice set bonds large enough to cover all these items. Frequently the bond is set in the amount of the accrued rent at the time of the judgment. The judge will be influenced by the various "human" factors in the case.

The defendant may move for waiver of the appeal bond if he or she is indigent. The court is required by the rules to schedule a hearing on the motion within 3 days. This may not happen automatically as it is supposed to. If it does not your office may have to follow up to get the motion marked and heard and keep the case moving. If the bond is waived the court will set a monthly payment which must be paid by the defendant as rent during the appeal. Very often this amount will be the contract rent. However the defendant may argue that the tenancy has been terminated so there is no contract rent, and that the poor condition of the premises reduces the value of use and occupancy and that a lesser amount should be paid. If the defendant is unhappy with the action of the district court on the appeal bond he or she may appeal to the appellate division of that court for review. In the housing court or superior court this appeal would be to the single justice of the Appeals Court. This appeal must be taken within 6 days of notice of the decision of the district court. It appears from the language of the statute that the defendant can appeal either the denial of the waiver or the amount of the periodic payment, while the plaintiff can only appeal the amount of the payment. After all appeals are exhausted the defendant must pay the bond amount or the periodic payment amount into court within 5 days or the appeal will be dismissed.

Step 15. If the court decides against you, you have 10 days to enter your notice of appeal. (*See* Volume 6, Chapter 14, Form 110.)

§ 14.03　Summary Process/Evictions Representing the Tenant

§ 14.03[1]　Prior to Court Hearing

Step 1. Get the basic information from the client which is necessary to complete the Information List—Summary Process, Volume 6, Chapter 14.

Step 2. Review possible affirmative defenses and counterclaims. If the likely value of viable counterclaims exceeds $25,000 consider whether you want to bring them in this forum. Consider whether you wish to claim a trial by jury of six. Even at this late date it is wise to consider a request for an inspection by the local health officer if you believe that there are substantial sanitary code violations in the premises, although it may be difficult to get local officials to act quickly enough. (*See* 13.06 *supra.*)

Step 3. Draft and file your Answer on or before the Monday next preceding the hearing date shown on the Summons. (Volume 6, Chapter 14, Form 111.)

Step 4. Decide whether discovery is needed. If so, file a Demand for Discovery on the plaintiff, with a copy to the clerk, at the same time your Answer is served. (Volume 6, Chapter 14, Form 112.)

Be sure to read and comply with Rule 7 of the Summary Process Rules, respecting discovery.

Step 5. After receiving response to Demand for Discovery, review possible defenses and counterclaims with other information in the file to develop a strategy for establishing each.

§ 14.03[2]　At the Court Hearing

Step 6. Make the presentation of your client's case as well organized and succinct as possible. Avoid cumulative witnesses and overly exhaustive direct or cross-examination. If your client has defenses make it clear that these are advanced in good faith and not as the excuses of a deadbeat.

Step 7. If the plaintiff prevails on the issue of possession, and the termination was for a reason other than nonpayment, request a stay of execution, if no appeal is contemplated.

You may use the following checklist for entering the tenant's case in evidence:

Defenses:
- — Nonreceipt of Notice to Quit
- — Improper or insufficient Notice to Quit
- — Notice to quit not filed with complaint
- — Complaint not served or served before Notice period expired

— Complaint entered late
— Improper venue
— Rent control or condominium conversion requirements not met
— Statutory cure by tenant, through payment or otherwise
— Improper notice of rent increase
— Rent tendered and accepted after Notice to Quit
— Statutory rent withholding
— Amount unpaid is not rent, but other debts or fees
— G.L. c. 239, § 8A offset where damages suffered are equal or greater than rent owed, including counterclaim damages
— Cause alleged in complaint is not good cause
— Lease violation alleged not material or has been cured
— Lease contains illegal provisions
— Where housing is public or subsidized, grievance procedure not complied with, or improperly conducted
— Violation of covenant of quiet enjoyment Counterclaims:
— Violation of Consumer Protection Act, M.G.L. c. 93A, § 9
— Discrimination, Race, etc., M.G.L. c. 151B, §§ 4, 6–11, 13, 18
— Breach of Quiet Enjoyment, M.G.L. c. 186, § 14
— Retaliatory Eviction, M.G.L. c. 186, § 18
— Violation of Security Deposit and Last Month's Rent Requirements, M.G.L. c. 186, § 15B
— Breach of Warranty of Habitability

§ 14.03[3]   After the Court Hearing

Step 8. If your client can afford to appeal on the issues of rent, possession, and/or any counterclaims, and wishes to do so, file the notice of appeal within 10 days after entry of the judgment. (Volume 6, Chapter 14, Form 110.)

Post the required appeal bond under G.L. c. 239, § 5.

Step 9. If your client is indigent as defined in G.L. c. 261, § 27A and cannot afford to post an appeal bond, file a motion to waive the appeal bond, along with supporting affidavits signed by your client and others with personal knowledge of his or her situation.

These documents should be filed along with the notice of appeal. (Volume 6, Chapter 14, Forms 113, 114.) *See* the discussion of waiver of appeal bonds at § 13.09.

Step 10. If the motion for waiver is denied, file a request for review with the clerk within 6 days of receipt of notice of the decision of the court. Argue the motion before the reviewing court.

Step 11. Comply with the decision of the reviewing court on the appeal bond within 5 days of receiving it.

Step 12. If and when the landlord obtains final judgment in the case, apply to the Court for a stay of execution and contact the opposing attorney to try to arrange time for voluntary departure by your client. Remember, it is very expensive and time-consuming to remove a tenant and his or her possessions involuntarily, so you have some leverage even if you lose your motion for a stay.

CHAPTER 15

THE CHARACTERISTICS AND USES OF NOMINEE REALTY TRUSTS—GENERAL PRINCIPLES OF LAW

Synopsis

§ 15.01   **Generally**

§ 15.02   **Common Provisions of Nominee Trusts**

§ 15.03   **Reasons for Using Nominee Trust**

§ 15.04   **Liability to Third Persons**
        § 15.04[1]   **Liability of Trustees**
        § 15.04[2]   **Liability of Beneficiaries**

§ 15.05   **Relationship Between Trustee and Beneficiary**

§ 15.06   **Maintaining Pass-Through Tax Status of Nominee Trusts**

§ 15.01   Generally

In recent years the nominee trust has come into ever more common use as a vehicle for the ownership of real property. Many lawyers, and even non-lawyers, such as brokers and builders, have developed or obtained standard form nominee trusts which they use over and over again. One lawyer even advised this writer that he regularly uses nominee trusts as substitutes for homestead exemptions to protect the principal dwellings of clients against creditors.

Given the widespread use of these instruments as vehicles for real estate ownership, there is a surprising amount of misunderstanding as to their nature and effect.[1]

§ 15.02   Common Provisions of Nominee Trusts

Most nominee trusts are only a few pages long, because the relationship between the beneficiaries is usually set out at length in an off-record document or documents. While there are of course drafting differences between them depending on individual circumstances, the main or core provisions of all nominee trusts tend to be quite similar.

The trust instrument will nearly always contain provisions according to the following tenor:

1) A declaration by one or more persons that they hold property as trustees for one or more undisclosed beneficiaries whose names appear on a Schedule of Beneficial Interests signed by the trustees and beneficiaries and filed with the trustees.

2) The trustees have no power to distribute principal or income or otherwise to deal in or with the trust property except as directed by the beneficiaries.

3) Notwithstanding any other provisions of the trust instrument, third persons may rely on the certificate of one or more persons who appear from the records to be trustees of the trust as to the existence or nonexistence of any fact or facts which constitute conditions precedent to acts by the trustee or are in any other way relevant to the affairs of the trust.

4) The beneficiaries, or any one of them, may at any time terminate the trust by notice in writing to the trustees in which case the trustees shall transfer legal title to the beneficiaries as tenants in common in proportion to their respective interests.

5) In some instruments it is also provided that a trustee may be a beneficiary of the trust and nevertheless exercise all rights of a beneficiary.

---

[1] *See* Birnbaum and Monahan, *The Nominee Trust in Massachusetts. Real Estate Practice*, 60 M.L.Q. 364 (1976).

The trust is usually recorded in the registry of deeds for each district in which the trust holds land. Title is held in the name of "X and Y, as trustees of the ABC Realty Trust, under a certain declaration of trust recorded with Z Registry of Deeds at Book _____, Page _____."

The beneficiaries of the trust are often listed on the unrecorded schedule of Schedule of Beneficial Interests as follows:

Beneficiary	Proportionate Interest
John Jones	50%
Samuel Smith	40%
Judy Jones	10%

This type of arrangement, although simple, is not recommended in most cases because it does not supply the specifics of the relationship between the beneficiaries which are left out of the trust instrument itself. The better practice is to name the trustee of another trust or a corporation as the 100% beneficiary of the nominee trust.

§ 15.03 Reasons for Using Nominee Trust

There are a number of advantages in using nominee trusts some or all of which may be important in a given transaction.

The most obvious advantage is that the beneficial owners of the trust property do not appear in the public records and may thereby protect their identity from creditors, ex-spouses, and others who do not wish them well.[1] Although, as pointed out below, in appropriate circumstances the identity of the beneficiaries may be discovered through judicial procedures.

With a nominee trust the beneficial interest or interests in the property may be sold by an off-record transfer assigning the seller's interest in the trust to the purchaser. The trustees of the trust may then be replaced if required by the purchaser. This type of off-record transfer may avoid triggering the due-on-sale clause of a mortgage, where the trustees are not in fact changed, although this very much depends on the language of the specific clause sought to be avoided.

Nominee trusts are often used in condominium, time share, or other commercial real estate projects where there are many owners and/or many documents must be signed on a regular basis.

---

[1] The enactment of G.L. c. 184, § 35 in 2003 has eliminated the need to record the entire trust document in the registry of deeds in order for the trustee to be able to give clear title to trust property. So this reason for the use of a nominee trust has lost some force.

And the use of such a trust with a partnership or limited partnership as beneficiary will avoid the difficulties and inconveniences associated with holding and transferring real property when owned directly by those entities.

Where corporate real property is held through a nominee trust the problem of obtaining evidence at the time of sale of the authority of the signatory officers to mortgage or sell the property is eliminated. Many lawyers believe the need to obtain the tax waiver required upon the sale of all or substantially all of a corporation's assets is eliminated as well. But there is substantial disagreement on this point, and some lawyers not only believe the waiver is required but insist on a trustee's certificate to the effect that the beneficiary is not a corporation or, if it is, that the sale does not involve all or substantially all of the corporate beneficiary's assets.

Because the exact identity of trustee and beneficiary could render the nominee trust a nullity many lawyers require a statement in the Trustee's Certificate that the trustee and beneficiary are not the same person.[2]

§ 15.04   Liability to Third Persons

It seems that, under applicable Massachusetts case law, for most purposes a nominee trust is not really a trust at all, but in fact is a an agency agreement that is using an agent or agents to hold legal title to real property.[1] The crucial difference in the two types of legal relationship is that in the "true" trust the trustees are masters over the property with the beneficiaries having only the right to receive income or principal, while in the nominee trust the beneficiaries have total control over all aspects of the ownership and management of the property. It seems that the draftsman of the trust can affect whether the nominee trust will be treated as an agency by the extent to which he limits the discretionary powers of the trustee. However nothing seems to be certain with this centaur of legal instruments, and how the courts treat it may very well be fact-driven, on a case-by-case basis.[2]

§ 15.04[1]   Liability of Trustees

In the case of a true trust the liability of trustees to third persons has been

---

[2] Druker v. State Tax Com., 374 Mass. 198, 372 N.E.2d 208 (1978).

[1] Williams v. Milton, 215 Mass. 1, 102 N.E. 355 (1913); Penta v. Concord Auto Auction, Inc., 24 Mass. App. 635 (1987). *But see* Roberts v. Roberts, 419 Mass. 685, 646 N.E.2d 1061 (1995), where the Court treated a nominee trust as a trust rather than an agency, and pointed out that a nominee trust could be an agency in some contexts and a trust in others. The facts of the case are such that it may be a hard case making bad law.

[2] *See* Williams v. Milton, 215 Mass. 1, 102 N.E. 355 (1913); Penta v. Concord Auto Auction, Inc., 24 Mass. App. 635 (1987). *But see* Roberts v. Roberts, 419 Mass. 685, 646 N.E.2d 1061 (1995). *See also* Zuroff v. First Wis. Trust Co., 41 Mass. App. 491, 671 N.E.2d 982 (1996), wherein a recorded lien against an individual who was trustee and a 51% beneficiary of a nominee trust was held not to reach the trust assets.

controlled by statute since January 1, 1978.[3] Unless otherwise provided in the contract, the trustee is not liable on a contract properly entered into on behalf of the trust unless he/she failed to reveal his representative capacity and identify the trust estate in the contract. He is liable in tort only if he was personally at fault.[4]

This seems little more than a codification of well-established common law rules relating to the liability of agents to third parties. That is, the agent of an undisclosed or partially disclosed principal is liable on a contract along with his master absent a specific exculpatory provision.[5] But his tort liability is unaffected by the fact that he is acting as an agent at the time of the tortious incident,[6] and he is bound only if he is personally at fault.

The Appeals Court has held that the statutory exemption from liability given to trustees by G.L. c. 203, § 14A "does not encompass the case of trustees who are trustees for themselves in the conduct of business affairs or are trustees of a nominee trust."[7] The Supreme Judicial Court has gone further and held that the statute does not apply to any trustees other than those acting under the donative type of trust associated with probate practice.[8]

§ 15.04[2]   Liability of Beneficiaries

In general, the beneficiaries of a true trust are not personally liable to trust creditors, including judgment creditors.[9] In the case of nominee trusts, if they are in fact principal/agent relationships, the beneficiaries would be liable as partially disclosed principals.[10] Although in the case of contracts an exculpatory clause in the trust instrument,[11] (if the other party is aware of it), or in the contract, or in the specific facts of a given transaction,[12] can limit liability to the trust assets only, there would appear to be no way of preventing tort liability based on the usual agency principles.[13]

The trust estate in a true trust is protected from the creditors of individual

---

[3] G.L. c. 203, § 14A, added by St. 1976, c. 515 and St. 1977, c. 76.

[4] G.L. c. 203, § 14A, added by St. 1976, c. 515 and St. 1977, c. 76.

[5] Mechem, Outlines of Law of Agency, (4th ed.) §§ 294–295; Sylvia v. Johnson, 44 Mass. App. 483 (1998). *But Cf.* Rogaris v. Albert, 431 Mass. 833 (2000).

[6] Mechem, §§ 343 *et seq.*

[7] Apahouser Lock & Secur. Corp. v. Carvelli, 26 Mass. App. 385, 528 N.E.2d 133 (1988), *review denied*, 403 Mass. 1104, 530 N.E.2d 797.

[8] First Eastern Bank, N.A. v. Jones, 413 Mass. 654, 602 N.E.2d 211 (1992).

[9] Scott, The Law of Trusts, (3rd ed.) § 267.

[10] Mechem, op. cit. n.4, *supra.*

[11] Sylvia v. Johnson, 44 Mass. App. 483 (1998).

[12] FDIC v. Porter, 46 Mass. App. 241 (1999).

[13] Scott, The Law of Trusts, (3rd ed.) §§ 349 *et seq.* Morrison v. Lennett, 415 Mass. 857, 616 N.E.2d 92 (1993), summary opinion at (Mass) 21 M.L.W. 3124.

beneficiaries. In the case of a spendthrift trust even the equitable interest of the beneficiary may be protected from creditors while the beneficiary is allowed to enjoy and even assign his right to benefits under the trust.[14] But a discretionary or spendthrift trust may not be created by a person for his or her own benefit as a way of defeating creditors.[15]

It seems most unlikely that a spendthrift provision in a nominee trust would be given effect by the courts, given the fact that they are unlikely to treat the trust as a true trust. In any case, a better method if this type of protection is desired would be to use a traditional trust with spendthrift provisions as the beneficiary of the nominee trust.[16]

§ 15.05   Relationship Between Trustee and Beneficiary

Since the nominee trust is not in fact a true trust the obligation of the trustee to the beneficiaries probably does not rise to the level of strictest fidelity imposed on a traditional trustee.[1] However, the relationship between them is certainly a fiduciary one, as is the relationship between principal and agent. The trustee would at least have a duty of loyalty and fidelity to the interests of the beneficiaries, and could not place him or herself in a position where his own personal interests conflicted with those of his principal. Nor could the trustee act in any way adverse to the interests of the beneficiaries.[2]

The trustee has no standing, as such, to bring an action that is personal to one or more of the trust beneficiaries. The beneficiary could of course assign the claim to the trustee, who could then bring the action, unless it is a personal injury claim.[3]

§ 15.06   Maintaining Pass-Through Tax Status of Nominee Trusts

It seems clear that the nominee trust would be a pass-through entity for federal tax purposes given the power over the trust property given to or retained by the settlors and/or beneficiaries.[1]

There is more risk of creating such a trust as a taxable entity for state tax

---

[14] Boston Safe Deposit & Trust Co. v. Luke, 220 Mass. 484, 108 N.E. 64 (1915), *aff'd*, 240 U.S. 427, 60 L. Ed. 723, 36 S. Ct. 391.

[15] Ware v. Gulda, 331 Mass. 68, 117 N.E.2d 137 (1954).

[16] Shamrock, Inc. v. FDIC, 36 Mass. App. 162, 629 N.E.2d 344 (1994), summary opinion at 22 M.L.W. 1325 (Mass. App.) and *review denied*, 417 Mass. 1105, 635 N.E.2d 252, 22 M.L.W. 1790.

[1] Gardiner v. Rogers, 267 Mass. 274, 166 N.E. 763 (1929).

[2] Lanigan v. Scharton, 238 Mass. 468, 131 N.E. 223 (1921); Mechem, Outlines of Law of Agency, (4th ed.) § 500.

[3] Vittands v. Sudduth, 49 Mass. App. 401 (2000).

[1] I.R.C. §§ 674(a), 2036, 678, 2041(a)(2), 2514.

purposes.[2] It seems clear that trusts which are completely controlled by the beneficiaries are to be ignored for state tax purposes.[3]

---

[2] Birnbaum and Monahan, *The Nominee Trust in Massachusetts. Real Estate Practice*, 60 M.L.Q. 364 (1976).,at p. 369.

[3] Druker v. State Tax Com., 374 Mass. 198, 372 N.E.2d 208 (1978).

CHAPTER 16

THE CHARACTERISTICS AND USES OF NOMINEE TRUSTS—THE PRACTICE

Synopsis

§ 16.01   Drafting a Nominee Trust
            § 16.01[1]   Introduction
            § 16.01[2]   Establishment of Trust
            § 16.01[3]   Trustees' Powers
            § 16.01[4]   Termination of the Trust
            § 16.01[5]   Trustee Succession
            § 16.01[6]   Relations Between Trust and Third Persons
            § 16.01[7]   Limitation on Liability to Third Persons
            § 16.01[8]   Ancillary Documents

§ 16.01   Drafting a Nominee Trust

§ 16.01[1]   Introduction

This section is, in essence, an annotation of the form of nominee trust which appears as Form 124 in Volume 6, Chapter 16. An attempt is made in each section to explain the purposes and effect of the language contained in each paragraph of the form document.

Most nominee trusts that one sees in use are variations on the simple general type of Form 124. Of course complex or specialized real estate transactions may require a more elaborate document. However it seems counterproductive to make the recorded nominee trust any more complex than absolutely necessary, since the documents creating the partnership, trust, or corporation which may be made the beneficiary of the nominee trust are the proper place for any needed complexity or specificity.

§ 16.01[2]   Establishment of Trust

The first paragraph of the trust should contain language which declares the creation of the trust relationship by the original trustee(s), who first sign and record the instrument. The name of the trust is set out; and, most importantly, the beneficiaries are identified only as the persons whose names are set forth in a document identified as a "Schedule of Beneficial Interest" which is signed by the trustees, their proportionate interest being as set out in the Schedule.

§ 16.01[3]   Trustees' Powers

The trust should define carefully the powers of the trustee. Since the total control given to the beneficiaries over the trust property by the first few lines of this paragraph have the likely effect of turning the trust document into an agency document, it is important to be quite specific in setting out the agent's powers. There will be no powers implicitly given to the trustee under statute or common law to fill in any omissions.

The degree of control over the trustee given by the trust instrument to the beneficiaries will likely have a good deal of influence on how a court will treat the relationship between trustee and beneficiaries in particular contexts. For instance, will it be an agency or a trust relationship? A whole range of varieties can be conceived. At one extreme the instrument would give the trustee no power except to hold title, and at the other, the instrument would give the trustee all of the traditional trust powers with the reservation of one or a few crucial ones to the beneficiaries. Forms 124.1 and 124.2 in Volume 6, Chapter 16, contain paragraphs relating to the powers of the trustee which can be substituted into Form 124. The first form is an example of the totally powerless trustee, who seems clearly an agent for all purposes. The second form is an example of a trustee who has the traditional powers but can only distribute principal and income, or convey the property when and as directed by all the beneficiaries. This will likely be considered to create a trust relationship in nearly all contexts.

§ 16.01[4] Termination of the Trust

It is customary to provide that any one or more of the beneficiaries may terminate the trust upon written notice to the trustees; and that all of the trustees may join together to terminate the trust by written notice to the beneficiaries.

It is also customary to provide language in the nature of a perpetuities saving clause to the effect that the trust will terminate in any case twenty years after the death of the survivor of the trustees named in the trust. Given the unlikelihood of the nominee trust being in fact treated as a trust by the courts this language seems of little consequence for purposes of trust law. However it may be useful in helping to assure the status of the trust as a pass-through entity for federal tax purposes in that it assures that the entity does not have perpetual or indefinite life.

Upon termination of the trust, by whichever means, the trustees must convey the trust property to the beneficiaries as tenants in common in proportion to their respective interests.

§ 16.01[5] Trustee Succession

Paragraph 4 of Form 124 has the more common provisions respecting trustee succession found in realty trusts, whether nominee trusts or not. There is also language allowing the beneficiaries to appoint and remove trustees, and also to add to the number of trustees by a written instrument signed by all of them. Either this instrument or a trustees' certificate must be recorded in the appropriate registries of deeds.

Since one of the main purposes for using a nominee trust is to assure the anonymity of the beneficiaries there will naturally be some reluctance to record an instrument signed by them. In cases where all trustees have resigned or left office it will be impossible to use a trustees' certificate. Therefore, provision for a set or two of successor trustees is made in the trust instrument itself.

§ 16.01[6] Relations Between Trust and Third Persons

The most important provision of the nominee trust with respect to its relationship with third persons is that respecting trustees' certificates. It is always provided that persons dealing with trust property or trustees may rely on the written certification of any trustee as to any matter germane to the affairs of the trust. Such a certificate is thus conclusive with respect to the trust in favor of any person relying upon the same. The trustee may not act except upon and in accordance with the direction of the beneficiaries, who are unknown to third persons. Therefore the trustee's certificate that his actions are duly authorized is an essential pre-condition to the willingness of third persons to deal with the trust.

As is seen in paragraph 5 of Form 124, Volume 6, Chapter 16, nominee trusts usually contain, in addition the traditional trust language limiting the liability of third persons dealing with the trustee and of the trustee to the beneficiaries.

§ 16.01[7]   Limitation on Liability to Third Persons

As discussed above, the idea of limited liability for trustees and beneficiaries of nominee trusts is probably more chimera than fact, the one exception to this being liability arising out of contracts containing specific exculpatory clauses. Attempts to limit liability based on language contained in the trust instrument itself are not liable to be any more successful in the case of nominee trust than they were in the case of other types of trusts prior to the enactment of G.L. c.203, § 14A.

However there is no harm done in putting the language in the trust. Paragraph 6 of Form 124, Volume 6, Chapter 16, is an example of this kind of language.

§ 16.01[8]   Ancillary Documents

Since the trustees may not act without the specific direction of the trustees, it is customary to prepare a specific written Direction of Beneficiaries authorizing each significant transaction. This protects the trustees, and persons dealing with them will sometimes be able to insist on seeing the Direction. (Volume 6, Chapter 16, Form 125)

Whenever the trust deals with third persons on any matter of significance, they will insist on having, and where appropriate recording, a trustee's certificate which will attest to all matters of importance such as the existence of the trust and the authority of the trustees to act. (Volume 6, Chapter 16, Form 126)

Of course, a Schedule of Beneficiaries is an integral part of any nominee trust. This is a fairly simple document which binds the beneficiaries to the trustees in a fiduciary relationship in accordance with the trust terms. (Volume 6, Chapter 16, Form 127)

Where an interest in a nominee trust is transferred from one entity to another, this is accomplished through a written but off-record transaction. Whether this kind of transaction is a transfer of an interest in real estate requiring the affixing of excise tax stamps to the document is a matter of dispute among conveyancing attorneys. (Volume 6, Chapter 16, Form 128)

CHAPTER 17

REAL ESTATE TAX ABATEMENTS AND EXEMPTIONS

Synopsis

§ 17.01   **Generally**

    § 17.01[1]   **Definition of Real Property**

    § 17.01[2]   **Owner with Multiple Parcels**

    § 17.01[3]   **Land and Buildings Are Taxed Together**

    § 17.01[4]   **Real Estate Under "Permanent Restriction"**

    § 17.01[5]   **Property with Multiple Owners of Fractional Interests**

    § 17.01[6]   **Taxation of "Brownfields" Property**

    § 17.01[7]   **Generally**

    § 17.01[8]   **If Tax Is Invalidated by Error or Irregularity**

    § 17.01[9]   **Effect of Clerical Errors**

    § 17.01[10]   **If Property Is Omitted from Annual Assessment**

    § 17.01[11]   **Generally**

    § 17.01[12]   **Personal Liability for Tax**

    § 17.01[13]   **If Real Estate Is Divided or Sold Before Tax Is Paid**

    § 17.01[14]   **Deceased Persons or Persons Unknown**

    § 17.01[15]   **Mortgagees**

    § 17.01[16]   **Condominium Owners**

    § 17.01[17]   **Planned Unit or Cluster Developments**

    § 17.01[18]   **Lessees of Public Property**

    § 17.01[19]   **Returns Filed by All Taxpayers**

    § 17.01[20]   **Returns by Organizations Claiming Charitable Exemption**

    § 17.01[21]   **Returns by Other Persons Claiming Exemption**

    § 17.01[22]   **Effect of Failure to Furnish List**

    § 17.01[23]   **Assessors' Right to Question Taxpayers by Questionnaire**

§ 17.01[24]   Assessors' Right to Question Businesses As to Profit/Loss
§ 17.01[25]   Generally
§ 17.01[26]   Public Access to Records of Assessors

§ 17.02   Introduction
§ 17.02[1]   Time for Application and Qualification
§ 17.02[2]   Generally
§ 17.02[3]   The United States
§ 17.02[4]   The Commonwealth
§ 17.02[5]   One Municipality Owning Property Located in Another
§ 17.02[6]   Generally
§ 17.02[7]   Definition of Charitable Organization
§ 17.02[8]   Use of Property for Noncharitable Purposes
§ 17.02[9]   Generally
§ 17.02[10]   Houses of Worship and Effect of Non-Religious Use on Exemption
§ 17.02[11]   Parsonages
§ 17.02[12]   Cemeteries
§ 17.02[13]   Nonprofit Hospitals and Other Medical Organizations
§ 17.02[14]   Urban Redevelopment Corporations
    § 17.02[14][a]   Payments by Urban Redevelopment Corporation in Lieu of Taxes
    § 17.02[14][b]   Project Developed in Separate Stages
    § 17.02[14][c]   Valuation of Property—Right to Appeal
    § 17.02[14][d]   Determination of Fair Cash Value Prior to Construction
§ 17.02[15]   Housing and Redevelopment Authorities
§ 17.02[16]   Veterans
§ 17.02[17]   Surviving Spouses, Orphans and Poor Persons
§ 17.02[18]   Aged Homeowners
§ 17.02[19]   Living in Multi-family Dwelling
§ 17.02[20]   Owning Less than Entire Property
§ 17.02[21]   Deferral of Tax
§ 17.02[22]   Manufactured Homes
§ 17.02[23]   Forest Land
§ 17.02[24]   Obtaining the Exemption
§ 17.02[25]   Appeal of State Forester's Decisions
§ 17.02[26]   Keeping the Exemption
§ 17.02[27]   Taxation of Classified Forest Land
§ 17.02[28]   Appeal of Assessment of Tax
§ 17.02[29]   Withdrawal from Classification
§ 17.02[30]   Conversion to Nonforest Use: First Refusal Option
§ 17.02[31]   Agricultural and Horticultural Land
§ 17.02[32]   Agricultural Land—Definition
§ 17.02[33]   Horticultural Land—Definition

§ 17.02[34]   **Minimum Area and Dollar Sales**

§ 17.02[35]   **Application for Eligibility**

§ 17.02[36]   **Valuation**

     § 17.02[36][a]   **Taxation of Farmhouses and Other Structures**

     § 17.02[36][b]   **Special or Betterment Assessments**

     § 17.02[36][c]   **Valuation for Other than Assessment Purposes**

§ 17.02[37]   **Effect of Sale or Change of Use**

     § 17.02[37][a]   **Conveyance Tax**

     § 17.02[37][b]   **Roll-back Tax**

     § 17.02[37][c]   **Conveyance and Roll-back Taxes—Relationship to One Another**

§ 17.02[38]   **Municipality's Option to Purchase Upon Sale or Conversion**

§ 17.02[39]   **Sale or Conversion of a Portion of Qualified Lands**

§ 17.02[40]   **Appeals from Determinations of Assessors**

§ 17.02[41]   **Agricultural Preservation Restrictions**

§ 17.02[42]   **Recreational Land**

§ 17.02[43]   **Recreational Land—Definition**

§ 17.02[44]   **Application for Eligibility**

§ 17.02[45]   **Valuation**

     § 17.02[45][a]   **Taxation of Dwelling Houses and Associated Structures**

     § 17.02[45][b]   **Special or Betterment Assessments**

§ 17.02[46]   **Effect of Sale or Change of Use**

     § 17.02[46][a]   **Conveyance Tax**

     § 17.02[46][b]   **Roll-back Tax**

     § 17.02[46][c]   **Conveyance and Roll-back Taxes—Relationship to One Another**

§ 17.02[47]   **Municipality's Option to Purchase Upon Sale or Conversion**

§ 17.02[48]   **Sale or Conversion of a Portion of Qualified Land**

§ 17.02[49]   **Appeals from Determinations of Assessors**

§ 17.02[50]   **Other Exempt Classes of Property**

§ 17.02[51]   **Generally**

§ 17.03   **Generally**

     § 17.03[1]   **Who Applies**

     § 17.03[2]   **When**

     § 17.03[3]   **Unusual Relief for Late Applications**

     § 17.03[4]   **To Whom—Form of Application**

     § 17.03[5]   **Assessors' Right to Inspection and Information Prior to Hearing**

     § 17.03[6]   **Hearings—Evidence Taxpayer Should Introduce**

     § 17.03[7]   **Non-income Producing Property**

     § 17.03[8]   **Income Producing Property**

§ 17.03[9]   Notice of Decision or Non-action
§ 17.03[10]   General Rules for Appeals
§ 17.03[11]   Late Appeals
§ 17.03[12]   Payment of Tax as Prerequisite to Appeal
§ 17.03[13]   Inability to Pay—Tax-Effect on Appeal
§ 17.03[14]   Assessors' Right to Remove from County Commissioners
§ 17.03[15]   Interest on Abated Taxes
§ 17.03[16]   Taxpayers Right to Certificate of Abatement
§ 17.03[17]   Effect if Property Sold or Taken for Non-payment of Taxes During Pendency Appeal

§ 17.04   Generally
§ 17.04[1]   Structure of the Board
§ 17.04[2]   Publication of Decisions
§ 17.04[3]   Right of Appeal to the Board
§ 17.04[4]   Jurisdiction
§ 17.04[5]   The Formal Procedure—Taxpayer's Petition
§ 17.04[6]   Assessors' Answer
§ 17.04[7]   The Informal Procedure—Taxpayer's Statement
§ 17.04[8]   Assessors' Answer
§ 17.04[9]   Assessors' Right to Elect the Formal Procedure
§ 17.04[10]   Discovery
§ 17.04[11]   Motion Practice
§ 17.04[12]   Telephone Motions
§ 17.04[13]   Continuances
§ 17.04[14]   Pre-hearing Conferences
§ 17.04[15]   Hearings
§ 17.04[16]   Taking of Views
§ 17.04[17]   Stenographic Reports of Proceedings
§ 17.04[18]   Costs of Suit
§ 17.04[19]   Appeals from Decisions of the Appellate Tax Board
§ 17.04[20]   Insuring Full Review on Appeal
§ 17.04[21]   Evidence Necessary to Sustain the Decision of the Board on Appeal

§ 17.05   Introduction
§ 17.05[1]   The Concept of Highest and Best Use
§ 17.05[2]   Replacement Cost
§ 17.05[3]   Generally
§ 17.05[4]   The Market Sales Comparison Method
§ 17.05[5]   The Cost Minus Depreciation Method (Depreciated Reproduction Cost)
§ 17.05[6]   Replacement Cost
§ 17.05[7]   Accrued Depreciation
§ 17.05[8]   The Capitalization of Income Method

§ 17.05[8][a]   Capitalization Rate

§ 17.05[8][b]   Interest Rate

§ 17.05[8][c]   Depreciation Rate

   § 17.05[8][c][i]   Straight Line Depreciation

   § 17.05[8][c][ii]   Sinking Fund Depreciation

   § 17.05[8][c][iii]   Annuity Depreciation

   § 17.05[8][c][iv]   Relative Merits of Three Depreciation Methods

§ 17.06   The Generally Accepted Valuation Methods

   § 17.06[1]   Definition

   § 17.06[2]   Rental Value as Evidence of Fair Cash Value

   § 17.06[3]   Rental Value of Owner-occupied Property

   § 17.06[4]   Rental Value of Other, Comparable Properties

   § 17.06[5]   Capitalizing Net Rental Value for Tax Purposes

   § 17.06[6]   Original Cost of Property as Evidence of Fair Cash Value

   § 17.06[7]   Sales of Other Comparable Properties as Evidence of Fair Cash Value

   § 17.06[8]   Depreciated Reproduction or Replacement Cost as Evidence of Fair Cash Value

   § 17.06[9]   Valuing Contaminated Property For Tax Purposes

   § 17.06[10]   Generally

   § 17.06[11]   Owners

   § 17.06[12]   Expert Witnesses

   § 17.06[13]   Other Persons

§ 17.07.   Generally

   § 17.07[1]   Assessment in Excess of Fair Market Value

   § 17.07[2]   Proving Assessment in Excess of Fair Market Value

   § 17.07[3]   Assessment of Different Kinds of Property at Different Percentages of Value (Disproportion)

   § 17.07[4]   Proving Disproportion

      § 17.07[4][a]   Can There Be a Class Within a Class?

   § 17.07[5]   Improper Classification

§ 17.08   Generally

   § 17.08[1]   How Classification Works

   § 17.08[2]   The Residential Exemption

   § 17.08[3]   The Small Commercial Exemption

   § 17.08[4]   Effect of Classification on Abatements and Exemptions

WHAT IS TAXED?

§ 17.01 Generally

The basic approach taken by the statute which creates the Massachusetts property tax[1] is to impose a tax on all property within the constitutional reach of the legislature, and then to carve out certain limitations, exceptions and exemptions. Thus, unless expressly made exempt, all property, whether real or personal, situated within the borders of the Commonwealth is subject to taxation.[2] If property is not exempt by statute the assessors cannot by contract with the owner make it exempt.[3] Nor can the assessors, or any other municipal officials, make any contract with a taxpayer which varies the taxpayer's rights or remedies under the law or otherwise deals with the subject of taxation.[4]

§ 17.01[1] Definition of Real Property

Real property for purposes of the local property tax is defined by the statute as all land, and any buildings or other things erected on or affixed to land.[5] Mortgages (unless the property is tax-exempt) are also supposed to be taxed as real estate.[6]

The statute requires that the mortgagor and mortgagee must each be assessed and taxed only for their respective interests in the property. Thus a $50,000 piece of property with a $25,000 mortgage should be assessed one-half to the mortgagor and one-half to the mortgagee.

However, a failure by the assessors to do so divide the tax does not make it invalid unless the mortgagor or mortgagee brings in a sworn statement of all of the mortgages held by the mortgagee, including a statement of the full amount remaining unpaid upon the subject mortgage and the mortgagee's interest therein.[7] These provisions relating to the separate assessment of mortgagors and mortgagees have been little observed in Massachusetts.[8]

It is important to realize that the traditional common law definitions of real and personal property are not necessarily applicable to taxes. In one reported case the assessors were attempting to tax certain large structures (a silo, bagging machine,

---

[1] G.L. c. 59.

[2] G.L. c. 59, § 2.

[3] Mahony v. Board of Assessors of Watertown, 362 Mass. 206, 285 N.E.2d 403 (1972); *but see* G.L. c. 121A, § 10.

[4] Town of Saugus v. Refuse Energy Systems Co., 388 Mass. 822, 448 N.E.2d 716 (1983).

[5] G.L. c. 59, § 2A.

[6] *See* G.L. c. 59, §§ 11–12B and particularly §§ 12 and 12A.

[7] *See* § 103.4, *infra*.

[8] Worcester v. City of Boston, 179 Mass. 41, 60 N.E. 410 (1901).

sand bin, dump bucket sixty-eight feet high and track and switches) as realty. The statute exempts from taxation the machinery of a domestic corporation engaged in manufacturing, so the dispute was whether the structures were exempt machinery or taxable realty. The Court found that the machinery was exempt, in the following language: "We now hold that even if the machinery by reason of its bulk or its peculiar method of affixation to the buildings themselves constituting real estate could be regarded as having become part of the real estate for some purposes, its predominant aspect for purposes of [the property tax] remains that of machinery ..."[9]

§ 17.01[2]   Owner with Multiple Parcels

When a taxpayer owns more than one parcel in a particular town there sometimes arises a disagreement between the taxpayer and the assessors as to whether the parcels are to be assessed and taxed as separate units or all together as one unit.

"There is no hard and fast rule that can be applied universally to guide assessors in determining as to whether different parcels of land are to be assessed separately or together."[10] This depends on the factual circumstances in each case, such as the physical proximity of the various parcels, whether or not they are used by the owner as a single unit, and other similar factors.

Where the assessors based their assessment on a subdivision plan which had been filed in their office but not recorded in the registry of deeds, the Supreme Judicial Court held the assessment to be valid. "There is no statutory definition of the lot or parcel of land that is the lawful unit for the creation of a tax. Contiguous parcels of land, though divided upon a plan for purposes of sale, may often be assessed as a unit. In like manner contiguous parcels of land owned by the same person may be assessed as a unit. But the several lots or parcels may also be assessed separately. The question whether the method of assessment is reasonable is in each case largely a question of fact..."[11]

Since the tax lien attaches only to the parcel assessed and not to the taxpayer's other property within the municipality, in a delinquency situation whether or not the property is assessed as one or two parcels can be a matter of great consequence to the taxpayer.[12] Note, however, that, although the tax lien attaches only to the parcel assessed, the collector can proceed against the taxpayer by suit and eventually levy on his other property.[13]

---

[9] Board of Assessors of Swampscott v. Lynn Sand & Stone Co., 360 Mass. 595, 277 N.E.2d 97 (1971).

[10] Town of Lenox v. Oglesby, 311 Mass. 269, 41 N.E.2d 45 (1942).

[11] City of Boston v. Boston Port Development Co., 308 Mass. 72, 30 N.E.2d 896 (1941).

[12] City of Marlborough v. Poorvu, 305 Mass. 124, 25 NW2d 189 (1940).

[13] G.L. c. 60, § 35.

§ 17.01[3]   Land and Buildings Are Taxed Together

Although the statute requires that land and buildings thereon be "valued" separately, they must be taxed as a single unit.[14] For abatement purposes the taxpayer cannot attack just the land valuation or just the building valuation.[15]

A structure erected on land is taxable as real estate regardless of private agreements between lessor and lessee or the degree of physical attachment to the land.[16] But the structure cannot be taxed as real estate except in connection with the land to which it is affixed."[17]

Similarly, in accordance with familiar common law principles, nursery stock growing on land, although belonging to a lessee who has a right to remove it, is part of the real estate for purposes of taxation.[18]

Probably the leading case in this area is *McGee v. City of Salem*.[19] In that case, greenhouses were assessed to their owner (the lessee of the real estate) as real estate, separate from the land on which they stood (which was assessed to another person who was the owner of the real estate). The owner of the greenhouses went bankrupt and they were sold to a third person. The tax collector tried to enforce a lien for taxes against the new owner of the greenhouses.

The Court held that the new owner was not liable. Although the statute requires separate valuation of land and buildings, they are one unit for tax purposes and cannot be taxed separately. Thus, the tax levied on the greenhouses was invalid and the tax lien did not follow the buildings to the new owners. Since only the person assessed is personally responsible for the tax, the new owners were not liable in any way.

Although the case does not reach this point, it would seem that no one would have been liable for this tax since it was improperly assessed. However, it could have been reassessed as a single tax on both land and buildings to either the landowner, or to the original owner of the greenhouses as the person in possession on the tax date.[20]

§ 17.01[4]   Real Estate Under "Permanent Restriction"

Real estate permanently restricted under the Scenic Rivers Protective Act, the

---

[14] G.L. c. 59, § 46; Newton Building Co. v. Comm. of Corp. and Taxation, 285 Mass. 471, 189 N.E. 543 (1934).

[15] Buckley v. Board of Assessors of Duxbury, 12 Mass. App. Tax Bd. Rep. 114 (1990).

[16] Board of Assessors of Darthmouth v. B.A. Simeone, Inc. , 269 N.E.2d 663 (1971).

[17] *See* McGee v. City of Salem, 149 Mass. 238, 21 N.E. 386 (1889).

[18] *See* Board of Assessors of Weston v. Paine, 297 Mass. 173, 7 N.E.2d 584 (1937).

[19] 149 Mass. 238, 21 N.E. 386 (1889).

[20] G.L. c. 59, §§ 11 and 77.

Coastal Wetlands Act, the Inland Wetlands Act, and/or under Conservation, Preservation and Agricultural Restrictions[21] must be assessed as a separate parcel.[22] This statutory requirement would presumably take precedence over the rules discussed earlier[23] relating to taxation of multiple parcels of a single owner. Taxation as a separate parcel must begin on January 1 next following the date of the restrictions. Other types of restrictions than those cited above, such as easements, will only reduce the value of the property for tax purposes.[24] There is no requirement of a separate assessment.

§ 17.01[5]   Property with Multiple Owners of Fractional Interests

Where a single piece of property is divided into multiple estates or interests (such as life estates and remainders, leasehold estate and fee, etc.), the tax thereon, regardless of to whom it is assessed, is a tax and lien on the entire estate and not just on the interest of the person taxed. For example, the statute permits taxes to be assessed to a tenant who is in possession of the property on the tax date. A sale for nonpayment of taxes assessed to that tenant in possession will divest the landlord of his title as well. The tax lien is paramount to all other interests in the property, regardless of which owner is actually assessed.[25]

As a corollary of this principle it is important to realize that Massachusetts law has traditionally held that an attempt to assess a tax on anything less than the entire interest in a parcel of real estate will result in the tax being held invalid.[26] There is but one tax assessed on any parcel, and that is a tax on the entire interest.

There is, however, a curious statutory provision[27] which appears to modify this traditional rule, and to allow the Commissioner of Revenue to authorize local assessors to split the assessment among the owners of different interests in the same parcel. In *Squantum Gardens, Inc. ,*[28] the Court referred to this statutory language as "ambiguous" but did not find it necessary to decide to what extent, if any, it permits the commissioner to authorize the assessment of taxes on less than the entire interest in a parcel of real estate, and thereby modifies the traditional rule. This statute is of little practical consequence at the present time.

---

[21] *See* G.L. c. 21, § 17B; c. 130, § 105; c. 131, § 40A; c. 184, 31.

[22] G.L. c. 59, § 11.

[23] *See* 17.01[2], *supra.*

[24] Lodge v. Inhabitants of Swampscott, 216 Mass. 260, 103 N.E. 635 (1913).

[25] G.L. c. 60, § 56; Donovan v. Haverhill, 247 Mass. 69, 141 N.E. 564 (1923).

[26] G.L. c. 60, § 56; Donovan v. Haverhill, 247 Mass. 69, 141 N.E. 564 (1923).

[27] "…whenever the Commissioner [of Revenue] deems it proper he may, in writing, authorize the assessment of taxes upon any present interest in real estate to the owner of such interest on January 1, and taxes on such interest may thereupon be assessed to such person." G.L. c. 59, § 11.

[28] 335 Mass. 140, 140 N.E.2d 482 (1957).

§ 17.01[6] Taxation of "Brownfields" Property

The so-called "Brownfields Bill," enacted in 1998, included a local option provision that allows municipalities to make agreements regarding the payment of outstanding real estate taxes, interest and penalties, including abatement of those amounts needed to make cleanup and redevelopment of a polluted property economically feasible. These agreements must:

Cover a property contaminated with oil or hazardous material and zoned for commercial or industrial use.

. Be entered into with an eligible owner under G.L. c. 21E, § 2. Eligible owners are new, innocent, purchasers who did not own the site at the time the oil or hazardous material was released and did not cause or contribute to its release.

. Specify the details agreed to regarding payment of any outstanding obligations, including abatements granted.

. Be signed by the chair of the city council or board of selectmen and the property owner, notarized and attested by the city or town clerk.

. Authorized by a vote of the municipal legislative body through the adoption of an ordinance or bylaw.

WHEN IS IT TAXED?

§ 17.01[7] Generally

Property taxes are assessed as of January 1 of each year for the succeeding fiscal year. (The fiscal year runs from July 1 to June 30.) The assessors are required to prepare and transmit a tax list and warrant to the collector. The collector must then send a separate tax bill to each person assessed, for each parcel of real estate.[29] The tax bill must sufficiently identify the parcel assessed, by street and number or otherwise, and separately state the assessed value of land, buildings and the total parcel, must state the classification of the property, the residential exemption if any, and the tax due and payable.[30]

The tax is based on the ownership, use and condition of the property as of the tax date (January 1). Traditionally, changes to the property occurring within the same calendar year have not affected the tax posture of the property. For example if the property is damaged by fire or other casualty on January 14, the taxpayer does not have any right to an abatement of his taxes for the year. It has been held that taxes are assessed annually, but not for any period of time; rather they are assessed as of a fixed tax date. The fact that the property suffers a temporary diminution of

---

[29] G.L. c. 59, §§ 21, 53, 54; c. 60, § 3.
[30] G.L. c. 60, § 3A.

value during the period between two tax dates is not ground for abatement.[31] This rule has also meant that improvements made during the year would not be taxed until the following January, so that many persons who built or altered structures would, if feasible, arrange for commencement or completion of the project to occur immediately after the January tax date, rather than immediately before. However, the enactment of two statutes since 1989 have given municipalities the option of avoiding the consequences of the traditional rule. Municipalities which accept the third sentence of G.L. c. 59, § 2A(a) can tax improvements to real estate made between January 2 and June 30 as if they had been in existence on the tax date. The statute offers no countervailing reduction for improvements that are destroyed in the same period.[32] Municipalities that accept § 2D of G.L. c. 59 can make a pro rata assessment on the value of certain improvements to real estate for which an occupancy permit was issued after the January 1 tax date. The assessment is calculated by applying the tax rate to the value of the improvement and prorating that amount over the portion of the fiscal year remaining after the permit was issued. If the permit is issued between January 1 and June 30, an assessment is imposed for the following year as well. Unlike § 2A(a), § 2D provides for a countervailing abatement of taxes whenever a parcel of real estate loses 50% or more of its value after January 1 due to fire or other natural disaster.

Likewise, if the property is not exempt as of July 1, the date for determining eligibility for exemption under G.L. c. 59, § 5, it will be taxed for that year even though it becomes exempt prior to the following July. Conversely, if the property is exempt on July 1, it may not be taxed for that year even if it becomes non-exempt prior to the next eligibility date.[33]

§ 17.01[8]   If Tax Is Invalidated by Error or Irregularity

There are cases where an error or irregularity in the assessment of a tax results in its being invalid and/or not a valid lien on the land taxed. In these cases, the tax may be reassessed, if it has not been paid in full, or if it has been recovered back by the owner, or if it has been paid under such circumstances that it can be recovered back.[34] Although the statute is not completely clear, the "errors" and "irregularities" contemplated appear to be those other than overvaluation, disproportionate valuation or any of the other grievances which could form the basis of an application for abatement. Instead, errors such as billing the wrong person or misi-

---

[31] Sarris v. Board of Assessors of Swampscott, 350 Mass. 613, 215 N.E.2d 892 (1974).

[32] This provision has been upheld as constitutional by the SJC in a case which holds that the requirement of "proportional" taxation applies only with respect to properties within the same municipality as the property in question.

[33] Board of Assessors of Hamilton v. Iron Rail Fund of Girls' Clubs of America, 367 Mass. 301, 325 N.E.2d 568 (1973).

[34] G.L. c. 59, § 77.

dentifying the property, or any mistakes which could form the basis of an action in contract to recover back taxes are what the statute is directed to.[35]

The statutory language also indicates that in making the reassessment the assessors should assess the tax in the manner that would have been correct on the tax date and should forward the tax to the collector as part of the original tax warrant for the year in question.[36]

The corrected, reassessed tax becomes a lien on the property "for the same period and under the same conditions as the original tax, if it had constituted a valid lien, would be, except where the reassessment is made after such period has expired."[37] In order to understand this language, it is necessary to be familiar with the provisions of G.L. c. 60, § 37. This section provides, in substance, that the lien for taxes assessed upon land shall attach as of January 1 of the year of assessment and shall terminate at the expiration of three years from October 1 of that year, provided that during such period the land has been alienated by a recorded instrument. If such alienation does not occur during the three-year period, then the lien shall continue until alienation takes place. Thus it would appear that, according to the statute, the reassessed tax would constitute a lien on the property for the remainder of the three-year lien period if the property has been alienated, and if it has not been alienated, then for any additional period beyond the three-year period until a recorded alienation takes place.[38] Where the lien period running from the original assessment has expired, then by the terms of the statute, the reassessed tax would not constitute a lien on the land.

It is not clear from the statute or cases what effect the alienation of a portion of the premises after the expiration of the three-year period would have on the lien. The Land Court has held that a lien for the entire tax will exist on the remaining portion of the premises still in the hands of the taxpayer.[39]

§ 17.01[9]   Effect of Clerical Errors

Tax assessments are not invalidated by minor spelling, typographical or other clerical errors in the taxpayer's name or address, nor by minor errors in the description of the property in the valuation lists, provided the interests of the taxpayer are not materially prejudiced thereby. It is enough if the assessment fairly designates the property intended to be taxed to the person liable therefor.[40] In

---

[35] Sawyer v. Mackie, 149 Mass. 269, 21 N.E. 307 (1889); Hunt v. Perry, 165 Mass. 287, 43 N.E. 103 (1896).

[36] G.L. c. 59, §§ 77 and 78.

[37] G.L. c. 59, §§ 77 and 78.

[38] City of Worcester v. Bennett, 310 Mass. 400, 38 N.E.2d 647 (1942).

[39] Town of Southwick v. Clark, Mass. Lawyers Weekly, December 12, 1977, p. 18.

[40] City of Lowell v. Marden and Murphy, 321 Mass. 597, 74 N.E.2d 666 (1947), *cert. denied,*

general, it may be said that where there is a merely technical error in the assessment or billing of the tax the courts make every possible effort to avoid finding that the mistake invalidated the tax.[41]

§ 17.01[10]   If Property Is Omitted from Annual Assessment

"If any parcel of real property or the personal property of a person has been unintentionally omitted from the annual assessment of taxes due to clerical or data processing errors or other good faith reason...," the assessors shall, in accordance with rules promulgated by the Commissioner of Revenue, assess the proper person for the omitted property. But in no event may such assessment be made later than June 20th of the taxable year or ninety days after the date on which the tax bills are mailed, whichever is later.[42]

The problems and consequent litigation under this part of the statute have usually arisen when the assessors have attempted to raise substantially the valuation of property previously assessed. Recent revisions to the statute seem to have resolved any ambiguity which may have previously existed on this point.[43] The assessors are now required to treat cases where property has been erroneously undervalued under a different section of the statute, rather than attempting to treat it as omitted property. Where property has been improperly valued or classified due to clerical or data processing error, or other good faith reason the assessors must revise the valuation or classification and assess any additional tax, all in accordance with the procedures set out in G.L. c. 59, § 75.[44]

The Court gave some guidance in determining what is "omitted" property for purposes of the statute in *Sears v. Town of Nahant*[45] which involved personal property. The assessors knew of the existence of the property, but it was not assessed until December of the tax year. The taxpayer claimed that since the assessors had no more knowledge with respect to the property in December than they had had on the tax date it was not "newly discovered" property and could not be assessed under the statute providing for late assessment of property omitted from the original tax list.

The Court said that the statute relating to omitted assessments "does not require that the property be newly discovered in the sense of coming for the first time to the knowledge of the assessors, in order that it may be legally assessed. If the

---

appeal dismissed, 322 U.S. 850, 68 S. Ct. 354; McManus v. City of Boston, 320 Mass. 585, 70 N.E.2d 819 (1947).

[41] City of Springfield v. Schaffer, 12 Mass. App. Ct. 277, 423 N.E.2d 797 (1981).

[42] G.L. c. 59, § 75.

[43] St. 1989, c. 398, § 1.

[44] G.L. c. 59, § 76.

[45] 215 Mass. 329, 102 N.E. 494 (1913).

assessors, through want of knowledge of facts, or ignorance of the law or their duty, or for any other honest reason, have failed to include property in the annual assessment, it is omitted property within the meaning of that section, and, in the exercise of good faith, they may include it in a supplemental assessment."[46]

Finally, it should be noted that a tax assessed on omitted property is not a new tax but part of the original tax and relates back to the original tax date. It should therefore be assessed and billed to the person who would have been liable for it as of the tax date, even if the property has since been sold.[47]

WHO IS TAXED?

§ 17.01[11]   Generally

The statute[48] requires that the tax on real estate be assessed to "the person who is the owner on January 1." The person who is the record owner as of January 1 "shall be held to be the true owner thereof." A person properly assessed as of January 1 can thus be held personally liable for the tax even if he sells the property on January 2.[49]

However, if the Commissioner of Revenue (who has general supervision over local property taxation) deems it proper, he can authorize in writing that the person in possession on January 1 be assessed and that person is "thereupon held to be the true owner thereof for the purposes of this section."[50]

If a rent-paying tenant in possession is taxed under the above statute he is allowed to make appropriate deductions from his rent or to bring suit against his landlord to recover the taxes paid, unless the parties have a contrary agreement.[51]

The courts have generally construed the statute as giving the assessors the widest possible latitude in determining to whom the tax should be assessed. In making this determination, they are charged with notice of what appears in the records of the registries of deeds and probate.[52] In fact, they may rely on such records in assessing the tax even though the actual facts as to ownership are different than the records indicate, and even if they have knowledge of those facts.[53] On the other hand, the

---

[46] Sears v. Town of Nahant, 215 Mass. 329, 102 N.E. 494, 496.

[47] Barlett v. Tufts, 241 Mass. 96, 134 N.E. 630 (1922).

[48] G.L. c. 59, § 11.

[49] Southeastern Regional Planning and Economic Development District v. Dartmouth, 6 Mass. App. Ct. 209, 374 N.E.2d 350 (1978), and cases cited therein.

[50] G.L. c. 59, § 11.

[51] G.L. c. 59, § 15.

[52] Conners v. City of Lowell, 209 Mass. 111, 95 N.E. 412 (1911).

[53] Assessors of Boston v. John Hancock Mutual Life Ins. Co., 323 Mass. 242, 81 N.E.2d 366

assessors are not bound by the record ownership and they may assess the actual owner if they know his identity even though he does not appear as owner in the records.[54] But they are not required to look outside the records to determine if there are persons who do not appear in the records but who have an interest in the land.[55]

The statutory language quoted above, to the effect that the record owner "shall be held to be the true owner" has been construed by the Court to be mandatory as respects the taxpayer but merely directory as respects the assessors. Thus record ownership would preclude the taxpayer from defending against liability on the ground that he was not in fact the owner, but would not serve as a defense against liability to an actual owner who was not the owner of record.[56]

§ 17.01[12]   Personal Liability for Tax

The person to whom the tax is properly assessed is primarily, and personally, liable for it whether or not he actually owns the property. If the person assessed is not in fact the owner, the actual owner will hold the property subject to a lien for the payment of the tax. However the actual owner would not be personally liable for the tax.[57] "Taxes on real estate are assessed, not to the estate, but to the person who is the owner or in possession on [the tax date]."[58] So, if the tax were properly assessed to A who was the person in possession on the tax date, and if B were the actual owner, B would not be primarily or personally liable for the tax, but B's title would be divested by a subsequent tax sale. However, if the proceeds of the sale were insufficient to pay the taxes due, then the tax collector could proceed against A in contract to recover the deficiency, but he could not so proceed against B.[59]

§ 17.01[13]   If Real Estate Is Divided or Sold Before Tax Is Paid

As discussed above,[60] real estate is assessed on each January 1, referred to as the tax date, and its status on that date determines its status for tax purposes until the following January 1.[61]

(1948); Hardy v. Jaeckle, 358 N.E.2d 769 (1977).

[54] City of Boston v. Quincy Market Cold Storage and Warehouse Co., 312 Mass. 638, 45 N.E.2d 959 (1943).

[55] Hardy v. Jaeckle, 358 N.E.2d 769 (1977).

[56] City of Boston v. Quincy Market Cold Storage and Warehouse Co., 312 Mass. 638, 45 N.E.2d 959 (1943).

[57] Town of Milton v. Ladd, 348 Mass. 762, 206 N.E.2d 161 (1965).

[58] Richardson v. City of Boston, 148 Mass. 508, 20 N.E. 166 (1889); City of Boston v. Gordon, 342 Mass. 586, 175 N.E.2d 311 (1961); Rogers v. Gookin, 198 Mass. 434, 85 N.E. 405 (1908).

[59] Richardson v. City of Boston, 148 Mass. 508, 20 N.E. 166 (1889); City of Boston v. Gordon, 342 Mass. 586, 175 N.E.2d 311 (1961); Rogers v. Gookin, 198 Mass. 434, 85 N.E. 405 (1908).

[60] *See* 17.01[7], *supra.*

[61] Municipalities that have accepted St. 1989, c. 653, § 40 may assess additions to the property

It will be obvious to the reader that this concept of an assessment date is something of a legal fiction. Municipal assessors of course do not spend each New Year's Day trudging through the snows assessing all the properties in town. Instead, much of the assessing process as it relates to the valuation of property takes place in the typical assessors' office over a period of months. The actual assessment of the tax in dollar figures cannot take place until the rate is set, something which occurs in the period from late Fall to early Spring in most cities and towns. There is thus a kind of "relation back" effect at work, the tax being assessed as of January 1 only in the sense that the determination of the final dollar amount at a later time is given legal effect retroactive to January 1.

Where, subsequent to the statutory assessment date (and by implication prior to the date when the tax is paid), a parcel of real estate is sold, mortgaged or otherwise divided, by a recorded instrument, the owner or mortgagee of any portion thereof may request in writing that the assessors apportion the tax and any interest or costs among the various portions into which the parcel has been divided.[62]

If the assessors receive such a request for apportionment at any time before the real estate has been advertised for sale for nonpayment of taxes they are required to apportion the tax among the various owners according to the value of their respective interests. After the apportionment each owner is liable only for the amounts attributable to his portion, and the lien on his portion is only for those amounts.[63]

Any person aggrieved by the apportionment may, within seven days, appeal to the County Commissioners or the Appellate Tax Board as in the case of a claimed over-assessment.[64] However, the decision of the Commissioners or Board shall be final in such appeals. "No apportionment can be demanded unless made in time for a lien effective for the practical purposes of a tax collector to remain upon the several parcels after the apportionment shall have been made."[65]

The court in *Rogers v. Gookin*[66] described the effect of the apportionment statute as follows: "It [the statute] recognizes the validity of the first assessment, but shifts its point of incidence from the person who is either the owner or in possession on [the tax date] so that it will rest upon the several parcels into which said real estate has been divided, and it releases the original owner from all personal liability for

made between January 2 and June 30. Eligibility for charitable exemption is determined as of July 1.

[62] G.L. c. 59, § 78A.
[63] G.L. c. 59, § 78A.
[64] G.L. c. 59, § 81.
[65] Salisbury Beach Assoc. v. Evans, 225 Mass. 399, 114 N.E. 675 (1917).
[66] 198 Mass. 434, 85 N.E. 405 (1908); *see also* Morrison v. Assessors of Brookline, 313 Mass. 746, 49 N.E.2d 237 (1943).

the tax upon any parcel to which he has no title at the time of apportionment."

§ 17.01[14]   Deceased Persons or Persons Unknown

"The undivided real estate of a deceased person may be assessed to his heirs or devisees, without designating any of them by name, until the names of such heirs or devises appear in the probate court records ..."[67] Thus the tax bill may be sent to "the heirs or devisees of John Doe" for each year until the names of the heirs or devisees appear in the probate records.[68] The statute makes the heirs and devisees severally liable for the entire tax with a right of contribution among themselves.[69] It is not clear, however, whether the liability of the heirs for taxes attaches before they are named in the assessment or only afterward. The statute appears to be creating personal liability on the part of the heirs and it would seem somewhat unfair to do this without requiring that they be named individually in the tax bill and receive timely notice thereof.

The use of the word "undivided" in the statute is also a little puzzling. When a person dies intestate then of course his heirs take undivided fractional interests in his realty. If he dies testate and the will devises all his real estate, in general terms, to more than one person, those persons could also be held to take undivided fractional interests. In these cases, it appears clear that the real estate of the deceased is undivided, and that the statute applies until the heirs or devisees make conveyances to divide the property among themselves. There would appear to be some question as to whether two specific, identifiable parcels devised to two different persons with neither person owning any interest in the land of the other could be considered undivided real estate. And, if it is not, to whom should such land be assessed? The answer may lie in G.L. c. 59, § 11, which allows the assessors to assess the record owner on January 1, even if that person is deceased. Section 11 and section 16, when read together, appear to give the assessors the option in such cases of assessing either the deceased record owner, or his heirs or devisees.

When the right or title to a deceased person's property is "doubtful or unascertained by reason of litigation concerning the will of the deceased" then the tax may be assessed "in general terms to his estate" (i.e., "The Estate of John Doe").[70]

And, it is settled that land may be assessed to "persons unknown" or to "John Doe, a fictitious person" if the assessors are unable to learn by reasonable inquiry who the owner is.[71] Such an assessment will create a valid tax lien and the land

---

[67] G.L. c. 59, § 12D.

[68] G.L. c. 59, § 12D. *See also* Hardy v. Jaeckle, 358 N.E.2d 769.

[69] G.L. c. 59, § 12D. *See also* Hardy v. Jaeckle, 358 N.E.2d 769.

[70] G.L. c. 59, § 12E.

[71] Town of Franklin v. Metcalfe, 307 Mass. 386, 30 N.E.2d 262 (1940); McDonough v. Everett, 237 Mass. 378, 129 N.E. 681 (1927).

may subsequently be taken by the collector. This rule, although already established by case law, was added to the statute in 1971, with the requirement that the Commissioner of Revenue authorize such assessments in writing.[72] Taxes on the estates of deceased or unknown persons which are not assessed according to the foregoing rules are invalid.[73]

Finally, when real estate has been unassessed because title thereto is doubtful, and the town conducts a search and determines title, the expense of such search is a lien on the land.[74]

§ 17.01[15]   Mortgagees

The statute[75] contains provisions instructing the assessors, under certain circumstances, to divide the assessed tax on a single piece of property between the mortgagor and any mortgagee according to their respective interests. However, these provisions have little practical significance today, because they are almost totally disregarded by both property owners and assessors. Indeed, indications are that they have had little practical significance for the past century.[76] The following discussion is included more out of a desire for thoroughness than out of a conviction that a knowledge of the workings of these provisions is essential to the modern practitioner.

The assessors are, as indicated, commanded by statute to divide the assessment on mortgaged property between the mortgagor and any mortgagees according to their interests. The mortgagee's interest should be valued at the face amount of the mortgage in such cases unless he files with the assessors a sworn statement of all mortgages on property within the municipality held by him, and a statement of the balance owing on the mortgage on the property being assessed. If he brings in such a list he will be assessed based on the balance owing on the mortgage. But the statute also states[77] that the assessors' failure to so divide the tax will not affect its validity, unless the mortgagor or mortgagee has delivered to the assessors, for each year in question, within the time provided for, the return of property lists by taxpayers,[78] a sworn statement of the amount secured by each and every mortgage on the particular parcel, together with the name and address of every person who holds an interest in it, either as mortgagor or mortgagee.

It would seem that, by necessary implication from the statutory language, where

---

[72] *See* G.L. c. 59, § 11, ¶ 3.
[73] Tobin v. Gillespie, 152 Mass. 219, 25 N.E. 88 (1890).
[74] G.L. c. 59, § 12F.
[75] *See* G.L. c. 59, §§ 12, 12A, and 12B.
[76] Worcester v. City of Boston, 179 Mass. 41, 60 N.E. 410.
[77] G.L. c. 59, § 34.
[78] G.L. c. 59, § 29.

a list pursuant to statute is brought in and the assessors fail to recognize the interest of the mortgagee in the assessment, the tax would be invalid. An invalid tax creates no lien, and the property may then be sold free of liability for any unpaid tax and an attempted tax sale may also be defeated.[79]

Apparently during the middle of the nineteenth century, local assessors developed the custom of assessing the mortgagor for the entire value of the property and also taxing the mortgagee of the same property an amount based on the face value of the mortgage. In 1882, the above provisions relating to the separate assessment of mortgagors and mortgagees were added.[80] The intent of the legislature was to abolish what was considered to be a form of double taxation.[81] Since the addition of these provisions, the goal of avoiding double taxation has been achieved by the universal custom among assessors of failing to assess the mortgagee for the sum represented by the mortgage.

Yet it may be that these rather archaic provisions still have some small bit of potential vitality left. It has been held in Massachusetts, virtually since the founding of the republic, that the tax on a parcel of real estate, whether assessed to the owner of record, mortgagee, tenant in possession, or whomever, is a tax and lien on the whole estate and not merely on the interest of the person taxed.[82] Thus, the owner of any one fractional interest would always be required, ultimately, to pay the entire tax in order to protect his own interest in the property.

However, in a case decided in 1937,[83] the Supreme Judicial Court reiterated the "general" rule that the tax reaches the whole estate; but in listing examples of where the general rule applies it used the following language: "These principles are applicable, for example, to mortgaged real estate—if a statement of the mortgagee's interest has not been filed, *see* G.L. c. 59, §§ 11–14."[84] It would seem by implication from this language that the general rule does not apply where a statement of the mortgagee's interest has been filed.

If this is indeed the law then one could make the argument that the mortgagee who files the required statement and pays the tax attributable to his interest should be able to prevent his rights to the property from being extinguished by any subsequent taking and sale by the tax collector resulting from the mortgagor's failure to pay the taxes assessed to his interest. This is, of course, the opposite of the normal situation where the tax taking and sale cuts off the interests of every owner or lienor regardless of whether or not the tax was assessed to him.

---

[79] *See* Abbott v. Frost, 185 Mass. 398, 70 N.E. 478 (1904).

[80] St. 1882, c. 175 and c. 304.

[81] Worcester v. City of Boston, 179 Mass. 41, 60 N.E. 410.

[82] Parker v. Baxter, 2 Gray 185; Donovan v. Haverhill, 247 Mass. 69, 141 N.E. 564 (1923).

[83] Crocker-McElwain v. Board of Assessors of Holyoke, 296 Mass. 338, 5 N.E.2d 558 (1937).

[84] Crocker-McElwain v. Board of Assessors of Holyoke, 296 Mass. 338, 5 N.E.2d 558, at 562.

§ 17.01[16] Condominium Owners

An exception to the rule, noted above, that the real estate tax is a tax upon the entire estate and not only upon the interest of the person taxed is made by statute with respect to condominiums. Under the provisions of G.L. c. 183A, each unit of a condominium is to be assessed as an individual piece of real estate which piece includes its proportional share of common areas and facilities. The common areas and facilities are not themselves deemed to be a taxable parcel.

Condominium developers frequently build their projects in so-called "phases." If economic conditions are such that it is decided to defer construction of one or more of the phases authorized by the master deed, the developer will usually reserve the right to build these later phases when it sells the units already built. Municipal assessors have sometimes attempted to tax these phasing rights as present interests in real estate under G.L. c. 59, § 11. However, the appeals court has firmly turned aside these efforts, and the parcels subject to phasing rights must be assessed to the present unit owners as part of the common elements. The value of the rights themselves goes untaxed.[85]

However, betterment assessments, annual sewer use charges, water rates and charges, and all rates, charges and assessments of every nature due to a city, town or district with respect to the condominium or any part of it, other than real estate taxes, may be charged to the organization of unit owners, but any lien for such charges provided by law shall attach to the individual units in proportion to their interests in the common areas.[86]

§ 17.01[17] Planned Unit or Cluster Developments

With respect to planned unit of cluster developments the statute provides as follows:[87] "Provided further that in cluster developments or planned unit developments, as defined in section 9 of chapter 40A, the assessment of taxes on the common land, so-called, the beneficial interest in which is owned by the owners of lots or residential units within the plot, may be included as an additional assessment to each individual lot owner in the cluster if authorized in writing by the Commissioner [of Revenue] and in such manner as prescribed by him." Accordingly, cluster development owners are taxed in a manner similar to condominium owners.

§ 17.01[18] Lessees of Public Property

In general, real estate owned or held in trust for the benefit of the United States,

---

[85] Spinnaker Island and Yacht Club Holding Trust v. Assessors of Hull, 49 Mass. App. 20 (2000); First Main Street Corp. v. Assessors of Acton, 49 Mass. App. 25 (2000).

[86] G.L. c. 183A, § 14.

[87] G.L. c. 59, § 11.

the Commonwealth, or a county, city or town, or an instrumentality thereof, if used in connection with a business conducted for profit or leased or occupied for other than public purposes is assessed and taxed annually as of January 1 to the user, lessee or occupant to the same extent as if he were the owner.[88] The fact that the lease or other occupancy arrangement with the governmental entity restricts the use of the property will not entitle the lessee to an abatement of the tax assessed thereon.[89] However, it should be noted that property of the United States is subject to taxation by states and their subdivisions only to the extent permitted by Congress,[90] and that lessees of some lands owned by the Commonwealth or its instrumentalities are made exempt from taxation by special statutes.[91]

HOW ASSESSORS LOCATE TAXABLE PROPERTY

§ 17.01[19]   Returns Filed by All Taxpayers

The statute[92] sets up a reporting system whereby the assessors are required to post a notice in one or more public places notifying all persons subject to taxation to bring into the assessors, by a certain date, a list of all their property not exempt from taxation. The property owning citizenry, individual and corporate, resident and nonresident, is then required to complete such list, in the form prescribed by the Commissioner of Revenue, and to return it to the assessors. To facilitate such reporting, the assessors are required by statute to furnish to any person subject to taxation a blank list in the form prescribed by the Commissioner under G.L. c. 58, § 5.

Whether such list should contain only personal property or both real and personal property is a matter of some doubt. Section 29 states that the assessors shall secure from the taxpayer a list "containing the items required by the Commissioner in the form prescribed by him under section 5 of Chapter 58." It also states that such list shall contain all the taxpayers' personal property subject to taxation and may or may not be required to contain a list of the taxpayers' real property.

However, G.L. c. 58, § 5, states that the Commissioner, in exercising his duty to prescribe the forms required under G.L. c. 59, § 29, "shall prescribe forms therefor so arranged that the statement of the person bringing in such a list will include all assessable property held by him."

---

[88] G.L. c. 59, § 2B; Dehydrating Process of Gloucester, Inc. v. City of Gloucester, 334 Mass. 287; 135 N.E.2d 20 (1956).

[89] Sisk v. Assessors of Essex, 426 Mass. 651 (1998).

[90] Quincy v. Squantum Gardens, Inc. , 335 Mass. 440, 140 N.E.2d 482 (1957); see also G.L. c. 59, § 3E.

[91] Board of Assessors of Newton v. Pickwick, Ltd., 351 Mass. 621, 223 N.E.2d 388 (1967).

[92] G.L. c. 59, §§ 29–37.

In practice, this conflict is not of major significance. This is because the assessors usually have their town's real estate mapped in some fashion, and most plots of land are assigned to some person as taxpayer. They therefore have no real need to have each taxpayer bring in a list of his real estate, as they might have had in 1785 when the law was first enacted. So the lists normally relate only to personal property.

§ 17.01[20]   Returns by Organizations Claiming Charitable Exemption

Although the return provisions of the statute play a relatively minor role in the local property tax system with respect to most taxpayers, they play a crucial role with respect to those who claim a charitable exemption from the tax.

The statute requires all persons (except Fraternal Benefit Societies reporting to the Commissioner of Insurance) to bring in to the assessors before a date specified by them (which date must be not later than March 1, unless for cause shown the assessors extend the deadline a reasonable later time in no event to be later than 30 days after the mailing of the tax bills for the fiscal year to which the filing relates), the following information: 1) a complete, itemized list of all property, real and personal, held for literary, educational, temperance, benevolent, charitable or scientific purposes on the January 1 next preceding the filing of the return, (or in the case of a corporation, it may elect to report as of the last day of its fiscal year next preceding the said first day of January); 2) any information required to comply with regulations issued by the State Department of Revenue pursuant to its duty to guide local assessors as to the information necessary and the criteria to be used in determining the eligibility of an organization for a charitable exemption; 3) a statement of receipts and expenditures for charitable purposes during the preceding year; and 4) copies of federal tax returns containing unrelated business income taxable under § 511, of the Internal Revenue Code.

Failure to file the required return and information will have disastrous consequences for a charitable organization, because the statute provides that a charitable organization "shall not be exempt for any year in which it omits to bring in to the assessors the list, statements, and affidavit required by section 29 [of Chapter 59] and a true copy of the report for such year required by section 8F of Chapter 12 to be filed with the division of public charities in the department of the attorney general ..." Such a filing is a jurisdictional issue in any later appeal of the tax.[93]

A charitable corporation can thus be taxed for any year in which it fails to file the required returns.

---

[93] G.L. c. 59, § 5(3)(b); Children's Hosp. v. Assessors of Boston, 388 Mass. 832, 448 N.E.2d 788 (1983).

§ 17.01[21]   Returns by Other Persons Claiming Exemption

Persons claiming a surviving spouse's exemption, hardship exemption or veteran's exemption may be required to furnish the assessors a full list of their taxable property, both real and personal.[94]

§ 17.01[22]   Effect of Failure to Furnish List

If the taxpayer fails to furnish such a list, the assessors are required to estimate as nearly as possible, the particulars of his personal and real estate and the just value of the same.[95] Once such an estimate is made by the assessors, it is "conclusive" on the taxpayer unless he shows "a reasonable excuse" for his failure to furnish a list.[96]

In spite of the implications of this language, the taxpayer who fails to bring in a list does not thereby lose his right to an abatement of the tax on real property. (However, such a list is still required in order to receive a full abatement on personal property.)[97] Originally the provisions of the statute made the timely filing of such a list a prerequisite to applying for any abatement. That provision was amended in 1931 and the courts have held since that the taxpayer may appeal the denial of an abatement on real property irrespective of whether or not he has filed a list.[98]

In practice, most assessors still post the notices required by the statute, and they send blank lists to some but not all taxpayers, requiring a return as to taxable personal property. Mainly the lists are sent to businesses, some boat owners and, in resort communities, to persons who own vacation homes.

§ 17.01[23]   Assessors' Right to Question Taxpayers by Questionnaire

The assessors also have broad investigatory and discovery power.[99] They may send to the owner of any real property, subject to taxation a request for "such information as may reasonably be required by them to determine the actual value of such property." If they utilize this procedure at all, boards of assessors generally send questionnaires only to owners of investment and commercial real estate, often including therein a request for an income and expense statement on the property.

Upon receiving such a questionnaire or other request for information, the taxpayer is required to respond, in writing and under oath, within 60 days. If he fails to respond within that time he loses his right to apply for an abatement of the taxes

---

[94] G.L. c. 59, § 29.
[95] G.L. c. 59, § 36.
[96] G.L. c. 59, § 37.
[97] G.L. c. 59, § 61.
[98] Wynn v. Board of Assessors, 281 Mass. 245, 183 N.E.2d 528 (1932).
[99] G.L. c. 59, § 38D and § 38E.

assessed against his real property for that year, unless his failure to reply was for reasons beyond his control. A taxpayer who knowingly makes a false statement of material fact on his return will also bar any appeal of the tax assessed. In addition, if any taxpayer fails to reply to a request for information in a timely fashion and in the prescribed form fifty dollars may be added to the tax levied on the property in the next fiscal year, provided the taxpayer was notified of this penalty at the time of the request.

After receiving the taxpayer's return the assessors can, if they wish, require him to appear before them and give testimony under oath relative to his return.

The assessors may also request the same kind of information from the taxpayer under a different statutory provision[100] after an application for abatement has been filed, and during the pendency of the abatement proceedings. They may also request that the property be identified and exhibited to them. The time limit for response by the taxpayer under this latter statute is 30 days. Failure to respond will also result in loss of the right to appeal, unless such failure was for reasons beyond the taxpayer's control, or he attempted to comply in good faith. Since there are no statutory guidelines as to what constitutes information "reasonably required" to determine the fair cash value of the property, a taxpayer refuses such a request at his peril. The question will not be tested until the assessors file a plea in bar at the Appellate Tax Board. If the reasonableness issue goes against the taxpayer it will be too late to comply and the appeal will be doomed.[101]

§ 17.01[24]   Assessors' Right to Question Businesses As to Profit/Loss

Many assessors, to the outrage of local businessmen, have attempted to require those businesses which own and occupy real estate for business purposes to provide the assessors with detailed profit and loss statements, mortgage balances, and other financial information, using the above cited statute as their authority for doing so.

Language contained in *Assessors of Quincy v. Boston Consol. Gas Co.*[102] casts some doubt on the legitimacy of this practice of assessors. The Court had this to say with respect to the proper method of valuing real estate owned and occupied by a commercial enterprise: "The capacity of the land to produce income may be shown by testimony as to how it has actually been employed. But the general rule is that the profits from a business located upon the land are not a fair measure of the value of the land, because the financial returns from a commercial undertaking are dependent on so many material factors having no real relation to the land itself that the profit cannot be said to be derived from the land. This general rule ought

---

[100] G.L. c. 59, § 61A.
[101] *See* Brown v. Assessors of Bedford, 398 Mass. 1010, 500 N.E.2d 286 (1986).
[102] 309 Mass. 60, 34 N.E.2d 623 (1941).

not to be relaxed except where the profit in the main results from some peculiarity of the land."

On the other hand, *Jordan Marsh Co. v. Board of Assessors of Malden*,[103] which was concerned with establishing the value of owner-occupied business realty, seems to imply that, in some cases at least, the operating results, particularly gross sales, of businesses are properly considered in arriving at the value of the property which they occupy. But the matter of the limits of assessor inquiry under the new discovery provisions must still be considered uncertain.

If property is held by an owner merely as an investment and is rented or held for rental to another person then it is difficult to conceive of any information relative to its operation which would not have to be provided to the assessors upon request. (This assumes, of course, that the request is not entirely freakish or outlandish.) But where the property in question is owner-occupied commercial or industrial property and detailed information respecting the financial condition and operations of the occupying business is requested, and this is often the case, the owner may be able to avoid providing the assessors with much of the information requested.

However, taxpayers who are considering withholding such information should be advised at the outset that under the present state of the law they are running a certain amount of risk. As discussed in the preceding section, property owners who refuse proper requests for information by the assessors lose their right to appeal their tax assessment for the year in question. So the owner must decide if attempting to preserve his business privacy is worth the risk of refusing what may later be found to be its proper request. Very often the owners of small, privately held, local companies are willing to incur a substantial risk of this nature in an attempt to keep from providing what they perceive as gossipy local officials with the financial details of their business operations.[104]

In view of the broad statutory language, a simple refusal to answer is not wise, even where the client is determined not to provide the information requested. The assessors may respond by raising the assessment dramatically and the client will have no right to appeal unless he can convince the Appellate Tax Board or the Supreme Judicial Court that the information requested was not reasonably required as part of the valuation process.

Although the Supreme Judicial Court has yet to rule on such a case, the Appellate

---

[103] 359 Mass. 106, 267 N.E.2d 912 (1971).

[104] Note that it is now provided by statute that information supplied in response to requests under G.L. c. 59, § 38D, 38E, and 61A, as well as 8A of c. 58A is open only to taxing officials and other officials whose duty requires it. G.L. c. 59, § 52B.

Tax Board has decided[105] that a taxpayer who owned and occupied business property and who refused to answer a request for information on the ground that the income and expense data for the real estate and the business which occupied it were not separable, and that the assessors had no right to business data, had lost his right to appeal the eventual assessment.

If, however, the taxpayer pursues a course of creative noncompliance, rather than outright refusal, he may avoid both the unhappy result of the *Cantor* case and the embarrassment of disclosing his private affairs.

As noted above, it has been settled law in Massachusetts for some time that the profitability of a business located on a parcel of real estate is not relevant to prove its value, unless the location or other peculiarity of the real estate makes it a major factor in the profitability of the business. So it does not seem that in the usual case the assessors should be able to require detailed financial disclosure from a business which owns and occupies its own real estate, since such information is not "reasonably required to determine value" under Massachusetts law.

However, it does seem that the assessors would have the right to require from the owner information about his operations sufficient for them to make an estimate of the fair rental value of the real property exclusive of the business occupying it, this being a recognized basis for determining assessed value.

Therefore, it is suggested that the proper response to the assessors is to have the client develop a figure for the fair rental value of his property, based on the rentals paid for similar properties in the area. (If rentals in the client's industry are tied to certain operating results: for example, percentages of gross sales as in the retail industry, then those particular operating results for the client's business would have to be provided to the assessors to support the fair rental value figure.)

From the fair rental value estimate thus developed would be subtracted the actual expenses incurred by the client in operating the real estate, with evidence that these expenses are typical in the area for buildings of the type involved. The resulting net income figure should then be capitalized to obtain the fair cash value of the real estate exclusive of the business occupying it.

This type of analysis can be obtained for a modest fee from a local appraiser. It has been approved by the Appeals Court as a valuation method in an analogous situation, and it utilizes methods which should be familiar to the assessor.

Once this material has been submitted, counsel at least has a basis for further discussion with the assessors. He can point out that his client has undertaken a considerable effort to provide the assessors with the information they need to do

---

[105] William Cantor and Michael Cantor, Trs. v. Board of Assessors of Newton, (1977) ATB 83059.

their job, and that he is naturally concerned about any disclosure of his business secrets to the public, and particularly to his competitors. Perhaps the matter can be resolved at this point; but if not, the property owner is in the best position he can be to resist a later claim that his appeal is barred for failure to comply with the assessors' request for information.

RECORDS KEPT BY ASSESSORS

§ 17.01[25] Generally

The record keeping requirements imposed on the assessors of the several cities and towns are detailed in G.L. c. 59, §§ 43–52 and 60. These record keeping requirements are directory and not mandatory, and the failure of the assessors to comply will not invalidate the tax.[106] Once again we are dealing with statutory provisions which are yellow with age, which have been amended frequently, and which often seem unrelated, out of sequence, or in actual conflict with one another.

Briefly, the assessors are required, by various statutes, to keep books, in the form prescribed by the Commissioner of Revenue, which show, with respect to each taxpayer, the following information: a.) the total value of his taxable personal property; b.) the value of each kind of taxable personal property he owns; c.) the valuation, classification and assessment of his total estate; d.) his name and address or such description of him as can be given and the valuation, classification and assessment of his real property; e.) the value of each building assessed, exclusive of the land and any machinery in the building; and f.) the tax on his estate.

At the end of the book there must be a summary listing the total valuation of each classification of property, and a list and description, with fair cash value of all property exempt from taxation under certain statutory provisions.

The assessors are also required to keep a record of all abatements granted. This record must be signed by a majority of the board and show plainly the name in which the tax stands, the year in which the tax was assessed, the total amount of the tax, the date of the abatement, the amount abated, and, in the case of an abatement based on a statutory exemption, an exact reference to the statutory provision under which the abatement is granted.[107]

Finally, the assessors are required to insert in the book, and to sign, a statutorily prescribed oath to the effect that the book contains a listing of all persons and property subject to taxation and the fair cash value of all such property, to the best of the assessors' knowledge and belief.

---

[106] Westhampton v. Searle, 127 Mass. 502 (1879).
[107] G.L. c. 59, § 60.

§ 17.01[26]   Public Access to Records of Assessors

Many records kept by assessors have been open to public inspection for years.[108] However, a 1973 reform of the laws relating to public access to public records resulted in virtually all of their records including so-called "field assessment cards" being, at least prima facie, open to inspection by taxpayers or their counsel.[109]

The present law defines "public record" as any "documentary materials or data, regardless of physical form or characteristics, made or received by any officer or employee of any agency, executive office, department, board, commission, bureau, division or authority of the commonwealth, or of any political subdivision thereof, or of any authority established by the general court to serve a public purpose ..."[110] Certain exemptions are made from this general definition, but ultimately all records are presumed public and the burden is on the custodian who would deny access to place the record within one of the statutory exemptions.[111] It will be noted from a reading of the statute that the exemptions are narrowly drawn. If the taxpayer is wrongly denied access to a record he may proceed in the Supreme Judicial Court or the Superior Court to compel its disclosure.[112]

As a final note it should be pointed out that there are certain types of records kept by assessors which are not accessible to the public. These are applications for abatements, and information collected through requests for information filed under §§ 38D, 38E, 61A of c. 59, and § 8A of c. 58A, which are by statute available only to certain designated public officials.[113] Also exempt from disclosure is so much of the return filed by the taxpayer under G.L. c. 59, § 29, as relates to a list of his personal estate.[114]

EXEMPTIONS FROM THE TAX IN GENERAL

§ 17.02   Introduction

The property tax statute begins with the imposition of a broad, all-encompassing tax on real property in its first section[1] and then, in the next few sections, carves

---

[108] G.L. c. 59, §§ 43 and 60.

[109] *See* Attorney General v. Board of Assessors of Woburn, 375 Mass. 430, 378 N.E.2d 45 (1978).

[110] G.L. c. 4, § 7(26).

[111] G.L. c. 66, § 10(c).

[112] G.L. c. 66, § 10(b).

[113] *See* G.L. c. 4, § 7(26)(a), G.L. c. 59, § 60 and G.L. c. 59, 52B.

[114] G.L. c. 59, § 32.

[1] G.L. c. 59, § 2.

out exceptions to and exemptions from that tax. Over the years more and more organizations, types of property and individuals have been added to the rolls of the exempt, until, at the present time, there are at least fifty exemption provisions in the law.[2] The fundamental principle with regard to exemptions is that taxation is the general rule and exemptions therefrom are to be strictly construed.[3] Exemptions from taxation are a matter of grace extended by the sovereign and are to be recognized only where the property clearly falls within the express words of legislative command.[4] The burden is always on the taxpayer to show that he is entitled to exemption.[5]

For the most part, exemptions from taxation are fairly intricately drawn, and the taxpayer who would place himself or his property within them must examine the relevant statutory provision very carefully to see if he or his property meets the requirements.

§ 17.02[1]   Time for Application and Qualification

The statute specifically provides that exemption applications by veterans, surviving spouses and children, blind persons, and the elderly may be filed up until December 15 of the year to which the tax relates, or if the bill or notice of tax is first sent after September 15 of such year, within three months after the bill or notice was sent.[6]

Whether there is any time limit for applying for the other exemptions is not clear, but the taxpayer would be well advised to file within thirty days after the date his tax bill was mailed.

The date of determination as to age, ownership or other factors necessary to qualify for exemption is July 1 of each year unless the relevant exemption clause specifies otherwise.[7]

GOVERNMENT PROPERTY

§ 17.02[2]   Generally

The property of one governmental entity located within the jurisdictional bounds

---

[2] G.L. c. 59, §§ 3E and 5.

[3] Children's Hospital Medical Center v. Board of Assessors of Boston, 353 Mass. 35, 227 N.E.2d 908 (1967); Town of Milton v. Ladd, 348 Mass. 762, 206 N.E.2d 101 (1965); Sylvester v. Assessors of Braintree, 344 Mass. 263, 182 N.E.2d 120 (1962).

[4] Boston Chamber of Commerce v. Assessors of Boston, 315 Mass. 712, 54 N.E.2d 199.

[5] Boston Chamber of Commerce v. Assessors of Boston, 315 Mass. 712, 54 N.E.2d 199.

[6] G.L. c. 59, § 59.

[7] G.L. c. 59, § 5.

of another governmental entity is usually exempt from taxation except to the extent that specific statutory language provides otherwise. Thus, if the assessors would tax a particular parcel of real estate within their community owned by another governmental body they must look for statutory authorization to do so.

§ 17.02[3]   The United States

Property of the United States Government or its agencies located in the Commonwealth is completely exempt from local taxation, except where Congress has granted permission for such taxation.[8] Taxation of such property must be strictly in compliance with congressional permission. This compliance has two aspects. "It means both (1) that the state tax statute must authorize a tax of the character permitted by Congress, and (2) that the administrative action of assessment and collection must comply with congressional and state statutory authorization."[9]

Thus, in order to determine if a tax on Federal property is valid, one must examine the appropriate Federal statute to see if taxation of such property is permitted, then the State statute must be examined to see if it authorizes a tax of the type permitted, and finally the actions of the assessors in levying and collecting the tax to see that they conform to both Federal and State mandates. (G.L. c. 59, § 3E is an example of a statute which attempts to meet the above outlined requirements for the taxation of Federal property.)

§ 17.02[4]   The Commonwealth

Property of the Commonwealth is exempt from local taxation, with the following exceptions: (a) real estate of which the Commonwealth is in possession under a mortgage for condition broken, (b) certain tidal flats located in Boston and Provincetown, specifically identified in the statute, and certain wharves and piers erected thereon, (c) certain structures erected by lessees under G.L. c. 75, § 26 (leased to employees of the University of Massachusetts), (d) property taxable under St. 1920, c. 575 (State-owned and MDC-held public reservation in Hull, leased or occupied for business purposes) and (e) structures erected on land in state forests, parks and reservations by persons occupying such land under authority conferred by the commissioner of environmental management, (f) real estate taxable under the former G.L. c. 59, § 3A[10] (now § 2B), (state-owned property leased to private business).

---

[8] G.L. c. 59, § 5(1), Note also G.L. c. 59, § 3E. *See also* U.S. v. City of Springfield, 22 F Supp 672 (D.c. 1938); Assessors of Wilmington v. Avco Corp. 357 Mass. 704, 260 N.E.2d 170 (1970); Small Business Administration v. Board of Assessors of Falmouth, 345 Mass. 294, 186 N.E.2d 917 (1962); Squantum Gardens, Inc. v. Assessors of Quincy, 335 Mass. 440, 140 N.E.2d 482 (1957).

[9] Squantum Gardens, Inc. v. Assessors of Quincy, 335 Mass. 440, 140 N.E.2d 482 (1957).

[10] G.L. c. 59, § 5(2); Corcoran v. City of Boston, 193 Mass. 586, 79 N.E. 829 (1907).

The most important statutory provision allowing taxation of State-owned property is G.L. c. 59, § 2B which provides, in substance, that real estate owned by the Commonwealth (or its subdivisions, or their instrumentalities) if used in connection with a business conducted for profit or if leased or occupied for other than public purposes might be taxed to the user, lessee, or occupant, as if he were the owner.

Exceptions to this general rule providing for the taxation of State property leased or occupied for other than public purposes, and therefore not taxable are "(1) a use, lease or occupancy which is reasonably necessary to the public purpose of a public airport, port facility, Massachusetts Turnpike, transit authority or park which is available to the use of the general public; (2) easements, grants, licenses or rights of way of public utility companies and (3) property of the United States in respect of which payments in lieu of taxes are made or which is occupied by a manufacturing corporation."[11]

The statute giving permission for local taxation of State and Federal property was rewritten in 1974, partly in response to the substantial amount of litigation that had arisen over attempts to tax Federal property and over the meaning of the words "use for other than a public purpose," contained in the statute, so pre-1974 cases construing these provisions should be read with this in mind.[12]

§ 17.02[5]   One Municipality Owning Property Located in Another

Property held by a city, town, district or the Massachusetts Water Resources Authority in another town for the purpose of water supply, protection of water sources, or of sewage disposal, or of a public airport, if yielding no rent, is exempt from taxation; but the municipality which owns the property must pay an annual amount in lieu of taxes equal to the taxes the other municipality would have received from the property. The amount to be paid is based on the average assessed values of the land, excluding structures, for the three years immediately preceding the acquisition of the property by the owning municipality. However, the value of any structures will be included in the valuation where the land is taken for the purpose of protecting an existing water supply.

If the land is part of a larger tract which has been assessed as a whole, its assessed valuation in any year will be that proportional part of the valuation of the whole tract which the valuation of the land acquired, exclusive of buildings, bore in that year to the value of the entire estate.

If rent is received from any part of the property, that part is subject to tax. The

---

[11] G.L. c. 59, § 3A.

[12] *See* Dehydrating Process Co. of Gloucester, Inc. v. Gloucester, 334 Mass. 287, 135 N.E.2d (1956); Atlantic Refining Co. v. Assessors of Newton, 342 Mass. 200, 172 N.E.2d 827 (1961).

assessors are required by statute to fix the average value of such land within one year of its acquisition. In addition to the foregoing in-lieu payment, the owning entity must pay to the locus municipality a stumpage fee equal to eight percent of the stumpage value of all forest products cut from the tract.[13]

Also, land acquired by a municipality or district after January 1, 1946, located in another municipality and held on January 1 of any year for any public purpose shall not be subject to taxation. But the owning municipality or district must make a payment, in lieu of taxes, equal to the tax on the average assessed value of the acquired land and buildings on the three assessment dates next preceding acquisition. There is also an eight percent stumpage fee on all forest products cut from the land.[14] The difference between this exemption and that discussed above for water/sewage projects and airports is that in the latter the value of buildings is not usually included in determining the in lieu payment.

Although the requirement of an in lieu payment is strictly statutory, the exemption of this kind of property from taxation is not dependent on statute but on "general principles of propriety, justice and expediency."[15]

CHARITABLE ORGANIZATIONS

§ 17.02[6] Generally

General Laws c. 59, § 5(3) provides in relevant part that "real estate owned by or held in trust for a charitable organization and occupied by it or its officers for the purposes for which it is organized" shall be exempt from taxation. Charitable organizations are defined by the statute as trusts or corporations dedicated to literary, benevolent, charitable, scientific or temperance purposes.[16]

The statutory language requires that a charitable corporation be incorporated in Massachusetts or that, if it is a charitable trust, that the trust be executed in Massachusetts or that its trustees be appointed by Massachusetts Courts and its principal activities be carried out in Massachusetts.[17] However, a Supreme Judicial Court decision, handed down in 1975,[18] held that the denial of the exemption to a foreign charitable corporation was invalid as violative of the Equal Protection

---

[13] G.L. c. 59, §§ 5D and 5E; Board of Gas and Electric Comm'rs of Middleborough v. Board of Assessors of Lakeville, 355 Mass. 387, 245 N.E.2d 249 (1969); Middlesex County v. City of Waltham, 278 Mass. 514, 180 N.E. 318 (1932).

[14] G.L. c. 59, § 5F.

[15] Middleborough v. Board of Assessors of Lakeville, 355 Mass. 387, 245 N.E.2d 249 (1969).

[16] G.L. c. 59, § 5(3).

[17] G.L. c. 59, § 5(3).

[18] Mary C. Wheeler School, Inc. v. Board of Assessors of Seekonk, 368 Mass. 344; 331 N.E.2d 888 (1975).

clause of the 14th Amendment to the United States Constitution. Presumably the same reasoning would apply to foreign trusts.

§ 17.02[7] Definition of Charitable Organization

Just what constitutes "charitable" organizations and activities has been the subject of a fair amount of litigation. In general, it can be said that the decisions have provided no clear cut formula or established litmus test to determine if an organization is dedicated to charitable or benevolent purposes.[19] The words "literary, benevolent, charitable, scientific or temperance society" in the statute are interpreted broadly by the Court, and are held not to be limited to activities such as almsgiving or the relief of poverty or distress.[20] Instead they embrace any activity which goes toward advancing the public interest or improving the lot or happiness of mankind.[21] Notwithstanding the breadth of these definitions, under Massachusetts law taxation is the general rule, and statutes granting exemption from taxation are strictly construed. The burden of proof is on the property owner to show that it comes within the terms of the charitable exemption claimed. Doubts will be resolved against the claim of exemption.[22]

Whether or not an institution is charitable for purposes of exemption depends both on the language of its charter and bylaws, and on its actual manner of operation.[23] If the dominant purpose of the organization is to benefit its own members or a very limited class of people it will not be exempt."[24] However the beneficiaries of the charity can be limited to some extent, and it is not necessary that the whole of mankind be benefited for the organization to be exempt.[25] In addition to being a charitable organization, the entity claiming exemption must show that the property claimed to be exempt is being used directly for the fulfillment of its charitable purposes.[26] And such direct use means something more

---

[19] Assessors of Dover v. Dominican Fathers Province of St. Joseph, 334 Mass. 530; 137 N.E.2d 225 (1956).

[20] Boston Symphony Orchestra v. Board of Assessors of Boston, 294 Mass. 248, 1 N.E.2d 6 (1936).

[21] New England Sanitarium v. Inhabitants of Stoneham, 205 Mass. 335; 91 N.E. 385 (1910).

[22] Board of Assessors of Boston v. Boston Pilot's Relief Society, 311 Mass. 232 (1942).

[23] Assessors of Boston v. World Wide Broadcasting Foundation, 317 Mass. 598, 59 N.E.2d 188 (1945); Jacob's Pillow Dance Festival v. Assessors of Becket, 320 Mass. 311, 69 N.E.2d 463 (1946).

[24] Massachusetts Medical Society v. Assessors of Boston, 340 Mass. 327, 164 N.E.2d 325 (1960); Western Massachusetts Lifecare Corp. v. Board of Assessors of Springfield, 434 Mass. 96, 747 N.E.2d 97 (2001) (while continuing care retirement community was not expressly designed to meet needs of indigent and its fees were substantial did not automatically defeat claim for charitable exemption; exemption properly denied where services were not accessible to sufficiently large and indefinite class of beneficiaries).

[25] Y.M.H.A. v. Board of Assessors, 2 Mass. B.T.A. 127 (1934).

[26] Burr v. City of Boston, 208 Mass. 537, 95 N.E. 208 (1911).

than mere ownership and possession, it must be an active appropriation to the immediate uses of the charitable cause for which the charity was organized.[27]

It is also important that the activities of the organizations are not carried on for private profit, although the fact that an institution is self-supporting or even makes a profit, if used for charitable purposes, will not necessarily make it noncharitable."[28] Within the bounds of reasonableness and good faith, the taxpayer can determine what uses of its real estate will directly promote its charitable purposes,[29] but use of the real estate merely to earn money to be applied to the charitable purpose is not sufficient.

The Supreme Judicial Court has held that the so-called "continuing care" retirement community, a relatively recent phenomenon, is not entitled to a charitable exemption, regardless of whether or not it is organized under G.L. c. 180 or qualified under I.R.c. 501(c)(3). In the particular case before the court, the property owner provided housing and services to elderly residents who, depending on their condition, lived in either "independent living units," "assisted living units" or a "skilled nursing facility." Common facilities included formal and informal dining rooms, recreation rooms, lounges, library, beauty shop, convenience store, coffee shop and gift shop. There was an asset test for entrance to the community. This fact was used by the court as the basis for deny exemption. It held that the persons who could benefit from the use of the property were a too limited class, the well-off elderly, for it to qualify for exemption.[30]

As long as the dominant purpose of the taxpayer in using the real estate is to accomplish directly its charitable purposes, the fact that profit results from a use less directly related to those purposes is not fatal to the right to exemption.[31] But the more substantial the non-charitable use of the property or, the less direct the appropriation to the organization's main purpose, the more difficult the exemption will be to sustain.[32]

---

[27] Boston Symphony Orchestra v. Board of Assessors of Boston, 294 Mass. 248, 1 N.E.2d 6 (1936); Board of Assessors of New Braintree v. Pioneer Valley Academy, 355 Mass. 610, 246 N.E.2d (1969); President, etc. of Williams College v. Assessors of Williamstown, 167 Mass. 505, 46 N.E. 394 (1897); *see also* Cardinal Cushing College v. Board of Assessors of Brookline, ATB 81989 (10/20/78).

[28] Board of Assessors of Boston v. Garland School of Homemaking, 296 Mass. 378, 6 N.E.2d 374 (1937)—A leading case.

[29] Assessors of Dover v. Dominican Fathers Province of St. Joseph, 334 Mass. 530; 137 N.E.2d 225 (1956).

[30] Jewish Geriatric Services, Inc. v. Assessors of Longmeadow, 61 Mass. App. Ct. 73 (2004).

[31] Board of Assessors of Boston v. Garland School of Homemaking, 296 Mass. 378, 6 N.E.2d 374 (1937).

[32] Trustees of Boston University v. Board of Assessors of Brookline, 11 Mass. App. Ct. 325, 416 N.E.2d 510 (1981); Brockton Knight of Columbus Bldg. Assn. v. Assessors of Brockton, 321

Although it can be said that the substantial use of property for purposes other than those directly connected with the organization's charitable purposes will destroy the right to exemption,[33] applying this rule can be quite difficult in practice. For example, just how much use is "substantial"? Or, is complete nonuse for any purpose a kind of non-charitable use?[34] Generally speaking, these are questions of fact which must be decided by the assessors or the Tax Board based on the circumstances of each case.[35]

The statute also provides for a two-year exemption period for "real estate purchased by a charitable organization with the purpose of removal thereto." However, only the portion of the property intended to be directly appropriated to the charitable uses of the organization will be entitled to exemption.[36]

§ 17.02[8] Use of Property for Noncharitable Purposes

Where parts of the same property are used for charitable and non-charitable purposes but the parts are separate and distinct, the taxpayer has a right to a proportional exemption with respect to the part applied exclusively to charitable use.[37] And, indeed, in some cases such a partial exemption has been given by local assessors.[38] However, since the well-settled rule is that the dominant use of the real estate is controlling,[39] the intensive use of the non-charitable portion could defeat the right to exemption of the charitable portion unless the separation of the charitable and non-charitable parts of the property is absolute.

As a final note on the qualification of a charitable organization for exemption

---

Mass. 110, 72 N.E.2d 406 (1947); Boston Symphony Orchestra v. Board of Assessors of Boston, 294 Mass. 248, 1 N.E.2d 6 (1936).

[33] Trustees of Boston University v. Board of Assessors of Brookline, 11 Mass. App. Ct. 325, 416 N.E.2d 510 (1981); Brockton Knights of Columbus Bldg. Assn. v. Assessors of Brockton, 321 Mass. 110, 72 N.E.2d 406 (1947); Boston Symphony Orchestra v. Board of Assessors of Boston, 294 Mass. 248, 1 N.E.2d 6 (1936). *See also* Phi Beta Epsilon Corp. v. Boston, 182 Mass. 457, 65 N.E. 824 (1903).

[34] *See* Boston Lodge of Elks v. City of Boston, 217 Mass. 176, 104 N.E. 453 (1914); Assessors of Dover v. Dominican Fathers Province of St. Joseph, 334 Mass. 530; 137 N.E.2d 225 (1956); Society of Redemptorist Fathers v. City of Boston, 129 Mass. 178 (1880).

[35] Fisher School v. Assessors of Boston, 325 Mass. 529, 91 N.E.2d 657 (1950).

[36] Mt. Auburn Hospital v. Board of Assessors of Watertown, 55 Mass. App. Ct. 611, 620 (2002).

[37] Lynn Hospital v. Board of Assessors of Lynn, 383 Mass. 14, 417 N.E.2d 14 (1981); Assessors of Framingham v. First Parish in Framingham, 329 Mass. 212, 107 N.E.2d 309 (1952).

[38] Assessors of Dover v. Dominican Fathers Province of St. Joseph, 334 Mass. 530, 137 N.E.2d 225 (1956).

[39] Brockton Knights of Columbus Bldg. Assn. v. Assessors of Brockton, 321 Mass. 110, 72 N.E.2d 406 (1947); Boston Symphony Orchestra v. Board of Assessors of Boston, 294 Mass. 248, 1 N.E.2d 6 (1936).

purposes, the statute specifically provides that if any of the income of a charitable organization is divided among the stockholders, members or trustees, or is used for non-charitable purposes, or if such persons would receive its assets upon dissolution, then it will not be exempt.[40] Also, contrary to some earlier case law, the statute provides that real property of an educational institution coming within the definition of a charitable organization "which is used wholly or principally as residences for officers of such institution and which is not part of or contiguous to real estate which is the principal location of such institution shall not be exempt."[41] Examples of organizations which have been held exempt are: Gloucester Community Pier Assoc. , Y.M.C.A., Y.M.H.A., Newton Center Woman's Club, Molly Varnum Chapter, D.A.R., Franklin Square House, Garland School of Homemaking, Harvard College, Perkins School for the Blind, and Suffolk Law School.

Examples of non-exempt organizations are: Massachusetts Medical Society, Boston Chamber of Commerce, Boston Pilots' Relief Assoc. , and Boston Lodge of Elks. These latter organizations usually failed to qualify because their charitable activities were held to be incidental or peripheral to a main purpose which was not charitable for exemption purposes.

OTHER EXEMPT ORGANIZATIONS

§ 17.02[9]   Generally

Also exempt is: certain property of incorporated horticultural and agricultural societies (notably the various "Fair" grounds around the state);[42] property up to the value of $200,000 (or $400,000 if a local option statute is accepted by the municipality) owned by incorporated veterans' organizations;[43] certain property of volunteer militia organizations;[44] the personal property of fraternal lodges which provide life, accident and health insurance, or other benefits for members;[45] the property of certain annuity, pension, endowment and retirement associations;[46] the personal property of religious associations if the principal or income is used or appropriated for religious purposes;[47] houses of worship and their associated parsonages;[48] cemeteries, tombs and rights of burial so long as dedicated to the

---

[40] G.L. c. 59, § 5(3)(a).
[41] G.L. c. 59, § 5(3)(e).
[42] G.L. c. 59, §§ 5(4) and (5)(4A).
[43] G.L. c. 59, § 5(5) and (5A).
[44] G.L. c. 59, § 5(6).
[45] G.L. c. 59, § 5(7).
[46] G.L. c. 59, §§ 5(8) and 5(9).
[47] G.L. c. 59, § 5(10).
[48] G.L. c. 59, § 5(11).

burial of the dead, and buildings of non-profit cemetery corporations used exclusively in the administration of the same;[49] real estate owned by an economic development corporation whose purpose is to retain and expand job opportunities, and which is organized under G.L. c. 180 (charitable corporation), for seven years or until the property is rented, leased or otherwise disposed of, whichever occurs first. However, if such real estate is used for other than the purposes of the corporation and if the corporation derives any income from that property, then so much of the property as is used for such purposes shall not be exempt.[50]

§ 17.02[10]   Houses of Worship and Effect of Non-Religious Use on Exemption

It is a common practice among churches of all denominations to rent or loan their facilities, particularly parish halls, to groups, often non-church groups, for purposes unrelated to religion. A question may arise as to whether such practice will jeopardize the organization's religious exemption with respect to that portion of its property.

The leading case in this area[51] involved an attempt by the assessors to tax a portion of a building owned by, adjacent to, and used in conjunction with a church. The building contained a parsonage, and certain other rooms used by various church clubs, Sunday schools and so forth, but also on occasion used by secular groups, some but not all of which made contributions to the church. Any such contributions were voluntary and no users were billed by the church.

The assessors exempted that part of the building used as a parsonage, but attempted to tax the remainder. The Appellate Tax Board gave the church an additional exemption on the ground that the rooms which were occasionally loaned to secular groups were nonetheless "appropriated for religious instruction in conjunction with the adjacent church." The Supreme Judicial Court upheld the Board saying, "The occasional use of the rooms by various secular organizations which does not appear to have interfered with their regular use for religious purposes does not, we think, constitute an appropriation for other purposes ... The right of exemption from taxation, which depends on the dominant purpose for which the rooms are maintained and their actual use for that purpose was therefore not affected."

It appears that much of what was said above in the section on charitable exemptions would be equally applicable here. It is the dominant purpose for which the property is used which determines its eligibility for exemption as church

---

[49] G.L. c. 59, §§ 5(12) and 5(13).

[50] G.L. c. 59, § 5(46).

[51] Assessors of Framingham v. First Parish in Framingham, 329 Mass. 212, 107 N.E.2d 309 (1952).

property.[52] Therefore the use of associated church buildings for secular purposes should be intermittent and not regular or permanent, and should not interfere with the primary religious purpose of the property.[53]

§ 17.02[11]   Parsonages

The provisions exempting parsonages from taxation up to a certain value have caused few problems. It is worthy of note however that the tax exemption is not limited to one parsonage per church.[54]

§ 17.02[12]   Cemeteries

The exemption for cemeteries has caused difficulties where large amounts of property are owned by the cemetery but where only a portion is actually used as a graveyard. In *Board of Assessors of Sharon v. Knollwood Cemetery*,[55] the Court said, "[The statute] cannot be interpreted as requiring that, to qualify for exemption, all land acquired ... for burial purposes must be developed at one time. It must be expected that a cemetery corporation, in making land purchases, will anticipate its future needs for a period of time and that it will prudently develop its property in an orderly fashion as the need for doing so arises." Note that the fact that the corporation is for profit will not affect the right to exemption of the land. However, administrative buildings of cemeteries must be owned by non-profit organizations to be exempt.[56]

§ 17.02[13]   Nonprofit Hospitals and Other Medical Organizations

Non-profit hospital service corporations, medical service corporations and medical service plans are, by statute, declared to be charitable corporations and are made exempt[57] from the local real estate tax.

Hospital service corporations are organizations such as Blue Cross, where subscribers or their employers pay a regular, periodic subscription fee, and in exchange are reimbursed by the corporation for fees charged to them for services rendered by hospitals which have a contract with the corporation.

Medical service corporations are organizations, such as Blue Shield, where

---

[52] Emerson v. Milton Academy, 185 Mass. 414, 70 N.E. 442 (1904).

[53] *See* William T. Stead Memorial Center of New York v. Wareham, 299 Mass. 235, 12 N.E.2d 725 (1938).

[54] Assessors of Boston v. Old South Society in Boston, 314 Mass. 364, 50 N.E.2d 51 (1943).

[55] 355 Mass. 584, 246 N.E.2d 660 (1969).

[56] Board of Assessors of Sharon v. Knollwood Cemetery, 355 Mass. 584, 246 N.E.2d 660 (1969); *see also* G.L. c. 59, § 5(12) and Blue Hill Cemetery v. Assessors of Braintree, 2 Mass. App. Ct. 602, 317 N.E.2d 831.

[57] G.L. c. 176A § 19; G.L. c. 178; G.L. c. 176C, § 14.

subscribers have a similar arrangement with the corporation with respect to physicians' services rendered to them.

Medical service plans are organizations, known as health maintenance organizations, which collect a fee from subscribers in exchange for which the subscriber has a right to secure certain specified medical services from the designated physicians who have contracted with the organization to provide such services.

However, physician group practices set up by hospitals as charitable corporations have not been successful in obtaining exemption from the local property tax.[58]

§ 17.02[14]   Urban Redevelopment Corporations

Real and personal property owned by an urban redevelopment corporation, (G.L. c. 121A), is exempt from the local property tax for a period of fifteen years after the date of organization of such corporation, and such exemption may be extended by the Department of Community Affairs for additional periods of time, but the total period of exemption cannot exceed forty years.[59] Qualifying low and moderate income housing projects are given the full forty-year exemption as of right.

Real and personal property of an urban redevelopment corporation which is leased from a housing authority, redevelopment authority, municipality, or corporation wholly owned or controlled by a municipality, is also exempt from the property tax for a period of fifteen years from the date of organization of the corporation.[60]

However, real property leased by such a corporation from a person or entity other than one of those listed above is subject to taxation in the same manner and to the same extent as if it were wholly owned and occupied by a private person. But all buildings and other things erected by the urban redevelopment corporation upon real estate leased from such private persons are for purposes of taxation deemed to be the tangible personal property of the redevelopment corporation.[61] Thus, if an urban redevelopment corporation leases real estate from a private person and proceeds to erect buildings thereon, the real estate owner would be liable to taxation by the municipality on the fair cash value of the real estate only, while the buildings erected on the property by the corporation would be exempt, so long as the fifteen-year exemption period and

---

[58] Sturdy Memorial Foundation, Inc. v. Assessors of No. Attleborough, 60 Mass. App. Ct. 573 (2004).
[59] G.L. c. 121A § 10. *See generally* G.L. c. 121A, § 1 *et seq.* and Dodge v. Prudential Ins. Co. of America, 179 N.E.2d 234 (1962).
[60] G.L. c. 121A § 10 (¶ 1).
[61] G.L. c. 121A § 10 (¶ 6).

any extensions thereof have not expired.

§ 17.02[14][a]   Payments by Urban Redevelopment Corporation in Lieu of Taxes

Although the property of urban redevelopment corporation is exempt from local taxation for a period of fifteen years after its organization, such a corporation must pay "in each calendar year to the commonwealth with respect to its corporate existence at any time within the preceding calendar year"[62] an excise tax, which the Commonwealth then distributes to the city or town where the redevelopment project is located.

This excise tax is an amount equal to the sum of (a) 5% of the corporation's gross income from all sources during the calendar year preceding that in which the tax becomes payable, and (b) an amount equal to $10 per thousand based upon the fair cash value of all the exempt real and personal property of the corporation as of January 1 of the year in which the excise tax becomes payable.

However, the statute also imposes a floor or minimum excise tax which the corporation must pay in each year regardless of what amount it would otherwise have been liable for based on the foregoing formula.

This minimum tax is equal to the lesser of: (a) the amount which the city or town would have received in taxes from the property if it were not exempt, or (b) the amount which the city or town would receive if the current tax rate[63] were applied to the average assessed valuation of the property on the three assessment dates next preceding the date of its acquisition by the redevelopment corporation, unless the property was acquired from a housing authority, redevelopment authority, city, town, or corporation wholly owned or controlled by a city or town, in which case the relevant assessment dates are the three dates immediately preceding the acquisition of the property by such entity.

In addition to the foregoing in lieu payments, the corporation can be required to make certain additional payments, up to the amount which would have been payable had the property not been exempt, if the gross receipts from the project in any year exceed certain specified limits.[64]

Where the statutory formula, and the contract entered into by the property owner pursuant to it, eventually results in a higher tax than would have been assessed if the property were not subject to G.L. c121A, the property owner is nevertheless

---

[62] G.L. c. 121A § 10 (¶ 3).

[63] The rate which is applied is the rate for the fiscal year beginning in the calendar year prior to that in which the tax is payable. Mass. Mutual Ins. Co. v. Comm'r of Corp. and Taxation, 363 Mass. 685, 296 N.E.2d 805 (1973); G.L. c. 121A, § 10 (¶ 3).

[64] G.L. c. 121A, § 15.

bound to pay the higher amount. The statute assures the municipality of receiving a minimum amount of revenue in lieu of taxes; it does not guarantee the owner will not pay more than it otherwise would have paid.[65]

§ 17.02[14][b]   Project Developed in Separate Stages

"Whenever [an urban redevelopment] project shall be developed in stages, any excise payable with respect to corporate existence in a calendar year ending before construction of the last stage of the project is completed shall be computed as though each stage constituted a separate project owned by a separate corporation."[66]

§ 17.02[14][c]   Valuation of Property—Right to Appeal

On or before March 1 in each year, the assessors of the municipality in which an urban redevelopment project is located must determine the fair cash value of all exempt property of the urban redevelopment corporation as of January 1 of that year, and certify that value to the Commissioner of Revenue and to the owning redevelopment corporation.

If the corporation is aggrieved by the valuation of the assessors it has until April 1 next ensuing, or thirty days after the receipt of the certificate of valuation from the assessors, whichever is later, to appeal the question to the Appellate Tax Board. The Board is required to hear and decide the matter and to give notice of its decision to the Commissioner of Revenue, the assessors and the corporation.[67]

§ 17.02[14][d]   Determination of Fair Cash Value Prior to Construction

The assessors of a city or town in which a redevelopment project is to be located may, and upon request of the Department of Community Affairs they shall, determine for purposes of the excise tax the maximum fair cash value of any proposed project or of any stages of such a project. Such determination may be made prior to the construction of the project or any stage thereof and in every fifth year thereafter. These determinations then become the upper limits of valuation by the assessors for purposes of computing the excise under c. 121A once the project is actually constructed, except when it can be shown that real estate or tangible personal property has been acquired which was not included in the project as

---

[65] Anderson Street Associates v. Boston, 442 Mass. 812 (2004).

[66] G.L. c. 121A, § 10 (¶ 4).

[67] G.L. c. 121A, § 10 (¶ 2). Note that all other matters relating to the administration of the tax imposed on redevelopment corporations are governed by G.L. c. 62C, so far as pertinent and consistent. See G.L. c. 121A, § 10 (¶ 5).

proposed.[68] The obvious purpose of this provision is to give the developer some indication of his probable tax liability when he is planning the project in order that he can make financial projections and other planning decisions with as much certainty as possible.

§ 17.02[15]   Housing and Redevelopment Authorities

The real estate and tangible personal property of housing and redevelopment authorities created under the provisions of G.L. c. 121B is exempt from taxation. However such entities are subject to assessment of an in lieu payment which is not in excess of the amount that could have been assessed on the real estate at the current tax rate based on the average assessed valuation for the three years immediately preceding acquisition of the property by the authority. This in lieu payment is held constant thereafter, regardless of subsequent general revaluations by the municipality.[69]

EXEMPT INDIVIDUALS

§ 17.02[16]   Veterans

There are a number of provisions granting exemptions to veterans who are disabled.[70] Generally speaking, the greater the veteran's disability, the larger the exemption.

Exemptions range from a $2,000 reduction in assessed value or $175 credit against tax due, (whichever results in the greatest reduction in taxes), for veterans with a 10% disability or who have received the purple heart, to a $10,000 reduction or $875 credit for veterans who are 100% disabled with specially adapted housing.

Within this range are a number of progressively larger exemptions based on various criteria. For example, certain persons crippled in service and recipients of the Congressional Medal of Honor, Air Force Cross, Navy Cross or Distinguished Service Cross are entitled to exemptions of $4,000 valuation or $350 credit against tax.

In every case, the veteran must be a legal resident of Massachusetts, not dishonorably discharged, who was domiciled in this State for at least six months prior to entering service or who has resided here for at least five years prior to filing for an exemption.

---

[68] G.L. c. 121A, § 10 (¶ 7); Pequot Assoc. v. Board of Assessors of Salem, 376 Mass. 270, 380 N.E.2d 648 (1978).

[69] G.L. c. 121B, § 16.

[70] G.L. c. 59, §§ 5, (22)(a), 5(22)(b), 5(22)(c), 5(22)(d), and 5(22)(e).

The wives or widows of veterans entitled to the exemption may also claim it, as may the widows or parents of men killed in action.

In one case, a taxpayer was denied a veteran's exemption by the assessors because the statute (G.L. c. 59, § 5, preamble) provides: "... any person who receives an exemption under the provisions of clause ... 22 [veteran's exemption] ... [or] 37 [blind person's exemption] ... shall not receive an exemption on the same property under any other provision of this section," and the taxpayer's wife was receiving a blind person's exemption on the same property. The Court reversed holding that a man and wife are not one person for purposes of this statute so both exemptions must be granted, even though the property is held by them as tenants by the entirety.[71]

A person who meets the requirements for the veteran's exemption may not be denied the exemption because he is a conscientious objector.

§ 17.02[17]   Surviving Spouses, Orphans and Poor Persons

There is another group of exemptions which, although not placed together in the law itself, are spiritually related because they each represent an attempt by the legislature to grant relief to persons who are under economic pressure as the result of advanced age, poverty, ill-health, or the loss of a breadwinner.

Real estate owned and occupied as a domicile by a surviving spouse, or a minor whose parent is deceased, or by a person over 70 years old who has owned and so occupied the property for at least ten years, is exempted to the extent of $2,000 in valuation or $175 in credit toward the tax due. This exemption may only be claimed by persons whose entire estate does not exceed $20,000.[72] Further, the exemption under this clause is limited to one for each domicile so that a widow with three children could not get four exemptions on one property.[73]

The assessors may, in their discretion, exempt any portion of the estate of a person who by reason of advanced age, infirmity, or poverty is, in their judgment, unable to contribute fully to the public charges (the so-called "hardship" exemption).[74]

The real estate of a blind person, occupied as his domicile, is exempted in the amount of $5,000 valuation or $437.50 credit toward the tax.[75]

---

[71] De Cenzo v. Board of Assessors of Framingham, 372 Mass. 523, 362 N.E.2d 913 (1977).

[72] G.L. c. 59, § 5(17); the amounts of income or assets which an applicant may possess and still qualify may be increased by local acceptance of § 5(17C) or § 5(17C 1/2).

[73] Sylvester v. Assessors of Braintree, 344 Mass. 263, 182 N.E.2d 120 (1962).

[74] G.L. c. 59, § 5(18).

[75] G.L. c. 59, § 5(37); by local acceptance of § 5(37A) this amount may be increased to $500.

Finally, a full exemption from taxes is given to the unmarried widow or surviving minor children of a fireman or policeman killed in the line of duty.[76]

§ 17.02[18]   Aged Homeowners

In an effort to mitigate the effect of rapidly escalating real estate taxes on older residents living on fixed incomes, the legislature has in recent years added specific provisions providing exemptions to elderly persons whose incomes are limited but who are not truly impoverished. These provisions for exemptions to elderly homeowners are rather complex, and the statute should always be consulted when a particular case arises. However they may be summarized as follows:

An exemption of $4,000 valuation or $500 credit, whichever results in the greater reduction in taxes, is granted if the taxpayer (a) is a joint tenant with his spouse and either is 70 or older, or is 70 or older and a joint tenant with anyone else, or is 70 or older and a sole owner and (b) if he occupies the property as his domicile and (c) if he has been domiciled in Massachusetts for the preceding ten years, and (d) if he has owned, and occupied as his domicile, real property in the Commonwealth for at least five years or is a surviving spouse who holds the property by inheritance and has occupied real property in the Commonwealth as his domicile for at least five years and (e) if the taxpayer's gross receipts from all sources in the previous year were less than $6,000 if he is single, or if married the combined receipts of both spouses totaled less than $7,000 (in computing gross receipts for this purpose the taxpayer subtracts from the total his ordinary business expenses and losses, but not personal and family expensed, and also an amount equal to the minimum Social Security payment then payable to a retired worker over 70 or a retired couple over 70, whichever is applicable), and finally (f) if the taxpayer's total estate, exclusive of the non income generating portion of real estate occupied as his domicile, is not in excess of $17,000 if single or $20,000 if mar ried. The taxpayer may elect to include his domicile in computing his total estate, in which case such total estate may not exceed $40,000 if single or $45,000 if married.[77]

It should also be noted that if the taxpayer holds the property jointly with a person not his spouse, then all other joint tenants must meet gross income and total estate criteria similar to those outlined above in order for the 70-year-old taxpayer to get the exemption.

The statute also provides that, in the case of the over-70 taxpayer who holds jointly with a non-spouse, "the amount of his exemption shall be that proportion of [the full exemption] which the amount of his interest in such property bears to the whole tax due."

---

[76] G.L. c. 59, §§ 5(42) and 5(43).

[77] G.L. c. 59, § 5(41). By local option, the income and asset tests to qualify for elderly exemption may be somewhat relaxed. See G.L. c. 59, § 5(41B) and (41C).

This language seems confused. Obviously it is intended that some sort of pro rata approach be taken where the over-70 taxpayer owns less than the whole property. Equally obviously, in order to take a pro rata approach, it is necessary to derive some fractional amount of the full exemption. What is not so obvious, however, is just which fraction the legislature wishes to use in this case.

The law refers to that proportion "which the amount of his interest in such property bears to the whole tax due." If the dollar amount of the whole tax due is to be the denominator of the fraction, as seems likely, then the numerator is the "amount of his [the taxpayer's] interest in such property." Surely the "amount" referred to is not the taxpayer's share of assessed value because in the vast majority of cases this would be larger than the tax due, making the numerator of the fraction larger than the denominator. Neither would it appear logical to express the tax-payer's interest as a percentage of the whole, since this would result in a miniscule abatement in every case.

It is this writer's opinion that the law should read something like "that percentage of the full exemption which is equal to his percentage interest in such property." So read, the statute extends the benefits which the legislature wished to confer on the elderly homeowner in a consistent and logical way to those elderly persons who occupy homes in which they own less than the entire fee interest. Read the way it is written, it merely succeeds in adding a touch of incomprehensibility to an intensely intricate section of the law. Unfortunately, at the present time there is no case law construing this section.

Any person who receives an elderly exemption may not receive any other exemption on the same property except a hardship exemption.

§ 17.02[19]   Living in Multi-family Dwelling

Where the elderly taxpayer owns and occupies one unit of a multiple unit building as his domicile he is entitled to the full exemption and not a proportion thereof.[78]

§ 17.02[20]   Owning Less than Entire Property

Occasionally, where the aged property owner has owned less than the entire interest in the property, as, for instance, a life estate, the assessors have attempted to deny him the statutory exemption.

Where the elderly taxpayer conveyed the property to an amendable, revocable trust of which he was the beneficiary he lost the exemption. The Court said that

---

[78] Board of Assessors of Everett v. Formosi, 349 Mass. 727, 212 N.E.2d 210 (1965).

to qualify for the exemption the taxpayer must have legal title and a beneficial interest in the property.[79]

But where the taxpayer conveyed to a straw, then immediately took back title as life tenant with the remainder in his children, he had a right to the full exemption since he still had both legal title and beneficial interest in the property.[80]

And, where the taxpayers conveyed to a straw and immediately took back title as trustees with a beneficial life interest in themselves, remainder to their children, they did not lose the exemption. The Court said that conveyance to a straw did not break the five-year statutorily required holding period, and that the taxpayers had sufficient legal title and beneficial interest to satisfy the statute.[81] A settlor who names himself as trustee need not be the sole trustee in order to hold sufficient legal interest to fulfill the exemption requirement.[82] However in the case of some of the elderly exemptions the other trustees will have to satisfy the income and total asset requirements of the statute, and even if they do the total exemption available may be reduced.[83] Although there appears to be no similar disadvantage where there are other beneficiaries than the elderly person, it does seem clear that the beneficial interest of the elderly person should be substantial.

Obviously, counsel for elderly taxpayers should use care in making these kinds of quasi-testamentary conveyances of property.

§ 17.02[21]   Deferral of Tax

The exemption for the elderly discussed in the preceding section was supplemented in 1974 by another provision which reaches a much broader class of elderly persons. These persons are allowed to defer payment of their property tax from year to year, at 8% interest per annum, until the total amount of deferred taxes for all years, plus interest, equals 50% of the full and fair cash value of the elderly taxpayer's interest in the property.[84]

In order to take advantage of this provision: (a) the tax-payer must be at least 65 years old or, if married, one of the spouses must be 65 and the property owned jointly, and (b) the 65-year-old taxpayer must occupy the property as his or her domicile, and (c) the taxpayer must have been domiciled in the Commonwealth for the preceding ten years, and (d) he must either have owned and occupied as his domicile real estate in the Commonwealth for five years or be a surviving spouse

---

[79] Kirby v. Board of Assessors of Medford, 350 Mass. 386, 215 N.E.2d 99 (1966).

[80] Coroa v. Board of Assessors of Fall River, 354 Mass. 235, 236 N.E.2d 875 (1968).

[81] Board of Assessors of Cambridge v. Bellissimo, 357 Mass. 198, 257 N.E.2d 463 (1970).

[82] Board of Assessors of Cambridge v. Bellissimo, 357 Mass. 198, 257 N.E.2d 463 (1970).

[83] See G.L. c. 59, § 5(41), (41B), (41C).

[84] G.L. c. 59, § 5(41)(a).

who holds by inheritance and has occupied real property in the Commonwealth as his or her domicile for five years, and (e) the gross receipts from all resources of the taxpayer and his spouse, reduced by ordinary business expenses and losses, must not be in excess of $20,000 (by local option this amount may be increased to $40,000). In computing the taxpayer's gross receipts for purposes of eligibility for deferral, ordinary business expenses and losses may be deducted, but not personal and family expenses.

Qualifying taxpayers may, on or before December 15 of each year, apply to the assessors for an exemption of all or part of the tax on their domicile for that year. The assessors are required to grant the requested exemption, provided the tax payer enters into a tax deferral and recovery agreement with the assessors on behalf of the city or town.

The law specifies in some detail what must be contained in such an agreement. However, the main points are that the deferred taxes will bear interest at 8%, that the total deferred amount plus interest will not exceed 50% of the fair cash value of the property, that the deferred tax will be paid off if the property is sold or if the taxpayer dies, (except that a surviving spouse can continue the deferred agreement during her life), that any joint tenant or mortgagee must give prior written approval of the agreement, that the assessors shall record in the registry of deeds a statement indicating the name of the owner, a description of the property and the fact that a tax deferral agreement exists. This statement creates a lien on the land for the amount of the deferred taxes to the same extent as if a taking for nonpayment of taxes had been recorded, except that, (a) interest accrues at the rate set in the deferral statute, (b) the lien may not be assigned, and (c) the lien may not be foreclosed until six months after the conveyance of the property or the death of the person whose taxes have been deferred (if there is no surviving spouse).

In the case of the over-65 taxpayer who is a joint tenant with one not his spouse, the law provides for a proportional deferral. Unfortunately, the phraseology providing for a deferral equal to the ratio that "the amount of the taxpayer's interest in such property bears to the whole tax due" used in the section providing for an exemption for the elderly, discussed above, is used in this section as well, and the discussion of the problem of interpretation of that section would be equally applicable here. (*See* § 17.02[18] above.)

The usefulness of the over-65 tax deferral privilege will vary from taxpayer to taxpayer. Unlike the over-70 exemption, there is no total asset limitation and the $20,000 income limitation seems high enough to include a substantial majority of retired homeowners. Also, unlike the exemption provisions, the deferral scheme has certain financial planning potential which may or may not have been intended by the legislature.

One effect of utilizing the tax deferral provision is that the taxpayer eases the burden of current living expenses on himself and shifts that burden to his estate and heirs. Another is that he can, at least with respect to himself, consume up to 50% of a real estate asset without the necessity of selling it. Of course with respect to his heirs the real estate would not be consumed, absent a provision in the will that the deferred taxes be paid by the recipients of the real estate, since otherwise the deferred taxes would be paid out of his personal estate. Another effect would be that, if the taxpayer has been paying his real estate taxes out of current income and if he continues to spend all his current income, he would be reducing the size of his estate subject to death taxes.

EXEMPT CLASSES OF PROPERTY

§ 17.02[22] Manufactured Homes

The statute exempts from taxation "Manufactured homes located in manufactured housing communities subject to the monthly license fee provided for under c. 140, § 32G ..."[85] An amendment to the statute enacted in 1991 changed the word "mobile" to "manufactured."[86] This may have the effect of ending a rather recurrent argument between assessors and residents of what were formerly called mobile home parks. An argument which often prompted owners of mobile homes which were never intended to be mobile to install hidden wheels on their homes in order to avoid the local real estate tax.

In *Ellis v. Board Assessors of Acushnet*,[87] a case decided under the old form of the statute, the taxpayers claimed that their mobile home was exempt from the real estate tax by virtue of this provision. However, the assessors disagreed and so did the Appellate Tax Board which held that the property was real estate and taxable as such. The Supreme Judicial Court affirmed. It was agreed that the taxpayers' mobile home was elaborately and sturdily constructed. It was on a permanent poured concrete foundation built over a cellar which contained a furnace and water heater. The Court found that "in almost every practical respect" the property looked like and served the purpose of a conventional home.

However, it was also clear that the property satisfied the definition of "mobile home" contained in G.L. c. 140.

The Court said that the definition of mobile home contained in c. 140 was not controlling for purposes of taxation; and that to hold otherwise would create a dual standard of taxation which was constitutionally not permissible.[88]

The *Ellis* case seemed to imply that one had to look at each so-called mobile

---

[85] G.L. c. 59, § 5(36).

[86] St. 1991, c. 481, § 8.

[87] 265 N.E.2d 491 (1970).

[88] *Cf.* Board of Selectmen of Hatfield v. Garvey, 362 Mass. 821, 291 N.E.2d 593 (1972).

home on its own merits. The less substantial, wheel mounted, transient types would tend to be found exempt, while the more elaborate types intended to function as permanent dwellings would be taxable. Presumably the change in the statute will eliminate the need for this type of analysis.

§ 17.02[23]   Forest Land

Forest land which is being cultivated or which is burdened with agricultural preservation restrictions is eligible to be taxed on a more favorable basis than other real estate.[89]

§ 17.02[24]   Obtaining the Exemption[90]

The provisions for the taxation of forest lands are contained in G.L. c. 61. In order to secure the benefit of these provisions the taxpayer must own land which meets the requirements of the statute, and he must apply in the manner outlined therein to have his property classified and taxed as forest land.

In order to be eligible for classification as forest land under the statute, the land in question must:

1) be at least sixteen and seven-tenths percent stocked;

2) contain at least seven and five-tenths square feet of basal area per acre of forest trees of any size; or

3) have formerly had such tree cover and not be currently developed for non-forest use; or

4) be a plantation containing at least five hundred trees per acre.

An application to have such land classified as forest land must be submitted to the state forester prior to July first in any year. The application must be accompanied by a "Forest Management Plan," on a form provided by the forester, which provides for a ten year program of forest management. If the management plan is approved by the forester he shall sign it and certify the land as forest land for purposes of exemption from the property tax.

After certification by the forester, the property owner must, by September first of the same year, submit a written application for classification as forest land to the assessors. Such application must be accompanied by the certification of the state forester and the approved forest management plan.

---

[89] *See generally* G.L. c. 184, §§ 31 and 32; G.L. c. 132A, §§ 11A, 11B, 11C, and 11D; G.L. c. 61; G.L. c. 61A; and G.L. c. 59, § 11 (¶ 4).

[90] *See generally* G.L. c. 61, §§ 1–8 for provisions creating forest land exemption.

Upon receipt of a proper application, other than their right of appeal discussed below, the assessors appear to be given no discretion by the statute and must so classify the land by filing a statement of classification in the registry of deeds on a form approved by the Commissioner of Revenue. This statement creates a lien on the land for the payment of taxes levied under chapter 61. Classification takes effect on the following January 1.

As part of the certification process the state forester is required to inspect the land. During such inspection he must determine if any cutting has occurred within the previous two years. If such cutting has occurred the forester must determine the "stumpage value"[91] of the forest products cut and notify the assessors in writing of such value. The assessors must then assess a tax on such products in accordance with the formula discussed below, and the payment of such tax is a condition of classification.[92]

Buildings and other structures and the land on which they stand or which is accessory to their use, which are part of an otherwise qualified parcel, may not be taxed as forest land.

Where a single parcel of land is part forest land and part other land the forest land portion may be eligible to be classified as forest land if it contains at least ten contiguous acres and otherwise complies with the statute.[93]

§ 17.02[25]   Appeal of State Forester's Decisions[94]

If the assessors believe land which is the subject of an application for forest land classification, or which is presently so classified, does not qualify under the statute, they may on or before December first in any year appeal to the state forester to have the classification denied or withdrawn. The state forester on his own motion may deny initial classification, or withdraw classified status, or grant or continue classification subject to conditions. In any case, the forester must take action by March first.

Parties aggrieved by the decision of the forester must, by April fifteenth, give him notice of a claim of appeal. Thereafter, on or before May fifteenth, the forester must convene in the region in which the land is located an appellate panel composed of three members. One member shall be named by the forester, one member by the assessors, and one member by the forester and assessors together. (It does not appear that the property owner participates in the selection process even when he or she has taken the appeal.)

---

[91] *See* § 17.02[27], *infra.*

[92] G.L. c. 61, § 2.

[93] G.L. c. 61, § 2.

[94] G.L. c. 61, § 2 (¶ 7).

The panel must hold a duly noticed hearing and render a decision within ten days after the close of such hearing. Persons aggrieved by the decision of the panel may appeal either to the superior court or the appellate tax board, within 45 days after receipt of its decision. The status of the land will not change until the appeal is decided.

§ 17.02[26] Keeping the Exemption

Once land has been classified as forest land it remains so classified for ten years, unless it is voluntarily withdrawn or converted to other uses, or unless the assessors or state forester commence a proceeding to remove it. Such removal proceedings are of course subject to review as outlined in the proceeding section. In order to keep the land classified, the owner must manage it in accordance with the approved plan, and must not use it for purposes incompatible with forest production.[95] At the end of each ten year period the owner must apply to the state forester for recertification. The forester or his designee has authority to enter on private land to make investigations to assure compliance with the management plan and the other statutory provisions.

§ 17.02[27] Taxation of Classified Forest Land[96]

Land classified under the provisions of the statute is exempt from the real estate tax (imposed by G.L. c. 59). However the owner of classified forest land must pay a forest products tax equal to 8% of the fair market value immediately prior to cutting (stumpage value) of any forest products cut from the land.

The owner is required to notify the assessors of all cutting, and the forester is required to file with the assessors all cutting plans filed with him.

On or before April first of each year the assessors must notify the landowner that a products tax is due. The owner must respond on or before May first by filing a return on a form approved by the state forester which shows the amount of forest products cut during the preceding calendar year. The assessors then assess the tax on the basis of this return. If the owner fails to file a return the assessors must send him or her a notice of delinquency. If the return is still not filed twenty days thereafter they can proceed to calculate and assess the products tax, subject to the owner's right to apply for abatement.[97] There is also a penalty of five dollars per day for each day that the return is not filed. But the total amount of this penalty tax must not exceed the amount of the products tax itself.[98]

---

[95] G.L. c. 61, § 2 (¶ 7).
[96] G.L. c. 61, § 3.
[97] G.L. c. 61, § 4.
[98] G.L. c. 61, § 6.

In addition to the products tax, the owner must pay a land tax assessed at the commercial property rate based on 5% of its fair cash value.

Classified forest lands are subject to special and betterment assessments, but, with the exception of assessments for water pipes to improve fire protection for the forest land, these are not due and payable until the land is removed from classification.[99]

§ 17.02[28]   Appeal of Assessment of Tax

Any person aggrieved by the assessment of the products or land tax may apply to the assessors for abatement within 60 days of notice of the tax. Such application must be in writing on a form approved by the Commissioner of Revenue. The assessors must provide a hearing before acting on the application. Further appeal may be taken to the Appellate Tax Board within 30 days after the date of notice of the assessors' decision or three months from the date of application for abatement, whichever is later.[100] Note that this appeal is from the assessment of the alternative tax itself rather than based on any quarrel over proper classification of the land.

§ 17.02[29]   Withdrawal from Classification

When the owner of classified forest land voluntarily withdraws such land from classification, or where there is otherwise a final determination that the land should be withdrawn from classification, the owner must pay to the municipality where the land is located an amount equal to the difference between the tax which would have been paid if the land had not been classified as forest land and the taxes actually paid from the last classification date, or during the last five years, whichever period is longer. Annual interest is added at the amount set by § 32 of c. 62c.

Note that no credit for taxes paid is given where the land is withdrawn after a final determination that it was improperly classified or not managed according to the approved management plan, or if it is voluntarily withdrawn by the owner at any time other than the end of a certification period.[101]

§ 17.02[30]   Conversion to Nonforest Use: First Refusal Option[102]

Where land is classified and taxed as forest land under c. 61 and the owner wishes to sell or convert it for use as residential, commercial or industrial land he must provide to the city or town where the land is located a notice of intention to so sell

---

[99] G.L. c. 61, § 5.

[100] G.L. c. 61, § 3. Note that three months in the case of this statute means 90 days. W.D. Cowls, Inc. v. Board of Assessors, 34 Mass. App. 944, 613 N.E.2d 930 (1993).

[101] G.L. c. 61, § 7.

[102] G.L. c. 61, § 8.

or convert. For a period of 120 days after notice the city or town has a right of first refusal to meet any bona fide offer to purchase the land, or to buy the land at its appraised fair market value in the case of a conversion without a sale. If the city or town does not wish to purchase the land itself it may assign its rights, after public hearing, to a nonprofit conservation organization, for the purpose of maintaining the land in use as forest land. (Interestingly, the city or town is not required to maintain the forest use if it purchases the land while a nonprofit assignee from the city or town must.)

The land may not be sold or converted until the notice has been given and the option period has expired, or the landowner has been notified in writing by the mayor or board of selectmen that the option will not be exercised. The notice requirements and registry recording requirements which apply to these first refusal rights are detailed and specific and the statute should be consulted and followed carefully.

The right of first refusal does not apply to foreclosing mortgagees. But they must give notice of sale to the city or town in the manner set out in the statute at least 90 days prior to the foreclosure sale.

Note that the right of first refusal only attaches if sale or conversion occurs while the property is being taxed as forest land. If it is withdrawn from classification prior to sale the right would not arise. However, voluntary withdrawal will trigger the penalty tax, and voluntary withdrawal prior to the end of a certification period will prevent the owner from receiving credit against the penalty tax for products and land taxes paid during classification.[103]

§ 17.02[31]　Agricultural and Horticultural Land

In an effort to arrest the steady decline in the number of farms and the total farm acreage in Massachusetts, the legislature, in 1973, adopted G.L. c. 61A, which provides that such land shall be taxed based on its value for agricultural or horticultural purposes. The following is a summary and overview of the statutory scheme.

§ 17.02[32]　Agricultural Land—Definition[104]

For purposes of the statute agricultural land is defined as that used primarily and directly in raising animals or in a related manner which is incidental to such use and represents a customary and necessary use in raising such animals and preparing them or the products derived from them for market.

---

[103] *See* G.L. c. 61, § 7.
[104] G.L. c. 61A, § 1.

§ 17.02[33]   Horticultural Land—Definition[105]

For purposes of the statute horticultural land is defined as that used primarily and directly in:

1) raising fruits, berries, vegetables, nuts and other foods for human consumption; or

2) raising feed for animals, tobacco, flowers, sod, trees, nursery or greenhouse products, and ornamental plants and shrubs for the purpose of selling such products in the ordinary course of business; or

3) raising forest products under a program certified by the state forester to be a planned program to improve the quantity and quality of a continuous crop for the purpose of selling such products in the regular course of business; or

4) a related manner which is incidental to the foregoing uses and is a customary and necessary use in raising such products and preparing them for market.

§ 17.02[34]   Minimum Area and Dollar Sales[106]

In order to be eligible for taxation under the provisions of G.L. c. 61A, land which meets the statutory definitions of agricultural and horticultural land must be at least five acres in area, and the gross sales of the agricultural and/or horticultural products of such land together with any amounts payable under Federal or State soil conservation or pollution abatement programs must total at least $500 per year. If the $500 minimum is not met, then the land may still be eligible, provided the owner can "clearly prove" that the use of the land during the year was for the purpose of achieving an annual total of at least $500 from product sales and government program payments within the "product development period." This product development period is established by the "farmland valuation advisory commission," which is a new body created by the statute, composed of the heads of various state agencies or their designees and an assessor appointed by the governor. Where the parcel proposed for exemption is more than five acres in area the gross sales and program payment standards are increased at the rate of five dollars per acre for the land over the initial five acres.

Contiguous land of the same owner located in more than one municipality is not required to satisfy the minimum acreage requirement in each town but is considered as one unit for such purposes. Thus if an owner had a five-acre parcel with one acre in each of five towns, the entire piece would, if otherwise eligible, be taxed under G.L. c. 61A, with each town taxing that portion of the property that lies within

---

[105] G.L. c. 61A, § 2.
[106] G.L. c. 61A, § 3.

its borders.[107] Only half the total contiguous acreage need be actively devoted to agricultural/horticultural use, provided none of the acreage is devoted to residential, commercial or industrial use.[108] The contiguous land not actively devoted to agricultural/horticultural use is not considered in calculating the per acre revenue when determining if the minimum statutory standards for exemption have been met.[109]

§ 17.02[35]   Application for Eligibility

Eligibility of land to be taxed pursuant to G.L. c. 61A is determined separately for each tax year and the landowner must therefore apply for eligibility each tax year. Such application must be on a form approved by the Commissioner of Revenue and must be submitted by October 1 of the year preceding the tax year for which the eligibility is requested.[110] Where a revaluation is completed in time for the upcoming fiscal year but not in time for the taxpayer to apply by October 1, then he may apply within 30 days after the mailing of the tax bill containing the new valuation.)

The board of assessors must either allow or disallow the landowner's application within three months from the date it is filed. Failure to act within the three-month period is deemed to be an allowance of the application.

The assessors are commanded by the statute to disallow any application where in their judgment the land does not qualify for taxation under G.L. c. 61A, or where they determine that the application is submitted "for the purpose of evading the payment of full and proper taxes."[111]

Within ten days after they make their decision, the assessors must send to the landowner, by certified mail, written notice of the allowance or disallowance of his application, together with the reasons therefor and a notice of the owner's right to appeal.[112] In the case of a partial disallowance, the landowner has a right to file an amended application, presumably covering only the land which the assessors have found qualified.

If the application is allowed, and it is the first application relating to a particular parcel which has been approved, or if it is a reapplication for land which for a period of time has not been taxed under chapter 61A, then the assessors are required to file a statement of their action in the registry of deeds. This statement constitutes

---

[107] G.L. c. 61A, § 5.
[108] G.L. c. 61A, § 4.
[109] Nashawena Trust v. Board of Assessors of Gosnold, 398 Mass. 821, 501 N.E.2d 506 (1986).
[110] G.L. c. 61A, §§ 6, 8.
[111] G.L. c. 61A, §§ 6, 9.
[112] G.L. c. 61A, § 9.

a lien upon the land for any taxes which may be levied under G.L. c. 61A.[113] When the land ceases to be valued under c. 61A, the assessors are also required to file a statement to that effect in the registry.

§ 17.02[36]   Valuation

Land which has been devoted to qualified agricultural and/or horticultural uses during the tax year in issue as well as during the two immediately preceding tax years, and has been approved as eligible by the assessors pursuant to the provisions of the statute, shall be assessed based only upon its value as agricultural and/or horticultural land. The assessors in determining such value must be guided by the list of ranges of value published by the "farmland advisory commission,"[114] and by their personal knowledge, judgment and experience as to local land values.[115] Thus, while consideration of the values published by the farmland advisory commission is mandatory, the assessors may also consider other more traditional methods of valuation, appropriately modified. For example, comparable sales may be considered where the buyer purchased the land for agricultural use. Similarly the assessors may use a capitalized income approach which is limited to the ability of the land to produce income derived from agricultural use.[116]

§ 17.02[36][a]   Taxation of Farmhouses and Other Structures

All buildings located on qualified agricultural or horticultural land and all land occupied by a dwelling or regularly used for family living must be assessed and taxed in the same manner as other taxable property. Thus, buildings such as barns and sheds, used in the operation of the farm are not eligible for the favorable tax treatment provided by G.L. c. 61A. Neither is a dwelling house with its associated land and buildings eligible.[117]

§ 17.02[36][b]   Special or Betterment Assessments[118]

Qualified agricultural or horticultural land is subject to special assessments or betterment assessments only to the "pro rata extent" that the service or facility financed by the assessment is used for "improving the agricultural or horticultural use capability" of the land or for "the personal benefit" of the owner of the land.

This provision seems ambiguous enough to be a fruitful source of litigation.

---

[113] G.L. c. 61A, § 9.
[114] See § 8.02[36], *supra*, for description of this commission.
[115] G.L. c. 61A, §§ 4 and 10.
[116] Mann v. Board of Assessors of Wareham, 387 Mass. 35, 438 N.E.2d 826 (1982).
[117] G.L. c. 61A, § 15.
[118] G.L. c. 61A, § 18.

Any special or betterment assessment must be suspended, upon application of the landowner, during the period that the land is in agricultural or horticultural use, provided that the interest on the suspended amount is paid annually. When the use of the land is changed the suspended assessment becomes due and payable.

§ 17.02[36][c]   Valuation for Other than Assessment Purposes

For any purpose other than the determination of the proper substitute tax under G.L. c. 61A, including eligibility for exemptions under G.L. c. 59, qualified agricultural and horticultural land will be valued and deemed to have been assessed on the same basis as other taxable property.[119]

§ 17.02[37]   Effect of Sale or Change of Use

§ 17.02[37][a]   Conveyance Tax[120]

If land which has been assessed and taxed as agricultural or horticultural land is sold for the purpose of being put to other use, the statute imposes a "conveyance tax" on the seller. This tax is at the rate of 10% of the sale price if the land is sold during the first year of ownership, 9% if sold during the second year of ownership, 8% if sold during the third, and so on, the rate declining 1% for each year of ownership until, following the end of the tenth year of ownership, no conveyance tax is imposed on the seller. The tax is payable by the seller at the time of transfer of the property. The conveyance tax will apply if the property is sold during the ten year period even if the property is not qualified under G.L. c. 61A during the year of sale.[121] Thus the property owner cannot avoid the conveyance tax merely by failing to apply for c. 61A assessment in the year of sale.

If the purchaser files with the assessors an affidavit to the effect that he intends to continue the agricultural and/or horticultural use of the land, then no conveyance tax will be imposed on the seller. But, if the purchaser does not in fact continue such use, then he will be liable for the conveyance tax which would have been paid by the seller. However, there are ten special types of conveyances, such as mortgage foreclosures, tax deeds, and deeds between husband and wife or parent and child where no consideration is received, which are exempt from the conveyance tax.[122] The practitioner should consult the statute to determine if his or her particular transaction is exempt. Where there is a nonexempt transfer after an exempt transfer, the holding period for purposes of calculating the conveyance tax runs from the date of the last nonexempt transfer; except where the grantor acquired the property

---

[119] G.L. c. 61A, § 20.
[120] G.L. c. 61A, § 12.
[121] McKenney v. Board of Assessors of Sterling, 13 Mass. App. Tax Bd. Rep. 167 (1991).
[122] G.L. c. 61A, § 12.

from a foreclosing mortgage the holding period runs from the date of such acquisition.

If land taxed under the statute as agricultural or horticultural land is changed to another use by its owner within a period of ten years from the time of its acquisition by the owner, or the earliest date of its uninterrupted use by the owner in agriculture or horticulture, whichever date is earlier, it is subject to the conveyance tax to the same extent as if it had been sold. In such cases, the tax is based on the fair market value of the land as determined by the assessors, based on the same valuation standards that they would use in assessing any other piece of property. In other words, the property is not valued for purposes of the conveyance tax based solely on its value as farmland but is valued as any other piece of property would be.

§ 17.02[37][b]   Roll-back Tax.[123]

Whenever land which is valued and assessed as agricultural or horticultural land no longer qualifies for such status, it becomes subject to an additional tax, called a "roll-back" tax. The roll-back tax applies in the year that the disqualification occurs and in those of the four immediately preceding tax years in which the land was taxed as agricultural or horticultural land. Thus if land is valued and taxed as agricultural and/or horticultural land in 1988 and in each subsequent year until 1993, during which year it becomes no longer qualified, the owner will be liable for the roll-back tax for the years 1989, 1980, 1991, 1992 and 1993. If the land had not been taxed as agricultural/horticultural land in any one of the four preceding years, then it would not be liable for the roll-back tax in that year.

The roll-back tax is equal to the difference, for each year, between the taxes paid or payable on the land as qualified agricultural or horticultural land and the taxes that would have been paid or payable if the land had not been so qualified.[124]

The statute also provides that, "If at a time during a tax year when a change in land use has occurred the land was not then valued, assessed and taxed under the provisions of this chapter then such land shall be subject to roll-back taxes only for such of the five immediately preceding years in which the land was valued, assessed and taxed thereunder."[125]

This provision appears to contemplate a situation where a parcel had been qualified and taxed under G.L. c. 61A as agricultural or horticultural land, and had subsequently ceased to be so taxed for one or more years, at which point the

---

[123] G.L. c. 61A, § 13.

[124] Where the municipality has adopted different tax rates for different classes of property the assessors can apply the commercial rate in calculating the roll back tax rate. Hill v. Board of Assessors of Sudbury, Appellate Tax Board Docket # 212972 (1994).

[125] G.L. c. 61A, § 13.

roll-back tax is levied and billed. Since the roll-back tax attaches as soon as the land no longer qualifies as "actively devoted" to agricultural and/or horticultural use[126] and since the landowner must apply each year for qualified status, this situation would probably only arise in practice when the owner of previously qualified land simply stopped applying for the special tax status, and the assessors began billing him for taxes on the same basis as other property. If a subsequent change in use were to occur and the assessors were at that time to attempt to assess a roll-back tax, they could only look back to the five years immediately preceding the change in use for the purpose of assessing such a tax.[127]

For example, in 1988, a landowner applies for and receives qualified status for a particular parcel. In 1989 and 1990, he also applies for and receives qualified status. In 1991, 1992, 1993, and 1994, even though his land would qualify, he does not apply for such status and the land is taxed on the same basis as all other property in town. In 1994, he sells his land to a developer. He will only be liable for rollback taxes for 1989 and 1990; the tax saving for 1988 remains his. The liability for the roll-back tax falls on the person who owns the land when it ceases to be actively devoted to agricultural or horticultural use.

The statutory language indicates quite clearly that the operative date for roll-back tax purposes is the date when the change of use occurs, not when the tax is assessed. For instance, if in the above example the assessors did not assess the tax until 1995, the taxpayer would not thereby escape paying the roll-back tax for 1989. The assessors would still look at the five years immediately preceding 1994, when the change of use occurred.

The assessment, collection, apportionment and payment of roll-back taxes is governed by the provisions of G.L. c. 59, § 75, relating to the assessment of omitted property, except that the time limits on the imposition of taxes contained in that section do not apply.[128]

§ 17.02[37][c]   Conveyance and Roll-back Taxes—Relationship to One Another

The conveyance and roll-back taxes discussed in the preceding two sections are actually alternative taxes. In the event of the sale or change of use of previously qualified agricultural or horticultural land, it is necessary to compute the tentative conveyance and roll-back taxes applicable to the property. The larger of the two

---

[126] G.L. c. 61A, § 13. Note that the mere failure to apply for qualification under c. 61A will not cause roll-back tax liability to attach. Rather it is the actual use of the land which controls on this point. G.L. c. 61A, § 16.

[127] G.L. c. 61A, § 13.

[128] G.L. c. 61A, § 19.

taxes is the only one which is actually assessed to the landowner.[129]

The conveyance tax is made inapplicable to any conveyance to or by the city or town in which the land is located. The roll-back tax, on the other hand, is inapplicable if the land is purchased by the city or town in which it is located, for a public purpose.[130] There appears to be no obvious reason for this distinction, given the close interrelationship of the two taxes.

Although the statutory language is not entirely clear on this point, it seems that the legislative intent is that a discontinuance of the agricultural/horticultural use of the land, even though it is not converted to residential or commercial use, is a sufficient "change of use" to invoke the roll-back or conveyance tax. This view is given support by the language of the statutory provision which gives the municipality a right to purchase land which is about to be converted from qualified agricultural/horticultural land to residential, commercial, or industrial use. This provision specifically states that the discontinuance of a qualified use shall not be considered a conversion of use.[131] However, this kind of language is not contained in the sections of the statute which create the conveyance and roll-back taxes.

The longer an owner has held his land, the less of a conveyance tax he will have to pay upon its sale or conversion to non-qualified uses, until, after he has owned the property for ten years, there is no conveyance tax at all.

The roll-back tax, on the other hand, will always apply regardless of how long the land is owned. Except where the owner has only held for a short period, the potential dollar amount of a roll-back tax is going to be much larger than that of a conveyance tax.

Through the use of this alternative tax system the legislature seems to be saying that in no way does it want developers and land speculators to hide their holdings from taxation by means of minimal, sham farming operations. So the conveyance tax is imposed on short term owners. (Note that criminal penalties are provided for those who use the statute as a means for "evading the payment of full and proper taxes."[132] But the chances of a reasonably cautious landowner having to suffer criminal sanctions seem negligible.)

The legislature is also saying that a legitimate farmer who has taken advantage of the tax benefits conferred by the statute, even if not liable for a conveyance tax, will be required to pay a full tax, as on non-farm land, for the five years immediately preceding the sale or conversion of the property. He may do this either by repaying

---

[129] G.L. c. 61A, §§ 12 and 13.
[130] G.L. c. 61A, §§ 12 and 13.
[131] G.L. c. 61A, § 14.
[132] G.L. c. 61A, § 23.

to the town the difference between the normal property tax and the special tax he has paid under G.L. c. 61A for the five years preceding the sale, or by foregoing the special tax status for the five years preceding the year in which he intends to sell.

§ 17.02[38] Municipality's Option to Purchase Upon Sale or Conversion[133]

Where land is valued and taxed pursuant to G.L. c. 61A, it may not be sold for or converted to residential, industrial or commercial use while so valued and taxed unless the city or town in which the property is located has been notified of the intent to so sell or convert. A narrowly divided Supreme Judicial Court, in *Town of Sudbury v. Scott*,[134] has decided that the "intent" to convert is a question of fact, and that it can refer to the intent of either the buyer or seller. The duty to send the 120-day notice arises when the intent is conceived and the option period will not begin to run until the notice is given. Where the buyer or seller mislead the municipality as to their intention to continue the land in qualified use, the municipality's option price will relate back to the time the intent to convert was formed. This could either be a sale price or an appraised value. In the *Scott* case, the buyer had taken a number of steps indicating that he intended to convert the property to a residential subdivision. However he certified to the assessors that he intended to continue the c. 61A use and filed for continued eligibility for one year after acquiring the property. The Court held that Sudbury's 120-day option did not begin to run until notice of the earlier formed "intent" had been sent to it. Further the option price was the price the defendant had paid for the property, not a much higher price at which he later agreed to sell it. This case should be required reading for counsel engaged in the purchase or sale of c. 61A or c. 61B. The notice must be sent by the landowner, via certified mail, to the mayor and council of a city, or to the board of selectmen of a town, and to the assessors, planning board and conservation commission, if any, of either a city or a town.

The city or town has a 120-day first refusal option to meet a bona fide offer to purchase, or, in the case of intended conversion not involving a sale, an option to purchase the land at its full and fair market value as determined by an independent appraiser. The bona fide offer can include contingencies, including a contingency tied to the number of lots the prospective purchaser is able to obtain permits for, even though the municipality would not be likely to pursue such permits if it acquired the land.[135] The effect of this in practice is that the option price will be the maximum price payable under the contingencies. Or in the case of non-price

---

[133] G.L. c. 61A, § 13.

[134] 439 Mass. 288 (2003).

[135] Town of Franklin v. Wyllie, 443 Mass. 187 (2005).

contingencies the municipality may have to waive the escape provisions benefiting the private buyer. If it does not wish to exercise the option itself it may, after public hearing, assign its option to a nonprofit conservation organization for the purpose of continuing the major portion of the property in agricultural or horticultural use. Note again that, as in the case of converted forest land, the municipality may purchase the land for any purpose, but the assignee must keep at least the "major portion" of the land in agricultural use. The notice and recording provisions of the statute relating to these options are specific and detailed and the statute should be consulted carefully. The option period begins to run on the day following the date that the last of the required notices was mailed. Thus if the selectmen are notified on July 1, and the other boards on July 5, the option period will begin to run on July 6. Note that the sale or conversion must occur "while" the land is being valued and taxed pursuant to G.L. c. 61A.[136] Thus it would seem that the owner could prevent the option in favor of the municipality from arising if he failed to apply for qualified status for the year in which he intends to sell or convert, provided there have been no objective manifestations of his intention that could bring the principles of *Sudbury v. Scott* into play.

The discontinuance of the use of qualified land for agricultural or horticultural purposes will not be deemed a conversion giving rise to the purchase option. Neither will the option arise in the case of a foreclosure sale by a mortgagee. However, the mortgagee must give notice to the above named boards and officials as to the time and place of the sale, at least 90 days before the sale.

§ 17.02[39]   Sale or Conversion of a Portion of Qualified Lands

When the owner of land which is valued and taxed under G. L. c. 61A wishes to sell or convert a portion of it for other uses, he is free to do so. However, he will be liable for conveyance and roll-back taxes with respect to that portion.[137] It would seem that the municipality would also have a 120 day option to purchase that portion of the qualified parcel being converted.[138] The conversion of a portion of qualified land will not affect the right of the landowner to have the remainder of his land retain its qualified status.

§ 17.02[40]   Appeals from Determinations of Assessors[139]

Any person who is aggrieved by any determination or assessment by the assessors under provisions of G.L. c 61A may within sixty days of the "date of notice

---

[136] G.L. c. 61A, § 14.
[137] G.L. c. 61A, § 17.
[138] *See* discussion at § 17.02[38], *supra*.
[139] G.L. c. 61 A, § 19.

thereof" apply in writing to the assessors for a modification of their determination or an abatement of the tax assessed.[140]

If the assessors refuse to modify their determination or abate the tax, or if they fail to act upon the application, then any person aggrieved by such refusal or failure to act may appeal to the Appellate Tax Board within thirty days "after the date of notice of their decision," or within three months of the date of application, whichever date is later. Whether the "date of notice" referred to by the statute means the date of mailing or the date of receipt of the notice of the assessors' action by the landowner is unclear. However, the Supreme Judicial Court has construed an analogous provision in G.L. c. 59 to mean the date notice is received.[141]

If the appeal relates to the annual general property tax, then the assessed tax must be paid in full as a condition to the right to appeal. If the appeal relates to an asserted conveyance or roll-back tax, no payment is required as a condition of appeal. However, the municipality may still proceed with a tax taking or other collection procedure while the appeal of the conveyance or roll-back tax is pending. Such collection procedures may be stayed by the payment of up to one-half of the assessed tax.

While the statute does not outline the nature and extent of this right of appeal or the manner in which it must be prosecuted, it seems safe to assume that such appeals would be analogous to those taken from the actions of assessors under G.L. c. 59.

§ 17.02[41]   Agricultural Preservation Restrictions

Land which is subject to an agricultural preservation restriction (as defined by G.L. c. 184, § 31),[142] while actively devoted to agricultural and/or horticultural uses (as defined by G.L. c. 61A), must be assessed for general property tax purposes at values no greater than its value as agricultural land, in the same manner as if it had qualified under c. 61A.[143]

Thus if the landowner is willing to encumber his property with an agricultural preservation restriction, he has a right to the favorable tax treatment of G.L. c. 61A, so long as he actively devotes the land to agricultural or horticultural uses. It is not clear from the statute whether the owner of such restricted land would be required

---

[140] The taxpayer cannot appeal the refusal of the assessors to grant c. 61A status directly to the Appellate Tax Board. He must first apply to the assessors for modification of their determination, or for abatement of the tax. Only upon denial of this second application to the assessors can he appeal. Gargano v. Assessors of Barnstable, 2003 WL 22110464 (Mass. App. Tax Bd. 2003).

[141] Berkshire Gas Co. v. Board of Assessors of Williamstown, 281 N.E.2d 602 (1972).

[142] See definition of such restrictions below.

[143] G.L. c. 132A, § 11D. See also G.L. c. 61A, § 10.

to apply for qualified status each year, as the owner applying under G.L. c. 61A must.

The statutory language seems to contemplate that the restriction would be sold, or given, by the landowner to a governmental body or to a charitable organization.[144] There is thus some question as to whether land subject to a valid agricultural preservation restriction created between private owners would be entitled to the favorable tax treatment. It would seem that it should, but the question is not likely to arise often.

A landowner should be very cautious in giving or selling an agricultural preservation restriction to a governmental body or charitable organization because it will be very difficult for him to secure the release of the restriction should he wish to convert the land to non-farm use.[145]

An agricultural restriction is defined by the statute[146] as "a right, whether or not stated in the form of a restriction, easement, covenant or condition, in any deed, will, or other instrument executed by or on behalf of the owner of the land appropriate to retaining land or water areas predominately in their agricultural farming or forest use, to forbid or limit any or all (a) construction or placing of buildings except for those used for agricultural purposes or for dwellings used for family living by the landowner, his immediate family or employees; (b) excavation, dredging or removal of loam, peat, gravel, soil, rock or other mineral substance in such a manner as to adversely affect the land's overall future agricultural potential; and (c) other acts or uses detrimental to such retention of the land for agricultural use. Such agricultural preservation restrictions shall be in perpetuity except as released under the provisions of section 32 [of chapter 184]. All other customary rights and privileges of ownership shall be retained by the owner including the right to privacy and to carry out all regular farming practice."

§ 17.02[42]   Recreational Land

In 1979, the legislature added chapter 61B to the General Laws, giving to "recreational land" as defined in the statute a favorable tax treatment similar to that provided for agricultural and horticultural land. The overall structure of the two statutes is similar, but the tax treatment afforded recreational land is not as favorable as is the case with agricultural and horticultural land.

§ 17.02[43]   Recreational Land—Definition

For purposes of the statute qualified recreational land is of two types, which may

---

[144] *See* G.L. c. 184, § 32.
[145] See requirements for release of such restrictions outlined in G.L. c. 184, § 32.
[146] G.L. c. 184, § 31.

be described as passive and active, although the statute does not so categorize them.

Passive recreational land is land not less than five acres in area "... retained in substantially a natural, wild, or open condition or in a landscaped condition in such a manner as to allow to a significant extent the preservation of wildlife and other natural resources ..."[147]

Active recreational land is land not less than five acres in area devoted primarily to recreational use which "does not materially interfere with the environmental benefits which are derived from said land, and is available to the general public or to members of a non-profit organization including a corporation organized under chapter 180." It would seem that the first part of the quoted general definition of active recreational land is rendered largely superfluous by a further provision which specifically enumerates the uses which may be considered recreational for purposes of c. 61B. Those uses are: hiking, camping, nature study and observation, boating, golfing, horseback riding, hunting, fishing, skiing, swimming, picnicking, private non-commercial flying, including hang gliding, archery and target shooting.

This specific enumeration also seems to render superfluous the statute's exclusion of "horse racing, dog racing, or any sport normally undertaken in a stadium, gymnasium or similar structure" as qualified recreational uses.[148]

§ 17.02[44]   Application for Eligibility

Eligibility of land to be taxed pursuant to G.L. c. 61B is determined separately for each tax year and the landowner must therefore apply for eligibility each tax year. Such application must be under the pains and penalties of perjury on a form approved by the Commissioner of Revenue and must be submitted by October 1 of the year preceding the tax year for which the eligibility is requested. (Where a revaluation is completed in time for the upcoming fiscal year but not in time for the taxpayer to apply by October 1, then he may apply within 30 days after the mailing of the tax bill containing the new valuation.)[149] Any application covering leased land must be accompanied by a written statement signed by the lessee of his intention to use the land for the purposes set forth in the application.[150]

The board of assessors must either allow or disallow the landowner's application within three months from the date it is filed. Failure to act within the three-month period is deemed to be an allowance of the application.[151]

The assessors are commanded by the statute to disallow any application where

---

[147] G.L. c. 61B, § 1.

[148] G.L. c. 61B, § 1 (¶¶ 2 and 3).

[149] G.L. c. 61B, § 5.

[150] G.L. c. 61B, § 3.

[151] G.L. c. 61B, § 6.

in their judgment the land does not qualify for taxation under G.L. c. 61B, or where they determine that the application is submitted "for the purpose of evading the payment of full and proper taxes."

Within ten days after they make their decision, the assessors must send to the landowner, by certified mail, written notice of the allowance or disallowance of his application, together with the reasons therefor and a notice of the owner's right to appeal. In the case of a partial disallowance, the landowner has a right to appeal. In the case of a partial disallowance, the landowner has a right to file an amended application, presumably covering only the land which the assessors have found qualified.[152]

If the application is allowed, and it is the first application relating to a particular parcel which has been approved, or a reapplication after a period during which the land has not been taxed under chapter 61B, then the assessors are required to file a statement of their action in the registry of deeds. This statement constitutes a lien upon the land for any taxes which may be levied under G.L. c. 61B. When the land ceases to be valued under c. 61B, the assessors are also required to file a statement to that effect.

§ 17.02[45]   Valuation

Recreational land which is approved for taxation under the provisions of G.L. c. 61B is taxed based on its actual use, (no issue here of highest and best use), in accordance with guidelines established by the Commissioner of Revenue, but in no event in excess of 25% of its fair market value.[153] The property is taxed at the class three, commercial, rate based on the value so established.

§ 17.02[45][a]   Taxation   of   Dwelling   Houses   and   Associated Structures

Dwelling houses and other buildings "regularly used for family living," and the land upon which they are located, which are contained within a parcel otherwise qualified for taxation under chapter 61B are taxed as any other similar property, and not as recreational property.[154]

§ 17.02[45][b]   Special or Betterment Assessments

Property qualified for taxation under chapter 61B is subject to special assessments or betterment assessments only "to such pro rata extent as the service or facility financed by such assessment is used for improving the recreational use

---

[152] G.L. c. 61B, § 6.

[153] G.L. c. 61B, § 2.

[154] G.L. c. 61B, § 10.

capability of said land or for the personal benefit of the owner thereof." Even assessments which are properly chargeable to classified recreational land may, upon application, during the time the land is so classified, as long as the interest on the assessment is paid annually.[155] It would seem that the use of the word "may" gives the municipality discretion to decide whether or not to suspend the assessment. Although there is no reported case on this point, the analogous provision of chapter 61A uses the word "shall" where chapter 61B uses the word "may."[156]

§ 17.02[46]   Effect of Sale or Change of Use

§ 17.02[46][a]   Conveyance Tax[157]

If land which has been assessed and taxed as recreational land is sold, for the purpose of being put to other use, the statute imposes a "conveyance tax" on the seller. This tax is at the rate of 10% of the sale price if the land is sold during the first five years of it first being so classified; and 5% if sold during the second five years of it first being so classified. Following the end of the tenth year of it first being classified, no conveyance tax is imposed on the seller. The tax is payable by the seller at the time of transfer of the property.

If the purchaser files with the assessors an affidavit to the effect that he intends to continue the recreational use of the land, then no conveyance tax will be imposed on the seller. But, if the purchaser does not in fact continue such use, then he will be liable for the conveyance tax, which would have been paid by the seller. Where there is a nonexempt transfer after an exempt transfer, the holding period for purposes of calculating the conveyance tax runs from the date of the last nonexempt transfer; except where the grantor acquired the property from a foreclosing mortgage the holding period runs from the date of such acquisition.

If land taxed under the statute as recreational land is changed to another use by its owner within a period of ten years from the date of its classification for recreational use by the owner, it is subject to the conveyance tax at the time of such change to the same extent as if it had been sold. In such cases, the tax is based on the fair market value of the land as determined by the assessors, based on the same valuation standards that they would use in assessing any other piece of property. In other words, the property is not valued for purposes of the conveyance tax based solely on its value as recreation land but is valued as any other piece of property would be.

---

[155] G.L. c. 61B, § 13.
[156] *See* G.L. c. 61A, § 18.
[157] G.L. c. 61B, § 7.

§ 17.02[46][b]   Roll-back Tax[158]

Whenever land which is valued and assessed as recreational land no longer qualifies for such status, it becomes subject to an additional tax, called a "roll-back" tax. The roll-back tax applies in the year that the disqualification occurs and in those of the nine immediately preceding tax years in which the land was taxed as recreational land. Thus if land is first valued and taxed as recreational land in 1988 and in each subsequent year until 1998, during which year it becomes no longer qualified, the owner will be liable for the roll-back tax for the years 1989 through 1998, but not for 1988. If the land had not been taxed as recreational land in any one of the nine preceding years, then it would not be liable for the roll-back tax in that year.

The roll-back tax is equal to the difference, for each year, between the taxes paid or payable on the land as qualified recreational land and the taxes that would have been paid or payable if the land had not been so qualified.

The statute also provides that, "If at a time during a tax year when a change in land use has occurred the land was not then valued, assessed and taxed under the provisions of this chapter then such land shall be subject to roll-back taxes only for such of the ten immediately preceding years in which the land was valued, assessed and taxed thereunder."

This provision appears to contemplate a situation where a parcel had been qualified and taxed under G.L. c. 61B as recreational land, and had subsequently ceased to be so taxed for one or more years, at which point the roll-back tax is levied and billed. Since the roll-back tax attaches as soon as the land no longer qualifies as "classified recreational land," and since the landowner must apply each year for qualified status,[159] this situation would probably only arise in practice when the owner of previously qualified land simply stopped applying for the special tax status, and the assessors began billing him for taxes on the same basis as other property. If a subsequent change in use were to occur and the assessors were at that time to attempt to assess a roll-back tax, they could only look back to the ten years immediately preceding the change in use for the purpose of assessing such a tax.

For example, in 1988, a landowner applies for and receives qualified status for a particular parcel. In 1989 and 1990, he also applies for and receives qualified status. Thereafter, even though his land would qualify, he does not apply for such status and the land is taxed on the same basis as all other property in town. In 1999,

---

[158] G.L. c. 61B, § 8.

[159] Note that the mere failure to apply for qualification under c. 61B in any given year will not cause the roll-back tax to attach. It is the actual use of the land which controls on this point. G.L. c. 61B, § 11.

he sells his land to a developer. He will only be liable for roll-back taxes for 1989 and 1990; the tax saving for 1988 remains his.

The statutory language indicates quite clearly that the operative date for roll-back tax purposes is the date when the change of use occurs, not when the tax is assessed. For instance, if in the above example the assessors did not assess the tax until 2000, the taxpayer would not thereby escape paying the roll-back tax for 1989. The assessors would still look at the ten years immediately preceding 1999, when the change of use occurred. The obligation for the roll-back tax falls on the person who owns the land when the disqualification occurs.[160]

The assessment, collection, apportionment and payment of roll-back taxes is governed by the provisions of G.L. c. 59, § 75, relating to the assessment of omitted property, except that the time limits on the imposition of taxes contained in that section do not apply.[161]

§ 17.02[46][c]   Conveyance and Roll-back Taxes—Relationship to One Another

The conveyance and roll-back taxes discussed in the preceding two sections are actually alternative taxes. In the event of the sale or change of use of previously qualified recreational land, it is necessary to compute the tentative conveyance and roll-back taxes applicable to the property. The larger of the two taxes is the only one which is actually assessed to the landowner. The roll-back tax is inapplicable if the land is purchased by the city or town in which it is located, for a public purpose. There is no similar exemption from the conveyance tax.[162]

§ 17.02[47]   Municipality's Option to Purchase Upon Sale or Conversion[163]

Where land is valued and taxed pursuant to G.L. c. 61B, it may not be sold for or converted to residential, industrial or commercial use while so valued and taxed unless the city or town in which the property is located has been notified of the owner's intention to so sell or convert. The notice must be sent by the landowner, via certified mail, to the mayor and council of a city, or to the board of selectmen of a town, and to the assessors, planning board and conservation commission, if any, of either a city or a town.

The city or town has a 120-day first refusal option to meet a bona fide offer to

---

[160] G.L. c. 61B, § 11.

[161] G.L. c. 61B, § 14.

[162] *But see* Coz v. Board of Assessors of Grafton, 13 Mass. App. Tax Bd. Rep. 137 (1991), for a case where the Appellate Tax Board found a way to avoid applying the conveyance tax where c. 61B qualified land was sold to the municipality.

[163] G.L. c. 61B, § 9.

purchase, or, in the case of an intended conversion not involving a sale, an option to purchase the land at its full and fair market value as determined by an independent appraiser. A narrowly divided Supreme Judicial Court, in *Town of Sudbury v. Scott*,[164] has decided that the "intent" to convert is a question of fact, and that it can refer to the intent of either the buyer or seller. The duty to send the 120-day notice arises when the intent is conceived and the option period will not begin to run until the notice is given. Where the buyer or seller mislead the municipality as to their intention to continue the land in qualified use, the municipality's option price will relate back to the time the intent to convert was formed. This could either be a sale price or an appraised value. In the *Scott* case, the buyer had taken a number of steps indicating that he intended to convert the property to a residential subdivision. However he certified to the assessors that he intended to continue the c. 61A use and filed for continued eligibility for one year after acquiring the property. The Court held that Sudbury's 120-day option did not begin to run until notice of the earlier formed "intent" had been sent to it. Further the option price was the price the defendant had paid for the property, not a much higher price at which he later agreed to sell it. This case should be required reading for counsel engaged in the purchase or sale of c. 61A or c. 61B. If it does not wish to exercise the option itself it may, after public hearing, assign its option to a nonprofit conservation organization for the purpose of continuing the major portion of the property in recreational use. Note again that, as in the case of converted agricultural land, the municipality may purchase the land for any purpose, but the assignee must keep at least the "major portion" of the land in recreational use. The notice and recording provisions of the statute relating to these options are specific and detailed and the statute should be consulted carefully. The option period begins to run on the day following the date that the last of the required notices was mailed. Thus if the selectmen are notified on July 1, and the other boards on July 5, the option period will begin to run on July 6. The bona fide offer can include contingencies, including a contingency tied to the number of lots the prospective purchaser is able to obtain permits for, even though the municipality would not be likely to pursue such permits if it acquired the land.[165] The effect of this in practice is that the option price will be the maximum price payable under the contingencies. Or in the case of non-price contingencies the municipality may have to waive the escape provisions benefiting the private buyer. Note that the sale or conversion must occur "while" the land is being valued and taxed pursuant to G.L. c. 61B. Thus it would seem that the owner could prevent the option in favor of the municipality from arising if he failed to apply for qualified status for the year in which he intends to sell or convert, provided there have been no objective manifestations of his intention that could bring the principles of *Sudbury v. Scott* into play.

---

[164] 439 Mass. 288 (2003).
[165] Town of Franklin v. Wyllie, 443 Mass. 187 (2005).

The discontinuance of the use of qualified land for agricultural or horticultural purposes will not be deemed a conversion giving rise to the purchase option. Neither will the option arise in the case of a foreclosure sale by a mortgagee. However the mortgagee must give notice to the above named boards and officials as to the time and place of the sale, at least 90 days before the sale.

§ 17.02[48]   Sale or Conversion of a Portion of Qualified Land

When the owner of land which is valued and taxed under G.L. c. 61B wishes to sell or convert a portion of it for other uses, he is free to do so. However, he will be liable for conveyance and roll-back taxes with respect to that portion.[166] It would seem that the municipality would also have a 120 day option to purchase that portion of the qualified parcel being converted.[167] The conversion of a portion of qualified land will not affect the right of the landowner to have the remainder of his land retain its qualified status.

§ 17.02[49]   Appeals from Determinations of Assessors[168]

Any person who is aggrieved by any determination or assessment by the assessors under the provisions of G.L. c. 61B may within sixty days of the "date of notice thereof" apply in writing to the assessors for a modification of their determination or an abatement of the tax assessed.

If the assessors refuse to modify their determination or abate the tax, or if they fail to act upon the application, then any person aggrieved by such refusal or failure to act may appeal to the Appellate Tax Board within thirty days "after the date of notice of their decision," or within three months of the date of the application, whichever date is later. Whether the "date of notice" referred to by the statute means the date of mailing or the date of receipt of the notice of the assessors' action by the landowner is unclear. However, the Supreme Judicial Court has construed an analogous provision in G.L. c. 59 to mean the date notice is received.[169]

If the appeal relates to the annual general property tax, then the assessed tax must be paid in full as a condition to the right to appeal. If the appeal relates to an asserted conveyance or roll-back tax, no payment is required as a condition of appeal. However, the municipality may still proceed with a tax taking or other collection procedure while the appeal of the conveyance or roll-back tax is pending. Such collection procedures may be stayed by the Appellate Tax Board, which as a condition of such stay may require the payment of up to one-half of the assessed tax.

---

[166] G.L. c. 61B, § 12.

[167] *See* discussion at § 17.02[38], *supra*.

[168] G.L. c. 61B, § 14.

[169] Berkshire Gas Co. v. Board of Assessors of Williamstown, 361 Mass. 873, 281 N.E.2d 602 (1972).

While the statute does not outline the nature and extent of this right of appeal or the manner in which it must be prosecuted, it seems safe to assume that such appeals should be for the most part analogous to those taken from the actions of assessors under G.L. c. 59. The Appellate Tax Board has held that the application for abatement of the tax need not be on a "form approved by the commissioner" as is the case in standard appeals, and that after an application is deemed denied by the passage of time the assessors lose power to act on it.[170]

§ 17.02[50]　　Other Exempt Classes of Property

Property used to abate or prevent industrial waste or industrial air pollution as those terms are defined in the statute;[171] hydropower facilities construction of which was commenced after January 1, 1979, for a period of 20 years, if the owner of the facility has entered into an agreement with the city or town to make in lieu payments of at least 5% of its gross income in the preceding calendar year;[172] property owned by an economic development corporation organized under c. 180 whose purpose is to retain and expand job opportunities, for the period between the time when the property is acquired and it is leased or disposed of, but not to exceed seven years;[173] if accepted by the city or town, improvements made to a dwelling of three or less units occupied by the applicant as his or her domicile for the purpose of providing housing to a person who is at least 60 years old, not to exceed $500 in taxes due.[174]

Legislation adopted in 1993 establishes two local property tax exemptions intended to function as incentives for economic development. A municipality may grant either exemption to a business in conjunction with a comprehensive plan for the development of economically distressed areas proposed by the community and approved by the Economic Assistance Coordinating Council (EACC). Economically distressed areas are referred to in the legislation as economic target areas (ETAs). Those parts of an ETA that are suitable for commercial or industrial development can be designated as economic opportunity areas (EOAs). Real estate projects within an EOA are eligible for the exemptions, but only one of the exemptions can be granted to any particular parcel.

The first type of exemption authorized is called a special tax assessment and is contained in General Laws Ch. 23A, § 3E. It provides a four-year declining exemption equal to 100% of a parcel's value in the first year, 75% of its value in

---

[170] Apple Country Club, Inc. v. Board of Assessors of Chelmsford, 11 Mass. App. Tax. Bd. Rptr. 13 (1989).

[171] G.L. c. 59, § 5(44).

[172] G.L. c. 59, § 5(45).

[173] G.L. c. 59, § 5(46).

[174] G.L. c. 59, § 5(50).

the second year, 50% in the third year and 25% in the fourth and final year.

The statutory framework for the other new exemption—the so-called tax increment financing or TIF exemption—is set out in G.L. Ch. 59, § 5 Clause 51 and in G.L. Ch. 40, § 59. The TIF exemption is an exemption of a percentage of the increase in a parcel's value over its base value in the year before the exemption was granted. The exemption can last for up to twenty years, and the percentage of the increased value that will be exempt can be up to 100%. Both the duration of the exemption and the percentage of increased value that will be exempt are fixed by the municipal vote that adopts the TIF plan. There is an adjustment to a parcel's base value to insure that the exemption applies only to increases in a parcel's value that exceed the ordinary inflationary increases in the value of other commercial and industrial property in the community. TIF exemption may be authorized for parcels in TIF zones within an EOA or within an area designated by the Secretary of Economic Affairs as presenting exceptional opportunities for increased economic development. Personal property situated on a parcel receiving a TIF exemption will also be exempt. Communities may also grant parcels receiving TIF exemptions whole or partial exemptions from betterments or special assessments.

Detailed regulations have been issued by the Executive Office of Communities and Development (EOCD) (751 Code of Massachusetts Regulations (CMR) 11.00) and the EACC (402 CMR 200) governing the applications process for the designation of ETAs and EOAs, and for the approval of real estate projects eligible for either of the exemptions.

By adoption of a local bylaw or ordinance a municipality may establish a policy for the favorable assessment of restored, owner-occupied residential buildings listed in the state register of historic places. Under this policy, any increased value attributable to the restoration will be assessed on a phased in basis over five years. In order to be eligible, the restoration must conform to the standards of the Massachusetts Historical Commission. The Secretary of State is given authority to promulgate regulations to carry out the program.[175]

APPEALS FROM DENIAL OF EXEMPTION

§ 17.02[51]   Generally

A taxpayer may appeal to the Appellate Tax Board only, if that right has been given to him by statute. If an abatement is requested based on a claimed overvaluation of the taxpayer's property, and if that abatement is refused, the right of the taxpayer to appeal the decision to the Appellate Tax Board is clear.[176] But where

---

[175] G.L. c. 59, § 5J.
[176] G.L. c. 59, § 65.

a claimed exemption under one of the clauses of G.L. c. 59, § 5 is denied, the right of appeal is less clear.

The reason for this is that the Board is a creation of the legislature rather than a traditional common law court. As such, it has only that jurisdiction specifically conferred upon it by statute.[177] The statute which defines the jurisdiction of the Board,[178] empowers it to hear appeals from the denial of real estate tax exemptions only where the claim of exemption is based on the exemption for the elderly, the exemption for veterans, or the exemption of municipally owned land; or where jurisdiction is specifically conferred on the Board by some other statute.

A statutory amendment,[179] for example, now allows appeals to the Board where the denied claim is for a charitable exemption. Such appeals from the granting or denial of a charitable exemption however are permitted only to the individual, corporation or trust which applied for the exemption, or an individual, corporation or trust engaged in a business activity in direct competition with an activity conducted by the applicant for exemption.[180]

The Board also has statutory authority to hear appeals from decisions of assessors under G.L. c. 61 (forest land exemption), under G.L. c. 61A (agricultural land exemption), G.L. c. 61B (recreational land exemption) and under G.L. c. 121A (exemption for urban redevelopment corporations).

Since § 5 itself does not provide for appeals to the Appellate Tax Board, in all other cases the taxpayer who is denied an exemption and who wishes to appeal that denial must find some other statutory authorization for an appeal to the Board, if he is to have one at all.[181]

The most likely remedy available to the taxpayer who cannot appeal to the Tax Board and who wishes to challenge the denial of exemption directly would appear to be a petition for review in the nature of certiorari under G.L. c. 249, § 4, filed in the Superior Court.[182] However, a petition for declaratory judgment may also be an appropriate remedy, at least in some cases.[183]

---

[177] Board of Assessors of Saugus v. Baumann, 370 Mass. 36, 345 N.E.2d 360 (1976); Lorantos v. Board of Assessors of Medfield, 372 Mass. 865, 361 N.E.2d 1253 (1977).

[178] G.L. c. 58A, § 6.

[179] G.L. c. 59, § 5B, added by St. 1977, c. 992, § 3.

[180] The Appellate Tax Board reversed its previous rulings and now holds that taxpayers appealing under this statute need not comply with the procedural requirements of G.L. c. 59 §§ 59–65D. The Trustees of Reservations v. Board of Assessors of Windsor, ATB 159046 (1991).

[181] Lorantos v. Board of Assessors of Medfield, 372 Mass. 865, 361 N.E.2d 1253 (1977); Board of Assessors of Saugus v. Baumann, 370 Mass. 36, 345 N.E.2d 360 (1976).

[182] Board of Assessors of Saugus v. Baumann, 370 Mass. 36, 345 N.E.2d 360 (1976).

[183] G.L. c. 231A, § 1 *et seq.*; Meenes v. Goldberg, 331 Mass. 688; 122 N.E.2d 356 (1954); Sydney v. Commissioner of Corporations and Taxation, 371 Mass. 289, 356 N.E.2d 460 (1976).

Probably the simplest approach is to apply for abatement based on the claimed exemption and appeal the denial by the assessors to the Appellate Tax Board under G.L. c. 59, §§ 59–65D.[184]

THE BOARD OF ASSESSORS AND APPEALS THEREFROM APPLICATION FOR ABATEMENT

§ 17.03   Generally

For the taxpayer who feels himself to be unfairly, excessively or disproportionately assessed, Massachusetts law provides an exclusive remedy through the abatement procedure.[1] Under this procedure, the taxpayer's appeal for relief moves entirely outside the traditional court system, with the exception of a conditional right to final review as to errors of law by the Supreme Judicial Court.

The procedural requirements for seeking an abatement are laid out in great detail by statute, and compliance with those requirements is absolutely essential if the taxpayer is to have any chance of prevailing.[2] Even though these requirements as to the form, time and manner of the application to the assessors or the appeal to the Tax Board are procedural in their nature, the effect of these procedural requirements is clearly substantive. This is because the Supreme Judicial Court has consistently refused to regard flaws in these areas as matters which may be waived by the parties, or disregarded by the courts, and the failure of the applicant to comply with them is considered to oust the jurisdiction of the assessors to grant an abatement, or the Tax Board to hear any later appeal.[3]

§ 17.03[1]   Who Applies[4]

The following persons are permitted to apply for abatements: (1) The person upon whom the tax has been assessed, or the executor, administrator or trustee under his will if aggrieved by the tax, may apply. An executor who is named in

---

[184] Children's Hospital Medical Center v. Board of Assessors of Boston, 393 Mass. 266, 471 N.E.2d 67 (1984); Children's Hospital Medical Center v. Assessors of Boston, 388 Mass. 832, 448 N.E.2d 748 (1983).

[1] Bates v. City of Boston, 59 Mass. 93 (1849); American Hyde and Leather Co. v. Commissioner, 252 Mass. 345, 147 N.E. 839 (1925); Board of Assessors of Brookline v. Prudential Insurance Co. 310 Mass. 300, 38 N.E.2d 145 (1941); Codman v. Assessors of Westwood, 309 Mass. 433, 35 N.E.2d 262 (1941).

[2] Assessors of Boston v. Neal, 311 Mass. 192, 40 N.E.2d 893 (1942).

[3] Old Colony R.R. Co. v. Assessors of Boston, 309 Mass. 439 (1941); Board of Assessors of Boston v. Suffolk Law School, 295 Mass. 489 (1936); G.L. c. 59, §§ 61, 64.

[4] G.L. c. 59, § 59.

the will but who has not yet been appointed by the probate court may apply for and obtain an abatement on behalf of his decedent. However, he cannot actually be reimbursed in the amount of the abatement until he has been appointed by the Court, because he has no right to receive money due the estate until he is appointed.[5] (The use of the word "aggrieved" in various places in § 59 is a little puzzling. The Supreme Judicial Court has defined the word, as used in this statute, to mean a person whose pecuniary interests are or may be affected.[6] This definition would appear to apply to all the classes of persons allowed to apply for abatement. Therefore any requirement that the applicant be aggrieved in addition to being a member of one of the classes of persons mentioned in G.L. c. 59, § 59, would appear to be redundant. However, a number of cases have mentioned, in connection with the use of the word in G.L. c. 59, § 64, that a person who does not fulfill the statutory requirements for applying for abatement is not "aggrieved" for purposes of the statute.)[7] (2) A rent paying tenant who is obligated to pay more than one-half of the taxes may apply. (3) If a person other than the person to whom the tax is assessed is the owner of the real estate, or has an interest in it, or is in possession of it, and if that person pays the tax, he may thereafter prosecute an application for abatement of the tax in his own name.[8] It will be noted that payment of a part or all of the tax is a condition precedent to the right of this class of persons to apply to the assessors for abatement, while other classes of persons may apply without prepayment. The persons who must prepay are those who were given the right to apply for abatements in their own names by amendments to the original § 59.[9] The general rule had previously been that only a person upon whom the tax had been assessed or a rent paying tenant could apply.[10] It may very well be that in conferring standing on persons in a more peripheral relationship to the property the legislature imposed the prepayment requirement to prevent the assessors from being over-burdened with marginal applications from persons who may have only a tenuous interest in the property. At any rate, the prepayment requirement is strictly enforced where it applies. (4) The holder of a mortgage on the property who has paid not less than one-half of the tax thereon may apply for abatement, provided the person assessed has not already applied for an abatement. If the mortgagee applies first, then the person assessed cannot apply. (5) Any person who acquires title to real estate after January 1 in any year may also apply. A 1977 amendment to the statute permits such persons for purposes of standing to apply for abatement, to be treated

---

[5] Miller v. Board of Assessors of Wenham, 350 Mass. 629, 216 N.E.2d 87 (1966).

[6] Hough v. City of North Adams, 196 Mass. 290, 82 N.E. 46 (1907).

[7] *See* Board of Assessors of Boston v. Suffolk Law School, 295 Mass. 489 (1936), and cases cited therein.

[8] *See* Canron v. Board of Assessors of Everett, 366 Mass. 634, 322 N.E.2d 83 (1975).

[9] *See* St. 1933, c. 165, § 1 and St. 1939, c. 250, § 1.

[10] Boston Five Cent Savings Bank v. Assessors of Boston, 311 Mass. 415, 41 N.E.2d 283 (1942).

as persons upon whom the tax has been assessed.[11] This provision appears to be addressed to the situation where title to real estate is taken subsequent to the assessment date and where by virtue of the purchase and sale agreement, or otherwise, the seller rather than the buyer pays the tax. Under prior law the buyer in such cases had no standing to prosecute an application for abatement in his own name.

§ 17.03[2]   When

An application for abatement must be made on or before October 1 of the year to which the tax relates, or, if the bill was sent after September 1, on or before the thirtieth day after which the bill was sent. However, if a mortgagee applies, he must apply between September 20 and October 1 of the year to which the tax relates.[12] These time deadlines are strictly enforced and they apply equally to every person who has the right to file for an abatement.[13] However, query what happens when the tax bill is sent subsequent to October 1 and the mortgagee attempts to apply for abatement.

Note also that persons assessed under omitted property assessments,[14] revised assessments,[15] or reassessments of invalid taxes[16] may apply for abatement up until three months after the bill for the additional taxes is sent.[17] Applications should be sent certified mail, return receipt requested, or hand carried to the assessors' office where a date-stamped copy of the application should be obtained. Where the application is made by mail, counsel should in his letter request that a date-stamped copy of the application be returned to him.

Since timely filing of the application with the assessors is a prerequisite to the right to appeal to the Appellate Tax Board, counsel should be sure he has definite proof of timely filing.

Failure of the taxpayer to receive his tax bill because of mail delays or other reasons will not excuse any subsequent failure to file the abatement application on time.[18] Thus, if the bills have been mailed and the taxpayer has not received his, he should go to the assessors' office, get a duplicate of his bill, and file his

---

[11] St. 1977, c. 198, amending G.L. c. 59, § 59.

[12] G.L. c. 59, § 59.

[13] Canron v. Board of Assessors of Everett, 366 Mass. 634, 322 N.E.2d 83 (1975).

[14] G.L. c. 59, § 75.

[15] G.L. c. 59, § 76.

[16] G.L. c. 59, § 77.

[17] G.L. c. 59, § 59.

[18] City of Boston v. DuWors, 340 Mass. 402, 164 N.E.2d 311 (1960); M. & J. Realty v. Board of Assessors of Walpole, 14 Mass. App. Tax Bd. Rep. 44 (1992).

application on time.[19]

G.L. c. 59, § 59, has been amended to provide that any abatement application delivered to the assessors by the post office after the abatement due date is deemed to have been received by them as of the postmark date on the envelope. This rule applies only to those applications mailed to the proper address of the assessors, first class postage prepaid, with postmarks made by the United States Postal Service.

G.L. c. 58, § 7 and c. 59, §§ 64–65 are also amended to make the above postmark rule applicable to appeals of assessors' abatement decisions that are mailed to and received by county commissioners or the Appellate Tax Board.

§ 17.03[3]   Unusual Relief for Late Applications

Where the taxpayer has failed to apply for abatement and the time for such action has expired, there remains one possible remedy open to him. This remedy is available only where both the assessors and the Commissioner of Revenue agree that the tax should be abated. In such cases, the Commissioner is empowered by statute[20] to authorize the assessors to grant the abatement. This administrative procedure is limited to very unusual cases where the need for relief is clear and there is no other remedy available. It is discretionary with both assessors and Commissioner and is infrequently used.

Also, a Bankruptcy Court can abate unpaid municipal property taxes if there is proof of overassessment, as long as that issue has not previously been adjudicated by an administrative or judicial tribunal, even if the time for application for abatement has expired under state law.[21]

§ 17.03[4]   To Whom—Form of Application

Application for an abatement must be made in writing, on a form approved by the Commissioner of Revenue, and directed to the board of assessors. Use of the approved form of application is jurisdictional. But the approved form in use for many years, and still in use by many assessors as of this writing, asked for information from the taxpayer which was not a prerequisite to consideration of the appeal. The failure to provide information on an application form which is not required by statute will not defeat the right to abatement.[22] An approved application

---

[19] *See* Adeline Owens v. Board of Assessors of Mashpee, ATB 85879 (2/23/77); Mutual Benefit Life v. Assessors of Boston, ATB 83748 (8/1/77).

[20] G.L. c. 58, § 8.

[21] 11 USCS 505(a)(b); *In re* New England High Carbon Wire Corp., 39 B.R. 886, 1984 Bankr. LEXIS 5635 (Bankr. D. Mass. 1984); *In re* St. John's Nursing Home, Inc., 154 B.R. 117, 1993 Bankr. LEXIS 709 (Bankr. D. Mass. 1993), summary op at 21 M.L.W. 2928 (B.C. D.C. Mass) and *aff'd*, 169 B.R. 795 (D.C. Mass).

[22] MacDonald v. Board of Assessors of Mashpee, 381 Mass. 724, 412 N.E.2d 336 (1980).

form may be obtained from the assessors. Although failure to apply on an approved form will be enough to defeat any right to appeal the decision of the assessors, filing on the approved form will not, in and of itself, assure that the application will not be defective as to form. This is because the application must also contain "a sufficient description of the particular real estate as to which abatement is requested."[23] If the application does not contain such a description, then the statute itself prohibits the assessors from granting the abatement initially or the Appellate Tax Board from granting the abatement on appeal.[24]

The statutory language quoted above was added by a 1931 amendment[25] which eliminated, with respect to real estate, the rule that taxpayers who had failed to provide the assessors with a list of their property pursuant to the requirements of the statute[26] could not appeal the assessors' denial of an abatement. The "sufficient description" required by the statute has been defined by the Supreme Judicial Court as one which conveys to the assessors a reasonable understanding of the extent and nature of the property.[27]

Once they receive an application in the proper form, the assessors are required by law to make a "reasonable abatement" if they find that the applicant has been taxed at more than his "just proportion" or taxed "upon an assessment of his property in excess of its fair cash value." The interpretation of these latter two phrases is the foundation of the vast majority of litigation in the area of tax abatements.

HEARINGS

§ 17.03[5]   Assessors' Right to Inspection and Information Prior to Hearing

When he files his application for abatement the taxpayer must upon request not only identify with certainty the property to which it relates; he must also, if requested, show the property to the assessors and furnish them, under oath, with such written information as may be reasonably required by them to determine the fair cash value of the property, including information as to the rents received from the property and the expenses of maintaining it.[28] Under a separate statute the assessors can also require such information prior to the filing of an application for

---

[23] G.L. c. 59, §§ 61 and 64.

[24] G.L. c. 59, §§ 61 and 64.

[25] St. 1931, c. 150, § 3.

[26] G.L. c. 59, § 29.

[27] Board of Assessors of Brookline v. Prudential Insurance Co., 310 Mass. 300, 38 N.E.2d 145 (1941).

[28] G.L. c. 59, § 61A.

abatement.[29] The two statutory provisions are now quite similar. Although prior to 1989 it seemed that the assessors might have had fewer discovery powers after an application for abatement had been filed than before. After the filing of written responses by the taxpayer, under either statute the assessors may require the taxpayer to testify under oath concerning his or her written return.[30]

The sanctions for failure to supply information "reasonably required" by the assessors are quite severe, mainly loss of all rights to appeal the tax assessed. Accordingly the taxpayer should be extremely careful before refusing to provide information on the ground that the request is unreasonable. The issue of reasonableness will not be decided until the case is before the Appellate Tax Board, long after the time to respond to the assessors' discovery requests has passed.

§ 17.03[6]   Hearings—Evidence Taxpayer Should Introduce

The statute is not explicit on whether or not the assessors are required to give an applicant for abatement a hearing prior to making a decision. However the cases hold that, although the applicant has no due process right to a hearing before the assessors because the statute provides for a full de novo hearing before the Tax Board,[31] "the statutes regulating proceedings for abatement of taxes are to be construed as contemplating hearings before the assessors upon applications for abatement."[32] The Court thus seems to be admonishing the assessors to hold hearings, while at the same time telling them that their failure to do so will not adversely affect their position on appeal. Since the failure of the assessors to grant any hearing at all will not be sufficient grounds to invalidate their action on appeal, then it would seem to follow logically that if they do hold a hearing the taxpayer cannot hope to prevail on appeal by contending that the hearing was in some way flawed, or inadequate.

In practice, hearings before local assessors tend to be extremely informal and would perhaps be better characterized as "discussions." Counsel should not, however, discount the importance of these hearings. They are a valuable opportunity to lay the groundwork for an eventual negotiated settlement of the dispute, either before or after an appeal to the Tax Board is taken, and it should be remembered that the vast majority of abatement cases are settled before trial. Local boards and agencies of every description tend to become markedly stiff and less forthcoming when the citizen before them is represented by counsel, and assessors are no exception to this rule. Counsel should not therefore exacerbate an already delicate

---

[29] G.L. c. 59, § 38D.

[30] G.L. c. 59, § 38E.

[31] Lincoln Hotel v. Assessors of Boston, 317 Mass. 595, 59 N.E.2d 1 (1945).

[32] Board of Assessors of Brookline v. Prudential Insurance Co. 310 Mass. 300, 38 N.E.2d 145 (1941).

situation by condescension to the Board or by overfrequent reference to cases or statutes which allegedly support his position.

This is not to say that counsel should not present facts and law in support of his client's position. But it is important to remember that this stage of an abatement proceeding may be closely analogized to negotiating the settlement of a tort case with an insurance adjuster, or pretrial plea bargaining with a prosecutor, in that the breaking down of barriers of suspicion and mistrust and the creation of some basic human rapport will go a good deal further in securing a favorable outcome for the client than all the legal knowledge in the world.

With respect to a record of the proceedings before the assessors, if a stenographic transcript or other record is kept by the Board itself then the taxpayer would have the right to a copy of this.[33] If the Board does not keep a record of the hearing, then the taxpayer may wish to have such a record made at his own expense, either stenographically or by means of a tape recorder, and he would have a statutory right to do this.[34] Whether it is tactically proper for the taxpayer to record the hearing is an open question. The assessors could make some damaging admissions at the hearing which might be useful at a later trial for impeachment or other purposes. However, the presence of a stenographer or tape recorder under the control of the taxpayer's counsel may so poison the atmosphere that settlement negotiations will be more difficult. Also it is important to remember that in the event of an appeal to the Tax Board the taxpayer will, if he chooses the formal procedure,[35] have the right to pretrial discovery and might perhaps get the same damaging admissions in this way. On the other hand, if taxpayer's counsel intends to choose the informal procedure[36] on appeal, he would have no such opportunity for discovery or to secure admissions, and he might view the problem differently.

§ 17.03[7]   Non-income Producing Property

The property under discussion at the meetings with the assessors will be either non-income producing property or income property. If it is non-income property (usually single family owner-occupied residential property) the discussions are very likely to center around whether the property is over-assessed compared to other similar property. In most communities, even those which purport to value property at fair cash value, the assessed value will tend to be under the likely sale value in the case of single family homes, although this is by no means always true.

Where the property in a municipality is legitimately at or near 100% valuation, the taxpayer must content himself with trying to show the assessors that his property

---

[33] G.L. c. 4, § 7(26) and G.L. c. 66, § 10.
[34] *See* G.L. c. 39, § 23B.
[35] *See* § 17.04[5], *infra*.
[36] *See* § 17.04[7], *infra*.

is actually worth less on the open market than it is assessed for. In the case of non-income property, this is usually accomplished by locating a number of recent sales of comparable property in the municipality and comparing their sales prices to the assessed value of the taxpayer's property. The taxpayer might also have an appraisal of his property done by a local real estate broker or appraiser, if this is financially feasible.

Where it can be shown, or is generally agreed, that the community assesses property at a discount from fair cash value the taxpayer's burden is a little lighter. In such cases, even where his property is assessed at less than its fair cash value he can still establish his right to an abatement if he can show that his property is assessed at a greater percentage of fair cash value than other comparable properties in the municipality. Here again he will want to develop a list of sales of comparable properties, and it will also be helpful to get an appraisal of the market value of his own property if such is financially feasible. Again, he may wish to obtain the equalized valuation calculations for the town made by the Department of Revenue. These will show the average assessment/fair cash value ratios for the class to which his property belongs. Once this information has been gathered the taxpayer will be able to show the average or median ratio of assessed value to fair cash value for properties comparable to his own and he has a right to have his property assessed at that same ratio. An even simpler method that the single family property owner can use to show that he has been disproportionately assessed is by merely pointing out to the assessors a significant number of comparable properties which are assessed at amounts lower than his own, without going into the issue of fair cash value or assessment/sales ratios.

In making the foregoing kinds of presentations to the assessors, the taxpayer will want to have a good eight to twelve comparable properties to point out in support of his contentions. The requirement of comparability cannot be overemphasized. Close attention must be paid to such things as house styles, lot sizes, number of square feet of living space, neighborhood, age, amenities, and so on. The properties should be as comparable in these respects as possible. There should also be a substantial disparity in the valuations of the taxpayer's property and the other comparable properties, since the assessors will tend to dismiss small variances.

The theory of disproportion cases and the methods of proving the same are discussed in detail later in this chapter. However, where non-income property is involved, it is rarely economically feasible to incur the expense required to establish a full-fledged disproportionate assessment case as outlined in this chapter. For that matter, it is rarely economically feasible in such cases to purchase the kind of expert appraisal needed to establish properly a simple claim of overvaluation. Therefore, the methods outlined in the preceding paragraphs are usually the only ones practically available to the small, non-income property owner.

§ 17.03[8]   Income Producing Property

Where income property is the subject of the abatement application it may be expected that the assessors will look closely at the income generating capacity of the property. The attorney who represents clients seeking real estate tax abatements is under a serious handicap if he does not understand at least the fundamentals of real estate appraisal theory. He will encounter in the assessors of the various cities and towns persons whose knowledge of appraisal theory runs the gamut from near total ignorance to great sophistication; and he must be able to adjust his presentation and negotiating tactics to fit the level of knowledge of the assessors with whom he is dealing in any particular case.

Most assessors, however, can be expected to have some knowledge of, and preference for, the methods of valuing income property based on the income generated by the property. At the stage when the abatement application is before the assessors, the taxpayer will not normally have had a formal appraisal of the property made. Therefore, it will be up to the taxpayer and his counsel to develop and present a proper statement of the gross income, expenses, net income and capitalized value of the property.

Once the taxpayer's presentation has been made, the discussion with the assessors may be expected to center around the issues of the difference between "fair rental value" of the property and its actual rental, the proper amount of expenses to be allocated to the operation of the property and the proper capitalization rate to be applied to net income.

If the property is partly or wholly vacant or rented at rates below market value, the assessors will often try to base the tax on "potential" rather than actual income. Again, the expenses claimed by the taxpayer as a deduction from gross income may be disallowed or reduced if they do not conform to established real estate industry guidelines. For example, the Institute of Real Estate Management is a trade association that puts out an annual Apartment Buildings, Income-Expense Analysis which gives standard ranges for each item of expense commonly associated with residential income property. To the extent that the expenses claimed by the taxpayer fall outside these ranges they are liable to be disallowed.

The selection of a proper capitalization rate, is, within reasonable parameters, very much a matter of judgment. The judgment of taxpayer and assessor may well differ on this point and it remains simply a matter for negotiation.

If the assessors and the taxpayer are able to agree on figures for gross income, expenses, net income and capitalization rate, they have yet one more question to resolve before assessed value can be determined. That question is the proper "tax factor" to be applied to the property. Tax factors are used in the valuation process as follows:

Fair Cash Value = Net Income Before Taxes and Depreciation Allowance/Capitalization Rate and Tax Factor

Thus, if net income before taxes and depreciation were $100,000, the capitalization rate 12%, and the tax rate $90 per thousand (9%), the proper assessed value would be: $100,000/(.12 + .09) = ($100,000/.21) = $476,190. Tax = ($90. × $476.19) = $42,857.

The foregoing calculations assume that the assessors value all property at 100% of fair cash value. If widespread underassessment is practiced in the municipality, it is necessary to reduce the tax factor proportionately. Thus if the tax rate is $90 per thousand or 9% and property is valued at 50% of fair market value, the tax factor will be 4.5% according to the formula: Tax Factor = Tax Rate × Disproportion Ratio. So, in the previous example, if the assessors value all property at 50% of fair cash value, the valuation formula would be: $100,000/(.12 + .045) = $100,000/.165 = $606,060 (fair cash value).

Note that in the disproportion case the formula yields fair cash value not assessed value, while where there is no disproportionate assessment the formula yields assessed value. To derive assessed value in the disproportion case it is necessary to perform the additional step of multiplying the fair cash value figure produced by the formula by the disproportion ratio, as follows: $606,060 × .50 = $303,030 (the assessed value). Then the tax = .09 × $303,030 = $27,272.

§ 17.03[9]   Notice of Decision or Non-action

After the assessors have made a decision on the application for abatement they are required to mail to the applicant notice of that decision within ten days. If they fail to act on the application within three months, without the written consent of the applicant, it is deemed denied, and the assessors are required to mail to the applicant notice of their inaction within ten days after the expiration of the three-month period. Such notice must indicate the date of the decision or the date the application was deemed denied, and must inform the applicant of his right to appeal.[37] The Department of Revenue provides the assessors of the various municipalities with forms to be used to notify taxpayers of action or inaction on petitions for abatement.

Even though the assessors may have denied an application for abatement, or failed to act on it so that it is deemed denied, they still retain the power to grant an abatement or modify their prior determination during the time allowed for the taking of an appeal and during the pendency of an appeal before the appellate Tax Board or the Supreme Judicial Court. It should be noted that the statute provides that if the assessors grant an abatement during the period for taking an appeal but

---

[37] G.L. c. 59, § 63.

before an appeal is entered, it must be in final settlement of the case;[38] but the statute imposes no such final requirement if an abatement is granted when an appeal has been entered into the case and is actually pending before the Tax Board or the Appeals Court.[39]

Therefore, in order to comply with the statute, counsel for the assessors should be careful to secure a waiver of appeal from the taxpayer as a condition to granting an abatement, even if the appeal period appears to have already run. If the matter is already pending before the Appellate Tax Board, assessors' counsel should secure a withdrawal of the appeal from taxpayer's counsel as a condition to granting an abatement. The reason for this is that if the abatement given is not satisfactory to the taxpayer, he will still be able to proceed with his appeal. In such cases, at the Tax Board the new, abated tax will be the starting point for negotiations in the mind of any Board member who deals with the case; the originally assessed tax will have become virtually irrelevant. The tactical disadvantage to the assessors in such a situation is obvious.

APPEALS

§ 17.03[10] General Rules for Appeals

If the assessors refuse the taxpayer's application for an abatement, the taxpayer can go next either to the County Commissioners, or other county board which has been authorized to hear such disputes, or he can go to the Appellate Tax Board.[40] If he goes to the County Commissioners for review, his action is called a Complaint; if he goes to the Appellate Tax Board, it is called an Appeal. Virtually all appeals from the assessors are taken to the Appellate Tax Board rather than to the Commissioners, since the Commissioners as a rule have little or no expertise in this area.

Appeals from the decision of the assessors must be taken within three months after the date of the assessors' decision. If the assessors fail to act on the application within three months from the date of filing, without the applicant's written consent to the delay, then the application is deemed denied. The applicant has three months from the date of the deemed denial to file an appeal. Thus, in the case where the assessors take no action, the time between the date of filing the application for abatement with the assessors and the last day for filing an appeal would be six months. The time during which an appeal from the decision of the assessors must be filed begins to run at midnight of the day on which the assessors' decision is made, or the last day on which the assessors could act, and expires three complete

---

[38] G.L. c. 59, § 64 and G.L. c. 58A, § 6.

[39] G.L. c. 58A, § 7.

[40] G.L. c. 59, §§ 64 and 65.

calendar months thereafter at midnight.[41] Where the last day for action by either the assessors or taxpayer falls on a Saturday, Sunday or legal holiday, then performance of such act on the next business day is timely.[42]

Where the assessors continue to consider an application for abatement after it is deemed denied by the passage of time this does not extend the time limit for the taxpayer to appeal to the Appellate Tax Board.[43] Similarly, where the application is deemed denied by the passage of time the subsequent sending of a notice of refusal to abate by the assessors will not extend the statutory time for taking an appeal.[44]

Finally, where the taxpayer appeals to the Appellate Tax Board before the time for action by the assessors has expired, and the time later expires without action by the assessors, the Board holds that it has jurisdiction of the appeal.[45]

G.L. c. 59, § 59, has been amended to provide that any abatement application delivered to the assessors by the post office after the abatement due date is deemed to have been received by them as of the postmark date on the envelope. This rule applies only to those applications mailed to the proper address of the assessors, first class postage prepaid, with postmarks made by the United States Postal Service.

G.L. c. 58, § 7 and c. 59, §§ 64–65 are also amended to make the above postmark rule applicable to appeals of assessors' abatement decisions that are mailed to and received by county commissioners or the Appellate Tax Board.

§ 17.03[11]　Late Appeals

If the assessors fail to take action on the taxpayer's application for three months from the date it is filed, without his written consent to the delay, then the application is deemed denied, and the assessors must send written notice to the applicant of their inaction within ten days of the date of the deemed denial. If they fail to send such notice to the applicant, and if by mistake or accident the applicant fails to enter his appeal with the Appellate Tax Board within the time limit provided by statute, he may petition the Tax Board to allow the late entry of his appeal. Such petition for late entry must be filed with the Board within two months after the deadline for filing the appeal has passed. After notice and hearing, and upon such terms as

---

[41] Berkshire Gas Co. v. Board of Assessors of Williamstown, 361 Mass. 873, 281 N.E.2d 602 (1972).

[42] Fort Howard Cup Corp. v. Board of Assessors of Somerville, 12 Mass. App. Tax Bd. Rep. 91 (1990).

[43] Franklin County Realty Trust v. Board of Assessors of Greenfield, 391 Mass. 1018, 463 N.E.2d 554 (1984).

[44] Lenson v. Board of Assessors of Brookline, 395 Mass. 178, 478 N.E.2d 954 (1985).

[45] Daniels v. Board of Assessors of Everett, 12 Mass. App. Tax Bd. Rep. 80 (1990).

it wishes, the Board may allow the taxpayer to enter his appeal.[46] Such petitions are usually allowed by the Board.

Upon reflection it will be seen that the effect of the assessors notice of inaction is to cut off the taxpayer's right to file for late entry. Counsel for taxpayers should note that if the failure of the assessors to act on an application for three months results in it being deemed to be denied, the taxpayer can only file for late entry where the assessors do not send the required notice of inaction. Where the notice is sent, after the expiration of the three-month period from the date of deemed denial, the taxpayer's right of appeal is completely foreclosed.

Counsel for taxpayers should also keep in mind that, even where a notice of inaction is not sent, the right to file for late entry is not limitless. A petition for late entry must be filed within five months of the date the application for abatement is deemed denied or the taxpayer is out of court.

It is easy to imagine the following scenario occurring in a busy law office: Application for abatement is filed. The assessors take no action for three months and the application is deemed denied. No notice of inaction is sent. Another three months passes during which time the taxpayer has called his attorney to ask if there is anything new on his abatement. The attorney's secretary has called the assessors' office a few times but has been told that no decision has been reached. At the end of this second three-month period the taxpayer's appeal as of right expires. Two more months pass, a total of eight since the application for abatement was filed, and still no decision by the assessors. The application for abatement is deemed denied and the taxpayer's right of appeal is now irrevocably foreclosed. The taxpayer's attorney will probably face a malpractice claim.

This kind of situation can be avoided if taxpayer's counsel gives permission, in writing, on the original application for the assessors to delay their decision for an extended period: one year, for example. In this way, the failure of the assessors to act on the application will not result in it being deemed to be denied, and the statute of limitations on the right to appeal will be tolled.[47] Of course this procedure could cause problems if the assessors refuse to act on the application and counsel cannot harass or cajole them into a decision. In such cases, taxpayer's counsel would not have any right to appeal until the additional time period expired.

§ 17.03[12] Payment of Tax as Prerequisite to Appeal

If the tax on a parcel of real estate for the full fiscal year is more than $3,000, then in addition to all other statutory requirements, if the taxpayer wishes to appeal the decision, or non-action, of the assessors to the County Commissioners or to the

---

[46] G.L. c. 59, § 65c.
[47] *See* G.L. c. 59, § 64 and G.L. c. 58A, § 6.

Appellate Tax Board, he must pay either: (a) "the full amount of said tax due without the incurring of any interest charges;" or (b) instead of paying the assessed tax he may pay, without incurring interest, as a "substitute" or "deemed" tax an amount not less than the average of the tax assessed, reduced by abatements, if any, for the three years next preceding the year of assessment, (but a year in which no tax was due shall not be used in computing such average, and if no tax was due in any of the three preceding years then the substitute tax provision will not apply). One-half of either the tax actually assessed or the "substitute" tax would then have to be paid by the November installment date in order for the taxpayer to have the right to appeal.[48] Where betterments or other non-tax charges have been added to the tax bill these may be disregarded when calculating the substitute tax. Also, if such items have been added to the tax, the taxpayer should specifically direct that his payments be applied first to the outstanding taxes. Otherwise the tax collector may apply payments in such a manner as to create an underpayment of the tax, resulting in the incurring of interest and possible loss of the right to appeal.[49]

The requirement that one-half of the tax be paid as a prerequisite to appeal in cases where the tax is greater than $3,000 has been upheld over the argument that the provision is violative of the due process and equal protection clauses of the 14th Amendment to the United States Constitution and Part 1, Article 11 of the Massachusetts Constitution.[50] It has also been held that the averaging provisions of the statute apply in computing the substitute tax even if there has been a substantial improvement in the property during the three-year averaging period.[51] Thus, if the property were raw land during two of the three years preceding the tax year at issue and contained a hotel in the third year, the substitute tax would still be based on the average of the three years' valuations.

Where the municipality issues preliminary tax bills under G.L. c. 59, § 23D the incurring of interest on such bills will not, under a number of holdings by the Appellate Tax Board, defeat the right to apply for abatement or appeal to the Board.[52]

§ 17.03[13] Inability to Pay Tax—Effect on Appeal

If the taxpayer is appealing a decision of the assessors to the Appellate Tax Board, and the tax due is more than $3,000, he must, its indicated in the preceding

[48] G.L. c. 59, § 64.

[49] Cressey Dockham & Co. v. Board of Assessors of Andover, 11 Mass. App. Tax Bd. Rep. 41 (1989).

[50] Old Colony R. R. Co. v. Assessors of Boston, 309 Mass. 439, 35 N.E.2d 246 (1941); City of Lowell v. Marden and Murphy, 321 Mass. 597, 74 N.E.2d 666 (1947).

[51] Altman v. Board of Assessors of Randolph, 372 Mass. 276, 361 N.E.2d 1252 (1977).

[52] Soep v. Board of Assessors of Boston, 13 Mass. App. Tax Bd. Rep. 172 (1991).

section, make timely payment of either the tax assessed or the "substitute tax" provided for in the statute before he will be allowed to maintain his suit before the Board.

Thus, if the appeal were filed in December, the November installment would have to have been paid when due; and if the appeal were still pending when the April installment came due, the taxpayer would normally have to pay that install-ment on time in order to prevent his suit from being dismissed.

Possibly to alleviate hardship on a taxpayer with a meritorious case who is unable to pay the balance of the tax due by the second installment date, the law allows the Tax Board some discretion to defer that second payment.

If the taxpayer has paid one-half of the tax due, or one-half of the tax deemed to be due for purposes of appeal, he may, on or before the due date of the next installment, file a motion with the Board requesting that payment of the balance of the tax be excused or deferred. The motion must allege and be supported by evidence that the taxpayer has met all the other requirements for an appeal and that he is actually financially unable to pay the balance of the tax.[53] The Board has absolute discretion as to whether or not to grant the taxpayer's request.[54] As a measure of the very broad discretion which the Board has in this area, in one case the taxpayer had obtained an extension for filing the second half fiscal year taxes to a date certain. The taxpayer failed to either pay the tax or move for a further extension prior to the expiration of the first extension period. Two months thereafter the taxpayer applied to the Board for a further extension of time to pay the second half taxes. The Board granted this request; and its authority to do so was later upheld.[55]

If the Board grants the motion, it may impose upon the taxpayer such conditions as it deems proper, including the requirement that he pay the balance of the tax, in whole or by installments, as a condition precedent to a hearing on the merits. If the taxpayer subsequently fails to comply with any of the conditions imposed by the order, his appeal may, upon motion, be dismissed.[56]

§ 17.03[14]   Assessors' Right to Remove from County Commissioners

The aggrieved taxpayer has the right to Appeal the decision of the assessors to either the County Commissioners or the Appellate Tax Board. If he does the former, the assessors may elect to have the appeal heard by the Appellate Tax Board. This election must be made within thirty days from the date the assessors receive a

---

[53] G.L. c. 59, § 65B.

[54] Currens v. Board of Assessors of Boston, 370 Mass. 249, 346 N.E.2d 849 (1976).

[55] Board of Assessors of Boston v. Duddy's, Inc. , 382 Mass. 686, 409 N.E.2d 1302 (1980).

[56] G.L. c. 59, § 65B.

certified copy of the complaint from the clerk of the County Commissioners. If the assessors make such an election, then the matter is transferred to the clerk of the Board by the clerk of the County Commissioners. The appeal will then be heard by the Tax Board according to its "formal" procedure.

However, if the appeal involves real property valued at $20,000 or less, used by the taxpayer as his dwelling, containing no more than three dwelling units, and not used for any other purpose, then it will be heard according to the "informal" procedure, unless the taxpayer elects the formal procedure, which election must be made within ten days of receipt by him of the notice of transfer.[57]

TAXPAYER'S RIGHTS IF HE WINS

§ 17.03[15]   Interest on Abated Taxes

If the taxpayer succeeds and is granted an abatement, the town must reimburse him in the amount of the abatement allowed plus any interest and charges which he has been required to pay, other than legal costs.[58] He must also be paid interest at the rate of 8% per annum on the sum abated from the time the tax was paid until it is refunded. But no refund will be paid on account of an abatement where there is an outstanding balance due on the tax to which the abatement relates, nor will any interest be paid for any period during which any part of the tax, net of the abatement, was unpaid.[59]

§ 17.03[16]   Taxpayer's Right to Certificate of Abatement

Where an abatement has been granted by the assessors, the Appellate Tax Board or other authority, the taxpayer has a right to receive a certificate of abatement from the abatement-granting authority.[60] He also has a right to have the tax collector and the municipal accountant notified of the abatement.[61]

§ 17.03[17]   Effect if Property Sold or Taken for Non-payment of Taxes During Pendency Appeal

If an application for abatement is filed prior to the institution of proceedings for the sale or taking of the subject property for non-payment of taxes, any subsequent sale or taking will not affect the proceedings on the application for abatement.

Where the property has been sold by the municipality to a third party and the

---

[57] G.L. c. 59, § 64 (¶ 2).
[58] G.L. c. 59, § 69. *See* G.L. c. 59, § 62.
[59] G.L. c. 59, § 69.
[60] G.L. c. 59, § 70.
[61] G.L. c. 59, § 70A.

original owner/applicant is found to be entitled to an abatement, he will be entitled to relief in the same manner and in the same amount as if the payment made by the purchaser of his property to the city or town for the property had been made instead as a direct payment of the taxes the non-payment of which caused the property to be sold. For example, suppose the tax assessed on a property is $1,000. The property owner neglects to pay and applies for abatement. During the pendency of his application the property is sold by the tax collector for nonpayment. The sale price is $1,000. Subsequently the taxpayer is granted an abatement of $500. He would have a right to receive $500 from the town with interest at the statutory rate from the date of payment of the purchase price of the property.[62] Provided his right to redeem had not been foreclosed, he could then proceed to recover the property from the purchaser.[63]

If the property is taken or purchased by the city or town for non-payment and has not yet been sold to a third party, the taxpayer is entitled to have the amount which he must pay the city or town to redeem the property reduced to the amount he would have had to pay if the abatement had become effective before the taking or purchase of the property by the municipality.[64]

THE APPELLATE TAX BOARD
AND APPEALS THEREFROM THE APPELLATE TAX BOARD

§ 17.04   Generally

A taxpayer who is unhappy with the decision of the assessors on his application for an abatement may have a complete new hearing before either the County Commissioners or the Appellate Tax Board. The latter alternative is usually preferred by both taxpayers and assessors on the theory that the Board was specifically created and designed to handle this type of case and has great expertise in the area of local taxation.

The following paragraphs will outline the mechanics of prosecuting an appeal to its conclusion before the Appellate Tax Board, and will discuss the scope of review which decisions of the Board will receive before the Appeals Court.

§ 17.04[1]   Structure of the Board

The Appellate Tax Board is a part of the Department of Revenue, but is in no way subject to the control of that agency.

---

[62] G.L. c. 59, § 65A.
[63] *See* G.L. c. 60, § 62; G.L. c. 59, § 65A.
[64] G.L. c. 59, § 65A.

It is composed of five members who are appointed by the Governor, with the approval of the Executive Council. One member is designated as Chairman of the Board.

The members serve six-year terms and are required to be full-time employees. Not more than three members of the Board can belong to the same political party. Although normally a majority of the members of the Board must be present to constitute a quorum for the conduct of business, a single member is authorized by statute to decide:

(a) Cases on appeal from a board of assessors where the assessed value of the property involved does not exceed $500,000.

(b) Cases on appeal from a board of assessors where the assessed value exceeds $500,000 but does not exceed $750,000 when the property owner and the assessors consent in writing.

(c) Cases heard under the informal procedure in which the assessed value is less than $1,000,000.

However, the Appellate Tax Board has, by rule,[1] limited further the appeals which may be decided by a single member by providing that, in addition to the monetary limitations, there must be no issue raised in the pleadings other than the over-valuation of the property. Thus a disproportionate assessment case could not be decided by a single member regardless of the assessed value of the property involved. In any case where a single member is authorized to decide the case, he may, in his discretion, submit the case to the full Board for decision.[2] In practice, in those cases where a single member is not authorized to decide the case it will usually be heard by a single member and formally decided by the full Board. However, while it is not the practice of the full Board to rubber stamp the views of the member who heard the case, his view will carry a great deal of weight with the other members. If a case is difficult or unusual it will often be discussed by the Board until a decision is reached. Sometimes in such cases the members who did not hear the case will read the transcript prior to such discussions.

§ 17.04[2]   Publication of Decisions

The Board is authorized by statute to publish such of its reports and opinions as are, in its opinion, of public interest.[3] All decisions of the Board that are accompanied by findings and opinion are published on a regular basis in the Massachusetts Appellate Tax Board Reporter, and are noted by the Massachusetts

---

[1] Rule 20, Rules of Practice of the Appellate Tax Board (ATB).

[2] Rule 20, Rules of Practice of the Appellate Tax Board (ATB).

[3] G.L. c. 58A, § 3.

Lawyers Weekly, a legal newspaper. The decisions are also available in county law libraries, at the Massachusetts Bar Association library and at the office of the Board.

PROCEDURE

§ 17.04[3]   Right of Appeal to the Board

The statutory prerequisites to an appeal from a decision of the assessors to the Appellate Tax Board are discussed at length in §§ 17.03[10]–[13], *supra*, and reference is made to that discussion. In general, it is important to remember that all the statutory requirements for initiating and prosecuting an appeal before the Tax Board must be complied with strictly, because the Board has no jurisdiction to entertain proceedings begun or prosecuted in a different manner than is pre-scribed by statute.[4] Additionally, the Supreme Judicial Court has held that the taxpayer who has not complied with the statutory requirements for appeal has no standing before the Board since he is not a person "aggrieved" for purposes of the statute.[5]

§ 17.04[4]   Jurisdiction

Since the Appellate Tax Board is a creation of the legislature rather than a traditional common law court it has only that jurisdiction specifically conferred upon it by statute.[6] With respect to the local real estate tax, the Board has statutory jurisdiction to hear appeals related to: claimed excess or disproportionate valua-tions and improper classification,[7] claims of exemption by the elderly and by veterans,[8] disputes over valuation, for purposes of in-lieu-of-tax payments, of land held by one municipality and located in another,[9] disputes over the apportionment of the tax on land divided after assessment,[10] and claims of charitable exemption.[11] The Board also has statutory jurisdiction of certain appeals under the statutes relating to taxation of qualified forest land,[12] taxation of qualified agricultural and

---

[4] Singer Sewing Machine Co. v. Assessors of Boston, 341 Mass. 513, 170 N.E.2d 342 (1936).

[5] Board of Assessors of Boston v. Suffolk Law School, 295 Mass. 489, 4 N.E.2d 342 (1936).

[6] Board of Assessors of Saugus v. Baumann, 370 Mass. 36, 345 N.E.2d 360 (1976); G.L. c. 58A, § 6.

[7] G.L. c. 59, §§ 64 and 65.

[8] G.L. c. 59, §§ 5(17) and 5(22).

[9] The provisions relating to such in-lieu payments were formerly contained in G.L. c. 59, §§ 7-7A. They are now found in G.L. c. 59, §§ 5D–5G. However, the proper technical correction has not as of this writing been made in G.L. c. 58A, § 6, which creates the jurisdiction of the Board. Presumably, the repeal of §§ 7 and 7A was not intended to eliminate the jurisdiction of the Board of these types of appeals, which are rather rare.

[10] G.L. c. 59, § 81.

[11] G.L. c. 59, §§ 5(3) and 5B.

[12] G.L. c. 61, § 3.

horticultural land,[13] taxation of qualified recreational land,[14] and taxation of urban redevelopment corporation and housing authority properties.[15]

In accordance with well-settled judicial principles, the matter of the jurisdiction of the Board may be raised at any stage of the proceedings by any party or by the Board itself.[16] This is so, even though Rule 16 of the Rules of Practice of the Board appears to make the filing of a plea in bar based on a lack of jurisdiction not apparent on the pleadings a matter of discretion with the Board once the issues are joined. Obviously neither the Tax Board nor any other judicial tribunal can confer jurisdiction upon itself where such does not exist merely by the promulgation of a court rule.[17] Thus it seems clear that the Board could not refuse to hear a plea alleging lack of jurisdiction no matter at what stage of the proceeding it is made.

§ 17.04[5]   The Formal Procedure—Taxpayer's Petition

There are two kinds of procedure before the Tax Board: formal and informal. A taxpayer who wishes to appeal a decision of the assessors to the Board under the formal procedure must, within three months after receiving notice of the decision or, if the assessors fail to act on his application for three months and it is thereby deemed denied, within three months from the date of the deemed denial,[18] file a petition with the clerk of the Board, sending a copy of the petition by registered mail, postage paid, to the assessors, their agent, or attorney of record. This filing must be timely. A petition is deemed filed upon its receipt by the Board.[19] When a filing deadline is near, the papers should be hand delivered to the Board. A petition must contain: (a) A caption in approved form. (b) A clear and concise statement of the nature of the tax or other matters in controversy and of the facts on which the petitioner relies, giving the date of notice of the decision or determination appealed from. If the appeal is from the refusal to abate a tax, describe the property or commodity taxed and state the valuation made by the taxing authority, the rate and amount of the tax, the year for which it was assessed, the amount and date of any payment made, and the date and manner of application for abatement to the taxing authority. (c) A clear and concise statement of the petitioner's objections to the decision appealed from, and of any contentions of law which the petitioner desires to raise. (d) A prayer setting forth the relief sought. (e) The name and address of the petitioner and his attorney for purposes of service of pleadings.

---

[13] G.L. c. 61A, § 19.

[14] G.L. c. 61B, § 14.

[15] G.L. c. 121A, § 10, G.L. c. 121B, § 16.

[16] Cohen v. Assessors of Boston, 344 Mass. 268, 182 N.E.2d 138 (1962).

[17] Cohen v. Assessors of Boston, 344 Mass. 268, 182 N.E.2d 138, at 140.

[18] *See* § 17.03[10], *supra*, for fuller discussion of filing deadlines. *See also* Timetable for Lawyers, *infra*.

[19] Doherty v. Board of Assessors of Northboro, 13 Mass. App. Tax Bd. Rep. 74 (1990).

Appeals involving taxes for more than one year may not be included in the same petition.[20] The statute provides that where two or more parcels are included in one decision by the assessors the Board "may" require that each parcel be the subject of a separate petition. It makes no reference to cases where two or more parcels are the subject of multiple decisions of the assessors. The Supreme Judicial Court has held that in the absence of a general rule of practice of the Board prohibiting it, two or more parcels which were the subject of multiple decisions of the assessors may be combined in one petition to the Board.[21]

The Board has developed standard forms for the use of parties practicing before it, among which are petitions for review under both the formal and informal procedures. These forms are helpful in many cases, but they assert only the ground of overvaluation as a basis for relief. If the taxpayer is basing his appeal on additional, or other grounds, he must amend the form to show these grounds or he may have a defective appeal.[22] However, the Board has been liberal in allowing amendments to pleadings.

Under the Rules of Practice of the Board, the person filing the appeal has ten days after filing to submit to the clerk either a signed acknowledgment of service, or a certificate of service with the appropriate post office receipts attached to it.[23] The assessors then have thirty days from the receipt of notice of the appeal to file an answer to the petition with the Board, and to send a copy of the answer by registered mail to the taxpayer.[24]

§ 17.04[6]   Assessors' Answer

The answer of the assessors under the formal procedure should contain the following:[25] (a) A specific admission or denial of each allegation of fact contained in the petition. (b) A clear and concise statement of any facts upon which the assessors rely. (c) A clear and concise statement of each finding of fact and ruling of law made by the assessors with respect to the tax or determination in issue. (d) A statement of the usual place of business of the assessors designating a municipal building by name and any other building by street and number.

The assessors are not required to file an answer if the only issue the taxpayer is raising by his petition is that his property was overvalued or improperly classified. If the assessors exercise their option not to file an answer, then the claim of

---

[20] G.L. c. 58A, § 7. Rule 3, Rules of Practice of the ATB.

[21] Mann v. Board of Assessors of Wareham, 387 Mass. 35, 438 N.E.2d 826 (1982).

[22] Board of Assessors of Brookline v. Prudential Insurance Co. of America, 310 Mass. 300, 38 N.E.2d 145 (1941).

[23] Rule 4, Rules of Practice of the ATB.

[24] Rule 12, Rules of Practice of the ATB.

[25] G.L. c. 58A, § 7; Rule 12, Rules of Practice of the ATB.

overvaluation or improper classification is considered to have been denied and all other factual allegations in the taxpayer's petition are considered to have been admitted.[26] It is extremely important to note that the statute creating the formal procedure provides that the Board shall not consider any issue of fact or law not raised by the taxpayer's petition or the assessors' answer unless, "equity and good conscience require."[27] Experience has shown that equity and good conscience are rarely deemed by the Board to apply.

§ 17.04[7]   The Informal Procedure—Taxpayer's Statement

In an effort to eliminate some of the costs and delays attendant upon an appeal to the Board, the legislature has directed the Board to establish a so-called "informal" procedure.[28] This procedure, insofar as is practicable, attempts to eliminate the formalities of pleading, practice and evidence that are associated with hearings under the formal procedure. The Board is also authorized, in its discretion, to eliminate any and all costs except the entry fee.

Where both parties elect the informal procedure the hearing will be so conducted. Otherwise the taxpayer files notice of his Election of the informal procedure when he files his Statement.

In addition to the Election and the Statement, the taxpayer must file a written Waiver of his right to appeal the decision of the Board except upon questions of law raised by the pleadings, or by an agreed statement of facts, or shown by the report of the Board. So, in order to obtain a speedy, inexpensive and uncomplicated hearing before the Board, the taxpayer must give up his right to comprehensive review of the Board's decision.

The taxpayer's Statement Under the Informal Procedure must contain:[29] (a) A caption. (b) The full name of each appellant. (c) A statement of the facts involved in the case. (d) A statement of the amount claimed in abatement. (e) An address for service of pleadings. (f) Such other information as the clerk may require (rarely invoked).

The statute provides that no statement under the informal procedure shall relate to an assessment on more than one parcel of real estate, except where the Board

---

[26] G.L. c. 58A, § 7.

[27] G.L. c. 58A, § 7. Note that the Board must on its own motion admit into evidence the report prepared by the Commissioner of Revenue under the provisions of G.L. c. 58, § 10C, which contains the sales/assessment ratios of the various classes of property in the municipality for the tax years in question. This report is prima facie evidence of the assessment practices in the municipality, and the Board may grant an abatement based on this report, if it shows disproportionate assessment, even if that issue was not raised by the pleadings. G.L. c. 58A, § 12c.

[28] G.L. c. 58A, § 7A; see also Rules 6 and 7, Rules of Practice of the ATB.

[29] Rule 7, Rules of Practice of the ATB.

"shall specifically permit otherwise."[30] The Board has adopted a rule which requires that the appellant obtain its permission to combine two or more parcels in one statement.[31] Nevertheless, the Appeals Court has held that the inclusion of more than one parcel in a single statement without first obtaining the permission of the Board does not defeat an appeal. Because, in the absence from the Board's rules of a statement of a reasonable and readily understood method specifying the time and manner of obtaining the Board's permission to include more than one parcel in a single appeal, there was no adequate negation of the Board's statutory discretion to allow such inclusion.[32]

The Board makes available two forms which if filled out properly will satisfy these threshold prerequisites for the informal procedure. If the assessed value of the property in question is $20,000 or less, the law requires that the forms be completed for the taxpayer/petitioner, if he so requests, by an employee of the Board.

§ 17.04[8]   Assessors' Answer

Once the forms have been completed, the clerk of the Board serves a copy of the taxpayer's Statement Under the Informal Procedure on the assessors. If the only defense that the assessors wish to assert is that the property was not overvalued or not improperly classified, then they are not required to file an answer; otherwise they must file their answer, similar to that required under the formal procedure, within thirty days.

The answer under the informal procedure should contain in substance the following: (a) A specific admission or denial of each allegation of fact contained in the Statement of taxpayer. (b) A clear and concise statement of any other facts upon which the appellee relies. (c) A clear and concise statement of each finding of fact or ruling of law made by the assessors with respect to the tax or determination in issue. (d) A statement of the usual place of business of the assessors, designating a municipal building by name and any other building by street and number, if any. If no Answer is filed, the allegation of overvaluation or improper classification is held to be denied and all other material facts alleged in the Statement are held to be admitted.

§ 17.04[9]   Assessors' Right to Elect the Formal Procedure

Even though the taxpayer files his appeal under the informal procedure, if the assessed value of the property exceeds $20,000, the assessors may elect to have the case heard under the formal procedure, provided they do so within thirty days

---

[30] G.L. c. 58A, § 7A.
[31] Rule 7, Rules of Practice of the ATB.
[32] Phifer v. Board of Assessors of Cohasset, 28 Mass. App. Ct. 552, 553 N.E.2d 234 (1990).

after receiving a copy of the taxpayer's petition.[33]

If the assessors fail to elect the formal procedure in such cases, they are deemed to have made the same waivers with respect to their right to review of the Board's decision as the taxpayer does when he elects the informal procedure. That is, the appellate courts will only review questions of law raised by the pleadings, by an agreed statement of facts, or shown by the report of the Board if one is made.[34]

Note that where the assessed value of the property is $20,000 or less and the taxpayer files his appeal under the informal procedure the assessors cannot elect the formal procedure. In such cases, an anomalous situation exists where the taxpayer will have only the limited right of review on appeal provided by the informal procedure while the assessors will have an unlimited right of review.[35] Until the unrealistically low removal threshold is increased this anomaly will be of only academic interest.

§ 17.04[10] Discovery

As indicated, a hearing before the Board may be conducted according to the formal procedure or the informal procedure, depending on the circumstances of the case and the wishes of the parties.

Under either procedure the taxpayer is required, before the hearing on the appeal, to allow the assessors or their experts, agents or attorneys to enter upon and examine the property in question.[36]

In the case of an appeal relating to property classified as residential greater than eight units, commercial or industrial, that is assessed for more than $200,000 in the previous fiscal year, upon motion made by the assessors and granted by the Board, the taxpayer must file with the Board an audited income and expense statement for the most recent year, within forty days from the date of taking the appeal.[37]

At least thirty days prior to the hearing, upon motion made and granted by the Board, the parties must exchange appraisal reports.[38]

Some of the other more usual and familiar types of discovery, normally associated with trials in the courts, such as interrogatories, motions to inspect and so

---

[33] G.L. c. 58A, § 7A.

[34] Board of Assessors of Kingston v. Sgarzi, 367 Mass. 840, 329 N.E.2d 121 (1975).

[35] Board of Assessors of Kingston v. Sgarzi, 367 Mass. 840, 329 N.E.2d 121 (1975). *See also* discussion at § 17.04[20].

[36] G.L. c. 58A, § 8A.

[37] G.L. c. 58A, § 7.

[38] G.L. c. 58A, § 8A.

on, are available but are limited to the formal procedure.[39] The Massachusetts Rules of Civil Procedure do not apply to the Appellate Tax Board. Instead, the statutory rules relative to discovery which pertained in the courts of the Commonwealth prior to the adoption of the Massachusetts Rules of Civil Procedure still apply.[40]

In spite of the fact that its Rules provide for them, the Board has not favored the use of depositions. The reason for this is that the deposition has not been conceived as a discovery tool in Board practice, but rather as a means for securing the testimony of a witness who would not otherwise be available. This is pointed up by the Board Rule that a deposition will be introduced into evidence by the party taking it.[41]

Note that the older practice regarding interrogatories bid out by G.L. c. 231, §§ 61–67, was somewhat different than the practice under the new Rules, in that only one set of interrogatories could be served without leave of court, answers were required to be served within twenty days and the interrogated party, could refuse to provide certain kinds of information.

Other forms of discovery provided for by the earlier rules of practice, such as demands for inspection of documents named in the pleadings, or motions for bills of particulars, have no real relevance to practice before the Board.

§ 17.04[11] Motion Practice

Motions must be "seasonably" made and, except when made during the hearing, must be in writing with a copy given to opposing counsel. Request for hearing on a motion may be made by either party at least seven days before the date suggested for the hearing.[42] Motions which are assented to by opposing counsel need not be marked for hearing. Motions for continuances agreed to by both parties still need the assent of the Board, which is usually given. Motions are heard on Mondays between 10 and 12 A.M.

§ 17.04[12] Telephone Motions

The Board allows motions to be argued via a telephone conference call hookup with the Chairman of the Board. Telephone motions must be in writing and filed with the Board and served on opposing counsel at least five days before they are to be heard. Telephone motions are usually heard at 2 P.M. on Mondays but may be scheduled for other afternoons. When a request for a telephone motion is

---

[39] In matters of discovery, much must be left to the discretion of the Board. Vara-Sorrentino v. Board of Assessors of Provincetown, 369 Mass. 692, 341 N.E.2d 649 (1976).

[40] *See* third sentence of G.L. c. 58A, § 8A, making §§ 61–70 inclusive of G.L. c. 231 applicable to the formal procedure. *See also* Rule 25, Rules of Practice of the ATB.

[41] Rule 26(i), Rules of Practice of the ATB.

[42] Rule 16, Rules of Practice of the ATB.

received, the clerk will assign a time for it to be heard.

§ 17.04[13]   Continuances

The official Board policy is to allow continuances only for good cause shown upon timely written request. However a reasonable number of continuances of a hearing date will usually be granted. This can vary from member to member and it is not unheard of for a member to insist that a case go forward absent "good cause."

Appeals will not be continued generally, but must be continued to a date certain or placed on a reserve list when the cause is, for example, to await the decision in some other case. Continuances can be granted only by the Chairman or a member, not by a clerk or other agency personnel.

A request for continuance based on the absence of a material witness must be supported by the same kind of affidavit required by Rule 40 of the Massachusetts Rules of Civil Procedure.

§ 17.04[14]   Pre-hearing Conferences

In some complex cases, the Board makes use of pre-hearing conferences similar to those provided for by Rule 16 of the Massachusetts Rules of Civil Procedure. The member conducting the conference tries to obtain as many stipulations of fact and law from the parties as is possible. He also tries in any other way possible to simplify the trial or other disposition of the case. Very often he will try to facilitate a settlement of the case without the need for a hearing. A pre-hearing conference may be scheduled at the request of a party or at the discretion of the Board.

§ 17.04[15]   Hearings

The law provides that the Board must grant a public hearing on an appeal if any party so requests and that either a party by motion, or the Board itself, may have a matter set down for hearing.[43]

In practice, the clerk of the Board routinely assigns dates for hearing all appeals that are filed, regardless of whether the parties have made a request for one. The Chairman assigns each hearing to a particular Board member with no advance notice to the parties. Except in cases which come under the purview of Rule 20,[44] the decision of the case must be made by a majority of the Board.[45]

The clerk of the Board maintains hearing lists of cases ripe for hearing under each

---

[43] G.L. c. 58A, § 8.
[44] *See* discussion at § 17.04[1], *supra.*
[45] *See* discussion at § 17.04[1], *supra.*

of the procedures, and, unless the Board directs otherwise, cases are heard in numerical order.[46] Hearing delays are lengthy, although a request for speedy hearing will often get a case on the trial list sooner.

Issues of fact or law which are sufficient in themselves to determine the decision of the Board may be heard and disposed of separately from the case in chief.[47] Such situations are not common, but they do occur.[48] Opening statements are not customary except in unusual or complex cases, and then are expected to be succinct and to the point in view of the presumed expertise of the tribunal hearing the case. Members prefer that a case be presented in its essentials and as expeditiously as possible.

During the hearing before the Board an original or copy of the following documents should be introduced in evidence:[49]

(a) The tax return or list, if any, filed by the taxpayer, so far as it is material to the controversy.

(b) The original assessment, or other original determination, so far as material.

(c) The tax bill or notice of tax, with date of payment, if paid, and the amount of interest paid.

(d) The application for abatement or other petition filed with the assessors, with the date of filing.

(e) The notice from the assessors of their decision on the application or petition, with the date when the decision was made, or the fact that no decision was made.

The parties may stipulate in writing as to the existence of any relevant fact and either may summon witnesses by subpoena or require the production of papers as they would at a trial in the courts.[50]

Provision is made in the Rules of Practice of the Board for the filing of Requests

---

[46] Rule 19, Rules of Practice of the ATB.

[47] Rule 22, Rules of Practice of the ATB.

[48] In Roda Realty Trust v. Board of Assessors of Belmont, 385 Mass. 493, 432 N.E.2d 522 (1982), the assessors filed a motion to dismiss for lack of jurisdiction based on untimely filing, with an affidavit as to the time of mailing of the tax bills. The taxpayer filed a counter affidavit raising (it thought) an issue of material fact. The Appellate Tax Board allowed the motion and dismissed the case. The taxpayer appealed alleging as error the summary disposition of the case without a hearing in the face of disputed material facts. The Court affirmed, apparently because the taxpayer had failed to request an evidentiary hearing before the Board and could not raise the issue for the first time on appeal.

[49] Roda Realty Trust v. Board of Assessors of Belmont, 385 Mass. 493, 432 N.E.2d 522 (1982).

[50] Rules 23 and 24, Rules of Practice of the ATB; *see also* G.L. c 58A, § 11.

for Findings of Fact and Rulings of Law, as is customary in the trial of civil cases in the district courts.[51] These should be ready for filing at the conclusion of the hearing.

The parties are also allowed to file with the Board briefs in support of their position, prior to the Board's decision.[52] In general, unless specifically, provided otherwise, the procedure before the Board should conform to that prevailing in civil actions in the courts, with the exception that under the informal procedure the member hearing the case may and usually does eliminate all formal rules of pleading, procedure and evidence to the extent that he deems practicable.[53]

This relaxation of the rules of evidence in the informal procedure will often mean that the member hearing the case will allow in hearsay or other incompetent evidence, and counsel should be well aware that his decision to do so will not be reviewable on appeal. It should be noted that the vast majority of appeals filed with the Board are settled before hearing.

§ 17.04[16]   Taking of Views

Views of the property will be taken, in the discretion of the member hearing the case, upon motion of either party. However, the Board generally regards views as appropriate only in those cases where the property is for some reason out of the ordinary. The burden is on the moving party to convince the member hearing the case that a view is necessary.

§ 17.04[17]   Stenographic Reports of Proceedings

Official stenographic reports of proceedings before the Appellate Tax Board are made only if one of the parties requests such a report before the taking of any evidence. Notice of the request should be given to the Board and all parties at least twenty-four hours in advance. The requesting party is required to deposit with the clerk of the Board an amount equal to the cost of the report, as estimated by the clerk. The requesting party should inquire of the clerk as to the amount of deposit required. The clerk arranges for a stenographer to be present at the hearing.

If neither party requests a stenographic report, then the scope of appellate review of the Board's decision afforded to the parties is diminished. If no report is requested, the parties are deemed to have waived their right to appeal upon questions as to the admission or exclusion of evidence, or as to whether a finding was warranted by the evidence.[54]

---

[51] Rule 29, Rules of Practice of the ATB.
[52] Rule 30, Rules of Practice of the ATB.
[53] Rule 37, Rules of Practice of the ATB.
[54] G.L. c. 58A, § 10.

The statute does provide, however, that in such cases "the right of appeal upon questions of law raised by the pleadings or by an agreed statement of fact or shown by the report of the Board shall not be deemed to be waived."[55]

One should not be misled by the similarity between this statutory language and that in the section relating to the informal procedure.[56] The appellant who has elected the formal procedure but has failed to request a stenographic report is not in exactly the same position as the appellant who has elected the informal procedure. In the former case, the appellant retains his right to review all matters of law save those relating to the admission or exclusion of evidence or whether the finding was supported by substantial evidence;[57] in the latter case the appellant has no right to any review except upon questions of law raised by the pleadings, an agreed statement of fact, or shown by a report of the Board if the Board chooses to make one.[58]

Even if no party requests an official stenographic report of the proceedings, the Board may, on its own motion, have one made. But this will be unofficial and for the Board's own use only. The transcript will not be made available to a party for inspection or for purposes of appeal.

Since 1994, the Board has been authorized by statute to employ transcription methods other than stenographic, including, without limitation, electronic transcription equipment to record its proceedings. When a part requests that the proceedings be officially recorded the choice of methods of recording and transcription is made by the Board.[59]

§ 17.04[18]   Costs of Suit

Normally the Board has discretion to assess only witness fees and service of process fees against the unsuccessful party in any case. In the usual case, these costs, are not awarded.

However, in those cases where the property in question has been before the Board once and the Board has made a determination as to its value, and where the assessors have increased the assessment to an amount greater than that value, if an appeal is taken to the Board for either of the next two fiscal years, then the burden is on the assessors to show that the increased assessment was justified. If the assessors fail to carry this burden, the Board may, in its discretion, award to the

---

[55] G.L. c. 58A, § 10.

[56] G.L. c. 58A, § 7A.

[57] Board of Assessors of Kingston v. Sgarzi, 367 Mass. 840, 329 N.E.2d 121 (1975).

[58] *See* Coomey v. Board of Assessors of Sandwich, 376 Mass. 836, 329 N.E.2d 117 (1975); Board of Assessors of Kingston v. Sgarzi, 367 Mass. 840, 329 N.E.2d 121 (1975).

[59] G.L. c. 58A, § 10; *see also* Rule 28, Rules of Practice of the ATB.

taxpayer all or part of his reasonable expenses in the preparation and trial of the case. On the other hand, if the Board finds that the increase was warranted, it may award the same costs to the assessors.[60]

This provision may have been an attempt by the Legislature to prevent any individual or small group of taxpayers from being harassed by a hostile board of assessors.

APPEALS

§ 17.04[19]   Appeals from Decisions of the Appellate Tax Board

A party aggrieved by a decision of the Appellate Tax Board may appeal to the Appeals Court.[61] Either party may take an appeal as to all questions of law, including the question of whether the evidence as a matter of law will support the Board's decision, unless he has actually or constructively waived his right to appeal as to some questions of law.[62] The Appeals Court cannot consider any question of law which does not appear to have been raised before the Board, with the exception of matters related to the Board's jurisdiction,[63] and the decision of the Board as to findings of fact is final.[64]

Appeals are taken from the Board pursuant to the Massachusetts Rules of Appellate Procedure.[65] Those Rules provide that an appeal is taken by filing a claim of appeal with the clerk of the Tax Board "within 30 days of the date of the entry of the judgment appealed from."[66] However, with respect to appeals from decisions of the Appellate Tax Board of cases heard under the formal procedure, the thirty–day period does not begin to run until the Board files its findings of fact and report, if the same have been requested.[67] Where the case is heard under the informal procedure, the appeal period begins to run when the decision is entered.

Historically the delays between the time a written findings and report is requested and the time it is issued by the Board have been lengthy. A 1999 statutory amendment has imposed time limits of a sort for the issuance of decisions and

---

[60] G.L. c. 58A, § 12A; Johnson v. Board of Assessors of Lunenburg, 14 Mass. App. Tax Bd. Rep. 39 (1992).

[61] G.L. c. 58A, § 13.

[62] G.L. c. 58A, § 13; see also G.L. c. 58A, §§ 7A and 10.

[63] G.L. c. 58A, § 13; see also Coomey v. Board of Assessors of Sandwich, 367 Mass. 836, 329 N.E.2d 117 (1975), and cases cited therein.

[64] New Bedford Gas and Edison Light Co. v. Board of Assessors of Dartmouth, 368 Mass. 745, 335 N.E.2d 897 (1975).

[65] G.L. c. 58A, § 13.

[66] Mass. R. App. P. 4.

[67] Forte Inv. Fund v. State Tax Commission, 369 Mass. 786, 343 N.E.2d 420, at 421, n.1.

findings by the Board. The time limits are as follows:

(a) Where the hearing has not been officially recorded, decision is due three months from the close of evidence, including submission of briefs.

(b) Where the evidence has been officially recorded, decision is due six months from the close of evidence, including the submission of briefs.

(c) In cases heard under the formal procedure, the above time limits for decision apply. But if a timely request for findings and report is made the Board has an additional three months to issue that. In its discretion, the Board may extend this period to six months, upon written notice to the parties setting forth the reason for the extension.

(d) In extraordinary circumstances, or with the consent of all parties, the Board may have an unlimited time to issue its findings and report.[68]

When a party claims an appeal, the clerk of the Tax Board will assemble the record, including the docket sheet, report, and findings of fact and will deliver the same to the clerk of the Appeals Court. Once the case has been entered in the Court, it proceeds as would any other appeal.

§ 17.04[20]   Insuring Full Review on Appeal

The party to a proceeding before the Appellate Tax Board who wishes to preserve his right to the fullest review of the actions of the Board allowed by law must begin with four basic steps:

(1) Elect Formal Procedure

First, if he is the taxpayer, he must make certain that the hearing before the Board is conducted under the formal procedure, since the waiver of comprehensive review is a precondition to the informal procedure.[69]

From the point of view of the assessors their counsel should be certain, if the assessed value of the property which is the subject of the appeal is greater than $20,000, that he exercises his option to elect the formal procedure where the taxpayer has brought the petition under the informal procedure. Failure to do so will result in the assessors being deemed to have waived their right to appeal except upon questions of law raised by the pleadings or by an agreed statement of facts or shown by the report of the Board, if one is made. If the assessed value of the property is $20,000 or less, the assessors cannot elect the formal procedure when the taxpayer files under the informal procedure but they, unlike the taxpayer, will have a right to full review.

---

[68] G.L. c. 58A, § 13.
[69] G.L. c. 58A, § 7A.

Briefly stated, the rule is that in appeal from a decision of the Tax Board of a case heard under the informal procedure is limited to questions of law raised by the pleadings or an agreed statement of facts, or shown by the report of the Board only in those cases where the appellant before the Appeals Court was the appellant before the Tax Board, or where the assessed valuation of the subject property is greater than $20,000 and the assessors did not elect the formal procedure. In all other cases, an appeal as to all matters of law may be taken by any party to the proceedings who has not waived his right to appeal.[70]

(2) Request Stenographic Report

Having taken the first step of insuring, if he can, that the case is heard under the formal procedure, the party desiring to preserve his rights to full appellate review must next be certain he has requested that the hearing before the Board be officially reported by a stenographer. He should also be certain that all requirements of the Board for having such a report made have been satisfied, particularly the requirement that an amount equal to the estimated cost of the report has been deposited with the clerk of the Board.[71] If no stenographic report is requested, then the parties, are deemed to have waived their right to review on questions of the admission or exclusion of evidence or on whether the decision was warranted by the evidence.[72]

Of course, where the hearing has been held under the formal procedure, even if he fails to request a stenographic report of the proceedings before the Board, the party seeking review may still require the Board to make a written report of its findings of fact.[73] If he is unusually fortunate, it may be that the findings will not adequately support the decision. Or it may be that certain documentary evidence introduced before the Board may show the reviewing court that the Board's decision was wrong as a matter of law. So the appellant from a decision made after a hearing under the formal procedure who has neglected to request a stenographic report is in a better position than he would have been had the hearing been held under the informal procedure. But his right to review has nonetheless been drastically circumscribed, and in the very areas where he would have the greatest chance of showing error by the Board.

In cases filed by the taxpayer under the informal procedure where the assessed value of the property is $20,000 or less, counsel for the assessors cannot elect the formal procedure. However, if he or she has some reason to believe that an appeal might be taken in connection with such a low value property, assessors' counsel

---

[70] G.L. c. 58A, § 7A; Board of Assessors of Kingston v. Sgarzi, 367 Mass. 840, 329 N.E.2d 121 (1975); Board of Assessors of Holbrook v. Dennehy, 357 Mass. 243, 258 N.E.2d 31 (1970).

[71] G.L. c. 58A, § 10; Rule 28, Rules of Practice of the ATB.

[72] G.L. c. 58A, § 10; Coomey v. Board of Assessors of Sandwich, 367 Mass. 836, 329 N.E.2d 117 (1975).

[73] G.L. c. 58A, § 13.

should still request a stenographic report of the proceedings in such cases, since failure to do so will prevent the assessors from later challenging the Board's decision on the ground that, as a matter of law, the evidence before the Board did not warrant its finding.[74]

Under the informal procedure the Board is not required to make findings of fact and a report thereon even if the parties request the same.[75] Without a stenographic report, if the Board declines to make a written report of findings the assessors will have only the most limited kind of appellate review. Where there is no statement of agreed facts, report by the Board, or transcript, the entry of a decision by the Board carries the same effect as the entry of a decree by a judge sitting in equity and under the same prior practice when no transcript or report of material facts was made. The decision itself imports a finding of all subsidiary facts necessary to support it. The only question then open on review is the power of the Board to enter a judgment on any evidence which might have been presented.[76]

(3) File Requests for Rulings of Law

Having elected the formal procedure where possible, and having requested and met the requirements for a stenographic report of the proceedings, the party desiring to preserve his right to full review must next be sure that all questions of law which he wishes to have reviewed by the Supreme Judicial Court are shown on the record to have been raised before the Tax Board.[77] The proper way to do this is to file appropriate and timely requests for rulings with the Board.[78] An obvious analogy is to the steps the attorney takes at the trial of a civil matter in the District Court in order to lay the foundation for an appeal to the Appellate Division of that Court.

(4) Request Report by the Board

Finally, the party intending to seek review should request, within ten days after the Board makes its decision, that the Board make findings of fact and a written report thereon if the decision is not accompanied by findings of fact. It should be noted that if the hearing is held under the formal procedure, and none of the parties makes a request for findings and report, then the Board is required only to make

---

[74] Board of Assessors of Kingston v. Sgarzi, 367 Mass. 840, 329 N.E.2d 121 (1975); Coomey v. Board of Assessors of Sandwich, 367 Mass. 836, 329 N.E.2d 117 (1975); *see also* Carlson v. Board of Assessors of Topsfield, 389 Mass. 1004, 453 N.E.2d 380 (1983), which holds that Rule 8(c) of the Mass. R. App. P. may not be used to remedy the lack of reported evidence.

[75] G.L. c. 58A, § 13. Leen v. Board of Assessors of Boston, 345 Mass. 494, 188 N.E.2d 460 (1963); Board of Assessors of Saugus v. Leo, 363 Mass. 47, 292 N.E.2d 676 (1973).

[76] Board of Assessors of Kingston v. Sgarzi, 367 Mass. 840, 329 N.E.2d 121 (1975).

[77] Assessors of Everett v. Albert N. Parlin House, Inc. , 331 Mass. 359, 118 N.E.2d 861 (1954).

[78] Beardsley v. Board of Assessors of Foxborough, 369 Mass. 855, 343 N.E.2d 359 (1976). *See also* Rule 29, Rules of Practice of the ATB.

a decision and may or may not make a report of findings, in its discretion.[79] If such report is not requested and is not in fact made by the Board, then the parties are again deemed to have waived all right to review upon questions as to the admission or exclusion of evidence or as to whether a finding was warranted by the evidence.[80]

In summary then, the decisions of the Board as to findings of fact are final, its decisions or questions of law are reviewable but will be considered by the Court only where: (a) the issue appears to have been raised before the Board, (b) the Board has made findings and a written report thereon, and (c) the record contains all the evidence which is necessary for the Court to consider the question.[81]

§ 17.04[21]　Evidence Necessary to Sustain the Decision of the Board on Appeal

In excess of 95% of all cases brought to the Tax Board turn on the question of the proper valuation of a piece of property. This is almost invariably a question of fact. Since by statute[82] the decision of the Board is final as to findings of fact, the most likely avenue of appeal of a party aggrieved by a decision of the Board will be one based on a claim that the Board's finding of fact as to value was not supported by sufficient evidence as a matter of law.[83] The following discussion deals with the problem of just how much evidence is legally sufficient to support the Board's finding as to value in any given instance.

Prior to 1968, review of decisions of the Appellate Tax Board was governed by the provisions of the State Administrative Procedure Act,[84] which required that its decisions be supported by "substantial evidence."[85] Substantial evidence is defined by the Act as "such evidence as a reasonable mind might accept as adequate to support a conclusion."[86]

However, in 1968, G.L. c. 30A was amended so as to exempt the Board from

---

[79] G.L. c. 58A, § 13. However, *see* Board of Assessors of New Braintree v. Pioneer Valley Academy, Inc., 358 Mass. 610, 246 N.E.2d 792 (1969), where the Court said that in cases likely to be appealed the Board should find facts upon which it relies to support its conclusions and report the same, even if neither party so requests, in order to enable the Court to decide justly the issues presented to it.

[80] *Id.*

[81] Beardsley v. Board of Assessors of Foxborough, 369 Mass. 855, 343 N.E.2d 359, at 360, n.3.

[82] G.L. c. 58A, § 13.

[83] New Bedford Gas and Edison Light Co. v. Board of Dartmouth, 368 Mass. 745, 335 N.E.2d 897 (1975); Singer Sewing Machine Co. v. Assessors of Boston, 341 Mass. 513, 170 N.E.2d 687 (1961).

[84] G.L. c. 30A, §§ 1 *et seq.*

[85] G.L. c. 30A, § 14(8)(e).

[86] G.L. c. 30A, § 1(6).

the Administrative Procedure Act,[87] thus eliminating the statutory requirements against which previous Board decisions had been measured. The Supreme Judicial Court responded by, in effect, reenacting the "substantial evidence" language, quoted above, in its decisions. In *New Bedford Gas and Edison Light Co. v. Board of Assessors of Dartmouth*,[88] the Court said that, even though it was no longer subject to the Administrative Procedure Act, the Board was still bound by the "general principles affecting administrative decisions and judicial review of them. In accordance with such principles, findings of fact by the Board must be supported by substantial evidence."

Of course there is a great deal of difference between knowing that the decision of the Board must, as a matter of law, always be supported by substantial evidence and knowing if the evidence in one's own particular case is "substantial" enough to support the Board's decision on appeal.

The taxpayer may attack the valuation of the assessors either by exposing flaws or errors in their methods, and/or by introducing affirmative evidence of value which undermines the assessors' valuation.[89] In making its report of findings of fact, the Board is not permitted simply to find the ultimate facts in the case. Instead, it must find the supporting subsidiary facts and set forth reasons for its conclusions.[90] However, the Board is not required to specify the exact manner in which it reaches its conclusions.[91] Yet it must be sufficiently specific as to the subsidiary facts it finds, its calculations, and the reasons for its conclusions so that "appellate review is meaningful."[92] In arriving at its decision, it may believe only portions of the testimony of each witness, so that its conclusions do not coincide with any one witness or party, and its decision may still be found to be supported by substantial evidence.[93] This is so, says the Supreme Judicial Court, because the "value of property must ultimately rest in the realm of opinion, estimate and judgment."[94] On the other hand, unrebutted and corroborated testimony may not be rejected without a basis for such rejection in the record. "If the proponent has presented the best available evidence which is logically adequate, and is neither

---

[87] St. 1968, c. 120.

[88] 368 Mass. 745, 335 N.E.2d 897 (1975); *see also* Schlaiker v. Board of Assessors of Great Barrington, 310 N.E.2d 602 (1974).

[89] Donlon v. Assessors of Holliston, 389 Mass. 848, 453 N.E.2d 395 (1983).

[90] Board of Assessors of Lynnfield v. New England Oyster House, Inc. , 362 Mass. 696, 290 N.E.2d 520 (1972); Leen v. Board of Assessors of Boston, 345 Mass. 494, 188 N.E.2d 460 (1963).

[91] Board of Assessors of Lynnfield v. New England Oyster House, Inc. , 362 Mass. 696, 290 N.E.2d 520 (1972); Leen v. Board of Assessors of Boston, 345 Mass. 494, 188 N.E.2d 460 (1963).

[92] Alstores Realty Corp. v. Board of Assessors of Peabody, 391 Mass. 60, 460 N.E.2d 1276 (1984).

[93] Assessors of Quincy v. Boston Consol. Gas Co., 309 Mass. 60, 34 N.E.2d 623 (1941); Jordan Marsh Co. v. Board of Assessors of Malden, 359 Mass. 106, 267 N.E.2d 912 (1971).

[94] Jordan Marsh Co. v. Board of Assessors of Malden, 359 Mass. 106, 267 N.E.2d 912 (1971).

contradicted nor improbable, it must be credited..."[95] And, disbelief of any particular evidence does not constitute substantial evidence to the contrary.[96]

These rules are based on familiar principles of appellate review. The reviewing court is always going to be reluctant to disturb the factual conclusions of the trial court, and the appellant who bases his appeal on the claim that the Board's decision is not supported by substantial evidence should be prepared to carry a very heavy burden if he expects to prevail. Just how heavy that burden can be is illustrated by two cases.

In *Board of Assessors of Holbrook v. Dennehey,*[97] the assessors appealed a decision of the Board granting an abatement on a single family residence. The only evidence supporting the $12,000 valuation determined by the Board was the owner's opinion that this was the value of the property. The Court held that since the owner of property assumed, under long standing common law principles, to be able to estimate intelligently the value of his property, his opinion was competent evidence sufficient to support the Board's decision.

(In the *Dennehey* case, the Court refers to "evidence" rather than "substantial evidence" in its discussion of what is necessary to sustain the Board's decision. With all due deference to common law principles, it is suggested that the opinion of an owner involved in a tax abatement proceeding as to the value of his property is perhaps not the kind of "evidence" that reasonable minds would accept, in and of itself, as sufficient to form the basis of a decision.)

In another case, *Schlaiker v. Board of Assessors of Great Barrington,*[98] the taxpayer was appealing a decision of the Board sustaining the valuation placed on his property by the assessors. The language of the decision indicates that there was very little creditable and competent evidence adduced at the hearing before the Board in support of the assessor's valuation figure, while the taxpayer introduced extensive testimony from a qualified appraisal expert in support of his position. Because of technical flaws the Board found in the methodology of the taxpayer's expert, it discounted the testimony determined by the assessors. In response to the taxpayer's argument on appeal that the Board's decision was not supported by substantial evidence, the Supreme Judicial Court said that it was indeed true that decisions of the Board were required as a general rule to be supported by substantial evidence. However, where the Board concludes that the taxpayer has offered no persuasive evidence whatsoever in support of his position it may find against him

---

[95] New Boston Garden Corp. v. Board of Assessors of Boston, 383 Mass. 456, 420 N.E.2d 298 (1981).

[96] Salisbury Water Supply Co. v. Department of Public Utilities, 344 Mass. 716, 184 N.E.2d 44 (1962).

[97] 357 Mass. 243, 258 N.E.2d 31 (1970).

[98] 310 N.E.2d 602 (1974).

even though the assessors have offered no evidence at all. This is so, said the Court, because a conclusion that the presumptively correct valuation of the assessors must stand is not such an affirmative finding as to require substantial evidence to support it.[99]

This principle is applicable not only when the assessors test the adequacy of the taxpayer's case by declining to present any evidence when the taxpayer rests, but also when the assessors present their own affirmative evidence that is disbelieved by the Board.[100]

It is clear from the language of the *Schlaiker* decision, which refers in a number of places to the taxpayer's failure to "sustain the burden of proof" that the "presumption" of validity which attaches to the valuation of the assessors is one of that class of presumptions which are the strongest of all the rebuttable presumptions.

These are referred to as presumptions which allocate the burden of proof by one writer,[101] and as continuing presumptions by another.[102] However denominated, they describe situations where the introduction of some evidence contrary to the presumption does not nullify or neutralize the effect of the presumption. Instead, the presumption continues with full vitality until the party with the burden of proof proves it wrong by at least a fair preponderance of credible evidence, even where the other party introduces no evidence in support of it.[103]

In some kinds of civil cases, the Massachusetts courts have imposed an even greater burden of proof than that of a fair preponderance of the evidence. In such cases, the standard of proof required seems to be somewhere between fair preponderance and the criminal standard of reasonable doubt. Phrases such as "full, clear and decisive" or "clear and convincing" are used to describe this standard.[104] It is submitted that the *Schlaiker* case and the *Judson Freight Forwarding Co.* case,[105] cited therein, use language which at least implies the imposition of this

---

[99] Schlaiker v. Board of Assessors of Great Barrington, 310 N.E.2d 602, at 604 n.2; *Accord*: Northwest Assoc. v. Board of Assessors of Burlington, 392 Mass. 593, 467 N.E.2d 176 (1984). *See also* Hampton Associates v. Board of Assessors of Northampton, 52 Mass. App. Ct. 110, 751 N.E.2d 437 (2001) (principle applicable when assessors test adequacy of taxpayer's case by declining to present any evidence when taxpayer rests and when assessors present their own affirmative evidence, thus even if board relied on assessor's opinion after concluding that taxpayer had not met its burden, that reliance would not invalidate ultimate decision in assessors' favor).

[100] Hampton Assoc. v. Board of Assessors of Northhampton, 52 Mass. App. 110 (2001).

[101] Liacos, Brodin and Avery, Handbook of Massachusetts Evidence (6th ed. 1994), at 229.

[102] Swartz, Trial Handbook for Massachusetts Lawyers (1972), at §§ 207–210.

[103] Rocha v. Alber, 302 Mass. 155, 18 N.E.2d 1018 (1939).

[104] *See* Swartz, Trial Handbook for Massachusetts Lawyers (1972), § 101, and cases cited therein.

[105] Judson Freight Forwarding Co. v. Commonwealth, 242 Mass. 47, 136 N.E. 375 (1922).

higher burden of proof on taxpayers who wish to overcome the presumptive validity of the assessors' valuation. Those cases require that the taxpayer make out his right to abatement of the tax "as a matter of law."[106] The use of the quoted phrase and the actual disposition of the issue on appeal in the *Schlaiker* case certainly imply at least the requirement of very high standard of proof from the taxpayer.[107]

So what does this mean for the practitioner? It means that, technically speaking, when the taxpayer and the assessors go before the Tax Board it is not a situation where each side begins on an equal footing and tries to convince the Board that its determination as to value is the proper one; rather, it is a situation where the taxpayer must make a showing that the valuation of the assessors is plainly wrong. The assessors, on the other hand, need offer no evidence at all in support of their position and they may still prevail; and if they do offer evidence in support of their position, the presumption of validity is there to reinforce their case.[108]

It may be argued that this is an overly technical and unrealistic view of the proceedings before the Board, and that in fact the Board will approach the average case without any overpowering bias in favor of the valuation figure of the assessors. However that may, be, the subject of this discussion is the amount of evidence necessary to sustain a decision of the Board on appeal Or, looked at another way, it is a discussion of when the attorney who has lost before the Board may reasonably believe he has a chance of overturning the Board on appeal based on the claim that the decision was not supported by substantial evidence. In such circumstances, the workings of these rather technical rules about presumptions become quite important.

So, if the attorney has lost before the Board, after a hearing in which he introduced two or three times as much substantial evidence as the assessors or in which the assessors offered virtually no evidence, he should not begin the appeal process sure and certain as to his eventual vindication. Instead, he should ask himself whether it appears from the record below that he made a clear and convincing showing before the Board that the valuation of the assessors was incorrect, and whether that showing was based on competent, credible oral and written testimony that was accepted by the Board, or at least not specifically rejected by it. He should answer these questions calmly and dispassionately, giving

---

[106] Judson Freight Forwarding Co. v. Commonwealth, 242 Mass. 47, 136 N.E. 375, at 379.

[107] One may legitimately wonder whether the taxpayer in *Dennehy* in fact met the burden of proof imposed by the Court on the taxpayer in *Schlaiker*.

[108] At the end of taxpayer's case, the assessors may test its sufficiency by a motion to dismiss similar to that provided for in 801 CMR 1.01(7)(d)(1). If such motion is denied, the assessors have the option of resting and then appealing on the sole issue of whether the taxpayer has met his or her burden of production. If the assessors offer evidence after the denial of such a motion then they waive any right to appellate review of that denial. General Electric Co. v. Board of Assessors of Lynn, 393 Mass. 591, 472 N.E.2d 1329 (1984).

no thought to the amount or quality of the evidence presented by the assessors in support of their position. Only then should he decide whether or not to take an appeal based on the contention that the decision of the Board was not warranted by the evidence.[109]

In short, it should be clearly understood by counsel that, except in those few cases where there has been a clear error of law by the Board, or where its decision is against the overwhelming weight of evidence, the chances of overturning its decision on appeal would have to be described as poor.[110]

APPRAISAL THEORY: GENERAL PRINCIPLES

§ 17.05   Introduction[1]

The question at the center of every abatement petition is: What is the proper amount of tax to be levied on this property? Since the property tax is a tax based on value, that question becomes what is the proper valuation of this property for tax purposes?

A body of theory has been developed defining the proper methods of determining the value of a parcel of real estate. This body of theory, known as real estate appraisal theory, provides the foundation and background upon, and against which, the abatement proceedings are set. However, it should be clearly understood that the Massachusetts courts have not imported the whole body of traditional real estate theory, pure and intact, into the common law. Instead, that theory has been modified, even in some cases distorted, to fit the exigencies of local assessing practices, judicial prejudices or decisional precedent.

Nonetheless, the attorney who wishes to represent his client effectively in a real estate tax abatement matter should have a firm grasp on the fundamentals and the language of appraisal theory. It is recommended that this chapter and the following chapter, dealing with valuation theory in the courts, be read together.

---

[109] It perhaps should be emphasized, at least parenthetically, that counsel who contemplates an appeal on the ground that the decision of the Board was not warranted by the evidence should be certain to file a Request for Ruling to this effect before the Board. This is, after all, a question of law which must be raised before the Board in order to be reviewed on appeal. *See* G.L. c. 58A, § 13.

[110] *See, e.g.*, Olympia & York State Street Co. v. Assessors of Boston, 428 Mass. 236 (1998).

[1] *See generally* as to all matters in this chapter: The Appraisal of Real Estate, American Institute of Real Estate Appraisers, Chicago, Illinois; *see also* The Valuation of Real Estate (2d ed. 1970) by Alfred A. Ring, Prentice-Hall, Inc. , Englewood Cliffs, N.H.; and Encyclopedia of Real Estate Appraising, Edith J. Friedman ed., Prentice-Hall, Inc. 1968.

§ 17.05[1]   The Concept of Highest and Best Use

A fundamental concept of real estate appraisal is that of the highest and best use of land. Appraisal theory assumes that any given parcel of land, whether developed or not, only has one highest and best use.

In beginning any evaluation, whether of land or land and buildings, and no matter which of the valuation methods he is using, it is necessary for the appraiser to determine what is the highest and best use of the land involved. This use is defined in various terms by different writers, but the essence of all these definitions is the same. What is sought to be determined is that use of the land whereby it is developed to the maximal economically feasible extent.

In short, the appraiser is supposed to determine whether if a different kind of structure were put on the land the percentage return on the total investment would be higher. For example, is a pig farm, representing a total investment of $30,000 and producing a net income of $1,500 or 5%, located on prime commercial property? Could a commercial structure be erected on the property for $1,000,000 which would produce a net income of $100,000 or 10%? If the answer is yes, then the pig farm is not the highest and best use of the land.

In economic terms, the highest and best use of land occurs at the point where the law of diminishing returns takes effect: that is, when an additional dollar invested in development will yield only that amount of return necessary to offset the investment.

In making a determination as to highest and best use, the appraiser must take no cognizance of what, if anything, is already on the land. When land is overimproved or underimproved in relation to its highest and best use a charge must be made against the value of the improvements, as a form of depreciation or obsolescence. If the appraiser goes ahead and values an improved property without dealing with the problem of the highest and best use of the land, his report will be seriously flawed.

In abatement cases tried before the Tax Board, the real estate expert will usually be asked about his understanding of highest and best use as he is being qualified by the party calling him. It is also common for a real estate expert to state in his testimony whether or not the present use of the particular property is its highest and best use. However, in the case of real estate taxation, unlike that of eminent domain, more lip service is paid to the concept of highest and best use than anything else.

Under Massachusetts law, in any case, highest and best use is to be considered only for its bearing on the market value of a property. In practice, the assessors and the Appellate Tax Board concern themselves with the proper valuation and taxation of what is in fact there, rather than hypothesizing about what is not there.

Only in the case of egregious over- or under-improvement would highest and best use become an important factor in an abatement case.[2]

§ 17.05[2] Replacement Cost

Replacement cost in appraisal theory is the expense necessary to create a property which would satisfy the same wants as the property being valued. This cost is considered to be the absolute ceiling of value of the subject property, based on the fairly obvious proposition that no one will pay any more for the property than he could have to spend to replace it. It functions as a check on the generally accepted valuation methods discussed below, because if one of these methods is applied to the property and yields a value higher than the replacement cost, such a value could be given little weight.

FOUR METHODS OF VALUATION

§ 17.05[3] Generally

There are a great many methods employed by real estate appraisers to determine the value of real estate; far too many to discuss here. The most common, and most generally accepted are: (1) the market sales comparison method, which involves analyzing a number of recent sales of properties comparable to the one being valued; (2) the capitalization of income method, which involves determining the total value in present dollars of the net income which the building can be expected to generate over its useful life; (3) the depreciated reproduction cost method, which involves estimating the cost to reproduce the building new, and then reducing that cost figure by an amount which reflects the loss in value suffered by the property as a result of physical, functional and economic obsolescence, in order to arrive at present value; and (4) the gross income multiplier method, which is a shorthand formula for converting the income generated by a property into a sum representing its market value.

§ 17.05[4] The Market Sales Comparison Method[3]

The market sales comparison method requires that the appraiser locate, verify and analyze a number of relatively recent sales of properties comparable to the one being valued. These are referred to as index properties. In choosing properties as index sales, the appraiser attempts to find properties which are as physically comparable to the property being valued as is possible. The appraiser next has to examine the circumstances of each of the index sales to see if there were any unusual factors affecting the prices. Among the factors which can make the price

---

[2] Ford v. Worcester, 339 Mass. 657, 162 N.E.2d 264 (1959).
[3] Ring, op. cit., n.1, p. 131.

of a piece of property higher or lower than the appraiser might expect are: a family relationship between buyer and seller, the condition of the market at the time of sale (real estate being a very cyclical business), and the fact that the sale occurred a number of years ago. If such factors exist the index property sale price must be adjusted to reflect them.

Once this adjustment is made, the appraiser should next adjust the index sale prices to reflect differences in lot and building size, quality of construction, aesthetics and neighborhood characteristics between the index properties and the property being valued. For example, if the sale price of the index property was $20,000 but it had been sold two years ago, its price might be adjusted upward 15% to reflect inflation. Similarly, if the index property had a much larger lot than the property being valued, then its price would have to be adjusted downward to reflect this.

Disagreements frequently arise among appraisers as to the proper way to make these adjustments. Generally speaking, there are two approaches. The first approach is very specific and detailed. Here, the appraiser analyzes each construction detail of the property being valued and each construction detail of each index property. Then a comparison is made between the index properties and the subject property with respect to each detail. Appropriate positive or negative adjustments are then made to the sale price of the index property, depending upon whether the construction of that detail is better or worse in the index property than in the property being valued.

The second adjustment approach is more general, less expensive, and more commonly used. Here, the appraiser only examines the overall features of each property, such as lot size, location, age, amenities, condition and so forth. He then rates each of these factors comparatively between the various index properties and the subject property, making positive or negative percentage adjustments to the sale prices of the index properties based on whether the index property is better or worse than the subject property in each of the broad categories. Remember that the purpose of these adjustments is to make the index properties as comparable to the property being valued as possible.

Once the index prices have been adjusted to reflect the differences between the various properties, whether by the specific or the general method, the final step is to weight the various index prices. This is accomplished by multiplying the index prices, as adjusted, by a percentage factor, which is chosen based on the degree of similarity or dissimilarity of the index properties to the subject property.

The choice of correlation factors is entirely within the judgment of the appraiser, as are the adjustments to the various index sale prices. As a general rule, the more the appraiser has had to adjust the index sale price to reflect the differences between the index property and the property being valued, the lower should be the correlation factor of that sale.

The strengths and weaknesses of this valuation approach are fairly apparent. The use of arms-length sales of similar properties as standards of value is the best feature of the method. The discretion given to the appraiser in weighing the necessary adjustments and in weighing the sales is its most serious weakness.

§ 17.05[5]　The Cost Minus Depreciation Method (Depreciated Reproduction Cost)[4]

In the second commonly accepted method of real property valuation, the appraiser develops a valuation figure by first determining the cost of replacing the property new, and then subtracting the estimated accrued depreciation from that cost to arrive at the value of the property in its present state.

A great deal of confusion in discussions of this method is caused by the terms "replacement cost" and "reproduction cost." Although court decisions, and even the literature of appraisal, often use these terms interchangeably, they properly refer to two distinct concepts. "Reproduction cost" refers to the expense which would have to be incurred in order to produce an exact replica of the building being valued. "Replacement cost," on the other hand, is defined as the expense which would have to be incurred to create a building having the same amenities and economic utility.[5]

For example, if a nineteenth century building with twenty-four inch thick walls and ten foot thick concrete footings were being valued, reproduction cost would have to include the cost of actually recreating these archaic construction features, even though they would never in practice be used in modern construction.

If, instead, the replacement cost for such a building were to be developed it would only include the cost of constructing a similar building using the latest construction methods, substituting, for instance, eight or ten inch ferro-concrete walls for two foot brick ones.

When the appraiser begins with reproduction cost he must add to the estimate of accrued depreciation a charge against the value of the property to account for the obsolescent construction. The actual amount which must be subtracted from the value of the building because of obsolescence is always a judgment call on the part of the appraiser.

If the appraiser uses replacement cost instead he avoids the uncertainty involved in assigning a dollar value to obsolete construction features and is able to rely on a relatively more certain estimate of the cost of building a modern building using modern methods. If the appraiser uses replacement cost instead of reproduction cost he must be careful not to include an allowance for obsolete construction when he

---

[4]　Ring, op. cit., chapters 11, 12 and 13.
[5]　Ring, op. cit., p. 45.

develops his estimate of accrued depreciation, since he has already accounted for this in developing his cost figure.

§ 17.05[6]　Replacement Cost

In applying the cost less depreciation method, the appraiser must begin by having an engineer or construction expert estimate the replacement cost of the building in current dollars. One way he may do this is by compiling a complete inventory of every item of material and labor which would go into a replacement or reproduction building, assigning a cost to each, and then adding up all these costs to arrive at a value for the building.

A less cumbersome method is to determine the cost per square foot of recently completed similar buildings and multiply this unit cost by the number of square feet in the building being valued. However the tendency of each building to be unique as well any passage of time since the completion of the index building can cause problems with this latter method.[6] To alleviate these problems, attempts have been made to develop "standard unit costs" for a typical or "base" building of each common type: apartment, single family, industrial, and so forth.

Using these standard unit costs as a starting point, the construction expert then attempts, by making adjustments, depending on the deviation of the subject building from the base building, to develop an appropriate unit cost for the subject building. There are various commercial cost services available which provide current information, on a regional basis, with respect to the unit cost of typical industrial and commercial buildings. The F. W. Dodge Division of McGraw-Hill Co. is probably the most prominent of these.

§ 17.05[7]　Accrued Depreciation

Once the replacement cost has been established it is necessary to derive a dollar value for accrued depreciation, which can then be subtracted to arrive at present value.

Loss in present value, from any cause, as measured by the difference between replacement cost in current dollars and the market value of the same property, is classified as depreciation.

It is axiomatic that an estimate of value via the cost approach is no more accurate than the underlying estimate of accrued depreciation, for it is this estimate that converts the fairly objective measure of cost into the measure of value that will be utilized by investors, assessors and courts. Unfortunately, this estimate is very dependent on the subjective judgment and experience of the appraiser.

---

[6] *See* Board of Assessors of Lynnfield v. New England Oyster House, Inc. , 362 Mass. 696, 290 N.E.2d 520 (1972).

Accrued depreciation can be estimated by the engineering observation approach, or by the accounting/mathematical approach. In using the accounting method, the appraiser first chooses one of the systems of asset write-off that have been developed for bookkeeping purposes and applies this to the property being valued. He notes the age of the property, and looks to see where on the depreciation curve applicable to the chosen accounting method that age falls. He will then be able to ascertain what percentage of the cost new will have been depreciated at the point in the property's life at which the appraisal is being done. For example, if the straight-line method of depreciation is chosen and the building is ten years old, with a total useful life of thirty years, then accrued depreciation will be one-third of the cost new.

Most appraising authorities caution against the use of this method, on the ground that straight line, sum-of-the-years-digits and the other depreciation conventions of accounting were developed as ways of amortizing an investment for bookkeeping purposes rather than to measure the actual decline in value of a particular asset. Clearly if an appraiser is going to use one of these methods he should try to choose the one that conforms most closely to the economic life cycle of the property itself. Thus, if the property tends to depreciate at a very even rate throughout its life, it would be most inappropriate to use an accelerated depreciation method to estimate accrued depreciation.

When the appraiser is using the preferred method of actual observation to estimate accrued depreciation, a construction expert must actually go to the site to see how much physical deterioration has set in and to estimate the cost of labor and materials necessary to restore the property. The appraiser must also estimate the loss in value due to obsolescence caused by outmoded facilities, such as exceptionally high ceilings, poorly planned wall or window layout, old fashioned toilets or exposed plumbing, and how much it would cost to correct those problems. Finally, he must estimate the loss in value due to incurable deterioration or obsolescence and to legal, environmental, sociological and economic changes which have affected the property.

The depreciated reproduction cost method is extremely difficult to apply in practice and is most useful when the property being valued is of fairly standard design. It is considered to be the weakest of the commonly accepted valuation methods.

§ 17.05[8]   The Capitalization of Income Method

Although all methods of real property valuation are as much art as science, the capitalization of income method is believed by many to be the most reliable of all, particularly with respect to investment or income property. It is the method most often relied on in tax abatement cases. This method begins with the assumption, common to all modern financial analysis, that when a person buys investment property, whether it be a corporate bond or an apartment building, what he is actually buying is the right to receive the future income stream which will be generated by that property. If this is the case, then it follows that the value of the property to the prospective purchaser will be exactly equal to the value of that income stream. So one simply uses the mathematics of finance to determine the capitalized, or present value of the future income flows and assigns this amount as the value of the property.

The crucial thing to remember about the capitalization method is that it is based on the premise that, over the useful life of the property, an investor wishes to receive an amount of income sufficient to return his investment to him and to pay him a fair return on the money he has invested. The property may be compared to a trust fund or bank account in this respect. At the end of an accounting period one expects to have his principal intact as well as a certain amount of interest. (Naturally, the investor expects a greater return from the relatively more risky real estate investment than he does from a bank account.) The capitalization method, in essence, is merely a mathematical measurement of the amount of money a reasonable and prudent real estate investor would pay to own the right to receive the income to be generated by a piece of property over its useful life.

In utilizing this method, there are three areas where the appraiser must exercise his judgment and knowledge of the particular type of property involved. First, he must estimate the net income that the property will generate over each of the remaining years of its useful life. To do this he must determine, through market knowledge, the appropriate gross rental the building may be expected to generate. From this amount he subtracts the appropriate allowances for vacancies, collection losses, reserves for the replacement of capital equipment, and normal operating expenses. (Note that the taxing authorities will only allow expenses to be deducted to the extent that they are within industry norms.) The amount remaining after these deductions will be the net income figure which will be capitalized to yield the value of the property.[7] The following is a simplified income and expense statement of the type used in real property appraisal:

Revenue	$28,000
Less: Vacancy and Collection Losses — 5%	1,400
Effective Gross Revenue	26,600
Operating Expenses:	
Fixed:	
Taxes[8]	3,000

---

[7] *See* Ring, op. cit., p. 223.

Insurance	500
Variable:	
Management — 10%	2,800
Janitor	3,000
Heat	1,600
Water	150
Electricity	350
Misc. — Supplies	100
Misc. — Repairs	250
Reserve for Repairs and Replacements:	
Appliances, Fixtures, Carpets, etc.	3,000
Total Expenses	$14,750
Net Income before depreciation and interest expense:	$13,250

Note that interest expense on the mortgage, while a legitimate expense for accounting and income tax purposes, should not be included as a deduction from net income for valuation purposes. The reason for this is that what is sought to be determined is the ability of the property to generate income. The financial arrangements that any particular owner has had to make to purchase the property are irrelevant for these purposes. Mortgage interest is thus a personal expense of the owner, not a legitimate charge against the income-generating capacity of the property.

Note also that the vacancy and collection allowance of 5% of gross revenue is a standard deduction among real estate professionals when they estimate potential revenue. However, some assessors will require that the actual revenue from the preceding year be used rather than subtracting the 5% vacancy allowance from the total potential revenue. If the preceding year was atypical, then such a practice can have a very distortive effect on ultimate valuation. Also, the practitioner should be aware that the various real estate owners' trade associations publish annual surveys of standard expenses for various types of properties. To the extent that the expenses on a property exceed these averages the assessors may disallow them.

The hazards involved in projecting the income and expenses likely to be associated with a piece of property over a period of twenty years will be apparent to anyone. Attempts are often made to adjust the expected income flows to reflect the fact that as it ages a building tends to generate less rent and to cost more to keep up. This kind of adjusting can of course easily turn the whole process into mere guesswork.

---

[8] When income/expense statements are drafted for tax purposes no deduction is made for real estate taxes. Instead, a tax factor is added to the capitalization rate.

Fortunately, in the case of investment real estate we have a relatively stable kind of property with a lot of history on which to base projections of future income flows. So a study of the income life cycles of similarly situated properties should give the appraiser a reasonably sound foundation from which to make his projections.

Having determined the projected income flows, the appraiser must then determine the appropriate rate at which these flows should be capitalized, the capitalization process being the way that an estimated future income flow is converted into a sum of present value. In order to capitalize an income flow one divides the yearly net income by a predetermined capitalization rate. For example, in the income and expense statement above the yearly net income was $13,250. If the proper capitalization rate is determined to be 10%, then $13,250/.10 = $132,500 (the value of the property).

§ 17.05[8][a]   Capitalization Rate[9]

The capitalization rate is a percentage which is the sum of the percentage interest rate and the percentage rate at which the investment is to be depreciated. For example, a depreciation rate of 3% and an interest rate of 5% will give a capitalization rate of 8%. Both of the component rates are determined by the appraiser in his best judgment. There are well defined parameters within which that judgment must operate, but the fact remains that the choice of the appropriate capitalization rate is an area of common disagreement between appraisers, especially when they are hired by rival interests. The significance of the capitalization rate can be seen in the following example: If a building generates $1,000 per year in net income and the capitalization rate is 8%, it will be valued at $12,500; if the rate is 10%, the value will be only $10,000. ($1,000/.08 = $12,500) ($1,00/.10 = $10,000).

§ 17.05[8][b]   Interest Rate

The interest rate is the wage paid for the use of money. This wage is determined by supply and demand in general, and specifically by the myriad factors that affect our capital markets over both the long and short term. The basic or floor interest rate would be that paid on Treasury Bills or guaranteed deposits in savings institutions. This is the rate of return which can be earned on a completely liquid, riskless investment that requires no management expense or expertise.

The interest rate charged for the use of funds invested in properties which are more or less illiquid, entail some degree of risk, and require some management, would go up commensurately as the risk, illiquidity and management requirements

---

[9] Ring, op. cit., p. 232. One occasionally sees the capitalization rate called, incorrectly, the interest rate.

went up. So, if the interest rate of Treasury Bills or in the local bank is 5%, and if the rate of return on highly speculative oil drilling ventures is 20%, then the appraiser must decide where in this range of risk the real estate he is evaluating fits.

There are a number of methods for doing this currently in use by professional appraisers. For the most part these methods require that the appraiser have an in depth knowledge of the various rates of interest prevailing in the marketplace with respect to properties such as the one he is evaluating.

For instance, in one of the accepted methods for determining the proper interest rate, the Board of Investment Method, the appraiser develops a weighted, average interest cost which reflects as nearly as possible conditions prevailing in capital markets with respect to the financing requirements of properties similar to the one being evaluated. This weighted rate is then assigned as the interest component of the capitalization rate. For example, if the appraiser knew that first mortgages on comparable properties could be obtained at interest rates of 8% for amounts up to 70% of value, that second mortgages could be obtained at rates of 10% for up to 15% of value and that the return on equity capital required by owners of similar properties was 16%, he would develop the weighted interest rate as follows:

$$.70 \times .10 = .056$$
$$.15 \times .10 = .015$$
$$.15 \times .16 = .024$$

Average .095

The interest rate used for capitalization purposes would thus be 9.5% in the foregoing example. Other methods of deriving the appropriate interest rate are similar amalgams of appraiser knowledge and judgment.[10] For instance, in the Summation Method the interest rate might be derived as follows:

6.0%—Rate for safe investment
1.0%—For lack of liquidity
1.0%—For need for management
1.5%—For risk
9.5% Interest Rate

In the Market Data Method the appraiser tries to locate a number of recent sales of similar property, discover the sale prices and net incomes of the properties, and from this deduce the correct capitalization rate and interest rate.

It will be seen that the first two methods are somewhat subjective, while the third

---

[10] *See* Ring, op. cit., p. 243.

will only be able to be used in those very unusual situations where the necessary information is available.

§ 17.05[8][c]   Depreciation Rate

Since land does not depreciate it is not necessary to include a depreciation factor when the income which it produces is capitalized. The interest rate and the capitalization rate are thus the same, so one simply divides the appropriate interest rate into the annual income attributable to the land to derive the capitalized value (Income = $5,000; Interest rate = 9%; Value $5,000/.09 = $45,000). Only when valuing improvements to the land, which have a finite life, is it necessary to add a depreciation factor to the interest rate in order to get the capitalization rate. Logically then, when the appraiser values property composed of both land and improvements, he should capitalize the income flows attributable to the land and buildings separately and then add the results to determine the total value of the property. Or, he must develop a weighted overall capitalization rate.[11]

In appraisal practice, only three methods of depreciation calculation are in common use: the straight line, sinking fund and annuity methods. The use of one of these methods by the appraiser is made even more likely by the fact that each of the three so-called "factor tables" which have been developed for appraisers is based on one of these methods.

The basis of depreciation theory is that, in addition to receiving a "wage," in the form of interest, for the use of his money, the investor should also recover back the entire amount of his original investment over the period of useful life of the property, just as he would have if he had invested the money in a bank account. The assumption is that a portion of each installment of net income which the property generates is a partial repayment of the owner's original investment.

A problem, and potential disagreement, arises when it is attempted to determine how much of each income installment should be allocated to depreciation. Obviously the larger the amount allocated to depreciation, the less will remain to be allocated as a return on investment and, ultimately, the lower the valuation of the property.

Generally speaking, the straight line method results in the largest charge against income, the sinking fund method results in the next largest, and the annuity method in the least.

§ 17.05[8][c][i]   Straight Line Depreciation

The straight line method is applied by first dividing the number of years of useful

---

[11] *See* § 8.05[9], *supra*.

life of the property into the purchase price, the resulting figure is then subtracted for, each year's operating income as a "provision for depreciation." Thus, if one were to depreciate a $10,000 building over its estimated useful life of forty years by the straight line method, assuming zero salvage value, he would subtract $10,000/40 = $250 from each year's income.

The straight line method takes no account of any interest that might be earned on the sums recaptured each year as depreciation. This failure is sometimes justified by the observation that income generated by a property will tend to decline over the years and this decline is not accounted for in the capitalization method, which assumes a level flow of income over the years of useful life. The overstatement of income which results is presumed to be offset by the failure to take account of interest earned on depreciation payments.

§ 17.05[8][c][ii]   Sinking Fund Depreciation

The sinking fund method differs from the straight line in that it is based on the premise that the amounts set aside each year as provision for depreciation are placed in a fund over which the investor has no control. These funds are further assumed to be earning compound interest at a so-called "safe rate." Traditionally that rate has been 3%. Since the fund is earning interest, to depreciate a $10,000 investment over forty years using this method requires $132.62 annually, only a little more than half that required under the straight line method.[12]

§ 17.05[8][c][iii]   Annuity Depreciation

The third method, called the annuity method, is similar in concept to the sinking fund method. However, under this method there is no assumption that the depreciation payments are placed in a fund and unavailable to the investor. Instead, these funds are assumed to be available for immediate reinvestment at a compound rate of return equal to that being generated by the property itself. Returning to our example of a $10,000 investment over forty years, if the property is generating a 7% return, then using the annuity method the annual provision for depreciation necessary to depreciate a $10,000 investment over forty years is $50.09, less than half that required under the sinking fund method and only one-fifth of that required under straight line.[13]

With both the sinking fund and annuity methods the fact that the depreciation fund is assumed to be earning interest is the basis for the smaller annual depreciation provision. Every dollar that the fund earns in interest is one less dollar that must be taken from the income produced by the property to pay back the owner's investment.

---

[12] $10,000 sinking fund factor at 3% for 40 years (.013262) = $132.62.
[13] $10,000 sinking fund factor at 7% for 40 years (.005009) = $50.09.

§ 17.05[8][c][iv]   Relative Merits of Three Depreciation Methods

There is a great deal of theoretical debate among appraisers as to which of the foregoing three methods gives the most accurate approximation of economic reality. All the methods are vulnerable to the criticism that they are based on artificial assumptions or conventions which are designed to be the foundations of general rules and which may have an extremely distortive effect in any given instance.

Is it realistic, for instance, to assume, as in the straight-line method, that the yearly depreciation payments thrown off by the property are held at no interest?

Is it realistic to assume, as in the sinking fund method, that depreciation payments are held in a special low interest fund unavailable to the investor?

Or is it realistic to assume, as in the annuity method, that the relatively small annual depreciation payments can be reinvested at a rate as favorable as that earned by the property as a whole, when experience shows that only rarely can small sums of money be placed at rates as attractive as those earned by large sums?

Arguing the relative merits of depreciation methods is more than a mere academic exercise. The choice of one or another of them can have a profound effect on the figure ultimately arrived at as the valuation of the property.

As an example, take a building which produces income of $1,000 per year and has an estimated useful life of forty years. Determine its value using capitalization rates based on the three different methods, assuming an interest rate of 8%. It will be seen that the value under the straight line method is $9,523; under the sinking fund method, $10,722; and under the annuity method, $11,924.

So, by changing nothing except the depreciation method, we can generate a range of valuations for the same property that vary over 25% from the lowest to the highest. Clearly then, since the choice of depreciation methods has so dramatic an effect on ultimate valuation, the appraiser should be prepared to justify his choice of one or the other in every instance.

LEGAL RULES FOR ESTABLISHING FAIR MARKET VALUE

§ 17.06   The Generally Accepted Valuation Methods

IN GENERAL

The vast majority of abatement cases are settled before trial. However, there are inevitably some that must be tried. The attorney who has such a case should prepare himself for it in much the same way he would prepare himself for a land damage case under G.L. c. 79. The central issue will be the correct value of the property for tax purposes and each party may be expected to call real estate experts whose testimony will be evaluated in accordance with established legal standards.

In evaluating property, real estate appraisers will normally use one or more of three generally accepted methods to determine the value of real estate. They are: the market sales comparison method,[1] which involves analyzing a number of recent sales of properties comparable to the one being valued; the capitalization of income method,[2] which involves determining the total value in present dollars of the net income which the building can be expected to generate over its useful life; and the depreciated reproduction cost method,[3] which involves estimating the cost to reproduce the building new, and then reducing that cost figure by an amount which reflects the loss in value suffered by the property as a result of physical, functional and economic obsolescence, in order to arrive at present value.

Each of these methods is fully recognized within the real estate community as a reliable valuation method, although the depreciated reproduction cost method is considered to be the weakest of the three.[4]

However, the Massachusetts courts have not adopted and imported the entire body of contemporary real estate appraisal theory into the law of the Commonwealth. Instead, the courts have evolved their own rules as to the proper way to establish the value of real estate for purposes of taxation or otherwise. These rules rely heavily on the methods of valuation discussed in the preceding chapter, but they also modify those methods in many cases, sometimes drastically.

Therefore, it is necessary for the practitioner to have an understanding of the basics of real estate appraisal theory as well a thorough knowledge of the permissible ways in which that theory may be used in the prosecution of a case before the Appellate Tax Board. For example, the market sales comparison valuation method uses so-called index sales of comparable properties to establish value. However, the law limits the kinds and location of the properties which may be used as index sales.

In view of the foregoing it is recommended that this and the preceding chapter be read together.

FAIR CASH VALUE

---

[1] *See* § 17.05[4], *supra* for a fuller discussion of this method.
[2] *See* § 17.05[8], *supra* for a fuller discussion of this method.
[3] *See* § 17.05[5], *supra* for a fuller discussion of this method.
[4] Ring, The Valuation of Real Estate (2d ed. 1970), Prentice-Hall.

§ 17.06[1] Definition

The assessors are mandated by statute[5] to value all property or tax purposes at its "fair cash value." And, since 1975, the statute has contained language specifically requiring the use of one or a combination of all generally accepted methods for determining values of such property, including a comparison of sales prices, capitalization of income and replacement cost less depreciation."

The Massachusetts cases defining the words "fair cash value" are legion. While the language of some of the decisions varies, the sense of all of them is the same, and that is that fair cash value is the dollar value which the property would bring if sold on the open market in a voluntary, arms-length transaction.[6] In *Tremont and Suffolk Mills v. City of Lowell*,[7] the Court said, "... Fair cash value is ascertained by a consideration of all those elements which make property attractive for valuable use to one under no compulsion to purchase but yet willing to buy for a fair price, attributing to each element of value the amount which it adds to the price likely to be offered by such a buyer." Again defining "fair cash value," in *Boston Gas Co. v. Assessors of Boston*,[8] the Court said, "The standard of valuation of property subject to local taxation is fair cash value. This means fair market value ... A valuation limited to what the property is worth to the purchaser is not market value ... [but] in determining fair cash value, the value of such property for any special purpose together with its value for all purposes for which it is reasonably adapted may be shown." However the assessors may not make valuations based on hypothetical or conjectural uses of the property. Attempts to value multi family rental properties based on their assumed conversion to condominiums and sale have not been successful, where the owner has not actually embarked on such a course.[9]

And where property is known to be subject to a deed restriction or to a governmentally-imposed restriction affecting its earning power, that fact should be considered in any determination of its fair cash value.[10] But where part of a multi family building had been converted to condominiums and the remaining units where restricted from such conversion, the Appellate Tax Board upheld the assessors when they assessed the restricted units at a value based on the recent sales of the unrestricted units.[11]

---

[5] G.L. c. 59, § 38.

[6] Assessors of Quincy v. Boston Consol. Gas Co., 309 Mass. 60, 34 N.E.2d 623 (1941).

[7] 271 Mass. 1; 170 N.E. 819 (1930).

[8] 334 Mass. 549; 137 N.E.2d 462 (1956).

[9] Board of Assessors of Newton v. Iodice, 29 Mass. App. Ct. 1014 (1991); Iodice v. Board of Assessors of Newton, 11 Mass. App. Tax Bd. Rep. 95 (1989); LaRovere v. Board of Assessors of Everett, 11 Mass. App. Tax Bd. Rep. 58–62 (1989).

[10] Boston Edison Co. v. Board of Assessors of Boston, 387 Mass. 298, 439 N.E.2d 763 (1982), *appeal after remand,* 393 Mass. 511, 471 N.E.2d 1312.

[11] Zuker v. Board of Assessors of Brookline, 9 Mass. App. Tax Bd. Rep. 37 (1987).

Just as a property's fair market value is not necessarily what it happens to be worth to any one particular purchaser, neither is it necessarily what it happens to be worth to any one particular owner. For example, the sentimental value of property to an owner is not a proper consideration in determining fair market value.[12]

What is sought then is the price the property would bring if exposed in the open market, in normal conditions, to prospective purchasers unmotivated by special concerns other than the desire to own a valuable piece of property. As an aid to the trier of fact in determining this price, the property owner may show the value of the property for any special purpose,[13] as well as for any other use to which it might be profitably put.[14]

§ 17.06[2]   Rental Value as Evidence of Fair Cash Value

Fair market value is to be ascertained from a consideration of all the factors that ought to influence the judgment of a seller and buyer in reaching a fair price.[15] Since the rental seller value of a property is one of the factors which buyers and sellers would consider in setting a price, it follows that it should be, and is, admissible on the question of fair-cash value.[16] Note that the fair rental value rather than the rental value based on actual rents received from the property is relevant here. The theory on which this rule is based, at least with respect to taxation, is that the taxing authorities will not reward the inefficient property owner with a lower tax. But as long as the actual rents adequately reflect earning capacity they will be used in determining fair market value, and the Appellate Tax Board will ordinarily use the actual rents unless the assessors introduce evidence to show that they are not the economic rents.[17]

However actual rents should not be used where those rents were not arrived at through arms-length bargaining, and are not related to actual marketplace rents.[18] For example, the existence of an outstanding lease at an unrealistically low rental for a long term, not representing the fair rental value of the property, is not to be

---

[12] Maher v. Commonwealth, 291 Mass. 343, 197 N.E. 78 (1935).

[13] *See* §§ 17.05[9] and 17.06[8] for discussion of "special purpose" properties.

[14] Assessors of Quincy v. Boston Consol. Gas Co., 309 Mass. 60, 34 N.E.2d 623 (1941). *See also* Lodge v. Inhabitants of Swampscott, 216 Mass. 260, 103 N.E. 635 (1913), which holds that any restriction on land use is also relevant in determining fair cash value.

[15] *Id.*

[16] Lincoln v. Commonwealth, 164 Mass. 368, 41 N.E. 489 (1895); Levenson v. Boston El. Ry. Co., 191 Mass. 75; 77 N.E. 635 (1906).

[17] La Rovere v. Board of Assessors of Everett, 11 Mass. App. Tax Bd. Rep. 62 (1989); R.A. Carye, Trustee v. Board of Assessors, 394 Mass. 1001, 474 N.E.2d 159 (1985).

[18] Alstores Realty Corp. v. Board of Assessors of Peabody, 391 Mass. 60, 460 N.E.2d 1276 (1984).

used as the basis for sharply reducing the value of the property for tax purposes.[19] Conversely, where the amount of rent that the property owner may receive is fixed below market rates by law or regulations the assessors must consider this in determining fair market value.[20] Typically government subsidized low or moderate income housing projects limit the rentals which may be charged by the owner. This must be taken into account by the assessors, but they may also take this into account when determining the proper capitalization rate for the property. The Appellate Tax Board rejected a claim by a taxpayer that fair market value should be determined by capitalizing the reduced rentals using an ordinary market capitalization rate. Instead, it required that the taxpayer use in the capitalization rate the rate of return set by the subsidy program.[21]

Property which is actually used for single tenant occupancy should be valued based on that use. And it is improper to use rents charged for buildings which are newer than, or in other respects not comparable to the property being valued. It is also improper to use rents of small separate properties, without adjustment, in attempting to value a large, single tenant property.[22]

The usual, modern practice is to "capitalize" the fair net rental value of a property by dividing that income by a percentage "capitalization rate." This mathematical process yields a valuation figure which represents the present value of the right to receive the future rental income to be generated by the property, and this is deemed to be the fair cash value of the property.[23] (i.e., net income = $10,000, capitalization rate = 10%) ($10,000/.10 = $100,000 fair cash value). The capitalization of income method of valuation is approved by the courts and the Appellate Tax Board[24] as a method to convert rental income into a fair cash valuation figure. Note that a distinction must always be made between the income generated by the real estate itself as rent for its use and any income which might be generated by a business conducted on the property.[25]

---

[19] Pepsi Cola Bottling Co. v. Board of Assessors of Boston, 397 Mass. 447, 491 N.E.2d 1071 (1989).

[20] Community Development Co. of Gardner v. Board of Assessors of Gardner, 377 Mass. 351, 385 N.E.2d 1376 (1979); Everett Sq./Glendale Court Associates v. Board of Assessors of Everett, 9 Mass. App. Tax Bd. Rep. 68 (1987).

[21] President Village Co. v. Board of Assessors of Fall River, 8 Mass. App. Tax Bd. Rep. 29 (1987).

[22] Avco Manufacturing Co. v. Assessors of Wilmington, 12 Mass. App. Tax Bd. Rep. 132 (1990).

[23] *See* § 17.05[8], *supra,* for full explanation of capitalization process.

[24] *See* Assessors of Quincy v. Boston Consol. Gas Co., 309 Mass. 60, 34 N.E.2d 623 (1941); Jordan Marsh Co. v. Board of Assessors of Malden, 359 Mass. 106, 267 N.E.2d 912 (1971).

[25] *Id.*

§ 17.06[3]   Rental Value of Owner-occupied Property

It often happens that it is necessary to determine the fair market value of owner-occupied property, particularly business property. In such cases, the owner of the property is either the occupying business itself or a controlled subsidiary. In the former case, no rent payments are made at all, and in the latter case the rental payments are not the result of a negotiated arms-length transaction. In either situation, it is not possible to capitalize the net rental income of the land to arrive at a realistic estimate of fair cash value, as can be done where the property is not owner-occupied.

However, it is still possible to introduce evidence of the "fair rental value" of such owner-occupied property for purposes of showing market value.[26] The logic of this rule becomes obvious when one considers that even where a property is earning rent it is the earning capacity, or "fair rental value," of property rather than its "actual income" which is relevant to its fair market value. In cases where an arms-length lease is negotiated, there is good reason to believe that rental income is identical to "fair rental value"[27] or earning capacity. But even in the arms-length lease it may be that for some reason the net rental income is higher or lower than it should be, and the actual rental income and "fair rental value" are not identical.

Since a threshold inquiry into the rental value of a property should be made according to the cases even where the property is presently earning rent under an arms-length lease, there would seem to be no greater unreliability involved in making the same inquiry as to the rental value of a property which is earning no actual rental payments.

In estimating the rental value of owner-occupied properties, it is important to remember the general rule that the relative prosperity or profitability of a business located on the property is "… not a fair measure of the value of the land because the financial returns from a commercial undertaking are dependent on so many material factors having no real relation to the land itself that the profit cannot be said to be derived from the land. This general rule ought not to be relaxed except in those comparatively rare instances where the profits in the main result from some peculiar characteristic of the land, and where the exclusion of such evidence would virtually deprive one [the owner] of proving the fair market value of his land."[28]

So the general rule is that the profitability of a business located on the land is relevant to prove the rental value of that land only where the land, by virtue of its location or some other peculiarity, is a major factor in the profitability of the

---

[26] *Id.*

[27] Assessors of Quincy v. Boston Consol. Gas Co., 309 Mass. 60, 34 N.E.2d 623 (1941).

[28] Assessors of Quincy v. Boston Consol. Gas Co., 309 Mass. 60, 34 N.E.2d 623 (1941); *see also* Revere v. Revere Const. Co., 285 Mass. 243, 189 N.E. 73 (1934).

business. (Land located next to a natural phenomenon such as the Grand Canyon and used for a hotel/resort business might be an example of this type of property.)

In spite of the foregoing, modern business practices have begun to cause another exception to be carved from the general rule. It is commonplace for a retail business to be required to pay a certain percentage of its gross sales to the property owner as a part of the rent for the property. In the modern shopping center lease, a rental based on a percentage of gross sales subject to a stated minimum is nearly universal. Obviously, where the rental income generated by a property is dependent on the gross sales of a business tenant, then, contrary to the general rule, the rental value and hence the value of the property is going to be dependent on the prosperity of the tenant business. In such cases, the profitability of the business actually occupying the property should be very relevant to the rental value of the property since the rent generated by the property will usually be tied to the sales of whatever store happens to be the tenant.

One case, *Jordan Marsh, Inc. v. Board of Assessors of Malden*,[29] at least impliedly, recognizes this fact. The property involved consisted of two interconnected buildings which contained offices and stores. The property owner applied for abatement, was denied, and appealed to the Tax Board. At the hearing before the Board both parties called experts who gave opinions as to the fair cash value of the property. Both experts used the "capitalization of net income"[30] method to determine value.

The assessors' expert arrived at a value of $1,500,000; the taxpayer's expert at a value of $880,928. The disparity between the two results arose mainly from the difference in rental value attributed by the experts to the department store portion of the premises, which was owner-occupied.

The Board found a fair cash value of $1,250,000. The assessors appealed, based in part on the claim that it was error for the Board to admit into evidence a periodic publication entitled "Operating Results of Department and Specialty Stores," by one Malcolm P. McNair (commonly called the McNair reports).

The Court held that the Board was "entitled to receive evidence as to the relationship among rental values, store size, gross sales, and other operating figures for stores of this general type." In a footnote to its decision,[31] the Court notes with seeming approval that the Board considered the "operating figures" of the owner-occupant department store.

Thus notwithstanding the general rule that the business income of a business

---

[29] 359 Mass. 106, 267 N.E.2d 912 (1971).
[30] *See* § 17.05[8], *supra* for explanation of this method.
[31] Jordan Marsh Co. v. Board of Assessors of Malden, 359 Mass. 106, 267 N.E.2d 912 (1971).

located on the property is not relevant in valuing the property, there are various special circumstances involving specialized types of property where the rule does not apply.[32]

§ 17.06[4]   Rental Value of Other, Comparable Properties

While evidence of recent, arms-length sales of properties similar to the one being valued is admissible to show the fair market value of the property,[33] evidence of the rental value of other comparable properties is not admissible for this purpose.[34]

In *Wenton*,[35] the property owner attempted to introduce evidence of the rent she was receiving on another parcel, similar to the parcel which was the subject of the litigation, for the purpose of showing the rental value of the latter parcel. The trial court allowed this evidence in.

On appeal, the Supreme Judicial Court said: "This evidence of rental value of other land should have been excluded. While the rental value of a parcel the market value of which is in issue may be received as some indication of the fair market value of that parcel, the rental value of similar premises, as distinguished from actual sales near in time, is not sufficiently relevant to warrant the extension of the field of controversy and fact finding which is entailed in its admission. [citations]"

A recent Appeals Court case includes language which appears at first to modify the holding of *Wenton*.[36] In that case, the Court said: "While the raw rental income derived from property similar to that taken is generally inadmissible to show the value of the property taken [citing *Wenton*], the capitalization of rental income determined from the rental income of comparable property is a valid method for estimating the fair market value of the property taken. This is especially so when the property is itself not rented, and there are no sales of comparable property on which to base an estimate of fair market value. A rule allowing the use of fair rental value of comparable property as a basis of determining fair rental value of property taken is very little different from a computation of fair market value based on comparable sales, since a rental can be viewed as a short term sale. The capitalization of the net income of the property taken, arrived at by deducting the

---

[32] General Dynamics Corp. v. Board of Assessors of Quincy, 388 Mass. 24, 444 N.E.2d 1266 (1983); Boston Edison Co. v. Assessors of Watertown, 387 Mass. 298, 439 N.E.2d 763 (1982); Leominster Nursing Home, Inc. v. Board of Assessors of the City of Leominster, 13 Mass. App. Tax Bd. Rep. 119 (1991).

[33] Iris v. Town of Hingham, 303 Mass. 401, 22 N.E.2d 13 (1939); H. E. Fletcher Co. v. Commonwealth, 350 Mass. 316, 214 N.E.2d 721 (1956).

[34] Wenton v. Commonwealth, 335 Mass. 78, 138 N.E.2d 609 (1956).

[35] 335 Mass. 78, 138 N.E.2d 609 (1956).

[36] Correia v. New Bedford Redevelopment Authority, 5 Mass. App. Ct. 289, 362 N.E.2d 538 (1977), *reversed on other grounds*, Correia v. New Bedford Redevelopment Authority, 375 Mass. 360, 377 N.E.2d 909 (1978).

reasonable expenses of operating that property from the gross rental income determined in the manner set forth above, is thus an acceptable method of determining the fair market value of that property."

The Appeals Court is not in this writer's opinion saying in the *Correia* case that evidence as to the rental income of comparable properties is not admissible to show market value but evidence of the capitalized rental income of comparable properties is. Such a holding would clearly make little sense. Instead, what the Court appears to be saying is that the appraiser may develop a hypothetical or pro forma estimate of the gross rental income that a property should generate, based on that generated by other comparable properties, from which he may subtract the estimated reasonable expenses of operating the subject property to arrive at a potential fair rental value figure, which is then capitalized.

For example, if the appraiser knows the gross rentals of a number of properties similar to the one in issue, he may use this knowledge as a basis for forming an opinion as to the gross rental income likely to be generated by the property in issue. He must then deduct from the estimated gross income "the reasonable expenses of operating the property." (The Court does not make clear upon what this estimate of expenses should be based.) The net income thus derived is then capitalized to arrive at a valuation figure. (Note that this method could be very useful in estimating the value of owner-occupied property.)

If the *Correia* case is interpreted as outlined in the preceding paragraphs it falls neatly into line with well-settled Massachusetts law on the admissibility of sales prices of comparable property as evidence of the market value of the property in issue.[37]

Notwithstanding the law as set out above, and as applied in the courts of the Commonwealth, the Appellate Tax Board will receive into evidence and review the actual rents of the comparable properties used by the appraiser, provided a proper foundation is laid on the comparability issue.

§ 17.06[5]   Capitalizing Net Rental Value for Tax Purposes

The steps involved in capitalizing income to determine the proper assessed value and tax are:

---

[37] *See* Hunt v. Boston, 152 Mass. 168, 25 N.E. 82 (1890), Manning v. City of Lowell, 173 Mass. 100, 53 N.E. 160 (1899), and R.H. White Realty Co., Inc. v. Boston Redevelopment Auth. 3 Mass. App. Ct. 505, 334 N.E.2d 637 (1975), for cases indicating that sales of property not sufficiently comparable to come in as direct evidence of value may be used as support and background for the opinion of an expert. Note also, however, that the Supreme Judicial Court specifically refrained from agreeing or disagreeing with the Appeals Court on this question of the admissibility of capitalized rental income based on that of comparable properties when it reversed the *Correia* case.

1. Determine fair rental value of property. (This may or may not be the same as actual rental income, as discussed above.)

2. Determine proper operating expenses to be subtracted from income. (These will usually have to be within accepted real estate industry guidelines even if actual expenses are greater.)

3. Determine net income before taxes and depreciation. (Fair rental value less operating expenses. See § 17.05[8], *supra* for a sample income and expense statement prior to adjustment for use in determining fair cash value for tax purposes. As indicated, no deduction is made for real estate taxes nor is any deduction made for mortgage interest. Where the actual rent roll is used there will ordinarily be no deduction for a vacancy allowance. If a so-called triple net lease is involved the only deductions from income would be a small expense allowance, a vacancy allowance and a reserve for equipment replacement.)[38]

4. Determine capitalization rate. (See § 17.05[8][a] *et seq.* There is no requirement that the rate be derived directly from the market sought to be analyzed. The only requirement is that the rate derived should reflect the return on investment necessary to attract investment capital.)[39]

5. Determine the proper tax factor. (In municipalities which value at 100% of fair cash value this will be the same percentage as the tax rate: i.e., tax rate = $100 per thousand; tax factor = 10%. Where property in the municipality is valued at less than fair cash value, for example, 50%, then the tax factor must be proportionately reduced: i.e., tax rate = $100 per thousand; disproportion rate = 50%; tax factor = .50 × 10%, or 5%. In the case of a triple net lease, no tax factor is used, since the tenant pays the taxes.)[40]

6. Determine fair cash value as follows:

Fair cash value = Net income before taxes and depreciation/Capitalization rate + Tax factor

7. Determine assessed value. (If the community is at 100%, valuation, fair cash value in step 6 and assessed value are the same. Where property is assessed at less than 100% it will be necessary to multiply the fair cash value obtained in step 6 by the disproportion ratio: for example, if step 6 yields a fair cash value of $100,000 and property is assessed at 50% of market value, then assessed value will be .50 × $100,000 = $50,000.)

---

[38] New England Telephone and Telegraph v. Assessors of Framingham, 10 Mass. App. Tax Bd. Rep. 6 (1988).
[39] Board of Assessors of Brookline v. Buehler, 396 Mass. 520, 487 N.E.2d 493 (1986). This case implicitly approves the "band of investment" method described above.
[40] General Electric Co. v. Board of Assessors of Lynn, 393 Mass. 591, 472 N.E.2d 1329 (1984).

8. Multiply assessed value by the tax rate to obtain amount of tax.

In § 17.05[8], *supra*, as part of the discussion of the mechanics of the capitalization of income method, an example was given of a standard form "Statement of Operating Income and Expenses," used for general real estate appraisal purposes.

It will be seen that in that Statement real estate taxes payable were deducted as an operating expense before net income was capitalized. While this is an entirely proper procedure when the valuation is being made for purposes unrelated to taxation, it is not acceptable for the purpose of determining value for tax purposes.

In *Board of Assessors of Lynnfield v. New England Oyster House, Inc.*,[41] the issue before the Court was the proper treatment of the real estate tax expense in applying the capitalization method. The taxpayer maintained that the local real estate taxes attributable to the property should be treated as an operating expense and subtracted from the figure for net income before that figure was capitalized. The Appellate Tax Board's position was that net income should be capitalized without making any deduction for local taxes, and that provision should be made in the capitalization rate for local taxes.

The Supreme Judicial Court agreed with the Appellate Tax Board, noting that since the amount of local taxation turns on the very point in dispute, the fair cash value of the property, it cannot logically be used as a component in arriving at that value. Instead, the Court said, the net income should be capitalized without any allowance for local taxes, with the capitalization rate increased to yield the investor's expected return plus the local taxes payable."[42]

A further modification of this principle which will apply in cash value municipalities which value at less than 100% of fair cash value was handed down in the Shop-Lease case,[43] decided in 1974. Here, it was agreed by all parties that the proper way to account for local taxes was to make an adjustment to the capitalization rate. The question before the Court was how the adjustment should be made when the assessors admittedly assessed all property at substantial discounts from fair cash value.

---

[41] 362 Mass. 696, 290 N.E.2d 520 (1972).

[42] This would be accomplished as follows: 1) determine net rental income before taxes and depreciation; 2) determine percentage capitalization rate; 3) determine percentage rate of local tax (tax factor); 4) add the capitalization rate and the percentage rate of local tax together; and 5) divide the sum into net income. The result is the assessed value.

[43] Board of Assessors of Lynn v. Shop-Lease Co., Inc. , 364 Mass. 569, 307 N.E.2d 310 (1974). *See also* City of New Brunswick v. State of New Jersey Div. of Tax Appeals, 39 N.J. 537, 189 A.2d 702 (1963), cited with approval by the Supreme Judicial Court in the *New England Oyster House* case, *supra*, where the New Jersey Court said that fair rental value rather than the actual rent payable under an existing lease should control in determining the proper amount to be capitalized.

It was determined that the net annual income from the property in question was $154,450, before allowance for local real estate taxes. The local tax rate was $200 per thousand or 20%, and the Tax Board used a capitalization rate of 10%. It was agreed that the assessors valued all property at 30% of fair cash value.

In capitalizing the income stream, the Tax Board used the full 20% rate as a tax factor as follows $154,450/(.20 + .10) = $514,800. The Board then reduced this figure by 70% to reflect the underassessment practices of the assessors, arriving at an assessed value of $154,440.

The assessors complained that the tax factor should have been 30% of 20%, or 6%, to reflect properly the city's under-assessment practices. The Supreme Judicial Court agreed, saying, "The purpose of a tax factor, in a formula for capitalization of earnings, is to reflect the tax which will be payable on the assessed value produced by the formula. If fair cash value is to be reduced in arriving at assessed value, tax factors must be proportionately reduced."

§ 17.06[6]   Original Cost of Property as Evidence of Fair Cash Value

The original cost, recently incurred, of a property is a legitimate factor to be considered by the trier of fact in determining cash value.[44] There would appear to be some discretion on the part of a tribunal in deciding whether or not to admit such evidence.[45] However, although the cases are not completely clear on the point, that discretion should not be as broad as it is in the case of the admissibility of sales prices of comparable properties.[46] A very recent arms-length purchase price is very powerful evidence of value, and at least before the Appellate Tax Board, will usually carry the day in the face of evidence of value developed by other methods.[47] Where the sale of the property in issue occurred many years previously, or where the sale was not an arms-length transaction, or where there has been a dramatic change in the physical or economic circumstances of the property since the sale, the Board would be justified in excluding evidence of the sale price.[48] However,

---

[44] Jordan Marsh Co. v. Assessors of Quincy, 368 Mass. 322, 331 N.E.2d 61 (1975). The sale price recited in the deed is not conclusive evidence of fair cash value. The sale must be arms length, and the recited sale price must be arrived at the same way. Where the property is sold as part of a larger sale of a business the sale price on the deed may very well be disregarded. Foxboro Assoc. v. Board of Assessors of Foxboro, 385 Mass. 679, 433 N.E.2d 890 (1982).

[45] Levenson v. Boston El. Ry. Co., 191 Mass. 75, 77 N.E. 635 (1906); Lembo v. Town of Framingham, 330 Mass. 461, 115 N.E.2d 370 (1953); Ramacorti v. Boston Redevelopment Auth., 341 Mass. 377, 170 N.E.2d 323 (1960).

[46] See Brush Hill Development, Inc. v. Commonwealth, 338 Mass. 359, 155 N.E.2d 170 (1959) and Iris v. Town of Hingham, 303 Mass. 401, 22 N.E.2d 13 (1939).

[47] Board of Assessors of Boston v. Diab, 396 Mass. 560, 487 N.E.2d 491 (1986).

[48] See Ramacorti v. Boston Redevelopment Auth., 341 Mass. 377, 170 N.E.2d 323 (1960); Lembo v. Town of Framingham, 330 Mass. 461, 115 N.E.2d 370 (1953).

according to the cases, the better practice in the less extreme cases would be to admit the evidence, subject to cross-examination of the witness and any rebuttal testimony, and leave the decision of the weight to be given to the cost of the property to the trier of fact.[49] In any case, where evidence of the cost of the property is admitted it is not in any sense dispositive of the issue of fair market value but is to be weighed along with all the other evidence of value.[50]

Notwithstanding the foregoing, the Appellate Tax Board has given very strong weight to the construction cost of a recently completed building, holding that it outweighs valuations derived from the capitalized income approaches to value which are normally favored.[51] Similarly a recent arms length purchase, followed by substantial rehabilitation expenses may result in a valuation at the combined acquisition and rehabilitation costs as against a lower value derived on the capitalized income basis.[52]

§ 17.06[7] Sales of Other Comparable Properties as Evidence of Fair Cash Value

"Actual sales of property shown to be similar to the property [at issue] and within a reasonable time of the taking are admissible in evidence for the purpose of showing the value of the premises in question. No two pieces of property are exactly alike, and much must be left to the discretion of the presiding judge, who, in the first instance, is to determine whether there is such general similarity between the land sold and the land [at issue] that the selling price of the former will furnish a fair criterion of the market value of the latter. In other words, he is to decide whether the evidence of the sale of such land will aid and assist the jury properly to fix the value of the land in controversy; or whether, on the whole, the land sold was not shown to be sufficiently similar to the land in question and, therefore, the introduction of evidence of the actual sale of such land would tend only to mislead and confuse the jury. The discretion of the judge is not unlimited, and his decision when affirmatively shown upon the record to be manifestly erroneous will be reversed."[53]

The quoted language fairly sums up the law with respect to the admissibility of evidence of sales of comparable property to show the market value of the property in issue. The essence of the law is that the judge, or in the case of an abatement petition, the Tax Board, has broad discretion as to the admissibility of such evidence

[49] *See* Brush Hill Development, Inc. v. Commonwealth, 338 Mass. 359, 155 N.E.2d 170 (1959); Manning v. City of Lowell, 173 Mass. 100, 53 N.E. 160 (1899).

[50] Manning v. City of Lowell, 173 Mass. 100, 53 N.E. 160 (1899).

[51] Blakeley v. Board of Assessors of Boston, 391 Mass. 473, 462 N.E.2d 278 (1984).

[52] Longwood Towers Realty Limited Partnership v. Board of Assessors of Boston, 11 Mass. App. Tax Bd. Rep. 115 (1989).

[53] Iris v. Town of Hingham, 303 Mass. 401, 22 N.E.2d 13 (1939).

and will not be reversed except upon a showing of manifest error.[54]

In the exercise of its discretion, the Board should be guided by the similarity or lack thereof between the properties in the areas of size, location, topography, neighborhood characteristics, accessibility, amenities, and so forth.[55] It is most important that the comparable sale properties be located as near as possible to the property in issue,[56] and that the sales be noncompulsory[57] and sufficiently near in time to the tax year at issue.[58] In the case of tax abatement hearings, the Appellate Tax Board has considerable discretion in deciding whether a sale was freely made and presents a comparable sale worthy of consideration.[59]

Just how near in time and geographic location the comparable sales must be is not definitely set out by the cases and is a matter of discretion with the trial court.[60] There would appear to be two outer limits to the Board's discretion: one consisting of sales which are so far removed in time and location as to be clearly inadmissible, and the other consisting of very recent free market sales of contiguous or nearly contiguous similar property which are clearly admissible.[61]

§ 17.06[8] Depreciated Reproduction or Replacement Cost as Evidence of Fair Cash Value

Whatever the relative importance or usefulness of the three generally accepted methods of real estate valuation to the real estate profession,[62] they have not been viewed as equally applicable or interchangeable under the law as the Massachusetts

---

[54] H. E. Fletcher Co. v. Commonwealth, 350 Mass. 316, 214 N.E.2d 721 (1956).

[55] Lyman v. City of Boston, 164 Mass. 99; 41 N.E. 127 (1895); Leen v. Board of Assessors of Boston, 345 Mass. 494, 188 N.E.2d 460 (1963).

[56] Epstein v. Boston Housing Authority, 317 Mass. 297, 58 N.E.2d 135 (1944); McCabe v. Chelsea, 265 Mass. 494, 163 N.E. 255 (1929).

[57] A foreclosure sale inherently suggests compulsion, and the proponent of the sale must rebut this suggestion. DSM Realty v. Board of Assessors of Andover, 391 Mass. 1014, 462 N.E.2d 114 (1984). The SJC has a very narrow definition of a sale made under compulsion, it being one made under "duress, fraud or imperative need for cash at any cost." The Westwood Group, Inc. v. Board of Assessors of Revere, 391 Mass. 1012, 462 N.E.2d 115 (1984).

[58] *Id.*

[59] The Westwood Group, Inc. v. Board of Appeals of Revere, 391 Mass. 1012, 462 N.E.2d 115 (1984).

[60] *See* Ramacorti v. Boston Redevelopment Auth., 341 Mass. 377, 170 N.E.2d 323 (1960); Lembo v. Town of Framingham, 330 Mass. 461, 115 N.E.2d 370 (1953); Iris v. Town of Hingham, 303 Mass. 401, 22 N.E.2d 13 (1939); Levenson v. Boston El. Ry. Co., 191 Mass. 75, 77 N.E. 635 (1906).

[61] R. H. White Realty Co., Inc. v. Boston Redevelopment Authority, 334 N.E.2d 637 (1975); Hunt v. Boston, 152 Mass. 168, 25 N.E. 82 (1890). *Compare* Correia v. New Bedford Redevelopment Authority, 5 Mass. App. Ct. 289, 362 N.E.2d 538 (1977), *reversed on other grounds,* 375 Mass. 360, 377 N.E.2d 909 (1978).

[62] These are the market sales comparison method, the capitalization of income method and the

courts have interpreted it.[63] More specifically, the market sales comparison and the capitalization of income methods have been considered the usual or normal valuation methods while the depreciated reproduction cost method is allowed only in those "special situations" where the other two methods cannot be reliably used.[64] The special situations referred to usually arise where the property in issue is adapted for a specialized use such that there is no active market for properties of the type and its value cannot therefore be shown by reference to sales of nearby comparable property.[65] In most cases, the property is owner-occupied or unrented and there is no ready rental market for such properties, making a capitalized income approach problematical as well.

Although some of the older cases indicated that the depreciated reproduction cost method could come in only where it was "impossible" to prove the value of the property by the other methods,[66] a more recent case relaxes this rule considerably. In *Correia v. New Bedford Redevelopment Authority*,[67] the Court reiterated the rule of "disfavoring" the depreciated reproduction cost method, but said that "the rule should be viewed as one of need, not impossibility," and that the trial court, "should be allowed to exercise sound discretion in determining when special conditions exist so as to justify the use of such data."

A fair statement of the law at the present time is that evidence of the depreciated reproduction cost of a property is not admissible to show its fair cash value except in those cases where proof of value by the other methods is impossible or highly conjectural and the Court, in the exercise of sound discretion, determines that the admission of such evidence is needed in order for the trier of fact to make an informed decision as to value.[68] Such evidence may be received where the structures remain reasonably well adapted for the special purposes for which they are employed and have not been shown to be in such condition as to make reproduction

---

depreciated reproduction or replacement cost method. *See* fuller discussion of these methods at § 17.05, *et seq., supra.*

[63] Correia v. New Bedford Redevelopment Authority, 375 Mass. 360, 377 N.E.2d 909 (1978).

[64] Correia v. New Bedford Redevelopment Authority, 375 Mass. 360, 377 N.E.2d 909 (1978).

[65] Correia v. New Bedford Redevelopment Authority, 375 Mass. 360, 377 N.E.2d 909 (1978); Silk v. Commonwealth, 1 Mass. App. 149, 294 N.E.2d 480 (1973); Commonwealth v. Mass. Turnpike Auth., 352 Mass. 143, 224 N.E.2d 186 (1967); Newton Girl Scout Council, Inc. v. Mass. Turnpike Auth., 335 Mass. 189, 138 N.E.2d 769 (1956); Tigar v. Mystic River Bridge Auth., 329 Mass. 514, 109 N.E.2d 148 (1952); Cochrane v. Commonwealth, 175 Mass. 299, 56 N.E. 610 (1900).

[66] *See* Cochrane v. Commonwealth, 175 Mass. 299, 56 N.E. 610 (1900); Tigar v. Mystic River Bridge Auth., 329 Mass. 514, 109 N.E.2d 148 (1952).

[67] 5 Mass. App. Ct. 289, 362 N.E.2d 538 (1977), *reversed on other grounds*, 375 Mass. 360, 377 N.E.2d 909 (1978).

[68] *See* cases cited at n.65, *supra*, and Correia v. New Bedford Redevelopment, 5 Mass. App. Ct. 289, 362 N.E.2d 538 (1977), *reversed on other grounds*, 375 Mass. 360, 377 N.E.2d 909 (1978).

unlikely or imprudent. It is only necessary that reproduction of essentially the same type of structure be reasonable. It is enough that the final adjusted figure tends to show what the owner would have to pay to obtain approximately the same still desirable and useful structure after taking into account age, wear and tear, and observed obsolescence.[69]

Even when such evidence is admitted, it is appropriate for the trier of fact to weigh it, mindful of the fact that depreciated reproduction cost is considered under Massachusetts law to have only a very inconclusive relation to fair market value.[70]

The burden is always on the party introducing the evidence to show that the circumstances justify dispensing with the usual rule and admitting evidence of depreciated reproduction cost.[71]

When such evidence is to be admitted, the proponent must call a trained and experienced construction expert or engineer to testify as to construction costs; a real estate appraiser will not be permitted to testify as to such costs.[72]

The Appellate Tax Board is not favorably disposed to attempts to prove fair cash value by the depreciated reproduction cost method.

§ 17.06[9]   Valuing Contaminated Property For Tax Purposes

As the environmental effects of the inadequate and improper waste disposal practices of past years have become apparent, courts have begun to be presented with a new, and very difficult, problem in tax valuation. The passage of enforced cleanup legislation at both the State and Federal level has had a disastrous effect on the marketability of properties contaminated with industrial wastes. Property owners have responded by seeking tax abatements to reflect what they perceive to be the sharply reduced value of their property, often seeking tax valuations of zero on the theory that contaminated land is unmarketable and has no "fair cash value." Municipal assessors on the other hand have argued that cleanup costs are burdens which are personal to the property owner and, like financing costs, should not be chargeable against the value of the land for assessment purposes. They argue that allowing a tax abatement to reflect the cost of cleaning up improperly disposed of waste effectively transfers the cost to the wrongdoing of the property owner, or his predecessor in title, to the other taxpayers in the community.

The main issue in this dispute was settled by the Supreme Judicial Court in

---

[69] Foxboro Assoc. v. Board of Assessors of Foxboro, 385 Mass. 679, 433 N.E.2d 890 (1982).

[70] Bachelder Truck Sales v. Commonwealth, 350 Mass. 270, 214 N.E.2d 36 (1966); Lipinski v. Lynn Redevelopment Auth., 355 Mass. 550, 246 N.E.2d 429 (1969).

[71] Tigar v. Mystic River Bridge Auth., 329 Mass. 514, 109 N.E.2d 148 (1952).

[72] Maryland Cup Corp. v. Board of Assessors of Wilmington, 10 Mass. App. Tax Bd. Rep. 45 (1988).

1991.[73] The Court held that the law of the Commonwealth obliges assessors to recognize the effects of proven environmental damage on the fair cash value of property, whether or not the landowner is subject to a court or regulatory cleanup mandate. This rule applies even if the landowner negligently, recklessly, or even intentionally caused the environmental damage to its property. However, because of the factual posture of the case, the Court was not required to deal with the subsidiary, and even more difficult, issue of how precisely one goes about adjusting the tax valuation of contaminated property. The Court states only the general proposition that the taxpayer has the burden of producing evidence to show "how the cost to cure a present defect would affect the value of the property to a potential buyer."[74] Although no specific methodology for doing this has been approved, the methodology which is probably most attractive to property owners has been disapproved by the Appellate Tax Board. The taxpayer may not simply value the property without the contamination and then subtract the cost of cleanup from the value so determined.[75] Further, any methodology which takes into account the cost of cleanup must also recognize the increase in the value of the property which would result from that cleanup.[76]

The practice of the Appellate Tax Board in many cases over the past few years involving contaminated property has been to reduce net income by an amount equal to any recurring costs added by the contamination, and by adding one percent to the total capitalization rate to reflect the market effect of the contamination.[77]

WITNESSES AS TO VALUE

§ 17.06[10]   Generally

Evidence of the fair cash value of property in an abatement case is normally going to consist of the opinions of witnesses called by the parties. These witnesses will fall into three categories: owners, real estate or, in some cases, construction experts, and other persons who are sufficiently familiar with the property to be able to testify as to its value.

-----

[73] *See* Reliable Electronic Finishing Co. v. Board of Assessors of Canton, 410 Mass. 381, 573 N.E.2d 959 (1991).

[74] Reliable Electronic Finishing Co. v. Board of Assessors of Canton, 410 Mass. 381, 573 N.E.2d 959 (1991). *See* Inmar Assocs., Inc. v. Borough of Carlstadt, 112 NJ 593, 549 A2d 38 (1988), cited by the SJC in the *Reliable Electronic Finishing* case, for a thoughtful and insightful discussion of the difficulties inherent in this process.

[75] Berkshire Life Insurance Co. v. Board of Assessors of Pittsfield, 12 Mass. App. Tax Bd. Rep. 34 (1989).

[76] Reliable Electronic Finishing Co. v. Board of Assessors of Canton, 13 Mass. App. Tax Bd. Rep. 1 (1990).

[77] *See, e.g.,* 23 West Bacon Corp. v. Assessors of Plainville, ATB 2000 678, 703 (2000).

§ 17.06[11]   Owners

An owner of real estate[78] or an officer of a corporation[79] which owns real estate may testify as to its fair cash value, provided that he has knowledge, apart from his ownership or mere holding of an office, which qualifies him to express an opinion as to its value. The determination of whether he has the requisite knowledge is a preliminary question of fact for the Court.[80]

The trial court's finding on this question will not be disturbed absent a clear abuse of discretion.[81] Note that the owner's opinion as to value may be contradicted by other witnesses, and he is also subject to cross-examination as to the basis of his opinion.[82]

§ 17.06[12]   Expert Witnesses

Once he has been properly qualified, an expert may testify as to the value of real property within the limits of his expertise.[83] Note, for example, that a real estate dealer or appraiser should not be allowed to testify as to the reproduction cost of a building and that such testimony should come from an engineer, architect or construction expert.

"Ordinarily a real estate dealer or appraiser may testify as to the value of property, whether or not he has seen it or sold land in the neighborhood, if he possesses sufficient experience and knowledge of values of other similar real estate in the particular locality. And it has been held to be reversible error not to permit such a witness to testify where he has shown sufficient knowledge of and experience with

---

[78] Rubin v. Town of Arlington, 327 Mass. 382, 99 N.E.2d 30 (1951).

[79] Winthrop Products v. Elroth Co., Inc. , 331 Mass. 83, 117 N.E.2d 157 (1964).

[80] Board of Assessors of Holbrook v. Dennehy, 357 Mass. 243, 258 N.E.2d 31 (1935); Newton Girl Scout Council, Inc. v. Mass. Turnpike Auth., 335 Mass. 189, 138 N.E.2d 769 (1956); Maher v. Commonwealth, 197 N.E. 78 (1935); Menici v. Orton Crane & Shovel Co., 285 Mass. 499, 189 N.E. 839 (1934).

[81] Rubin v. Town of Arlington, 327 Mass. 382, 99 N.E.2d 30 (1951).

[82] Carlson v. Town of Holden, 358 Mass. 22, 260 N.E.2d 666 (1970).

[83] Lee Lime Corp. v. Mass. Turnpike Auth., 337 Mass. 433, 149 N.E.2d 905 (1958); R. H. White Realty Co., Inc. v. Boston Redevelopment Authority, 334 N.E.2d 637 (1975); Klous v. Commonwealth, 188 Mass. 149, 74 N.E. 330 (1905). *See also* Western Massachusetts Lifecare Corp. v. Board of Assessors of Springfield, 434 Mass. 96, 747 N.E.2d 97 (2001). In *Lifecare*, the taxpayer operated a continuing care retirement community and its expert witness had expertise in the operation and management of long-term care facilities, such as nursing homes and could assess the value of a long-term care enterprise. The expert, however, had no training or experience in real estate or real estate valuation. For that reason, an objection was raised to the witness's qualifications. The board reserved ruling on that issue and allowed the expert to testify. The expert stated no opinion of the value of the real estate and at the conclusion of the testimony, a motion to strike was made which the board took under advisement, but in its findings of fact and report, it ultimately ruled that the expert was not qualified.

the particular type of real estate involved in the litigation. But it is not sufficient that a real estate dealer or appraiser may have a general knowledge of real estate values. He should possess knowledge and experience regarding the particular type of property involved ..."

An expert may testify on direct as to the reasons for his opinion, although his opinion is admissible without the reasons therefore. The expert may testify as to such reasons if the reasons are based on hearsay, but "this should be even done in such terms that inadmissible hearsay is not introduced in a manner prejudicial to a party." Thus the expert should not testify as to the terms of a particular transaction which formed the basis of his opinion unless a party to the sale is produced and subjected to cross-examination. However it is not indispensable that an expert witness actually observe all comparable properties. He is entitled to draw conclusions in part from information learned from inquiries made and answers given.

If the expert's opinion is based partly on such legally incompetent matter it may still be considered by the trier of fact. Only where the opinion is based wholly on such matter should it be excluded or stricken upon motion of the opposing party. The motion to strike the expert's testimony must be made as soon as it becomes apparent that the opinion is wholly based on incompetent matter. At the Appellate Tax Board it is customary for the appraiser's report to be introduced into evidence. Where cross examination reveals that such report is wholly or partially incompetent a motion should be made to strike all, or the offending parts, of the report from the record.

In the case of properties adapted for specialized use, such as mill sites, refrigeration plants, country clubs, etc. , the rules concerning the qualification of an expert to testify as to value are somewhat different. In such cases, "it will frequently be necessary to allow much greater flexibility in the, presentation of evidence than would be necessary in the case of properties having more conventional uses. In such cases ... detailed knowledge by ... witnesses of local prices of land for ordinary residential or commercial use may be far less helpful than knowledge of conditions (relevant to the particular type of property) over a wide geographical area and of the demand for and use of comparable specialized properties by a particular industry or class of users or customers." Thus, in the case of specialized use properties the expert must still show sufficient knowledge of and experience with the particular type of real estate involved in the litigation as is the case with conventional property, but he need not necessarily have knowledge of local real estate conditions.

Where a preferred expert has been found not qualified and has not been allowed to testify, it is not necessary for the party calling him to make an offer of proof to preserve his rights on appeal.

§ 17.06[13]   Other Persons

Persons who are neither owners of the property in issue nor real estate or construction experts may testify as to the property's value, provided they can show themselves to be sufficiently familiar with the property. However, "caution should be exercised by the trial judge in the admission of opinion testimony from such witnesses and its admission rests largely upon his sound judicial discretion."

DISCRIMINATORY VALUATION AS A BASIS FOR ABATEMENT

§ 17.07   Generally

When the taxpayer applies for an abatement of his real estate tax he can base his claim on one or more of the following theories: (1) He may claim simply that his property is over-assessed in that it is valued for tax purposes at an amount in excess of what it is actually worth; or (2) he may claim that his property is over-assessed because the assessors have implemented a scheme of assessment whereby a large number of properties are valued at amounts less than their fair cash value,[1] and that his property is assessed at a greater percentage of cash value than some others, (disproportionate assessment); or (3) he may claim that his property is exempt from taxation; or (4) he may claim that his property has been improperly classified.

§ 17.07[1]   Assessment in Excess of Fair Market Value

If the taxpayer's property can be shown to be valued for purposes of taxation at an amount in excess of its fair cash value, then the law is clear, and the taxpayer has an unquestioned right to abatement. The central issue in the case is very similar to the central issue in a land damage case filed under G.L. c. 79, § 14: i.e., what is the actual fair market value of the property, (and what are the legally permissible methods which may be used by the parties in attempting to prove that value to the trier of fact?)[2]

The proceedings before the Tax Board will thus revolve around the testimony of the assessors, the owner, the real estate experts called by the assessors and the

---

[1] "Fair cash value" and "fair market value" mean the same thing. Garebedian v. City of Worcester, 338 Mass. 48, 153 N.E.2d 622 (1958).

[2] "Fair market value" in real estate tax abatement cases, as in eminent domain cases, means the highest price which a hypothetical willing buyer would pay to a hypothetical willing seller in a free market and in the absence of peculiar or special circumstances. Epstein v. Boston Housing Auth., 317 Mass. 297, 58 N.E.2d 135 (1945); Maher v. Commonwealth, 291 Mass. 343, 197 N.E. 78 (1935).

owner, and the method of valuation used by each. Experience shows that the opinions of the rival experts as to the fair market value of the real estate which is the subject of the petition will often tend to be widely divergent.

After hearing their testimony, and the rest of the evidence, the Board must make a decision as to the correct valuation of the property. Experience also shows that the Board's conclusion as to value will often be different than that of all the experts, and will often fall somewhere between the positions of the two parties.

It is important to remember that real estate appraisal is as much art as science and that, within certain parameters, the exact market value of a property must rest in the realm of opinion and judgment rather than of certainty.[3] Therefore, unless the taxpayer shows clearly that the assessors' valuation figure is unreasonable, everything militates toward the Tax Board upholding the assessors.

First, there is the traditional legal rule making the actions of public officials presumptively regular and correct.[4] Second, there is the fact that there is no scientific way to establish, beyond doubt, the absolute fair market value of property. Third, there is the practical consideration that the Appellate Tax Board does not exist to fine tune every assessment made by local officials or to substitute its judgment for theirs. Rather, it exists to correct situations where the assessors have made a more egregious error of fact or law.

A leading case[5] illustrates this, and delineates the legal position of the taxpayer who has failed to convince the Board that his property is overvalued. In the *Schlaiker* case, the taxpayer was disputing a valuation of $812,000 placed on his property by the assessors. Taxpayer's own expert, using the capitalization of income method,[6] had arrived at a value of $573,000. At the hearing before the Board the chairman of the Great Barrington assessors, who was not a qualified real estate appraiser, testified that the assessors had used the "reproduction cost less depreciation" method of valuation.

The language of the Supreme Judicial Court decision indicates that other than this statement very little evidence was adduced before the Tax Board by the assessors in support of their valuation figure, particularly in comparison to the presentation of the taxpayer's expert. The Board's findings indicated that it had placed great reliance on the tax stamps on the deed which indicated that the taxpayer had recently purchased the property for an amount in excess of $950,000. This was clearly hearsay, however, and there was no other competent evidence of the purchase price introduced at the hearing.

---

[3] Jordan Marsh Co. v. Assessors of Malden, 359 Mass. 106, 267 N.E.2d 912 (1971).

[4] American Employers' Insurance Co. v. Comm'r of Ins., 298 Mass. 161, 10 N.E.2d 76 (1937).

[5] Schlaiker v. Board of Assessors of Great Barrington, 310 N.E.2d 602 (1974).

[6] *See* § 17.05[8], *supra*.

The Tax Board upheld the valuation of the assessors. It expressly dismissed the valuation by the taxpayer's expert on the ground that his methods were flawed, in that he failed to show that a nursing home was the highest and best use of the property, failed to show that the nursing home was being operated efficiently, and failed to justify some of the operating, expenses shown on the taxpayer's income statement.

But, even conceding the fact that the expert's testimony contained some rather careless gaps, there was substantially more evidence before the Board supporting the taxpayer's valuation figure than that of the assessors. Indeed, there was virtually no competent evidence before the Board supporting the assessors' valuation, and it seems fair to assume that the Board relied heavily on the tax stamps in reaching its decision. Yet the Supreme Judicial Court affirmed the action of the Board in denying the taxpayer's appeal.

What the Court's decision in *Schlaiker* suggests is that a hearing before the Appellate Tax Board, even though it is a de novo proceeding, with the taking of evidence and so on, is not, at least from a purely legal viewpoint, a contest where each side begins on a more or less equal basis and may prove its case by a preponderance of the evidence, as in an ordinary law suit. Rather, it is a contest where the assessors are presumed to be correct and must prevail absent a clear and convincing showing by the taxpayer that he is entitled to an abatement as a matter of law.[7] Thus, according to the Supreme Judicial Court, it is "proper for the Board to presume that the valuation of the property by the assessors is valid, unless the taxpayer has clearly proved the contrary"[8] In a margin note to the *Schlaiker* decision, the Court points out that while among the general principles of administrative law applicable to the Appellate Tax Board is the requirement that its findings "must be supported by substantial evidence on the record as a whole, where as here there is no persuasive evidence on the part of the party carrying the burden of proof, a conclusion that a presumptively valid assessment must stand is by its nature not such an affirmative finding as to require substantial evidence to support it."[9]

This language is really quite compelling. *Schlaiker* reminds us that it is entirely within the power of the Board, as the trier of fact, simply to disbelieve the taxpayer's witnesses"[10] (although unrebutted and corroborated testimony may not be rejected without a basis for such rejection in the record)[11] and, even if the

---

[7] Judson Freight Forwarding Co. v. Commonwealth, 242 Mass. 47, 136 N.E. 375 (1922).

[8] Schlaiker v. Board of Assessors of Great Barrington, 310 N.E.2d 602, at 604.

[9] Schlaiker v. Board of Assessors of Great Barrington, 310 N.E.2d 602.

[10] Lindenbaum v. New York, N.H. & H. Ry. Co., 197 Mass. 314, 84 N.E. 129 (1908).

[11] Salisbury Water Supply Co. v. Department of Public Utilities, 344 Mass. 716, 184 N.E.2d 44 (1962).

assessors offer no evidence whatever in support of their valuation, the presumption of validity which attaches to their assessment can be enough to carry the day.[12]

Since by statute the decision of the Board as to findings of fact is final, the refusal to believe the taxpayer's evidence would not be reviewable, unless clearly arbitrary and unreasonable.[13] Given the fairly subjective nature of all real estate appraisal methods, in most cases the Tax Board should be able to find a sufficient number of reasons for disagreeing with the taxpayer's expert to prevent a finding of arbitrariness on its part.[14]

The lesson for the taxpayer is clear. Since in the case of claimed overvaluation he bears such a heavy burden of proof before the Board, he should have his evidence as to value carefully thought out and prepared according to judicially accepted appraisal principles, with each element that involves an exercise of discretion by the appraiser fully justified.

He should plan if he has income property to use the capitalization of income method of proving valuation if at all possible, since the discretion allowed his expert in determining the proper figure for net income and the proper capitalization rate will facilitate the presentation of evidence favorable to the taxpayer's position, and since it has become more and more favored in recent years as a method of valuing income property.

And, he should realize that unless he is able to show the Board clearly that the valuation of the assessors is substantially off the mark he will probably lose, and that if he does lose, his chances of overturning the Board on appeal on the valuation question are virtually nil.

§ 17.07[2]   Proving Assessment in Excess of Fair Market Value

Once the assessors have denied his application, the appeal to the Board is merely the continuation by the taxpayer of his disagreement with the assessors, in another forum. The ultimate issue remains the same: has the taxpayer's property been assessed at an amount in excess of its fair market value? Where there is no claim of disproportionate assessment, this may very likely be the only issue.[15]

The taxpayer/appellant is thus usually in the position of simply gathering up his

---

[12] Newcomb v. Board of Aldermen, 271 Mass. 565, 171 N.E. 826 (1930).

[13] G.L. c. 58A, § 13; New Bedford Gas & Edison Light Co. v. Board of Assessors of Dartmouth, 355 N.E.2d 897 (1975).

[14] Jordan Marsh Co. v. Board of Assessors of Malden, 359 Mass. 106, 267 N.E.2d 912 (1971).

[15] Prior to the passage of St. 1979, c. 383 in July of 1979, adding § 12C to M.G.L. c. 58A, the Tax Board could not consider any issue of fact or law not raised in the petition or answer unless "equity and good conscience so required." It now seems, although the point is not completely clear, that the Board must consider the disproportion issue on its own motion in every case.

arguments and proofs and proceeding, to the Board for a de novo hearing on the valuation question. However, since his appeal constitutes an escalation of his dispute with the assessors, and since the assessors are presumed to be correct in their valuation, absent a clear showing by the taxpayer that they are not, it would be wise for taxpayer's counsel to review thoroughly his or her evidentiary position.

The evidence that he submitted before the assessors on the fair cash value of his property, and the fair cash value and assessed value of other comparable properties may have been unsystematic, sketchy and unsupported by expert testimony. Such evidence may have been entirely adequate to form the basis of negotiations with the assessors. It may very well be inadequate to support an appeal before the Tax Board.

The Board has expressed in a number of its opinions the desire that the taxpayer be afforded a meaningful appeal and that he not be denied that right because of the imposition of overly burdensome or prohibitively expensive standards of proof. It may therefore be expected that the Board will require less in the way of proof from the taxpayer who appeals the tax on his own home than would be expected from the taxpayer who appeals the tax on a 300-unit apartment house. Nevertheless, it belabors the obvious to suggest that the taxpayer, small and large alike, should prepare the best case on the issue of valuation that the circumstances will allow, rather than relying on the indulgence of the Board.

If at all feasible, the taxpayer should enlist at this point the services of a qualified, professional real estate appraiser. At the very least he should hire a local broker to assist him.

Where income property is the subject of the appeal, the capitalization of income method will most often be the primary basis for establishing the value of the property, and income property owners who proceed before the Board without the services of an expert appraiser have good reason to be less than hopeful about the outcome.

A seasoned appraiser will know how to prepare a proper report based on the various valuation methods without much assistance. But counsel for the taxpayer should be certain that the appraiser is prepared to justify his conclusions on the comparability of index sales where the market comparison valuation method is used, and his conclusions on fair rental value, appropriate expenses and proper capitalization value where the capitalization method is used.[16]

Where non-income property, particularly single-family residential property, is involved it will usually not be feasible to hire an appraiser. In such cases, the

---

[16] *See* discussions at § 17.05[8] *et seq.* herein, which explain method of proving value of income real estate by capitalization of the income flow.

taxpayer should consider hiring an experienced local broker to evaluate his property. He should also expand his research into recent sales of comparable properties in the municipality. A well-prepared survey of comparable properties with sales and assessment figures, photographs, and charts showing in detail the similarities and dissimilarities of the taxpayer's property and the comparable properties will be of immeasurable assistance to the taxpayer in carrying his burden before the Board. At the very least the taxpayer should have a survey of other comparable properties with photographs, assessor's field records and assessed values. Assessed values of comparable properties are specifically made admissible by statute.[17]

§ 17.07[3]   Assessment of Different Kinds of Property at Different Percentages of Value (Disproportion).

A second theory upon which the taxpayer can base his petition for abatement is that of the claimed existence of a scheme of disproportionate assessment which discriminates against him. Such a scheme exists when different classes of property are deliberately assessed at different percentages of fair market value. For example, residential property may be assessed at 40% of market value, commercial property at 70% of market value, industrial property at 85%, and so on. Such a practice has been repeatedly declared to be illegal.[18]

The importance of disproportionate assessment claims in tax abatement practice has been sharply diminished during the 1980's and 1990's through the implementation of triennial revaluations by municipalities. Many municipalities also utilize valuation adjustments between revaluations, called "factoring," based on computer programs which key on sales/assessment ratios of properties sold during the interim period. Where a municipality has been certified by the Department of Revenue (DOR) as assessing its real property at 100% of fair cash value, the principles discussed in this section will likely be useful only where the taxpayer's attorney believes that some kind of intra class disproportion can be shown, as where residential condominiums are systematically assessed at a greater proportion of fair cash value than single family homes. Even then, the taxpayer trying to make out a disproportion claim in a DOR certified municipality faces a very difficult burden indeed.[19]

If the taxpayer can demonstrate that he has been the victim of a scheme of discriminatory, disproportionate assessment, he must be granted an abatement which will make his assessment proportional to other assessments. In order to obtain this relief, the taxpayer must first establish that there has been improper

---

[17] G.L. c. 58A, § 12B

[18] Bettigole v. Board of Assessors of Springfield, 343 Mass. 223, 178 N.E.2d 10 (1961); Town of Sudbury v. Comm'r of Corporations and Taxation, 366 Mass. 558, 321 N.E.2d 641 (1974).

[19] Brown v. Assessors of Brookline, 43 Mass. App. 327 (1997).

assessment of such a number of properties at less than fair cash value, and on a basis discriminating against him, as to support an inference that there was a deliberate scheme of such an assessment.[20]

Once this is established, the burden of going forward shifts to the assessors and they must introduce evidence to show that there was no such scheme. "… Sustaining that burden requires that the assessors make an affirmative showing of a reasonable effort to apply the statutory standard of full and fair cash value … The assessment process should be shown to be more than the mere exercise of judgment or whim of individual assessors following visual examination of each particular property."[21] If the assessors fail to carry this burden, then the taxpayer has a right to have his assessment reduced.

Where the Board finds that the taxpayer has been assessed disproportionately, it must determine the measure of damages as follows:

1. Compute an equalized tax rate by dividing the total taxes assessed for that city or town for the year for which the finding was made by the fair cash value of the city or town, which fair cash value shall not be higher than the equalized value determined pursuant to G.L. c. 58, § 10C for the next preceding year.

2. Apply the equalized tax rate to the fair cash value of the property to determine the taxes that should have been paid.

3. Subtract the amount of taxes that should have been paid from those actually paid or assessed. The difference is the abatement due the taxpayer.

4. Provided however, where the municipality has implemented property classifications, the measure of damages shall be computed based on the tax rate of the class in which the property has been or should have been assessed.[22]

§ 17.07[4]   Proving Disproportion

In order to establish the existence of a disproportionate assessment scheme in a particular city or town, it is necessary for the taxpayer to introduce before the Board reliable, admissible evidence of the fact that there is a widespread disparity between the valuation of property for tax purposes and its actual fair cash value.

The methods employed by taxpayers over the years to prove the existence of disproportionate assessment schemes to the Appellate Tax Board have been

---

[20] Shoppers' World, Inc. v. Board of Assessors of Framingham, 348 Mass. 366, 203 N.E.2d 811 (1965).

[21] First National Stores v. Somerville, 358 Mass. 554, 265 N.E.2d 848 (1971).

[22] G.L. c. 58A, § 14.

diverse, to say the least;[23] and presentations have run the gamut from exhaustive preparation and sophistication to ignorant blundering.[24]

The formidable problems of proof which taxpayers once faced in trying to establish a disproportion case have been substantially mitigated by the passage of a statute[25] which requires that the Appellate Tax Board admit into evidence, on its own motion, the reports of the Commissioner of Revenue to the legislature relative to the assessment/fair cash value ratios of each class of property in each of the several cities and towns. The statute further provides that such report "shall be prima facie evidence of the assessment practices of the city or town and the ratios at which property is assessed ..."[26]

There has thus been a dramatic reduction in the burden of proof imposed upon a taxpayer who seeks an abatement based on a claim of disproportionate assessment. The Tax Board must now consider the assessment/fair cash value ratios determined by the Commissioner of Revenue in every appeal whether or not the taxpayer introduces them into evidence. If the ratios show the existence of widespread, discriminatory underassessment, then the burden shifts to the assessors to adduce evidence of their efforts to assess properties fairly. If they fail, the taxpayer sustains his burden of proof by showing that the assessment/fair cash value ratio for his own property is higher than that of the most favored class. This showing can be made by introducing expert testimony to prove the value of taxpayer's property, and by introducing the tax bill showing its assessed value. If the assessment/fair cash value ratio thus established is greater than the average ratio for the most favored class of property as shown by the report of the Commissioner, then the taxpayer is entitled to abatement.

§ 17.07[4][a]   Can There Be a Class Within a Class?

What if the taxpayer is himself the owner of residential property, assessed at perhaps 55% of fair market, while other residential property owners are assessed at 25% or 30% of market value? What are the rights of this taxpayer once he establishes the existence of a disproportionate assessment scheme? Does he have the right to be assessed at the median or average percentage valuation of the entire class of residential property? Or, can he attempt to establish the existence of a separate "class within a class" of residential properties and to have his assessment made equal to that class?

In one case,[27] the taxpayer was able to establish the existence of two sub-classes

---

[23] *See*, for example, Chomerics, Inc. v. Board of Assessors of Woburn, 6 Mass. App. Ct. 394.
[24] *See* H.L. Kavet et al. v. Board of Assessors of Watertown, Appellate Tax Board 1978-61.
[25] St. 1979, c. 383.
[26] G.L. c. 58A. § 12c.
[27] Beardsley v. Board of Assessors of Foxborough, 369 Mass. 855, 343 N.E.2d 359 (1976).

of residential properties and the fact that these sub-classes were assessed at different percentages of fair cash value: he was granted an abatement sufficient to make the assessment on his residence proportional to the favored residential sub-class.

The taxpayer carried his burden of proof by introducing an exhibit showing the assessed valuations and sale prices of all properties sold in the particular subdivision where his property was located during the years 1970-1973.

The properties were divided into two groups, with all Capes and Garrisons in one group and all Splits and Ranches in the other. The exhibit was based on six sales in 1970, six sales in 1971, fifteen sales in 1972, and ten sales in 1973, and it indicated that in each year the Cape/Garrison group was assessed at a higher percentage of aggregate sale price than was the Split/Ranch group.

The assessors also introduced evidence showing that the assessment/sales ratios of Capes and Garrisons sold in the subdivision during 1971, 1972, and 1973 were higher than the ratio for all single family houses sold in the town in those years. (It is difficult to conceive of what purpose the assessors could have had in introducing this evidence since it supports the inference of improper assessment rather than rebutting it.)

Based on the foregoing evidence, the owners of houses in the Cape/Garrison group were given abatements to the level of the Split/Ranch group.

The *Beardsley* case seems pretty clearly to stand for the proposition that intraclass discriminatory disproportionate assessment can be a ground for abatement.

Thus, if a residential property owner can show that the property in a particular section of the municipality is more favorably assessed than that in other sections, or if he can show older houses are more favorably assessed than newer houses, he should have a right to abatement.[28]

§ 17.07[5] Improper Classification

Improper classification claims have not generated much litigation. This is probably because a case decided by the Supreme Judicial Court in 1986 pretty much reads the classification guidelines issued by the Department of Revenue into the statute.[29] The guidelines, which are contained in a publication entitled Guidelines for Classification and Taxation of Property According to Use, break down the four statutory classifications into over two hundred sub-classes. Whenever a dispute does arise it can usually be settled locally by reference to these guidelines. Where

---

[28] *See* Olympia & York State Street Co. v. Assessors of Boston, 428 Mass. 236 (1998), where the SJC approved a finding by the Appellate Tax Board of the existence of a sub-class of "Class A +" office towers in the City of Boston.

[29] McNeill v. Board of Assessors of West Springfield, 396 Mass. 603, 487 N.E.2d 849 (1986).

the property does not clearly fall into one of the categories set out in the guidelines it may be expected that the Appellate Tax Board will use them as a basis for reasoning by analogy in deciding any case which comes before it.

VALUING PROPERTIES ACCORDING TO USE

§ 17.08 Generally

In November of 1978, the voters of the Commonwealth approved an Amendment to the State Constitution by virtue of which the legislature is permitted to classify real property according to its use, for purposes of taxation. This is, of course, contrary to the previous long standing rule that all property be assessed and taxed at the same rate and at 100% of fair cash value.

The 1978 Classification Act was held constitutional by the Supreme Judicial Court on July 6, 1979.[1] In November of 1979, the legislature passed a second Classification Act[2] which repealed the 1978 Act and substituted an entirely different scheme of taxation based on use.

The statute provides that the classification of real property shall apply to the assessment of taxes on property for fiscal years beginning on or after July 1, 1980. However classification cannot be implemented in any city or town until the Commissioner of Revenue has certified in writing to the assessors that they have assessed all property at full and fair cash value and that a majority of the assessors are qualified to classify the property according to use.[3]

§ 17.08[1] How Classification Works

Under classification all real property is divided into four main categories:

1. Class one, residential—property used or held for human habitation containing one or more dwelling units including rooming houses with facilities designed and used for living, sleeping, cooking and eating on a non-transient basis. Such property includes accessory land, buildings or improvements incidental to such habitation and used exclusively by the residents of the property or their guests, land in a residential zone which has been subdivided into residential lots and land used for the purpose of a manufactured housing community. Such property shall not include a hotel, or motel. Such property may be exempt from taxation under other pro-

---

[1] Associated Industries of Massachusetts, Inc. v. Commissioner of Revenue, 378 Mass. 657, 393 N.E.2d 812.

[2] St. 1979, c. 797.

[3] G.L. c. 59, § 2A.

visions of law. The portion of any property which is operated as a child care facility pursuant to G.L. c. 40A, § 9C shall be classified as residential.[4]

2. Class two, open-space—land which is not otherwise classified and which is not taxable under the provisions of chapter sixty-one, sixty-one A, or sixty-one B, or taxable under a permanent conservation restriction, and which land is not held for the production of income but is maintained in an open or natural condition and which contributes significantly to the benefit and enjoyment of the public.

3. Class three, commercial—property used or held for use for business purposes and not specifically includible in another class, including but not limited to any commercial, business, retail, trade, service, recreational, agricultural, artistic, sporting, fraternal, governmental, educational, medical or religious enterprise, for non-profit purposes. Such property may be expressly exempt from taxation under other provisions of this chapter.

4. Class four, industrial—property used or held for use for manufacturing, milling, converting, producing, processing or fabricating materials; the extraction or processing of materials unserviceable in their natural state to create commercial products or materials, the mechanical, chemical or electronic transformation of property into new products and any use that is incidental to or an integral part of such use, whether for profit or non-profit purposes: and property used or held for use for the storage, transmitting and generating of utilities regulated by the department of public utilities. Such property may be exempt from taxation under other provisions of law.

Where real property is used or held for use for more than one purpose and such uses result in different classifications, the assessors must allocate to each classification the percentage of the fair-cash valuation of the property devoted to each use according to the guidelines issued by, the Commissioner of Revenue.

Once all the real property in a community has been valued at 100% of its full and fair cash value and has been assigned to one of the four statutory classes it is necessary to determine the "class percentage" for each class.[5] This is the percentage of the total tax levy for the fiscal year which must be borne by such class. These percentages are determined biennially on or before May 1, by the assessors with the approval of the selectmen in towns, and by the mayor with the approval of the city council in cities.

Before determining the class percentages, however, the selectmen or mayor, as the case may be, must first adopt a "residential factor." This factor determines what

---

[4] 3.1 G.L. c. 59, § 3F.
[5] St. 1979, c. 797, § 1, adding § 56 to G.L. c. 40.

percentage of its pro rata share of the tax burden will be borne by residential property.

The residential factor set by the municipality is subject to a minimum set by the Commissioner of Revenue. It must always be at least 65% and it must be even higher if that is necessary to assure that no class of property pays more than one and one-half times its proportionate share of the total tax levy.

In other words, if commercial property accounts for only 10% of total assessed value it cannot be responsible for more than 15% of the total tax levy, and the minimum residential factor must be raised high enough by the Commissioner to assure this.

Once the various percentages are determined for each class the assessors will set the tax rate for that class based on the total cash value of the property, and the amount of tax dollars which must be contributed by it.

§ 17.08[2] The Residential Exemption

At the option of the board of selectmen, or the mayor with the approval of the city council, as applicable, there is an exemption for the principal residence of a taxpayer equal to twenty percent of the average assessed value of all class one residential parcels.[6] So if there are 100 residential parcels in the community and the total assessed value of all residential property is $1,000,000, then the residential exemption is equal to $2,000 per parcel.

However, since the total tax dollars which must be contributed by residential property owners will have already been fixed according to the formula illustrated above, the exemption can only have the effect of shifting the residential tax burden from lower to higher value homes.

For example, if $50,000 of the tax levy had to be raised from taxing residential property and total value of such property was $500,000 then the tax rate would be 10%. But if $50,000 is removed from total assessed value by exemptions then the same $50,000 in taxes must be raised from a residential tax base of $450,000 and the tax rate would be 11.1%. Since the first $5,000 in taxable valuation is removed from each parcel, the more expensive homes will suffer a higher percentage exposure to the increased rate.

§ 17.08[3] The Small Commercial Exemption

At the option of the board of selectmen, or the mayor with the approval of the

---

[6] G.L. c. 59, § 5c. This exemption is unavailable where the taxpayer's residence is held in trust by an entity other than the taxpayer. Moscatiello v. Board of Assessors, 36 Mass. App. 622, 634 N.E.2d 147 (1994), summary op at 22 M.L.W. 2044 (Mass. App.).

city council, as applicable, there is an exemption of up to ten percent of the value of Class Three, Commercial, parcels with a fair cash value of less than one million dollars that are occupied by businesses with an average annual employment of no more than ten people at all locations during the previous calendar year, as certified by the Commissioner of the Department of Employment and Training. Like the residential exemption, the small commercial exemption is a reduction in the taxable valuation of the property made by the assessors before setting the tax rate. If adopted, it has the effect of reducing property taxes on properties occupied by small businesses and shifting those taxes onto other commercial and industrial properties.[7]

§ 17.08[4]   Effect of Classification on Abatements and Exemptions

Even though a parcel of real estate may be exempt from taxation, in most cases it must still be classified into one of the four statutory classes. This being the case, the inclusion of exempt property in a particular class will be a matter of concern to the non-exempt members of that class, since the effect of the classification statute is that they will be required to pay the entire tax burden that would otherwise be borne by the exempt property.

The sole exceptions to this rule of inclusion are forest land and agricultural/horticultural land which has qualified for special taxation under G.L. c. 61 and c. 61A, and recreational land taxed under G.L. c. 61B.

It does not appear that urban redevelopment projects have been excluded from being classified. This seems odd because like qualified agricultural property these properties pay a substitute tax whereas other exempt property pays nothing. Thus it seems unfair to the other members of the class in which they are included for urban renewal properties to add to the tax burdens of the class, with no offset for the in lieu excise payments made to the municipality.

With respect to abatements, there is now, of course, the additional ground of improper classification as a basis of appeal. There is also the effect of classification on disproportionate assessment cases. Under the taxation scheme embodied in the 1979 Classification Act all property must be assessed at full and fair cash value and a different tax rate is then applied to each class. Any policy by the assessors whereby one class of property is purposely undervalued or valued at a lower percentage of full value than other classes will result in disproportion as surely as it does where classification is not in effect.

Additionally, the constitutional amendment[8] which made classification possible requires that property within each class be taxed "proportionately." So it would

---

[7] G.L. c. 59, § 5I.
[8] Amend. Art. 112, amending Art. 4 of c. I of Part the Second of the Constitution.

seem that a taxpayer who could prove a pattern of discriminatory assessment within his class should also have a right to abatement.

CHAPTER 18

REAL ESTATE TAX ABATEMENTS AND EXEMPTIONS—THE PRACTICE

Synopsis

§ 18.01   Obtaining Real Estate Tax Abatements
    § 18.01[1]   Preliminary Information
    § 18.01[2]   Evaluate the Case
    § 18.01[3]   File the Appropriate Applications
    § 18.01[4]   Appeal Unfavorable Action By Assessors to the Appellate Tax Board
    § 18.01[5]   Determine Whether to Utilize the Limited Discovery Available
    § 18.01[6]   The Hearing
    § 18.01[7]   Real Estate Tax Abatement Timetable

§ 18.01   Obtaining Real Estate Tax Abatements

§ 18.01[1]   Preliminary Information

Step 1. Obtain the basic information from the client necessary to complete the Information List—Abatement of Real Estate Tax.

Step 2. Determine without delay the various statutory time limits applicable to the client's abatement rights, and whether those time limits have been adhered to.

Step 3. Obtain copies of all documents have been received from or filed with the assessors.

Step 4. Determine whether or not a professional appraisal of the property has been completed recently. If so, obtain a copy of the same.

Step 5. Obtain any other information the client may have about the history and condition of the property.

Step 6. Obtain any information the client may have about assessments of other comparable properties in the same municipality. Disgruntled property owners will often obtain this information on their own, and it is sometimes useful.

§ 18.01[2]   Evaluate the Case

Step 7. Using the actual assessed value, the applicable tax rate and the likely assessed value after any abatement, determine the potential recovery in the case. This is crucial to determining whether it is worth your while and your client's while for you to take on the case. Persons who feel overtaxed often develop a sense of outrage out of all proportion to the money involved. This evaluation process is an important reality check for everyone involved.

§ 18.01[3]   File the Appropriate Applications

Step 8. Beginning with fiscal year 1998, an application for abatement must be made on or before the last day for payment of the first installment of the actual tax bill issued upon the establishment of the tax rate for the fiscal year to which the tax relates. This is a recent change from the decades old rule that application had to be filed within thirty days from the date the tax bill was mailed, a rule that caused frequent confusion and lost rights on the part of taxpayers. The bill must also have printed upon it the last date for the assessed owner to apply for abatement or exemption under provisions other than those listed in c. 59. If a bill or notice contains an erroneous payment or abatement application date that is later than the date established under c. 59, the date printed on the bill or notice shall be the deadline for payment or applying for abatement or exemption. (Volume 6, Chapter 18, Form 143).

Step 9. Be sure to make a timely response to reasonable requests for information about the property received from the assessors. Failure to do so may result in the loss of the right of appeal to the Appellate Tax Board.

§ 18.01[4]   Appeal Unfavorable Action By Assessors to the Appellate Tax Board

Step 10. If the client has received an abatement unsatisfactory in amount (Volume 6, Chapter 18, Form 144) or a denial of any abatement whatsoever (Volume 6, Chapter 18, Form 145), it will be necessary to file an appeal to the Appellate Tax Board.

Step 11. Appeal to Appellate Tax Board under either Formal Procedure (Volume 6, Chapter 18, Form 146), or Informal Procedure (Volume 6, Chapter 18, Forms 146 and 147), must be filed to be received no later than 3 months after the date the assessors acted.

Step 12. If no response to the application for abatement has been received from the assessors check to see if 3 months have elapsed since the date of filing of the application. If so, file an appeal with the Appellate Tax Board as provided above.

The taxpayer's right to appeal to the Appellate Tax Board automatically expires 6 months from the date of filing the application for abatement with the assessors.

Step 13. If more than 6 months has passed since the date of filing of the application for abatement with the assessors, and the client has not received a timely notice of deemed denial, file a Petition for Late Entry of An Appeal (Volume 6, Chapter 18, Form 149).

If the Petition is allowed, as most are, file your appeal with the Tax Board.

Step 14. Be sure that the taxes for the first half of the fiscal year are paid on time without incurring any interest. If client can demonstrate financial hardship which makes him/her/it unable to pay the second half tax bill the Tax Board may, on motion, grant an extension of time to pay. Subsequent requests for extension should be made to the Board prior to the expiration of the current extension period.

§ 18.01[5]   Determine Whether to Utilize the Limited Discovery Available

Step 15. Tax Board practice does not contemplate the kind of extensive discovery typical of civil actions in the courts. In many cases there is not formal discovery whatsoever. (*See* Volume 6, Chapter 18, Form 150 for sample interrogatories).

A fairly recent statutory amendment allows the Board, upon motion, to order an exchange of appraiser's reports. The desirability of obtaining the opponent's report must be weighed against the necessity of turning over your own.

§ 18.01[6]   The Hearing

Step 16. Request a stenographer at least one day prior to the hearing if the case is being heard under the Formal procedure.

Step 17. Be prepared to introduce your appraisal report into evidence.

Step 18. Be ready to file requests for findings of fact and rulings of law at the conclusion of the hearing and prior to oral argument, or prior to submission without oral argument.

Step 19. Briefs may be filed before or at the time of hearing, or within a time thereafter set by the Board member hearing the case.

Step 20. If an appeal to the Appeals Court is contemplated file a Request for Report within 10 days after the Board makes its decision.

§ 18.01[7]   Real Estate Tax Abatement Timetable for Lawyers

July 1–June 30	Municipal Fiscal Year
January 1	Assessment Date-Property is assessed based on its ownership and condition as of this date. Tax for next succeeding fiscal year based on this assessment. Municipalities which have accepted certain local option statutes can assess improvements made after January 1.

June 20, or 90 days after tax bills are mailed, whichever is later.

	Deadline for assessment of omitted property by assessors pursuant to G.L. c. 59, § 75.
July 1	Eligibility for exemptions under G.L. c. 59, § 5, determined as of this date
Sept. 20–Oct. 1	The holder of a mortgage who has paid not less than one-half of the tax on the property must if it wishes to apply for abatement do so during this period.

July 1–June 30	Municipal Fiscal Year
October 1	Applications for abatement must be filed by this date if (actual as opposed to preliminary) tax bill was mailed on or before September 1. Otherwise, application for abatement must be filed on or before the 30th day after the date on which the bill was mailed, or the last date for payment of tax without interest printed on the tax bill, whichever is later.
November 1	If the tax is greater than $3000, one-half of assessed tax must be paid by this date to prevent the incurring of interest and to preserve the right to appeal to Appellate Tax Board. However, if the tax bill is mailed after October 1, then one-half the assessed tax must be paid on or before the 30th day after the date on which the bill was mailed or by the last date for payment without interest printed on the tax bill, whichever is later. But see G.L. c. 59, § 64 for provisions allowing payment of tax based on average valuation of three preceding years.
30 Days after Tax Bill is Mailed	Taxes based on omitted or revised assessments (G.L. c. 59, §§ 75 & 76) must be paid by this date to prevent incurring of interest. In municipalities which have accepted the quarterly billing statute these bills are due 30 days after mailing or May 1, whichever is later.
December 15	Application for exemption for surviving spouses, hardship, veterans, blind persons surviving spouses and children of police or firemen killed in the line of duty, and elderly persons must be made on or before this date, if the bill was first sent after September 1, otherwise within 3 months after the bill is sent.

July 1–June 30	Municipal Fiscal Year
February 1	Notice of second half of taxes for fiscal year due to be sent.
May 1	If the tax is more than $3000, second half of taxes for fiscal year must be paid to prevent incurring of interest and to preserve right to appeal, even if appeal pending at appellate tax board, unless that board grants an extension.
3 Months After Tax Bill Is Sent To Taxpayer	
	Time during which taxpayer aggrieved by omitted, revised or reassessed tax (G.L. c. 59, §§ 75, 76, 77) may apply for abatement.

3 Months After Date of Denial of Application for Abatement

> Time limit during which taxpayer may appeal assessors' denial to County Commissioners or Appellate Tax Board.

6 Months After Date of Filing of Application for Abatement

> Time limit for filing appeal to the County Commissioners or Appellate Tax Board where assessors fail to act on application for abatement, unless applicant has consented to delay in writing. Otherwise application deemed denied 3 months after filing if no action. Appeal period runs 3 months after deemed denial. Notice of denial sent by assessors more than three months after filing application will not extend period for appeal to tab board. A late denial is held by the board to be invalid.

8 Months After Date of Filing of Application for Abatement

July 1–June 30

Municipal Fiscal Year
Time limit for filing petition for late entry of appeal with Appellate Tax Board where assessors fail to act on application for abatement and fail to send Notice of Inaction to taxpayer, provided taxpayer had not earlier given timely written consent to assessors' delay. If assessors send Notice of Inaction within 10 days after the application is deemed to be denied then taxpayer's right to file for late entry is foreclosed.

CHAPTER 19

DRAFTING A COMMERCIAL LEASE—THE PRACTICE

Synopsis

§ 19.01   Introduction

§ 19.02   Identify Parties

§ 19.03   Describe Premises and Appurtenances Fully

§ 19.04   Set Forth Warranties of Title and Authority

§ 19.05   Set Forth Lease Term and Base Rent With Specificity

§ 19.06   Define Conditions Under Which Lease Agreement May Be Extended or Renewed

§ 19.07   Include Provisions for Any Automatic Rent Escalators Agreed to By Parties

§ 19.08   Provide for Security Deposit to be Held by Lessor

§ 19.09   Provide for Payment of Utilities

§ 19.10   Describe Any Limitations on Use of Premises

§ 19.11   Describe Any Limitations on Assignment or Sublease

§ 19.12   Define Duties of the Parties with Respect to Maintenance and Repair

§ 19.13   Signs

§ 19.14   Define Rights of the Parties with Respect to Structural Alteration or Additions to Premises

§ 19.15   Set Forth Respective Obligations of Parties To Make Repairs

§ 19.16   Set Forth the Responsibilities of Parties With Respect to Indemnity and Insurance

§ 19.17   Define Rights of the Parties in Event Property is Partially Destroyed or Taken by Eminent Domain

§ 19.18   Subrogation in Event of Casualty Loss

§ 19.19   Set Forth Events of Default Under Lease

§ 19.20   Subordination of Subsequent Mortgages

§ 19.21   **Miscellaneous Provisions**

§ 19.01 Introduction

The purpose of this chapter is to illustrate the considerations that go into the drafting of a lease for a smaller commercial tenant. This is done through the presentation of three sample forms of commercial lease, Lease A (Volume 6, Chapter 19, Form 115), which is a standard lessors' form of lease, Lease B (Volume 6, Chapter 19, Form 116), which is the same form modified to be somewhat gentler to the lessee and Lease C (Volume 6, Chapter 19, Form 116.1), which is a somewhat more complex lease, dealing with the same issues dealt with in the first two leases in more detail and providing terms for "build-out" of the leased space to suit the lessee's requirements..

It should be clear that all the leases are somewhat favorable to the Lessor. But unless he, she, or it is a major, key tenant, lessee cannot ordinarily hope to negotiate dramatic changes to the usual lessor-oriented lease, and must be content with attempting to ameliorate some of the harsher clauses.

§ 19.02 Identify Parties

It is best to identify all parties to the lease fully, with designation of form of legal entity and address of principal office. All lease forms use similar language.

§ 19.03 Describe Premises and Appurtenances Fully

While any description which identifies the premises with certainty is sufficient, the better practice is to include a full legal description of the property. There should also be a full and clear description of lessee's right to use appurtenant rights of ways, parking spaces, alleyways, and so on. Lease Forms A and B assume that this will be done through the use of an attachment to the lease designated as "exhibit A." Lease Form C uses a preliminary "Reference Data" paragraph that spells out parking and signage rights in writing. The use of this type of paragraph also allows the major terms of the lease to be placed up front in one place where the non-lawyer persons involved in the transaction can review them conveniently. Finally the paragraph makes it easier to use the lease as a template because most changes needed to be made from lease to lease are concentrated in one place. If the tenant is concerned that common areas, such as lobbies or yards, remain as they are when the lease is signed, this should be specifically provided for. The landlord may of course resist this. Lease C has a provision giving the lessee a first option on contiguous space in the building should it become available.

§ 19.04 Set Forth Warranties of Title and Authority

Leases often contain a warranty by the lessor that it has good record title to the property and sufficient interest therein to allow it to convey the leasehold to Lessee. Where a corporation, LLC, trust, or similar entity is involved, creating an issue as to the authority of the person signing the lease, appropriate votes, or other documentation of authority should be attached.

§ 19.05   Set Forth Lease Term and Base Rent With Specificity

It will be noted that the sample lease forms define the lease term through the use of both dates and times. This eliminates potential confusion with respect to the first and last day of the term. Where the premises are not empty, or are otherwise unready for occupancy at the time the lease is signed the lessee will want the commencement of the lease term to be deferred until occupancy is obtained. Forms B & C contain language to this effect.

The "base rent," which is the rent without additional payments which may be required by tax or operating expense escalators, is also carefully set out with reference to the lease term. Also set out are the rent payment periods and whether payments are to be in advance or in arrears. Lease Form C is substantially more precise with respect to the so-called "Additional Rent" escalators.

§ 19.06   Define Conditions Under Which Lease Agreement May Be Extended or Renewed

The sample forms contain "extension" clauses which contemplate a continuation of the lease for an additional period on the same terms, except to the extent that the clause provides for renegotiation of certain items. The agreed rental is of course the most common item made subject to renegotiation in an extension clause.

Note that lease Form A requires the Lessee to give notice to lessor of his or her intention to extend on or before a certain date, while Form B contains an automatic extension clause.

Also, in Form A, if the parties cannot agree on a rental price for the extended term the extension will never take effect. In Form B, if there is no agreement, the matter is submitted to binding arbitration. In Form C, the rental price is to be the "prevailing market rate," subject to specified maximums.

§ 19.07   Include Provisions for Any Automatic Rent Escalators Agreed to By Parties

The most common forms of rent escalators are tax escalators and operating expense escalators. While lessee can sometimes resist the inclusion of an operating expense escalator if the lease provides for base rent increases each year of the term, tax escalators are almost inevitable.

The tax escalator contained in both lease Forms A & B assumes that the lessee is occupying the entire premises. Where this is not the case language must be added to the effect that the lessee will "pay as additional rent" that percentage of the tax increase "equal to the percentage of the total rentable floor area of the entire building which is represented by the floor area leased by lessee under this Agreement." Lease Form C contains this type of pro rata clause.

With respect to operating expense escalators, it will be noted that lease Forms A & C contain such a clause while lease Form B does not. The clause in Form A assumes once again that the lessee is occupying the whole building. Where this is not the case the clause will have to be modified to provide that the lessee will pay "a percentage of such increase equal to the percentage of the total rentable floor area of the entire building which is represented by the floor area leased by lessee under this Agreement." Lease Form C contains this type of pro rata clause.

Lessees will want to be careful that the base fiscal year's taxes and expenses are based on full assessment and full operation, respectively. Lessor may want to add a provision requiring increases in operating costs to be paid by lessee as they occur, rather than being paid as additional rent at the end of the year.

§ **19.08**   **Provide for Security Deposit to be Held by Lessor**

Security deposits of at least one month's rent are of course commonplace in leases of smaller commercial properties. Note that lease Form B has a provision giving lessee a right to a return of part of his or her security deposit at the end of each year in which there has been no material default by lessee. Conversely, lease Form C requires that lessee replenish the security deposit if it is wholly or partly used to cure a default by lessee.

§ **19.09**   **Provide for Payment of Utilities**

Since both sample leases A & B assume that the lessee is occupying the entire premises a "net" lease approach is taken with respect to heat, electricity, and other utilities even though the leases are not pure net.

Where more than one tenant occupies the premises the landlord will customarily pay for utilities serving the common areas and will rely on an additional rent clause for reimbursement of such costs, with an operating expense escalator as a way of passing increased costs on to the tenants. Lease Form C contains an example of this approach with respect to some but not all utilities. It also specifies in more detail the lessor's obligations respecting utilities serving the common areas.

Where the landlord is paying for common utilities, structures or access and the tenant has special needs or concerns in this area, the lease should state specifically the landlord's obligations in this regard and the tenant's rights upon breach of those obligations. For example the tenant may demand the right to repair common area failures which substantially interfere with its business, and to charge the cost against rent.

§ **19.10**   **Describe Any Limitations on Use of Premises**

Unless the uses to which the leased premises may be put are limited by the terms of the lease, lessee may use the premises for any lawful purpose.

Few lessors are willing to surrender totally their control over the property. In addition there will often be other tenants on the property who will object to having inconsistent business activities going on next to them. So lessor will usually want to limit the use of the leased premises to one, or a few, uses. This is usually agreeable to lessee.

However, there is often a great deal of negotiation over just how narrow the restrictions on use will be. Obviously it is in the lessee's interest to have the limitation phrased as broadly as possible. From the point of view of negotiation strategy it is best to view this provision and the one restricting the right of assignment as two parts of one whole. A liberal right of assignment will be much less valuable if only one or two uses are allowed under the base.

All the lease forms contain clauses limiting use of the premises. Lease Form B contains a warranty by Lessor that the contemplated use is allowed under applicable zoning and other regulations. Lease Form C spells out use limitations in more detail and contains a clause indemnifying the lessor against liability for improper use or disposal of hazardous materials on the leased premises.

§ 19.11 Describe Any Limitations on Assignment or Sublease

If there is no provision in a lease restricting assignment or sublease then the lessee may do either as it chooses.

Since the lessor is naturally concerned with the nature and identity of any tenant of his or her property, limitations on, and frequently prohibitions of, assignments or subleases are common.

It will be recalled that an assignment transfers lessee's entire interest while a sublease transfers a smaller, or at least different, interest. In lease Form A, both assignment and subleases are prohibited. Lease Form B allows a portion of the premises to be sublet.

Rather than the outright prohibition on assignment or subletting contained in Form A, or the subletting by right contained in Form B, the lease may provide that assignment or sublease are allowed only with the written consent of lessor. The lessee will usually want a provision that such consent will not be unreasonably withheld.[1]

---

[1] In National Union Fire Ins. Co. v. Rose, 53 Mass. App. Ct. 910, 760 N.E.2d 791 (2002), the lease contained a typical clause providing that "As long as no Default of Tenant is outstanding, Landlord shall not unreasonably withhold or delay Landlord's prior consent to sub-lettings by Tenant of all or parts of the Demised Premises." However, the lease also provided:

If the rent received by Tenant on account of a sublease of all or any portion of the Demised Premises exceeds

Such language is very advantageous to the lessee in cases where a dispute over assignment arises. Often the proposed assignee is objectionable to the lessor for certain reasons but is not manifestly unsuitable. The question of the "reasonableness" of the lessor in withholding consent will then end up forming the basis of a claim or counterclaim by the lessee which has as its object the avoidance of some or all of the obligations of the lease. A possible compromise, if the lessor feels that it must compromise this important point, is to specify the objective criteria upon which proposed assignees will be judged.

Lease Form C gives the lessee the right to assign or sublease with the consent of lessor, such consent not to be unreasonably withheld. The Lessor has the right to receive certain information about the proposed assignee/sublessee before making a decision. The lessor also has the right to terminate the lease within ten days of receipt of the requested information, or to release the lessee from the lease with respect to the portion of the leased premises proposed to be sublet. This of course prevents the lessee from benefiting from a substantial rise in prevailing rents by assignment or sublease, if the lessor is willing to release lessee from its obligations under the lease or portion thereof.

§ 19.12 Define Duties of the Parties with Respect to Maintenance and Repair

All forms of lease contain a recitation of the common law duty imposed upon the lessee not to commit waste. Lease Form A places the primary burden for maintenance and repair of the premises on the lessee, as is typical in leases which contemplate that the lessee will be the sole occupant of the property.

Where there is multiple occupancy of the property, maintenance and repair responsibilities in the non-net lease will be divided between lessor and lessee.

---

the Annual Fixed Rent and Additional Rent allocated to the space subject to the sublease in the proportion of the area of such space to the area of the entire Demised Premises, plus actual out-of-pocket expenses incurred by Tenant in connection with Tenant's subleasing of such space, including without limitation reasonable attorney's fees, brokerage commissions and the cost of preparing such space for occupancy by the subtenant, Tenant shall pay to Landlord seventy-five (75) percent of such excess, monthly as received by Tenant.

The tenant attempted to sublease a portion of the premises with rent terms identical to those in its own lease. The Landlord withheld consent arguing that the tenant could sublease only at market rents—which had gone up—and that if it did not do so, it would be denying the Landlord its percentage of excess rent due under the sublease. The trial court disagreed saying that withholding consent was unreasonable because the clear language of the profit sharing sublease provision did not obligate the tenant to sublease at market rents, but was operative only if the sublease rent exceeded the tenant's rent, which it did not. The appeals court affirmed and added that the landlord's reliance on an earlier case was misplaced because that case involved a percentage of profits lease conferring expectations on the landlord the National Union lease did not. *See* Worcester-Tatnuck Square CVS, Inc. v. Kaplan, 33 Mass. App. Ct. 499, 601 N.E.2d 485 (1992).

Lessor is customarily responsible for common areas and facilities with lessee being responsible for the premises leased by it. Lease Form C takes this approach, and also contains a simple provision relating to "build-out" of the leased premises. These are matters for negotiation and a simple clause can be drafted to reflect the agreement of the parties.

§ 19.13   Signs

Lessee will usually be very concerned about its right to erect or attach signs. This is a frequent source of controversy, and the rights of the parties should be clearly spelled out in the lease.

Lease Form A gives lessor total control over signs while lease Forms B & C give lessee certain minimum rights to signage.

§ 19.14   Define Rights of the Parties with Respect to Structural Alteration or Additions to Premises

All lease forms contain the standard language prohibiting lessee from making structural or permanently affixed changes and/or additions to the leased premises without the permission of the lessor, and further providing for title to any such alterations or additions to pass to lessor at the end of the lease term. Lease Form C gives the lessor the option of taking ownership of the additions or requiring the lessee to remove them and restore the premises. Lessee has the right to remove additions that may be removed without causing substantial damage.

Lease Form B simply softens some of the language from the point of view of lessee. It is important for lessee to at least leave open the possibility of negotiating for the right to remove, or be compensated for any expensive additions to the premises.

It is not uncommon for disagreements to arise over what are "structural," or "permanently affixed" as opposed to "nonstructural," or "temporarily affixed" changes. If substantial changes by the lessee are foreseeable during the lease term it may be useful to essay the difficult task of defining these terms.

§ 19.15   Set Forth Respective Obligations of Parties To Make Repairs

All lease forms give the lessor the right to enter upon the leased premises for the purpose of making inspections and, in appropriate cases, repairs. Lease Form B substantially cuts down the lessors powers and eliminates the exculpatory language contained in lease Form A. Also, Form B does not provide that expenditures for repairs made by lessor shall be deemed additional rent owing forthwith from lessee, thereby cutting down lessors leverage in extracting such payments, and perhaps cutting down also his tendency to make unjustified repairs.

§ 19.16   Set Forth the Responsibilities of Parties With Respect to Indemnity and Insurance

Lessee customarily indemnifies lessor from liability for any loss arising out of the use or occupancy of the leased premises. Since these risks are customarily insured against the indemnity clause will not be the source of much controversy. Instead most discussion will center on the amount and nature of the insurance to be purchased by the parties, and who will pay the premiums.

Lessor will normally insure the building in the multiple occupancy non-net lease situation; otherwise the lessee provides such insurance.

Lease Form A requires that the lessee provide fire and extended coverage insurance on the building, with a company reasonably acceptable to the lessor, in an amount equal to the replacement value of the building. Lease Form B requires the lessor to provide such insurance, while lessee covenants not to permit any use of the premises which will make any insurance voidable, and to pay any increase of premium caused by its use of the premises. Lease Form C, being for less than the entire building requires lessee to carry commercial general liability insurance with respect to the leased premises, while the lessor is required to obtain such coverage, as well as casualty insurance for the land and buildings.

Lessee's counsel will often request that the indemnities be mutual, and Form B is charged to reflect this mutuality. However, the indemnity in Form A is more gentle to lessee than that found in many leases. The indemnities in Form C run in both directions but are spelled out in more detail.

§ 19.17   Define Rights of the Parties in Event Property is Partially Destroyed or Taken by Eminent Domain

Lease Forms A & C differ markedly from lease Form B in their treatment of the partial taking or casualty loss of the property. Partial destruction can be characterized as being of either a substantial or non-substantial nature. Substantial damage renders the property unsuitable for the use contemplated in the agreement; non-substantial damage on the other hand leaves the lessee with the beneficial use of the premises, even though that use may be somewhat impaired.

Lease Forms A & B impose no obligation on the lessor with respect to non-substantial damage or taking. Presumably the practicalities of the situation would force the tenant to make the necessary repairs himself.

Lease Form B requires that the lessor commence forthwith to repair any casualty damage up to the extent of any insurance proceeds, and that such repairs be completed as quickly as possible. It also provides a bright line definition of just what kind of damage is to be considered substantial and to give rise to termination rights. Form B also allows the lessee to retain its right to receive so-called "special" damages such as moving expenses in the event of an eminent domain taking.

§ 19.18   Subrogation in Event of Casualty Loss

If either party receives insurance proceeds as the result of a loss occasioned by the negligence of the other or those for whom he or she is responsible the insurer may be subrogated to the insured's rights against the negligent party. Lease Forms B & C each contain a clause of a type frequently found in commercial leases which prevents subrogation rights from attaching.

Note that while in residential tenancies, absent an express lease provision providing tenant liability for a loss from a negligently triggered fire, the landlord's insurance is deemed to be held for the mutual benefit of both parties,[1] the Supreme Judicial Court has explicitly refused to extend that rule to commercial tenancies.[2] The Court will continue to look to the terms of the lease and other any evidence to ascertain the intent of the parties.

§ 19.19   Set Forth Events of Default Under Lease

It is customary for the lease to specify just what events constitute a default by lessee under the lease and the consequences of such default.

A major difference between the three lease forms in this area is that lease Forms B & C require notice of default from lessor to lessee, except in case of nonpayment of rent, before lessor's remedies for the default mature.

Additionally, the measure of damages after termination for default is much harsher toward lessee in lease Forms A & C as are lessor's remedies for default by lessee which does not result in termination.

§ 19.20   Subordination of Subsequent Mortgages

Often times there will be negotiations between the parties on the question of subordinating the lease to subsequent mortgages. This kind of a clause is essential to the lessor and will nearly always be insisted upon by it.

In response lessee will usually request a non-disturbance agreement, which in essence provides that lessor will obtain mortgage terms from the mortgagee that require lessee's rights to be recognized in the event of foreclosure. Forms B & C contain examples of such attornment subordination and nondisturbance clauses.

Lessors will sometimes resist a non-disturbance clause except in the case of very important tenants. Length of lease and amount of space taken are crucial here. In

---

[1] Peterson v. Silva, 428 Mass. 751, 704 N.E.2d 1163 (1999).
[2] Seaco Ins. Co. v. Barbosa, 435 Mass. 772, 761 N.E.2d 946 (2002).

this light, an important tenant may also raise the question of non-disturbance agreements from existing mortgagees.

§ 19.21   Miscellaneous Provisions

Most leases contain a collection of miscellaneous provisions at the end relating to, *inter alia*: the place to which rent and notices are to be mailed, the rights of lessor if lessee fails to remove property from the premises at the end of the lease term, integration and severability of the agreement, binding effect of the document on heirs and assigns, choice of law, regulation of recording of the lease or notice of lease.

The three lease forms contain many of the same of these so-called miscellaneous provisions. Lease Form B eliminates certain of these clauses that are almost invariably found in leases drafted by lessors' counsel.

CHAPTER 20

REGISTRATION AND CONFIRMATION OF TITLE TO REAL ESTATE—THE PRACTICE

Synopsis

§ 20.01   Preliminary Considerations—Registration or Con-
           firmation
§ 20.02   Prepare to File Complaint
§ 20.03   Prepare Filing Documents
§ 20.04   File Documents in Court
§ 20.05   Follow Up Regularly with the Court
§ 20.06   Petitions Subsequent to Registration
§ 20.07   Voluntary Withdrawal of Land from Registration

§ 20.01   Preliminary Considerations—Registration or Confirmation

Step 1. You should thoroughly understand the title problem before deciding to pursue land court proceedings. If a complete title examination has not been done you should order one. It may save your client money if you hire an examiner who is a certified land court examiner. This way when you later file your complaint you can suggest to the court that the same person be appointed the court examiner for the case. It would seem that the examiner should give your client some credit on the charges for the official examination based on the fact that some of the work will have been done already. This could be discussed with the examiner at the very outset.

Where the title problem involves boundaries, easements, area or other surveying or engineering problems all available plans should be studied. Some preliminary engineering work may be arranged to get a fuller understanding of the problem before undertaking the significant expense of a plan which meets land court requirements. This engineering investigation can be crucial in the decision to go forward. Because the land court is in effect guaranteeing the correctness of the title and plan its staff people will be very particular that all regulatory issues affecting the property and disclosed by the plan have been complied with. For example, if the plan shows a man-made structure protruding into wetlands or tidal lands, or into navigable waters, the court will want assurances that all local and state permits and licenses have been obtained. If your client has, as is often the case, constructed improvements without the necessary permits, he or she will be required to obtain those permits before proceeding. The necessity of, for example, undertaking a Chapter 91 license proceeding prior to filing in the land court may very well be dispositive in the client's mind as to whether it makes sense to go forward.

A decision must be made on the likelihood of success of any land court proceeding, and which proceeding should be undertaken. The plaintiff must usually establish either record title or title by adverse possession. The existence of potential defendants who may appear and actively contest the complaint should be seriously investigated and considered. A contested proceeding to establish title will be extremely lengthy, costly, and very possibly unsuccessful.

There is substantial disagreement among practitioners as to the relative desirability of registration as opposed to confirmation. A judgment of registration results in title and boundaries established by the court, and it gives the owner the benefits of the assurance fund. Title is evidenced by a certificate of title which contains all exceptions and encumbrances upon it. All future transactions involving the land must take place in the registered land section of the local registry of deeds. Confirmation results in an in rem decree that title to the land is in the plaintiff's name as of a certain date according to an accompanying plan, subject to the encumbrances listed in the judgment. The land stays on the unregistered side of the registry of deeds. The documentary submissions, proof, and time involved are about the same for registration and confirmation.

The greatest advantage of the registered title over the confirmed title is that its certainty carries forward into the future, while the confirmed title just goes back to being unregistered land and gradually loses some of the credibility it had as of the date of confirmation, with respect to events which may have occurred subsequently. On the other hand registered land can be cumbersome to deal with. For example, many kinds of transfers require land court approval before the registry of deeds will allow them to be recorded, e.g. deeds under license of court, deeds by limited partnership, conveyances by trustee for nominal consideration. The court will not allow the use of exception clauses in deeds of registered land. Further subdivisions of registered land require new approvals by the engineering department of the court, with consequent delays and expense.

Ultimately the facts of the particular situation should determine which procedure is used.

§ 20.02   Prepare to File Complaint

Step 2. Make a preliminary estimate of the likely costs of the case and discuss this thoroughly with your client, so that there are no misunderstandings and possible hard feelings down the road. The costs will be court fees, engineering/surveying fees, fees for the land court title examiner, and attorneys' fees.

The fees charged by the court are listed in attachment A at the end of the chapter. Engineering fees are by far the most significant and will vary with the size and character of the land. At least three surveyors should be approached for quotes. Determine whether the surveyor is willing to appear as a witness if the proceeding becomes a contested one. Find out what will be the charge for court appearances.

Next, a discussion should be had with the person proposed to be the land court title examiner. Some estimate of cost should be obtained; ideally, a fixed fee should be negotiated. The estimate should be obtained for both a contested and uncontested case. This of course can be very difficult for an examiner who has never seen the title. However this problem is partly obviated if the examiner was the person who did the prefiling examination for the attorney. Less ideal, but still very helpful, is having the examiner review the prefiling examination done by another prior to estimating his or her charges. Once again the examiner's willingness to appear as a witness should be explored.

The final element of cost to be considered is the attorneys' fees for the case. These will of course vary widely depending on whether or not the case is contested, something which is often not determinable at the outset. Even uncontested cases consume a great deal of time in meetings, trips to assessor's office, visits to land court, review of plans and title reports, and so on. While the client will be very anxious to have a fixed upside limit on fees, especially if the case is uncontested, the attorney should be very cautious in giving an absolutely fixed number. Registration/confirmation cases have a tendency to be much more complicated and time consuming than they first appear.

Step 3. Have the plan prepared by a registered land surveyor in accordance with the most recent land court Manual of Instructions for Surveyors, which is available at the engineering department of the court. The surveyor should be familiar with these requirements and the details can be left to him or her.

Step 4. Review the plan to be sure that the record title respecting easements, stone walls, encroachments, etc. is reflected on the plan. Items of this nature which exist on the ground but are not of record should also be shown, especially if the court will be asked to deal with them.

Step 5. You and your surveyor should take the plan in to the land court engineering department for review prior to completing the remaining filing documents. It is not in the least uncommon for the engineering department to raise concerns, request additional information on the plan, require changes to the plan, etc. Issues which surface at this review may cause significant delays in the actual filing of the complaint, or may result in a reduction in the size, or change in the configuration of the land which your client decides to proceed to try to register. If the other documents have been completed they will have to be done again.

The plan should be signed and stamped by the surveyor and dated within six months of filing. If it is dated over six months previously it must be re-certified by the surveyor. The plan must also have the endorsement of the municipal planning board as an approved subdivision or an approval not required plan, which endorsement must be within six months of the filing date or be re-certified by the planning board. A so-called "chapter 380" certification by a registered surveyor will be accepted in lieu of the planning board endorsement only if a single lot is involved and the plaintiff does not own any abutting unregistered land. Deficiencies in the plan are usually indicated on a form of the type included at the end of the chapter as attachment C.

§ 20.03   Prepare Filing Documents

Step 6. Complete Information List—Registration or Confirmation of Land Title, and prepare the land court complaint and pink copy of same. (Volume 6, Chapter 20, Forms 134 and 135.) It will be seen that the forms are identical except for color, the pink copy being sent to the title examiner by the court. This form is straightforward and easy to complete. The following comments are numbered in accordance with the paragraph of the complaint to which they relate:

Paragraph 1) Do not use a deed or plan description or a running description. The court wants a metes and bounds description.

Paragraph 2) If your client claims the right to use a private way that claim should be stated here. If such a claim is made the filing plan, or an attachment or supplement to it, will have to have a sketch by the engineer showing the claim and the names and addresses of all the owners on both sides of the private way, from the locus to the public way to which it connects. All of these persons will have to receive notice and are potential respondents who may contest the asserted right. If the locus is already shown on a recorded plan it may be possible to avoid the necessity of adding all these parties by simply relying on the statutory right of a lot owner to use the ways shown on the plan creating the lost (G.L. c. 183, § 58. In such a case no claim would be made in paragraph 2 of the complaint.)

Paragraph 4) This paragraph should be include, in addition to the interests requested, any denial of rights which the plaintiff wishes to assert. For example, if the plaintiff wishes to deny the rights of anyone to use a cart path shown on the filing plan, or to maintain an encroaching wall, then that should be stated here.

Paragraph 7) Although the form requests names and addresses of abutters "so far as known to the plaintiff," it is expected that this information will be obtained from the assessors and registry of deeds. Where the property is on a private way and claim is made of ownership to the center of it, the name of abutters across the way opposite the locus must be included. Where a claim of appurtenant right to use the private way to the public way is stated in paragraph 2 include the names and addresses of owners on the sketch plan as well.

Paragraph 8) If the locus abuts on a public way, it should be determined whether the taking for the way was in fee or only an easement. In the former case, strike out the language of paragraph 8 which relates to ownership of the land within the limits of the way.

Paragraph 9) In the usual case, the plaintiff will be claiming to the center of an adjoining private way. In some cases, the way may abut the locus but devolve from a different chain of title; and the locus may only have an easement over it, or no rights over it at all. The notarial acknowledgment on the form should be completed prior to filing.

Step 7. Prepare the Assessors' Certificate and submit it to the local assessors for completion. (Volume 6, Chapter 20, Form 136.) The space for the sketch on the front of the form may be filled in by the attorney based on the engineer's plan. Many assessors now charge a fee for completing this form.

§ 20.04   File Documents in Court

Step 8. Take the plan (linen and two prints), the completed complaint and pink copy, the completed Assessors' Certificate, suggestion of land court examiner and the appropriate filing fee in to the land court for filing. Although filing by mail is permitted, it is very much not recommended. After engineering has signed off and your other filing documents have been reviewed and approved your complaint will be accepted and a docket number assigned.

Step 9. Complete the Notice of Filing form and file it in the appropriate registry of deeds. Use the same description of the land used in the complaint. (Volume 6, Chapter 20, Form 137.) This notice may be signed by the attorney on behalf of the client. It is returned by the registry directly to the land court for filing with the papers in the case.

Step 10. Stay in touch with the examiner after a few months have passed to see how the examination is going. Delays by examiners in filing reports is one of the most persistent causes of the lengthy delays which often attend on the registration process.

Step 11. The land court examiner files his or her report. This report consists of the court reference to the examiner signed by him, the narrative report with abstract of title and signed opinion sheet, and the completed Assessors' Certificate.

From this point on, the process is entirely in the hands of court personnel and counsel can do nothing but check regularly on the progress of the case and respond promptly to requests from the court for additional information or submittals. If there is a transfer of ownership of all or part of the locus during the pendency of a registration proceeding then a Motion for Substitution or partial substitution must be filed. (Volume 6, Chapter 20, Form 138.) If it appears that a portion of the land may be successfully registered on an uncontested basis while the remainder will be contested, or perhaps may clearly belong to another, it is necessary to file a Motion to Sever and Retain Jurisdiction in Separate Cases or a Motion to Sever and Dismiss. (Volume 6, Chapter 20, Forms 141 and 142.)

§ 20.05   Follow Up Regularly with the Court

Step 12. Clerk examines all papers in case and determines if necessary information for required service is present. If not a letter will be sent to counsel requesting additional information. When the information is complete the court issues, and arranges for publication and service of the citation. Appearances and Answers must be filed with the court or appropriate registry district on or before the return day.

Step 13. If the case is contested then counsel must move to have it assigned for trial. After hearing the judge will issue findings and an order for judgment.

Step 14. If the case is uncontested, it will be assigned to a particular judge for reading. The judge's title examiner will examine the file and advise counsel for plaintiff of any missing items which must be supplied before the case can move on.

Step 15. An Order for Judgment enters and the case moves to the engineering department for preparation of the official plan. The engineering department reviews the entire file, reconciles the plan with other registered land, and supervises the setting of land court bounds on the locus by the plaintiff's surveyor. Problems can sometimes surface with the plan at this time requiring a return to an earlier step in the process.

Step 16. A copy of the judgment, judgment plan and a statement of the financial account for the case are sent to plaintiff's attorney, with a request for any final items needed to finish up the paperwork on the case.

Step 17. When all is in order the clerk's office sends the judgment, plan and other necessary documents to the appropriate registry of deeds, along with a run date taken from the examiner's report. The local registry runs the title to date. If there is no problem the process is then complete and the land is registered. If there has been some change in the title the case may have to be sent back to the court for further proceedings as outlined above. In the case of confirmation the judgment is recorded on the unregistered side of the registry of deeds and is thereafter dealt with as any other parcel of unregistered land.

§ 20.06   Petitions Subsequent to Registration

There are situations arising after the Judgment of Registration has entered which require further action of the Land Court. These are typically issuance of new certificates of title after death or wrongful refusal to surrender. Less frequently a petition to the Court is needed to correct or amend a certificate or the record plan, or to reflect the fact that an interest in the land covered by the certificate has expired or been released. The statute (G.L. c.185, § 115) requires that such petitions be filed as a part of the original case. Consequently they are docketed by the Court under the original case number with the suffix "S," and are referred to as "S Petitions." A generic form of such a petition is included as Form 142.1 (Volume 6, Chapter 20.) Other forms of 'S' petitions directed to specific purposes are also included as Forms 142.1, 142.3, 142.4, 142.5, 142.6, 142.7 and 142.8 in Volume 6, Chapter 20.

§ 20.07   Voluntary Withdrawal of Land from Registration

Dealing with registered land presents to the practitioner a good deal more in the way of procedural requirements, delays and plain "red tape" than is the case with unregistered land. While an owner of unregistered land could always choose whether or not to submit it to the registered system, once the land was registered subsequent owners were pretty much stuck in that system whether they liked it or not. It is now possible, under certain conditions, for owners to voluntarily withdraw their land from the registration system.[1]

Withdrawal is accomplished by filing a complaint with the Land Court seeking permission to withdraw a particular parcel. The court then appoints one of its approved title examiners to examine the title to the parcel. The examiner reports to the court the identities of the record owner and all mortgages and lessees with interests of record in the parcel. The court must approve the withdrawal if

1. the registered land constitutes less than 50% of a single parcel or of two or more contiguous parcels in common ownership; or

2. the registered land consists of less than 10% of the land area to which an original certificate pertained; or

3. the owners of the registered land have submitted it to condominium or time-share ownership; or

4. if the court finds that the owners have demonstrated "other good cause for withdrawal," and if no mortgagee or lessee of record files an objection. Even if such an objection is filed, the court may allow withdrawal unless it determines that there is good cause for the objection.

Notwithstanding the use of "shall" and "may" by the statute in the two categories contained in number 4 above, as a practical matter it would seem that where an applicant cannot meet the specific requirements of numbers 1–3 withdrawal is permissive.

If the complaint for withdrawal is approved by the court, the landowner files in the Land Court side of the appropriate registry of deeds a Notice of Voluntary Withdrawal endorsed with the approval of a land court judge.

Once the withdrawal process is complete, the withdrawn parcel moves to the unregistered side of the registry where it has the same status as a parcel the title to which has been confirmed without registration. It has been suggested that it would be practical to record the Notice of Voluntary Withdrawal on the unregistered side as well to create a kind of starting point for the title to the parcel on that side. The Land Court approved forms for use in this process are included as Forms 142.9, 143 and 144 in Volume 6, Chapter 20.

---

[1]　St. 2000, c.413.

Attachment A to Chapter 20

[Land Court Handout on Registration/Confirmation]

A. OUTLINE ON REGISTRATION/CONFIRMATION ONLY G.L., Chapter 185, § 1(a)

I. PREPARATION: (a) Plan of locus drawn to Land Court specifications by Land Court authorized surveyor (linen and two prints); (b) Drafting of Petition—Land Court Form No. LCP-8 Drafting of Pink Copy—Land Court Form No. LCP-9 Drafting of Notice of Petition—Land Court Form No. LCN-3 Completion of Assessor's Certificate—Land Court Form No. LCA-1

Provide portion of assessor's map if available showing locus;

Suggestion of Land Court Examiner. (c) Deposit-check payable to "Land Court."

(1) Registration—$335.00 plus 1/10th of 1% of assessed value (i.e., if value is $10,000.00, deposit of $345.00 required);

(2) Confirmation only—$335.00

II. THE FILING AT LAND COURT: (a) Engineering Department—plan checked; (b) Legal Department—petition checked and case number assigned; (c) Record notice of filing at local registry of deeds.

III. REPORT AND ABSTRACT OF TITLE: (a) Prepared by Land Court Examiner and filed with the Court.

IV. SERVICE AND NOTICE: (all done by Court) (a) Publication—3 successive weeks—local newspaper; (b) Certified Mail—return receipt requested to interested parties; (c) Posting—by deputy sheriff on locus.

V. RETURN DAY: (a) Clear case—assigned to Judge for reading; (b) Contested case—may be marked for hearing or settled by parties.

VI. ORDER FOR DECREE: (a) Affidavits or proof as required by Judge; (b) Case to Engineering Department for drafting of decree plan.

VII. PREPARATION OF DECREE AND FINAL CHECK WITH JUDGE

VIII. CLOSEOUT: (a) Attorney notified by receiving copy of decree, copy of plan, request for money needed—other legal documents (i.e., white military affidavit—Land Court Form No. LCA-4 and General Default—Land Court Form No. LCM-1) original mortgage and certified copy.

XI. FUNCTION OF LOCAL REGISTRY: (a) Attested copy of decree, plan, mortgages, filing fees are sent for final rundown—if record clear, land becomes registered and certificate of title will issue to owner(s) from local registered land district. If anything found on record, papers are returned to Land Court and update requested, so that decree can be updated. In confirmation, decree is recorded and land remains on the recorded side.

Attachment B to Chapter 20

[Land Court Engineering Department Handout on Registration/Confirmation Applies to Proceedings Subsequent to Original Registration Petition Only]

REGISTRATION/CONFIRMATION OF TITLE TO LAND

Guidelines for Submissions to Land Court Engineering Department

The Subdivision Section of the Engineering Division of the Land Court will conduct prefiling reviews and approval of subdivision and condominium site plans of registered land by APPOINTMENT ONLY.

The filing of original registration petitions and plans or the approval of deeds concerning lots on subdivision plans approved and filed but not sent to the local registry of deeds are not affected by this procedure and are reviewed on a first come, first served basis.

Appointments can be made by calling 227-7470, extension 49, between the hours of 9:00 A.M. and 4:00 P.M. Monday through Friday.

Appointments will be made for a specific time but not with a specific Land Court Engineer.

The caller should have the following information available when making an appointment.

1. The plan number and existing lots that are being subdivided.

2. The number of lots to be shown on the plan to be submitted.

The Owner or Owner's Attorney must bring the following to the Engineering Division of the Land Court at the appointed time to expedite the approval and filing procedure:

1. a) A recently attested copy of Certificate of Title, OR b) Owner's Duplicate Certificate of Title, OR c) (If the Owner's Duplicate Certificate of Title has not been issued) an attested copy of the prior Certificate of Title and an attested copy of the latest deed as filed showing the assigned Certificate number.

2. Letter of authorization signed by the Owner or Owner's Attorney, authorizing third party to file necessary documents with the Land Court IF not being filed by Owner or Owner's Attorney.

3. Plan (linen) prepared in accordance with the 1989 Land Court Manual of Instructions.

4. Two prints of the above mentioned plan.

5. Surveyor's computations and worksheets including: a) unbalanced field survey line closure; b) balanced field survey line closure; c) locus perimeter closure; d) individual lot closures and e) interior block closures, if applicable.

6. Complete attested copies of any Documents and plans of takings and easements noted on the encumbrance sheet of the outstanding Certificate of Title but not shown on the Land Court plan being subdivided. Fixed takings or easements should be reflected on the plan being submitted.

7. Check for the filing fee made payable to the Land Court. (Fee for filing is $15.00 plus $3.00 for each lot to be shown.)

8. Check for the registration fee made payable to the Registry of Deeds in which the land is located in the amount of $20.00 IF Planning Board endorsement is approved subject to Covenant to be filed with plan.

THE MORE COMPLETE THE PREFILING DATA—THE BETTER THE COURT CAN SERVE

CONDOMINIUM PLANS—A GUIDELINE For registered land condominiums, three (3) plans are necessary:

(1) A plan made for the Land Court in accordance with Instructions of 1989 conforming in all respects as a subdivision plan and also including:

(a) The exterior location of the building or buildings in the condominium completely enough so it could be relocated upon the ground if destroyed.

(b) The name or names of the buildings and the designation of the unit or units located therein.

(c) The type of construction of these buildings.

(d) A separate certification in addition to the certification in the 1989 Manual of Instructions in the following form: "I certify that this plan fully and accurately depicts the location and dimensions of the buildings as built and fully lists the units contained therein." Date _____Signed _____

(2) A set of floor plans which are filed with the master deed. The certification on the plans should be substantially as follows: "I certify that this plan fully and accurately depicts the layout, location, unit number and dimensions of the units numbered _____through _____inclusive, (name of buildings) as built." Date _____Signed _____

The certificate and seal of the signer must be on each sheet.

(3) A copy of a portion of the above plan is to be filed with the first unit deed. The certification on this plan should be substantially as follows:

"I certify that this plan shows unit _____being conveyed and the immediately adjoining units and that it fully and accurately depicts the layout, location, dimensions, approximate area, main entrance and immediate common are to which it has access, as built."

Date _____Signed _____

The date, signature and seal must be separately endorsed on each unit plan.

Attachment C to Chapter 20

[Land Court Engineering Department Handout on Change of Surveyor]

MEMORANDUM

CHANGE OF SURVEYOR

The Court may have only one Surveyor of record responsible for a pending case. Surveyor as used herein refers to a firm or an individual. If a change in Surveyor is to be made, one of the following procedures must be met, as a minimum.

1. NEW SURVEYOR—NEW PLAN

(a) The new Surveyor prepares a new plan in accordance with the presently effective LAND COURT MANUAL OF INSTRUCTIONS and said plan is filed in the Court as a subsequent plan.

2. NEW SURVEYOR—PRESENTLY FILED PLAN(S)

(b) A statement from the petitioner or attorney for the petitioner that the new Surveyor, identified by name and full business address, will be responsible Surveyor.

(c) A Certification of the new Surveyor that he has:

(i) reviewed filed plan(s),

(ii) made a field survey sufficient to verify the location of monuments and buildings,

(iii) accepts responsibility for plan(s) filed in Land Court Case No. _____,

(iv) that conditions on the ground are as shown on the Plan(s) with exceptions noted,

(v) signed by responsible Surveyor and

(vi) stamp of Surveyor affixed nearby signature.

This Certification, noted exceptions in red ink, the seal and signature of the new

Registered Land Surveyor to be made on a print of the filed plan(s) in the subject case.

If no exceptions exist, the above may be made in letter form by the New Surveyor.

CERTIFICATION BY NEW SURVEYOR

I certify that I have reviewed plan(s) filed, made a field survey sufficient to verify the location of monuments and buildings, that I accept responsibility for plan(s) filed in Land Court Case No. _____, and that conditions on the ground are as shown on the Plan(s). [with exceptions noted in red on print]

Signature _____Date _____PLS Stamp